FIXED INCOME AND EQUITY PORTFOLIO MANAGEMENT

CFA® Program Curriculum
2023 • LEVEL III • VOLUME 3

WILEY

© 2022, 2021, 2020, 2019, 2018, 2017, 2016, 2015, 2014, 2013, 2012, 2011, 2010, 2009, 2008, 2007, 2006 by CFA Institute. All rights reserved.

This copyright covers material written expressly for this volume by the editor/s as well as the compilation itself. It does not cover the individual selections herein that first appeared elsewhere. Permission to reprint these has been obtained by CFA Institute for this edition only. Further reproductions by any means, electronic or mechanical, including photocopying and recording, or by any information storage or retrieval systems, must be arranged with the individual copyright holders noted.

CFA®, Chartered Financial Analyst®, AIMR-PPS®, and GIPS® are just a few of the trademarks owned by CFA Institute. To view a list of CFA Institute trademarks and the Guide for Use of CFA Institute Marks, please visit our website at www.cfainstitute.org.

This publication is designed to provide accurate and authoritative information in regard to the subject matter covered. It is sold with the understanding that the publisher is not engaged in rendering legal, accounting, or other professional service. If legal advice or other expert assistance is required, the services of a competent professional should be sought.

All trademarks, service marks, registered trademarks, and registered service marks are the property of their respective owners and are used herein for identification purposes only.

ISBN 978-1-953337-13-9 (paper)
ISBN 978-1-953337-37-5 (ebk)

10 9 8 7 6 5 4 3 2 1

Please visit our website at
www.WileyGlobalFinance.com.

CONTENTS

How to Use the CFA Program Curriculum	vii
Background on the CBOK	vii
Organization of the Curriculum	viii
Features of the Curriculum	viii
Designing Your Personal Study Program	ix
CFA Institute Learning Ecosystem (LES)	x
Prep Providers	xi
Feedback	xii

Portfolio Management

Study Session 6	**Fixed-Income Portfolio Management (2)**	3
Reading 13	**Yield Curve Strategies**	5
	Introduction	5
	Key Yield Curve and Fixed-Income Concepts for Active Managers	6
	Yield Curve Dynamics	6
	Duration and Convexity	10
	Yield Curve Strategies	13
	Static Yield Curve	14
	Dynamic Yield Curve	19
	Key Rate Duration for a Portfolio	36
	Active Fixed-Income Management across Currencies	38
	A Framework for Evaluating Yield Curve Strategies	45
	Summary	48
	Practice Problems	51
	Solutions	56
Reading 14	**Fixed-Income Active Management: Credit Strategies**	59
	Introduction	60
	Key Credit and Spread Concepts for Active Management	60
	Credit Risk Considerations	61
	Credit Spread Measures	69
	Credit Strategies	84
	Bottom-Up Credit Strategies	84
	Top-Down Credit Strategies	92
	Factor-Based Credit Strategies	97
	Liquidity and Tail Risk	99
	Liquidity Risk	99
	Tail Risk	101
	Synthetic Credit Strategies	104
	Credit Spread Curve Strategies	110
	Static Credit Spread Curve Strategies	111
	Dynamic Credit Spread Curve Strategies	115
	Global Credit Strategies	120
	Structured Credit	124

◎ indicates an optional segment

	Fixed-Income Analytics	126
	Summary	129
	Practice Problems	132
	Solutions	140
Study Session 7	**Equity Portfolio Management (1)**	**145**
Reading 15	**Overview of Equity Portfolio Management**	**147**
	Introduction and the Role of Equities in a Portfolio	147
	The Roles of Equities in a Portfolio	148
	Equity Investment Universe	153
	Segmentation by Size and Style	153
	Segmentation by Geography	156
	Segmentation by Economic Activity	157
	Segmentation of Equity Indexes and Benchmarks	159
	Income Associated with Owning and Managing an Equity Portfolio	159
	Dividend Income	160
	Securities Lending Income	160
	Ancillary Investment Strategies	161
	Costs Associated with Owning and Managing an Equity Portfolio	161
	Performance Fees	162
	Administration Fees	162
	Marketing and Distribution Costs	163
	Trading Costs	163
	Investment Approaches and Effects on Costs	164
	Shareholder Engagement	164
	Benefits of Shareholder Engagement	165
	Disadvantages of Shareholder Engagement	166
	The Role of an Equity Manager in Shareholder Engagement	166
	Equity Investment Across the Passive-Active Spectrum	168
	Confidence to Outperform	168
	Client Preference	168
	Suitable Benchmark	169
	Client-Specific Mandates	169
	Risks/Costs of Active Management	170
	Taxes	170
	Summary	170
	Practice Problems	173
	Solutions	175
Reading 16	**Passive Equity Investing**	**177**
	Choosing a Benchmark: Indexes as a Basis for Investment	177
	Choosing a Benchmark	179
	Choosing a Benchmark: Index Construction Methodologies	182
	Choosing a Benchmark: Factor-Based Strategies	188
	Approaches to Passive Equity Investing: Pooled Investments	191
	Pooled Investments	192
	Approaches to Passive Equity Investing: Derivatives-Based Approaches & Index-Based Portfolios	195
	Separately Managed Equity Index-Based Portfolios	199

◉ indicates an optional segment

	Passive Portfolio Construction	**201**
	Full Replication	**201**
	Stratified Sampling	**203**
	Optimization	**204**
	Blended Approach	**205**
	Tracking Error Management	**205**
	Tracking Error and Excess Return	**206**
	Potential Causes of Tracking Error and Excess Return	**207**
	Controlling Tracking Error	**208**
	Sources of Return and Risk in Passive Equity Portfolios	**208**
	Attribution Analysis	**209**
	Securities Lending	**211**
	Investor Activism and Engagement by Passive Managers	**212**
	Summary	**214**
	Practice Problems	**217**
	Solutions	**222**
Study Session 8	**Equity Portfolio Management (2)**	**225**
Reading 17	**Active Equity Investing: Strategies**	**227**
	Introduction	**227**
	Approaches to Active Management	**228**
	Differences in the Nature of the Information Used	**230**
	Differences in the Focus of the Analysis	**231**
	Difference in Orientation to the Data: Forecasting Fundamentals vs. Pattern Recognition	**231**
	Differences in Portfolio Construction: Judgment vs. Optimization	**232**
	Bottom-Up Strategies	**233**
	Bottom-Up Strategies	**234**
	Top-Down Strategies	**240**
	Country and Geographic Allocation to Equities	**241**
	Sector and Industry Rotation	**241**
	Volatility-Based Strategies	**241**
	Thematic Investment Strategies	**242**
	Factor-Based Strategies: Overview	**243**
	Factor-Based Strategies: Style Factors	**247**
	Value	**248**
	Price Momentum	**248**
	Growth	**251**
	Quality	**252**
	Factor-Based Strategies: Unconventional Factors	**253**
	Activist Strategies	**257**
	The Popularity of Shareholder Activism	**258**
	Tactics Used by Activist Investors	**259**
	Typical Activist Targets	**260**
	Other Active Strategies	**264**
	Strategies Based on Statistical Arbitrage and Market Microstructure	**264**
	Event-Driven Strategies	**267**
	Creating a Fundamental Active Investment Strategy	**267**
	The Fundamental Active Investment Process	**268**

◉ indicates an optional segment

	Pitfalls in Fundamental Investing	270
	Creating a Quantitative Active Investment Strategy	274
	Creating a Quantitative Investment Process	274
	Pitfalls in Quantitative Investment Processes	277
	Equity Investment Style Classification	281
	Different Approaches to Style Classification	281
	Strengths and Limitations of Style Analysis	289
	Summary	290
	Practice Problems	293
	Solutions	299
Reading 18	**Active Equity Investing: Portfolio Construction**	**305**
	Introduction	305
	Building Blocks of Active Equity Portfolio Construction	306
	Fundamentals of Portfolio Construction	307
	Building Blocks Used in Portfolio Construction	309
	The Implementation Process: Portfolio Construction Approaches	318
	The Implementation Process: The Choice of Portfolio Management Approaches	319
	The Implementation Process: Measures of Benchmark-Relative Risk	322
	The Implementation Process: Objectives and Constraints	329
	Absolute vs. Relative Measures of Risk	334
	Absolute vs. Relative Measures of Risk	335
	Determining the Appropriate Level of Risk	340
	Implementation constraints	341
	Limited diversification opportunities	342
	Leverage and its implications for risk	342
	Allocating the Risk Budget	343
	Additional Risk Measures Used in Portfolio Construction and Monitoring	347
	Heuristic Constraints	347
	Formal Constraints	348
	The Risks of Being Wrong	350
	Implicit Cost-Related Considerations in Portfolio Construction	353
	Implicit Costs—Market Impact and the Relevance of Position Size, Assets under Management, and Turnover	354
	Estimating the Cost of Slippage	356
	The Well-Constructed Portfolio	360
	Long/Short, Long Extension, and Market-Neutral Portfolio Construction	365
	The Merits of Long-Only Investing	366
	Long/Short Portfolio Construction	368
	Long Extension Portfolio Construction	369
	Market-Neutral Portfolio Construction	370
	Benefits and Drawbacks of Long/Short Strategies	371
	Summary	375
	Practice Problems	379
	Solutions	384
	Glossary	**G-1**

◙ indicates an optional segment

How to Use the CFA Program Curriculum

Congratulations on your decision to enter the Chartered Financial Analyst (CFA®) Program. This exciting and rewarding program of study reflects your desire to become a serious investment professional. You are embarking on a program noted for its high ethical standards and the breadth of knowledge, skills, and abilities (competencies) it develops. Your commitment should be educationally and professionally rewarding.

The credential you seek is respected around the world as a mark of accomplishment and dedication. Each level of the program represents a distinct achievement in professional development. Successful completion of the program is rewarded with membership in a prestigious global community of investment professionals. CFA charterholders are dedicated to life-long learning and maintaining currency with the ever-changing dynamics of a challenging profession. CFA Program enrollment represents the first step toward a career-long commitment to professional education.

The CFA exam measures your mastery of the core knowledge, skills, and abilities required to succeed as an investment professional. These core competencies are the basis for the Candidate Body of Knowledge (CBOK™). The CBOK consists of four components:

- A broad outline that lists the major CFA Program topic areas (www.cfainstitute.org/programs/cfa/curriculum/cbok);
- Topic area weights that indicate the relative exam weightings of the top-level topic areas (www.cfainstitute.org/programs/cfa/curriculum);
- Learning outcome statements (LOS) that advise candidates about the specific knowledge, skills, and abilities they should acquire from readings covering a topic area (LOS are provided in candidate study sessions and at the beginning of each reading); and
- CFA Program curriculum that candidates receive upon exam registration.

Therefore, the key to your success on the CFA exams is studying and understanding the CBOK. The following sections provide background on the CBOK, the organization of the curriculum, features of the curriculum, and tips for designing an effective personal study program.

BACKGROUND ON THE CBOK

CFA Program is grounded in the practice of the investment profession. CFA Institute performs a continuous practice analysis with investment professionals around the world to determine the competencies that are relevant to the profession, beginning with the Global Body of Investment Knowledge (GBIK®). Regional expert panels and targeted surveys are conducted annually to verify and reinforce the continuous feedback about the GBIK. The practice analysis process ultimately defines the CBOK. The CBOK reflects the competencies that are generally accepted and applied by investment professionals. These competencies are used in practice in a generalist context and are expected to be demonstrated by a recently qualified CFA charterholder.

© 2021 CFA Institute. All rights reserved.

The CFA Institute staff—in conjunction with the Education Advisory Committee and Curriculum Level Advisors, who consist of practicing CFA charterholders—designs the CFA Program curriculum in order to deliver the CBOK to candidates. The exams, also written by CFA charterholders, are designed to allow you to demonstrate your mastery of the CBOK as set forth in the CFA Program curriculum. As you structure your personal study program, you should emphasize mastery of the CBOK and the practical application of that knowledge. For more information on the practice analysis, CBOK, and development of the CFA Program curriculum, please visit www.cfainstitute.org.

ORGANIZATION OF THE CURRICULUM

The Level III CFA Program curriculum is organized into six topic areas. Each topic area begins with a brief statement of the material and the depth of knowledge expected. It is then divided into one or more study sessions. These study sessions should form the basic structure of your reading and preparation. Each study session includes a statement of its structure and objective and is further divided into assigned readings. An outline illustrating the organization of these study sessions can be found at the front of each volume of the curriculum.

The readings are commissioned by CFA Institute and written by content experts, including investment professionals and university professors. Each reading includes LOS and the core material to be studied, often a combination of text, exhibits, and in-text examples and questions. End of Reading Questions (EORQs) followed by solutions help you understand and master the material. The LOS indicate what you should be able to accomplish after studying the material. The LOS, the core material, and the EORQs are dependent on each other, with the core material and EORQs providing context for understanding the scope of the LOS and enabling you to apply a principle or concept in a variety of scenarios.

The entire readings, including the EORQs, are the basis for all exam questions and are selected or developed specifically to teach the knowledge, skills, and abilities reflected in the CBOK.

You should use the LOS to guide and focus your study because each exam question is based on one or more LOS and the core material and practice problems associated with the LOS. As a candidate, you are responsible for the entirety of the required material in a study session.

We encourage you to review the information about the LOS on our website (www.cfainstitute.org/programs/cfa/curriculum/study-sessions), including the descriptions of LOS "command words" on the candidate resources page at www.cfainstitute.org.

FEATURES OF THE CURRICULUM

End of Reading Questions/Solutions *All End of Reading Questions (EORQs) as well as their solutions are part of the curriculum and are required material for the exam.* In addition to the in-text examples and questions, these EORQs help demonstrate practical applications and reinforce your understanding of the concepts presented. Some of these EORQs are adapted from past CFA exams and/or may serve as a basis for exam questions.

Glossary For your convenience, each volume includes a comprehensive Glossary. Throughout the curriculum, a **bolded** word in a reading denotes a term defined in the Glossary.

Note that the digital curriculum that is included in your exam registration fee is searchable for key words, including Glossary terms.

LOS Self-Check We have inserted checkboxes next to each LOS that you can use to track your progress in mastering the concepts in each reading.

Source Material The CFA Institute curriculum cites textbooks, journal articles, and other publications that provide additional context or information about topics covered in the readings. As a candidate, you are not responsible for familiarity with the original source materials cited in the curriculum.

Note that some readings may contain a web address or URL. The referenced sites were live at the time the reading was written or updated but may have been deactivated since then.

Some readings in the curriculum cite articles published in the *Financial Analysts Journal*®, which is the flagship publication of CFA Institute. Since its launch in 1945, the *Financial Analysts Journal* has established itself as the leading practitioner-oriented journal in the investment management community. Over the years, it has advanced the knowledge and understanding of the practice of investment management through the publication of peer-reviewed practitioner-relevant research from leading academics and practitioners. It has also featured thought-provoking opinion pieces that advance the common level of discourse within the investment management profession. Some of the most influential research in the area of investment management has appeared in the pages of the *Financial Analysts Journal*, and several Nobel laureates have contributed articles.

Candidates are not responsible for familiarity with *Financial Analysts Journal* articles that are cited in the curriculum. But, as your time and studies allow, we strongly encourage you to begin supplementing your understanding of key investment management issues by reading this, and other, CFA Institute practice-oriented publications through the Research & Analysis webpage (www.cfainstitute.org/en/research).

Errata The curriculum development process is rigorous and includes multiple rounds of reviews by content experts. Despite our efforts to produce a curriculum that is free of errors, there are times when we must make corrections. Curriculum errata are periodically updated and posted by exam level and test date online (www.cfainstitute.org/en/programs/submit-errata). If you believe you have found an error in the curriculum, you can submit your concerns through our curriculum errata reporting process found at the bottom of the Curriculum Errata webpage.

DESIGNING YOUR PERSONAL STUDY PROGRAM

Create a Schedule An orderly, systematic approach to exam preparation is critical. You should dedicate a consistent block of time every week to reading and studying. Complete all assigned readings and the associated problems and solutions in each study session. Review the LOS both before and after you study each reading to ensure that you have mastered the applicable content and can demonstrate the knowledge, skills, and abilities described by the LOS and the assigned reading. Use the LOS self-check to track your progress and highlight areas of weakness for later review.

Successful candidates report an average of more than 300 hours preparing for each exam. Your preparation time will vary based on your prior education and experience, and you will probably spend more time on some study sessions than on others.

You should allow ample time for both in-depth study of all topic areas and additional concentration on those topic areas for which you feel the least prepared.

CFA INSTITUTE LEARNING ECOSYSTEM (LES)

As you prepare for your exam, we will email you important exam updates, testing policies, and study tips. Be sure to read these carefully.

Your exam registration fee includes access to the CFA Program Learning Ecosystem (LES). This digital learning platform provides access, even offline, to all of the readings and End of Reading Questions found in the print curriculum organized as a series of shorter online lessons with associated EORQs. This tool is your one-stop location for all study materials, including practice questions and mock exams.

The LES provides the following supplemental study tools:

Structured and Adaptive Study Plans The LES offers two ways to plan your study through the curriculum. The first is a structured plan that allows you to move through the material in the way that you feel best suits your learning. The second is an adaptive study plan based on the results of an assessment test that uses actual practice questions.

Regardless of your chosen study path, the LES tracks your level of proficiency in each topic area and presents you with a dashboard of where you stand in terms of proficiency so that you can allocate your study time efficiently.

Flashcards and Game Center The LES offers all the Glossary terms as Flashcards and tracks correct and incorrect answers. Flashcards can be filtered both by curriculum topic area and by action taken—for example, answered correctly, unanswered, and so on. These Flashcards provide a flexible way to study Glossary item definitions.

The Game Center provides several engaging ways to interact with the Flashcards in a game context. Each game tests your knowledge of the Glossary terms a in different way. Your results are scored and presented, along with a summary of candidates with high scores on the game, on your Dashboard.

Discussion Board The Discussion Board within the LES provides a way for you to interact with other candidates as you pursue your study plan. Discussions can happen at the level of individual lessons to raise questions about material in those lessons that you or other candidates can clarify or comment on. Discussions can also be posted at the level of topics or in the initial Welcome section to connect with other candidates in your area.

Practice Question Bank The LES offers access to a question bank of hundreds of practice questions that are in addition to the End of Reading Questions. These practice questions, only available on the LES, are intended to help you assess your mastery of individual topic areas as you progress through your studies. After each practice question, you will receive immediate feedback noting the correct response and indicating the relevant assigned reading so you can identify areas of weakness for further study.

Mock Exams The LES also includes access to three-hour Mock Exams that simulate the morning and afternoon sessions of the actual CFA exam. These Mock Exams are intended to be taken after you complete your study of the full curriculum and take practice questions so you can test your understanding of the curriculum and your readiness for the exam. If you take these Mock Exams within the LES, you will receive feedback afterward that notes the correct responses and indicates the relevant assigned readings so you can assess areas of weakness for further study. We recommend that you take Mock Exams during the final stages of your preparation for the actual CFA exam. For more information on the Mock Exams, please visit www.cfainstitute.org.

PREP PROVIDERS

You may choose to seek study support outside CFA Institute in the form of exam prep providers. After your CFA Program enrollment, you may receive numerous solicitations for exam prep courses and review materials. When considering a prep course, make sure the provider is committed to following the CFA Institute guidelines and high standards in its offerings.

Remember, however, that there are no shortcuts to success on the CFA exams; reading and studying the CFA Program curriculum *is* the key to success on the exam. The CFA Program exams reference only the CFA Institute assigned curriculum; no prep course or review course materials are consulted or referenced.

SUMMARY

Every question on the CFA exam is based on the content contained in the required readings and on one or more LOS. Frequently, an exam question is based on a specific example highlighted within a reading or on a specific practice problem and its solution. To make effective use of the CFA Program curriculum, please remember these key points:

1 All pages of the curriculum are required reading for the exam.

2 All questions, problems, and their solutions are part of the curriculum and are required study material for the exam. These questions are found at the end of the readings in the print versions of the curriculum. In the LES, these questions appear directly after the lesson with which they are associated. The LES provides immediate feedback on your answers and tracks your performance on these questions throughout your study.

3 We strongly encourage you to use the CFA Program Learning Ecosystem. In addition to providing access to all the curriculum material, including EORQs, in the form of shorter, focused lessons, the LES offers structured and adaptive study planning, a Discussion Board to communicate with other candidates, Flashcards, a Game Center for study activities, a test bank of practice questions, and online Mock Exams. Other supplemental study tools, such as eBook and PDF versions of the print curriculum, and additional candidate resources are available at www.cfainstitute.org.

4 Using the study planner, create a schedule and commit sufficient study time to cover the study sessions. You should also plan to review the materials, answer practice questions, and take Mock Exams.

5 Some of the concepts in the study sessions may be superseded by updated rulings and/or pronouncements issued after a reading was published. Candidates are expected to be familiar with the overall analytical framework contained in the assigned readings. Candidates are not responsible for changes that occur after the material was written.

FEEDBACK

At CFA Institute, we are committed to delivering a comprehensive and rigorous curriculum for the development of competent, ethically grounded investment professionals. We rely on candidate and investment professional comments and feedback as we work to improve the curriculum, supplemental study tools, and candidate resources.

Please send any comments or feedback to info@cfainstitute.org. You can be assured that we will review your suggestions carefully. Ongoing improvements in the curriculum will help you prepare for success on the upcoming exams and for a lifetime of learning as a serious investment professional.

Portfolio Management

STUDY SESSIONS

Study Session 1	Behavioral Finance
Study Session 2	Capital Market Expectations
Study Session 3	Asset Allocation and Related Decisions in Portfolio Management
Study Session 4	Derivatives and Currency Management
Study Session 5	Fixed-Income Portfolio Management (1)
Study Session 6	Fixed-Income Portfolio Management (2)
Study Session 7	Equity Portfolio Management (1)
Study Session 8	Equity Portfolio Management (2)
Study Session 9	Alternative Investments Portfolio Management
Study Session 10	Private Wealth Management (1)
Study Session 11	Private Wealth Management (2)
Study Session 12	Portfolio Management for Institutional Investors
Study Session 13	Trading, Performance Evaluation, and Manager Selection
Study Session 14	Cases in Portfolio Management and Risk Management

This volume includes Study Sessions 6–8.

© 2021 CFA Institute. All rights reserved.

TOPIC LEVEL LEARNING OUTCOME

The candidate should be able to prepare an appropriate investment policy statement and asset allocation; formulate strategies for managing, monitoring, and rebalancing investment portfolios; and evaluate portfolio performance.

PORTFOLIO MANAGEMENT
STUDY SESSION

6

Fixed-Income Portfolio Management (2)

This study session covers yield curve and credit strategies for fixed-income portfolios. Fundamental concepts necessary for understanding yield curves and yield curve strategies are reviewed. Portfolio management strategies, which are based on the investor's expectations regarding the level, slope, and curvature of the yield curve, are presented. Strategies used to construct and manage fixed-income credit portfolios follow. Coverage includes various credit spread measures, bottom-up and top-down approaches to credit strategies, and credit-related risks.

READING ASSIGNMENTS

Reading 13	Yield Curve Strategies by Robert W. Kopprasch, PhD, CFA, and Steven V. Mann, PhD
Reading 14	Fixed-Income Active Management: Credit Strategies by Campe Goodman, CFA, and Oleg Melentyev, CFA

READING 13

Yield Curve Strategies

by Robert W. Kopprasch, PhD, CFA, and Steven V. Mann, PhD

Robert W. Kopprasch, PhD, CFA, is at Bates Group, LLC (USA). Steven V. Mann, PhD, is at the University of South Carolina (USA).

LEARNING OUTCOMES	
Mastery	The candidate should be able to:
☐	a. describe the factors affecting fixed-income portfolio returns due to a change in benchmark yields;
☐	b. formulate a portfolio positioning strategy given forward interest rates and an interest rate view that coincides with the market view;
☐	c. formulate a portfolio positioning strategy given forward interest rates and an interest rate view that diverges from the market view in terms of rate level, slope, and shape;
☐	d. formulate a portfolio positioning strategy based upon expected changes in interest rate volatility;
☐	e. evaluate a portfolio's sensitivity using key rate durations of the portfolio and its benchmark;
☐	f. discuss yield curve strategies across currencies;
☐	g. evaluate the expected return and risks of a yield curve strategy.

1. INTRODUCTION

The size and breadth of global fixed-income markets, as well as the term structure of interest rates within and across countries, lead investors to consider numerous factors when creating and managing a bond portfolio. While fixed-income index replication and bond portfolios that consider both an investor's assets and liabilities were addressed earlier in the curriculum, we now turn our attention to active bond portfolio management. In contrast to a passive index strategy, active fixed-income management involves taking positions in primary risk factors that deviate from those of an index in order to generate excess return. Financial analysts who can successfully

© 2021 CFA Institute. All rights reserved.

apply fixed-income concepts and tools to evaluate yield curve changes and position a portfolio based upon an interest rate view find this to be a valuable skill throughout their careers.

Prioritizing fixed-income risk factors is a key first step. In what follows, we focus on the yield curve, which represents the term structure of interest rates for government or benchmark securities, with the assumption that all promised principal and interest payments take place. Fixed-income securities, which trade at a spread above the benchmark to compensate investors for credit and liquidity risk, will be addressed later in the curriculum. The starting point for active portfolio managers is the current term structure of benchmark interest rates and an interest rate view established using macroeconomic variables introduced earlier. In what follows, we demonstrate how managers may position a fixed-income portfolio to capitalize on expectations regarding the level, slope, or shape (curvature) of yield curves using both long and short cash positions, derivatives, and leverage.

2. KEY YIELD CURVE AND FIXED-INCOME CONCEPTS FOR ACTIVE MANAGERS

a describe the factors affecting fixed-income portfolio returns due to a change in benchmark yields

The factors comprising an investor's expected fixed-income portfolio returns introduced earlier in the curriculum are summarized in Equation 1:

$$E(R) \approx \text{Coupon income} \quad (1)$$

$+/-$ Rolldown return
$+/- E\,(\Delta \text{ Price due to investor's view of benchmark yields})$
$+/- E\,(\Delta \text{ Price due to investor's view of yield spreads})$
$+/- E\,(\Delta \text{ Price due to investor's view of currency value changes})$

Sections 2 and 3 will focus on actively managing the first three components of Equation 1, and Section 4 will include changes in currency. Credit strategies driving yield spreads will be discussed in a later lesson. As active management hinges on an investor's ability to identify actionable trades with specific securities, our review of yield curve and fixed-income concepts focuses on these practical considerations.

2.1 Yield Curve Dynamics

When someone refers to "the yield curve," this implies that one yield curve for a given issuer applies to all investors. In fact, a yield curve is a stylized representation of the yields-to-maturity available to investors at various maturities for a specific issuer or group of issuers. Yield curve models make certain assumptions that may vary by investor or by the intended use of the curve, raising such issues as the following:

- Asynchronous observations of various maturities on the curve
- Maturity gaps that require interpolation and/or smoothing
- Observations that seem inconsistent with neighboring values

- Use of on-the-run bonds only versus all marketable bonds (i.e., including off-the-run bonds)
- Differences in accounting, regulatory, or tax treatment of certain bonds that may make them look like outliers

As an example, a yield curve of the most recently issued, or on-the-run, securities may differ significantly from one that includes off-the-run securities. Off-the-run bonds are typically less liquid than on-the-run bonds, and hence they have a lower price (higher yield-to-maturity). Inclusion of off-the-run bonds will tend to "pull" the yield curve higher.

This illustrates two key points about yield curves. First, although we often take reported yield curves as a "given," they often do not consist of traded securities and must be derived from available bond yields-to-maturity using some type of model. This is particularly true for constant maturity yields, shown in some of the following exhibits. A constant maturity yield estimates, for example, what a hypothetical 5-year yield-to-maturity would be if a bond were available with exactly five years to maturity. While some derivatives reference the daily constant maturity yield, the current on-the-run 5-year Treasury issued before today has a maturity of less than five years. Estimating a constant maturity 5-year yield typically requires interpolating the yields-to-maturity on actively traded bonds with maturities *near* five years. Different models and assumptions can produce different yield curves. The difference between models becomes more pronounced as yields-to-maturity are converted to spot and forward rates (as spot and forward rate curves amplify yield curve steepness and curvature).

Second, a tradeoff exists between yield-to-maturity and liquidity. Active management strategies must assess this tradeoff when selecting bonds for the portfolio, especially if frequent trading is anticipated. While off-the-run bonds may earn a higher return if held to maturity, buying and selling them will likely involve increased trading costs (especially in a market crisis).

Primary yield curve risk factors are often categorized by three types: a change in (1) level (a parallel "shift" in the yield curve); (2) slope (a flattening or steepening "twist" of the yield curve); and (3) shape or curvature (or "butterfly movement"). Earlier in the curriculum, principal components analysis was used to decompose yield curve changes into these three separate factors. Level, slope, and curvature movements over time accounted for approximately 82%, 12%, and 4%, respectively, of US Treasury yield curve changes. Although based upon a specific historical period, the consistency of these results over time and across global markets underscores the importance of these factors in realizing excess portfolio returns under an active yield curve strategy.

The following exhibits provide historical context for the three yield curve factors using constant maturity US Treasury yields. Exhibit 1 shows US 10-year constant maturity yield levels.

Exhibit 1   10-Year US Treasury Yield, 2007–2020 (%)

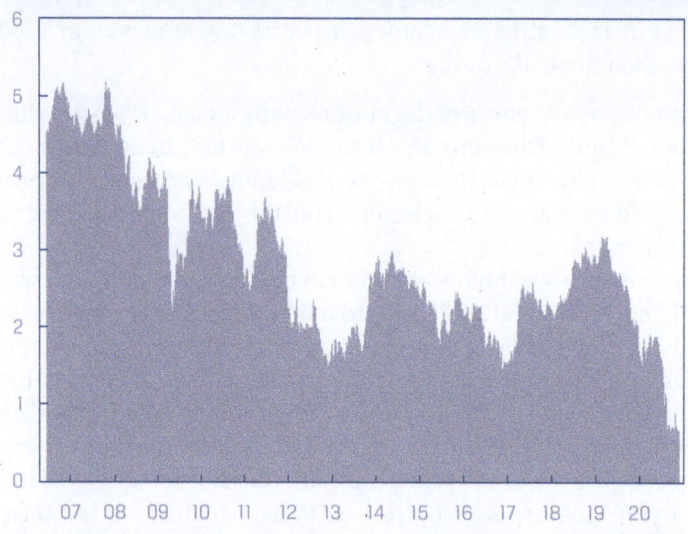

Source: US Federal Reserve.

During the period shown in Exhibit 1, 10-year US Treasury yields-to-maturity demonstrated significant volatility, falling to new lows in 2020 amid a flight to quality during the COVID-19 pandemic. Slower growth and accommodative monetary policy in the form of quantitative easing among global central banks since the 2008 global financial crisis years has driven government yields to zero and below. In 2020, negative yields were common on many Japanese, German, and Swiss government bonds, among others.

A change in yield *level* (or parallel shift) occurs when all yields-to-maturity represented on the curve change by the same number of basis points. Under this assumption, a portfolio manager might use a first-order duration statistic to approximate the impact of an expected yield curve change on portfolio value. This implies that yield curve changes occur only in parallel shifts, which is unreliable in cases where the yield curve's slope and curvature also change. Larger yield curve changes necessitate the inclusion of second-order effects in order to better measure changes in portfolio value.

Yield curve *slope* is often defined as the difference in basis points between the yield-to-maturity on a long-maturity bond and the yield-to-maturity on a shorter-maturity bond. For example, as of July 2020, the slope as measured by the 2s30s spread, or the difference between the 30-year Treasury bond (30s) and the 2-year Treasury note (2s) yields-to-maturity (1.43% and 0.16%, respectively), was 127 bps. Exhibit 2 shows the 2s30s spread for US Treasury constant maturity yields. As this spread increases, or widens, the yield curve is said to steepen, while a decrease, or narrowing, is referred to as a flattening of the yield curve. In most instances, the spread is positive and the yield curve is upward-sloping. If the spread turns negative, as was the case just prior to the 2008 global financial crisis, the yield curve is described as "inverted."

Exhibit 2: 2s30s US Yield Spread, 2007–2020 (%)

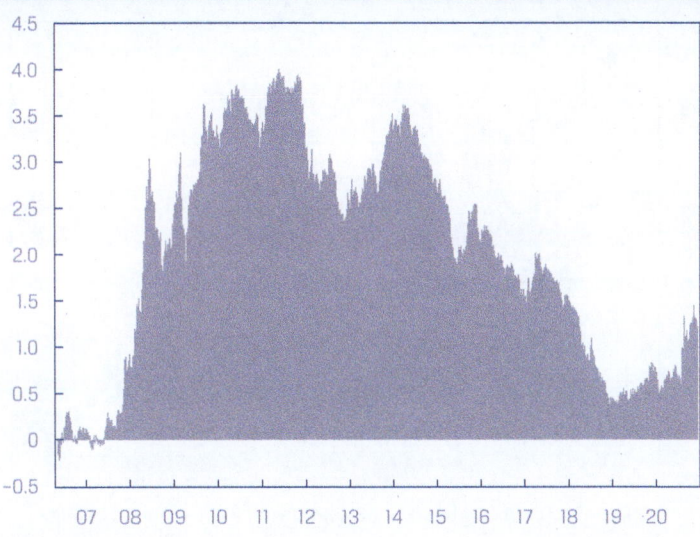

Source: US Federal Reserve.

Yield curve shape or *curvature* is the relationship between yields-to-maturity at the short end of the curve, at a midpoint along the curve (often referred to as the "belly" of the curve), and at the long end of the curve. A common measure of yield curve curvature is the **butterfly spread**:

$$\text{Butterfly spread} = -(\text{Short-term yield}) + (2 \times \text{Medium-term yield}) - \text{Long-term yield} \tag{2}$$

The butterfly spread takes on larger positive values when the yield curve has more curvature. Exhibit 3 displays this measure of curvature for the US Treasury constant maturity yield curve using 2-year, 10-year, and 30-year tenors. Curvature indicates a difference between medium-term yields and a linear interpolation between short-term and long-term yields-to-maturity. A positive butterfly spread indicates a "humped" or concave shape to the midpoint of the curve, while a "saucer" or convex shape indicates the spread is negative. The butterfly spread changes when intermediate-term yield-to-maturity changes are of a different magnitude than those on the wings (the short- and long-end of the curve). Note that as in the case of yield curve slope, the butterfly spread was generally positive until 2020, except for the period just prior to the 2008 global financial crisis.

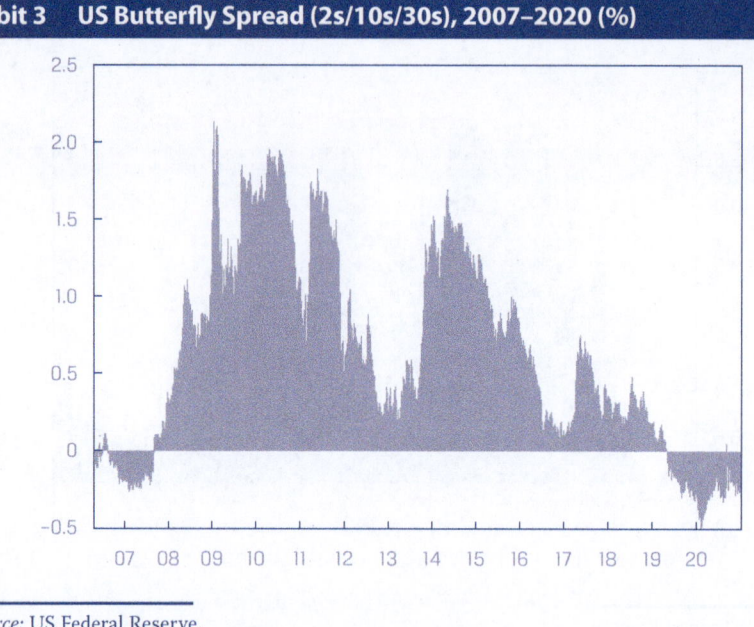

Exhibit 3 US Butterfly Spread (2s/10s/30s), 2007–2020 (%)

Source: US Federal Reserve.

2.2 Duration and Convexity

As active managers position their portfolios to capitalize on expected changes in the level, slope, and curvature of the benchmark yield curve, the anticipated change in portfolio value due to yield-to-maturity changes are captured by the third term in Equation 1—namely, the expected change in price due to investor's view of benchmark yields. The price/yield relationship for fixed-income bonds was established earlier in the curriculum as the combination of two factors: a negative, linear first-order factor (*duration*) and a usually positive, non-linear second-order factor (*convexity*), as shown in Exhibit 4.

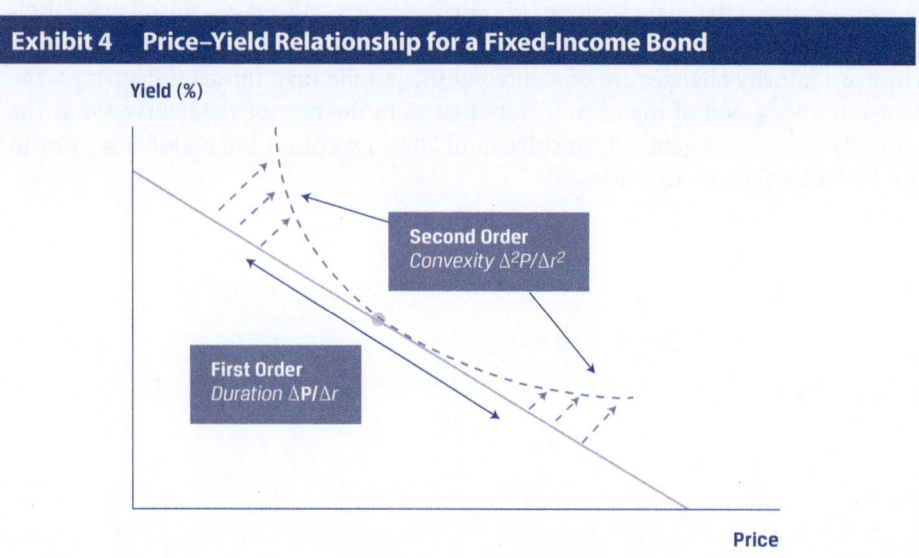

Exhibit 4 Price–Yield Relationship for a Fixed-Income Bond

The third term in Equation 1, E (Δ Price due to investor's view of benchmark yield), combines the duration and convexity effects in Equation 3 of the percentage change in the full price (%ΔPV^{Full}) for a single bond as introduced earlier:

$$\%\Delta PV^{Full} \approx -(ModDur \times \Delta Yield) + [½ \times Convexity \times (\Delta Yield)^2]. \quad (3)$$

Fixed-income portfolio managers often approximate changes in a bond portfolio's present value (PV) by substituting market value (MV)-weighted averages for modified duration and convexity into Equation 3.

$$AvgModDur = \sum_{j=1}^{J} ModDur_j \times \left(\frac{MV_j}{MV}\right) \quad (4)$$

$$AvgConvexity = \sum_{j=1}^{J} Convexity_j \times \left(\frac{MV_j}{MV}\right) \quad (5)$$

Active managers focus on the *incremental* effect on these summary statistics for a portfolio by adding or selling bonds in the portfolio or by buying and selling fixed-income derivatives. Duration is a first-order effect that attempts to capture a linear relationship between bond prices and yield-to-maturity. Convexity is a second-order effect that describes a bond's price behavior for larger movements in yield-to-maturity. This additional term is a positive amount on a traditional (option-free) fixed-rate bond for either a yield increase or decrease, causing the yield/price relationship to deviate from a linear relationship. Because duration is a first-order effect, it follows that duration management—accounting for changes in yield curve level—will usually be a more important consideration for portfolio performance than convexity management. This is consistent with our previous discussion of the relative importance of the yield curve level, slope, and curvature. As we shall see later in this lesson, convexity management is more closely associated with yield curve slope and shape changes.

All else equal, positive convexity is a valuable feature in bonds. If a bond has higher positive convexity than an otherwise identical bond, then the bond price increases more if interest rates decrease (and decreases less if interest rates increase) than the duration estimate would suggest. Said another way, the expected price change of a bond with positive convexity for a given rate change will be higher than the price change of an identical-duration, lower-convexity bond. This price behavior is valuable to investors; therefore, a bond with higher convexity might be expected to have a lower yield-to-maturity than a similar-duration bond with less convexity. All else equal, bonds with longer durations have higher convexity than bonds with shorter durations. Also, as noted earlier in the curriculum, convexity is affected by the *dispersion* of cash flows—that is, the *variance* of the times to receipt of cash flow. Higher cash flow dispersion leads to an increase in convexity. This is in contrast to Macaulay duration, which measures the weighted *average* of the times to cash flow receipt. Note that throughout this lesson, we will use "raw" versus scaled (or "raw" divided by 100) convexity figures often seen on trading platforms. We can see the convexity effect by comparing two bond portfolios:

> **EXAMPLE 1**
>
> ### US Treasury Securities Portfolio
>
> | Tenor | Coupon | Price | ModDur | Convexity |
> |-------|--------|-------|--------|-----------|
> | 2y | 0.250% | $100 | 1.994 | 5.0 |
> | 5y | 0.875% | $100 | 4.880 | 26.5 |
> | 10y | 2.000% | $100 | 9.023 | 90.8 |
>
> Consider two $50 million portfolios: Portfolio A is fully invested in the 5-year Treasury bond, and Portfolio B is an investment split between the 2-year (58.94%) and the 10-year (41.06%) bonds. The Portfolio B weights were chosen to (approximately) match the 5-year bond duration of 4.88. How will the value of these portfolios change if all three Treasury yields-to-maturity immediately rise or fall by 50 bps?
>
> Using Equation 3, we can derive the percentage value change for Portfolios A and B as well as the dollar value of each $50 million investment:
>
> | Portfolio | + 50 bps % Δ Price | + 50 bps Δ Price | – 50 bps % Δ Price | – 50 bps Δ Price |
> |-----------|--------------------|------------------|--------------------|------------------|
> | A | –2.407% | ($1,203,438) | 2.473% | $1,236,563 |
> | B | –2.390% | ($1,194,883) | 2.490% | $1,245,170 |
>
> For example, for the case of a 50 bp increase in rates:
>
> Portfolio A
>
> $$-2.407\% = (-4.880 \times 0.005) + [0.5 \times 26.5 \times (0.005^2)]$$
>
> Portfolio B
>
> $$-2.390\% = 0.5894 \times \{[-1.994 \times 0.005] + [0.5 \times 5 \times (0.005^2)]\} + 0.4106 \times \{[-9.023 \times 0.005] + [0.5 \times 90.8 \times (0.005^2)]\}$$
>
> Note that Portfolio B gains *more* ($8,607) than Portfolio A when rates fall 50 bps and loses *less* ($8,555) than Portfolio A when rates rise by 50 bps.

The first portfolio concentrated in a single intermediate maturity is often referred to as a **bullet** portfolio. The second portfolio, with similar duration but combining short- and long-term maturities, is a **barbell** portfolio. Although the bullet and barbell have the same duration, the barbell's higher convexity (40.229 versus 26.5 for the bullet) results in a larger gain as yields-to-maturity fall and a smaller loss when yields-to-maturity rise. Convexity is therefore valuable when interest rate volatility is expected to rise. This dynamic tends to cause investors to bid up prices on more convex, longer-maturity bonds, which drives changes in yield curve shape. As a result, the long end of the curve may decline or even invert (or invert further), increasing the curvature of the yield curve.

EXAMPLE 2

Portfolio Convexity

Portfolio convexity is a second-order effect that causes the value of a portfolio to respond to a change in yields-to-maturity in a non-linear manner. Which of the following best describes the effect of positive portfolio convexity for a given change in yield-to-maturity?

a Convexity causes a greater increase in price for a decline in yields-to-maturity and a greater decrease in price when yields-to-maturity rise.

b Convexity causes a smaller increase in price for a decline in yields-to-maturity and a greater decrease in price when yields-to-maturity rise.

c Convexity causes a greater increase in price for a decline in yields-to-maturity and a smaller decrease in price when yields-to-maturity rise.

The correct answer is c. Note that the convexity component of Equation 3 involves squaring the change in yield-to-maturity, or [½ × Convexity × $(\Delta Yield)^2$], making the term positive as long as portfolio convexity is positive. This adds to the overall portfolio gain when yields-to-maturity decline and reduces the portfolio loss when yields-to-maturity rise.

YIELD CURVE STRATEGIES

b formulate a portfolio positioning strategy given forward interest rates and an interest rate view that coincides with the market view

c formulate a portfolio positioning strategy given forward interest rates and an interest rate view that diverges from the market view in terms of rate level, slope, and shape

d formulate a portfolio positioning strategy based upon expected changes in interest rate volatility

e evaluate a portfolio's sensitivity using key rate durations of the portfolio and its benchmark

Earlier in the curriculum, we established that yield curves are usually upward-sloping, with diminishing marginal yield-to-maturity increases at longer tenors—that is, flatter at longer maturities. As nominal yields-to-maturity incorporate an expected inflation premium, positively sloped yield curves are consistent with market expectations of rising or stable future inflation and relatively strong economic growth. Investor expectations of higher yields-to-maturity for assuming the increased interest rate risk of long-term bonds also contribute to this positive slope. Active managers often begin with growth and inflation forecasts, which they then translate into expected yield curve level, slope, and/or curvature changes. If their forecasts coincide with today's yield curve, managers will choose active strategies that are consistent with a static or stable yield curve. If their forecasts differ from what today's yield curve implies about these future yield curve characteristics, managers will position the portfolio to generate excess return based upon this divergent view, within the constraints of their investment mandate, using the cash and derivatives strategies we discuss next.

3.1 Static Yield Curve

A portfolio manager may believe that bonds are fairly priced and that the existing yield curve will remain unchanged over an investment horizon.

The two basic ways in which a manager may actively position a bond portfolio versus a benchmark index to generate excess return from a static or stable yield curve is to increase risk by adding either duration or leverage to the portfolio. If the yield curve is upward-sloping, longer duration exposure will result in a higher yield-to-maturity over time, while the "repo carry" trade (the difference between a higher-yielding instrument purchased and a lower-yielding (financing) instrument) will also generate excess returns.

Starting with cash-based instruments, "buy-and-hold" is an obvious strategy if the yield curve is upward-sloping. In an active context, this involves buying bonds with duration above the benchmark without active trading during a subsequent period. If the relationship between long- and short-term yields-to-maturity remains stable over this period, the manager is rewarded with higher return from the incremental duration. "Rolling down" the yield curve, a concept introduced previously, differs slightly from the "buy-and-hold" approach in terms of the investment time horizon and expected accumulation. The rolldown return component of Equation 1 (sometimes referred to as "carry-rolldown") incorporates not only coupon income (adjusted over time for any price difference from par) but also additional return from the passage of time and the investor's ability to sell the shorter-maturity bond in the future at a higher price (lower yield-to-maturity due to the upward-sloping yield curve) at the end of the investment horizon. If the yield curve is upward-sloping, buying bonds with a maturity *beyond* the investment horizon offers a total return (higher coupon plus price appreciation) greater than the purchase of a bond with maturity *matching* the investment horizon if the curve remains static. Finally, a common strategy known as a repurchase agreement or repo trade may be used in an expected stable rate environment to add leverage risk to the portfolio. The repo market involves buying a long-term security and financing it at a short-term rate below the long-term yield-to-maturity—that is, earning a positive "repo carry." At the end of the trade, the bond is sold and the repo is unwound. These cash-based strategies are summarized in Exhibits 5 and 6.

Exhibit 5	Cash-Based Static Yield Curve Strategies		
Strategy	**Description**	**Income**	**Objective**
Buy-and-hold	Constant without active trading	Coupon income	Add duration beyond target given static yield curve view
Rolling down the yield curve	Constant, with Δ Price as maturity shortens	Coupon income +/− Rolldown return	Add duration and increased return if future shorter-term yields are below current yield-to-maturity
Repo carry trade	Finance bond purchase in repo market	(Coupon income +/− Rolldown return)— Financing cost	Generate repo carry return if coupon plus rolldown exceeds financing cost

Yield Curve Strategies

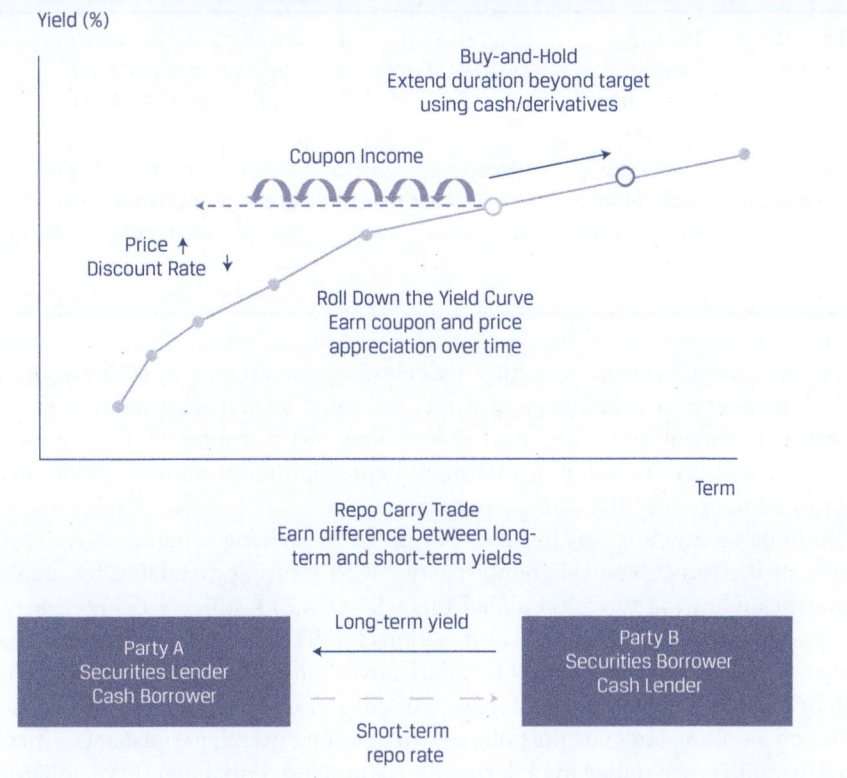

Exhibit 6 Carry, Rolldown, and Buy-and-Hold Strategies under a Static Yield Curve

Excess return under these strategies depends upon stable rate levels and yield curve shape. Note that a more nuanced "buy-and-hold" strategy under this scenario could also involve less liquid and higher-yielding government bonds (such as off-the-run bonds). The lack of portfolio turnover may make the strategy seem passive, but in fact it may be quite aggressive as it introduces liquidity risk, a topic addressed in detail later in the curriculum. The ability to benefit from price appreciation by selling a shorter-dated bond at a premium when rolling down (or riding) the yield curve hinges on a reasonably static and upward-sloping yield curve. Not only will the repo carry be maintained under this yield curve scenario, but it also will generate excess return due to the reduced cash outlay versus a term bond purchase.

Active managers whose investment mandate extends to the use of synthetic means to increase risk by adding duration or leverage to the portfolio might consider using the derivatives-based strategies in Exhibit 7 to increase duration exposure beyond a benchmark target. Although the long futures example is similar to rolling down the yield curve, it relies solely on price appreciation rather than bond coupon income. The receive-fixed swap, on the other hand, is similar to the cash-based repo carry trade, but the investor receives the fixed swap rate and pays a market reference rate (MRR), which is often referred to as "swap carry."

Exhibit 7 Derivatives-Based Static Yield Curve Strategies

Strategy	Description	Targeted Return	Goal
Long futures position	Purchase contract for future bond delivery	(Δ Price / Δ Bond yield) – Margin cost	Synthetically increase duration (up-front margin and daily mark-to-market valuation)
Receive-fixed swap	Fixed-rate receiver on an interest rate swap	(Swap rate – MRR) + (Δ Swap mark-to-market / Δ Swap yield)	Synthetically increase portfolio duration (up-front / mark-to-market collateral) + / – Swap carry

As mentioned previously in the curriculum, global exchanges offer a wide range of derivatives contracts across swap, bond, and short-term market reference rates for different settlement dates, and over the counter (OTC) contracts may be uniquely tailored to end user needs. Our treatment here is limited to futures and swaps and will extend to options in a later section.

Although margining was historically limited to exchange-traded derivatives, the advent of derivatives central counterparty (CCP) clearing mandated by regulatory authorities following the 2008 global financial crisis to mitigate counterparty risk has given rise to similar cash flow implications for OTC derivatives. Active managers using both exchange-traded and OTC derivatives must therefore maintain sufficient cash or eligible collateral to fulfill margin or collateral requirements. They must also factor any resulting foregone portfolio return into their overall performance. That said, since the initial cash outlay for a derivative is limited to initial margin or collateral as opposed to the full price for a cash bond purchase, derivatives have a high degree of implicit leverage. That is, a small move in price/yield can have a very large effect on a derivative's mark-to-market value (MTM) relative to the margin posted. Exhibit 8 shows these cash flow mechanics. This outsized price effect makes derivatives effective instruments for fixed-income portfolio management.

Exhibit 8 Derivatives Cash Flow Impact for a Fixed-Income Portfolio

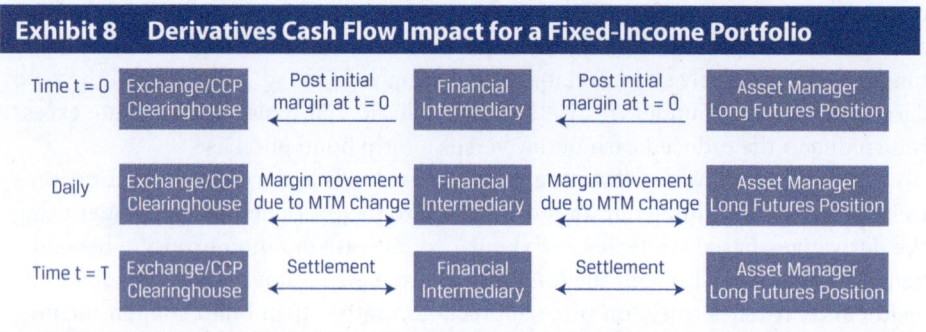

For example, bond futures involve a contract to take delivery of a bond on a specific future date. Changes in the futures contract value mirror those of the underlying bond's price over time, allowing an investor to create an exposure profile similar to a long bond position by purchasing this contract with a fraction of the outlay of a cash bond purchase. While futures contracts are covered in detail elsewhere in the curriculum, for our purposes here it is important to establish the basis point value (BPV) of a futures contract. Most government bond futures are traded and settled using the least costly or cheapest-to-deliver (CTD) bond among those eligible for future delivery. For example, the CME Group's Ultra 10-Year US Treasury Note Futures contract specifies delivery of an original 10-year issue Treasury security with not less than 9 years, five months and not more than 10 years to maturity with an assumed 6% yield-to-maturity and contract size of $100,000. The "duration" of the bond futures contract is assumed to match that of the CTD security. In order to determine the futures BPV, we use the following approximation introduced previously:

$$\text{Futures BPV} \approx \text{BPV}_{\text{CTD}} / \text{CF}_{\text{CTD}}, \tag{6}$$

where CF_{CTD} is the conversion factor for the CTD security. For government bond futures with a fixed basket of underlying bonds, such as Australian Treasury bond futures, the futures BPV simply equals the BPV of an underlying basket of bonds.

The manager in Example 1 can replicate the 10-year Treasury exposure using futures by matching the BPV of the cash bond. As explained elsewhere, the BPV of the $20.53 million (or 41.06% × $50 million) 10-year Treasury position equals the modified duration (9.023) multiplied by the full price (also known as the money duration) times one basis point, or $18,524. If the CTD security under the Ultra 10-Year Futures contract is a Treasury bond also priced at par but with 9.5 years remaining to maturity, modified duration of 8.84, and a conversion factor of 0.684, then each $100,000 futures contract has a BPV of $129.24 ($88.40/0.684). The manager must therefore buy approximately 143 futures contracts ($18,524/$129.24) to replicate the exposure. Note that as shown in Exhibit 8, this will involve an outlay of initial margin and margin movement due to MTM changes rather than investment of full principal.

An interest rate swap involves the net exchange of fixed-for-floating payments, where the fixed rate (swap rate) is derived from short-term market reference rates for a given tenor. As shown in Exhibit 9, the swap contract may be seen as a combination of bonds, namely a fixed-rate bond versus a floating-rate bond of the same maturity.

Exhibit 9   Swaps as a Duration Management Tool

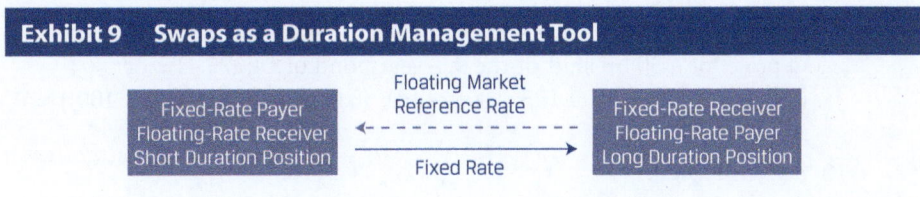

Note the similarities between the "carry" trade in Exhibit 5 and the receive-fixed interest rate swap position on the right in Exhibit 9. The fixed-rate receiver is "long" a fixed-rate term bond and "short" a floating-rate bond, giving rise to an exposure profile that mimics a "long" cash bond position by increasing duration. A swap's BPV may be estimated using Equation 7.

$$\text{Swap BPV} = \text{ModDur}_{\text{Swap}} \times \text{Swap Notional}/10{,}000. \tag{7}$$

The difference between the receive-fixed swap and long fixed-rate bond positions is best understood via an example.

EXAMPLE 3

Calculating Bond versus Swap Returns

Say a UK-based manager seeks to extend duration beyond an index by adding 10-year exposure. The manager considers either buying and holding a 10-year, 2.25% semi-annual coupon UK government bond priced at £93.947, with a corresponding yield-to-maturity of 2.9535%, or entering a new 10-year, GBP receive-fixed interest rate swap at 2.8535% versus the six-month GBP MRR currently set at 0.5925%. The swap has a modified duration of 8.318. We compare the results of both strategies over a six-month time horizon for a £100 million par value during which both the bond yield-to-maturity and swap rates fall 50 bps. We ignore day count details in the calculation.

Position	Income	Price Appreciation/MTM	Gain in 6 Months
10y UK bond	£1,125,000	£4,337,779	£5,462,778
10y GBP swap	£1,130,500	£4,234,260	£5,364,760

The relevant return components from Equation 1 are income, namely coupon income for the bond versus "carry" for the swap, and E (Δ Price due to investor's view of benchmark yield) in the form of price appreciation for the bond versus an MTM gain for the swap:

10-Year UK Government Bond:

Coupon income = £1,125,000, or (2.25%/2) × £100 million.

Price appreciation = £4,337,779. Using Excel, this is the difference between the 10-year, or [PV (0.029535/2, 20, 1.125, 100)], and the 9.5-year bond at the lower yield-to-maturity, or [PV (0.024535/2, 19, 1.125, 100)] × £1 million.

We can separate bond price appreciation into two components:

Rolldown return: The difference between the 10-year and 9.5-year PV with *no* change in yield-to-maturity of £262,363, or [PV (0.029535/2, 20, 1.125, 100)] − [PV (0.029535/2, 19, 1.125, 100)] × £1 million].

(Δ Price due to investor's view of benchmark yield): The difference in price for a 50 bp shift of the 9.5-year bond of £4,075,415, or [PV (0.029535/2, 19, 1.125, 100)] − [PV (0.024535/2, 19, 1.125, 100)] × £1 million.

10-Year GBP Swap:

Swap carry = £1,130,500, or [(2.8535% − 0.5925%)/2] × £100,000,000.

Swap MTM gain = £4,234,260. The swap MTM gain equals the difference between the fixed leg and floating leg, which is currently at par. The fixed leg equals the 9.5-year swap value given a 50 bp shift in the fixed swap rate, which is £104,234,260, or [PV(0.023535/2, 19, 2.8535/2, 100)] × £1 million, and the floating leg is priced at par and therefore equal to £100,000,000.

We can use Equation 7 to derive an approximate swap MTM change of £4,159,000 by multiplying swap BPV (8.318 × £100 million) by 50 bps. As in the case of a bond future, the cash outlay for the swap is limited to required collateral or margin for the transaction as opposed to the bond's full cash price. Note that for the purposes of this example, we have ignored any interest on the difference between the bond investment and the cash outlay for the swap.

While these strategies are designed to gain from a static or stable interest rate term structure, we now turn to portfolio positioning in a changing yield curve environment.

> **EXAMPLE 4**
>
> ### Static Yield Curve Strategies under Curve Inversion
>
> An investment manager who pursues the cash-based yield curve strategies described in Exhibit 5 faces an inverted yield curve (with a decline in long-term yields-to-maturity and a sharp increase in short-term yields-to-maturity) instead. Which of the following is the *least* likely portfolio outcome under this scenario?
>
> **a** The manager realizes a loss on a "buy-and-hold" position that extends duration beyond that of the index.
>
> **b** The manager faces negative carry when financing a bond purchase in the repo market.
>
> **c** The manager is able to reinvest coupon income from a yield curve roll-down strategy at a higher short-term yield-to-maturity.
>
> ### Solution:
>
> The correct answer is a. The fall in long-term yields-to-maturity will lead to price *appreciation* under the "buy-and-hold" strategy. The difference between long-term and short-term yields-to-maturity in b will fall, leading to negative carry if short-term yields-to-maturity rise sharply. As for c, higher short-term yields-to-maturity will enable the manager to reinvest bond coupon payments at a higher rate.

3.2 Dynamic Yield Curve

Exhibits 1 through 3 show that yield curves are dynamic over time, with significant changes in the level, slope, and curvature of rates across maturities. Unless otherwise specified, the sole focus here is on instantaneous yield-to-maturity changes affecting E(Δ Price due to investor's view of benchmark yields), the third component of Equation 1.

3.2.1 *Divergent Rate Level View*

The principal components analysis cited earlier underscores that rate level changes are the key driver of changes in single bond or bond portfolio values. The first term in Equation 3 shows that bond value changes result from yield-to-maturity changes multiplied by a duration statistic. For active fixed-income managers with a divergent rate level view, positioning the portfolio to increase profit as yield levels fall or minimizing losses as yield levels rise is of primary importance. To be clear, a divergent rate level view implies an expectation of a *parallel* shift in the yield curve, as shown in Exhibit 10.

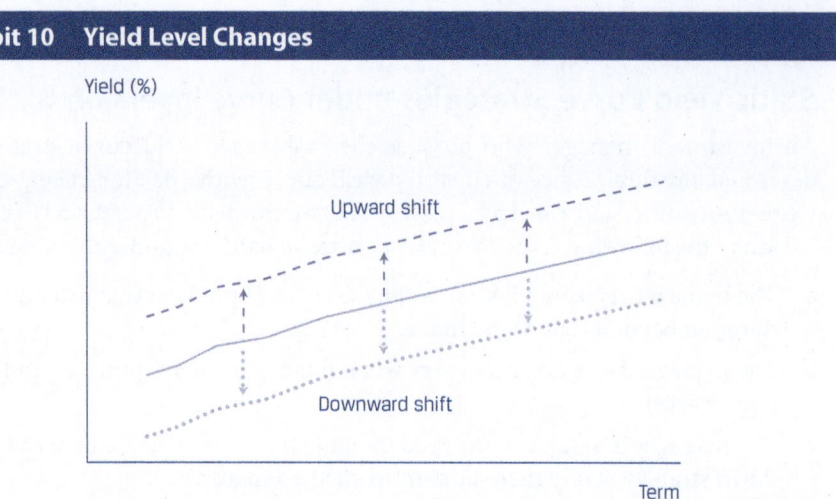

Exhibit 10 Yield Level Changes

Exhibit 1 shows a general decline in bond yield levels, referred to as a bull market, since 2007. This trend began in late 1981 when the 10-year US Treasury yield-to-maturity peaked at nearly 16%, a consequence of contractionary US Federal Reserve monetary policy in which the short-term federal funds rate was raised to 20% to combat double-digit inflation. Extending duration beyond a target index over this period was a winning active strategy, despite occasional periods of yield increases. Exhibit 11 summarizes the major strategies an active manager might pursue if she expects lower yield levels and downside risks.

Exhibit 11 Major Yield Curve Strategies to Increase Portfolio Duration

Strategy	Description	Expected Excess Return	Downside Risks
Cash bond purchase ("bullet")	Extend duration with longer-dated bonds	Price appreciation as yield-to-maturity declines	Higher yield levels
Receive-fixed swap	Fixed-rate receiver on an interest rate swap	Swap MTM gain plus "carry" (fixed minus floating rate)	Higher swap yield levels and/or higher floating rates
Long futures position	Purchase contract for forward bond delivery	Futures MTM gain – Margin cost	Higher bond yields and/or higher margin cost

Assume the "index" portfolio equally weights the 2-, 5-, and 10-year Treasuries priced at par from Example 1, while a higher duration "active" portfolio is weighted 25% for 2- and 5-year Treasuries, respectively, and 50% in 10-year Treasuries. Average portfolio statistics are summarized here:

Portfolio	Coupon	Modified Duration	Convexity
Index	1.042%	5.299	40.8
Active (25/25/50)	1.281%	6.230	53.3

We can see from this table that the active portfolio has a blended coupon nearly 24 bps above that of the index.

We now turn to the impact of a parallel yield curve shift on the index versus active portfolios. Assuming an instantaneous 30 bp downward shift in yields-to-maturity, the index portfolio value would rise by approximately 1.608%, or $(-5.299 \times -0.003) + 0.5 \times (40.8) \times (-0.003^2)$, versus an estimated 1.893% increase for the actively managed portfolio, a positive difference of nearly $285,000 for a $100 million portfolio.

EXAMPLE 5

Portfolio Impact of Higher Yield-to-Maturity Levels

Consider a $50 million Treasury portfolio equally weighted between 2-, 5-, and 10-year Treasuries using parameters from the prior example as the index, and an active portfolio with 20% each in 2- and 5-year Treasuries and the remaining 60% invested in 10-year Treasuries. Which of the following is closest to the active versus index portfolio value change due to a 40 bp rise in yields-to-maturity?

a Active portfolio declines by $181,197 more than the index portfolio

b Active portfolio declines by $289,915 more than the index portfolio

c Index portfolio declines by $289,915 more than the active portfolio

Solution:

The correct answer is b. First, we must establish average portfolio statistics for the 20/20/60 portfolio using a weighted average of duration (6.79 versus 5.299 for the index) and convexity (60.8 versus 40.8 for the index). Second, using these portfolio statistics, we must calculate $\%\Delta PV^{Full}$, as shown in Equation 3, for both the index and active portfolios, which are −2.087% for the index and −2.667% for the active portfolio, respectively. Finally, we multiply the difference of −0.58% by the $50 million notional to get −$289,915.

Receive-fixed swaps or long futures positions may be used in place of a cash bond strategy to take an active view on rates. Note that most fixed-income managers will tend to favor option-free over callable bonds if taking a divergent rate level view due to the greater liquidity of option-free bonds. An exception to this arises when investors formulate portfolio positioning strategies based upon expected changes in interest rate volatility, as we will discuss in detail later in this lesson.

As 2020 began, some analysts expected government yields-to-maturity to eventually rise following over a decade of quantitative easing after the 2008 global financial crisis. However, yields instead reached new lows during 2020 when the COVID-19 pandemic caused a sharp economic slowdown, prompting additional monetary and fiscal policy stimulus. If analysts expected a strong economic rebound to increase yield levels, they might seek to lessen the adverse impact of higher rate levels by reducing duration. Exhibit 12 outlines major strategies to achieve this goal.

Exhibit 12 Major Yield Curve Strategies to Reduce Portfolio Duration

Strategy	Description	Expected Excess Return	Downside Risks
Cash bond sale ("bullet")	Reduce duration with short sale/switch to shorter-dated bonds	Smaller price decline as yield-to-maturity increases	Lower yield levels
Pay-fixed (interest rate swap)	Fixed-rate payer on an interest rate swap	Swap MTM gain plus "swap carry" (MRR – Fixed swap rate)	Swap MTM loss amid lower swap yield levels and/or lower floating rates
Short futures position	Sell contract for forward bond delivery	Futures MTM gain – Margin cost	Futures MTM loss amid lower bond yields and/or higher margin cost

Returning to our "index" portfolio of equally weighted 2-, 5-, and 10-year Treasuries, we now consider an active portfolio positioned to reduce downside exposure to higher yields-to-maturity versus the index. In order to limit changes to the bond portfolio, the manager chooses a swap strategy instead.

EXAMPLE 6

Five-Year Pay-Fixed Swap Overlay

In this example, the manager enters into a pay-fixed swap overlay with a notional principal equal to one-half of the size of the total bond portfolio. We will focus solely on first-order effects of yield changes on price (ignoring coupon income and swap carry) to determine the active and index portfolio impact. As the pay-fixed swap is a "short" duration position, it is a negative contribution to portfolio duration and therefore subtracted from rather than added to the portfolio. Recall the $100 million "index" portfolio has a modified duration of 5.299, or (1.994 + 4.88 + 9.023)/3. If the manager enters a $50 million notional 5-year pay-fixed swap with an assumed modified duration of 4.32, the portfolio's modified duration falls to 3.139, or [(5.299 × 100) – (4.32 × 50)]/100. Stated differently, the bond portfolio BPV falls from $52,990 to $31,390 with the swap. For a 25 bp yield increase, this $21,600 reduction in active portfolio BPV reduces the adverse impact of higher rates by approximately $540,000 versus the "index" portfolio.

One point worth noting related to short duration positions is that with the exception of distressed debt situations addressed later in the curriculum, the uncertain cost and availability of individual bonds to borrow and sell short leads many active managers to favor the use of derivatives over short sales to establish a short bond position. Derivatives also facilitate duration changes without interfering with other active bond strategies within in a portfolio.

Portfolio managers frequently use average duration and yield level changes to estimate bond portfolio performance in broad terms. However, these approximations are only reasonable if we assume a parallel yield curve shift. As Exhibits 2 and 3 show, non-parallel changes, or shifts in the slope and/or shape of the yield curve, occur frequently and require closer examination of individual positions and rate changes across maturities.

3.2.2 Divergent Yield Curve Slope View

Exhibit 2 established that while a positively sloped yield curve prevails under most economic scenarios, this difference between long-term and short-term yields-to-maturity can vary significantly over time. Changes in monetary policy, as well as expectations for growth and inflation, affect yields differently across the term structure, resulting in an increase (steepening) or decrease (flattening) in this spread. Although the **barbell** strategy combining extreme maturities is often referred to in a long-only context as in Example 1, here we take a more generalized approach in which the short-term and long-term security positions within the barbell trade may move in opposite directions—that is, combining a "short" and a "long" position. This type of barbell is an effective tool employed by managers to position a bond portfolio for yield curve steepening or flattening changes, as shown in Exhibit 13.

Exhibit 13 Barbell Strategy for a Yield Curve Slope Change

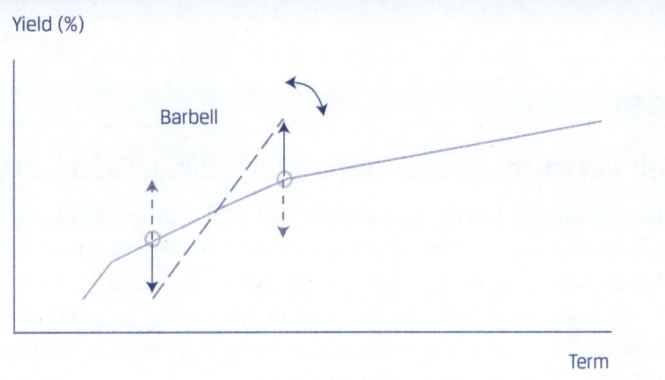

A manager could certainly use a bullet to increase or decrease exposure to a specific maturity in anticipation of a price change that changes yield curve slope, but a *combination* of positions in both short and long maturities with greater cash flow dispersion is particularly well-suited to position for yield curve slope changes or twists. Managers combine long or short positions in either maturity segment to take advantage of expected yield curve slope changes—which may be duration neutral, net long, or short duration depending upon *how* the curve is expected to steepen or flatten in the future. Also, in some instances, the investment policy statement may allow managers to use bonds, swaps, and/or futures to achieve this objective. Finally, while not all strategies shown are cash neutral, here we focus solely on portfolio value changes due to yield changes, ignoring any associated funding or other costs that might arise as a result.

Yield curve steepener strategies seek to gain from an increase in yield curve slope, or a greater difference between long-term and short-term yields-to-maturity. This may be achieved by combining a "long" shorter-dated bond position with a "short" longer-dated bond position. For example, assume an active manager seeks to benefit from yield curve steepening with a net zero duration by purchasing the 2-year Treasury and selling the 10-year Treasury securities from our earlier example, both of which are priced at par.

Tenor	Coupon	Position ($ MM)	Modified Duration	Convexity
Long 2y	0.25%	163.8	1.994	5.0
Short 10y	2.00%	−36.2	9.023	90.8

Note that here and throughout the lesson, negative portfolio positions reflect a "short" position. We can approximate the impact of *parallel* yield curve changes using portfolio duration and convexity. Portfolio duration is approximately zero, or [1.994 × 163.8/(163.8 − 36.2)] + [9.023 × −36.2/(163.8 − 36.2)], and portfolio convexity equals −19.34, or [5.0 × 163.8/(163.8 − 36.2)] + [90.8 × −36.2/(163.8 − 36.2). A 25 bp increase in *both* 2-year and 10-year Treasury yields-to-maturity therefore has no duration effect on the portfolio, although negative convexity leads to a 0.006%, or $7,712 decline in portfolio value, or $127,600,000 × 0.5 × −19.34 × 0.0025^2.

However, changes in the *difference* between short- and long-term yields-to-maturity are not captured by portfolio duration or convexity but rather require assessment of individual positions. For example, if yield curve *slope* increases from 175 bps to 225 bps due to a 25 bp *decline* in 2-year yields-to-maturity and a 25 bp *rise* in 10-year yields-to-maturity, the portfolio increases in value by $1,625,412 as follows:

2y: $819,102 = $163,800,000 × (−1.994 × −0.0025 + 0.5 × 5.0 × $−0.0025^2$)
10y: $806,310 = −$36,200,000 × (−9.023 × 0.0025 + 0.5 × 90.8 × 0.0025^2)

EXAMPLE 7

Barbell Performance under a Flattening Yield Curve

Consider a Treasury portfolio consisting of a $124.6 million long 2-year zero-coupon Treasury with an annualized 2% yield-to-maturity and a short $25.41 million 10-year zero-coupon bond with a 4% yield-to-maturity. Calculate the net portfolio duration and solve for the first-order change in portfolio value based upon modified duration assuming a 25 bp rise in 2-year yield-to-maturity and a 30 bp decline in 10-year yield-to-maturity.

First, recall from earlier in the curriculum that Macaulay duration (MacDur) is equal to maturity for zero-coupon bonds and modified duration (ModDur) is equal to MacDur/1+r, where r is the yield per period. We can therefore solve for the modified duration of the 2-year zero as 1.96 (= 2/1.02) and the 10-year zero as 9.62 (= 10/1.04), so net portfolio duration equals zero, or [124.6/(124.6 − 25.41) × 1.96] + [−25.4/(124.6 − 25.41) × 9.62].

We may show that the 2-year Treasury BPV is close to $24,430 (= 1.96 × 124,600,000/10,000) and the 10-year Treasury position BPV is also approximately $24,430 (= 9.61 × 25,410,000/10,000), but it is a short position. Therefore a 25 bp *increase* in 2-year yield-to-maturity *decreases* portfolio value by $610,750 (25 bps × $24,430), while a 30 bp *decrease* in the 10-year yield-to-maturity also *decreases* portfolio value (due to the short position) by an additional $732,900 (= 30 bps × $24,430), for a total approximate portfolio *loss* of $1,343,650.

The portfolio manager is indifferent as to whether the portfolio gain from a greater slope arises due to a greater change in value from short-term or long-term yield movements as the duration is matched between the two positions. Two variations of a steeper yield curve adapted from Smith (2014) are shown in Exhibit 14.

Exhibit 14 Yield Curve Slope Changes—Steepening

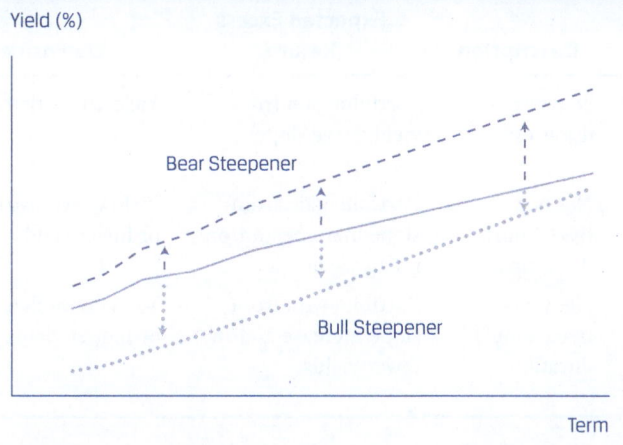

In an earlier lesson on establishing a rate view, we highlighted a **bull steepening** scenario under which short-term yields-to-maturity fall by more than long-term yields-to-maturity if the monetary authority cuts benchmark rates to stimulate economic activity during a recession. Exhibit 15 shows the bull steepening that occurred in the UK gilt yield curve amid the 2008 global financial crisis. After reaching a cycle peak of 5.75% in July 2007, the Bank of England cut its monetary policy base rate six times, down to 2.00% in early December 2008, due to weakening economic conditions and financial market stress.

Exhibit 15 UK Government Yields, 2007 versus 2008 (Year End)

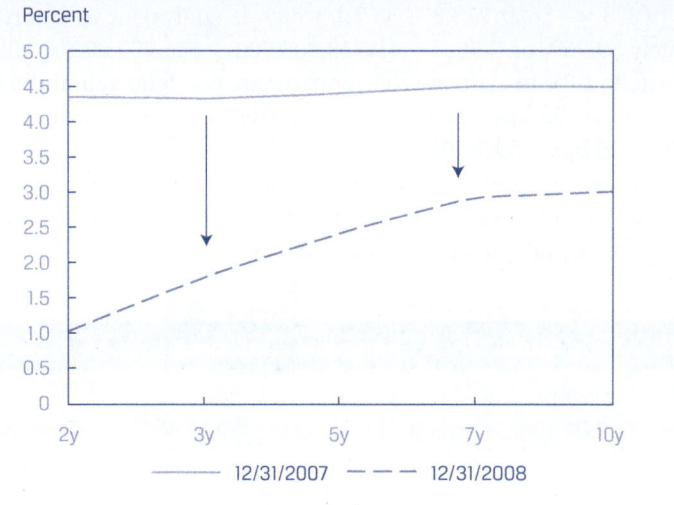

Source: Bloomberg.

On the other hand, a **bear steepening** occurs when long-term yields-to-maturity rise more than short-term yields-to-maturity. This could result from a jump in long-term rates amid higher growth and inflation expectations while short-term rates remain unchanged. In this case, an analyst might expect the next central bank policy change to be a monetary tightening to curb inflation.

Bull or bear steepening expectations will change the strategy an active fixed-income manager might pursue, as seen in Exhibit 16.

Exhibit 16 Yield Curve Steepener Strategies

Strategy	Description	Expected Excess Return	Downside Risks
Duration neutral	Net zero duration	Portfolio gain from yield curve slope increase	Yield curve flattening
Bear steepener	Net negative ("short") duration	Portfolio gain from slope increase and/or rising yields	Yield curve flattening and/or lower yields
Bull steepener	Net positive ("long") duration	Portfolio gain from slope increase and/or lower yields	Yield curve flattening and/or higher yields

For example, assume an active manager expects the next yield curve change to be a bull steepening and establishes the following portfolio using the same 2-year and 10-year Treasury securities as in our prior examples.

Tenor	Coupon	Position ($ MM)	Modified Duration	Convexity
Long 2y	0.25%	213.8	1.994	5.0
Short 10y	2.00%	−36.2	9.023	90.8

In contrast to the earlier duration-matched steepener, the bull steepener increases the 2-year long Treasury position by $50 million, introducing a net long duration position to capitalize on an anticipated greater decline in short-term yields-to-maturity. We can see this by solving for portfolio duration of 0.5613, or [1.994 × 213.8/(213.8 − 36.2)] + [9.023 × −36.2/(213.8 − 36.2)], which is equivalent to a portfolio BPV of approximately $9,969, or 0.5613 × [($213,800,000 − $36,200,000)/10,000]. We may use this portfolio BPV to estimate the approximate portfolio gain if the 2-year yield-to-maturity falls by 25 bps more than the 10-year yield-to-maturity, which is equal to $249,225 (= 25 bps × $9,969).

Yield curve flattening involves an anticipated narrowing of the difference between long-term and short-term yields-to-maturity, two basic variations of which are shown in Exhibit 17 and are adapted from Smith (2014).

Exhibit 17 Yield Curve Slope Changes—Flattening

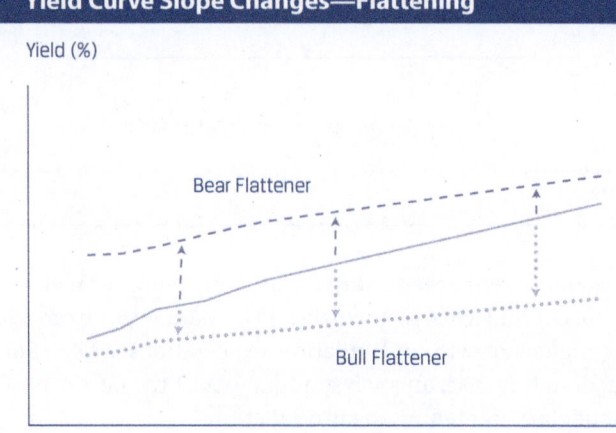

Yield Curve Strategies

A flatter yield curve may follow monetary policy actions due to changing growth and inflation expectations. For example, a **bear flattening** scenario might follow the bear steepening move seen in Exhibit 15 if policymakers respond to rising inflation expectations and higher long-term rates by raising short-term policy rates. It was established earlier in the curriculum that investors sell higher risk assets and buy default risk-free government bonds in a flight to quality during highly uncertain markets, a situation which often contributes to **bull flattening** as long-term rates fall more than short-term rates. Flattener strategies may use a barbell strategy, which reverses the exposure profile of a steepener—namely, a "short" short-term bond position and a "long" long-term bond position. The bull and bear variations of this strategy are summarized in Exhibit 18.

Exhibit 18 Yield Curve Flattener Strategies

Strategy	Description	Expected Excess Return	Downside Risks
Duration neutral	Net zero duration position	Portfolio gain from yield curve slope decrease	Yield curve steepening
Bear flattener	Net negative duration position	Portfolio gain from slope decrease and/or rising yields	Yield curve steepening and/or lower yields
Bull flattener	Net positive duration position	Portfolio gain from slope decrease and/or lower yields	Yield curve steepening and/or higher yields

Say, for example, a French investor expects the government yield curve to flatten over the next six months following years of quantitative easing by the European Central Bank through 2019. Her lack of a view as to whether this will occur amid lower or higher rates causes her to choose a duration neutral flattener using available French government (OAT) zero-coupon securities. She decides to enter the following trade at the beginning of 2020:

Tenor	Yield	Price	Notional (€ MM)	Modified Duration	Position BPV	Convexity
Short 2y	−0.65%	€101.313	−83.24	2.013	(€16,975)	6.1
Long 10y	0.04%	€99.601	17.05	9.996	€16,977	110

Note that as the Excel PRICE function returns a #NUM! error value for bonds with negative yields-to-maturity, we calculate the 2-year OAT zero-coupon bond price of 101.313 using $100/(1 - 0.0065)^2$. The initial portfolio BPV close to zero tells us that parallel yield curve shifts will have little effect on portfolio value, while the short 2-year and long 10-year trades position the manager to profit from a decline in the current 69 bp spread between 2- and 10-year OAT yields-to-maturity. After six months, the portfolio looks as follows:

Tenor	Yield	Price	Notional (€ MM)	Modified Duration	Convexity
Short 1.5y	−0.63%	€100.95	−83.24	1.51	3.8
Long 9.5y	−0.20%	€101.92	17.05	9.52	100.2

At the end of six months (June 2020), the sharp decline in economic growth and inflation expectations due to the COVID-19 pandemic caused the OAT yield curve to flatten as the 10-year yield-to-maturity fell. The six-month barbell return of €695,332 is comprised of rolldown return and yield changes, calculated as follows:

Rolldown Return Zero-coupon bonds usually accrete in value as time passes if rates remain constant and the yield-to-maturity is positive. However, under negative yields-to-maturity, amortization of the bond's premium will typically result in a negative rolldown. In our example, the investor is short the original 2-year zero and therefore realizes a positive rolldown on the short position. Rolldown return on the barbell may be shown to be approximately €277,924, as follows:

"**Short**" **2-year:** $-€83.24 \text{ MM} \times \{[1/(1 + -0.65\%)^{1.5}] - [1/(1 + -0.65\%)^{2}]\}$
"**Long**" **10-year:** $€17.05 \text{ MM} \times \{[1/(1 + 0.04\%)^{9.5}] - [1/(1 + 0.04\%)^{10}]\}$

Δ Price Due to Benchmark Yield Changes The yield difference falls from 69 bps to 43 bps, mostly due to a 24 bp decline in the 10-year yield-to-maturity. Note that the Excel DURATION and MDURATION functions also return a #NUM! error for negative yields-to-maturity. We may use either price changes, as shown next, or the modified duration and convexity statistics as of the end of the investment horizon, just shown, to calculate a return of €417,408 using Equation 3.

"**Short**" **2-year:** $-€83.24 \text{ MM} \times \{[1/(1 + -0.63\%)^{1.5}] - [1/(1 + -0.65\%)^{1.5}]\}$
"**Long**" **10-year:** $€17.05 \text{ MM} \times \{[1/(1 - 0.20\%)^{9.5}] - [1/(1 + 0.04\%)^{9.5}]\}$

As we have considered duration-neutral, long, and short duration strategies to position the portfolio for expected yield curve slope changes, average duration is clearly no longer a sufficient summary statistic. A barbell strategy has greater cash flow dispersion and is therefore more convex than a bullet strategy, implying that its value will decrease by less than a bullet if yields-to-maturity rise and increase by more than a bullet if yields-to-maturity fall. We therefore must consider portfolio convexity in addition to duration when weighing yield curve slope strategies under different scenarios.

3.2.3 Divergent Yield Curve Shape View

As described in Section 2.1, yield curve shape or curvature describes the relationship between short-, medium-, and long-term yields-to-maturity across the term structure. Recall from Equation 2 that we quantify the butterfly spread by subtracting both short- and long-term rates from twice the intermediate yield-to-maturity. Since the difference between short- and medium-term rates is typically greater than that between medium- and long-term rates, the butterfly spread is usually positive, as seen earlier in Exhibit 3.

What factors drive yield curve curvature changes as distinct from rate level or curve slope changes? The segmented markets hypothesis introduced previously offers one explanation: Different market participants face either regulatory or economic asset/liability management constraints that drive the supply and demand for fixed-income instruments within different segments of the term structure. For example, a potential factor driving the apparent butterfly spread volatility in Exhibit 3 is the active central bank purchases of Treasury securities at specific maturities under its quantitative easing policy.

The most common yield curve curvature strategy combines a long bullet with a short barbell portfolio (or vice versa) in what is referred to as a **butterfly strategy** to capitalize on expected yield curve shape changes. The short-term and long-term bond positions of the barbell form the "wings," while the intermediate-term bullet bond position forms the "body" of the butterfly, as illustrated in Exhibit 19. Note that unlike the steepener and flattener cases, the investor is either "long" or "short" *both* a short-term and long-term bond and enters into an intermediate-term bullet trade in the opposite direction.

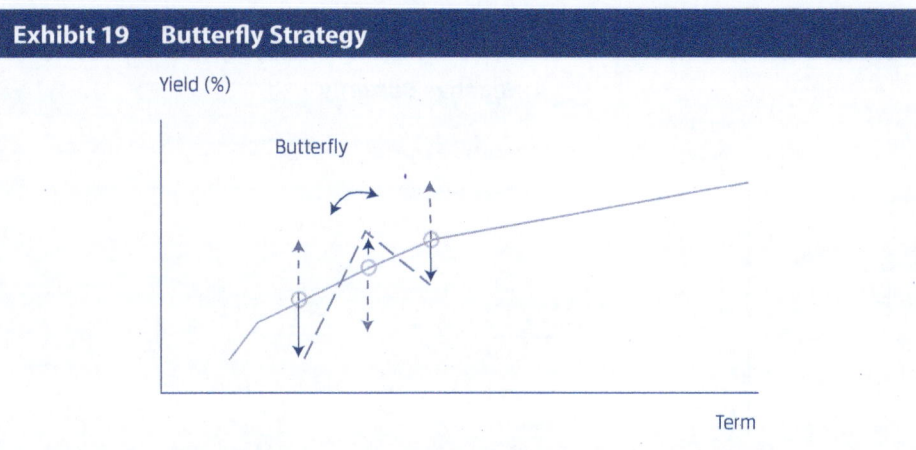

Exhibit 19   Butterfly Strategy

For example, consider a situation in which an active manager expects the butterfly spread to rise due to lower 2- and 10-year yields-to-maturity and a higher 5-year Treasury yield-to-maturity. Using the same portfolio statistics as in prior examples with bonds priced at par, consider the following combined *short* (5-year) bullet and *long* (2-year and 10-year) barbell strategy.

Tenor	Coupon	Position ($ MM)	Modified Duration	Position BPV	Convexity
Long 2y	0.25%	110	1.994	$21,934	5.0
Short 5y	0.875%	−248.3	4.88	($121,170)	26.5
Long 10y	2.00%	110	9.023	$99,253	90.8

While the sum of portfolio positions (−$28.3 MM) shows that the investor has a net "short" bond position, we can verify the strategy is duration neutral by either adding up the position BPVs or calculating the portfolio duration, or [1.994 × (110/−28.3)] + [4.88 × (−248.3/−28.3)] + [9.023 × (110/−28.3)] to confirm that both are approximately zero. The portfolio convexity may be shown as −139.9, or [5.0 × (110/−28.3)] + [26.5 × (−248.3/−28.3)] + [90.8 × (110/−28.3)].

How does this portfolio perform if 2- and 10-year Treasury yields-to-maturity fall by 25 bps each and the 5-year yield-to-maturity rises by 50 bps? A duration-based estimate multiplying each position BPV by the respective yield change gives us an approximation of $9,088,175, or (+25 bps × $21,934) + −(50 bps × −$121,170) + (+25 bps × $99,253). A more precise answer of $9,038,877 incorporating convexity for each position may be derived using Equation 3. You might ask why the precise portfolio value change is below our approximation. The answer lies in the relative *magnitude* of yield changes across the curve. Since the 5-year yield-to-maturity is assumed to increase by 50 bps rather than 25 bps, the convexity impact of the short bullet position outweighs that of the long barbell. Although the portfolio is nearly immune to parallel yield curve changes with a BPV close to zero, the portfolio gain in our example coincides with an increase in the butterfly spread from −50 bps to +100 bps.

This example shows that an active manager's specific view on *how* yield curve shape will change will dictate the details of the combined bullet and barbell strategy. Exhibit 20, adapted from Smith (2014), shows both the **negative butterfly** view just shown as well as a **positive butterfly**, which indicates a *decrease* in the butterfly spread due to an expected rise in short- and long-term yields-to-maturity combined with a lower medium-term yield-to-maturity. Note that a positive butterfly view indicates a decrease in butterfly spread due to a bond's inverse price–yield relationship.

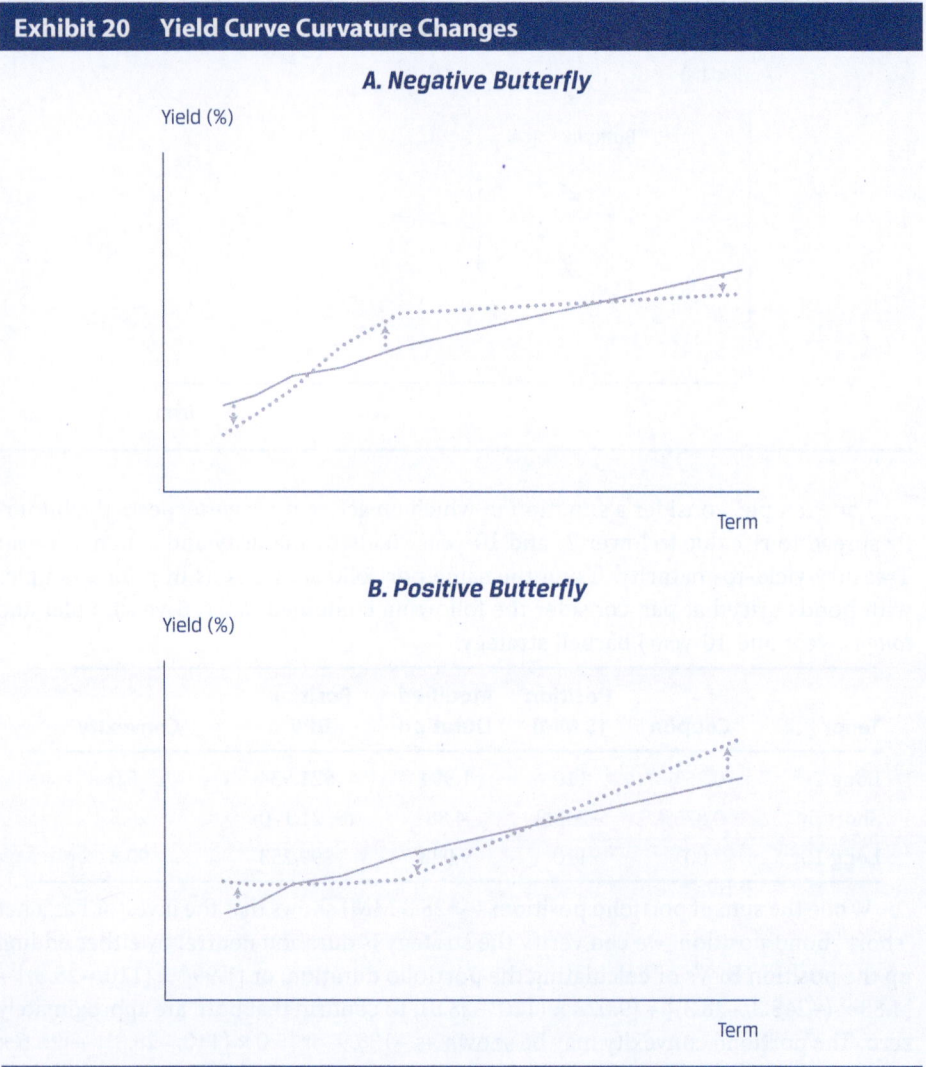

Exhibit 20   Yield Curve Curvature Changes

A. Negative Butterfly

B. Positive Butterfly

Note that as in the case of yield curve slope strategies, the *combination* of a short bullet and long barbell increases portfolio convexity due to higher cash flow dispersion, making this a more meaningful portfolio risk measure for this strategy than average duration (which remains neutral in the Exhibit 20 example). Exhibit 21 summarizes the two butterfly strategies.

Exhibit 21: Yield Curve Curvature Strategies

Expected Scenario	Investor's Expectation	Active Position
Negative butterfly	Lower short- and long-term yields, Higher medium-term yields	Short bullet, Long barbell (long positions in short- and long-term bonds)
Positive butterfly	Higher short- and long-term yields, Lower medium-term yields	Long bullet, Short barbell (short positions in short- and long-term bonds)

3.2.4 Yield Curve Volatility Strategies

While the prior sections focused on strategies using option-free bonds and swaps and futures as opposed to bonds with embedded options and stand-alone option strategies, we now explicitly address the role of volatility in active fixed-income management.

Option-only strategies play a more modest role in overall yield curve management. In markets such as in the United States where a significant portion of outstanding fixed-income bonds, such as asset-backed securities, have embedded options, investors use cash bond positions with embedded options more frequently than stand-alone options to manage volatility. For example, as of 2019 approximately 30% of the Bloomberg Barclays US Aggregate Bond Index was comprised of securitized debt, which mostly includes bonds with embedded options. As outlined earlier, the purchase of a bond call (put) option offers an investor the right, but not the obligation, to buy (sell) an underlying bond at a pre-determined strike price. An active manager's choice between purchasing or selling bonds with embedded call or put options versus an option-free bond with otherwise similar characteristics hinges upon expected changes in the option value and whether the investor is "short" volatility (i.e., has sold the right to call a bond at a fixed price to the issuer), as in the case of callable bonds, or "long" volatility (i.e., owns the right to sell the bond at a fixed price to the issuer), as for putable bonds. Exhibit 22 shows how callable and putable bond prices change versus option-free bonds as yields-to-maturity change.

Exhibit 22 Callable and Putable versus Option-Free Bonds

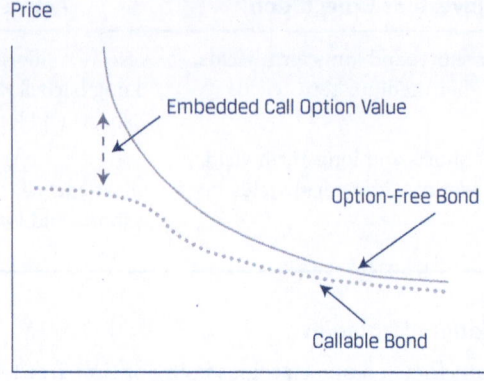

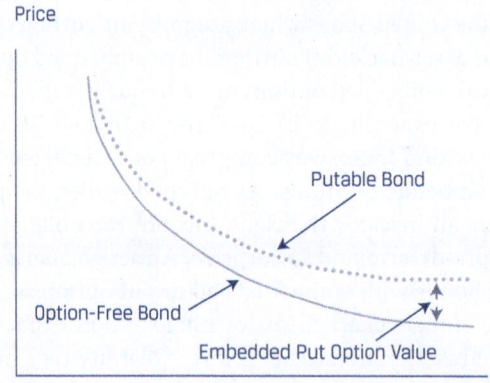

EXAMPLE 8

Option-Free Bonds versus Callable/Putable Bonds

An investment manager is considering an incremental position in a callable, putable, or option-free bond with otherwise comparable characteristics. If she expects a downward parallel shift in the yield curve, it would be most profitable to be:

a long a callable bond.
b short a putable bond.
c long an option-free bond.

Solution:

"C" is correct. The value of a bond with an embedded option is equal to the sum of the value of an option-free bond plus the value to the embedded option. The bond investor can be either long or short the embedded option, depending on the type of bond. With a callable bond, the embedded call option is owned by the issuer of the bond, who can exercise this option if yields-to-maturity decrease (the bond investor is short the call option). With a putable bond, the

> embedded put option is owned by the bond investor, who can exercise the option if yields-to-maturity increase. For a decrease in yields-to-maturity—as given in the question—the value of the embedded call option increases and the value of the embedded put option decreases. This means that a long position in a callable bond ("A") would underperform compared to a long position in an option-free bond. A short position in a putable bond ("B") would underperform a long position in an option-free bond primarily because yields-to-maturity were declining, although the declining value of the embedded put option would mitigate some of the loss (the seller of the putable bond has "sold" the embedded put).

As mentioned earlier in the curriculum, effective duration and convexity are the relevant summary statistics when future bond cash flows are contingent upon interest rate changes.

$$\text{Effective Duration}(\text{EffDur}) = \frac{(PV_-) - (PV_+)}{2 \times (\Delta \text{Curve})(PV_0)} \quad (8)$$

$$\text{Effective Convexity}(\text{EffCon}) = \frac{(PV_-) + (PV_+) - 2(PV_0)}{(\Delta \text{Curve})^2 \times (PV_0)} \quad (9)$$

In Equations 8 and 9, PV_- and PV_+ are the portfolio values from a decrease and increase in yield-to-maturity, respectively, PV_0 is the original portfolio value, and ΔCurve is the change in the benchmark yield-to-maturity.

Although cash-based yield curve volatility strategies are limited to the availability of liquid callable or putable bonds, several stand-alone derivatives strategies involve the right, but not the obligation, to change portfolio duration and convexity based upon an interest rate-sensitive payoff profile.

Interest rate put and call options are generally based upon a bond's price, not yield-to-maturity. Therefore, the purchase of a bond call option provides an investor the right, but not the obligation, to acquire an underlying bond at a pre-determined strike price. This purchased call option adds convexity to the portfolio and will be exercised if the bond price appreciates beyond the strike price (i.e., generally at a lower yield-to-maturity). On the other hand, a purchased bond put option benefits the owner if prices fall (i.e., yields-to-maturity rise) beyond the strike prior to expiration. Sale of a bond put (call) option limits an investor's return to the up-front premium received in exchange for assuming the potential cost of exercise if bond prices fall below (rise above) the pre-determined strike. Note that the option seller must post margin based on exchange or counterparty requirements until expiration.

An interest rate **swaption** involves the right to enter into an interest rate swap at a specific strike price in the future. This instrument grants the contingent right to increase or decrease portfolio duration. For example, Exhibit 23 shows a purchased payer swaption, which a manager might purchase to benefit from higher rates using an option-based strategy.

Exhibit 23 Purchased Payer Swaption

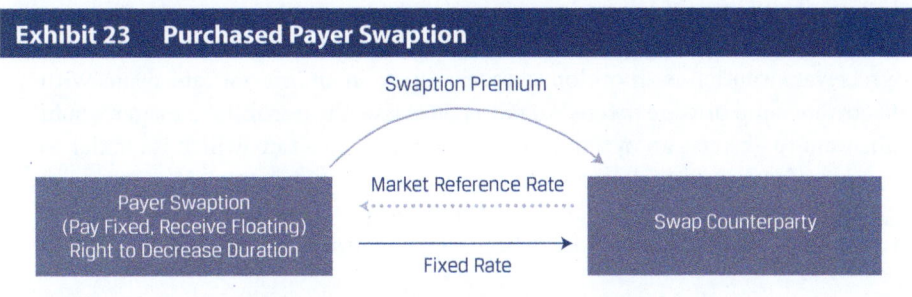

Options on bond futures contracts are liquid exchange-traded instruments frequently used by fixed-income market participants to buy or sell the right to enter into a futures position. Long option, swaption, and bond futures option strategies are summarized in Exhibit 24.

Exhibit 24 Long Option, Swaption, and Bond Futures Option Strategies

Strategy	Description	Targeted Return	Portfolio Impact
Long bond call option	Purchase right to take forward bond delivery	Max (Bond price at lower yield – Strike price, 0) – Call premium	Increase portfolio duration and convexity (up-front premium)
Long bond put option	Purchase right to deliver bond in the future	Max (Strike price – Bond price at higher yield, 0) – Put premium	Decrease portfolio duration and convexity (up-front premium)
Long payer swaption	Own the right to pay-fixed on an interest rate swap at a strike rate	Max (Strike rate – Swap rate, 0) – Swaption premium	Decrease in portfolio duration and convexity (up-front premium)
Long receiver swaption	Own the right to receive-fixed on an interest rate swap at a strike rate	Max (Swap rate – Strike rate, 0) – Swaption premium	Increase in portfolio duration and convexity (up-front premium)
Long call option on bond future	Own the right to take forward bond delivery at a strike price	Max (Bond futures price at lower yield – Strike price, 0) – Call premium	Increase in portfolio duration and convexity (up-front premium)
Long put option on bond future	Own the right to deliver bond in the future at a strike price	Max (Strike price – Bond futures price at higher yield, 0) – Put premium	Decrease in portfolio duration and convexity (up-front premium)

EXAMPLE 9

Choice of Option Strategy

A parallel upward shift in the yield curve is expected. Which of the following would be the best option strategy?

a Long a receiver swaption

b Short a payer swaption

c Long a put option on a bond futures contract

Solution:

C is correct. With an expected upward shift in the yield curve, the portfolio manager would want to reduce portfolio duration in anticipation of lower bond prices. A put option increases in value as the yield curve shifts upward, while the price of the underlying bond declines below the strike. A is incorrect because a receiver swaption is an option to receive-fixed in an interest rate swap. With fixed-rate bond prices expected to fall as rates rise, the portfolio manager would not want to exercise an option to receive a fixed strike rate, which is similar to owning a fixed-rate bond. B is incorrect because a payer swaption is an option to pay-fixed/receive-floating in an interest rate swap. A *long*, not a short, position in a payer swaption would benefit from higher rates.

In an expected stable or static yield curve environment, an active manager may aim to "sell" volatility in the form of either owning callable bonds (which is an implicit "sale" of an option) or selling stand-alone options in order to earn premium income, if this is within the investment mandate. The active portfolio decision here depends upon the manager's view as to whether future realized volatility will be greater or less than the implied volatility, as reflected by the price of a stand-alone option or a bond with embedded options. The manager will benefit if rates remain relatively constant and the bond is not called and/or the options sold expire worthless. Alternatively, if yield curve volatility is expected to increase, a manager may prefer to be long volatility in order to capitalize on large changes in level, yield curve slope, and/or shape using option-based contracts.

EXAMPLE 10

Option-Free versus Callable and Putable Bonds Amid Higher Yield Levels

Given a parallel shift upwards in the yield curve, what is the most likely ordering in terms of expected decline in value—from least to most—for otherwise comparable bonds? Assume that the embedded options are deep out-of-the-money.

a Callable bond, option-free bond, putable bond
b Putable bond, callable bond, option-free bond
c Putable bond, option-free bond, callable bond

Solution:

Answer: B is correct. The value of a bond with an embedded option may be considered as the value of an option-free bond plus the value of the embedded option. While the upward shift in the yield curve will cause the option-free component of each bond to depreciate in value, this change in yields-to-maturity will also affect the value of embedded options.

For a putable bond, the bond investor has the option to "put" the bond back to the issuer if yields-to-maturity rise. The more rates rise, the more valuable this embedded option becomes. This increasing option value will partially offset the decline in value of the putable bond relative to the option-free bond. This can be seen in the lower panel of Exhibit 22: The dotted line for the putable bond has a flatter slope than the solid line for the option-free bond; its price will decrease more slowly as yields-to-maturity increase.

For a callable bond, the bond issuer has an option to "call" the bond if yields-to-maturity decline; the more rates rise, the lower the call option value. Since the bond investor is short the embedded option and the value of the embedded option has fallen, this will partially offset the decline in the value of the callable bond relative to the option-free bond. The top panel of Exhibit 22 shows that the dotted line for the callable bond has a flatter slope than the solid line for the option-free bond.

As rates continue to increase, the embedded option for the putable bond rises in value more quickly at the margin as it shifts toward becoming an in-the-money option. In contrast, the deep out-of-the-money embedded call option moves further out-of-the-money as rates increase and the marginal impact of further rate increases declines.

3.3 Key Rate Duration for a Portfolio

So far, we have evaluated changes in yield curve level, slope, and curvature using one, two, and three specific maturity points across the term structure of interest rates, respectively. The concept of **key rate duration** (or partial duration) introduced previously measures portfolio sensitivity over a set of maturities along the yield curve, with the sum of key rate durations being identical to the effective duration:

$$\text{KeyRateDur}_k = \frac{1}{\text{PV}} \times \frac{\Delta \text{PV}}{\Delta r_k} \tag{10}$$

$$\sum_{k=1}^{n} \text{KeyRateDur}_k = \text{EffDur} \tag{11}$$

where r_k represents the kth key rate and PV is the portfolio value. In contrast to effective duration, key rate durations help identify "shaping risk" for a bond portfolio—that is, a portfolio's sensitivity to changes in the shape of the benchmark yield curve. By breaking down a portfolio into its individual duration components by maturity, an active manager can pinpoint and quantify key exposures along the curve, as illustrated in the following simplified zero-coupon bond example.

Compare a passive zero-coupon US Treasury bond portfolio versus an actively managed portfolio:

"Index" Zero-Coupon Portfolio

Tenor	Coupon	Annualized Yield	Price (per $100)	Position ($ MM)	ModDur	KeyRateDur
2y	0.00%	1%	98.03	98.03	1.980	0.738
5y	0.00%	2%	90.57	90.57	4.902	1.688
10y	0.00%	3%	74.40	74.40	9.709	2.747

Assume the "index" portfolio is simply weighted by the price of the respective 2-, 5-, and 10-year bonds for a total portfolio value of $263 million, or $1 million × (98.03 + 90.57 + 74.4). We can calculate the portfolio modified duration as 5.173, or [1.98 × (98.03/263)] + [4.902 × (90.57/263)] + [9.709 × (74.40/263)]. Or, we could calculate each key rate duration by maturity, as in the far right column. For example, the 2-year key rate duration (KeyRateDur$_2$) equals 0.738, or 1.98 × (98.03/263). Note that these three key rate duration values also sum to the portfolio value of 5.173.

"Active" Zero-Coupon Portfolio

Tenor	Coupon	Annualized Yield	Price (per $100)	Position ($ MM)	ModDur	KeyRateDur
2y	0.00%	1%	98.03	51.40	1.980	0.387
5y	0.00%	2%	90.57	−46.00	4.902	−0.857
10y	0.00%	3%	74.40	257.60	9.709	9.509

Yield Curve Strategies

As in the case of the "index" portfolio, the "active" zero-coupon portfolio has a value of $263 million, or [$1 million × (51.4 − 46 + 257.6)], but the portfolio duration is greater at 9.039, or [1.98 × (51.4/263)] + [4.902 × (−46/263)] + [9.709 × (257.6/263)]. Note that the short 5-year active position has a negative key rate duration of −0.857, or 4.902 × (−46/263).

By now, you may have noticed that our active manager is positioned for the combination of a negative butterfly and a bull flattening at the long end of the yield curve. However, a comparison of the active versus index portfolio duration summary statistic does not tell the entire story. Instead, we can compare the key rate or partial durations for specific maturities across the index and active portfolios to better understand exposure differences:

Tenor	Active	Index	Difference
2y	0.39	0.74	−0.35
5y	−0.86	1.69	−2.55
10y	9.51	2.75	6.76
Portfolio	9.04	5.17	−3.87

The key rate duration differences in this chart provide more detailed information regarding the exposure differences across maturities. For example, the negative differences for 2-year and 5-year maturities (−0.35 and −2.55, respectively) indicate that the active portfolio has lower exposure to short-term rates than the index portfolio. The large positive difference in the 10-year tenor shows that the active portfolio has far greater exposure to 10-year yield-to-maturity changes. This simple zero-coupon bond example may be extended to portfolios consisting of fixed-coupon bonds, swaps, and other rate-sensitive instruments that may be included in a fixed-income portfolio, as seen in the following example.

EXAMPLE 11

Key Rate Duration

A fixed-income manager is presented with the following key rate duration summary of his actively managed bond portfolio versus an equally weighted index portfolio across 5-, 10-, and 30-year maturities:

Tenor	Active	Index	Difference
5y	−1.188	1.633	−2.821
10y	2.909	3.200	−0.291
30y	11	8.067	2.933
Portfolio	12.72	12.9	−0.179

Assume the active manager has invested in the index bond portfolio and used only derivatives to create the active portfolio. Which of the following most likely represents the manager's synthetic positions?

a Receive-fixed 5-year swap, short 10-year futures, and pay-fixed 30-year swap

b Pay-fixed 5-year sap, short 10-year futures, and receive-fixed 30-year swap

c Short 5-year futures, long 10-year futures, and receive-fixed 30-year swap

> **Solution:**
>
> Answer: B is correct. The key rate duration summary shows the investor to be net short 5- and 10-year key rate duration and long 30-year key rate duration versus the index. A combines synthetic long, short, and short positions in the 5-, 10-, and 30-year maturities, respectively. C combines short, long, and long positions across the curve. The combination of a pay-fixed (short duration) 5-year swap, a short 10-year futures position, and a receive-fixed (long duration) 30-year swap is, therefore, the best answer.

4. ACTIVE FIXED-INCOME MANAGEMENT ACROSS CURRENCIES

f discuss yield curve strategies across currencies

The benefits of investing across borders to maximize return and diversify exposure is a consistent theme among portfolio managers. While both the tools as well as the strategic considerations of active versus passive currency risk management within an investment portfolio are addressed elsewhere, here we will primarily focus on extending our analysis of yield curve strategies from a single yield curve to multiple yield curves across currencies.

An earlier currency lesson noted that investors measure return in functional currency terms—that is, considering domestic currency returns on foreign currency assets, as shown in Equations 12 and 13.

$$\text{Single asset: } R_{DC} = (1 + R_{FC})(1 + R_{FX}) - 1 \tag{12}$$

$$\text{Portfolio: } R_{DC} = \sum_{i=1}^{n} \omega_i (1 + R_{FC,i})(1 + R_{FX,i}) - 1 \tag{13}$$

R_{DC} and R_{FC} are the domestic and foreign currency returns expressed as a percentage, R_{FX} is the percentage change of the domestic versus foreign currency, while ω_i is the respective portfolio weight of each foreign currency asset (in domestic currency terms) with the sum of ω_i equal to 1. In the context of Equation 1, R_{DC} simply combines the third factor, +/–E (Δ Price due to investor's view of benchmark yield), and the fifth factor, +/–E (Δ Price due to investor's view of currency value changes), factors in the expected fixed-income return model.

In a previous term structure lesson, we highlighted several macroeconomic factors that influence the bond term premium and required returns, such as inflation, economic growth, and monetary policy. Differences in these factors across countries are frequently reflected in the relative term structure of interest rates as well as in exchange rates.

For example, after a decade of economic expansion following the 2008 global financial crisis, the US Federal Reserve's earlier reversal of quantitative easing versus the European Central Bank through 2019 led to significantly higher short-term government yields-to-maturity in the United States versus Europe.

Against this historical backdrop, assume a German fixed-income manager decides to buy short-term US Treasuries to take advantage of higher USD yields-to-maturity. At the end of March 2019, a USD Treasury zero-coupon bond maturing on 31 March 2021 had a price at 95.656, with an approximate yield-to-maturity of 2.25%. Based upon the then-current USD/EUR spot rate of 1.1218 (that is, $1.1218 = €1), the manager pays €85,270,102 (= $95,656,000/1.1218) for a $100 million face value Treasury security, as seen in Exhibit 25.

Exhibit 25 USD/EUR Spot Trade and US Treasury Zero Purchase

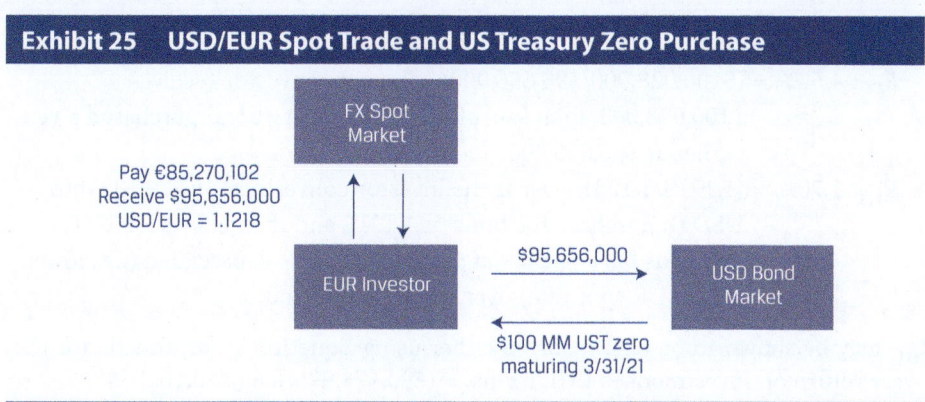

As in the single currency yield curve case, the investor will benefit from bond price appreciation if the US Treasury yield-to-maturity falls during the holding period. In addition, since her domestic returns are measured in EUR, she will also benefit if the USD she receives upon sale of the bond or at maturity buy more EUR per USD in the future—that is, if USD/EUR decreases (i.e., USD *appreciates* versus EUR).

In fact, the flight to quality induced by the COVID-19 pandemic in early 2020 led to a sharp decline in US Treasury yields-to-maturity. Exhibit 26 shows how the relationship between US and German government rates changed between March 2019 and March 2020.

Exhibit 26 US vs. German Government Yield Curves, 2019 and 2020

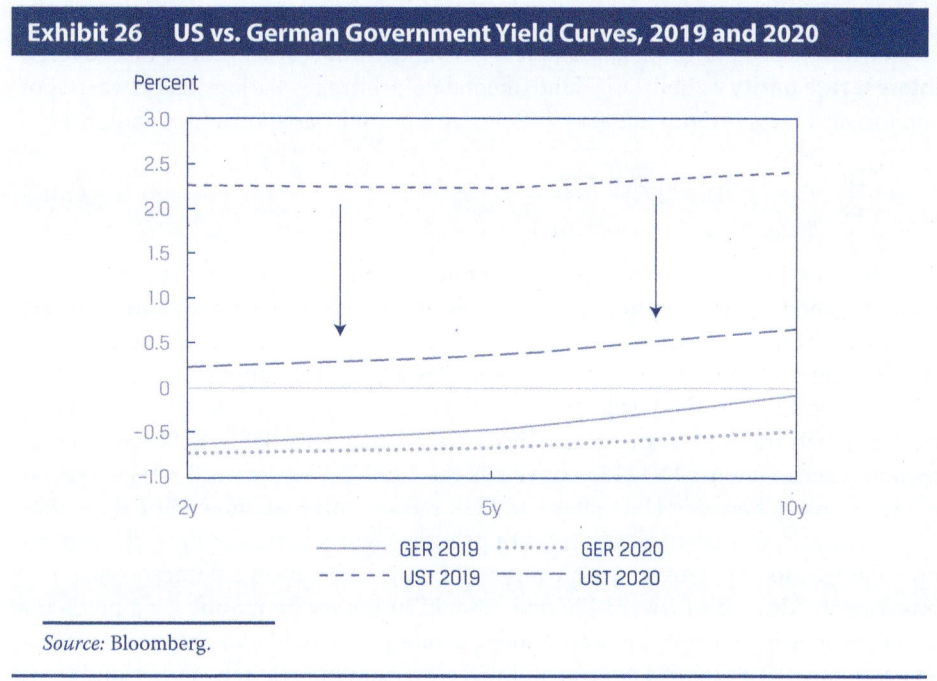

Source: Bloomberg.

As a result, one year after purchase (31 March 2020), the US Treasury zero-coupon bond maturing 31 March 2021 traded at a price of 100.028 and the USD/EUR spot was 1.1031.

Now we calculate the German investor's 1-year domestic currency return from holding the $100 million par value US Treasury zero-coupon bond.

Equation 12 separates this return into two key components:

R_{FC}: 4.57%, = ($100,028,000/$95,656,000) − 1, as the investor receives $100,028,000 upon sale of the US Treasury bond purchased a year earlier at $95,656,000.

R_{FX}: 1.70%, = (1.1218/1.1031 − 1), as the investor converted €85,270,102 into USD to purchase the bond at 1.1218 and then converted USD proceeds back to EUR at 1.1031. The EUR depreciated (i.e., lower USD/EUR spot rate) over the 1-year period.

R_{DC} may be shown to be 6.34%, solved either using Equation 12 or directly for the 1-year return on investment in EUR terms, = (€90,678,996/€ 85,270,102) −1.

In contrast to the *unhedged* 1-year example, let us now assume that the German manager fully hedges the foreign currency risk associated with the US Treasury bond purchase and holds it instead for two years, at which time she receives the bond's face value of $100,000,000. Specifically, the manager enters a 2-year FX forward agreement at the time of bond purchase to sell the future $100,000,000 payment upon bond maturity and buy EUR at the then current 2-year USD/EUR forward rate of 1.1870, locking in a certain €84,245,998, = $100,000,000/1.1870, in two years' time.

If fully hedged, the expected annualized return, R_{DC}, in EUR terms on the 2-year US Treasury zero-coupon bond hedged EUR investment over two years is equal to −0.60%, = (€84,245,998/€85,270,102)$^{0.5}$ − 1, which matches the 2-year annualized German government zero-coupon bond yield-to-maturity upon inception. This may also be calculated using Equation 12, with R_{FC} = 2.25% and R_{FX} = −2.785%, or (1.1218/1.1870)$^{0.5}$ − 1.

The fully hedged investment example is a reminder from earlier lessons that **covered interest rate parity** establishes a fundamental no-arbitrage relationship between spot and forward rates for individual cash flows in T periods, as shown in Equation 14.

$$F\left(\frac{DC}{FC}, T\right) = S_0(DC/FC)\frac{(1+r_{DC})^T}{(1+r_{FC})^T} \quad (14)$$

F denotes the forward rate; S is the spot rate; and r_{DC} and r_{FC} reflect the respective domestic and foreign currency risk-free rates. If an investor uses a forward contract to fully hedge foreign currency cash flows, she should expect to earn the domestic risk-free rate, as seen in our example. Recall also that this implies in general that a higher-yielding currency will trade at a forward discount, while a lower-yielding currency will trade at a premium. This is consistent with USD/EUR spot versus forward exchange rates (1.1218 spot versus the 1.187 2-year forward rate) as well as the relationship between USD rates and EUR rates in 2019, as shown in Exhibit 26.

In contrast, **uncovered interest rate parity** suggests that over time, the returns on unhedged foreign currency exposure will be the same as on a domestic currency investment. Although forward FX rates should in theory be an unbiased predictor of future spot FX rates if uncovered interest rate parity holds, in practice investors sometimes seek to exploit a persistent divergence from interest rate parity conditions (known as the **forward rate bias**) by investing in higher-yielding currencies, which is in some cases enhanced by borrowing in lower-yielding currencies.

This demonstrates that active fixed-income strategies across currencies must factor in views on currency appreciation versus depreciation as well as yield curve changes across countries. Our investor's USD versus EUR interest rate view in the previous example combined with an implicit view that USD/EUR would remain relatively stable led to the highest return in the unhedged case with a 1-year investment horizon. This stands in contrast to the relationship between USD/EUR spot and 2-year forward rates at the inception of the trade on 31 March 2019, when implied (annualized) EUR appreciation was 2.87%, = (1.187/1.1218)$^{0.5}$ − 1.

Active Fixed-Income Management across Currencies

The European fixed-income manager in our example might use leverage instead of cash by borrowing in euros when buying the 2-year US Treasury zero. This is an extension of the single currency repo carry trade shown in Exhibit 5, in which an investor borrows short-term in one currency and invests in another higher-yielding currency. This **carry trade across currencies** is a potential source of additional income subject to short-term availability if the positive interest rate differential persists for the life of the transaction. Given the preponderance of fixed-rate coupon versus zero-coupon bonds, our analysis turns next to these securities. As in the case of the fully hedged German investor in US Treasuries, we first establish the necessary building blocks to replicate a risk-free domestic currency return when investing in a foreign currency fixed-income coupon bond. We then consider how an active investor might deviate from this exposure profile to generate excess return.

Consider the example of a Japan-based investor who buys a fixed-rate USD coupon bond. In order to fully hedge JPY domestic currency cash flows for the foreign currency bond, as in the case of the earlier German investor, the investor must first sell Japanese yen (JPY) and purchase USD at the current spot rate to purchase the bond. At the end of each semi-annual interest period, the investor receives a USD coupon, which must be converted at the future JPY/USD spot rate (that is, the number of JPY required to buy one USD). At maturity, the investor receives the final semi-annual coupon and principal, which must be converted to JPY using the future JPY/USD spot rate to receive the final payment in domestic currency.

The fixed-rate foreign currency bond exposes the Japanese investor to a series of FX forward exposures that may be hedged upon purchase with a cross-currency swap, as seen in Exhibit 27 with the example of a par 10-year US Treasury bond with a 0.625% coupon issued in May 2020.

Exhibit 27 Fixed-Fixed Cross-Currency Swap Diagram and Details

Trade Details	JPY/USD Fixed-Fixed Cross-Currency Swap
Start date	15 May 2020
Maturity date	15 May 2030
Fixed USD payer	JPY Investor
Fixed JPY payer	Swap counterparty
Initial exchange	JPY investor pays JPY10.706 billion and receives USD100 million as of 15 May 2020
Fixed USD rate	0.625% Semiannual, Act/Act
Fixed JPY rate	−0.726% Semiannual, Act/365
Final exchange	JPY investor pays USD100 million and receives JPY10.706 billion as of 15 May 2030

Note that the fixed-fixed cross-currency swap components, shown in Exhibit 28, are a combination of three distinct hedging transactions: a receive-fixed JPY interest rate swap, a USD-JPY **cross-currency basis swap** involving the exchange of floating JPY for floating USD payments, and a pay-fixed USD interest rate swap.

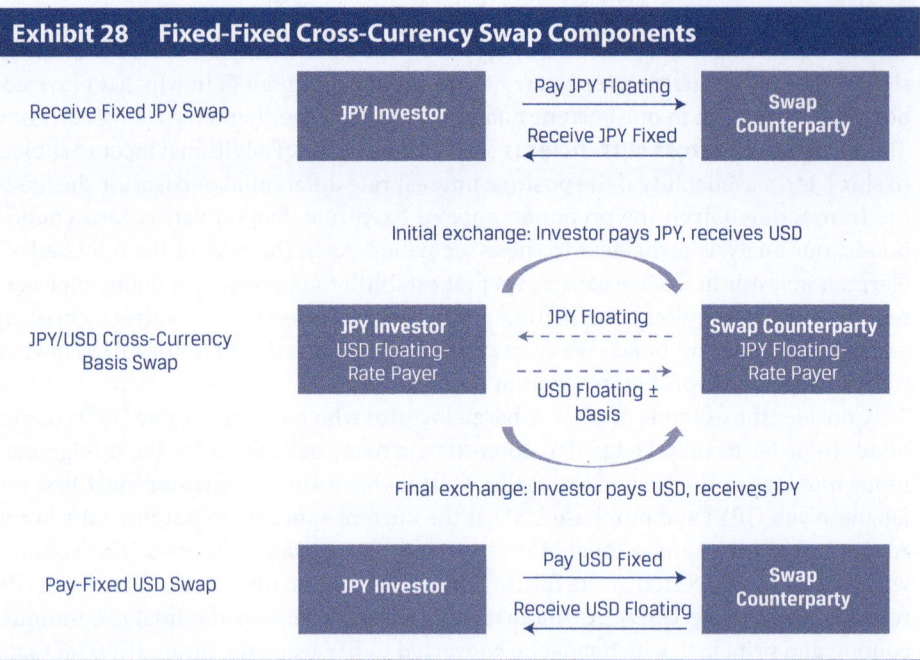

Exhibit 28 Fixed-Fixed Cross-Currency Swap Components

CROSS-CURRENCY BASIS AND COVERED INTEREST RATE PARITY

The "basis" or spread, as shown in the cross-currency basis swap, is the difference between the USD interest rate and the synthetic USD interest rate derived from swapping JPY into US dollars. A positive (negative) currency basis means that the direct USD interest rate is higher (lower) than the synthetic USD interest rate. While covered interest rate parity suggests that cross-currency basis should be close to zero, Exhibit 29 shows that the JPY and EUR cross-currency basis was persistently negative following the 2008 global financial crisis.

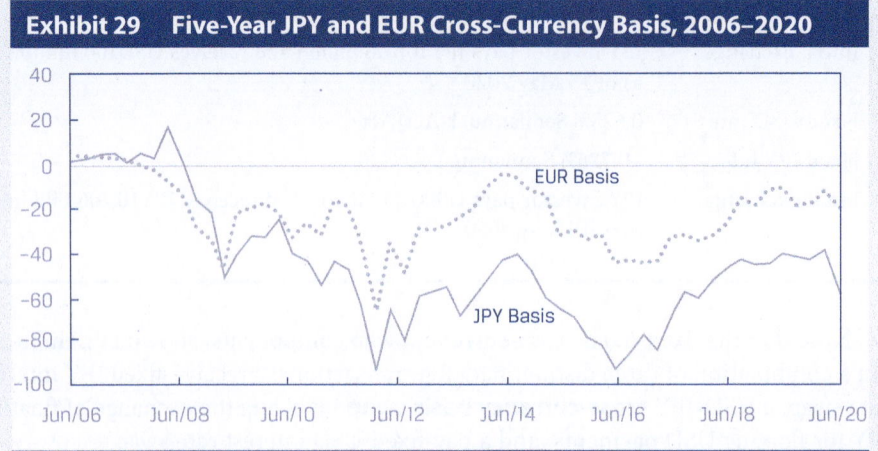

Exhibit 29 Five-Year JPY and EUR Cross-Currency Basis, 2006–2020

Cross-currency basis is widely seen as a barometer for global financial conditions. For example, greater credit and liquidity risk within the EU financial sector and the European Central Bank's aggressive quantitative easing have been cited as causes of the wider USD/EUR cross-currency basis.

> Du, Tepper, and Verdelhan (2018) investigate the persistent no-arbitrage violation of covered interest rate parity implied by wider cross-currency basis observed across G-10 countries and offer several explanations. First, higher financial intermediation costs since the 2008 global financial crisis, such as higher bank regulatory capital requirements, prevent market participants from taking advantage of basis arbitrage opportunities. Second, covered interest rate parity violations suggest international imbalances in the form of high demand for investments in high interest rate currencies and a large supply of savings in low interest rate currencies. These deviations are magnified by divergent monetary policies across jurisdictions.

The building blocks of the fixed-fixed cross-currency swap shown in Exhibit 28 offer an active fixed-income investor a simplified framework within which one can take interest rate or currency positions to deviate from a risk-free domestic currency return. For example, by foregoing the pay USD fixed swap, the JPY investor takes a USD rate view by earning the USD fixed coupon and paying USD floating while fully hedging the currency exposure via the cross-currency basis swap. Similar principles apply as in the single currency case—namely, to go long (or overweight) assets expected to appreciate and go short (or underweight) assets expected to decline in value or appreciate less. The overweight and underweight bond positions may now be denominated in different currencies, with the active strategy often using an underweight position in one currency to fund an overweight position in another. The resulting yield curve strategy faces three potential risks: (1) yield curve movements—level, slope, or curvature—in the overweight currency; (2) yield curve changes in the underweight currency; and (3) exchange rate changes.

Consider the following unhedged example of a higher- versus lower-yielding currency.

EXAMPLE 12

MXN Carry Trade

Consider the case of a portfolio manager examining a cross-currency carry trade between US dollar (USD) and Mexican peso (MXN) money market rates. The manager is contemplating borrowing in USD for one year and investing in 90-day Mexican treasury bills, rolling them over at maturity for the next 12 months. Assume that today's 1-year USD interest rate is 1.85%, the 90-day MXN interest rate is currently 7.70% (annualized), and the MXN/USD spot exchange rate is 19.15 (that is, it takes 19.15 MXN to buy one USD).

If the manager expected that Mexican money market rates and the MXN/USD exchange rate would remain stable, the expected profit from this carry trade is:

$(1 + 0.0770/4)^4 - (1 + 0.0185) \approx 6.08\%.$

However, money market and exchange rates are rarely stable; this trade is exposed to changes in both the 90-day MXN interest rate and the MXN/USD spot exchange rate. (The 1-year fixed-rate USD loan eliminates exposure to USD rate changes). Assume that 90-day MXN interest rates and exchange rates change as follows over the 12-month period.

Rate / Time	Today	90 Days	180 Days	270 Days	360 Days
90-day MXN rate	7.70%	7.85%	8.15%	8.20%	N/A
MXN/USD spot rate	19.15	18.05	19.05	18.80	19.65

Note that 90-day MXN yields-to-maturity rose and that MXN depreciated slightly versus USD over the 360-day period. If the manager had rolled over this trade for the full 12 months, the realized return would have been:

$$\left(1 + \frac{0.0770}{4}\right)\left(1 + \frac{0.0785}{4}\right)\left(1 + \frac{0.0815}{4}\right)\left(1 + \frac{0.082}{4}\right) \times \frac{19.15}{19.65} - (1 + 0.0185) \approx 3.61\%$$

While the cross-currency carry trade was ultimately profitable, it was exposed to risks over the horizon; moreover, despite the rise in 90-day MXN yields-to-maturity, a late-period MXN depreciation undercut the profitability of the trade. This underscores the fact that carry trades are unhedged and are most successful in stable (low volatility) markets: Unforeseen market volatility can quickly erase even the most attractive cross-currency carry opportunities. For example, in the first quarter of 2020 at the start of the COVID-19 pandemic, MXN depreciated against the USD by approximately 25% in just over a month.

While an endless number of unhedged strategies seeking to capitalize on a level, slope, or curvature view across currencies exist, Exhibit 30 summarizes several of these major strategies.

Exhibit 30 Active Cross-Currency Strategies

Strategy	Purchase	Sell / Borrow	Expected Unhedged Return
Receive-fixed/pay-fixed	High-yielding fixed-income asset	Lower-yield fixed-rate loan	Carry (higher yield minus lower yield) assuming uncovered interest parity does not hold
Receive-fixed/pay-floating	High-yielding fixed-rate asset	Short-term, lower yield floating-rate loan rolled over until maturity	Carry (higher yield minus lower yield) plus long- versus short-term rate differential for lower-yielding currency
Receive-floating/pay-fixed	High-yield floating-rate asset	Lower-yield fixed-rate loan	Carry (higher floating yield minus lower fixed yield)
Receive-floating/pay-floating	High-yield floating-rate asset	Short-term, lower yield floating-rate loan rolled over until maturity	Carry (higher floating yield minus lower floating yield)

EXAMPLE 13

Bear Flattening Impact

A fixed-income manager is considering a foreign currency fixed-income investment in a relatively high-yielding market, where she expects bear flattening to occur in the near future and her lower-yielding domestic yield curve to remain stable and upward-sloping. Under this scenario, which of the following strategies will generate the largest carry benefit if her interest rate view is realized?

a Receive-fixed in foreign currency, pay-fixed in domestic currency

b Receive-fixed in foreign currency, pay-floating in domestic currency

c Receive-floating in foreign currency, pay-floating in domestic currency

> **Solution:**
>
> The correct answer is C. If the higher-yielding foreign currency experiences a bear flattening in the yield curve as the manager expects, then foreign currency short-term yields-to-maturity will increase by more than long-term yields-to-maturity; thus she will want receive-floating in foreign currency. Given the upward-sloping domestic yield curve, we would expect the carry difference between receiving foreign currency floating rates and paying domestic currency floating rates to be the highest.

5. A FRAMEWORK FOR EVALUATING YIELD CURVE STRATEGIES

g   evaluate the expected return and risks of a yield curve strategy

The factors affecting the expected return of a fixed-income portfolio were summarized in Equation 1. The key underlying assumption in this calculation is that the inputs rely on the fixed-income manager's expectations under an active strategy. As we have seen earlier, unexpected changes to the level, slope, and shape of the yield curve as well as currency changes can impact a portfolio's value in a number of ways—as quantified by the use of portfolio duration and convexity statistics in Equation 3 for a single currency and in Equation 13 for a multicurrency portfolio.

Practitioners frequently evaluate fixed-income portfolio risk using **scenario analysis**, which involves changing multiple assumptions at once to assess the overall impact of unexpected market changes on a portfolio's value. Managers may use historical rate and currency changes or conduct specific stress tests using this analysis. For example, a leveraged investor might evaluate how much rates or currencies must move before she faces a collateral or margin call or is forced to unwind a position. Fixed-income portfolio models offer practitioners a variety of historical or user-defined scenarios. The following scenario analysis example shows how this may be done for the US Treasury portfolio seen earlier.

EXAMPLE 14

Scenario Analysis—US Treasury Securities Portfolio

Tenor	Coupon	Price	Modified Duration	Convexity
2y	0.25%	100	1.994	5.0
5y	0.875%	100	4.88	26.5
10y	2.00%	100	9.023	90.8

In Example 1, we compared two $50 million portfolios. Portfolio A is fully invested in the 5-year Treasury bond, while Portfolio B is split between 2-year (58.94%) and 10-year (41.06%) bonds to match a 5-year bond duration of 4.88. Rather than the earlier parallel yield curve shift, we now analyze two yield curve slope scenarios—namely, an immediate bear steepening and bull flattening of the US Treasury yield curve. The bear steepening scenario involves a 50 bp and 100 bp *rise* in 5- and 10-year yields-to-maturity, respectively, while the bull flattening is assumed to result from a 50 bp fall in 5-year rates and a 100 bp fall in 10-year rates. Using Equation 3, our scenario analysis looks as follows:

Scenario	Portfolio A % Δ Price	Portfolio A Δ Price	Portfolio B % Δ Price	Portfolio B Δ Price
Bear steepening	−2.407%	($1,203,437)	−3.518%	($1,759,216)
Bull flattening	2.473%	$1,236,563	3.891%	$1,945,628

We may conclude from our analysis that although Portfolios A and B have similar duration and therefore perform similarly if the yield curve experiences a parallel shift (except for the convexity difference) seen in Example 1, they perform very differently under various yield curve slope scenarios.

The fixed-income portfolio risk and return impact of rolldown return versus carry, changes in the level, slope, and shape of a single currency yield curve, and an extension to multiple currencies (where spot and forward FX rates are related to relative interest rates) are best illustrated with a pair of examples.

EXAMPLE 15

AUD Bullet versus Barbell

A US-based portfolio manager plans to invest in Australian zero-coupon bonds denominated in Australian dollars (AUD). He projects that over the next 12 months, the Australian zero-coupon yield curve will experience a downward parallel shift of 60 bps and that AUD will appreciate 0.25% against USD. The manager is weighing bullet and barbell strategies using the following data:

Statistic	Bullet	Barbell
Investment horizon (years)	1.0	1.0
Average bond price in portfolio (today)	98.00	98.00
Average portfolio bond price (in 1 year/stable yield curve)	99.75	100.00
Expected portfolio effective duration (in 1 year)	3.95	3.95
Expected portfolio convexity (in 1 year)	19.50	34.00
Expected change in AUD zero-coupon yields	−0.60%	−0.60%
Expected change in AUD versus USD	+0.25%	+0.25%

Solve for the expected return over the 1-year investment horizon for each portfolio using the step-by-step estimation approach in Equation 1.

Rolldown Return

The sum of coupon income (in %) and the price effect on bonds from "rolling down the yield curve." Since both portfolios contain only zero-coupon bonds, there is no coupon income and we calculate the rolldown return using $(PV_1 − PV_0) / PV_0$, where PV_0 is today's bond price and PV_1 is the bond price in one year, assuming no shift in the yield curve.

1 **Bullet:** 1.7857% = (99.75 − 98.00) / 98.00
2 **Barbell:** 2.0408% = (100.000 − 98.00) / 98.00

A Framework for Evaluating Yield Curve Strategies

E (Δ Price Due to Investor's View of Benchmark Yield)

The effect of the interest rate view on expected portfolio return may be estimated using Equation 3, using effective duration and convexity in one year's time to evaluate the expected 60 bp downward parallel yield curve shift:

1. **Bullet:** 2.4051% = (−3.95 × −0.0060) + [1/2 × 19.5 × (−0.0060)^2]
2. **Barbell:** 2.4312% = (−3.95 × −0.0060) + [1/2 × 34.0 × (−0.0060)^2]

$E(R)$ ≈ % Rolldown return + E (% Δ Price due to investor's view of benchmark yield) + E (% Δ Price due to investor's view of currency value changes)

In addition to rolldown return and expected price changes due to changes in yield-to-maturity, the expected 0.25% appreciation of AUD versus USD must be incorporated in order to arrive at the USD investor's domestic currency return. Using Equation 12, R_{FC} equals the sum of rolldown return and changes in price due to yield-to-maturity changes, while R_{FX} is 0.25%. Expected returns are as follows:

$E(R_1)$ = 4.4513%, or [(1 + 0.017857 + 0.024051) × (1.0025)] − 1

$E(R_2)$ = 4.7332%, or [(1 + 0.020408 + 0.024312) × (1.0025)] − 1

Overall, the barbell outperforms the bullet by approximately 28 bps. Rolldown return contributes most of this outperformance. Rolldown return contributed approximately 25.5 bps of outperformance (i.e., 2.0408% − 1.7857%) for the barbell, and the greater convexity of the barbell portfolio contributed just over 2.6 bps of outperformance (i.e., 2.4312% − 2.4051%). Currency exposure had the same impact on both strategies. The strong rolldown contribution is likely driven by the stronger price appreciation (under the stable yield curve assumption) of longer-maturity zeros in the barbell portfolio relative to the price appreciation of the intermediate zeros in the bullet portfolio as the bonds ride the curve over the 1-year horizon to a shorter maturity.

EXAMPLE 16

US Treasury Bullet versus Barbell

Assume a 1-year investment horizon for a portfolio manager considering US Treasury market strategies. The manager is considering two strategies to capitalize on an expected rise in US Treasury security zero-coupon yield levels of 50 bps in the next 12 months:

1. A bullet portfolio fully invested in 5-year zero-coupon notes currently priced at 94.5392.
2. A barbell portfolio: 62.97% is invested in 2-year zero-coupon notes priced at 98.7816, and 37.03% is invested in 10-year zero-coupon bonds priced at 83.7906.

Further assumptions for evaluating these portfolios are shown here:

Statistic	Bullet	Barbell
Investment horizon (years)	1.0	1.0
Average bond price in portfolio (today)	94.5392	92.6437

(continued)

Statistic	Bullet	Barbell
Average portfolio bond price (in 1 year/stable yield curve)	96.0503	94.3525
Expected portfolio effective duration (in 1 year)	3.98	3.98
Expected portfolio convexity (in 1 year)	17.82	32.57
Expected change in US Treasury zero-coupon yields	0.50%	0.50%

Solve for the expected return over the 1-year investment horizon for each portfolio using the step-by-step estimation approach in Equation 1.

Rolldown Return

The sum of coupon income (in %) and the price effect on bonds from "rolling down the yield curve." Since both portfolios contain only zero-coupon bonds, there is no coupon income and we calculate the rolldown return using ($PV_1 - PV_0$) / PV_0, where PV_0 is today's bond price and PV_1 is the bond price in one year, assuming no shift in the yield curve.

Bullet: (96.0503 − 94.5392) ÷ 94.5392 = 1.5984%
Barbell: (94.3525 − 92.6437) ÷ 92.6437 = 1.8445%

E (Δ Price Due to Investor's View of Benchmark Yield)

The effect of the interest rate view on expected portfolio return may be estimated with Equation 3, using effective duration and convexity in one year's time to evaluate the expected 50 bp upward parallel yield curve shift:

Bullet: −1.9677% = (−3.98 × 0.0050) + [1/2 × 17.82 × (0.0050)^2]
Barbell: −1.9493% = (−3.98 × 0.0050) + [1/2 × 32.57 × (0.0050)^2]

Expected total return in percentage terms for each portfolio is equal to:

$E(R)$ = % Rolldown return + E (% Δ Price due to investor's view of benchmark yield)

The total expected return over the 1-year investment horizon for the bullet portfolio is therefore −0.3693%, or 1.5984% − 1.9677%, and the expected return for the barbell portfolio is −0.1048%, or 1.8445% − 1.9493%.

If the manager's expected market scenario materializes, the barbell portfolio outperforms the bullet portfolio by 26 bps. The higher barbell convexity contributed just under 2 bps of outperformance, whereas the rolldown return contributed nearly 25 bps. Stronger price appreciation (under the stable yield curve assumption) resulted from a greater rolldown effect from the 10-year zeros in the barbell versus the 5-year zeros over one year.

SUMMARY

This reading addresses active fixed-income yield curve management using cash- and derivative-based strategies to generate returns which exceed those of a benchmark index due to yield curve changes. The following are the main points in the reading:

- A par yield curve is a stylized representation of yields-to-maturity available to investors at various maturities, which often does not consist of traded securities but must be extracted from available bond yields using a model.

- Primary yield curve risk factors may be categorized by changes in level (or a parallel "shift"), slope (a flatter or steeper yield curve), and shape or curvature.

Summary

- Yield curve slope measures the difference between the yield-to-maturity on a long-maturity bond and the yield-to-maturity on a shorter-maturity bond. Curvature is the relationship between short-, intermediate-, and long-term yields-to-maturity.
- Fixed-income portfolio managers can approximate actual and anticipated bond portfolio value changes using portfolio duration and convexity measures. Duration measures the linear relationship between bond prices and yield-to-maturity. Convexity is a second-order effect describing a bond's price behavior for larger rate movements and is affected by cash flow dispersion.
- A barbell portfolio combining short- and long-term bond positions will have greater convexity than a bullet portfolio concentrated in a single maturity for a given duration.
- Active managers seeking excess return in an expected static yield curve environment that is upward-sloping can use a buy-and-hold strategy to increase duration, roll down the yield curve, or use leverage via a carry trade in cash markets. Receive-fixed swaps and long futures positions replicate this exposure in the derivatives market.
- Derivatives offer the opportunity to synthetically change exposure with a far smaller initial cash outlay than cash strategies but require managers to maintain sufficient cash or eligible securities to fulfill margin or collateral requirements.
- Active fixed-income managers with a divergent rate level view increase duration exposure above a target if yields-to-maturity are expected to decline and reduce duration if expecting higher yields-to-maturity to minimize losses.
- Yield curve steepeners seek to gain from a greater spread between short- and long-term yields-to-maturity by combining a "long" short-dated bond position with a "short" long-dated bond position, while a flattener involves sale of short-term bonds and purchase of long-term bonds.
- Steepener and flattener strategies may be net duration neutral or net long or short duration depending upon a manager's view of how the yield curve slope will change—that is, the relative contribution of short- and long-term yield-to-maturity changes to the expected yield curve slope change.
- The butterfly strategy combining a long bullet with a short barbell portfolio (or vice versa) is commonly used to capitalize on expected yield curve shape changes.
- Active managers capitalize on a view as to whether future realized interest rate volatility will be greater or less than implied volatility by purchasing or selling bonds with embedded options or by using stand-alone interest rate options.
- Stand-alone interest rate put and call options are generally based upon a bond's price, not yield-to-maturity.
- Interest rate swaptions and options on bond futures are among the common tools used by active managers to alter portfolio duration and convexity subject to yield-to-maturity changes. An interest rate swaption involves the right to enter into an interest rate swap at a specific strike price in the future, while an option on a bond future involves the right, not the obligation, to buy or sell a futures contract.
- Key rate durations can be used in active fixed-income management to identify a bond portfolio's sensitivity to changes in the shape of the benchmark yield curve, allowing an active manager to quantify exposures along the curve.

- Fixed-income managers engaged in active yield curve strategies across currencies measure excess return from active management in functional currency terms—that is, considering domestic currency returns on foreign currency assets within a portfolio.
- Interest rate parity establishes the fundamental relationship between spot and forward exchange rates, with a higher-yielding currency trading at a forward discount and a lower-yielding currency trading at a premium.
- Covered interest rate parity involves the use of a forward contract to lock in domestic currency proceeds, while uncovered interest rate parity suggests that over time, the returns on unhedged foreign currency exposure will be the same as on a domestic currency investment.
- Active investors use the carry trade across currencies to take advantage of divergence from interest rate parity by borrowing in a lower-yield currency and investing in a higher-yield currency.
- A cross-currency swap enables investors to fully hedge the domestic currency value of cash flows associated with foreign currency bonds.
- Active managers deviate from fully hedged foreign currency bond cash flows by entering overweight and underweight bond positions denominated in different currencies, often using an underweight position in one currency to fund an overweight position in another.
- Investors evaluate the expected return on an active fixed-income portfolio strategy by combining coupon income and rolldown return with expected portfolio changes based on benchmark yield-to-maturity, credit, and currency value changes over the investment horizon.
- Unexpected market changes or risks to portfolio value are frequently evaluated using scenario analysis.

REFERENCES

Du, Wenxin, Alexander Tepper, and Adrien Verdelhan. 2018. "Deviations from Covered Interest Rate Parity." Journal of Finance 73 (3): 915–957. https://doi.org/10.1111/jofi.12620

Smith, Donald J. 2014. Bond Math: The Theory behind the Formulas, 2nd ed. Hoboken, NJ: John Wiley & Sons.

PRACTICE PROBLEMS

The following information relates to Questions 1–8

A Sydney-based fixed-income portfolio manager is considering the following Commonwealth of Australia government bonds traded on the ASX (Australian Stock Exchange):

Tenor	Coupon	Yield	Price	Modified Duration	Convexity
2y	5.75%	0.28%	110.90	1.922	4.9
4.5y	3.25%	0.55%	111.98	4.241	22.1
9y	2.50%	1.10%	111.97	8.175	85.2

The manager is considering portfolio strategies based upon various interest rate scenarios over the next 12 months. She is considering three long-only government bond portfolio alternatives, as follows:

Bullet: Invest solely in 4.5-year government bonds

Barbell: Invest equally in 2-year and 9-year government bonds

Equal weights: Invest equally in 2-year, 4.5-year, and 9-year bonds

1. The portfolio alternative with the *highest* modified duration is the:
   - A bullet portfolio.
   - B barbell portfolio.
   - C equally weighted portfolio.

2. The manager estimates that accelerated economic growth in Australia will increase the *level* of government yields-to-maturity by 50 bps. Under this scenario, which of the three portfolios experiences the *smallest* decline in market value?
   - A Bullet portfolio
   - B Barbell portfolio
   - C Equally weighted portfolio

3. Assume the manager is able to extend her mandate by adding derivatives strategies to the three portfolio alternatives. The best way to position her portfolio to benefit from a *bear flattening* scenario is to combine a:
   - A 2-year receive-fixed Australian dollar (AUD) swap with the *same* modified duration as the bullet portfolio.
   - B 2-year pay-fixed AUD swap with *twice* the modified duration as the 2-year government bond in the barbell portfolio.
   - C 9-year receive-fixed AUD swap with *twice* the modified duration as the 9-year government bond position in the equally weighted portfolio.

4. In her market research, the manager learns that ASX 3-year and 10-year Treasury bond futures are the most liquid products for investors trading and hedging medium- to long-term Australian dollar (AUD) interest rates. Although

© 2020 CFA Institute. All rights reserved.

neither contract matches the exact characteristics of the cash bonds of her choice, which of the following additions to a barbell portfolio *best* positions her to gain under a *bull flattening* scenario?

  A Purchase a 3-year Treasury bond future matching the money duration of the short-term (2-year) position.

  B Sell a 3-year Treasury bond future matching the money duration of the short-term bond position.

  C Purchase a 10-year Treasury bond future matching the money duration of the long-term bond position.

5 An economic slowdown is expected to result in a 25 bp decline in Australian yield *levels*. Which portfolio alternative will experience the largest gain under this scenario?

  A Bullet portfolio

  B Barbell portfolio

  C Equally weighted portfolio

6 The portfolio alternative with the *least* exposure to convexity is the:

  A bullet portfolio.

  B barbell portfolio.

  C equally weighted portfolio.

7 The current butterfly spread for the Australian government yield curve based upon the manager's portfolio choices is:

  A 83 bps.

  B 28 bps.

  C −28 bps.

8 If the manager has a positive butterfly view on Australian government yields-to-maturity, the *best* portfolio position strategy to pursue is to:

  A purchase the bullet portfolio and sell the barbell portfolio.

  B sell the bullet portfolio and buy the barbell portfolio.

  C purchase the equally weighted portfolio and sell the barbell portfolio.

---

9 An analyst manages an active fixed-income fund that is benchmarked to the Bloomberg Barclays US Treasury Index. This index of US government bonds currently has a modified portfolio duration of 7.25 and an average maturity of 8.5 years. The yield curve is upward-sloping and expected to remain unchanged. Which of the following is the *least* attractive portfolio positioning strategy in a static curve environment?

  A Purchasing a 10-year zero-coupon bond with a yield of 2% and a price of 82.035

  B Entering a pay-fixed, 30-year USD interest rate swap

  C Purchasing a 20-year Treasury and financing it in the repo market

10 A Dutch investor considering a 5-year EUR government bond purchase expects yields-to-maturity to decline by 25 bps in the next six months. Which of the following statements about the rolldown return is *correct*?

  A The rolldown return equals the difference between the price of the 5-year bond and that of a 4.5-year bond at the lower yield-to-maturity.

Practice Problems

    B The rolldown return consists of the 5-year bond's basis point value multiplied by the expected 25 bp yield-to-maturity change over the next six months.

    C The rolldown return will be negative if the 5-year bond has a zero coupon and is trading at a premium.

11 An investment manager is considering decreasing portfolio duration versus a benchmark index given her expectations of an upward parallel shift in the yield curve. If she has a choice between a callable bond which is unlikely to be called, a putable bond which is likely to be put, or an option-free bond with otherwise comparable characteristics, the most profitable position would be to:

    A own the callable bond.

    B own the putable bond.

    C own the option-free bond.

12 An active fixed-income manager holds a portfolio of commercial and residential mortgage-backed securities that tracks the Bloomberg Barclays US Mortgage-Backed Securities Index. Which of the following choices is the most relevant portfolio statistic for evaluating the first-order change in his portfolio's value for a given change in benchmark yield?

    A Effective duration

    B Macaulay duration

    C Modified duration

13 An active fund trader seeks to capitalize on an expected steepening of the current upward-sloping yield curve using option-based fixed-income instruments. Which of the following portfolio positioning strategies *best* positions her to gain if her interest rate view is realized?

    A Sell a 30-year receiver swaption and a 2-year bond put option.

    B Purchase a 30-year receiver swaption and a 2-year bond put option.

    C Purchase a 30-year payer swaption and a 2-year bond call option.

The following information relates to Questions 14–17

A financial analyst at an in-house asset manager fund has created the following spreadsheet of key rate durations to compare her active position to that of a benchmark index so she can compare the rate sensitivities across maturities.

Tenor	KeyRateDur^{Active}	KeyRateDur^{Index}	Difference
2y	−0.532	0.738	−1.270
5y	0.324	1.688	−1.364
10y	5.181	2.747	2.434
30y	1.142	2.162	−1.020
Portfolio	6.115	7.335	−1.220

14 Which of the following statements is true if yield *levels* increase by 50 bps?

    A The active portfolio will outperform the index portfolio by approximately 61 bps.

    B The index portfolio will outperform the active portfolio by approximately 61 bps.

C The index portfolio will outperform the active portfolio by approximately 21 bps.

15 Which of the following statements best characterizes how the active portfolio is positioned for yield curve changes *relative* to the index portfolio?

A The active portfolio is positioned to benefit from a bear steepening of the yield curve versus the benchmark portfolio.

B The active portfolio is positioned to benefit from a positive butterfly movement in the shape of the yield curve versus the index.

C The active portfolio is positioned to benefit from yield curve flattening versus the index.

16 Which of the following derivatives strategies would *best* offset the yield curve exposure difference between the active and index portfolios?

A Add a pay-fixed 10-year swap and long 2-year, 5-year, and 30-year bond futures positions to the active portfolio.

B Add a receive-fixed 30-year swap, a pay-fixed 10-year swap, and short positions in 2-year and 5-year bond futures to the active portfolio.

C Add a pay-fixed 10-year swap, a short 30-year bond futures, and long 2-year and 5-year bond futures positions to the active portfolio.

17 Which of the following statements best describes the forward rate bias?

A Investors tend to favor fixed-income investments in currencies that trade at a premium on a forward basis.

B Investors tend to hedge fixed-income investments in higher-yielding currencies given the potential for lower returns due to currency depreciation.

C Investors tend to favor unhedged fixed-income investments in higher-yielding currencies that are sometimes enhanced by borrowing in lower-yielding currencies.

The following information relates to Questions 18–20

A US-based fixed-income portfolio manager is examining unhedged investments in Thai baht (THB) zero-coupon government bonds issued in Thailand and is considering two investment strategies:

1 **Buy-and-hold:** Purchase a 1-year, THB zero-coupon bond with a current yield-to-maturity of 1.00%.

2 **Roll down the THB yield curve:** Purchase a 2-year zero-coupon note with a current yield-to-maturity of 2.00% and sell it in a year.

THB proceeds under each strategy will be converted into USD at the end of the 1-year investment horizon. The manager expects a stable THB yield curve and that THB will appreciate by 1.5% relative to USD. The following information is used to analyze these two investment strategies:

Practice Problems

Statistic	Buy and Hold	Yield Curve Rolldown
Investment horizon (years)	1.0	1.0
Bond maturity at purchase (years)	1.0	2.0
Yield-to-maturity (today)	1.00%	2.00%
Average portfolio bond price (today)	99.0090	96.1169
Expected average portfolio bond price (in 1 year)	100.00	99.0090
Expected currency gains (in 1 year)	1.5%	1.5%

18 The *rolldown returns* over the 1-year investment horizon for the Buy-and-Hold and Yield Curve Rolldown portfolios are closest to:

- **A** 1.00% for the Buy-and-Hold portfolio and 3.01% for the Yield Curve Rolldown portfolio, respectively.
- **B** 0.991% for the Buy-and-Hold portfolio and 3.01% for the Yield Curve Rolldown portfolio, respectively.
- **C** 0.991% for the Buy-and-Hold portfolio and 2.09% for the Yield Curve Rolldown portfolio, respectively.

19 The *total expected return* over the 1-year investment horizon for the Buy-and-Hold and Yield Curve Rolldown portfolios are closest to:

- **A** 2.515% for the Buy-and-Hold portfolio and 4.555% for the Yield Curve rolldown portfolio, respectively.
- **B** 2.42% for the Buy-and-Hold portfolio and 4.51% for the Yield Curve Rolldown portfolio, respectively.
- **C** 2.491% for the Buy-and-Hold portfolio and 3.59% for the Yield Curve Rolldown portfolio, respectively.

20 Which of the following statements best describes how the expected total return results would *change* if THB yields were to rise significantly over the investment horizon?

- **A** Both the Buy-and-Hold and Yield Curve Rolldown expected portfolio returns would *increase* due to higher THB yields.
- **B** Both the Buy-and-Hold and Yield Curve Rolldown expected portfolio returns would *decrease* due to higher THB yields.
- **C** The Buy-and-Hold expected portfolio returns would be *unchanged* and the Yield Curve Rolldown expected portfolio returns would *decrease* due to the rise in yields.

21 An active investor enters a duration-neutral yield curve flattening trade that combines 2-year and 10-year Treasury positions. Under which of the following yield curve scenarios would you expect the investor to realize the *greatest* portfolio gain?

- **A** Bear steepening
- **B** Bull flattening
- **C** Yield curve inversion

SOLUTIONS

1. B is correct. The modified duration of a fixed-income portfolio is approximately equal to the market value-weighted average of the bonds in the portfolio, so the barbell has a modified duration of 5.049, or (1.922 + 8.175)/2, which is larger than that of either the bullet (4.241) or the equally weighted portfolio (4.779, or (1.922 + 4.241 + 8.175)/3.

2. A is correct. The change in portfolio value due to a rise in Australian government rate levels may be calculated using Equation 3:

   $\%\Delta PV^{Full} \approx -(ModDur \times \Delta Yield) + [½ \times Convexity \times (\Delta Yield)^2]$,

   where ModDur and Convexity reflect portfolio duration and convexity, respectively. Therefore, the bullet portfolio declines by 2.093%, or −2.093% = (−4.241 × 0.005) + [0.5 × 22.1 × (0.005^2)], followed by a drop of 2.343% for the equally weighted portfolio, or −2.343% = (−4.779 × 0.005) + [0.5 × 37.4 × (0.005^2)], and a drop of 2.468% for the barbell portfolio, or −2.468% = (−5.049 × 0.005) + [0.5 × 45.05 × (0.005^2)].

3. B is correct. A bear flattening scenario is a decrease in the yield spread between long- and short-term maturities driven by higher short-term rates. The manager must therefore position her portfolio to benefit from rising short-term yields. Under A, the receive-fixed 2-year swap is a synthetic long position, increasing portfolio duration that will result in an MTM loss under bear flattening. The receive-fixed swap in answer C will increase duration in long-term maturities. In the case of B, the pay-fixed swap with twice the modified duration of the barbell will more than offset the existing long position, resulting in net short 2-year and long 9-year bond positions in the overall portfolio and a gain under bear flattening.

4. C is correct. A bull flattening is a decrease in the yield spread between long- and short-term maturities driven by lower long-term yields-to-maturity. Both A and B involve changes in portfolio exposure to short-term rates, while C increases the portfolio exposure to long-term rates to benefit from a fall in long-term yields-to-maturity.

5. B is correct. The portfolio value change due to lower Australian government rate levels may be calculated using Equation 3:

   $\%\Delta PV^{Full} \approx -(ModDur \times \Delta Yield) + [½ \times Convexity \times (\Delta Yield)^2]$,

   where ModDur and Convexity reflect portfolio duration and convexity, respectively. Therefore, the barbell portfolio rises by 1.276%, or (−5.049 × −0.0025) + [0.5 × 45.05 × (−0.0025^2)], followed by the equally weighted portfolio at 1.207%, or (−4.779 × −0.0025) + [0.5 × 37.4 × (−0.0025^2)], and the bullet portfolio at 1.067%, or (−4.241 × −0.0025) + [0.5 × 22.1 × (−0.0025^2)].

6. A is correct. The bullet portfolio has the same convexity as the 45.5-year bond, or 22.1. The barbell portfolio in B has portfolio convexity of 45.05, = (4.9 + 85.2)/2, while the equally weighted portfolio has portfolio convexity of 37.4, = (4.9 + 22.1 + 85.2)/3.

7. C is correct. The butterfly spread is equal to twice the medium-term yield minus the short-term and long-term yields, as in Equation 2, or −28 bps, or −0.28% + (2 × 0.55%) − 1.10%).

Solutions

8 A is correct. A positive butterfly view indicates an expected decrease in the butterfly spread due to an expected rise in short- and long-term yields-to-maturity combined with a lower medium-term yield-to-maturity. The investor therefore benefits from a long medium-term (bullet) position and a short short-term and long-term (barbell) portfolio. The portfolio in answer B represents the opposite exposure and benefits from a negative butterfly view, while in C, combining short barbell and long equally weighted portfolios leaves the investor with bullet portfolio exposure.

9 B is correct. The 30-year pay-fixed swap is a "short" duration position and also results in negative carry (that is, the fixed rate paid would exceed MRR received) in an upward-sloping yield curve environment; therefore, it is the least attractive static curve strategy. In the case of a.), the manager enters a "buy-and-hold" strategy by purchasing the 10-year zero-coupon bond and extends duration, which is equal to 9.80 = 10/1.02 since the Macaulay duration of a zero equals its maturity, and ModDur = MacDur/(1+r) versus 7.25 for the index. Under c.), the manager introduces leverage by purchasing a long-term bond and financing it at a lower short-term repo rate.

10 C is correct. Rolldown return is the difference between the price of the 5-year bond and that of a 4.5-year bond at the *same* yield-to-maturity. A 5-year zero-coupon bond trading at a premium has a negative yield. As the price "pulls to par" over time, the premium amortization will be a loss to the investor. A reflects the full price appreciation since it is calculated using the lower yield-to-maturity, while B equals E (Δ Price due to investor's view of benchmark yield).

11 B is correct. The value of a bond with an embedded option is equal to the sum of the value of an option-free bond plus the value to the embedded option. With a putable bond, the embedded put option is owned by the bond investor, who can exercise the option if yields-to-maturity increase, as in this scenario. Under A, the embedded call option is owned by the bond issuer, who is more likely to exercise if yields-to-maturity decrease (that is, the bond investor is short the call option). As for C, the option-free bond underperforms the putable bond given the rise in value of the embedded put option.

12 A is correct. Effective duration is a yield duration statistic that measures interest rate risk using a parallel shift in the benchmark yield curve (ΔCurve), as in Equation 8. Effective duration measures interest rate risk for complex bonds whose future cash flows are uncertain because they are contingent on future interest rates. Both Macaulay duration (B) and modified duration (C) are relevant statistics only for option-free bonds.

13 C is correct. A steepening of the yield curve involves an increase in the slope, or the difference between long-term and short-term yields-to-maturity. An optimal portfolio positioning strategy is one which combines a short duration exposure to long-term bonds and a long duration exposure to short-term bonds. Portfolio C involves the right (but not the obligation) to purchase a 2-year bond, which will increase in value as short-term yields fall with the right to pay-fixed on a 30-year swap, which increases in value if long-term yields rise. Portfolio A involves the sale of two options. Although they will expire unexercised in a steeper curve environment, the investor's return is limited to the two option premia. Portfolio B is the opposite of Portfolio C, positioning the investor for a flattening of the yield curve.

14 A is correct. Recall from Equation 11 that the sum of the key rate durations equals the effective portfolio duration. The approximate (first-order) change in portfolio value may be estimated from the first (modified) term of Equation 3, namely (–EffDur × ΔYield). Solving for this using the –1.22 effective duration difference multiplied by 0.005 equals 0.0061%, or 61 bps.

15 B is correct. A positive butterfly indicates a decrease in the butterfly spread due to an expected rise in short- and long-term yields-to-maturity combined with a lower medium-term yield-to-maturity. Since the active portfolio is short duration versus the index in the 2-year, 5-year, and 30-year maturities and long duration in the 10-year, it will generate excess return if the butterfly spread falls.

16 A is correct. A net positive key rate duration difference indicates a long duration position relative to the index, while a net negative duration difference indicates a short position. Relative to the index, the active portfolio is "short" in the 2-year, 5-year, and 30-year maturities and "long" the 10-year maturity versus the index. The pay-fixed 10-year swap and long 2-year, 5-year, and 30-year bond futures positions best offset these differences.

17 C is correct. Forward rate bias is defined as an observed divergence from interest rate parity conditions under which active investors seek to benefit by borrowing in a lower-yield currency and investing in a higher-yield currency. A is incorrect since lower-yielding currencies trade at a forward premium. B is incorrect due to covered interest rate parity; fully hedged foreign currency fixed-income investments will tend to yield the domestic risk-free rate.

18 A is correct. Since both strategies use zero-coupon bonds, the rolldown return is calculated from expected bond price changes from "rolling down" the THB yield curve, which is assumed to be static.

Buy and Hold: 1.00% = (100.00 – 99.009)/99.009

Yield Curve Rolldown: 3.01% = (99.009 – 96.1169)/96.1169

19 A is correct. Under a static yield curve assumption, expected returns are equal to rolldown return plus changes in currency over the investment horizon. Using Equation 12, we solved for R_{FC} for both portfolios in Question 18, and R_{FX} is 1.5%. Expected returns are:

Buy and Hold: $E(R)$ = 2.515%, or (1.01 × 1.015) – 1

Yield Curve Rolldown: $E(R)$ = 4.555%, or (1.0301 × 1.015) – 1

20 C is correct. In a higher THB yield scenario in one year, the Yield Curve Rolldown expected return would fall since a higher THB yield-to-maturity in one year would reduce the price at which the investor could sell the 1-year zero in one year. The Buy-and-Hold portfolio return will be unaffected since the 1-year bond matures at the end of the investment horizon.

21 C is correct. A duration-neutral flattening trade involves a short 2-year bond position and a long 10-year bond position, which have a "matched" duration or portfolio duration of zero. This portfolio will realize a gain if the slope of the yield curve—that is, the difference between short-term and long-term yields—declines. Yield curve inversion is an extreme version of flattening in which the spread between long-term and short-term yields-to-maturity falls below zero. The bear steepening in A involves an unchanged 2-year yield-to-maturity with a rise in the 10-year yield-to-maturity, causing a portfolio *loss*. The bull flattening in B combines a constant 2-year yield-to-maturity with lower 10-year rates, resulting in a gain on the 10-year bond position and an unchanged 2-year bond position.

READING
14

Fixed-Income Active Management: Credit Strategies

by Campe Goodman, CFA, and Oleg Melentyev, CFA

Campe Goodman, CFA, is at Wellington Management (USA). Oleg Melentyev, CFA, is at Bank of America Merrill Lynch (USA).

LEARNING OUTCOMES

Mastery	The candidate should be able to:
☐	a. describe risk considerations for spread-based fixed-income portfolios;
☐	b. discuss the advantages and disadvantages of credit spread measures for spread-based fixed-income portfolios, and explain why option-adjusted spread is considered the most appropriate measure;
☐	c. discuss bottom-up approaches to credit strategies;
☐	d. discuss top-down approaches to credit strategies;
☐	e. discuss liquidity risk in credit markets and how liquidity risk can be managed in a credit portfolio;
☐	f. describe how to assess and manage tail risk in credit portfolios;
☐	g. discuss the use of credit default swap strategies in active fixed-income portfolio management;
☐	h. discuss various portfolio positioning strategies that managers can use to implement a specific credit spread view;
☐	i. discuss considerations in constructing and managing portfolios across international credit markets;
☐	j. describe the use of structured financial instruments as an alternative to corporate bonds in credit portfolios;
☐	k. describe key inputs, outputs, and considerations in using analytical tools to manage fixed-income portfolios.

© 2021 CFA Institute. All rights reserved.

1. INTRODUCTION

Most fixed-income instruments trade at a nominal yield to maturity (YTM) that lies above that for an equivalent government or benchmark bond of similar maturity. This **yield spread** or difference compensates investors for the risk that they might not receive interest and principal cash flows as expected, whether as a result of a financially distressed corporate borrower, a sovereign issuer unable (or unwilling) to meet scheduled payments, or a deterioration in credit quality in an underlying pool of assets of a structured instrument such as an asset-backed security. A portion of the yield spread reflects the bid–offer cost of buying or selling a particular bond versus a government security, a liquidity premium that varies based on market conditions. Active managers of spread-based fixed-income portfolios take positions in credit and other risk factors that vary from those of an index to generate excess return versus passive index replication. Financial analysts who build on their foundational knowledge by mastering these more advanced fixed-income concepts and tools will broaden their career opportunities in the investment industry.

We begin by reviewing expected fixed-income portfolio return components with a particular focus on credit spreads. These spreads are not directly observable but rather derived from market information. Similar to benchmark yield curves, credit-spread curves are often defined by spread level and slope, and usually grouped by credit rating to gauge relative risk as well as to anticipate and act on expected changes in these relationships over the business cycle. We outline credit spread measures for fixed- and floating-rate bonds and quantify the effect of spread changes on portfolio value. Building blocks for active credit management beyond individual bonds include exchange-traded funds (ETFs), structured financial instruments, and derivative products such as credit default swaps (CDS). These tools are used to describe bottom-up and top-down active credit management approaches as well as how managers position spread-based fixed-income portfolios to capitalize on a market view.

2. KEY CREDIT AND SPREAD CONCEPTS FOR ACTIVE MANAGEMENT

a describe risk considerations for spread-based fixed-income portfolios

Managers seeking to maximize fixed-income portfolio returns will usually buy securities with a higher YTM (and lower equivalent price) than a comparable default risk-free government bond. The excess return targeted by active managers of spread-based fixed-income portfolios is captured in the fourth term of the now familiar fixed-income return equation:

$$E(R) \approx \text{Coupon income} \tag{1}$$

$$+/- \text{ Rolldown return}$$
$$+/- E (\Delta \text{ Price due to investor's view of benchmark yields})$$
$$+/- E (\Delta \text{ Price due to investor's view of yield spreads})$$
$$+/- E (\Delta \text{ Price due to investor's view of currency value changes})$$

Similar to the benchmark yield curve addressed earlier in the curriculum, yield spreads for a specific bond issuance over a comparable government bond cannot be directly observed but are rather derived or estimated from market information. This yield spread is a risk premium that primarily compensates investors for assuming credit and liquidity risks.

While credit risk for a specific borrower depends on both the likelihood of default and the loss severity in a default scenario, credit risk for a specific bond *issuance* also depends on the period over which payments are promised, the relative seniority of the debt claim, and the sources of repayment, such as the value of underlying collateral, among other factors.

Liquidity risk refers to an investor's ability to readily buy or sell a specific security. The YTM difference (or bid–ask spread) between the purchase and sale price of a bond depends on market conditions and on the specific supply-and-demand dynamics of each fixed-income security. As active fixed-income portfolio managers identify and pursue specific credit strategies, they must also consider trading costs when calculating expected excess returns.

2.1 Credit Risk Considerations

Yield spreads over default risk-free government bonds mostly compensate investors for the potential of not receiving promised cash flows (issuer default) and for the loss severity if a default occurs. Spreads range widely across ratings categories and time periods. For example, Exhibit 1 shows yield spreads as a percentage of total YTM for A-, BBB-, and BB rated US corporate issuers from mid-2009 to mid-2020.

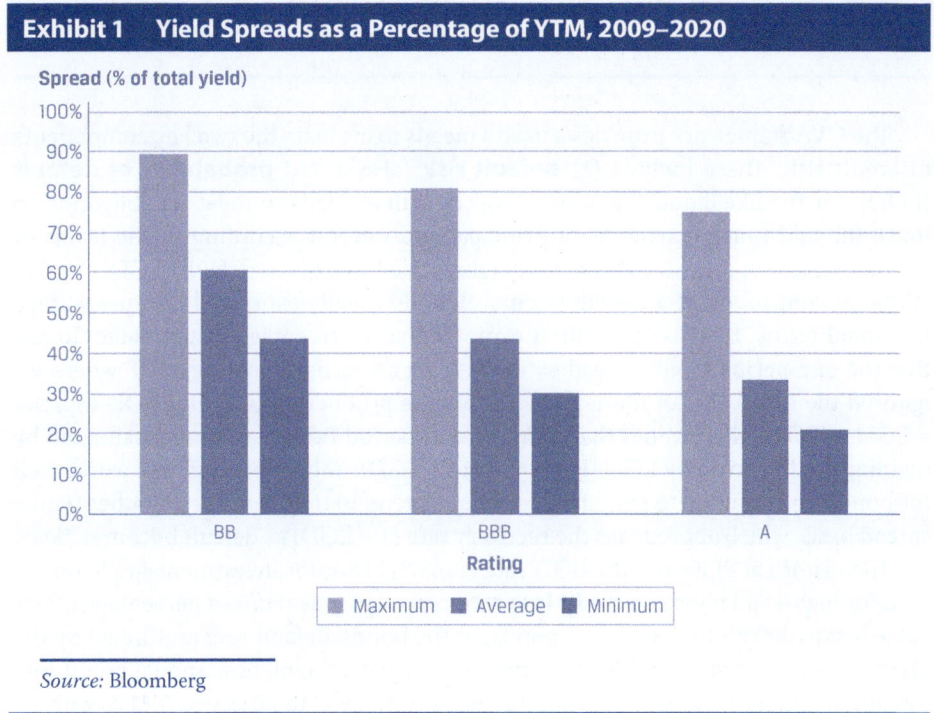

Exhibit 1   Yield Spreads as a Percentage of YTM, 2009–2020

Source: Bloomberg

On average, 60% of total YTM was attributable to yield spread for BB rated issuers versus 33% for A rated issuers over the period. This percentage was at a minimum for all rating categories in 2010 as the US economy recovered from the 2008–09 financial crisis and reached its peak in early 2020 during the economic slowdown due to the

COVID-19 pandemic. The higher average proportion of all-in yield attributable to credit risk warrants a greater focus on this factor among high-yield investors over the credit cycle.

2.1.1 Default Probabilities and Recovery Rates

The **credit valuation adjustment (CVA)** framework shown earlier in the curriculum and in Exhibit 2 comprises the present value of credit risk for a loan, bond, or derivative obligation.

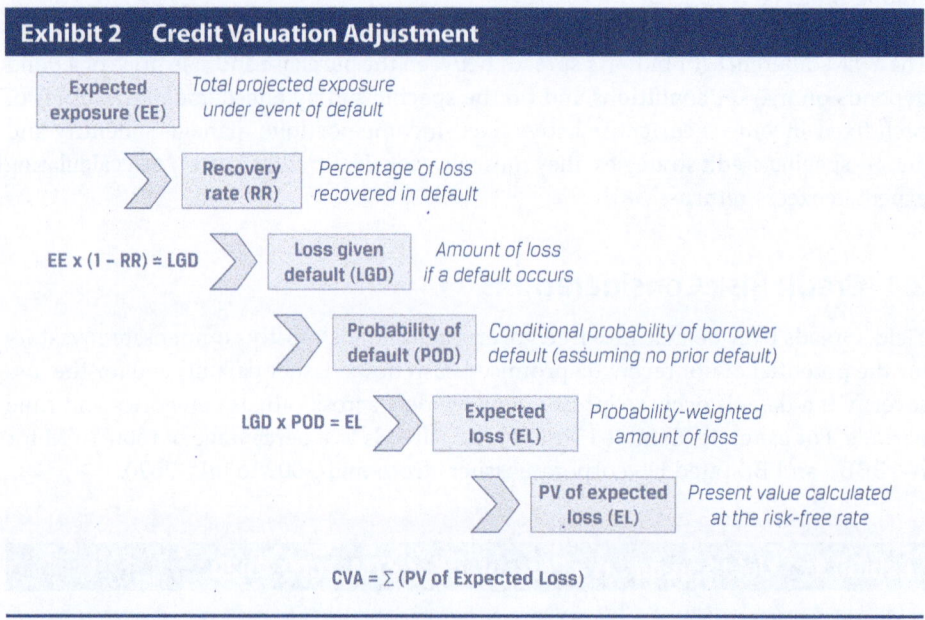

The CVA framework provides a useful means to evaluate the two key components of credit risk. These include (1) **default risk** (also called **probability of default** [POD]), or the likelihood that a borrower defaults or fails to meet its obligation to make full and timely payments of principal and interest according to the terms of the debt security; and (2) **loss severity** (also called loss given default [LGD]), which is the amount of loss if a default occurs. POD is usually expressed as a percentage in annual terms. LGD is most often expressed as a percentage of par value. Recall that the one-period credit spread estimate from an earlier lesson on CDS where we ignored the time value of money was simply the product of LGD and POD (Spread ≈ LGD × POD). This implies that a simple one-period POD can be approximated by dividing credit spread by LGD (POD ≈ Spread/LGD). While this estimate works well for bonds trading close to par, distressed bonds tend to trade on a price rather than a spread basis, which approaches the recovery rate (1 – LGD) as default becomes likely.

The historical POD and the LGD rate is much lower for investment-grade bonds than for high-yield bonds. A **credit loss rate** represents the *realized* percentage of par value lost to default for a group of bonds, or the bonds' default rate multiplied by the loss severity. According to Moody's Investors Service, the highest annual credit loss rate for US investment-grade corporate bonds from 1983 to 2019 was 0.41%, with an average of just 0.05%. For high-yield bonds, the average credit loss rate over the same period was 2.53%, and in several years, usually around economic recessions, losses exceeded 5%. Exhibit 3 shows global annual corporate default rates from S&P Global Ratings for a similar period.

Key Credit and Spread Concepts for Active Management

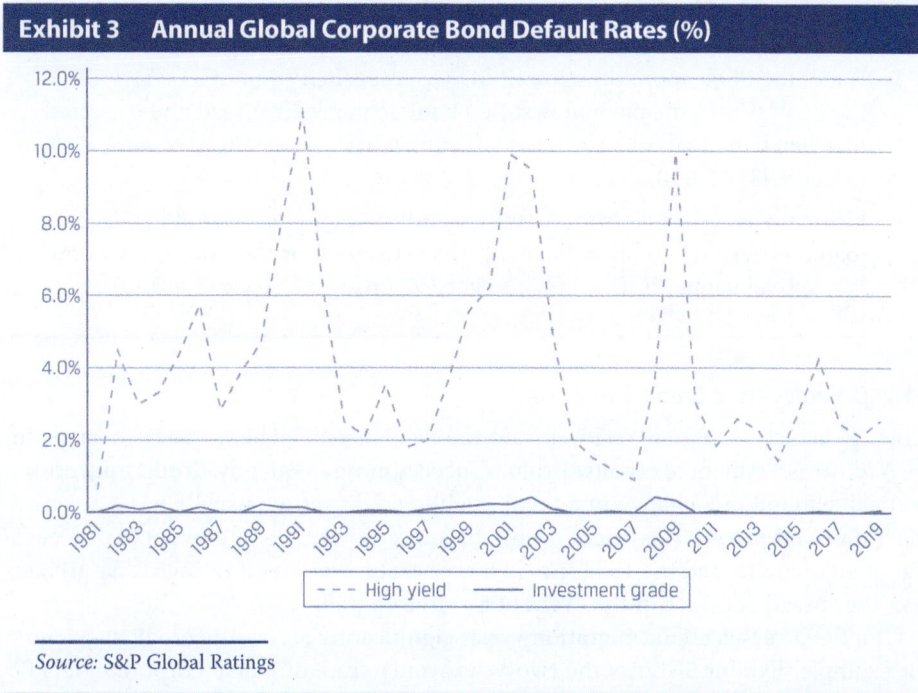

Exhibit 3 Annual Global Corporate Bond Default Rates (%)

Source: S&P Global Ratings

Exhibit 3 makes clear that the likelihood of default rises significantly as the economy slows, reaching peaks during the 1990–91, 2001, and 2008 recessions. The percentage of par value lost in a default scenario depends on a bond's (or loan's) relative position in the capital structure and whether it is secured or unsecured, as shown in Exhibit 4.

Exhibit 4 Average Volume Weighted US Corporate Debt Recovery Rates, 1983–2019

First lien bank loan	64%
Second lien bank loan	29%
Senior unsecured bank loan	44%
First lien bond	55%
Second lien bond	45%
Senior unsecured bond	35%
Senior subordinated bond	27%
Subordinated bond	28%
Junior subordinated bond	14%

Source: Moody's Investors Service

EXAMPLE 1

Estimating Credit Spreads Using POD and LGD

A bank analyst observes a first lien bank loan maturing in two years with a spread of 100 bps from an issuer considering a new second lien bank loan. Using average historical volume weighted corporate debt recovery rates (RR) as a guide, what is the estimated credit spread for the new second lien bank loan?

> **Answer:**
>
> 1. Using the POD approximation (POD ≈ Spread/LGD and LGD = (1 − RR)), the analyst uses the current first lien bank loan credit spread and expected first lien bank loan recovery rate to estimate the issuer's POD to be 2.778% (=1.00%/(1 − 0.64)).
>
> 2. Using the issuer POD from Answer 1 and the expected second lien bank loan recovery rate of 29%, the bank analyst solves for the expected second lien spread using (POD × LGD) to get 197 bps (=2.778% × (1 − 0.29)).

2.1.2 Default versus Credit Migration

Although actual defaults are relatively rare among higher-rated bond issuers, changes in the *relative* assessment of creditworthiness occurs more frequently. **Credit migration**, or the likelihood of a change in a bond's public credit rating, usually has a negative effect on bond prices. This effect occurs because the chance of downgrade exceeds that of an upgrade, and the yield spread increase at lower credit ratings is far greater than the spread decrease in the event of a credit upgrade.

The POD versus credit migration varies significantly across the credit spectrum. For example, Exhibit 5 shows the two-year average rate of global corporate default and one-notch downgrade.

Exhibit 5 Two-Year Average Global Corporate Default/Downgrade, 1981–2019

Statistic/Rating	AAA	AA	A	BBB	BB	B	CCC
Default Probability (%)	0.03	0.06	0.14	0.45	1.96	7.83	36.49
One Notch Downgrade (%)	16.22	13.79	8.81	5.66	9.82	5.22	

Source: S&P Global Ratings

Investors typically categorize credit risk using public debt ratings, distinguishing between investment-grade and high-yield market segments. Investment-grade bonds generally have higher credit ratings, lower default risk, and higher recovery in the event of default and offer lower all-in yields to maturity. High-yield bonds usually have higher yields to maturity as a result of lower (sub-investment or speculative grade) credit ratings, higher default risk, and lower recovery in the event of default. In an earlier yield curve strategies lesson, changes in the level, slope, and shape of the government bond term structure across maturities were established as primary risk factors. The level and slope of credit spread curves are often categorized by public credit rating to distinguish relative market changes across the credit spectrum.

For example, the relative historical yield spread *level* across public rating categories for US corporate borrowers is shown in Exhibit 6.

Key Credit and Spread Concepts for Active Management

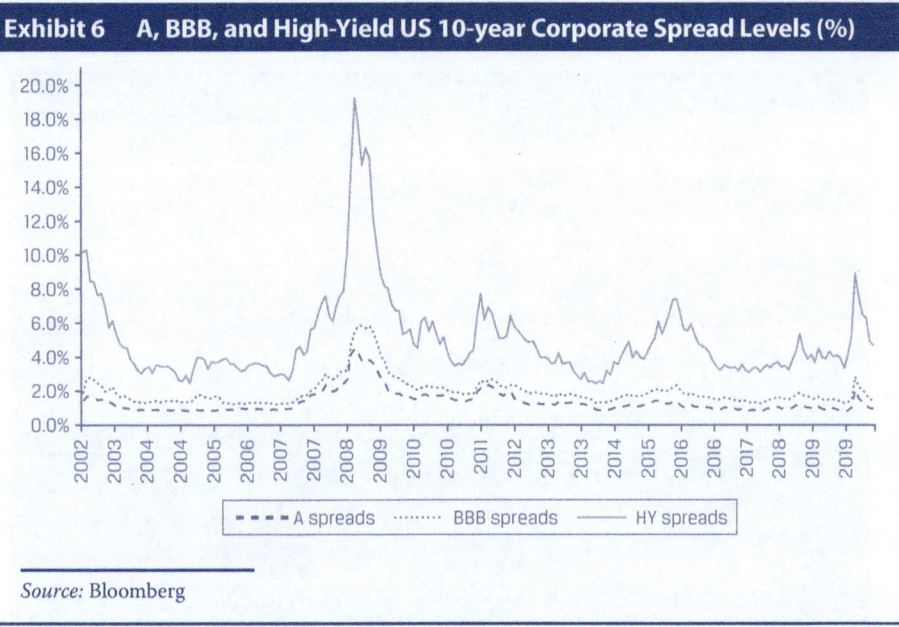

Exhibit 6: A, BBB, and High-Yield US 10-year Corporate Spread Levels (%)

Source: Bloomberg

Lower-rated bonds face a greater impact from adverse market events, as evidenced by the widening gap between BBB rated and high-yield bonds during the 2008 financial crisis and the COVID-19 pandemic in 2020.

2.1.3 Credit Spread Curves

Active managers often position spread-based portfolios to capitalize on expected credit spread curve changes in a way similar to the benchmark yield curve strategies seen in an earlier lesson. While frequent issuers with many bonds outstanding across maturities have their own issuer-specific credit curve, credit spread curves are usually categorized by rating, issuer type, and/or corporate sector. These curves are derived from the difference between all-in yields to maturity for bonds within each respective category and a government benchmark bond or swap yield curve, with adjustments for specific credit spread measures covered in detail later. For example, Exhibit 7 shows the decline in option-adjusted spreads for US BBB rated health care companies over a one-year period from the end of Q3 2019 to 2020, with the bar graph at the bottom showing the decrease for each maturity.

Exhibit 7 BBB Rated US Corporate Health Care Spreads, 2019–2020

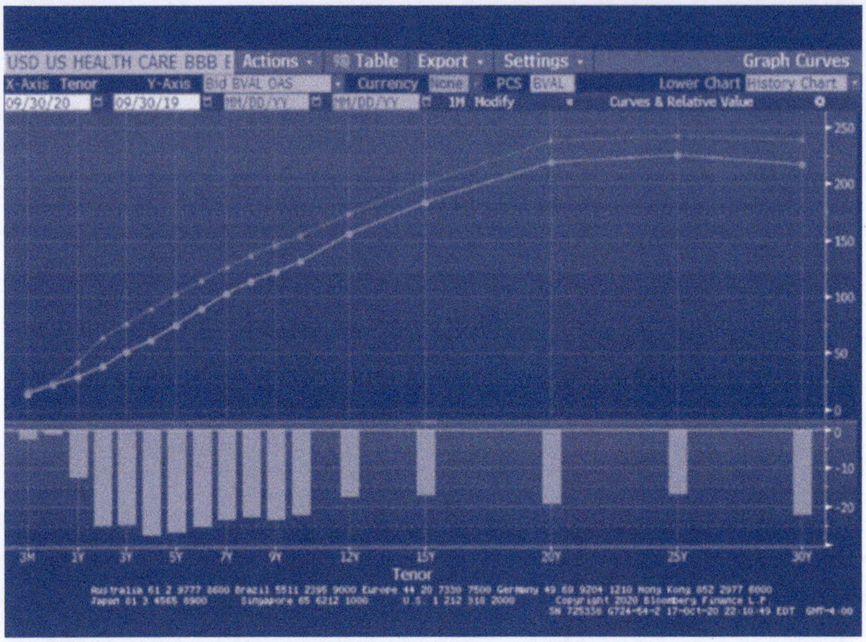

Source: Bloomberg

Primary credit risk factors for a specific issuer include the level and slope of the issuer's credit spread curve. For instance, ignoring liquidity differences across maturities, an upward-sloping credit spread curve suggests a relatively low near-term default probability that rises over time as the likelihood of downgrade and/or default increases. A flatter credit spread curve in contrast indicates that downgrade/default probabilities are equally likely in the near- and long-term.

Credit spread curve changes are broadly driven by the **credit cycle**, the expansion and contraction of credit over the business cycle, which translates into asset price changes based on default and recovery expectations across maturities and rating categories. Exhibit 8 outlines key credit cycle characteristics and the general effect on credit spread curve levels and slope for high- and low-rated issuers.

Exhibit 8 General Credit Cycle Characteristics

	Early Expansion (Recovery)	Late Expansion	Peak	Contraction (Recession)
Economic Activity	Stable	Accelerating	Decelerating	Declining
Corporate Profitability	Rising	Peak	Stable	Falling
Corporate Leverage	Falling	Stable	Rising	Peak
Corporate Defaults	Peak	Falling	Stable	Rising

Exhibit 8   (Continued)

	Early Expansion (Recovery)	Late Expansion	Peak	Contraction (Recession)
Credit Spread Level	Stable	Falling	Rising	Peak
Credit Spread Slope	Stable for high grade, inverted for low ratings	Steeper for both higher and lower ratings	Steeper for both higher and lower ratings	Flatter for high grade, inverted for low ratings

Exhibits 3 and 6 demonstrate the significant variability in annual credit loss rates and credit spread changes, respectively, across the ratings spectrum. Lower-rated issuers tend to experience greater slope and level changes over the credit cycle, including more frequent inversion of the credit curve, given their larger rise in annual credit losses during economic downturns. Higher-rated issuers, in contrast, face smaller credit spread changes and usually exhibit upward-sloping credit curves and fewer credit losses during periods of economic contraction. Credit spread differences *between* major ratings categories tend to narrow during periods of strong economic growth and widen when growth is expected to slow.

For example, consider the widening of BB versus single-A US corporate spreads during Q1 2020 shown in Exhibit 9. The difference between two-year BB spreads and A spreads for the same tenor more than tripled over this three-month period.

Exhibit 9   BB versus A Credit Spread Curve, 2019 versus 2020

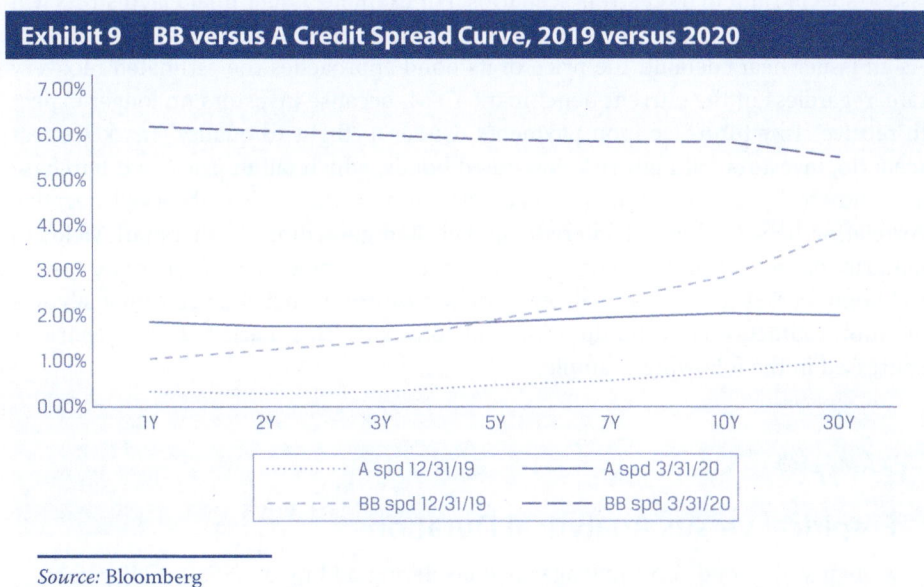

Source: Bloomberg

EXAMPLE 2

Credit Cycle and Credit Spread Curve Changes

Which of the following *best* describes the expected shape of the credit spread curve in an economic downturn?

A Investment-grade and high-yield issuers usually experience similar credit spread curve steepening because of declining corporate profitability.

B High-yield issuers usually experience more spread curve steepening than investment-grade issuers because higher leverage leads to a greater decline in profitability.

C High-yield issuers often experience more pronounced flattening or credit spread curve inversion in an economic downturn because the probability of downgrade or default is higher in the near term than the long term.

Solution:

The correct answer is C. While investment-grade and high-yield issuers both experience declining profitability in an economic downturn, as in answers A and B, this usually leads to a flatter credit spread curve for investment-grade issuers and often to credit spread curve inversion for high-yield issuers, given a rise in near-term downgrades and defaults.

Actual price movements of lower-rated bonds can be quite different from what analytical models based on benchmark rates and credit spreads would predict under issuer-specific and market stress scenarios. For example, issuer financial distress will cause a bond's price to diverge from what a model using benchmark rates would suggest. As an issuer nears default, the price of its bond approaches the estimated recovery rate, regardless of the current benchmark YTM, because investors no longer expect to receive risky future coupon payments. Under a "flight to quality" market stress scenario, investors sell high-risk, low-rated bonds, which fall in price, and purchase government bonds, which experience price appreciation. This observed negative correlation between high-yield credit spreads and government benchmark yields to maturity often leads fixed-income practitioners to use statistical models and historical bond market data to estimate **empirical duration** rather than rely on analytical duration estimates based on duration and convexity. This market stress scenario is addressed in the following example.

EXAMPLE 3

Empirical versus Analytical Duration

A high-yield bond fund manager is considering adding a US$50 million face value, five-year, 6.75% semiannual coupon bond with a YTM of 5.40% to an active portfolio. The manager uses regression analysis to estimate the bond's empirical duration to be 2.95. Calculate the bond's analytical duration, and estimate the difference in the expected versus actual market value change for this position, given a 50 bp decline in benchmark yields to maturity using these two measures.

Solution:

1 Solve for the bond's analytical duration by using the Excel MDURATION function (MDURATION(settlement, maturity, coupon, yield, frequency, basis)) using a settlement date of 1 January 2022, maturity of 1

Key Credit and Spread Concepts for Active Management

> January 2027, a 6.75% coupon, 5.40% YTM, semiannual frequency and basis of 0 (30/360 day count) to get 4.234. Note the analytical duration is greater than the observed empirical duration of 2.95.
>
> 2 The bond position value can be calculated using the Excel PRICE function (PRICE(settlement, maturity, coupon, yield, frequency, basis)) to solve for a price of 105.847 per 100 face value, or a price of US$52,923,500 for a US$50 million face value.
>
> 3 The difference in percentage market value change can be estimated using the 0.50% yield change multiplied by modified duration (−ModDur × ΔYield) for the two estimates. If the benchmark YTM declines by 50 bps, then
>
> > Analytical duration estimate: 2.117% = (−4.234 × −0.5%)
> >
> > Empirical duration estimate: 1.475% = (−2.95 × −0.5%)
> >
> > The analytical duration calculation overestimates the price gain versus the empirical duration estimate.
>
> 4 The difference is 0.642% (2.117% − 1.475%), or an expected US$339,769 (=0.642% × $52,923,500) value difference between the two measures.

While the concept of empirical duration emphasizes the *direction* of high-yield credit spread changes versus benchmark rates, as suggested earlier, the *magnitude* of credit spread changes is greater for lower- versus higher-rate bonds. As we will see later in the lesson, this empirical observation leads to the use of credit spread measure changes based on *percentage* as opposed to absolute credit spread changes for lower-rated issuers.

2.2 Credit Spread Measures

b discuss the advantages and disadvantages of credit spread measures for spread-based fixed-income portfolios, and explain why option-adjusted spread is considered the most appropriate measure

2.2.1 Fixed-Rate Bond Credit Spread Measures

The estimation of yield spreads from market information gives rise to several measures of the difference between a fixed-rate bond's YTM and a benchmark rate. Recall that the YTM is an internal rate of return calculation of all bond cash flows that assumes any earlier payments are reinvested at the same rate and the bond is held to maturity. Spread comparisons are accurate when comparing bonds with identical maturities but different coupons. Because bond maturities vary in practice, a mismatch arises that creates measurement bias if the yield curve is sloped. As a bond rolls down the curve, the benchmark security can also change over time. Finally, yield-based measures do not accurately gauge the return of carry-based strategies often used by active managers (for example, long a risky bond, short a default risk-free position in the repo market).

The yield spread (or benchmark spread) defined earlier as the simple difference between a bond's YTM and the YTM of an on-the-run government bond of similar maturity is easy to calculate and interpret for option-free bonds, and it is particularly useful for infrequently traded bonds. The yield spread also facilitates the approximation of bond price changes for a given benchmark YTM change, assuming a constant yield spread. That said, this simple government bond–based measure has both curve slope and maturity mismatch biases and lacks consistency over time because government benchmarks change as a bond nears maturity.

The **G-spread** uses constant maturity Treasury yields to maturity as the benchmark. Exhibit 10 shows the difference between yield spread and G-spread measures using the example of a bond with 12 years remaining to maturity. While the yield spread for this bond would likely be quoted over a 10-year government benchmark rate, the G-spread involves an interpolation between 10-year and 20-year government yields to maturity.

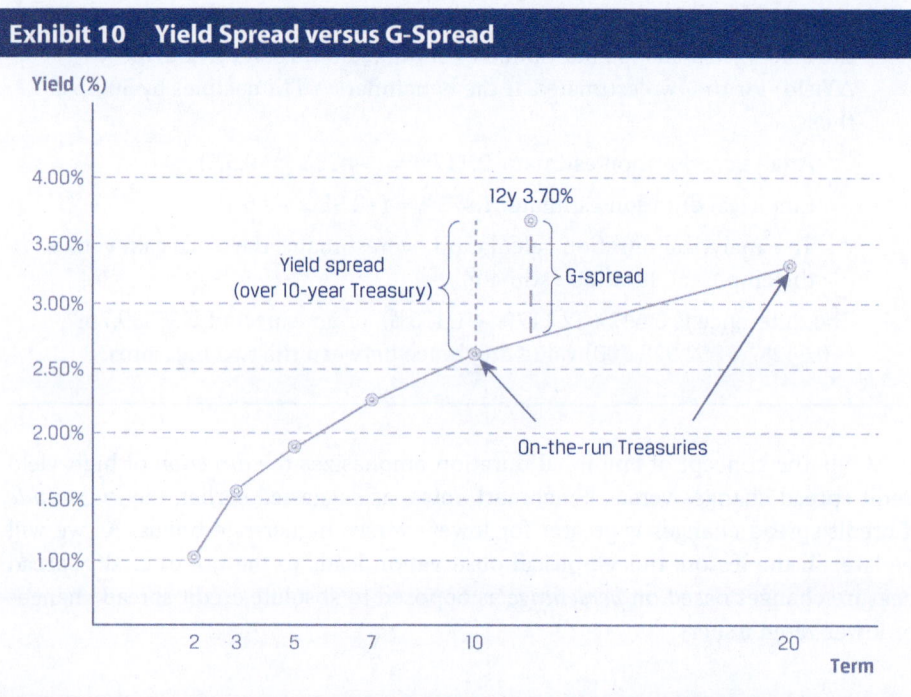

Exhibit 10   Yield Spread versus G-Spread

EXAMPLE 4

Yield Spread versus G-Spread

A portfolio manager considers the following annual coupon bonds:

Issuer	Term	Coupon	Yield	ModDur
Bank	8y	2.75%	2.68%	7.10
Government	7y	1.5%	1.39%	6.61
Government	10y	1.625%	1.66%	9.16

1   Calculate the yield spread and G-spread for the bank bond.
2   An increase in expected inflation causes the government yield curve to steepen, with a 20-point rise in the 10-year government bond YTM and no change in the 7-year government YTM. If the respective bank bond yield spread measures remain unchanged, calculate the expected bank bond percentage price change in each case, and explain which is a more accurate representation of the market change in this case.

Solution to 1:

Yield spread for the bank bond is 1.290%, or the simple difference between the 2.68% bank bond YTM and the 1.39% YTM of the nearest on-the-run government bond.

The G-spread is the difference between the bank bond YTM and a linear interpolation of the YTMs of the 7-year government bond (r_{7yr}) and the 10-year government bond (r_{10yr}). Calculate the approximate 8-year government rate as follows:

1. Solve for the weights of the 7-year and the 10-year bond in the interpolation calculation.

    7-year bond weight = w_7 = 66.7% (= (10 − 8)/(10 − 7))

    10-year bond weight = w_{10} = 33.3% (or (1 − w_7))

    Note that (w_7 × 7) + (w_{10} × 10 = 8).

2. The 8-year government rate is a weighted average of the 7-year bond rate and the 10-year bond rate using the weights in Step 1.

    $r_{8yr} = w_7 \times r_{7yr} + w_{10} \times r_{10yr}$

    = (66.7% × 1.39%) + (33.3% × 1.66%) = 1.48%

3. The G-spread, or the difference between the bank bond YTM and the 8-year government rate, equals 1.20% (= 2.68% − 1.48%).

Solution to 2:

For the yield spread measure, neither the 1.20% spread nor the 7-year government rate of 1.39% has changed, so an analyst considering only these two factors would expect the bank bond price to remain unchanged.

However, for the G-spread measure, the 20 bp increase in the 10-year government YTM causes the 8-year interpolated government YTM to change.

1. The 7-year and the 10-year bond weights for the interpolation are the same as for Question 1, w_7 = 66.7% and w_{10} = 33.3%.

2. The new 8-year government rate is a weighted average of the 7-year bond rate and the 10-year bond rate using the weights in Step 1.

    $r_{8yr} = w_7 \times r_{7yr} + w_{10} \times r_{10yr}$

    = (66.7% × 1.39%) + (33.3% × 1.81%) = 1.53%

3. The bank bond YTM has risen by 0.05% to 2.73% (=1.53% + 1.20%).

4. The bank bond price change can be estimated by multiplying the yield change by modified duration (−ModDur × ΔYield) as in earlier lessons. This change can be calculated as −0.355% (=−7.1 × 0.05%).

    Note that we can confirm this using the Excel PV function (=−PV (rate, nper, pmt, FV, type)) where "rate" is the interest rate per period (0.0268), "nper" is the number of periods (8), "pmt" is the periodic coupon (2.75), "FV" is future value (100), and "type" corresponds to payments made at the end of each period (0).

    Initial bank bond price: 100.50 (=−PV (0.0268, 8, 2.75, 100, 0))

    New bank bond price: 100.14 (=−PV (0.0273, 8, 2.75, 100, 0))

    Price change: −0.354% (= (100.14 − 100.50)/100.50)

> The G-spread calculation provides a more accurate representation of the estimated bank bond price change in this case because it incorporates the term structure of interest rates.

The **I-spread (interpolated spread)** uses interest rate swaps as the benchmark. Recall that swap rates are derived using short-term lending or market reference rates (MRRs) rather than default-risk-free rates, and unlike government bonds, they are quoted across all maturities. Short-term MRR were historically survey-based Libor rates and are transitioning to transaction-based, secured overnight funding rates. The spread over an MRR-based benchmark can be interpreted as a *relative* rather than absolute credit risk measure for a given bond issuer. An issuer might use the I-spread to determine the relative cost of fixed-rate versus floating-rate borrowing alternatives, while an investor can use the MRR spread to compare pricing more readily across issuers and maturities. Swap benchmarks have the added benefit of directly measuring all-in bond YTMs with an instrument that can be used both as a duration hedge and to measure carry return more accurately for a leveraged position. While the I-spread addresses the maturity mismatch of bonds and benchmarks as raised earlier, it incorporates yield levels using a point on the curve to estimate a risky bond's yield spread rather than the term structure of interest rates and is limited to option-free bonds as a credit risk measure.

Asset swaps convert a bond's periodic fixed coupon to MRR plus (or minus) a spread. If the bond is priced close to par, this spread approximately equals the bond's credit risk over the MRR. Exhibit 11 shows the mechanics of an asset swap.

Exhibit 11 Asset Swap Mechanics

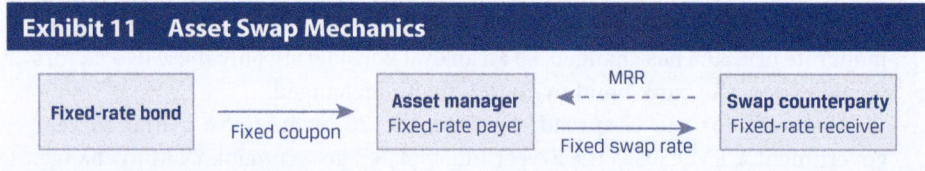

The **asset swap spread (ASW)** is the difference between the bond's fixed coupon rate and the fixed rate on an interest rate swap versus MRR, which matches the coupon dates for the remaining life of the bond. If we assume an investor purchases a bond at par, the asset swap transforms the fixed-rate coupon to an equivalent spread over MRR for the life of the bond. Note that under a bond default scenario, the asset manager would still face the mark-to-market settlement of the swap.

EXAMPLE 5

ASW versus I-Spread

Consider the information from the bank and government annual coupon bonds from the prior example:

Issuer	Term	Coupon	Yield	ModDur
Bank	8y	2.75%	2.68%	7.10
Government	7y	1.5%	1.39%	6.61
Government	10y	1.625%	1.66%	9.16

Key Credit and Spread Concepts for Active Management

Assuming that 7- and 10-year swap spreads over the respective government benchmark yields to maturity are 15 bps and 20 bps, calculate the ASW and the I-spread for the bank bond, and interpret the difference between the two.

Solution:

1. Solve for the weights of the 7-year and the 10-year bond in the interpolation calculation.

    7-year bond weight = w_7 = 66.7% (= (10 − 8)/(10 − 7)).

    10-year bond weight = w_{10} = 33.3% (or (1 − w_7)).

    Note that (w_7 × 7) + (w_{10} × 10) = 8.

2. The interpolated 8-year swap rate is a weighted average of the 7-year swap rate (1.54% = 1.39% + 0.15%) and the 10-year swap rate (1.86% = 1.66% + 0.20%).

    $r_{Swap8yr} = w_7 \times r_{Swap7yr} + w_{10} \times r_{Swap10yr}$

    (66.7% × 1.54%) + (33.3% × 1.86%) = 1.647%

3. The ASW equals the difference between the bank bond *coupon* of 2.75% and the 8-year swap rate of 1.647%, or 110.3 bps.

4. The I-spread is the difference between the bank bond's current YTM of 2.68% and the 8-year swap rate of 1.647%, or 103.3 bps.

The ASW is an estimate of the spread over MRR versus the bond's original coupon rate to maturity, while the I-spread is an estimate of the spread over MRR for a new par bond from the bank issuer, with the difference largely reflecting the premium or discount of the outstanding bond price.

While both the G-spread and I-spread use the same discount rate for each cash flow, a more precise approach incorporating the term structure of interest rates is to derive a constant spread over a government (or interest rate swap) spot curve instead. This spread is known as the **zero-volatility spread (Z-spread)** of a bond over the benchmark rate. The Z-spread formula shown in Equation 2 was introduced in an earlier reading.

$$PV = \frac{PMT}{(1 + z_1 + Z)^1} + \frac{PMT}{(1 + z_2 + Z)^2} + \ldots + \frac{PMT + FV}{(1 + z_N + Z)^N} \qquad (2)$$

Here the bond price (PV) is a function of coupon (PMT) and principal (FV) payments in the numerator with respective benchmark spot rates $z_1 \ldots z_N$ derived from the swap or government yield curve and a constant Z-spread per period (Z) in the denominator discounted as of a coupon date. While more accurate than either the G-spread or I-spread, this is a more complex calculation that is conducted by practitioners using either a spreadsheet or other analytical model.

Credit default swap (CDS) basis refers to the difference between the Z-spread on a specific bond and the CDS spread of the same (or interpolated) maturity for the same issuer. Recall from earlier in the curriculum that a CDS is a derivative contract in which a protection buyer makes a series of premium (or CDS spread) payments to a protection seller in exchange for compensation for credit losses (or the difference between par and the recovery rate) under a credit event. Negative basis arises if the yield spread is above the CDS spread, and positive basis indicates a yield spread in excess of the CDS market. Although spreads for a single issuer across bond and CDS markets should be closely aligned in principle, in practice, CDS basis arises because of such factors as bond price differences from par, accrued interest, and varying contract terms, among other items. As in the case of asset swaps, CDS basis is a pricing measure, but unlike ASW, a CDS contract is terminated and settled following a credit event with no residual interest rate swap mark-to-market exposure. Similar to the I-spread using swaps or the asset swap just mentioned, CDS basis is a useful credit measure for investors actively trading or hedging credit risk using CDS, as addressed in detail later.

The **option-adjusted spread (OAS)** is a generalization of the Z-spread calculation that incorporates bond option pricing based on assumed interest rate volatility. Earlier readings established the use of the term structure of zero rates combined with a volatility assumption to derive forward interest rates used to value bonds with embedded options. The OAS is the constant yield spread over the zero curve which makes the arbitrage-free value of such a bond equal to its market price as shown in Exhibit 12. Note that the Z-spread for an option-free bond is simply its OAS, assuming zero volatility.

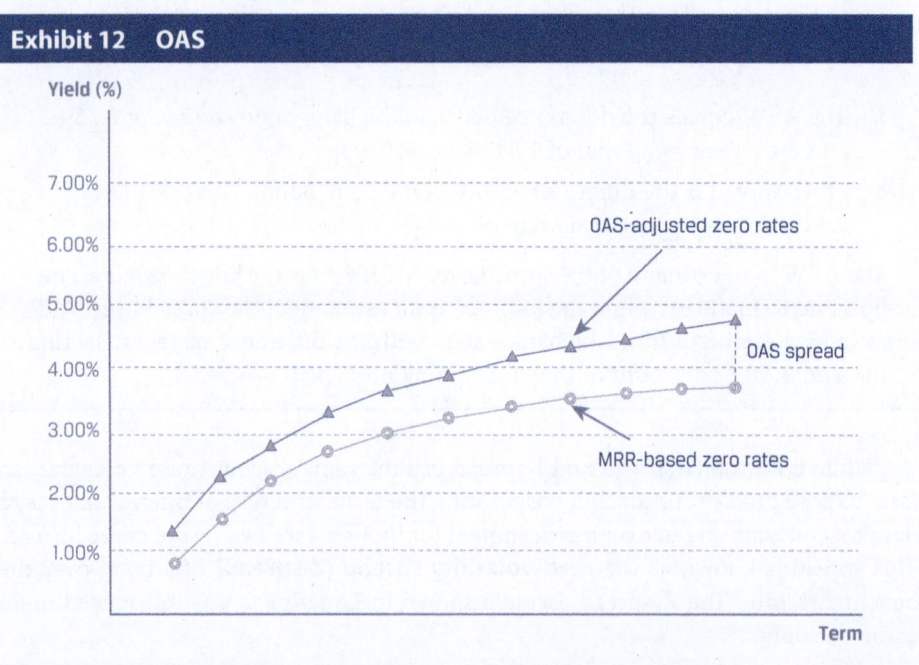

The OAS approach is the most appropriate yield spread measure for active fixed-income portfolio managers because it provides a consistent basis for comparing credit risk yield spreads for option-free, callable, putable, and structured fixed-income instruments. OAS calculations typically rely on fixed-income analytical models that incorporate the current term structure of interest rates, interest rate volatility, and term structure model factors introduced earlier in addition to the specific option-based features of a particular bond. Although OAS provides the best means to facilitate yield spread comparisons across different fixed-income securities, the main drawback of the OAS is that it is highly dependent on volatility and other model assumptions. For example, returns on structured financial instruments are highly dependent on prepayment versus extension risk, as outlined in an earlier lesson. While some analytical models calculate OAS using a standard or constant prepayment speed assumption, values based on historical or empirical analysis might provide very different and more accurate results. Also, the theoretical nature of the OAS calculation implies that bonds

Key Credit and Spread Concepts for Active Management

with embedded options are unlikely to realize the spread implied by the bond's OAS. Despite these shortcomings, OAS is the most widely accepted credit spread measure for comparing bonds with and without optionality across a fixed-income bond portfolio.

EXAMPLE 6

Portfolio OAS

A European portfolio manager is presented with the following information on a portfolio of two bonds. Calculate the OAS of the portfolio.

Issuer	Face Value	Price*	Accrued Interest*	OAS (bps p.a.)
Company A	€ 100,000,000	95	1.5	125
Company B	€ 200,000,000	97	2.0	150

*Per 100 of par value

Solution:

1. Solve for bond and portfolio values:
   - **A** Company A bond: €96,500,000 = €100,000,000 × (0.95 + 0.015)
   - **B** Company B bond: €198,000,000 = €200,000,000 × (0.97 + 0.02)
   - **C** Portfolio: €294,500,000 = €96,500,000 + €198,000,000
2. Solve for portfolio weights w_A and w_B:
   - **A** Company A (w_A): 32.8% = €96,500,000/€294,500,000
   - **B** Company B (w_B): 67.2% = €198,000,000/€294,500,000
3. Solve for portfolio OAS using $(OAS_A \times w_A) + (OAS_B \times w_B)$.

   OAS = 142 bps p.a. = (0.328 × 125 bps) + (0.672 × 150 bps)

Exhibit 13 summarizes these fixed-rate bond credit spread measures adapted from O'Kane and Sen (2005).

Exhibit 13: Key Fixed-Rate Bond Credit Spread Measures

Spread	Description	Advantages	Disadvantages
Yield spread	Difference between bond YTM and government benchmark of similar tenor	Simple to calculate and observe	Maturity mismatch, curve slope bias, and inconsistent over time
G-spread (Government spread)	Spread over interpolated government bond	Transparent and maturity matching default risk-free bond	Subject to changes in government bond demand

(continued)

Exhibit 13 (Continued)

Spread	Description	Advantages	Disadvantages
I-spread (Interpolated spread)	Yield spread over swap rate of same tenor	Spread versus market based (MRR) measure often used as hedge or for carry trade	Point estimate of term structure and limited to option-free bonds
ASW (Asset swap)	Spread over MRR of fixed bond coupon	Traded spread to convert current bond coupon to MRR plus a spread	Tradable spread rather than spread measure corresponding to cashflows and limited to option-free bonds
Z-spread (Zero volatility spread)	Yield spread over a government (or swap) spot curve	Accurately captures term structure of government or swap zero rates	More complex calculation limited to option-free bonds
CDS Basis	Yield spread versus CDS spread of same tenor	Interpolated CDS spread versus Z-spread	Traded spread rather than spread measure corresponding to cashflows and limited to option-free bonds
OAS	Yield spread using Z-spread including bond option volatility	Provides generalized comparison for valuing risky option-free bonds with bonds with embedded options	Complex calculation based on volatility and prepayment assumptions; bonds with embedded options are unlikely to earn OAS over time

EXAMPLE 7

Comparison of Fixed-Rate Bond Credit Spread Measures

1 An active manager observes a yield spread for an outstanding corporate bond that is above the G-spread for that same bond. Which of the following is the most likely explanation for the difference?

   A The government benchmark bond used to calculate the yield spread has a *shorter* maturity than the corporate bond, and the benchmark yield curve is *upward* sloping.

   B The government benchmark bond used to calculate the yield spread has a *shorter* maturity than the corporate bond, and the benchmark curve is *downward* sloping.

   C The government benchmark bond used to calculate the yield spread has a *longer* maturity than the corporate bond, and the benchmark yield curve is *downward* sloping.

2 An active manager is weighing the purchase of two callable bonds with similar credit risks and the same final maturity. Which of the two bonds is more likely to be called on the next call date?

Key Credit and Spread Concepts for Active Management

A The bond with the lower ASW
B The bond with the lower Z-spread
C The bond with the lower OAS

Solution to 1:

The correct answer is A. For a given all-in YTM, the lower the (on-the-run or interpolated) benchmark rate, the higher the relevant spread measure over the benchmark. Therefore, the higher yield spread versus G-spread most likely arises from the government benchmark having a shorter maturity than the bond and an upward sloping government yield curve. As for B and C, the yield spread would be lower than the G-spread for a downward sloping yield curve.

Solution to 2:

The correct answer is C. The OAS measure is best suited to compare the impact of embedded options on similar bonds because it incorporates a volatility assumption to account for the value of bond options. Answer A indicates the spread over MRR for an outstanding bond swapped versus the original coupon rate, while the Z-spread in B assumes zero volatility and therefore does not capture the value of bond options.

2.2.2 Floating-Rate Note Credit Spread Measures

In contrast to fixed-rate bonds, floating-rate notes (FRNs) pay a periodic interest coupon comprising a variable MRR plus a (usually) constant yield spread. While fixed- and floating-rate bonds both decline in price if credit risk rises, interest rate risk on these bond types differs, and the associated FRN credit spread measures warrant our attention.

An earlier reading provided a simplified framework for valuing a floating-rate bond on a payment date, shown in Equation 3:

$$PV = \frac{\left(\frac{(MRR + QM) \times FV}{m}\right)}{\left(1 + \frac{(MRR + DM)}{m}\right)^1} + \frac{\left(\frac{(MRR + QM) \times FV}{m}\right)}{\left(1 + \frac{(MRR + DM)}{m}\right)^2} + \ldots + \frac{\left(\frac{(MRR + QM) \times FV}{m}\right) + FV}{\left(1 + \frac{(MRR + DM)}{m}\right)^N} \quad (3)$$

Each interest payment is MRR plus the **quoted margin** (QM) times par (FV) and divided by m, the number of periods per year. Rather than a fixed YTM as for fixed-rate bonds, the periodic discount rate per period is MRR plus the **discount margin** (DM) divided by the periodicity (m), or (MRR + DM)/m. Note that for the purposes of Equation 3, MRR is based on current MRR and therefore implies a flat forward curve. The QM is the yield spread over the MRR established upon issuance to compensate investors for assuming the credit risk of the issuer. While some FRN bond indentures include an increase or decrease in the QM if public ratings or other criteria change, given that this spread is usually fixed through maturity, the QM does not reflect credit risk changes over time.

The discount (or required) margin is the yield spread versus the MRR such that the FRN is priced at par on a rate reset date. For example, assume an FRN issued at par value pays three-month MRR plus 1.50%. The QM is 150 bps. If the issuer's credit risk remains unchanged, the DM also equals 150 bps. On each quarterly reset date, the floater will be priced at par value. Between coupon dates, the flat price will be at a premium or discount to par value if MRR falls or rises. If on a reset date, the DM falls to 125 bps because of an issuer upgrade, the FRN will be priced at a premium above par value. The amount of the premium is the present value of the premium future cash flows. The annuity difference of 25 bps per period is calculated for the remaining life of the bond. Exhibit 14 summarizes the relationship between the QM versus DM and an FRN's price on any reset date.

Exhibit 14   FRN Discount, Premium, and Par Pricing

FRN price	Description	QM versus DM
Par	FRN trades at a price (PV) equal to its future value (FV)	QM = DM
Discount	FRN trades at PV < FV	QM < DM
Premium	FRN trades at PV > FV	QM > DM

EXAMPLE 8

Discount Margin

A London-based investor owns a five-year £100 million FRN that pays three-month MRR + 1.75% on a quarterly basis. The current MRR of 0.50% is assumed to remain constant over time. If the issuer's credit risk deteriorates and the DM rises to 2.25%, explain whether the FRN is trading at a discount or premium, and calculate the price difference from par.

Solution:

The FRN is trading at a discount because the QM is below the DM. We can solve for the price difference using the following steps.

1   Solve for the quarterly interest payment (=(MRR + QM) × FV/m) in the numerator and the discount rate (=(MRR + DM)/m) in the denominator of Equation 3 with QM = 1.75%, DM = 2.25%, MRR = 0.50%, and m = 4.

   A   Quarterly interest payment: £562,500 (= (0.50% + 1.75%) × £100,000,000/4)

   B   Discount rate: 0.6875% (= (0.50% + 2.25%)/4)

2   Solve for the new price using results from 1A and 1B with N = 20.

$$£97,671,718 = \frac{£562,500}{(1 + 0.6875\%)} + \frac{£562,500}{(1 + 0.6875\%)^2} + \frac{£562,500}{(1 + 0.6875\%)^3} + \ldots + \frac{£100,562,500}{(1 + 0.6875\%)^{20}}$$

3   The price difference is £2,328,282 (= £100,000,000 − £ 97,671,718).

The **zero-discount margin (Z-DM)** incorporates forward MRR into the yield spread calculation for FRNs. As in the case of the zero-volatility spread for fixed-rate bonds shown earlier, the Z-DM is the fixed periodic adjustment applied to the FRN pricing model to solve for the observed market price. As Equation 4 shows, this calculation incorporates the respective benchmark spot rates z_i derived from the swap or government yield curve for the Z-spread into the FRN pricing model shown earlier.

$$PV = \frac{\left(\frac{(MRR + QM) \times FV}{m}\right)}{\left(1 + \frac{(MRR + Z - DM)}{m}\right)^1} + \frac{\left(\frac{(z_2 + QM) \times FV}{m}\right)}{\left(1 + \frac{(z_2 + Z - DM)}{m}\right)^2}$$

$$+ \ldots + \frac{\left(\frac{(z_N + QM) \times FV}{m}\right) + FV}{\left(1 + \frac{(z_N + Z - DM)}{m}\right)^N}$$

(4)

As in the case of the Z-spread for fixed-rate bonds, the Z-DM will change based on changes in the MRR forward curve. For example, in an upward-sloping yield curve, the Z-DM will be below the DM. Also, the Z-DM assumes an unchanged QM and that the FRN will remain outstanding until maturity. Exhibit 15 summarizes FRN credit spreads as adapted from O'Kane and Sen (2005).

Exhibit 15 Key FRN Credit Spread Measures

Spread	Description	Advantages	Disadvantages
QM	Yield spread over MRR of original FRN	Represents periodic spread related FRN cash flow	Does not capture changes in credit risk over time
DM	Yield spread over MRR to price FRN at par	Establishes spread difference from QM with constant MRR	Assumes a flat MRR zero curve
Z-DM	Yield spread over MRR curve	Incorporates forward MRR rates in yield spread measure	More complex calculation and yield spread does not match FRN cash flows

EXAMPLE 9

Floating-Rate Credit Spread Measure

An Australian investor holds a three-year FRN with a coupon of three-month MRR + 1.25%. Given an expected strong economic recovery, she anticipates a rise in Australian MRR over the next three years and an improvement in the FRN issuer's creditworthiness. Which of the following credit spread measures does she expect to be the *lowest* as a result?

A QM

B DM

C Z-DM

Solution:

The correct answer is C. The QM will be above the DM if issuer creditworthiness improves. As MRRs rise over the next three years, the upward-sloping curve will cause the Z-DM to remain below the DM.

2.2.3 Portfolio Return Impact of Yield Spreads

We now turn from credit spread measures to their impact on expected portfolio return. The first and third variables in Equation 1, namely roll-down return and E (Δ Price due to investor's view of yield spreads), are directly relevant for active managers targeting excess return above a benchmark portfolio using credit strategies.

In the first instance, recall from earlier lessons that investors "rolling down" the yield curve accumulate coupon income and additional return from fixed-rate bond price appreciation over an investment horizon if benchmark rates are positive and the yield curve slopes upward. For fixed-rate bonds priced at a spread over the benchmark, roll-down return from coupon income is higher by the bond's original credit spread. The roll-down return due to price appreciation will also be higher than for an otherwise identical government security because the higher-yielding instrument will generate greater carry over time. Note that this higher return comes with greater risk and assumes all promised payments take place and the bond remains outstanding—that is, no default or prepayment occurs, and the bond is not called.

EXAMPLE 10

Corporate versus Government Bond Roll Down

A London-based investor wants to estimate roll-down return attributable to a fixed-rate, option-free corporate bond versus UK gilts over the next six months assuming a static, upward-sloping government yield curve and a constant credit spread. The corporate bond has exactly 10 years remaining to maturity, a semi-annual coupon of 3.25%, and a YTM of 2.75%, while the closest maturity UK gilt is a 1.75% coupon currently yielding 1.80%, with 9.5 years remaining to maturity.

1. Calculate the annualized roll-down return to the UK corporate bond versus the government bond over the next six months.

2. Describe how the relative roll-down return would change if the investor were to use an interpolated government benchmark rather than the actual 9.5-year gilt.

Solution to 1:

Solve for the annualized difference in roll-down return by calculating the change in price plus the coupon income for both the corporate bond and the government bond.

1. Calculate the corporate bond roll-down return per £100 face value. For price changes, use the Excel PV function (= –PV(rate, nper, pmt, FV, type)) where "rate" is the interest rate per period (0.0275/2), "nper" is the number of periods (20), "pmt" is the periodic coupon (3.25/2), "FV" is future value (100), and "type" corresponds to payments made at the end of each period (0).

    A. Initial price is 104.346 (= –PV (0.0275/2, 20, 3.25/2, 100, 0)).

    B. Price in six months is 104.155 (= –PV (0.0275/2, 19, 3.25/2, 100, 0)). Price *depreciation* is 0.18% (= (104.155 – 104.346)/104.346).

> **C** Six-month coupon income is 1.625 (= 3.25/2), or equal to 1.557% (=1.625/104.346), which combined (without rounding) with −0.18% from B results in a 1.375% six-month return (2.75% annualized).
>
> **2** Calculate the UK gilt price change and coupon income.
>
> **A** Initial price is 99.565 (= −PV (0.018/2, 19, 1.75/2, 100, 0)).
>
> **B** Price in six months is 99.586 (= −PV (0.018/2, 18, 1.75/2, 100, 0)). Price *appreciation* is 0.021% (= (99.586 − 99.565)/99.565).
>
> **C** Six-month coupon income is 0.875 (=1.75/2), or equal to 0.879% (0.875/99.565), which combined with +0.021% equals 0.9% for six months (1.80% annualized).
>
> The annualized roll-down return difference is the 2.75% corporate bond realized return less the 1.80% UK gilt realized return, or 0.95%.
>
> **Solution to 2:**
>
> The interpolated benchmark involves the use of the most liquid, on-the-run government bonds to derive a hypothetical 10-year UK gilt YTM. Because the UK gilt yield curve is upward sloping in this example, we can conclude that the relative roll-down return using an interpolated benchmark would be lower than the 0.95% difference in Question 1.

Active credit managers often view the E (Δ Price due to investor's view of yield spreads) term in Equation 1 on a stand-alone basis because they manage benchmark rate risks separately from credit. Equation 5 is similar to equations from earlier lessons quantifying the change in bond price for a given YTM change, but it is limited here to yield spread changes, or %ΔPV^{Spread} (= ΔPV/ΔSpread).

$$\%\Delta PV^{Spread} \approx -(EffSpreadDur \times \Delta Spread) + (\tfrac{1}{2} \times EffSpreadCon \times (\Delta Spread)^2) \tag{5}$$

where effective spread duration (EffSpreadDur) and effective spread convexity (EffSpreadCon) reflect spread rather than curve changes, and ΔSpread is typically defined as the change in OAS.

$$EffSpreadDur = \frac{(PV_-) - (PV_+)}{2 \times (\Delta Spread)(PV_0)} \tag{6}$$

$$EffSpreadCon = \frac{(PV_-) + (PV_+) - 2(PV_0)}{(\Delta Spread)^2 \times (PV_0)} \tag{7}$$

The first term of Equation 5 is sometimes simply referred to as **spread duration**, or, alternatively, as **OAS duration** when OAS is the underlying spread. Active managers approximate bond portfolio value changes due to spread changes by substituting market value–weighted averages for the duration and convexity measures in Equation 5. As noted earlier, spread changes for lower-rated bonds tend to be consistent on a proportional percentage rather than absolute basis; therefore, adjusting spread duration to capture this **Duration Times Spread (DTS)** effect is important, as in Equation 8.

$$DTS \approx (EffSpreadDur \times Spread) \tag{8}$$

A portfolio's DTS is the market value–weighted average of DTS of its individual bonds, and spread changes of a portfolio are measured on a percentage (ΔSpread/Spread) basis rather than in absolute basis point terms, as in the following example.

> **EXAMPLE 11**
>
> ### DTS Example
>
> A financial analyst compares a portfolio evenly split between two technology company bonds trading at par to an index with an average OAS of 125 bps.
>
> | Issuer | OAS | EffSpreadDur |
> |---|---|---|
> | A Rated Bond | 100 bps | 3.0 |
> | BB Rated Bond | 300 bps | 4.0 |
>
> Calculate the portfolio DTS, and estimate how the technology bond portfolio will perform if index OAS widens by 10 bps.
>
> **Solution:**
>
> Portfolio DTS is the market value–weighted average of DTS based on Equation 8, or $\sum_{i=1}^{n} w_i (\text{EffSpreadDur}_i \times \text{Spread}_i)$.
>
> 1 Portfolio DTS in this two-asset example is $w_A(\text{EffSpreadDur}_A \times \text{Spread}_A)$ + $w_{BB}(\text{EffSpreadDur}_{BB} \times \text{Spread}_{BB})$ with equal weights ($w_A = w_{BB} = 0.50$). Solve for portfolio DTS of 750 (= (0.5 × 100 bps × 3.0) + (0.5 × 300 bps × 4.0)).
>
> 2 Index spread widening of 10 bps is equivalent to 8% (10 bps/125 bps spread) on a ΔSpread/Spread basis. We can therefore calculate the estimated basis point change in the technology bond portfolio by multiplying the portfolio DTS of 750 by the 8% expected percentage spread change to get an expected 60 bps p.a. widening for the technology bond portfolio.

As active credit managers consider *incremental* effects of credit-based portfolio decisions, they often use spread duration–based statistics to gauge the first-order impact of spread movements. For example, Equation 9 approximates the annualized **excess spread** return for a spread-based bond:

$$\text{ExcessSpread} \approx \text{Spread}_0 - (\text{EffSpreadDur} \times \Delta\text{Spread}) \quad (9)$$

Spread_0 is the initial yield spread, which changes to (Spread_0/Periods Per Year) for holding periods of less than a year. Note that this calculation assumes no defaults for the period in question. While relatively rare, as an event of default grows more likely, expected future bond cash flows are impaired, and a bond's value instead approaches the present value of expected recovery. The annualized expected excess return shown in Equation 10 incorporates both default probability and loss severity:

$$E[\text{ExcessSpread}] \approx$$
$$\text{Spread}_0 - (\text{EffSpreadDur} \times \Delta\text{Spread}) - (\text{POD} \times \text{LGD}) \quad (10)$$

Equation 10 captures a key goal of active credit management, which is to maximize expected spread return in excess of the portfolio credit loss or realized percentage of par value lost to defaults over time.

Key Credit and Spread Concepts for Active Management

> **EXAMPLE 12**
>
> ### Excess Spread and Expected Excess Spread
>
> A corporate bond has an effective spread duration of five years and a credit spread of 2.75% (275 bps).
>
> 1. What is the approximate excess return if the bond is held for six months and the credit spread narrows 50 bps to 2.25%? Assume the spread duration remains at five years and that the bond does not experience default losses.
> 2. What is the instantaneous (holding period of zero) excess return if the spread rises to 3.25%?
> 3. Assume the bond has a 1% annualized expected POD and expected loss severity of 60% in the event of default. What is the expected excess return if the bond is held for six months and the credit spread is expected to fall to 2.25%?
>
> #### Solution to 1:
>
> Using Equation 9 ($Spread_0$ − (EffSpreadDur × ΔSpread)), the excess return on the bond is 3.875% = (2.75% × 0.5) − [(2.25% − 2.75%) × 5].
>
> #### Solution to 2:
>
> Using Equation 9, the instantaneous excess return on the bond is approximately −2.5% = (2.75% × 0) − [(3.25% − 2.75%) × 5].
>
> #### Solution to 3:
>
> Using Equation 10 ($Spread_0$ − (EffSpreadDur × ΔSpread) − (POD × LGD)), the expected excess return on the bond is approximately 3.575% = (2.75% × 0.5) − [(2.25% − 2.75%) × 5] − (0.5 × 1% × 60%).

Finally, we must address the difference in duration as an interest rate sensitivity measure for FRNs versus fixed-rate bonds. The periodic reset of MRRs in both the FRN numerator and denominator leads to a *rate* duration of near zero for floaters trading at par on a reset date (prior to MRR reset). As we saw in an earlier DM example, changes in *spread* (DM or Z-DM) are the key driver of price changes for a given FRN yield change. The respective FRN rate and spread duration measures are shown in Equations 11 and 12 and demonstrated in the following example.

$$EffRateDur_{FRN} = \frac{(PV_-) - (PV_+)}{2 \times (\Delta MRR)(PV_0)} \quad (11)$$

$$EffSpreadDur_{FRN} = \frac{(PV_-) - (PV_+)}{2 \times (\Delta DM)(PV_0)} \quad (12)$$

We return to the example of a five-year £100 million FRN at three-month MRR + 1.75%, with a DM of 2.25% and a 0.50% MRR priced at £97,671,718. We can derive the FRN's effective rate duration by first calculating PV_- and PV_+ using a spreadsheet by shifting MRR down and up by 0.05% as follows:

$$PV0 = £97,671,718 = \frac{£562,500}{(1 + 0.6875\%)} + \frac{£562,500}{(1 + 0.6875\%)^2} + \ldots + \frac{£100,562,500}{(1 + 0.6875\%)^{20}}$$

$$PV_- = £97,668,746 = \frac{£550,000}{(1+0.6750\%)} + \frac{£550,000}{(1+0.6750\%)^2} + \ldots + \frac{£100,550,000}{(1+0.6750\%)^{20}}$$

$$PV_+ = £97,674,685 = \frac{£575,000}{(1+0.7000\%)} + \frac{£575,000}{(1+0.7000\%)^2} + \ldots + \frac{£100,575,000}{(1+0.7000\%)^{20}}$$

Solving for $EffRateDur_{FRN}$, we arrive at a rate duration of –0.061, which is slightly negative because the floater trades at a discount. The spread duration statistic $EffSpreadDur_{FRN}$ is calculated in a similar manner by shifting DM down and up by 0.05%, with PV_- and PV_+ equal to £97,972,684 and £97,515,401 and $EffSpreadDur_{FRN}$ equal to 4.682.

3 CREDIT STRATEGIES

3.1 Bottom-Up Credit Strategies

c discuss bottom-up approaches to credit strategies

As active fixed-income managers consider the selection process for spread-based bond portfolio investments, they must assess different ways in which to maximize excess spread across the fixed-income issuer types, industries, and instruments within their prescribed investment mandate. A fundamental choice these investors face is whether to engage in an individual security selection process or bottom-up approach; a macro- or market-based, top-down approach in pursuing this objective; or a combination of both.

Fundamental credit analysis covered earlier in the curriculum considers the basis on which a specific issuer can satisfy its interest and principal payments through bond maturity. Analysts often assess unsecured corporate bonds using factors such as profitability and leverage to identify the sources and variability of cash flows available to an issuer to service debt. These measures are usually chosen and compared relative to an industry and/or the jurisdiction in which the issuer operates. In the case of a sovereign borrower, the relevant metric is the economic activity within a government's jurisdiction and the government's ability and willingness to levy taxes and generate sufficient revenue to meet its obligations. Alternatively, for a special purpose entity issuer with bonds backed by mortgage-based or other securitized cash flows, a credit measure of both the residential borrowers and underlying collateral value as well as internal credit enhancements are among the primary factors considered in the assessment.

While individual bonds across all these issuer types are usually rated by at least two of the major credit rating agencies, active managers typically conduct their own credit assessment of individual borrowers rather than relying on ratings, which are frequently used to define a mandate (e.g., investment grade versus high yield), categorize, or benchmark investments of similar credit quality.

3.1.1 Defining the Credit Universe

A bottom-up approach typically begins with a manager defining the universe of eligible bonds within a mandate and then grouping the universe into categories that allow consistent relative value analysis across comparable borrowers. For example, a corporate bond portfolio manager is likely to divide eligible bonds into industry sectors, such as media and telecommunications and industrials, as well as into subsectors and/or firms located in different jurisdictions. Media and telecommunications subsectors include firms in the cable and satellite industries, internet media, and telecommunications carriers. Within each sector or subsector based on either industry classification methodologies or a customized approach, she can use relative value analysis to determine the bonds that are attractively valued.

EXAMPLE 13

Dividing the Credit Universe

An investor is conducting a relative value analysis on global bond issuers in the health care sector. He is trying to decide whether the global health care sector is a sufficiently narrow sector for his analysis. Through his research, he has determined the following:

- Biotech and pharmaceutical companies are active globally across Europe, Asia, and the Americas.
- Health care facilities are typically local in nature and tend to sell into only one of these three regions.
- Medical equipment and devices is a more cyclical business, and many of these firms are part of multi-industry companies in which health care accounts for a smaller fraction of overall company sales.

Describe considerations that the investor can use in determining how to best divide the health care sector into comparable companies.

Solution:

An investor typically seeks to isolate a sector that contains a set of companies for which he expects company-level risks, rather than industry or macro risks, to be the dominant factors. Based on the investor's analysis, biotech and pharmaceutical companies differ meaningfully from health care facilities and medical equipment manufacturers. Health care facilities have a narrow regional focus in contrast to the global focus in biotech and pharma.

The investor might therefore want to divide the global health care sector into global biotech and global pharmaceuticals. Hospitals and other health care facilities warrant separate treatment given their narrow geographic focus and different industry drivers. He might want to consider a different approach to medical device companies given their multi-industry profiles.

3.1.2 *Bottom-Up Credit Analysis*

Once the credit universe has been divided into sectors and prospective bonds identified, the investor evaluates each issuer's implied credit risk comparing company-specific financial information to spread-related compensation for assuming default, credit migration, and liquidity risks for comparative purposes.

Beyond the prospects within a company's industry, its competitive position within that industry, and operating history, financial ratios are a valuable tool to compare creditworthiness across firms. Earlier lessons stressed the value of key ratios, including profitability and cash flow, leverage, and debt coverage, which are summarized in Exhibit 16.

Exhibit 16   Key Financial Ratios for Bottom-Up Credit Analysis

Ratio	Description	Advantages	Disadvantages
EBITDA/ Total Assets	**Profitability** Cash flow as a percentage of assets	Combines operating income with non-cash expense	Ignores capital expenditures and working capital changes
Debt/ Capital	**Leverage** Fraction of company's capital financed with debt	Direct measure of relative reliance on debt financing	More relevant for investment-grade than high-yield issuers
EBITDA/ Interest Expense	**Coverage** Cash flow available to service debt	Measures relative issuer ability to meet debt payments	Volatile measure for firms with high cash flow variability

While offering a relatively consistent basis for comparison across firms and over time, reliance on financial ratios based on publicly available accounting data alone is of limited value because of comparability issues across firms and industries as well as the historical nature of financial statements. Alternative measures combine several relevant financial ratios with market-based measures to establish a forward-looking approach to creditworthiness.

A previous lesson established that statistical credit analysis models to measure individual issuer creditworthiness can be categorized as either **reduced form credit models** or **structural credit models**. Reduced form models solve for **default intensity**, or the POD over a specific time period, using observable company-specific variables such as financial ratios and recovery assumptions as well as macroeconomic variables, including economic growth and market volatility measures. Structural credit models use market-based variables to estimate the market value of an issuer's assets and the volatility of asset value. The likelihood of default is defined as the probability of the asset value falling below that of liabilities.

An early example of the reduced form approach is the **Z-score** established by Altman (1968), which combined liquidity (working capital/total assets), profitability (retained earnings/total assets), asset efficiency (EBIT/ total assets), market versus book value of equity, and asset turnover (sales/total assets) factors weighted by coefficients to form a composite score. Each composite, or Z-score, was used to classify manufacturing firms into those expected to remain solvent and those anticipated to go bankrupt. Similar to credit scoring models, this multiple discriminant analysis reduces the dimensionality of the input variables to a single cutoff Z-score that represents the default threshold, as shown in the following example.

EXAMPLE 14

Z-Score Comparison of Two Firms

A United Kingdom–based financial analyst considers a Z-score model in evaluating two publicly traded non-manufacturing companies as follows:

$$\text{Z-Score Model} = 1.2 \times A + 1.4 \times B + 3.3 \times C + 0.6 \times D + 0.999 \times E,$$

where

    A is Working Capital/Total Assets
    B is Retained Earnings/Total Assets
    C is EBIT/Total Assets
    D is Market Value of Equity/Total Liabilities
    E is Sales/Total Assets

Firms with a Z-score greater than 3.0 are considered financially sound, those scoring between 3.0 and 1.8 are at greater risk of financial distress, and those with a Z-score below 1.8 are likely to face insolvency.

1. Calculate the Z-score for Firm 1 and Firm 2. Which has a higher likelihood of financial distress based on this measure?

Financial Data (GBP thousands)/Firm	Firm 1	Firm 2
Total Sales	23,110	15,270
EBIT	6,910	2,350
Current Assets	7,560	4,990
Total Assets	36,360	23,998
Current Liabilities	5,400	3,564
Total Liabilities	9,970	10,050
Retained Earnings	20,890	13,787
Market Value of Equity	29,000	18,270

2. Evaluate the most likely reasons for the difference in creditworthiness between the two firms based on the Z-score model factors.

Solution to 1:

First, calculate the respective ratios for both firms as follows, noting that working capital is equal to current assets minus current liabilities:

Z-Score Factors	Firm 1	Firm 2
Working Capital/Assets	0.059	0.059
Retained Earnings/Assets	0.575	0.575
EBIT/Total Assets	0.190	0.098
Market Value of Equity/Total Liabilities	2.909	1.818
Sales/Total Assets	0.636	0.636

Solving for the respective Z-scores, we find that Firm 1 has a Z-score of 3.883, while Firm 2 has a Z-score of 2.925. Firm 2 therefore has a greater likelihood of financial distress.

Solution to 2:

Comparing the respective Z-score ratios of Firm 1 and Firm 2, we find that Firm 2 has a far lower asset efficiency (EBIT/Total Assets of 9.8% versus 19% for Firm 1) and a lower relative equity market value (Market Value of Equity/Total Liabilities of 1.818 versus 2.909 for Firm 1) than Firm 1, while all other ratios are comparable.

Structural credit models used in practice include Moody's Analytics Expected Default Frequency (EDF) and Bloomberg's Default Risk (DRSK) models, both of which provide daily POD estimates for a broad range of issuers over a selected period. The EDF model estimates a forward-looking POD defined as the point at which the market value of assets falls below a firm's obligations. The model uses asset volatility to determine the likelihood of reaching the default point and is calibrated for different industries, regions, and observed credit market dynamics.

Bloomberg's DRSK model estimate for AbbVie Inc., as shown in Exhibit 17, includes a market-based asset value measure derived from equity market capitalization and equity volatility as well as a default threshold measured using the book value of liabilities. These and other DRSK model inputs in the left column of the screen can be defined by users and compared within and across industry sectors. In addition to the one-year POD estimate of 0.0413%, DRSK calculates a "model" CDS spread (upper left corner) which can be compared to the actual market CDS spread.

Exhibit 17 Bloomberg DRSK Model Estimate for AbbVie Inc.

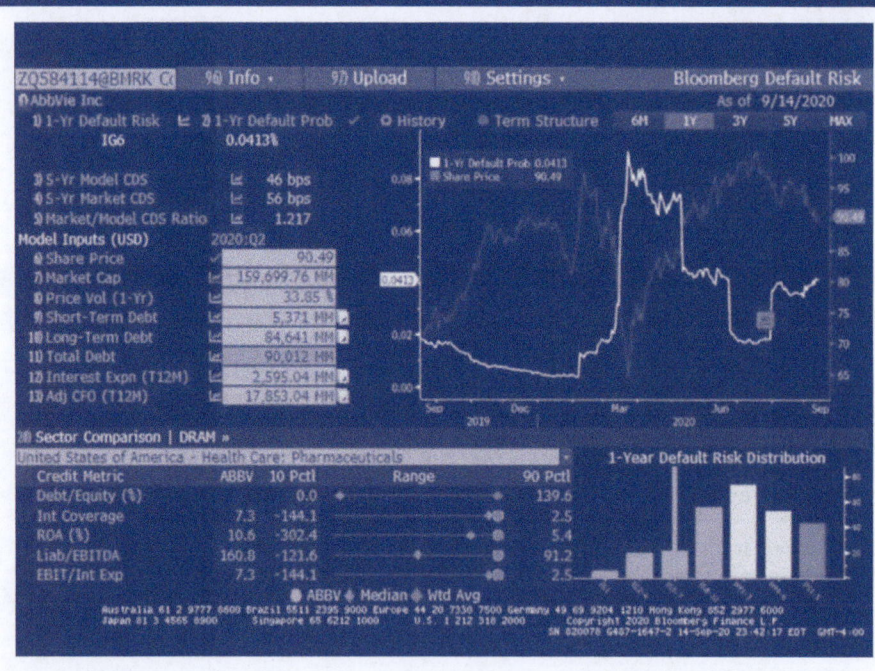

Source: Bloomberg

Both the EDF and DRSK approaches are sometimes referred to as "distance to default" models because a probability distribution is used to determine how far an issuer's current market value of assets is from the default threshold for a given period.

EXAMPLE 15

"Distance to Default" Models

An active manager is weighing an investment in the bonds of two issuers in the same industry with identical PODs using a structural credit model. Which of the following changes to the model inputs for one of the issuers would lead the analyst to expect an increase in the POD for that issuer?

A An increase in the issuer's coverage ratio

Credit Strategies

  B An increase in the volatility of the issuer's stock price

  C A decrease in the issuer's leverage ratio

Solution:

The correct answer is B. Higher equity volatility increases the likelihood that the market value of the issuer's assets will fall below the default threshold. A higher coverage ratio in A implies higher cash flow as a percentage of assets, increasing the issuer's ability to service its debt obligations. The decrease in the issuer's leverage ratio in C represents a decline in the amount of debt versus equity, reducing the issuer's likelihood of financial distress.

3.1.3 Bottom-Up Relative Value Analysis

Given two issuers with similar credit risk, the investor will typically choose bonds of the issuer with the higher yield spread, given the greater potential for excess returns. For issuers with different credit-related risk, the investor must decide whether the additional spread is sufficient compensation for the incremental exposure. The excess expected return calculation in Equation 10 captures the relationship between yield spreads and the components of credit risk, as seen in the following example.

EXAMPLE 16

Comparing Investments Using Expected Excess Return

A portfolio manager considers two industrial bonds for a one-year investment:

Issuer	Rating	EffSpreadDur	YTM	Z-Spread
A Rated Industrial	A2	5.0	4.0%	100 bps
B Rated Industrial	B2	7.0	6.5%	350 bps

 The manager observes a historical annual default probability of 0.27% for A2 rated issuers and 3.19% for B2 rated issuers and assumes a 40% recovery rate for both bonds.

1 Compute the estimated excess return for each bond assuming no change in spreads, and interpret whether the B rated bond spread provides sufficient compensation for the incremental risk.

2 Which bond is more attractive if spreads are expected to widen by 10%?

Solution to 1:

As per Equation 10,

$$E[\text{ExcessSpread}] \approx \text{Spread}_0 - (\text{EffSpreadDur} \times \Delta\text{Spread}) - (\text{POD} \times \text{LGD}).$$

 A rated expected excess return is 0.84% = 1% − (5 × 0) − (0.27% × 60%). B rated expected excess return is 1.59% = 3.5% − (7 × 0) − (3.19% × 60%). The B rated bond appears to provide sufficient compensation for the added risk.

Solution to 2:

Recalculate Equation 10 with ΔSpread of 10 bps for the A rated bond and 35 bps for the B rated bond.

 A rated excess return is 0.34% = 1% − (5 × 0.1%) − (0.27% × 60%).

 B rated excess return is −0.86% = 3.5% − (7 × 0.35%) − (3.19% × 60%).

> The A rated bond is more attractive under this scenario.

In practice, bonds from different issuers usually also have various maturity, embedded call or put provisions, liquidity, and other characteristics, so these additional features should be taken into account during the security selection process. For example, structural differences such as callability or priority within the capital structure must be factored in because they affect valuation. Also, bonds recently issued in larger tranches by frequent issuers will tend to have narrower bid–offer spreads and greater daily transaction volume, allowing investors to buy or sell the bond at a lower cost. This feature is likely to be of greater importance to investors who expect short-term spread narrowing and/or have a relatively short investment time horizon. Note that relative liquidity tends to decline over time, particularly if the same issuer returns to the bond market and offers a price concession for new debt. If, on the other hand, an investor has a longer investment horizon with the flexibility to hold a bond to maturity, he might be able to increase excess return via a greater liquidity premium. Finally, other factors driving potential yield spread differences to be considered include split ratings or negative ratings outlooks, potential merger and acquisition activity, and other positive or negative company events not adequately reflected in the analysis.

When deciding among frequent issuers with several bond issues outstanding, investors might consider using credit spread curves for these issuers across maturities to gauge relative value.

EXAMPLE 17

Using Spread Curves in Relative Value Analysis

A United States–based issuer has the following option-free bonds outstanding:

Outstanding Debt	Term	Coupon	Price	YTM
2-year issue	2	4.25%	106.7	0.864%
5-year issue	5	3.25%	106	1.984%
15-year issue	15	2.75%	91	3.528%

Current on-the-run US Treasury YTMs are as follows:

Tenor	Coupon	Price
2y	0.250%	100
5y	0.875%	100
10y	2.000%	100
20y	2.250%	100

An investor considers the purchase of a new 10-year issue from the company and expects the new bond to include a 10 bp new issue premium. What is the fair value spread for the new issue based on outstanding debt?

1 First, solve for the credit spreads for outstanding bonds as the difference in the YTM from an actual or interpolated government bond:

5-year spread: 110.9 bps (= 1.984% − 0.875%)

15-year spread: Solve for 10- and 20-year bond interpolation weights.

10-year weight: $w_{10} = 0.50\% (= (20 − 10)/(15 − 10))$

20-year weight: $w_{20} = 0.50\% (= (1 − w_{10}))$

Credit Strategies

> 15-year interpolated bond: 2.125% = (2.00% × 0.5) + (2.25% × 0.5)
>
> 15-year spread: 140.3 bps (= 3.528% − 2.125%)
>
> **2** Derive the implied 10-year new issue spread by interpolating the 5- and 15-year credit spreads using the same interpolation weights as for Treasuries and adding the 10 bp new issue premium.
>
> 10-year spread: 135.6 bps = 0.1% + (1.109% × 0.5 + 1.403% × 0.5)

Many issuers have several bond issues, each of which typically has a different maturity and duration. To reflect the various maturities, a spread curve can be developed for each issuer and can be useful in conducting relative value analysis. A spread curve is the fitted curve of credit spreads for similar bonds of an issuer plotted against the maturity of those bonds.

Exhibit 18 plots the Z-spread versus maturities for select outstanding bonds of two A2/A+ rated health care companies, Eli Lilly (LLY) and Bristol-Myers Squibb (BMS), which have similar probabilities of default.

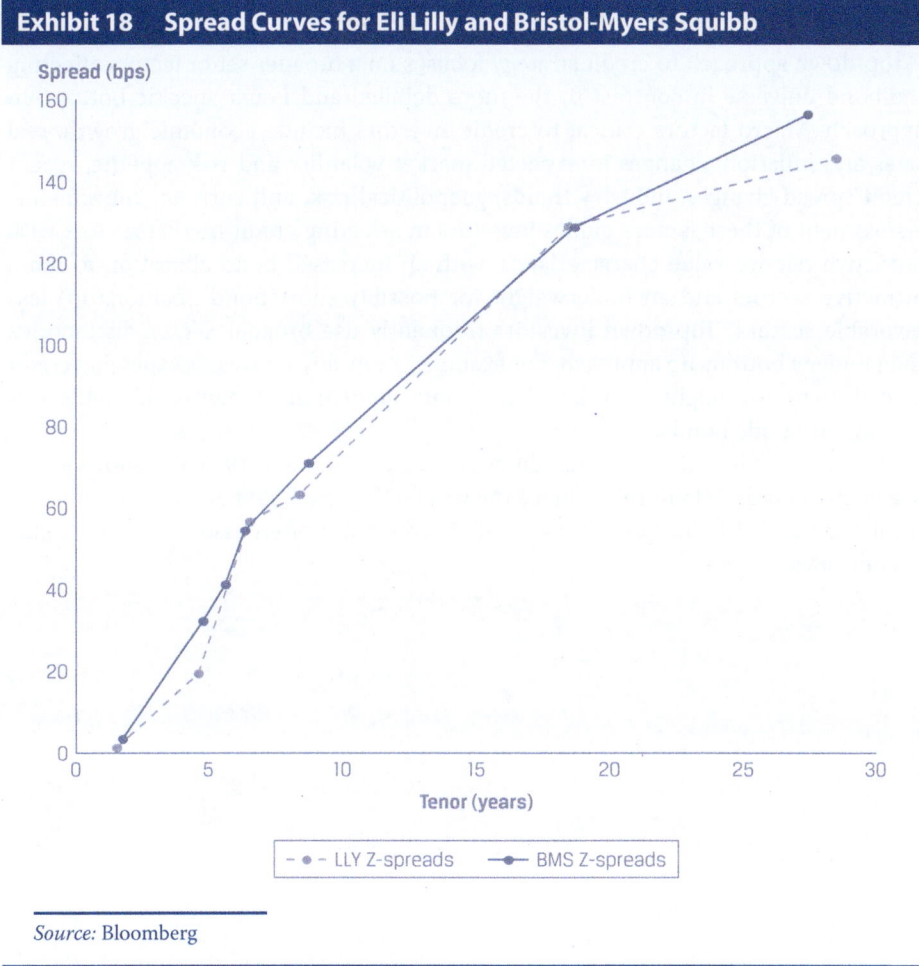

Exhibit 18 Spread Curves for Eli Lilly and Bristol-Myers Squibb

Source: Bloomberg

These spread curves are closely aligned except in roughly five-year and nearly 30-year maturities, where the BMS spreads are approximately 10 bps wider than those of LLY. If the bonds have similar features and liquidity, then a manager might conclude that the market perceives BMS credit risk to be slightly higher than that of

LLY. However, if the manager believes that BMS is the stronger credit, several actions are possible depending on portfolio objectives and constraints. For example, if the investment mandate is to outperform a benchmark using long-only positions, the manager might overweight BMS bonds and underweight LLY bonds relative to the benchmark. If the objective is to generate positive absolute returns, underweighting or avoiding LLY bonds is less appropriate because such actions are meaningful only in the context of a benchmark. If permitted, the manager could also consider a long–short CDS strategy outlined later.

Once a manager has identified specific issuers and bond maturities to actively over- or underweight versus a benchmark, the next important step is to quantify and track these active investments in the context of the primary indexing risk factors identified in an earlier lesson in the active portfolio construction process. For example, if an investor chooses to overweight specific health care industry issuers versus the respective sector and spread duration contributions of the benchmark index, the difference in portfolio weights between the active and index positions establishes a basis upon which excess return can be measured going forward.

3.2 Top-Down Credit Strategies

d   discuss top-down approaches to credit strategies

A top-down approach to credit strategy focuses on a broader set of factors affecting the bond universe in contrast to the more detailed and issuer-specific bottom-up approach. Macro factors critical to credit investors include economic growth, real rates and inflation, changes in expected market volatility and risk appetite, recent credit spread changes, industry trends, geopolitical risk, and currency movements. Assessment of these factors guides investors in selecting credit market sectors with attractive relative value characteristics, with an increased bond allocation to more attractive sectors and an underweight (or possibly short bond positions in) less favorable sectors. Top-down investors frequently use broader sector distinctions than under a bottom-up approach. For example, a top-down investor expecting credit spreads to narrow might favor the relative value opportunity of high-yield bonds over investment-grade bonds.

GDP growth is critical to the credit cycle, as seen in Exhibit 19, which shows global speculative-grade default rates versus the real GDP growth rate among G7 countries from 1962 to 2019. Sharp declines in GDP growth are often associated with rising default rates.

Exhibit 19 Global Speculative-Grade Default Rate and Real GDP Growth Rate for G7 countries, 1962–2019

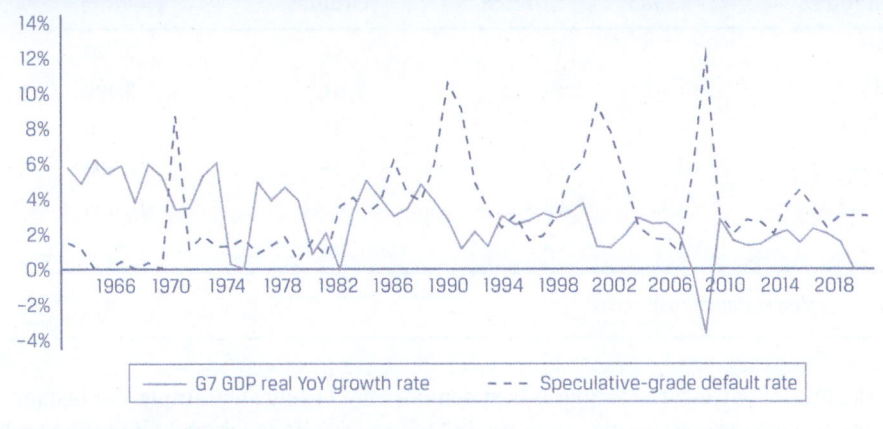

Sources: Moody's Investors Service, OECD (IHS Markit)

A portfolio manager or analyst might decide to factor this relationship into the investment decision-making process; for example, an above-consensus real GDP growth forecast might lead to an increased high-yield allocation if future defaults are expected to remain below market expectations.

3.2.1 Assessing Credit Quality in a Top-Down Approach

Active top-down and bottom-up credit managers frequently use public ratings to categorize and rank the credit quality of bonds within a portfolio. As investors compare investments across credit ratings, the fact that default risk rises more rapidly as ratings decline is important to consider. The use of weighted factors, such as those established by Moody's based on the likelihood of credit loss over a specific period versus ordinal factors across the credit spectrum, enables managers to capture this effect more accurately, as demonstrated in Exhibit 20.

Exhibit 20 Weighted Versus Ordinal Credit Rating Categories

Moody's	S&P	Fitch	Ordinal	Weighted
Aaa	AAA	AAA	1	1
Aa1	AA+	AA+	2	10
Aa2	AA	AA	3	20
Aa3	AA-	AA-	4	40
A1	A+	A+	5	70
A2	A	A	6	120
A3	A-	A-	7	180
Baa1	BBB+	BBB+	8	260
Baa2	BBB	BBB	9	360
Baa3	BBB-	BBB-	10	610
Ba1	BB+	BB+	11	940
Ba2	BB	BB	12	1,350
Ba3	BB-	BB-	13	1,766
B1	B+	B+	14	2,220

(continued)

Exhibit 20 (Continued)

Moody's	S&P	Fitch	Ordinal	Weighted
B2	B	B	15	2,720
B3	B-	B-	16	3,490
Caa1	CCC+	CCC+	17	4,770
Caa2	CCC	CCC	18	6,500
Caa3	CCC-	CCC-	19	10,000
Ca	CC	CC	20	

Source: Moody's Investors Service

The impact of weighted ratings is best demonstrated using an example. For instance, assume a manager is assessing credit quality for a portfolio in which half of the bonds are rated A1/A+ and the other half are rated Ba3/BB-. Using an ordinal scale, the average portfolio credit quality score is 9 (= 50% × 5 + 50% × 13), which corresponds to an average rating of Baa2/BBB in Exhibit 20. However, using the weighted scale at the far right, the portfolio's average credit quality score is 918 (= 50% × 70 + 50% × 1,766), or closer to Ba1/BB+, two levels (notches) below the average rating derived using an ordinal scale.

Earlier readings underscored the risks of relying on public credit ratings, in particular that ratings tend to lag the market's pricing of credit risk critical to an active investor. In addition, one should note that S&P's and Moody's ratings capture different types of risks, with S&P ratings focused on the POD, while Moody's focuses on expected losses, which could influence historical comparisons. The credit rating time horizon is also critical because ratings agencies issue both short-term and long-term ratings for specific issuers, which might warrant additional attention. For these reasons, active managers often prefer to use credit spread measures such as OAS to measure average portfolio credit quality. To calculate a portfolio's average OAS, each bond's individual OAS is weighted by its market value. A manager might also group bonds by OAS categories, which are sometimes mapped to public ratings for comparative purposes.

The use of spread-based rather than rating-based measures also facilitates the measurement of changes in portfolio value due to spread changes. As shown earlier, Equation 5 provides a framework to quantify portfolio value changes due to yield spread movements:

$$\%\Delta PV^{Spread} \approx -(EffSpreadDur \times \Delta Spread) + (½ \times EffSpreadCon \times (\Delta Spread)^2)$$

Smaller yield spread changes are often estimated using the first term in Equation 5. This analytical duration approach provides a reasonable approximation of the price–yield spread relationship for investment-grade bonds with low credit spreads. However, for bonds with greater default risk further down the credit spectrum, changes to both the EffSpreadDur and the ΔSpread terms might be required to accurately reflect empirical observations of how credit risk changes affect overall portfolio value.

In isolating portfolio value changes due to yield spread changes using EffSpreadDur, Equation 5 implicitly assumes that government bond YTMs and credit spreads are uncorrelated, independent variables. However, empirical duration estimates using statistical models often diverge from analytical duration calculations over time and in different interest rate environments. For instance, under a "flight to quality" scenario, the macroeconomic factors driving government bond YTMs *lower* will cause high-yield bond credit spreads to *rise* as the result of an expectation of a greater likelihood and higher severity of financial distress, as shown in Exhibit 21 during the COVID-19 pandemic in early 2020.

Credit Strategies

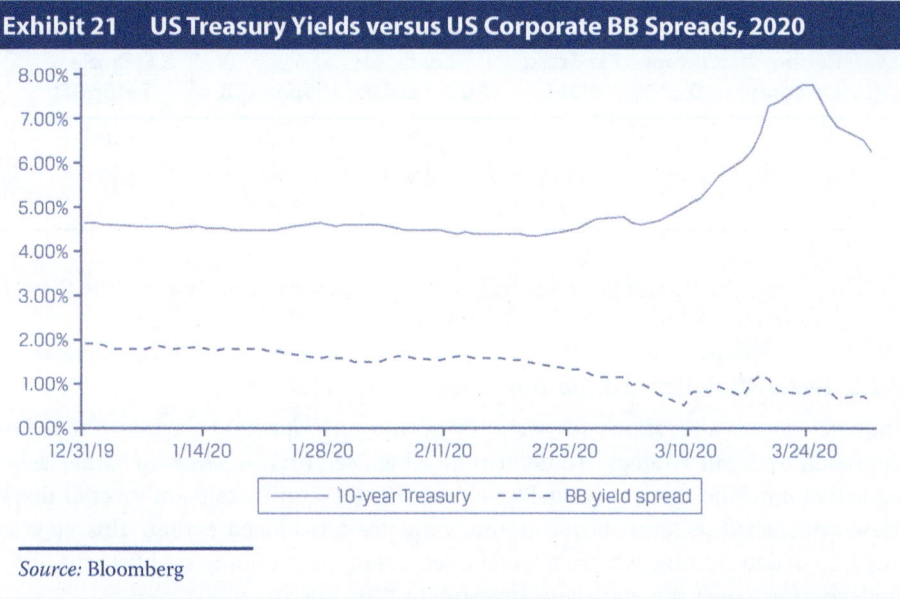

Exhibit 21: US Treasury Yields versus US Corporate BB Spreads, 2020

Source: Bloomberg

As for ΔSpread, recall the empirical observation that bonds trading at wider spreads usually experience larger spread changes, which are proportional to the DTS measure in Equation 8.

These greater changes in bond spread have an impact similar to that of the weighted Moody's credit rating categories in Exhibit 18.

EXAMPLE 18

Top-Down Excess Returns

An investor has formed expectations across four bond rating categories and intends to overweight the category with the highest expected excess return over the next 12 months. Evaluate which rating group is the most attractive based on the information in the following table and assuming no change in spread duration:

Rating Category	Current OAS	Expected ΔOAS	Expected Loss (POD × LGD)	EffSpreadDur
A	1.05%	−0.25%	0.06%	5.5
Baa	1.35%	−0.35%	0.30%	6.0
Ba	2.45%	−0.50%	0.60%	4.5
B	3.50%	−0.75%	3.00%	4.0

Solution:

The following table summarizes expected excess returns E [ExcessSpread] ≈ Spread_0 − (EffSpreadDur × ΔSpread) − (POD × LGD) for each of the four rating categories. For example, expected excess return for rating category A is 2.37% (=1.05% − (5.5 × −0.25%) − 0.06%).

Rating Category	Current OAS	Expected ΔOAS	Expected Loss (POD × LGD)	EffSpreadDur	E(Excess Return)
A	1.05%	−0.25%	0.06%	5.5	2.37%
Baa	1.35%	−0.35%	0.30%	6.0	3.15%

(continued)

Rating Category	Current OAS	Expected ΔOAS	Expected Loss (POD × LGD)	EffSpreadDur	E(Excess Return)
Ba	2.45%	−0.50%	0.60%	4.5	4.10%
B	3.50%	−0.75%	3.00%	4.0	3.50%

Given that the Ba category has the highest expected excess return, it is the most attractive rating category to overweight in the portfolio.

3.2.2 Sector Allocation in a Top-Down Approach

Industry sector allocations (or weightings) are an important part of a top-down approach to credit strategy. To determine which sector(s) to over- or underweight, an active portfolio manager usually begins with an interest rate and overall market view established using macroeconomic variables introduced earlier. This view is a key step in determining whether specific sectors of the economy are likely to over- or underperform over the manager's investment time horizon.

Quantitative methods such as regression analysis are often used in making industry allocation decisions. For example, the average spread of bonds within an individual industry sector and rating category might be compared with the average spread of the bonds with the same rating but excluding the chosen industry sector. Alternatively, a portfolio manager might also use financial ratios in comparing sector spreads and sector leverage. Generally speaking, higher leverage should imply higher credit risk and thus wider spreads. A portfolio manager could therefore compare sectors on a spread-versus-leverage basis to identify relative value opportunities.

Sector- and rating-specific spread curves are a useful tool in guiding decision making for top-down sector allocations. A comparison of curves combined with an investor's view could lead to credit portfolio positioning based on a view that a specific credit spread curve will flatten or steepen, or that two spread curves will converge or diverge. For example, Exhibit 22 shows the divergence in industrial versus health care spreads for BBB rated US issuers over the first half of 2020 during the COVID-19 pandemic. The flatter industrial credit spread curve reflects that sector's relatively weak credit outlook versus health care over the period.

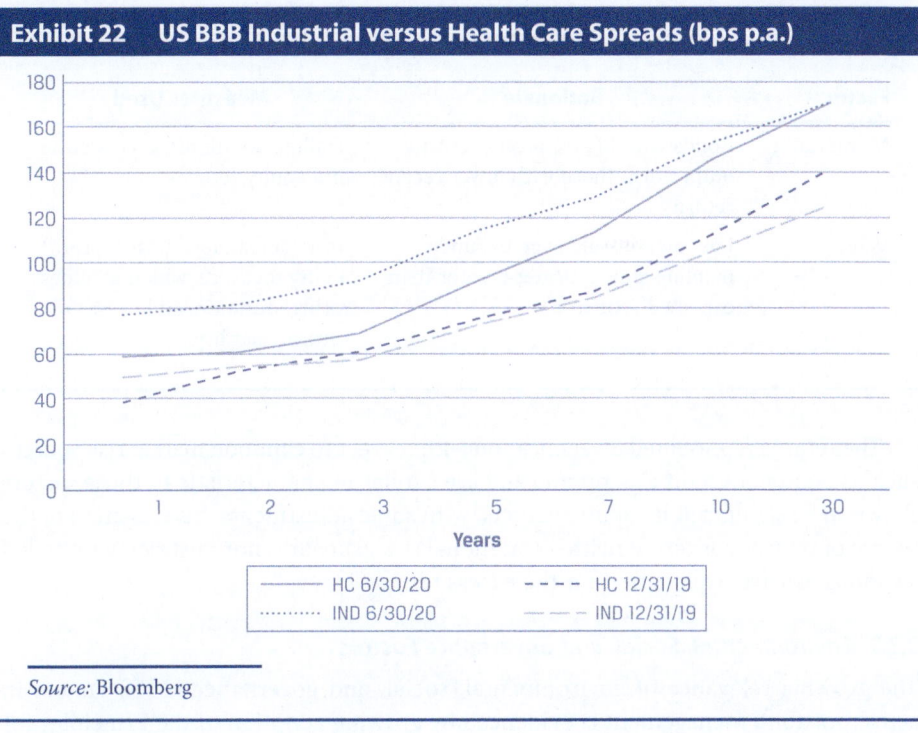

Exhibit 22 US BBB Industrial versus Health Care Spreads (bps p.a.)

Source: Bloomberg

3.3 Factor-Based Credit Strategies

While the top-down approach to fixed-income portfolio construction outlined in the previous section grouped investment choices by sector and public ratings, active credit investors are increasingly turning to strategies based on style factors.

3.3.1 *Key Factors Affecting Credit Spreads*

Factor investing has long been applied in equity markets as noted in earlier lessons, but the application of systematic risk factors such as size, value, and momentum in fixed-income markets is relatively new. For example, Israel, Palhares, and Richardson (2018) established a framework for evaluating excess corporate bond returns based on a number of characteristics, evaluating their significance in explaining fixed-income returns. The authors found strong evidence of positive risk-adjusted returns to measures of carry, defensive, momentum, and value. Exhibit 23 lists these four factors, their rationale, and the measures used in their analysis.

Exhibit 23 Selected Fixed-Income Factors

Factor	Rationale	Measures Used
Carry	Expected return measure if POD or aggregate risk premium is unchanged	OAS
Defensive	Empirical research suggests safer low-risk assets deliver higher risk-adjusted returns	Market-based leverage, gross profitability, and low duration

(continued)

Exhibit 23 (Continued)

Factor	Rationale	Measures Used
Momentum	Bonds with higher recent returns outperform those with lower recent returns	Trailing six-month excess bond and equity returns
Value	Low market value versus fundamental value indicates greater than expected return	Bond spread less default probability measure, which includes rating, duration, and excess return volatility

The returns represented diversification with respect to common market risk sources such as equity or credit risk premia and are similar in characteristic to those factors shown to be significant in equity markets, with some adjustments. Investigation of the source of returns suggested neither traditional risk exposures nor mispricing provided a comprehensive explanation for the excess returns.

3.3.2 Environmental, Social, and Governance Factors

The growing relevance of environmental, social, and governance (ESG) factors in active portfolio management is evidenced by growing adoption of the Principles for Responsible Investment. This independent body established in partnership with the United Nations to promote ESG factors in investing has more than 3,000 signatories worldwide with more than $100 trillion in assets under management.

Active credit investors usually incorporate ESG factors into portfolio strategies in one of three basic ways:

- The use of screens to either exclude specific industries with less favorable ESG characteristics, such as firearms, tobacco, or coal, or to rule out specific companies or sovereign issuers with ESG-specific ratings below a threshold
- Use of ESG ratings to target issuers within a given sector or rating category with relatively favorable ESG characteristics while matching a specific index risk and return
- Targeting fixed-income investments that directly fund ESG-specific initiatives

ESG-specific ratings for private and public issuers are a key element in the portfolio selection process. The wide range of quantitative and qualitative criteria used to measure ESG attributes and differences in methodology and weighting leads to greater dispersion in ESG versus credit ratings. That said, ESG and credit ratings tend to be positively correlated for two reasons. First, issuers with more financial resources are better able to meet more stringent ESG standards, while those with a greater likelihood of financial distress often face governance or other adverse risks. Second, major rating agencies now explicitly incorporate ESG risks into the traditional credit rating process. In 2019, Moody's cited ESG risks as a material factor in one-third of its credit rating actions among private sector issuers.

Green bonds are fixed-income instruments that directly fund ESG-related initiatives such as those related to environmental or climate benefits. This rapidly growing segment of the fixed-income market includes corporate, financial institution, and public issuers where bond proceeds are directed to projects that reduce air pollution, recycle post-consumer waste products, underwrite environmental remediation projects, and invest in alternative construction materials for environmentally sustainable buildings. Issuers frequently agree to voluntary guidelines such as the International Capital Market Association's Green Bond Principles (2018) to ensure that these securities meet investor ESG requirements. Although green bonds usually rank pari passu (or at the same level) with the issuer's outstanding senior unsecured bonds and therefore reflect similar pricing, the favorable ESG characteristics often result in greater investor demand than for standard debt issues. For example, in October 2020, the European Union issued €17 billion in new 10-year and 20-year debt in its first-ever offering of social bonds to finance its COVID-19 pandemic-related job support program. At nearly 14 times the issuance size, the €233 billion in investor orders for the new bonds represented the largest demand ever for a primary bond issuance.

LIQUIDITY AND TAIL RISK

e discuss liquidity risk in credit markets and how liquidity risk can be managed in a credit portfolio

f describe how to assess and manage tail risk in credit portfolios

4.1 Liquidity Risk

The feasibility and cost of buying and selling fixed-income instruments are important considerations for active investors. Trading volumes and bid–offer costs vary widely across fixed-income markets and regions. For instance, sovereign bonds in large developed markets are highly liquid, usually offering institutional bid–offer spreads in secondary markets for on-the-run securities of less than one basis point during trading hours. Smaller, off-the-run corporate bonds or structured notes, on the other hand, might command bid–offer spreads of 10 bps or more and take days to execute, given that many outstanding bonds do not trade at all on a given trading day.

Consider, for example, the US corporate bond market, wherein a single major issuer might have dozens of outstanding debt tranches of varying tenor, currency, or other feature, each separately traded and identifiable via a specific CUSIP or ISIN (International Securities Identification Number). As mentioned earlier in the curriculum, individual bond issuance and trading has historically taken place in over-the-counter (OTC) markets as opposed to on an exchange. OTC market liquidity rests with individual dealers, their specific portfolio and depth of inventory, and appetite to supply liquidity at a cost. Corporate bonds are traditionally traded on a request-for-quote basis, in which investors reach out to multiple dealers to request a fixed price quote for a specific trade size. The use of electronic trading platforms for bond trading has grown because higher regulatory capital requirements reduced bond inventories among dealers after the 2008–09 global financial crisis. While electronic trading platforms comprised less than one-third of individual corporate bond trading volume as of 2020, trading in bond portfolios and bond ETFs, addressed later in this lesson, has grown in importance.

Transaction cost estimates in bond markets vary significantly from those in equity markets because of market structure differences. Price discovery for infrequently traded individual bonds often begins with **matrix pricing (or evaluated pricing)** techniques introduced earlier in the curriculum using bonds from similar issuers and actively traded government benchmarks to establish a bond's fair value. For bonds quoted actively on a request-for-quote system by individual dealers, the effective spread transaction cost statistic introduced in an earlier lesson and shown in Equation 13 provides an estimate of trading cost.

$$\text{Trade size} \times \begin{cases} \text{Trade price} - (\text{Bid} + \text{Ask})/2 \text{ for buy orders} \\ (\text{Bid} + \text{Ask})/2 - \text{Trade price for sell orders} \end{cases} \quad (13)$$

However, the effective spread is an inadequate gauge of trading costs for positions that are traded in smaller orders over time and/or whose execution affects market spreads. A separate, ex-post liquidity gauge specific to the US corporate bond market is the TRACE (Trade Reporting and Compliance Engine) reporting system introduced in 2002 to track real-time price and volume reporting for bond transactions. Portfolio managers will often review recent TRACE trading activity to gauge the estimated cost of trading a bond position.

Active portfolio managers take several steps in managing the liquidity risk of bond portfolios, given the significant market risk involved in trading less liquid positions. First, active managers will usually favor on-the-run government bonds or most recently issued corporate or other bonds for short-term tactical portfolio positioning, while reserving relatively illiquid positions for buy-and-hold strategies or strategic positioning to minimize expected return erosion due to trading costs. Second, active managers might consider liquid alternatives to individual bond trades to close portfolio gaps where active management adds little value, or to react quickly to rapidly changing markets. These alternatives include CDS outlined later and bond ETFs.

Fixed-income ETFs are liquid, exchange-traded bond portfolios that create and redeem shares using an OTC primary market that exists between a set of institutional investors (or **authorized participants**) and the ETF sponsor. These ETF shares trade in the secondary market on an exchange, overcoming the liquidity constraints of individual OTC-traded bonds. Bond ETFs have enjoyed significant growth and are available across the credit spectrum as well as for different maturities and in different markets. Although the underlying cash flow exposures are similar, ETFs usually neither mature nor experience duration drift (with the exception of target maturity ETFs) as do individual bonds. As ETF sponsors target a specific index or profile, ETFs offer relatively constant portfolio duration and pay variable monthly interest based on the overall portfolio. Active credit managers use ETFs to quickly and efficiently overweight or underweight exposures in rapidly changing markets and to take on strategic exposure in segments of the market where individual or bottom-up bond selection is less of a focus.

When relatively illiquid bond positions are purchased or sold over longer periods, portfolio managers might consider hedging strategies such as asset swaps to mitigate the benchmark risk of a portfolio position as outlined in the following example.

EXAMPLE 19

Using Asset Swaps to Manage Liquidity Risk

Recall the earlier example of a United States–based issuer with the following option-free bonds outstanding:

Outstanding Debt	Term	Coupon	Price	YTM
2-year issue	2	4.25%	106.7	0.864%
5-year issue	5	3.25%	106.0	1.984%
15-year issue	15	2.75%	91.0	3.528%

Liquidity and Tail Risk

> Assume the investor instead holds a US$50 million face value position in the outstanding 15-year bond. Historical TRACE data suggest an average $5 million daily trading volume in the 15-year bond. Which of the following statements *best* describes how the issuer might use an asset swap to manage the benchmark interest rate risk associated with liquidating this bond position?
>
> **A** The investor should enter into an asset swap where he receives fixed and pays floating, unwinding the swap position once the bond position is sold.
>
> **B** The investor should enter into an asset swap where he pays fixed and receives floating, unwinding the swap position once the bond position is sold.
>
> **C** The investor should enter into an asset swap where he pays fixed and receives floating, unwinding the swap position over time in proportion to the amount of the bond sold.
>
> **Solution:**
>
> The correct answer is C. Because the investor's bond position represents a long position (i.e., long both spread duration and benchmark duration), the best hedge would be a short-duration (or pay-fixed swap) position rather than A. As for B, the hedge unwind occurs once the bond position is sold rather than over time, which exposes the investor to benchmark interest rate risk for the portion of the bond sold. The proportional swap unwind in C ensures that the offsetting swap position matches the benchmark interest rate risk of the bond.

4.2 Tail Risk

Extreme adverse outcomes that exceed those to be expected from a normally distributed portfolio are often referred to as tail events. In the context of active fixed-income management, the measurement and management of tail risk involves stress testing a portfolio's value based on the key fixed-income returns factors in Equation 1. In an earlier lesson on measuring and managing market risk, **value at risk (VaR)** was introduced as a measure of the minimum portfolio loss expected to occur over a given time period at a specific confidence level. For example, a 5% daily VaR of €8.7 million implies that a portfolio manager should expect a daily portfolio loss of *at least* €8.7 million on 5% of all trading days. Assuming normally distributed portfolio returns, the 5% confidence level translates to an outcome at least 1.65 standard deviations below the mean, while a 1% confidence interval lies at least 2.33 standard deviations below the mean. Risk managers often use expected returns, volatilities, and correlations to estimate parametric VaR in addition to either historical simulation or Monte Carlo methods. The following example shows a simple parametric VaR calculation for a bond position.

> **EXAMPLE 20**
>
> ### Fixed-Rate Bond VaR
>
> Consider the earlier case of an investor holding $50 million face value of a 15-year bond with a coupon of 2.75%, a current YTM of 3.528%, and a price of 91 per 100 of face value. What is the VaR for the full bond price at a 99% confidence interval for one month (assuming 21 trading days in the month) if daily yield volatility is 1.75% and we assume a normal distribution?

> **Solution:**
>
> First, we solve for the expected change in YTM based on a 99% confidence interval for the bond and a 1.75% yield volatility over 21 trading days, which equals 18.7 bps = (1.75% × 2.33 standard deviations × $\sqrt{21}$). We can quantify the bond's market value change using either a duration approximation or the actual price change as follows. We can use the Excel MDURATION function to solve for the bond's duration as 12.025. We can therefore approximate the change in bond value using the familiar (−ModDur × ΔYield) expression as $1,023,147 = ($50 million × 0.91 × (−12.025 × .00187)). We can also use the Excel PRICE function to directly calculate the new price of 88.982 and multiply the price change of 2.018 by the face value to get $1,009,000.

The simplicity and transparency of VaR can be misleading if it is used as a tool for quantifying tail risk for several reasons. First, VaR tends to underestimate the frequency and severity of extreme adverse events. It also fails to capture the downside correlation and liquidity risks associated with market stress scenarios. Finally, although VaR addresses *minimum* loss for a specific confidence level, it fails to quantify the *average* or expected loss under an extreme adverse market scenario. **Conditional value at risk** (CVaR), or expected loss, measures the average loss over a specific time period conditional on that loss exceeding the VaR threshold. While computationally more complex and beyond the scope of this lesson, CVaR is often measured using historical simulation or Monte Carlo techniques. Two related measures of portfolio VaR include incremental and relative measures. For example, an analyst seeking to measure the impact of adding or removing a portfolio position might use an **incremental VaR (or partial VaR)** calculation for this purpose. As mentioned in an earlier lesson, an investor could use **relative VaR** to measure the expected tracking error versus a benchmark portfolio by calculating VaR (or CVaR) based on a portfolio containing the active positions *minus* the benchmark holdings under a market stress scenario.

> **EXAMPLE 21**
>
> ### VaR Measures
>
> An active fixed-income manager is considering increasing an overweight portfolio allocation to BBB rated health care issuers versus a targeted index. Which of the following VaR measures is the most appropriate to evaluate the impact of this decision on overall portfolio VaR?
>
> A Incremental VaR
>
> B Relative VaR
>
> C CVaR
>
> **Solution:**
>
> The correct answer is A. Incremental VaR measures the impact of a specific portfolio position change on VaR, while relative VaR in answer B evaluates all active portfolio positions versus the benchmark index and could be important for an active fixed-income mandate that aims to beat an index once the portfolio change has been made. CVaR in C measures a portfolio's average loss over a specific time period conditional on that loss exceeding the VaR threshold.

Liquidity and Tail Risk

Tail risk assessment is typically conducted using one of the three methods summarized in Exhibit 24.

Exhibit 24: Methods to Assess Portfolio Tail Risk

Method	Description	Advantages	Disadvantages
Parametric Method	Uses expected value and standard deviation of risk factors assuming normal distribution	Simple and transparent calculation	Not well suited for non-normally distributed returns or option-based portfolios
Historical Simulation	Prices existing portfolio using historical parameters and ranking results	Actual results, accommodates options, with no probability distribution assumed	Highly dependent on historical period and repetition of historical market trends
Monte Carlo Analysis	Involves generating random outcomes using portfolio measures and sensitivities	Randomly generated results from a probability distribution, accommodates options	Highly dependent on model assumptions and less transparent

Hypothetical scenario analyses are often used to supplement these three methods of analysis to test portfolio vulnerabilities to specific portfolio parameter changes over time.

In addition to portfolio measures of duration and convexity as a basis for portfolio value changes, analytical models often rely on implied volatility parameters for benchmark interest rates and currencies, such as swaption volatility or currency option volatility, respectively, while reduced form or structural credit models incorporating CDS or equity volatility can be used to model expected spread volatility. Finally, term structure models introduced in an earlier lesson that incorporate interest rate volatility and drift in an equilibrium or arbitrage-free framework are frequently incorporated to simulate term structure changes over time.

Once tail risk under an extreme market scenario has been quantified, it is important to weigh this exposure against other binding portfolio constraints and to take steps to manage the downside risk. For example, a leveraged portfolio might face forced liquidation of certain bond positions beyond a certain tail risk threshold. Alternatively, a defined-benefit pension fund manager might be required to increase plan contributions if extreme market moves cause plan funding status to fall below a statutory minimum. Finally, a bank treasury officer could face increased regulatory capital requirements if adverse market changes under a stress test show significant portfolio losses.

A fixed-income portfolio manager can reduce tail risk by establishing position limits, risk budgeting, or using similar techniques designed to reduce portfolio concentration or to cap portfolio risk exposure to certain issuers, credit ratings, or regions. Alternatively, a portfolio manager might consider the use of derivatives to protect against downside portfolio risk. For example, the manager could consider purchasing a swaption (or the right to enter an interest rate swap at a pre-agreed rate in the future) or a credit default swaption (the right to purchase credit protection on an issuer or index at a strike rate in the future) to protect against the risk of benchmark YTM changes or credit spread changes, respectively. However, each of these strategies requires an upfront premium that will reduce excess portfolio spread over time. In addition, establishing these hedges in a distressed market will greatly increase hedging cost because of higher option volatility, so the manager must weigh these hedging costs against a risk mitigation strategy to determine the best course of action.

5. SYNTHETIC CREDIT STRATEGIES

g discuss the use of credit default swap strategies in active fixed-income portfolio management

As outlined in an earlier lesson, a CDS is the basic building block for strategies to manage credit risk separately from interest rate risk. CDS are often more liquid than an issuer's underlying bonds, enabling investors to take long or short positions, access maturities, and establish other exposures unavailable in cash markets with a smaller cash outlay than direct bond purchases.

Exhibit 25 shows CDS contract mechanics under which a protection "buyer" purchases credit protection from a protection "seller." Each contract references a specific issuer (or issuers) as well as credit event terms that, when triggered, lead to a settlement payment equal to the LGD multiplied by the contract notional amount from the seller to the buyer.

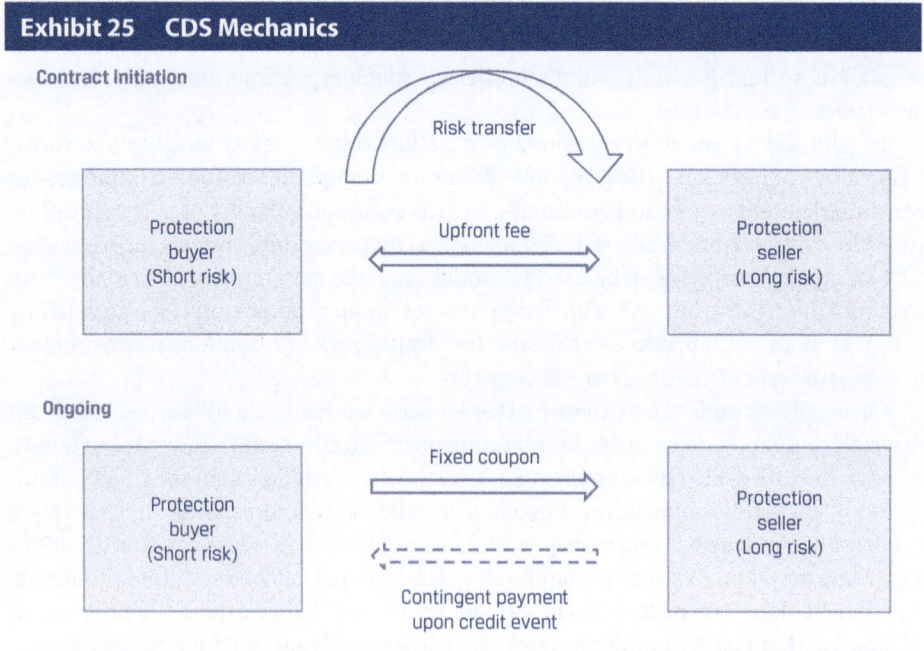

Exhibit 25 CDS Mechanics

CDS contracts are usually quoted on an issuer's CDS spread, which corresponds to a price equal to the present value difference between the CDS spread and a fixed coupon rate on the notional amount over the contract life. Fixed CDS coupon rates of 1% for investment-grade issuers and 5% for high-yield issuers were established when the International Swaps and Derivatives Association standardized CDS market conventions following the 2008 financial crisis. CDS pricing models discount future payments by the swap zero curve multiplied by the **hazard rate**, or the likelihood that an issuer credit event will occur given that it has not already occurred in a prior period.

Synthetic Credit Strategies

The CDS price at contract inception or on a coupon payment date as a percentage of notional can be approximated using Equation 14:

$$\text{CDS Price} \approx 1 + ((\text{Fixed Coupon} - \text{CDS Spread}) \times \text{EffSpreadDur}_{CDS}) \quad (14)$$

where CDS Spread is the issuer's current CDS market spread and $\text{EffSpreadDur}_{CDS}$ is the CDS contract's effective spread duration (sometimes referred to as CDS DV01). At contract inception, the protection buyer must either make a payment to or receive a payment from the protection seller equal to the CDS contract price difference from par, as shown in Exhibit 26.

Exhibit 26 Upfront Payment at CDS Contract Inception

Description	Upfront Premium
CDS Spread = Fixed Coupon	None
CDS Spread < Fixed Coupon	Protection buyer *receives* ((Fixed Coupon - CDS Spread) × $\text{EffSpreadDur}_{CDS}$)
CDS Spread > Fixed Coupon	Protection buyer *pays* ((CDS Spread - Fixed Coupon) × $\text{EffSpreadDur}_{CDS}$)

CDS contracts have similarities to both bonds and interest rate swaps. As with a cash bond priced at a discount when its coupon is below current market rates, the protection seller is entitled to an upfront payment in exchange for accepting a fixed coupon below the CDS market spread. As with a standard interest rate swap, a CDS contract priced at par has a zero net present value, and the notional is not exchanged but rather serves as a basis for spread and settlement calculations.

EXAMPLE 22

CDS Price and Price Changes

An investor seeks to purchase credit protection under a five-year CDS contract at a CDS market spread of 0.50% p.a. for an investment-grade issuer with an estimated effective spread duration ($\text{EffSpreadDur}_{CDS}$) of 4.75.

1 Determine whether the investor must pay or receive an upfront amount upon CDS contract inception and calculate the difference from par.
2 Calculate the change in contract price if the CDS spread rises to 0.60% p.a. and interpret the impact of the change on the protection buyer.

Solution to 1:

Because investment-grade CDS contracts have a fixed coupon of 1.00% p.a. versus the 0.50% p.a. CDS market spread, the investor buying protection should receive the difference from par upfront in exchange for paying an "above market" coupon under the contract. Calculate the estimated difference using Equation 14 ((Fixed Coupon − CDS Spread) × $\text{EffSpreadDur}_{CDS}$)) with CDS Spread of 0.50%, Fixed Coupon of 1.00%, and $\text{EffSpreadDur}_{CDS}$ equal to 4.75.

Upfront premium: 2.375% of CDS notional (= (1.00% − 0.50%) × 4.75).

Solution to 2:

Calculate the upfront premium using Equation 14 and a 0.60% spread.

Upfront premium: 1.90% of CDS notional (= (1.00% − 0.60%) × 4.75).

> The protection buyer realizes a mark-to-market gain equal to 0.475% (2.375% − 1.90%) of the CDS contract notional because of the wider CDS spread.

CDS price changes for a given CDS spread change can be quantified using the contract's effective spread duration:

$$\Delta(\text{CDS Price})/\Delta(\text{CDS Spread}) \approx -(\Delta(\text{CDS Spread}) \times \text{EffSpreadDur}_{\text{CDS}}) \quad (15)$$

Active fixed-income portfolio managers buy or sell CDS protection across issuers, maturities, and/or sectors to alter portfolio exposure, as illustrated in the following example.

EXAMPLE 23

Credit Underweight Using CDS

A European-based fixed-income manager intends to underweight exposure to a BBB rated French media and telecommunications issuer. She observes that the issuer's current on-the-run five-year CDS contract is trading at a spread of 110 bps p.a. with an EffSpreadDur$_{\text{CDS}}$ of 4.595. Which position should she take in the CDS market? Calculate the result if spreads widen to 125 bps for a €10 million notional position.

Solution:

The manager can underweight the issuer's credit by *purchasing* protection in the CDS market. This short risk position will realize a gain if the issuer's spreads widen. For example, if the issuer's credit spreads widen from 110 bps p.a. to 125 bps p.a., we can estimate the change in CDS contract value by multiplying (−Δ(CDS Spread) × EffSpreadDur$_{\text{CDS}}$) from Equation 15 by the CDS notional to get €68,925 (=−€10,000,000 × (−0.15% × 4.595)).

While CDS contracts are available across maturities, the five-year tenor is generally the most frequently traded contract. Exhibit 27 summarizes the most common CDS strategies used in practice.

Exhibit 27   Credit Derivative–Based Alternatives to Corporate Bonds

Instrument	Description	Targeted Return	Portfolio Impact
Single-Name CDS	Protection buyer pays premium to seller in exchange for payment if credit event occurs	Buyer gains and seller loses if single-name credit spread widens or credit event occurs	Short (buyer) or long (seller) single-name credit spread exposure
Index-Based CDS	Protection buyer pays premium in exchange for partial payment if credit event occurs for index member	Buyer gains and seller loses if index member spreads widen or if credit event occurs	Short (buyer) or long (seller) index-based credit spread exposure

Exhibit 27   (Continued)

Instrument	Description	Targeted Return	Portfolio Impact
Payer Option on CDS Index	Option buyer pays premium for right to buy protection ("pay" coupons) on CDS index contract at a future date	Max (CDS Credit Spread Strike – CDS Credit Spread at expiration, 0) – Option Premium	Short CDS index-based credit spread exposure
Receiver Option on CDS Index	Option buyer pays premium for right to sell protection ("receive" coupons) on CDS index contract at a future date	Max (Credit spread at expiration – CDS Credit Spread Strike, 0) – Option Premium	Long CDS index-based credit spread exposure

Single-name reference entities include both private corporations and sovereign borrowers. Several CDS indexes are available across regions and often also offer subindexes covering a particular sector or borrower type. For example, the Markit CDX North American Investment Grade index consists of 125 equally weighted CDS contracts on entities, including six subindexes (High Volatility, Consumer Cyclical, Energy, Financials, Industrial, and Telecom, Media, and Technology).

CDS strategies are commonly used by active fixed-income portfolio managers to over- or underweight credit spread exposure to individual issuers, specific sectors, or borrower types. As with benchmark yield curves, CDS portfolio positioning strategies are usually based on expected changes in the credit curve level, slope, or shape. The credit curve referred to here is the **CDS curve**, or the plot of CDS spreads across maturities for a single reference entity or index, rather than the fitted credit spread curves addressed earlier. This might involve an investor taking a long or short CDS position in one issuer or issuer type, or a long or short position overweighting one reference entity or group of entities and underweighting another. Investors using CDS strategies to hedge bond portfolios must always consider the potential impact of basis changes on the strategy over the investment horizon.

Fixed-income ETFs offer derivatives such as futures and options that are different from CDS contracts. As with bond futures, ETF futures are a contract to take future delivery of an ETF and trade on a price rather than a spread basis. Because underlying ETF prices are derived from all-in bond yields held by the fund, ETF derivative prices change with changes in both benchmark rates and credit spreads.

CDS long–short strategies based on spread level are appropriate for both bottom-up and top-down approaches. Assume, for example, that an investor believes that issuer A's credit spreads will likely narrow versus those of issuer B. To capitalize on this view in the cash market, the investor would first source A's individual bonds for purchase and then seek a duration-matched amount of issuer B's bonds to borrow and sell short. The existence of a liquid single-name CDS market for both issuers allows the investor to simply sell protection on A and purchase protection on B for the same notional and tenor.

> **EXAMPLE 24**
>
> ### CDS Long–Short Strategies
>
> Consider the investor from the prior example who sought to underweight a French media and telecommunications issuer. Assume instead that the investor seeks to maintain a constant media and telecommunications credit allocation by overweighting a BBB rated German media and telecommunications competitor. CDS contract details are as follows:
>
> | Issuer | Tenor | CDS Spread | EffSpreadDur$_{CDS}$ |
> |---|---|---|---|
> | French Media & Telecoms Issuer | 5 years | 110 bps | 4.697 |
> | German Media & Telecoms Issuer | 5 years | 130 bps | 4.669 |
>
> Describe an appropriate long–short CDS strategy to meet this goal, and calculate the investor's return if the French issuer's spreads widen by 10 bps and those of the German issuer narrow by 25 bps based on €10 million notional contracts.
>
> ### Solution:
>
> The manager purchases protection on the French issuer and simultaneously sells protection on the German issuer. Use $(-\Delta(\text{CDS Spread}) \times \text{EffSpreadDur}_{CDS})$ from Equation 15 multiplied by the CDS notional to solve for changes in the short and long risk positions:
>
> Short risk (French issuer): €46,970 (= €10,000,000 × (−0.10% × −4.697))
>
> Long risk (German issuer): €116,725 (= −€10,000,000 × (−0.25% × 4.669))
>
> The total gain on the long–short strategy is €163,695 (= €46,970 + €116,725).

A similar long–short strategy can be applied under a top-down approach. For example, an investor might overweight (underweight) a specific sector given an expectation of narrower (wider) spread levels versus the total portfolio by selling (buying) protection on a CDS subindex contract. Alternatively, assume an active manager expects a weaker economy and a widening of high-yield versus investment-grade credit spread levels. The manager can capitalize on this view by buying five-year protection on a high-yield CDS index and selling protection on an investment-grade CDS index for the same tenor. Standardized CDS contracts eliminate the impact of duration difference, liquidity, and other factors that arise under a similar strategy in the cash bond market.

CDS long–short strategies based on expected credit curve slope changes involve CDS curve trades. For example, an upward-sloping credit curve implies relatively low near-term expected default probability that rises over time. An investor might expect an issuer's CDS curve to steepen if its near-term default probability declines as a result of higher than expected profits and stable leverage. This investor can capitalize on this view by selling short-term protection using a single-name CDS contract and buying long-term protection on that same reference entity. As shown in the following example, capitalizing on spread changes for different maturities requires duration matching of the positions, as in the case of benchmark yield curve strategies.

Synthetic Credit Strategies

> **EXAMPLE 25**
>
> ### Duration-Weighted Single-Name CDS Curve Steepener
>
> Returning to our earlier example of the German media and telecommunications issuer, the investor decides instead to position her portfolio for a steepening of the issuer's credit curve using the CDS market. Details of on-the-run 5- and 10-year CDS contracts outstanding are as follows.
>
> | Issuer | Tenor | CDS Spread | $EffSpreadDur_{CDS}$ |
> |---|---|---|---|
> | German Media & Telecoms Issuer | 5 years | 130 bps | 4.669 |
> | German Media & Telecoms Issuer | 10 years | 175 bps | 8.680 |
>
> Describe an appropriate long–short CDS strategy to meet this goal assuming a €10,000,000 10-year CDS contract notional. Calculate the investor's return if the 5-year spreads rise 10 bps and the 10-year spreads rise 20 bps.
>
> ### Solution:
>
> A steeper credit curve implies that $((CDS\ Spread)_{10yr} - (CDS\ Spread)_{5yr})$ will increase. The appropriate long–short strategy to position for this change is to purchase protection based on the 10-year, €10,000,000 notional and to sell protection on an equivalent duration 5-year CDS contract.
>
> 1. Calculate the 5-year CDS contract notional that matches the basis point value (BPV) of a 10-year, €10,000,000 CDS ($BPV_{10yr} = EffSpreadDur_{10yrCDS}$ × notional) using the effective spread duration ratio of 1.859 ($EffSpreadDur_{10yrCDS}/EffSpreadDur_{5yrCDS}$ = 8.68/4.669) multiplied by €10,000,000 to get €18,590,000.
>
>   Confirm this equivalence by comparing BPV_{5yr} and BPV_{10yr}:
>
> BPV_{5yr}: €8,680 = €18,590,000 × 4.669/10,000
>
> BPV_{10yr}: €8,680 = €10,000,000 × 8.68/10,000
>
> 2. Calculate portfolio return for a 10 bp increase in 5-year CDS spreads and a 20 bp increase in 10-year CDS spreads using Equation 15 ($-\Delta(CDS\ Spread) \times EffSpreadDur_{CDS}$) multiplied by the CDS notional.
>
>   5 year (long risk): −€86,800 (= €18,590,000 × (−0.1% × 4.669))
>
>   10 year (short risk): €173,600 (= −€10,000,000 × (−0.2% × 8.68))
>
>   Net portfolio gain: €86,800 = €173,600 − €86,800

The same curve strategy just described applies to expected credit curve slope changes for a CDS index or subindex. For instance, an investor who believes the economy is nearing the end of a growth cycle might expect the CDS curve for industrial issuers to flatten amid rising near-term credit spreads. Under this expected scenario, an investor purchases short-term CDS subindex protection on industrials and sells long-term protection on the same subindex to capitalize on a flattening view. Alternatively, an investor taking a top-down approach who shares a similar bearish economic view might consider a flattening trade for an entire CDS index.

Additional CDS strategies seek to either capitalize on the basis difference between CDS and cash bonds or take advantage of specific events that affect CDS spreads and curves. As noted earlier, basis differences arise from a number of factors but are also due to differences in liquidity across derivative and cash markets, a detailed treatment of which is beyond the scope of this lesson. Corporate events that influence CDS spreads by affecting bondholders differently from shareholders include mergers and acquisitions and leveraged buyouts, both of which are addressed elsewhere in the curriculum.

6. CREDIT SPREAD CURVE STRATEGIES

h discuss various portfolio positioning strategies that managers can use to implement a specific credit spread view

Earlier in the lesson, we established that the credit cycle is a key driver of credit spread changes across maturities and ratings. The probability of issuer default and severity of loss over the cycle must be considered within the context of an overall market view. For example, positively sloped credit spread curves suggest relatively low near-term default probability, a view consistent with stable or rising future inflation and relatively strong expected economic growth. Investor demand for higher credit spreads for assuming the risk of downgrade or default for longer periods also contributes to a positive slope.

The level and slope of credit curves change over the economic cycle. Early in an expansion, as profits rise and defaults remain high, high-yield spreads remain elevated and well above investment-grade spreads, which often exhibit a flat to inverted spread curve. As an expansion progresses, lower defaults and increased profits cause short-term high-yield and investment-grade spreads to decline and credit spread curves to steepen. Credit curve steepening continues as economic growth peaks amid higher leverage and inflation expectations. As economic growth slows or the economy enters a recession, credit spreads rise, and spread curves flatten, with the high-yield curve inverting in some instances amid falling profitability and rising defaults. Although no two credit cycles are alike, Exhibit 28 presents a stylized view of these credit spread curve level and shape changes for investment-grade (IG) and high-yield (HY) issuers over the economic cycle.

Credit Spread Curve Strategies

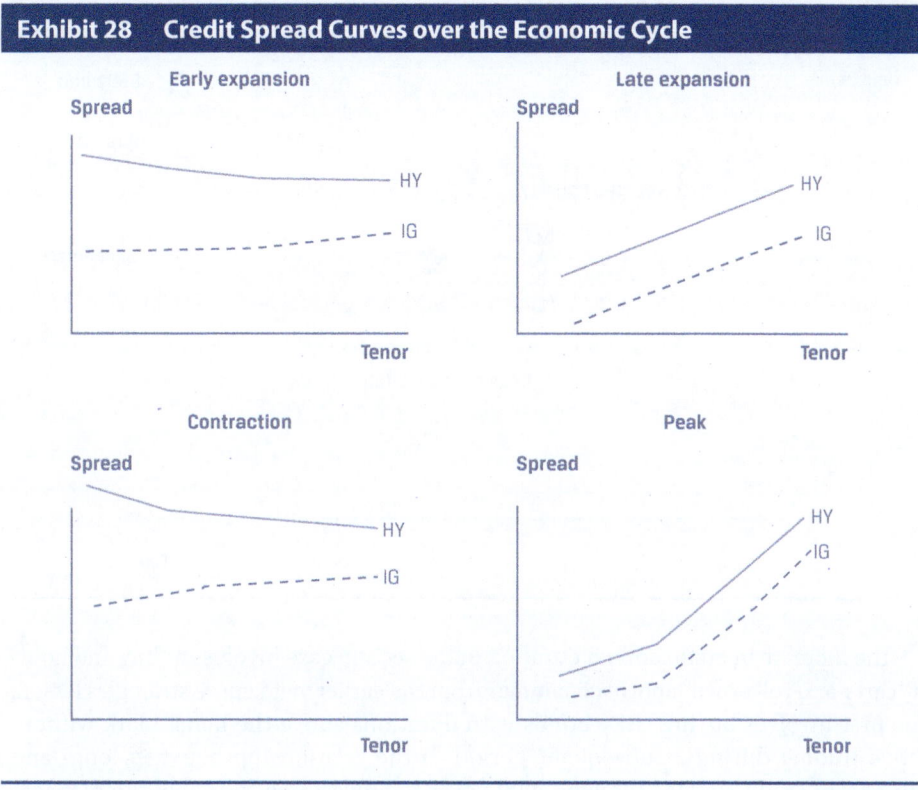

Exhibit 28 Credit Spread Curves over the Economic Cycle

Active credit managers often incorporate the credit cycle into economic growth and inflation forecasts, which are then translated into sector- and issuer-specific views driving specific credit curve level and slope expectations using the bottom-up or top-down approaches outlined earlier. If these forecasts coincide with current credit spread curves, managers will choose active credit strategies consistent with static or stable credit market conditions. However, if an investor's views differ from what today's credit curve implies about future defaults and the severity of credit loss, they will position the portfolio to generate excess return based on this divergent view within investment mandate constraints using the cash and derivative strategies outlined in the following section.

6.1 Static Credit Spread Curve Strategies

An active credit manager might believe that current credit spreads are reasonably priced and that credit curves will remain stable or unchanged over an investment horizon while credit defaults and annual loss rates remain low. Exhibit 29 shows that a manager could position a portfolio to generate excess return in this scenario by either lowering the portfolio's average credit rating or adding credit spread duration by investing in longer-dated bonds with a similar rating to the current portfolio.

In the first case, a portfolio tilt toward lower-rated bonds will increase expected spread return, as seen in Equation 10 (E [ExcessSpread] ≈ $Spread_0$ − (EffSpreadDur × ΔSpread) − (POD × LGD)) if Spread, POD, and LGD remain stable. The shift from an average A rated to BBB rated portfolio in Exhibit 29 is an extension of an earlier case (Example 10) that quantified corporate versus government bond roll-down returns as the YTM difference assuming constant spreads and default rates.

Exhibit 29 Buy-and-Hold Strategies under a Static Credit Curve

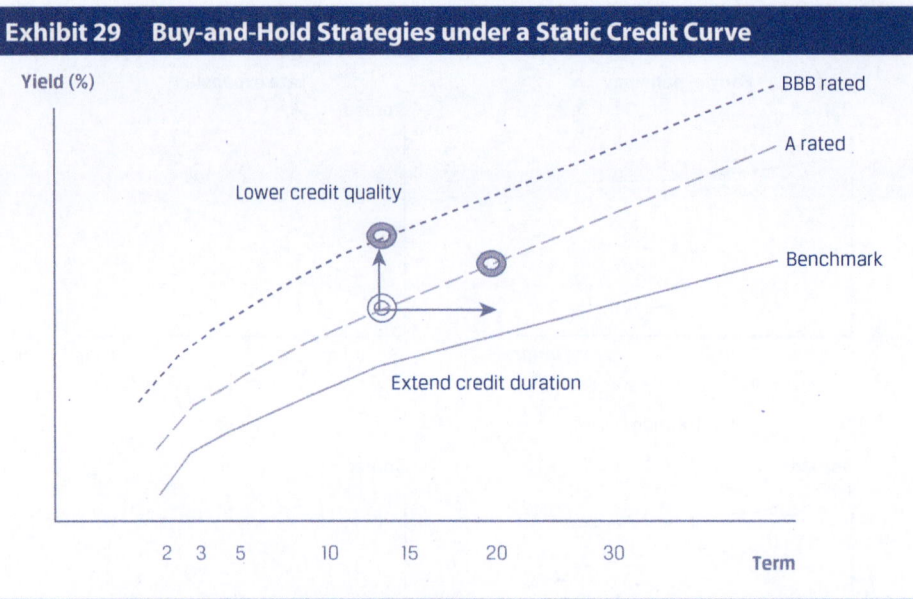

The increase in credit spread duration in the second case involves a "buy and hold" or "carry and roll down" approach familiar from the earlier yield curve strategies lesson. The first involves buying risky bonds with durations above the benchmark without active trading during a subsequent period. If the relationship between long- and short-term credit spreads remains stable over the investment horizon, the manager is rewarded with greater return from the higher spread duration. "Rolling down" the credit curve not only generates incremental coupon income (adjusted over time for any price difference from par) due to wider spreads but also adds return from the passage of time and the investor's ability to sell the shorter-maturity position in the future at a lower credit spread at the end of the investment horizon. The following example illustrates this second case, shown in Exhibit 29.

EXAMPLE 26

Adding Credit Duration under a Static Credit Curve

A Sydney-based investor notes the following available option-free bonds for an A rated Australian issuer:

Debt Term	Coupon	YTM	Price
5 years	1.00%	1.00%	100
10 years	1.35%	1.25%	100.937
15 years	2.00%	1.95%	100.648

The 5-year, 10-year, and 15-year Australian government bonds have YTMs and coupons of 0.50%, 0.75%, and 1.10%, respectively, and both corporate and government bonds have a semiannual coupon. As an active manager who expects stable benchmark yields and credit spreads over the next six months, the investor decides to overweight (by AUD50,000,000 in face value) the issuer's 15-year versus 10-year bond for that period. Calculate the return to the investor of the roll-down strategy in AUD and estimate the returns attributable to benchmark yield versus credit spread changes.

Credit Spread Curve Strategies

Solution:

To estimate credit curve roll-down returns, we must solve for the first two return components from Equation 1 (Coupon income +/− Roll-down return) and separate the impact of benchmark yield versus credit spread changes.

1. Solve for the respective 5-year, 10-year, and 15-year bond credit spreads. Yield spread and G-spread are reasonable approximations because the bonds are option-free, with maturities closely aligned to par government securities.

    5-year spread: 0.50% (= 1.00% − 0.50%)

    10-year spread: 0.50% (= 1.25% − 0.75%)

    15-year spread: 0.85% (= 1.95% − 1.10%)

2. Solve for 6-month expected returns of the 10-year versus 15-year bond:

    a. Incremental coupon income = $162,500 (= (2.00% − 1.35%)/2 × $50 million)

Debt Tenor	Coupon	Yield Spread	Total Coupon Income	Coupon (Benchmark Yield)	Coupon (Credit Spread)
10 years	1.35%	0.50%	$337,500	$187,500	$150,000
15 years	2.00%	0.85%	$500,000	$275,000	$225,000

    Divide incremental coupon into benchmark and credit spread components:

    Income due to benchmark yields: $87,500 = $275,000 − $187,500

    Income due to credit spreads: $75,000 = $225,000 − $150,000

    b. Price appreciation is determined by the bond's price today and in six months' time based on unchanged benchmark rates. In six months, the 10-year and 15-year positions will be 9.5-year and 14.5-year bonds, respectively, at a yield and yield spread point along the curve. Estimate all-in YTMs and yield spreads using interpolation to arrive at the following results:

Debt Tenor	Date	Coupon	All-In Yield	Benchmark Yield	Yield Spread
5 years	Today	1.00%	1.00%	0.50%	0.50%
10 years	Today	1.35%	1.25%	0.75%	0.50%
15 years	Today	2.00%	1.95%	1.10%	0.85%
9.5 years	In six months	1.35%	1.225%	0.725%	0.50%
14.5 years	In six months	2.00%	1.88%	1.065%	0.815%

Calculate price appreciation using the difference between current bond prices and those in six months using the Excel PV function (= −PV(rate, nper, pmt, FV, type)) where "rate" is the interest rate per period (0.01225/2), "nper" is the number of periods (19), "pmt" is the periodic coupon (1.35/2), "FV" is future value (100), and "type" (0) involves payments made at the end of each period.

10-year: Initial price: 100.937

Price in six months: 101.118 (= −PV (0.01225/2, 19, 1.35/2, 100, 0))

Price appreciation: $89,660 (= (101.118 − 100.937)/100.937 × $50 million)

Because the yield spread curve is flat at 0.50%, the full $89,660 price change in the 10-year is benchmark yield curve roll down.

15-year: Initial price: 100.648

Price in six months: 101.517 (= −PV (0.0188/2, 29, 1, 100, 0))

Price appreciation: $431,700 (= (101.517 − 100.648)/100.648 × $50 million)

Because the 0.07% decline in YTM is estimated to be equally attributable to benchmark yield and yield spread changes, each is assumed equal to $215,850.

3 Incremental income due to price appreciation is therefore $342,040 (=$431,700 − $89,660), of which $215,850 is attributable to credit spread changes.

In total, the incremental roll-down strategy generates $504,540 (=$342,040 + 162,500), of which $290,850 (= $215,850 + $75,000) is estimated to be due to credit spread curve roll down.

Derivative-based credit strategies to add credit spread duration or increase credit exposure include selling CDS single-name or index protection for longer maturities or lower credit quality or using a long–short approach to achieve a similar objective.

EXAMPLE 27

Using CDS for a Static Fixed-Income Credit Strategy

Returning to our earlier example of the investment-grade German media and telecommunications issuer, the investor decides instead to overweight exposure to this name by taking a long risk position in the single-name 10-year CDS market for one year. Details of today's 5-year and 10-year CDS contracts are as follows.

Issuer	Tenor	CDS Spread	EffSpreadDur$_{CDS}$
German Media & Telecoms Issuer	5 years	130 bps	4.669
German Media & Telecoms Issuer	10 years	175 bps	8.680

Describe the roll-down strategy using CDS and calculate the one-year return in euros on a €10,000,000 position assuming an annual coupon payment and a 9-year EffSpreadDur$_{CDS}$ of 7.91.

Solution:

The investor sells 10-year CDS protection on the German issuer to overweight exposure and terminates the position in one year. As with the bond example, the sold protection strategy generates coupon income if the issuer does not default and price appreciation if credit spreads decline over time.

1 The fixed coupon received at the end of one year equals the notional multiplied by the standard 1% investment-grade coupon for the period, or €100,000, or €10,000,000 × 1.00% for one year.

2 Estimate the CDS price change over one year by interpolating the 9-year issuer spread under a static credit curve assumption.

Credit Spread Curve Strategies

Solve for the 5-year and 10-year CDS spread weights in the 9-year spread interpolation calculation.

5-year CDS weight = w_5 = 20% (= (10 − 9)/(10 − 5))

10-year CDS weight = w_{10} = 80% (or (1 − w_5))

Note that (w_5 × 5) + (w_{10} × 10) = 9

The 9-year spread is a weighted average of 5- and 10-year CDS spreads.

CDS Spread$_{9yr}$ = w_5 × CDS Spread$_{5yr}$ + w_{10} × CDS Spread$_{10yr}$

1.66% (=1.30% × 0.2 + 1.75% × 0.8)

Estimate the CDS contract price change by multiplying the change in CDS price from Equation 14 (CDS Price ≈ 1 + ((Fixed Coupon − CDS Spread) × EffSpreadDur$_{CDS}$)) by the CDS notional.

10-year CDS per €1 par: 0.934 = (1 + (−0.75% × 8.68))

9-year CDS per €1 par: 0.947794 = (1 + (−0.66% × 7.91))

Calculate the price appreciation by multiplying the price change by the contract notional to get €128,940 (= (0.947794 − 0.9349) × €10,000,000).

Total return equals the sum of the coupon income and price appreciation, or €228,940 (= €100,000 + €128,940).

6.2 Dynamic Credit Spread Curve Strategies

Active credit managers seek to capitalize on divergent market views using cash-based or derivative strategies related to specific issuers, sectors, or the overall credit market over the credit cycle given anticipated credit curve changes across both maturities and rating categories. The following examples demonstrate how an active manager might position a credit portfolio in anticipation of these changes to generate excess return.

EXAMPLE 28

Tactical Credit Strategies – Economic Slowdown Scenario

An active credit portfolio manager considers the following corporate bond portfolio choices familiar from an earlier example:

Rating Category	Current OAS	Expected Loss (POD × LGD)	EffSpreadDur
A	1.05%	0.06%	5.5
Baa	1.35%	0.30%	6.0
Ba	2.45%	0.60%	4.5
B	3.50%	3.00%	4.0

The investor anticipates an economic slowdown in the next year that will have a greater adverse impact on lower-rated issuers. Assume that an index portfolio is equally allocated across all four rating categories, while the investor chooses a tactical portfolio combining equal long positions in the investment-grade (A and Baa) bonds and short positions in the high-yield (Ba and B) bonds.

1. Calculate excess spread on the index and tactical portfolios assuming no change in spreads over the next year (ignoring spread duration changes).
2. Calculate excess spread under an economic downturn scenario for the index and tactical portfolios where both OAS and expected loss rise 50% for investment-grade bonds and double for high-yield bonds.

Solution to 1:

The following table summarizes expected excess returns $E[\text{ExcessSpread}] \approx \text{Spread}_0 - (\text{EffSpreadDur} \times \Delta\text{Spread}) - (\text{POD} \times \text{LGD})$ for each of the four rating categories with no change in spreads. For example, expected excess return for rating category A is 0.99% (=1.05% − (5.5 × 0) − 0.06%).

Rating Category	Excess Spread
A	0.99%
Baa	1.05%
Ba	1.85%
B	0.50%

Solve for the equally weighted versus tactical portfolios as follows:

Equally weighted index: 1.10% (= (0.99% + 1.05% + 1.85% + 0.50%)/4)

Tactical portfolio: −0.16% (= (0.99% + 1.05%)/2 − (1.85% + 0.50%)/2)

Solution to 2:

The following table summarizes expected excess returns $E[\text{ExcessSpread}] \approx \text{Spread}_0 - (\text{EffSpreadDur} \times \Delta\text{Spread}) - (\text{POD} \times \text{LGD})$ for each of the four rating categories with the expected 50% increase in both OAS and expected loss under the slowdown scenario. For example, expected excess return for rating category A is −1.928% (=1.05% − (5.5 × 0.525%) − 0.09%).

Rating Category	E(OAS)	E(Expected Loss)	E(Excess Spread)
A	1.575%	0.09%	−1.928%
Baa	2.025%	0.45%	−3.150%
Ba	4.900%	1.20%	−9.775%
B	7.000%	6.00%	−16.500%

Solve for the equally weighted versus tactical portfolios as follows.

Equally weighted index: −7.84% = (−1.928% − 3.150% −9.775% − 16.500%)/4
Tactical portfolio: +10.6% = (−1.928% − 3.150%)/2 − (−9.775% − 16.500%)/2

This example assumes that an active manager is able to source and borrow the necessary Ba- and B rated bonds to sell short at no cost. However, in practice, the availability and cost of shorting bonds vary over the economic cycle, and shorting bonds is often far more difficult and costly during an economic slowdown. The synthetic, CDS-based strategy in the following example targets a similar objective.

EXAMPLE 29

Synthetic Credit Strategies: Economic Slowdown Scenario

As in the prior example, an active fixed-income manager anticipates an economic slowdown in the next year with a greater adverse impact on lower-rated issuers. The manager chooses a tactical CDX (credit default swap index) strategy combining positions in investment-grade and high-yield CDX contracts to capitalize on this view. The current market information for investment-grade and high-yield CDX contracts is as follows:

CDX Contract	Tenor	CDS Spread	EffSpreadDur$_{CDS}$
CDX IG Index	5 years	120 bps	4.67
CDX HY Index	5 years	300 bps	4.65

Assume that both CDX contracts have a $10,000,000 notional with premiums paid annually, and that the EffSpreadDur$_{CDS}$ for the CDX IG and CDX HY contracts in one year are 3.78 and 3.76, respectively.

1. Describe the appropriate tactical CDX strategy, and calculate the one-year return assuming no change in credit spread levels.
2. Calculate the one-year return on the tactical CDX strategy under an economic downturn scenario in which investment-grade credit spreads rise by 50% and high-yield credit spreads double.

Solution to 1:

The investor should buy protection on the CDX IG Index and sell protection on the CDX HY Index. Current CDS prices are estimated by multiplying EffSpreadDur$_{CDS}$ by the spread difference from the standard rates of 1% and 5%, respectively:

CDX IG: 99.066 per $100 face value, or 0.99066 (=1 + (−0.20% × 4.67))

CDX HY: 109.3 per $100 face value, or 1.093 (=1 + (2.00% × 4.65))

In one year, the return is measured by combining the coupon income with the price appreciation assuming no spread change. Because the investor is long CDX HY and short CDX IG, the net annual premium received is $400,000 (=$10,000,000 × (5.00% − 1.00%). The respective CDS prices in one year are as follows:

CDX IG: 99.244 per $100 face value, or 0.99244 (=1 + (−0.20% × 3.78))

CDX HY: 107.52 per $100 face value, or 1.0752 (=1 + (2.00% × 3.76))

The investor has a $17,800 gain from the CDX IG position (= (0.99244 − 0.99066) × $10,000,000) and a $178,000 gain from the short CDX HY position (1.0752 − 1.093) × −$10,000,000). Adding the $400,000 coupon income results in a one-year gain from the strategy of $595,800 with constant spreads.

Solution to 2:

Initial CDS prices are derived exactly as in Question 1:

CDX IG: 99.066 per $100 face value, or 0.99066 (=1 − (4.67 × 0.2%))

CDX HY: 109.3 per $100 face value, or 1.093 (=1 + (4.65 × 2.00%))

In one year, the return is measured by combining the coupon income with the price appreciation given the expected rise in the CDX IG spread to 1.80% and the CDX HY spread to 6.00%. In this case, the investor takes the opposite position to that of Question 1, namely long CDX HY and short CDX IG, so the net annual premium received is $400,000 (=$10,000,000 × (5.00% − 1.00%). Respective CDS prices in one year are as follows:

CDX IG: 96.976 per $100 face value, or 0.96976 (=1 − (3.78 × 0.8%))

CDX HY: 96.24 per $100 face value, or 0.9624 (=1 − (3.76 × 1.00%))

The investor has a $209,000 loss from the CDX IG position ((0.96976 − 0.99066) × $10,000,000) and a $1,306,000 gain from the short CDX HY position (0.9624 − 1.093) × −$10,000,000). Adding the $400,000 net premium results in a one-year gain from the strategy of $1,497,000 under this scenario.

The early expansion phase of the credit cycle is usually characterized by rising profits and falling leverage, as shown earlier in Exhibit 8, increasing cash flow coverage available to service outstanding debt. This reduction in the likelihood of near-term financial distress leads to both lower credit spread levels and a steeper credit curve, an effect that is more pronounced for lower-rated issuers in cyclical industries. The following examples illustrate how an active manager might capitalize on this credit cycle view in cash and synthetic markets.

EXAMPLE 30

Tactical Credit Strategies: Economic Recovery Scenario

A long-only active credit manager faces similar corporate bond portfolio choices to those in an earlier example:

Rating Category	OAS	EffSpreadDur	Expected Loss
A	1.40%	5.5	0.10%
Baa	2.00%	6.0	0.30%
Ba	3.75%	4.5	1.00%
B	5.50%	4.0	4.50%

Given an expectation that an economic rebound will cause both credit spreads and expected loss rates to fall by one-third, an active manager decides to tilt her credit portfolio toward high yield. Compare the impact of this rebound scenario on an active portfolio (33.3% invested in each of the Ba and B bond categories, with the remaining 33.3% split evenly between A and Baa) versus on an equally weighted passive portfolio.

Solution:

The economic rebound scenario results in the following new OAS and expected losses, with expected excess returns E [ExcessSpread] ≈ $Spread_0 - (EffSpreadDur \times \Delta Spread) - (POD \times LGD)$ in the far right column:

Rating Category	E(OAS)	E(Expected Loss)	E(Excess Spread)
A	0.933%	0.07%	3.898%
Baa	1.333%	0.20%	5.80%
Ba	2.50%	0.67%	8.705%
B	3.667%	3.00%	9.832%

Credit Spread Curve Strategies

Solve for the passive (equally weighted) portfolio returns versus tactical portfolio returns.

Passive portfolio return: 7.059% (= (3.898% + 5.80% + 8.705% + 9.832%)/4)

Tactical portfolio return: 7.795% (= 3.898%/6 + 5.80%/6 + 8.705%/3 + 9.832%/3).

EXAMPLE 31

Synthetic Credit Strategies: Economic Recovery Scenario

As in the prior example, an active fixed-income manager anticipates an economic rebound that is expected to cause high-yield credit curve steepening. The manager chooses a tactical CDX strategy combining 5-year and 10-year credit positions to capitalize on this view. Current market information for these high-yield CDX contracts is as follows:

CDX Contract	Tenor	CDS Spread	EffSpreadDur$_{CDS}$
CDX HY Index	5 years	450 bps	4.637
CDX HY Index	10 years	375 bps	8.656

Describe an appropriate duration-neutral portfolio positioning strategy to capitalize on this view using these CDX HY contracts. Calculate the return assuming that 5-year CDX spreads immediately fall by 175 bps and 10-year spreads decline by 25 bps for an equivalent $10,000,000 notional on the 10-year CDX index contract.

Solution:

The appropriate strategy is to sell protection on the 5-year CDX HY and buy protection on the 10-year CDX HY.

1. Calculate the 5-year CDS contract notional that matches the BPV of a 10-year, $10,000,000 CDS (BPV$_{10yr}$ = EffSpreadDur$_{10yrCDS}$ × notional) using the effective spread duration ratio of 1.8667 (EffSpreadDur$_{10yrCDS}$/EffSpreadDur$_{5yrCDS}$ = 8.656/4.637) multiplied by $10,000,000 to get $18,667,000.

   Confirm this equivalence by comparing BPV$_{5yr}$ and BPV$_{10yr}$:

   BPV$_{5yr}$: $8,656 = $18,667,000 × 4.637/10,000

   BPV$_{10yr}$: $8,656 = $10,000,000 × 8.656/10,000

2. Calculate portfolio return for a 175 bp decline in 5-year CDX HY spreads and a 25 bp decline in 10-year CDX HY spreads using Equation 15 (−Δ(CDS Spread) × EffSpreadDur$_{CDS}$) multiplied by the CDS notional as follows:

   CDX HY 5 year: $1,514,780 = (−1.75% × 4.637) × $18,667,000

   CDX HY 10-year: −$216,400 = (0.25% × 8.656) × −$10,000,000
   Portfolio gain: $1,298,380 = $1,514,780 − $216,400.

   Note that this equals the contract BPV of $8,656 multiplied by the 150 bp credit curve steepening.

7. GLOBAL CREDIT STRATEGIES

i. discuss considerations in constructing and managing portfolios across international credit markets

While yield curve strategies across currencies were covered in an earlier lesson, we now turn to cross-border fixed-income investments in which investors face the risk that they will not receive interest and principal cash flows as expected. Investors distinguish between international credit markets in developed market countries versus emerging or frontier markets. Fixed-income markets in developed countries usually have well-established and liquid derivative and other capital markets and feature a broad range of private and public debt issuers with bonds denominated in a freely floating domestic or other major currency. Emerging or frontier fixed-income markets on the other hand are often dominated by sovereign issuers, state-owned or controlled enterprises, banks, and producers operating in a dominant domestic industry such as basic commodities. As some emerging economies face concentrated risk to a particular commodity or industry, investments across sovereign, bank, and private sector debt could offer little to no diversification. While many emerging-market bonds are denominated in a restricted domestic currency with varying degrees of liquidity, the sovereign government and a select few domestic issuers often issue global bonds in a major foreign currency such as US dollars or euros.

Credit strategies across countries must take these and other individual market differences into consideration. For example, in the case of developed markets, sector composition differences exist. A far higher percentage of the US fixed-income market (and roughly one-third of the Bloomberg Barclays US Aggregate Bond Index) comprises mortgage-backed and other asset-backed instruments versus other developed markets. Investors in developed European and Asian markets seeking commercial or residential real estate exposure might instead consider covered bonds or indirect exposure via bank bonds in markets where securitization is less prevalent. International accounting standards differences between the International Accounting Standards Board's International Financial Reporting Standards and US GAAP in such areas as inventory recognition, restricted cash, and cash flow definitions require adjustment for financial ratio comparisons across jurisdictions. Finally, while most developed markets face common macroeconomic factors that influence the bond term premium and expected returns, such as inflation, monetary policy, and economic growth, differences in the timing and magnitude of market changes, as well as the credit cycle across countries, are often reflected in interest rate differentials, exchange rates, and credit spreads.

> **EXAMPLE 32**
>
> ### Credit Strategies across Developed Markets
>
> An active United States–based credit manager is offered similar US corporate bond portfolio choices to those in an earlier example:
>
> | Rating Category | OAS | EffSpreadDur | Expected Loss |
> |---|---|---|---|
> | A | 1.40% | 5.5 | 0.10% |
> | Baa | 2.00% | 6.0 | 0.30% |
> | Ba | 3.75% | 4.5 | 1.00% |
> | B | 5.50% | 4.0 | 4.50% |

As in the earlier case, the manager expects an economic rebound but now believes that European economies will experience a stronger recovery than the United States. In particular, European high-yield credit spreads are expected to narrow by 25% in the near term, the euro is expected to appreciate 1% against the US dollar, and all US credit spreads and expected loss rates are expected to decline just 10% over the same period. The euro-denominated 5-year European iTraxx Crossover index (iTraxx-Xover) of liquid high-yield issuers (with a 5% fixed premium) is currently trading at 400 bps with an EffSpreadDur$_{CDS}$ of 4.25.

Describe the position the manager would take in iTraxx-Xover to capitalize on the stronger European rebound, and calculate the expected excess return percentage assuming an equally weighted allocation to US corporate bonds and an iTraxx-Xover position that matches that of the US high-yield bond allocation.

Solution:

To capitalize on expected greater euro spread tightening, the manager would sell protection on the iTraxx-Xover index. To calculate expected return, first consider the US corporate bond portfolio. The economic rebound scenario results in the following new OAS and expected losses for the portfolio, with expected excess returns E [ExcessSpread] ≈ Spread$_0$ −(EffSpreadDur × ΔSpread) − (POD × LGD) in the far right column:

Rating Category	E(OAS)	E(Expected Loss)	E(Excess Spread)
A	1.26%	0.09%	2.08%
Baa	1.80%	0.27%	2.93%
Ba	3.38%	0.90%	4.54%
B	4.95%	4.05%	3.65%

Return on the equally weighted portfolio is equal to 3.30% (= (2.08% + 2.93% + 4.54% + 3.65%)/4). We can estimate the initial iTraxx-Xover price by subtracting the product of EffSpreadDur$_{CDS}$ and the difference between the standard coupon (5%) from the market premium of 400 bps as follows:

Original iTraxx-Xover 5-year: 95.75 per $100, or 0.9575 (=1 − (4.25 × 1.00%))

If European high-yield spreads tighten by 25%, the iTraxx-Xover premium narrows by 100 bps to 300 bps, and the protection seller realizes a gain:

New iTraxx-Xover 5-year: 91.50 per $100, or 0.9150 (=1 − (4.25 × 2.00%))

We can calculate the percentage return on the iTraxx-Xover investment in euro terms by dividing the price change by the initial price to get 4.439% (= (95.75 − 91.50)/95.75). For a United States–based investor, we must convert the euro return to US dollars as described in an earlier lesson:

$R_{DC} = (1 + R_{FC})(1 + R_{FX}) - 1$

R_{DC} and R_{FC} are the domestic and foreign currency returns in percent, and R_{FX} is the percentage change of the domestic versus foreign currency.

We solve for US dollar iTraxx-Xover returns as 5.483% (= (1 + 4.439%) × (1 + 1.00%) − 1). Given that iTraxx-Xover carries a weight equal to one-half of the US corporate bond portfolio, the strategy returns 6.04% (or 3.30% + 5.483%/2).

Emerging markets are characterized by higher, more volatile, and less balanced economic growth than developed markets, often in addition to greater geopolitical risk, currency restrictions, and capital controls. Sovereign credit risk is therefore a critical starting point in considering fixed-income investments in emerging markets, where both the ability and willingness of issuers to repay debt is of importance. An earlier lesson outlined in detail sovereign credit risk considerations such as a country's institutional and economic profile, use of monetary and fiscal policy, the exchange rate regime, and external debt status and outlook.

Institutional considerations include political stability, institutional transparency, and adherence to property rights and contract law. Geopolitical risks include such factors as potential conflicts and trade relations, which in some instances could have a greater impact on emerging markets whose economies are highly dependent on energy or other commodity exports. As mentioned earlier, ESG factors are key elements for sustainable, balanced, long-term economic growth.

As sovereign governments tax economic activity within their borders to repay interest and principal, key financial ratios used to assess and compare sovereign creditworthiness are usually measured as a percentage of GDP. For example, government debt to GDP and the annual government budget deficit (or surplus) as a percentage of GDP are common measures of indebtedness and fiscal stability, respectively, for both developed and emerging markets.

Finally, a country's exchange rate regime is a critical element of monetary and external flexibility. Freely floating currency regimes that allow a currency to be held in reserve outside the country enable sovereign governments to pursue an independent and flexible monetary policy. Restrictive or fixed-rate regimes limit policy effectiveness, magnifying the impact of economic crises and increasing the likelihood of financial distress. Emerging markets are usually characterized by non-reserve currency regimes with significant external debt denominated in major foreign currencies, leading analysts to incorporate external debt to GDP and currency reserves as a percentage of GDP as key leverage and liquidity measures of creditworthiness, respectively.

The Bloomberg Sovereign Risk (SRSK) model shown in Exhibit 30 combines quantitative and qualitative factors such as external debt to GDP, currency reserves, GDP growth, and political risk to estimate a sovereign issuer's one-year POD. Similar to the DRSK model discussed earlier, the SRSK model allows users to change model inputs and also derives a "model" CDS spread, which could be compared to the market CDS spread.

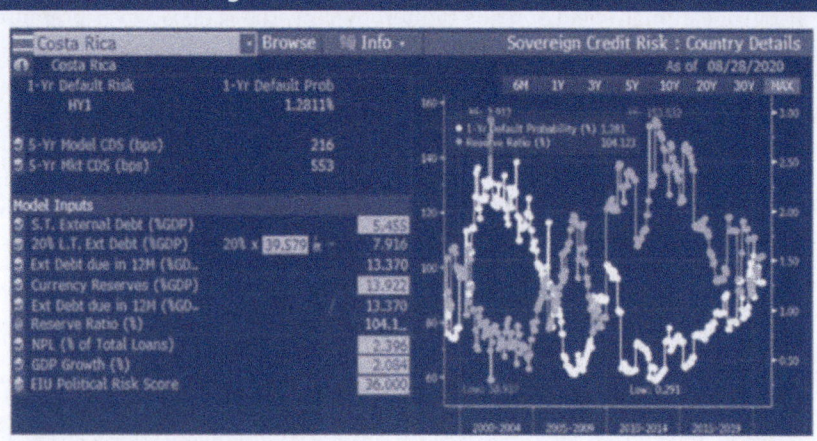

Exhibit 30   Bloomberg SRSK Screen

In this example, Costa Rica has a 1.28% one-year default risk and a model CDS spread well below the market CDS spread.

> **EXAMPLE 33**
>
> **Sovereign Risk Factors for Emerging Markets**
>
> A financial analyst is considering the likelihood that an emerging market sovereign issuer of US dollar–denominated bonds is able to meet its interest payments over the next 12 months. Which of the following financial ratios is most appropriate to assess the sovereign borrower's liquidity position?
>
> **A** Government budget deficit/GDP
>
> **B** External debt/GDP
>
> **C** Currency reserves/GDP
>
> **Solution:**
>
> The correct answer is C. The government budget deficit as a percentage of GDP is a gauge of fiscal stability for the domestic economy, while the external debt-to-GDP ratio is a measure of financial leverage to foreign lenders. Currency reserves as a percentage of GDP measure the available liquidity in foreign currency to meet external obligations.

Several additional considerations are important for investors in emerging market bonds issued by private companies. First, although some local companies might have partial private ownership and publicly traded equity, the sovereign government could exercise controlling influence on the business, including replacing management or ownership groups.

Credit quality in the emerging market credit universe exhibits a high concentration in lower investment-grade and upper high-yield ratings categories. This concentration of credit ratings is largely a reflection of the sovereign ratings of emerging markets but also reflects the fact that a "sovereign ceiling" is usually applied to corporate issuers globally. This ceiling implies that a company's rating is typically no higher than the sovereign credit rating of its domicile.

Finally, relative liquidity conditions and currency volatility are key considerations for international credit investors. In emerging markets, liquidity is often constrained because of a relatively small number of bonds that trade regularly, resulting in investors demanding higher premiums for holding emerging market credit securities. Local bond markets might seem highly liquid and can exceed the trading volume of the local stock exchanges, but such high trading volume could also be inflated by interbank trading by local banks and retail investors. Currency volatility can be particularly significant in emerging markets as a result of restrictive currency regimes and derivative markets. Higher YTMs available in emerging market currencies versus developed markets typically suggest that these emerging currencies will depreciate over time. That said, emerging markets offer investors the opportunity to exploit divergence from interest rate parity conditions (known as the forward rate bias) by investing in higher-yielding currencies, as addressed in earlier lessons. Although temporary deviations from a fixed exchange rate are possible under such regimes, what is more common during economic crises is exchange rate regime change, central bank intervention, and/or devaluation. The following example demonstrates how such factors are considered in emerging market credit strategies.

> **EXAMPLE 34**
>
> ### Emerging Market Credit Strategy
>
> An active United States–based investor is considering a portfolio allocation to the bonds of a major commodities producer headquartered in an emerging market economy. The issuer is a major exporter, and commodity exports comprise a significant proportion of the country's economic growth. Describe how the investor would decide between purchasing a higher-yielding, local-currency-denominated bond and a lower-yielding, US-dollar-denominated bond with otherwise similar features.
>
> ### Solution:
>
> A United States–based investor seeking to maximize US-dollar-denominated return must consider the relationship between the higher local currency bond YTM, the lower US dollar bond YTM, and the local currency's expected depreciation (or appreciation) versus the US dollar over the investment horizon. While uncovered interest rate parity suggests that local currency depreciation versus the US dollar would offset any benefit of a higher YTM, an investor with a bullish view of the emerging economy's growth prospects would benefit from forward rate bias and earn a higher return in US dollar terms from an unhedged investment in the local currency bond if the local currency were to depreciate less than expected under interest rate parity conditions.

8   STRUCTURED CREDIT

j   describe the use of structured financial instruments as an alternative to corporate bonds in credit portfolios

Active managers have access to a wide array of credit management tools beyond individual fixed-income securities that include structured financial instruments. These alternatives to direct bond investments in corporate bonds introduced in earlier lessons are summarized in Exhibit 31.

Exhibit 31   Structured Alternatives to Individual Bonds

Instrument	Description	Exposure	Portfolio Applications
Collateralized Debt Obligations (CDOs)	Fixed-income securities backed by a diversified pool of debt obligations	Redistribute portfolio debt cash flows across ratings spectrum	Create tailored portfolio-based debt exposure categories/profiles unavailable in the cash bond market
Collateralized Loan Obligations (CLOs)	Fixed-income securities backed by a diversified pool of floating-rate leveraged loan obligations	Redistribute portfolio loan cash flows across ratings spectrum	Create tailored portfolio-based loan and interest rate exposure profiles unavailable in the cash bond market
Mortgage-Backed Securities (MBS)	Fixed-income securities backed by a pool of commercial or residential mortgage loans	Provide portfolio-based exposure to real estate cash flows	Offer active managers exposure to real estate and to volatility (prepayment/extension risk) unavailable in the cash bond market

Exhibit 31 (Continued)

Instrument	Description	Exposure	Portfolio Applications
Asset-Backed Securities (ABS)	Fixed-income securities backed by a pool of credit card, auto, and other loans	Provide portfolio-based exposure to consumer loan cash flows	Offer active managers direct exposure to consumer loans and to volatility unavailable in the cash bond market
Covered Bonds	Senior debt obligations backed by pool of commercial/residential mortgages or public sector assets	Provide portfolio-based exposure to real estate cash flows with recourse to issuer	Offer active managers direct exposure to consumer loans and to real estate/public sector cash flows unavailable in the cash bond market

Structured financial instruments can offer active credit managers the ability to access fixed-income cash flows such as commercial or residential real estate, enhance returns by increasing portfolio exposure to interest rate volatility (via mortgage prepayment and extension risk), and add debt exposure created by the redistribution of default risk into different tranches across the credit spectrum. Exhibit 32 shows an illustrative example of the tranching that characterizes ABS and CDO transactions. In this case, the ABS issuer is a special purpose vehicle (SPV) that owns the underlying asset pool and issues debt across several tranches backed by the asset pool cash flows.

Exhibit 32   Illustrative Tranching Example

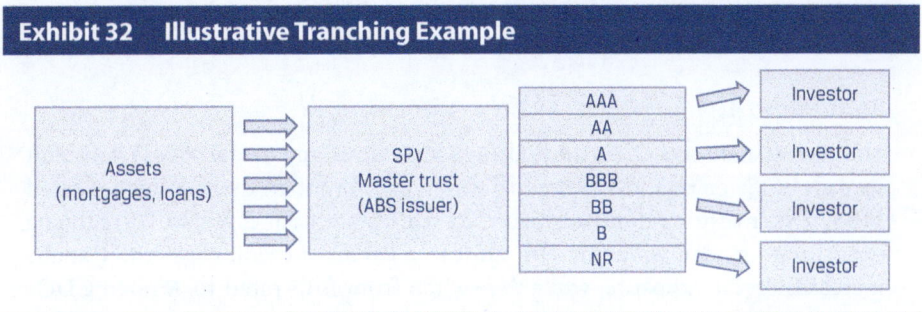

An earlier lesson addressed the redistribution of default risk from the underlying asset pool. This is achieved by establishing higher-rated tranches via internal credit enhancement or overcollateralization, with successively lower-rated tranches absorbing a greater proportion of the associated default risk. An active investor might overweight default risk by choosing a lower-rated ABS tranche based on a tactical view. For example, such an investor might anticipate lower-than-expected defaults or believe the credit cycle is in recovery mode and that lower-rated tranches will experience greater spread tightening than higher-rated tranches. Alternatively, a portfolio manager might underweight credit exposure using a higher-rated tranche in a downturn.

While covered bonds offer real estate cash flow exposure similar to that of ABS, given the dual recourse (i.e., to both the issuing financial institution and the underlying asset pool), as well as the substitution of non-performing assets, covered bonds usually involve lower credit risk and a lower yield. The following examples demonstrate the role of structured products in active credit portfolios.

> **EXAMPLE 35**
>
> ### The Role of Structured Products in Active Credit Management
>
> 1 An active credit manager anticipates an economic slowdown led by a decline in residential housing prices. Which of the following portfolio positioning strategies involving structured products is the most appropriate to consider under this scenario?
>   - **A** Shift exposure from an A rated tranche of a credit card ABS transaction to a BB rated tranche
>   - **B** Increase exposure to an A rated CDO tranche and reduce exposure to a BBB rated CDO tranche
>   - **C** Increase exposure to an A rated MBS tranche and decrease exposure to a BBB rated MBS tranche
>
> 2 An active fixed-income portfolio manager expects an economic recovery in the near term to be accompanied by rising short-term rates and a flatter benchmark yield curve. Which of the following strategies best positions an active manager to capitalize on this scenario?
>   - **A** Increase exposure to covered bonds and decrease exposure to MBS
>   - **B** Shift exposure from an A rated CDO tranche to a BBB rated CLO tranche
>   - **C** Shift exposure from a BB rated tranche of an automotive ABS transaction to a A rated tranche
>
> **Solution to 1:**
>
> The correct answer is C. As the housing sector slows and default rates rise, credit spreads of lower-rated MBS tend to widen by more than those of higher-rated MBS. The investor retains exposure to real estate cash flows while reducing exposure to spread widening. The shift to a BB rated credit card ABS tranche increases credit exposure, while the switch from BBB rated to A rated CDOs represents a reduction in overall market risk rather than a more targeted underweight, as in C.
>
> **Solution to 2:**
>
> The correct answer is B. Economic recovery is typically associated with lower defaults and greater credit spread tightening among lower-rated issuers and debt tranches. CLO tranches benefit more from short-term rate rises than CDOs because CLOs comprise leveraged loans based on MRRs plus a credit spread. As for A, a shift to covered bonds from MBS reduces credit risk because of the dual recourse and substitutability of collateral characteristics of covered bonds. In C, credit exposure is reduced, limiting the benefit from credit spread reduction within the portfolio.

9 FIXED-INCOME ANALYTICS

- k describe key inputs, outputs, and considerations in using analytical tools to manage fixed-income portfolios

Fixed-Income Analytics

Fixed-income analytical tools continue to adapt not only to technological change but also to the market and regulatory environment within which active fixed-income practitioners operate. The inputs and outputs of these models have become more complex as market participants integrate tasks across operational duties and portfolio decision making and execution. These tasks include portfolio construction, risk analytics, trading and settlement, cash and collateral management, daily valuation, portfolio accounting, and regulatory reporting.

Primary inputs for fixed-income models include all long and short cash bond and derivative positions, repurchase agreements, and cash across currencies. Fixed-income security inputs use CUSIP or ISIN identifiers to capture all relevant features such as interest and principal payment dates, day count conventions, and put–call features. Portfolio derivative and repo position inputs also include details of such agreements, such as settlement dates, option strike prices, and collateral terms necessary to satisfy derivative counterparty or clearing requirements based on market changes.

Real-time market data feeds usually sourced from vendors via application programming interfaces include spot and forward rates, credit curves, implied volatilities, and exchange rates that are used to value historical, existing, and potential future new portfolio positions. These tools value inactively traded fixed-income instruments using matrix pricing (or evaluated pricing) based on observable liquid benchmark YTMs of similar maturity and duration and credit spreads of actively traded bonds with comparable times to maturity, credit quality, and sector. Additional model inputs include index subscriptions, ESG and credit ratings, and issuer balance sheet data. In contrast to more static equity indexes, fixed-income indexes are subject to constant change as a result of both new debt issuance and bond maturities as well as ratings changes, bond callability, and prepayment.

Model assumptions include user-defined parameters such as term structure models, investment time horizon, VaR methodology, historical and/or specific market scenarios, and portfolio filters that could involve inclusion or exclusion of specific sectors or a minimum ESG rating threshold for consideration.

Fixed-income analytical model outputs support each stage of the active portfolio management process, namely portfolio selection and construction, risk analysis of existing and prospective portfolio positions, and trading and position management. A portfolio summary or landing page typically aggregates current portfolio risk and return across sectors, ratings, and currencies versus the benchmark index. Model applications supporting research and portfolio construction allow managers to assess the expected change in portfolio performance by including incremental long or short cash bond, derivative, or structured product positions. Portfolio risk dashboards embedded in these tools provide detailed insight into portfolio duration and convexity as well as tail risk. These statistics are often further disaggregated into key rate duration measures for benchmark rates and credit spreads by maturity. VaR and expected shortfall (or CVaR) are calculated based on user threshold and methodology settings. Finally, trading, cash, and position management outputs quantify existing cash positions, anticipated cash inflows and outflows from existing positions, and liquidity risk. Exhibit 33 summarizes the key elements of a fixed-income portfolio analytics tool.

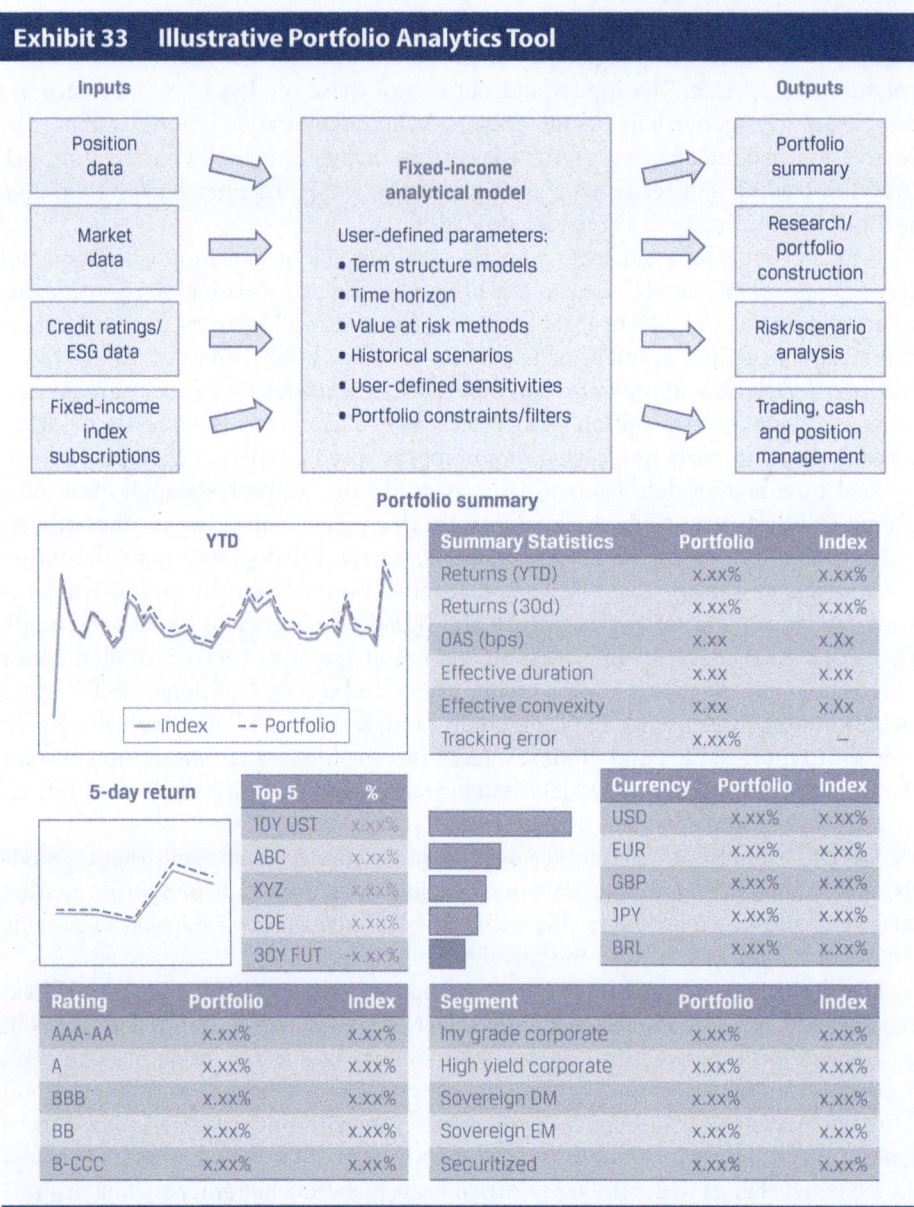

Exhibit 33 Illustrative Portfolio Analytics Tool

Key considerations for fixed-income analytical tools include both the accuracy of model inputs and assumptions and the degree of alignment between model outputs and specific fixed-income manager objectives.

Bond price and YTM calculations are affected by assumptions related to the term structure of benchmark rates and volatilities and how they change over time based on term structure models. Model outputs are often tailored to match an active manager's objectives. For example, an index fund manager might seek to minimize the tracking error defined earlier as the deviation of portfolio returns from an index. An active fixed-income manager with fewer constraints might maximize risk-adjusted returns, while estimating and categorizing how each position contributes to active risk taking. For example, performance attribution measures returns from credit, duration, sector, and currency tilts, among other factors. Finally, an active manager facing liability constraints usually models the fixed-income characteristics of obligations to maximize the expected surplus of assets over liabilities. Practitioners applying these tools must both recognize their limitations and anticipate and interpret model results, as in the following example.

EXAMPLE 36

Applying Fixed-Income Analytical Tools

An active fixed-income manager is conducting scenario analysis for the MBS component of a portfolio. Which of the following analytical model input changes is most likely to reduce the future value of the MBS subportfolio versus similar option-free bond holdings?

A An increase in benchmark yield curve volatility

B A decrease in benchmark yield curve volatility

C Upward parallel shift in the benchmark yield curve

Solution:

The correct answer is A. The value of a bond with an embedded option is equal to the sum of the value of an option-free bond plus the value to the embedded option. The value of the embedded call option owned by the issuer will increase as volatility rises, reducing the value of the MBS versus a similar option-free bond. Answers B and C are more likely to result in an increase in the value of MBS versus an option-free bond.

SUMMARY

Active spread-based, fixed-income portfolio management involves taking positions in credit and other risk factors that differ from those of an index to generate excess return. The main points of the reading are as follows:

- Yield spreads compensate investors for the risk that they will not receive expected interest and principal cash flows and for the bid–offer cost of buying or selling a bond under current market conditions.
- Two key components of a bond's credit risk are the POD and the LGD.
- Credit spread changes are driven by the credit cycle, or the expansion and contraction of credit over the business cycle, which causes asset prices to change based on default and recovery expectations.
- High-yield issuers experience greater changes in the POD over the credit cycle than investment-grade issuers, with bond prices approaching the recovery rate for distressed debt.
- While fixed-rate bond yield spread measures use actual, interpolated, or zero curve–based benchmark rates to capture relative credit risk, OAS allow comparison between risky option-free bonds and bonds with embedded options.
- FRNs pay periodic interest based on an MRR plus a yield spread.
- Spread duration measures the change in a bond's price for a given change in yield spread, while spread changes for lower-rated bonds tend to be proportional on a percentage rather than an absolute basis.
- Bottom-up credit strategies include the use of financial ratio analysis, reduced form credit models (such as the Z-score model), and structural credit models, including Bloomberg's DRSK model.

- Top-down credit strategies are often based on macro factors and group investment choices by credit rating and industry sector categories.
- Fixed-income factor investing incorporates such factors as size, value, and momentum to target active returns and also increasingly include ESG factors.
- Liquidity risk in credit markets is higher than in equities because of market structure differences and is often addressed using liquid bonds for short-term tactical positioning, less liquid positions for buy-and-hold strategies, and liquid alternatives where active management adds little value.
- Credit market tail risk is usually quantified using VaR or expected shortfall measures and is frequently managed using position limits, risk budgeting, or derivative strategies.
- Credit derivative strategies offer a synthetic liquid alternative to active portfolio managers as a means of over- or underweighting issuers, sectors, and/or maturities across the credit spectrum.
- Credit spread levels and curve slopes change over the credit cycle, with credit curve steepening usually indicating low near-term default expectations and higher growth expectations, while curve flattening, or inversion, suggests rising default expectations and lower future growth.
- Active credit managers can benefit under a stable credit curve scenario by adding spread duration for existing exposures and/or increasing average portfolio credit risk and can capitalize on divergent market views using cash- or derivative-based strategies related to specific issuers, sectors, or the overall credit market.
- Investors in international credit markets distinguish between developed and emerging markets. Developed markets face common macro factors, with market and credit cycle differences affecting relative interest rates, foreign exchange rates, and credit spreads. Emerging markets usually exhibit higher growth combined with greater sovereign and geopolitical risk, currency restrictions, and capital controls.
- Structured financial instruments offer active credit managers access to liquid bond portfolios, fixed-income cash flows derived from real estate and consumer loans, and enhanced returns by adding volatility and/or debt exposure via tranching across the credit spectrum.
- Key considerations for fixed-income analytical tools include the accuracy of model inputs and assumptions as well as alignment between model outputs and fixed-income manager objectives.

REFERENCES

Altman, Edward I. 1968. "Financial Ratios, Discriminant Analysis and the Prediction of Corporate Bankruptcy." *Journal of Finance* 23 (4): 589–609.

International Capital Markets Association (ICMA). 2018. "*Green Bond Principles. Voluntary Process Guidelines for Issuing Green Bonds*" (June). www.icmagroup.org/assets/documents/Regulatory/Green-Bonds/Green-Bonds-Principles-June-2018-270520.pdf.

Israel, Ronen, Diogo Palhares, and Scott Richardson. 2018. "*Common Factors in Corporate Bond Returns.*" Journal of Investment Management 16 (2), 17–46. www.aqr.com/-/media/AQR/Documents/Journal-Articles/Common-Factors-in-Corporate-Bond-Returns.pdfMoody's Investors Service. 2018. "Cross-Sector: Annual Default Study: Corporate Default and Recovery Rates, 1920–2017." Data report (15 February).

Nazeran, Pooya, and Douglas Dwyer. 2015. "*Modeling Methodology: Credit Risk Modeling of Public Firms: EDF9,*" Moody's Analytics Quantitative Research Group (June). www.moodysanalytics.com/-/media/whitepaper/2015/2012-28-06-public-edf-methodology.pdf.

O'Kane, Dominic, and Saurav Sen. 2005. "Credit Spreads Explained." *Journal of Credit Risk* 1 (2): 61–78.

S&P Global Ratings. 2020. "*Default, Transition and Recovery: 2019 Annual Global Corporate Default and Rating Transition Study*" (29 April). www.spglobal.com/ratings/en/research/articles/200429-default-transition-and-recovery-2019-annual-global-corporate-default-and-rating-transition-study-11444862.

PRACTICE PROBLEMS

1 Which of the following statements best describes empirical duration?
   A A common way to calculate a bond's empirical duration is to run a regression of its price returns on changes in a benchmark interest rate.
   B A bond's empirical duration tends to be larger than its effective duration.
   C The price sensitivity of high-yield bonds to interest rate changes is typically higher than that of investment-grade bonds.

2 A junior analyst considers a 10-year high-yield bond issued by EKN Corporation (EKN) position in a high-yield portfolio. The bond has a price of 91.82, a modified duration of 8.47, and a spread duration of 8.47. The analyst speculates on the effects of an interest rate increase of 20 bps and, because of a change in its credit risk, an increase in the EKN bond's credit spread of 20 bps. The analyst comments that because the modified duration and the credit spread duration of the EKN bond are equal, the bond's price will not change (all else being equal) in response to the interest rate and credit spread changes.

   Is the analyst's prediction correct that the EKN bond price will not change in response to the interest rate and credit spread changes, all else being equal?
   A Yes.
   B No, the bond price should decrease.
   C No, the bond price should increase.

3 Which of the following outcomes is most likely if the junior analyst revises the bond's original recovery rate higher?
   A An increase in the bond's POD
   B A decrease in the bond's POD
   C A decrease in the bond's credit spread

4 Which of the following observations on the risks of spread-based fixed-income portfolios is the most accurate?
   A Because credit spreads equal the product of the LGD and the POD, distinguishing between the credit risk and liquidity risk components of yield spread across all market scenarios is straightforward.
   B Given that frequent issuers with many bonds outstanding across maturities have their own issuer-specific credit curve, distinguishing between the credit spread and liquidity spread of all bonds for these issuers is straightforward.
   C The yield spread of a particular bond comprises both credit and liquidity risk and depends on market conditions and the specific supply-and-demand dynamics of each fixed-income security.

Practice Problems

The following information relates to Questions 5–8

An active portfolio manager observes the following market information related to an outstanding corporate bond and two on-the-run government bonds that pay annual coupons:

Issuer	Term	Coupon	Yield	ModDur
Corporate	12y	3.00%	2.80%	9.99
Government	10y	1.75%	1.85%	9.09
Government	20y	2.25%	2.30%	15.94

The portfolio manager also observes 10-year and 20-year swap spreads of 0.20% and 0.25%, respectively.

5 Calculate the G-spread of the corporate bond.
   A 0.860%
   B 0.725%
   C 0.950%

6 Calculate the I-spread of the corporate bond.
   A 0.85%
   B 0.65%
   C 0.95%

7 Calculate the ASW of the corporate bond.
   A 0.65%
   B 0.95%
   C 0.85%

8 Estimate the corporate bond's percentage price change if the government yield curve steepens, assuming a 0.20% increase in the 20-year YTM and no change to the 10-year government YTM or corporate G-spread.
   A −0.40%
   B 0.40%
   C −0.04%

9 Which of the following statements about credit spread measures is most accurate?
   A The DM is the yield spread over the MRR established upon issuance to compensate investors for assuming an issuer's credit risk.
   B The Z-DM will be above the DM if the MRR is expected to remain constant over time.
   C The yield spread for a corporate bond will be equal to the G-spread if the government benchmark yield curve is flat.

The following information relates to Questions 10–12

An active fixed-income manager is considering two corporate bond positions for an active portfolio. The first bond has a BBB rating with a credit spread of 2.75% and an effective spread duration of 6, and the second bond has a BB rating with a credit spread of 3.50% and an effective spread duration of five years.

10 What is the approximate excess return if the BBB rated bond is held for six months and the credit spread narrows by 40 bps, ignoring spread duration changes and assuming no default losses?

   A 3.775%

   B 2.35%

   C 2.40%

11 What is the instantaneous (holding period of zero) excess return for the BB rated bond if the spread widens by 50 bps?

   A 3.00%

   B −2.50%

   C 2.50%

12 What is the expected excess spread of the BBB rated bond for an instantaneous 50 bp decline in yields if the bond's LGD is 40% and the POD is 0.75%?

   A 1.95%

   B 2.45%

   C 2.70%

---

13 An active manager is considering the senior bonds of one of several corporate issuers. Holding other factors constant, which of the following key financial ratio changes would lead the manager to expect a decrease in the POD for that issuer?

   A An increase in the issuer's coverage ratio

   B An increase in the issuer's stock price volatility

   C An increase in the issuer's leverage ratio

14 Which of the following statements about statistical credit analysis models is most accurate?

   A Structural credit models solve for the POD using observable company-specific variables such as financial ratios and macroeconomic variables.

   B Reduced-form credit models use market-based variables to estimate an issuer's asset value and the volatility of asset value.

   C Structural credit models define the likelihood of default as the probability of the asset value falling below that of liabilities.

Practice Problems

The following information relates to Questions 15–17

An investor is faced with an active portfolio decision across three bond rating categories based on the following current market information:

Rating Category	Current OAS	Expected Loss (POD x LGD)	EffSpreadDur
A	1.00%	0.10%	7
BBB	1.75%	0.75%	6
BB	2.75%	2.50%	5

15 Which bond rating category offers the highest expected excess return if credit spreads remain stable under current market conditions?
   A   A rated bond category
   B   BBB rated bond category
   C   BB rated bond category

16 Which active bond portfolio maximizes expected excess return under a stable credit market assumption versus an equally weighted benchmark portfolio across the three rating categories?
   A   50% A rated bonds, 50% BBB rated bonds
   B   50% BBB rated bonds, 50% BB rated bonds
   C   50% A rated bonds, 50% B rated bonds

17 Which bond rating category offers the highest expected excess return if spreads instantaneously rise 10% across all ratings categories?
   A   A rated bond category
   B   BBB rated bond category
   C   BB rated bond category

---

18 Which of the following strategies best addresses the liquidity risk of a less frequently traded bond position in an active manager's portfolio?
   A   Enter into a receive fixed, pay floating asset swap, unwinding the swap position once the illiquid bond position is sold.
   B   Sell single-name CDS protection on the illiquid bond issuer, unwinding the CDS contract when the bond is sold.
   C   Allocate the illiquid bond to the buy-and-hold portion of the investment portfolio.

19 Which of the following statements best describes methods for assessing portfolio tail risk?
   A   Parametric methods use expected value and standard deviation of risk factors under a normal distribution and are well suited for option-based portfolios.
   B   Historical simulation methods use historical parameters and ranking results and are not well suited for option-based portfolios.
   C   Monte Carlo methods generate random outcomes using portfolio measures and sensitivities and are well suited for option-based portfolios.

The following information relates to Questions 20 and 21

An investor is considering the portfolio impact of a new 12-year corporate bond position with a $75 million face value, a 3.25% coupon, current YTM of 2.85%, modified duration of 9.887, and a price of 104.0175 per 100 of face value.

20 Which of the following VaR measures is most appropriate for the portfolio manager to use to evaluate how this position would affect portfolio tail risk?

   A CVaR

   B Relative VaR

   C Incremental VaR

21 What is the approximate VaR for the bond position at a 99% confidence interval (equal to 2.33 standard deviations) for one month (with 21 trading days) if daily yield volatility is 1.50% and returns are normally distributed?

   A $1,234,105

   B $2,468,210

   C $5,413,133

---

22 Which of the following statements best describes how a single-name CDS contract is priced at inception?

   A If the reference entity's credit spread trades below the standard coupon rate, the CDS contract will be priced at a premium above par because the protection buyer pays a "below market" periodic coupon.

   B If the reference entity's credit spread trades above the standard coupon rate, the CDS contract will be priced at a discount to par because the protection seller effectively receives a "below market" periodic premium.

   C Similar to fixed-rate bonds, CDS contracts are initially priced at par with a fixed coupon and a price that changes over time as the reference entity's credit spreads change.

The following information relates to Questions 23 and 24

An active portfolio manager seeking to purchase single-name CDS protection observes a 1.75% 10-year market credit spread for a private investment-grade issuer. The effective spread duration is 8.75 and CDS basis is close to zero.

23 What should the protection buyer expect to pay or receive to enter a new 10-year CDS contract?

   A The buyer should receive approximately 6.5625% of the notional.

   B The buyer should pay approximately 15.3125% of the notional.

   C The buyer should pay approximately 6.5625% of the notional.

24 Once the manager purchases CDS protection, the issuer's CDS spread immediately falls to 1.60%. What is the investor's approximate mark-to-market gain or loss for a contract notional of €10,000,000?

Practice Problems

    A The manager realizes an approximate loss of €131,250.

    B The manager realizes an approximate gain of €131,250.

    C The manager realizes an approximate gain of €525,000.

---

25 Which of the following credit portfolio positioning strategies is the most appropriate to underweight the financial sector versus an index?

    A Purchase protection on the CDX and sell protection on the CDX Financials subindex.

    B Sell protection on the CDX and purchase protection on the CDX Financials subindex.

    C Purchase a payer option on the CDX and sell protection on the CDX Financials subindex.

26 Which of the following phases of the credit cycle typically involves a decline in the number of issuer defaults?

    A Late expansion phase

    B Early expansion phase

    C Peak phase

27 Which of the following regarding the shape of the credit spread curve for high-yield issuers is most accurate?

    A High-yield credit spread curves change shape more over the cycle than investment-grade ones do and usually invert during the peak phase.

    B Investors should exercise caution in interpreting credit spread curve shape for distressed debt issuers because their bonds tend to trade on a price rather than credit spread basis as the likelihood of default increases.

    C High-yield credit spread curves often invert because of the empirical observation that DTS is the best way to measure high-yield bond price changes.

28 Which of the following statements best describes a credit curve roll-down strategy?

    A Returns from a credit curve roll-down strategy can be estimated by combining the incremental coupon from a longer maturity corporate bond with price appreciation due to the passage of time.

    B A synthetic credit curve roll-down strategy involves purchasing protection using a single-name CDS contract for a longer maturity.

    C A credit curve roll-down strategy is expected to generate a positive return if the credit spread curve is upward sloping.

The following information relates to Questions 29 and 30

An investor observes the following current CDS market information:

CDX Contract	Tenor (years)	CDS Spread	EffSpreadDur$_{CDS}$
CDX IG Index	5	85 bps	4.9
CDX IG Index	10	135 bps	8.9
CDX HY Index	5	175 bps	4.7
CDX HY Index	10	275 bps	8.7

29 Select the most appropriate credit portfolio positioning strategy to capitalize on an expected steepening of the investment-grade credit spread curve.

  A Sell protection on the 10-year CDX IG index and purchase protection on the 5-year CDX IG index using contracts of equal notional value.

  B Sell protection on the 10-year CDX IG index and purchase protection on the 5-year CDX IG index using a contract with a notional amount equal to 1.82 times that of the 10-year contract.

  C Buy protection on the 10-year CDX IG index and sell protection on the 5-year CDX IG index using a contract with a notional amount equal to 1.82 times that of the 10-year contract.

30 Which of the following is the most appropriate credit portfolio positioning strategy to capitalize on an expected economic contraction?

  A Buy protection on the 5-year CDX HY index and sell protection on the 5-year CDX IG index in approximately equal notional amounts.

  B Buy protection on the 10-year CDX IG index and sell protection on the 5-year CDX IG index using a contract with a notional amount equal to 1.82 times that of the 10-year contract.

  C Buy protection on the 10-year CDX HY index and sell protection on the 5-year CDX HY index using a contract with a notional amount equal to 1.85 times that of the 10-year contract.

31 Which of the following is the most accurate statement related to international credit markets?

  A Fixed exchange-rate regimes among emerging markets usually reduce the likelihood of financial distress because the domestic currency is tied to a major foreign currency.

  B Although many emerging economies have domestic bond markets that include sovereign, financial, and corporate issuers, investments across these bonds offer less diversification than similar investments in developed markets.

  C Higher domestic currency YTMs among emerging versus developed markets are due to expected currency appreciation resulting from higher economic growth.

The following information relates to Questions 32 and 33

An active United States–based credit manager faces the following US and European investment-grade and high-yield corporate bond portfolio choices:

Practice Problems

Rating Category	OAS	EffSpreadDur	Expected Loss
USD IG	1.25%	4.50	0.40%
USD HY	3.00%	5.50	2.25%
EUR IG	1.15%	4.75	0.50%
EUR HY	3.25%	6.00	2.50%

The EUR IG and EUR HY allocations are denominated in euros, and the euro is expected to depreciate by 2% versus the US dollar over the next year.

32 What is the approximate unhedged excess return to the United States–based credit manager for an international credit portfolio index equally weighted across the four portfolio choices, assuming no change to spread duration and no default losses occur?

   A −0.257%

   B −0.850%

   C 0.750%

33 Which of the following active portfolios is expected to have the highest excess return versus the index if European economies are expected to experience an earlier and much stronger credit cycle recovery than the United States?

   A EUR HY 50.0%, EUR IG 25.0%, USD IG 12.5%, USD HY 12.5%

   B EUR IG 50.0%, EUR HY 25.0%, USD IG 12.5%, USD HY 12.5%

   C EUR HY 33.3%, US HY 33.3%, EUR IG 16.7%, USD IG 16.7%

34 Which of the following statements about the role of structured products in an active credit portfolio is most accurate?

   A Covered bonds perform relatively well in a downturn versus other fixed-income bonds with real estate exposure because a covered bond investor also has recourse to the issuer.

   B Higher-rated ABS tranches are attractive for active investors seeking to overweight default risk when the credit cycle is in recovery.

   C CLO tranches are more advantageous than CDO tranches with similar ratings under an economic slowdown scenario.

35 An active fixed-income manager is evaluating the relative performance of an investment-grade corporate versus a high-yield corporate debt allocation in a fixed-income portfolio. Which of the following analytical model assumption changes is most likely to reduce the future value of the high-yield portfolio relative to the investment-grade holdings?

   A Steepening of the benchmark yield volatility curve

   B Decreased likelihood of an economic slowdown

   C Increased likelihood of a flight to quality associated with bullish benchmark yield curve flattening (long-term rates fall by more than short-term rates do)

SOLUTIONS

1. A is correct. A bond's empirical duration is often estimated by running a regression of its price returns on changes in a benchmark interest rate.

2. B is correct. An increase in interest rates results in a decrease in the bond price. An increase in the credit spread also results in a decrease in the bond price. For the EKN bond, its modified duration shows the effect of the 20 bp increase in interest rates. The approximate percentage price change resulting from the increase in interest rates is $-8.47 \times 0.0020 = -1.694\%$. The spread duration shows the effect of the 20 bp increase in the credit spread. The approximate percentage price change resulting from the increase in the credit spread is $-8.47 \times 0.0020 = -1.694\%$. The combined effect is a total change of -3.388%, or a price decrease of roughly 3.4%.

3. C is correct. An increase in a bond's recovery rate will lower the loss severity, or LGD, because LGD = (1 − RR). Recall the simple one-period relationship between credit spreads, LGD, and the POD as Spread ≈ LGD × POD. A lower LGD will result in a lower spread.

4. C is correct. A bond's yield spread includes both credit and liquidity risk. Liquidity risk depends on both market conditions and the specific supply-and-demand dynamics of each fixed-income security.

5. A is correct. The G-spread is the difference between the corporate bond YTM and a linear interpolation of the 10-year and 20-year government bond YTMs. To calculate the approximate 12-year government rate, solve for the weights of the 10-year bond as 80% (= (20 − 12)/(20 − 10)) and the 20-year bond as 20% (or (1 − 80%), noting that (80% × 10) + (20% × 20) = 12). The 12-year government rate is 1.94% (or (80% × 1.85%) + (20% × 2.30%)), and the difference between the corporate bond YTM and the 12-year interpolated government rate is 0.860%.

6. B is correct. The I-spread is an estimate of the corporate bond's spread over an interpolated swap benchmark. We can solve for the 10-year and 20-year swap rates as 2.05% (=0.20% + 1.85%) and 2.55% (=0.25% + 2.30%), respectively, by adding the swap spread to the respective government bond. The 12-year swap rate is 2.15% (or (80% × 2.05%) + (20% × 2.55%)), and the difference between the corporate bond YTM and the 12-year interpolated government rate is 0.80%.

7. C is correct. The ASW is an estimate of the spread over MRR versus the bond's original coupon rate to maturity, which is equal to the difference between the corporate bond coupon of 3.00% and the 12-year swap rate of 2.15%, or 0.85%.

8. A is correct. The 20 bp increase in the 20-year government YTM causes the 12-year interpolated government YTM to rise 4 bps to 1.98% (or (80% × 1.85%) + (20% × 2.50%)). The corporate bond percentage price change can be estimated based on the YTM change multiplied by modified duration (−ModDur × ΔYield) familiar from earlier lessons. This percentage price change can be calculated as −0.4% (=−9.99 × 0.04%).

9. C is correct. The yield spread is the simple difference between a bond's all-in YTM and a current on-the-run government bond of similar maturity, while the G-spread is an interpolation of government benchmark yields. If the government bond yield curve is flat, these two measures will equal one another.

Solutions

10. A is correct. Recall that ExcessSpread ≈ ($Spread_0$/Periods Per Year) − (EffSpreadDur × ΔSpread), so we combine the 6-month return with the spread duration–based price change estimate to get 3.775% (= (2.75% × 0.5) − (6 × −0.4%)).

11. B is correct. The instantaneous holding period return equals −EffSpreadDur × ΔSpread = −5 × 0.5% or −2.50%.

12. C is correct. The expected excess spread is equal to the change in spread multiplied by effective spread duration (−(EffSpreadDur × ΔSpread)) less the product of LGD and POD, which we can solve for to get 2.70% (=(−6 × 0.50%) − (0.75% × 40%)).

13. A is correct. The coverage ratio measures cash flow available to service debt, with a higher ratio indicating a lower probability of financial distress.

14. C is correct. Structural credit models use market-based variables to estimate an issuer's asset value and asset value volatility, defining the likelihood of default as the probability of the asset value falling below that of liabilities, with zero net assets defined as the default threshold.

15. B is correct. Recall that expected excess spread is defined as follows:

    $$E[ExcessSpread] \approx Spread_0 - (EffSpreadDur \times \Delta Spread) - (POD \times LGD)$$

    Because ΔSpread = 0, the expected excess spread is the simple difference between current OAS and expected loss, so E[ExcessSpread] is 0.90%, 1.00%, and 0.25% for the A-, BBB-, and B rated categories, respectively.

16. A is correct. E[ExcessSpread] from Question 15 is 0.90%, 1.00%, and 0.25% for the A-, BBB-, and B rated categories, respectively. The excess spread of the 50% A rated and 50% BBB rated portfolio is 0.95% (=(0.9% + 1.00%/2) versus the equally weighted portfolio expected excess return of 0.7167% (=(0.90% + 1.00% + 0.25%)/3) for a positive active return of 0.233%, while B and C return less than the equally weighted benchmark.

17. A is correct. If spreads rise 10% across all ratings categories, we can use E[ExcessSpread] ≈ $Spread_0$ −(EffSpreadDur × ΔSpread) − (POD × LGD) to solve for expected excess spread as follows:

Rating Category	Current OAS	New OAS	Expected Loss (POD × LGD)	EffSpreadDur	E(Excess Spread)
A	1.00%	1.100%	0.10%	7	0.200%
BBB	1.75%	1.925%	0.75%	6	−0.050%
BB	2.75%	3.025%	2.50%	5	−1.125%

18. C is correct. Both A and B represent "long" risk positions that would increase rather than offset the benchmark yield and credit spread risk to the portfolio manager related to the illiquid bond.

19. C is correct. Parametric methods in A are not well suited for non-normally distributed returns or option-based portfolios, while historical simulation assumes no probability distribution and accommodates options.

20. C is correct. The incremental VaR measures how the additional portfolio position would change the overall portfolio's VaR measure.

21. A is correct. The expected change in yield based on a 99% confidence interval for the bond and a 1.50% yield volatility over 21 trading days equals 16 bps = (1.50% × 2.33 standard deviations × √21). We can quantify the bond's market value change by multiplying the familiar (−ModDur × ΔYield) expression by bond price to get $1,234,105 = ($75 million × 1.040175 ☒ (−9.887 × .0016)).

22 B is correct. For example, if the reference entity's credit spread trades at 1.50% versus a standard coupon rate of 1.00%, the CDS contract will be priced at a discount equal to the 0.50% difference multiplied by the effective CDS spread duration times the contract notional. Under A, the contract is priced at a premium to par because the protection buyer is receiving an "above market" periodic premium.

23 C is correct. Because the market premium is 0.75% above the 1.00% standard investment-grade CDS coupon, the protection buyer must pay the protection seller 6.5625% (= EffSpreadDur$_{CDS}$ × ΔSpread, or 8.75 × 0.75%) of the fixed notional amount upon contract initiation; the initial CDS price is therefore 93.4375 per 100 of notional with a CDS spread of 175 bps.

24 A is correct. The CDS spread decline of 0.15% leads to a new CDS contract price of 94.75 per 100 face value (=1 − (EffSpreadDur$_{CDS}$ × ΔSpread) or (8.75 × 0.60%)). The protection buyer (short risk) position therefore realizes an approximate mark-to-market loss of €131,250 (=(94.75 − 93.4375)/100 × €10,000,000) because of the 0.15% decline in CDS spreads.

25 B is correct. Selling protection on the CDX index is a "long" credit spread risk position, while purchasing protection on the CDX Financials subindex is a "short" credit spread risk position, leaving the investor with a long index position without exposure to financial reference entities in the CDX index. Both A and C increase exposure to financial sector issuers.

26 A is correct. The late expansion phase is typically associated with accelerating growth, peak profits, stable leverage, and a decline in defaults.

27 B is correct. Investors should exercise caution in interpreting credit spread curve shape for distressed debt issuers because their bonds tend to trade at a price close to the recovery rate. A is incorrect because the high-yield spread curve tends to invert during a contraction, while C is incorrect because a high-yield curve inversion is related to the relationship between near-term and long-term default as opposed to DTS.

28 C is correct. A credit curve roll-down strategy will generate positive return only under an upward-sloping credit spread curve. As for A, the benchmark yield changes must be separated from changes due to credit spreads, and under B, a synthetic credit roll-down strategy involves selling protection using a single-name CDS contract for a longer maturity.

29 C is correct. The investor benefits from a short risk (as protection buyer) on the 10-year CDX IG index and long risk (as protection seller) on the 5-year CDX IG index, duration matching the notional value by increasing 5-year notional 1.82 times (=8.9/4.9) versus the 10-year.

30 A is correct. Because an economic contraction is often associated with a sharp rise in shorter-term high-yield spreads and spread curve flattening in investment grade and inversion in high yield, the most appropriate choice is to take a short risk (purchase protection) in five-year high-yield spreads and a long position (sell protection) in five-year investment-grade spreads. Answers B and C position the investor to benefit from a steeper investment-grade and high-yield spread curve, respectively.

31 B is correct. Fixed exchange rate regimes in A usually result in greater instability and a higher probability of financial distress, while higher domestic currency YTMs in emerging economies in C are a sign of expected currency depreciation, not appreciation, over time.

32 A is correct. We solve for the excess spread by subtracting Expected Loss from the respective OAS:

Solutions

Rating Category	OAS	EffSpreadDur	Expected Loss	E(Excess Spread)
USD IG	1.25%	4.5	0.40%	0.85%
USD HY	3.00%	5.5	2.25%	0.75%
EUR IG	1.15%	4.75	0.50%	0.65%
EUR HY	3.25%	6	2.50%	0.75%

Recall that the United States–based investor must convert the euro return to US dollars using $R_{DC} = (1 + R_{FC})(1 + R_{FX}) - 1$, so the USD IG and USD HY positions comprising half the portfolio return an average 0.80%, while the EUR IG and EUR HY positions return −1.314% in US dollar terms (= ((1 + ((0.65% + 0.75%)/2)) × 0.98) − 1), so −0.257% = ((0.80% − 1.314%)/2).

33. A is correct. Given that high-yield spreads are expected to fall the most in an economic recovery, the manager should choose the portfolio with the highest percentage of EUR HY credit exposure.

34. A is correct. Covered bonds perform relatively well in a downturn versus other fixed-income bonds with real estate exposure because the investor also has recourse to the issuer.

35. C is correct. Under a "flight to quality" scenario, macroeconomic factors driving government bond YTMs lower cause high-yield bond credit spreads to rise because of an increased likelihood of and expected higher severity of financial distress. This relationship is captured in the difference between empirical and analytical duration measures.

PORTFOLIO MANAGEMENT
STUDY SESSION

7

Equity Portfolio Management (1)

Because equity securities represent a significant portion of many investment portfolios, equity portfolio management is often an important component of overall investment success. This study session begins by explaining the role played by equity investments in portfolios, with consideration given to costs and shareholder responsibilities. It then discusses two approaches to equity portfolio management: passive or index-based investing and active equity strategies. The reading on passive equity investing addresses important issues such as alternative approaches to index replication and factor-based passive strategies. Tracking error, risk, and return considerations from an indexing perspective are examined.

READING ASSIGNMENT

Reading 15	Overview of Equity Portfolio Management by James Clunie, PhD, CFA, and James Alan Finnegan, CAIA, RMA, CFA
Reading 16	Passive Equity Investing by David M. Smith, PhD, CFA, and Kevin K. Yousif, CFA

© 2021 CFA Institute. All rights reserved.

READING 15

Overview of Equity Portfolio Management

by James Clunie, PhD, CFA, and James Alan Finnegan, CAIA, RMA, CFA

James Clunie, PhD, CFA, is at Jupiter Asset Management (United Kingdom). James Alan Finnegan, CAIA, RMA, CFA (USA).

LEARNING OUTCOMES	
Mastery	The candidate should be able to:
☐	a. describe the roles of equities in the overall portfolio;
☐	b. describe how an equity manager's investment universe can be segmented;
☐	c. describe the types of income and costs associated with owning and managing an equity portfolio and their potential effects on portfolio performance;
☐	d. describe the potential benefits of shareholder engagement and the role an equity manager might play in shareholder engagement;
☐	e. describe rationales for equity investment across the passive–active spectrum.

1. INTRODUCTION AND THE ROLE OF EQUITIES IN A PORTFOLIO

a   describe the roles of equities in the overall portfolio;

Equities represent a sizable portion of the global investment universe and thus often represent a primary component of investors' portfolios. Rationales for investing in equities include potential participation in the growth and earnings prospects of an economy's corporate sector as well as an ownership interest in a range of business entities by size, economic activity, and geographical scope. Publicly traded equities are generally more liquid than other asset classes and thus may enable investors to more easily monitor price trends and purchase or sell securities with low transaction costs.

This reading provides an overview of equity portfolio management. Section 1.1 discusses the roles of equities in a portfolio. Section 2 discusses the equity investment universe, including several ways the universe can be segmented. Sections 3 and 4 cover the income and costs in an equity portfolio. Section 5 discusses shareholder engagement between equity investors and the companies in which they invest. Section 6 discusses equity investment across the passive–active investment spectrum. A summary of key points completes the reading.

1.1 The Roles of Equities in a Portfolio

Equities provide several roles in (or benefits to) an overall portfolio, such as capital appreciation, dividend income, diversification with other asset classes, and a potential hedge against inflation. In addition to these benefits, client investment considerations play an important role for portfolio managers when deciding to include equities in portfolios.

1.1.1 Capital Appreciation

Long-term returns on equities, driven predominantly by capital appreciation, have historically been among the highest among major asset classes. Exhibit 1 demonstrates the average annual real returns on equities versus bonds and bills—both globally and within various countries—from 1967–2016. With a few exceptions, equities outperformed both bonds and bills, in particular, during this period across the world.

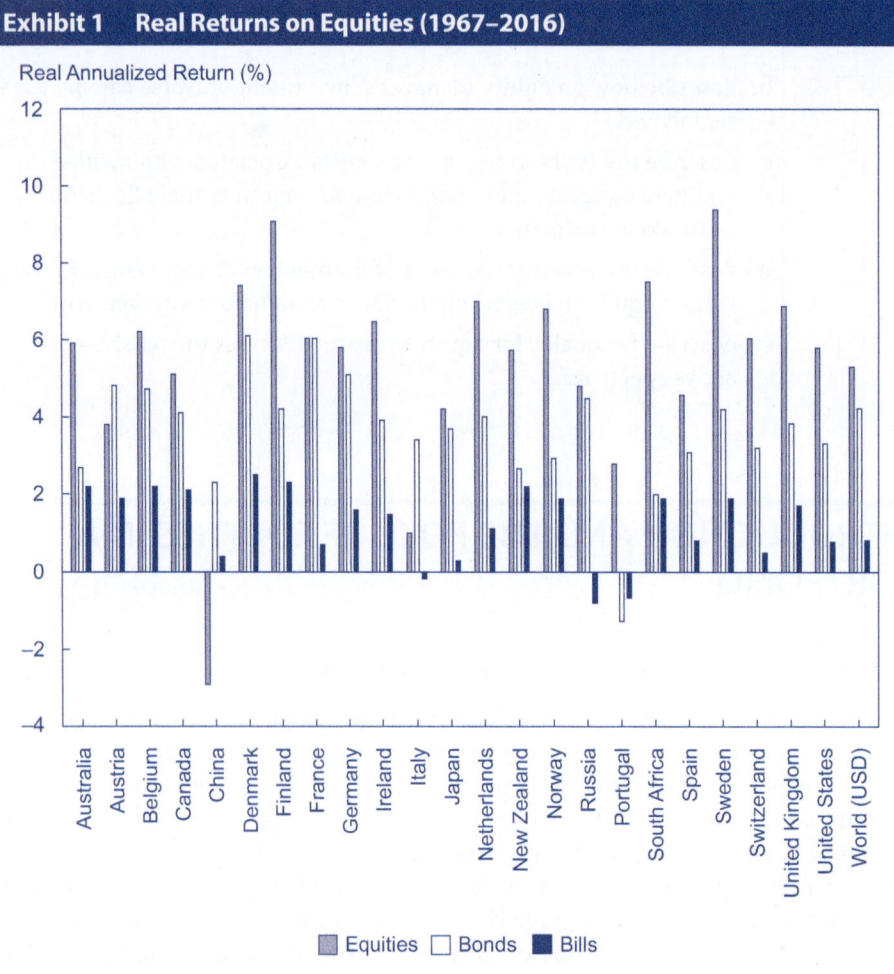

Exhibit 1 Real Returns on Equities (1967–2016)

* China data are from 1993 to 2016.
** Russia data are from 1995 to 2016.
Source: Credit Suisse Global Investment Returns Yearbook 2017, Summary Edition.

Introduction and the Role of Equities in a Portfolio

Equities tend to outperform other asset classes during periods of strong economic growth, and they tend to underperform other asset classes during weaker economic periods. Capital (or price) appreciation of equities often occurs when investing in companies with growth in earnings, cash flows, and/or revenues—as well as in companies with competitive success. Capital appreciation can occur, for example, in such growth-oriented companies as small technology companies as well as in large, mature companies where management successfully reduces costs or engages in value-added acquisitions.

1.1.2 Dividend Income

The most common sources of income for an equity portfolio are dividends. Companies may choose to distribute internally generated cash flows as common dividends rather than reinvest the cash flows in projects, particularly when suitable projects do not exist or available projects have a high cost of equity or a low probability of future value creation. Large, well-established corporations often provide dividend payments that increase in value over time, although there are no assurances that common dividend payments from these corporations will grow or even be maintained. In addition to common dividends, preferred dividends can provide dividend income to those shareholders owning preferred shares.

Dividends have comprised a significant component of long-term total returns for equity investors. Over shorter periods of time, however, the proportion of equity returns from dividends (reflected as dividend yield) can vary considerably relative to capital gains or losses. Exhibit 2 illustrates this effect of dividend returns relative to annual total returns on the S&P 500 Index from 1936 through 2016. Since 1990, the dividend yield on the S&P 500 has been in the 1–3% range; thus, the effect of dividends can clearly be significant during periods of weak equity market performance. Also note that the dividend yield may vary considerably by sector within the S&P 500.

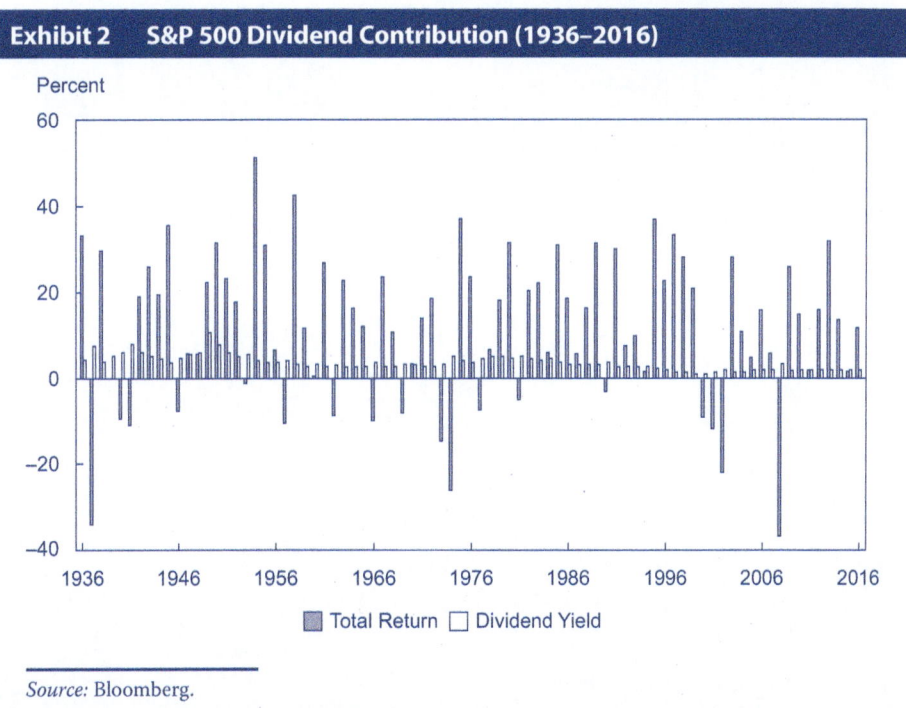

Exhibit 2 S&P 500 Dividend Contribution (1936–2016)

Source: Bloomberg.

1.1.3 Diversification with Other Asset Classes

Individual equities clearly have unique characteristics, although the correlation of returns among equities is often high. In a portfolio context, however, equities can provide meaningful diversification benefits when combined with other asset classes (assuming less than perfect correlation). Recall that a major reason why portfolios can effectively reduce risk (typically expressed as standard deviation of returns) is that combining securities whose returns are less than perfectly correlated reduces the standard deviation of the diversified portfolio below the weighted average of the standard deviations of the individual investments. The challenge in diversifying risk is to find assets that have a correlation that is much lower than +1.0.

Exhibit 3 provides a correlation matrix across various global equity indexes and other asset classes using total monthly returns from January 2001 to February 2017.[1] The correlation matrix shows that during this period, various broad equity indexes and, to a lesser extent, country equity indexes were highly correlated with each other. Conversely, both the broad and country equity indexes were considerably less correlated with indexes in other asset classes, notably global treasury bonds and gold. Overall, Exhibit 3 indicates that combining equities with other asset classes can result in portfolio diversification benefits.

It is important to note that correlations are not constant over time. During a long historical period, the correlation of returns between two asset classes may be low, but in any given period, the correlation can differ from the long term. Correlation estimates can vary based on the capital market dynamics during the period when the correlations are measured. During periods of market crisis, correlations across asset classes and among equities themselves often increase and reduce the benefit of diversification. As with correlations, volatility (standard deviation) of asset class returns may also vary over time.

---

[1] Monthly return data cover January 2001 to February 2017 for all indexes except the FTSE EPRA/NAREIT Global Real Estate Index (whose inception date was November 2008).

Introduction and the Role of Equities in a Portfolio

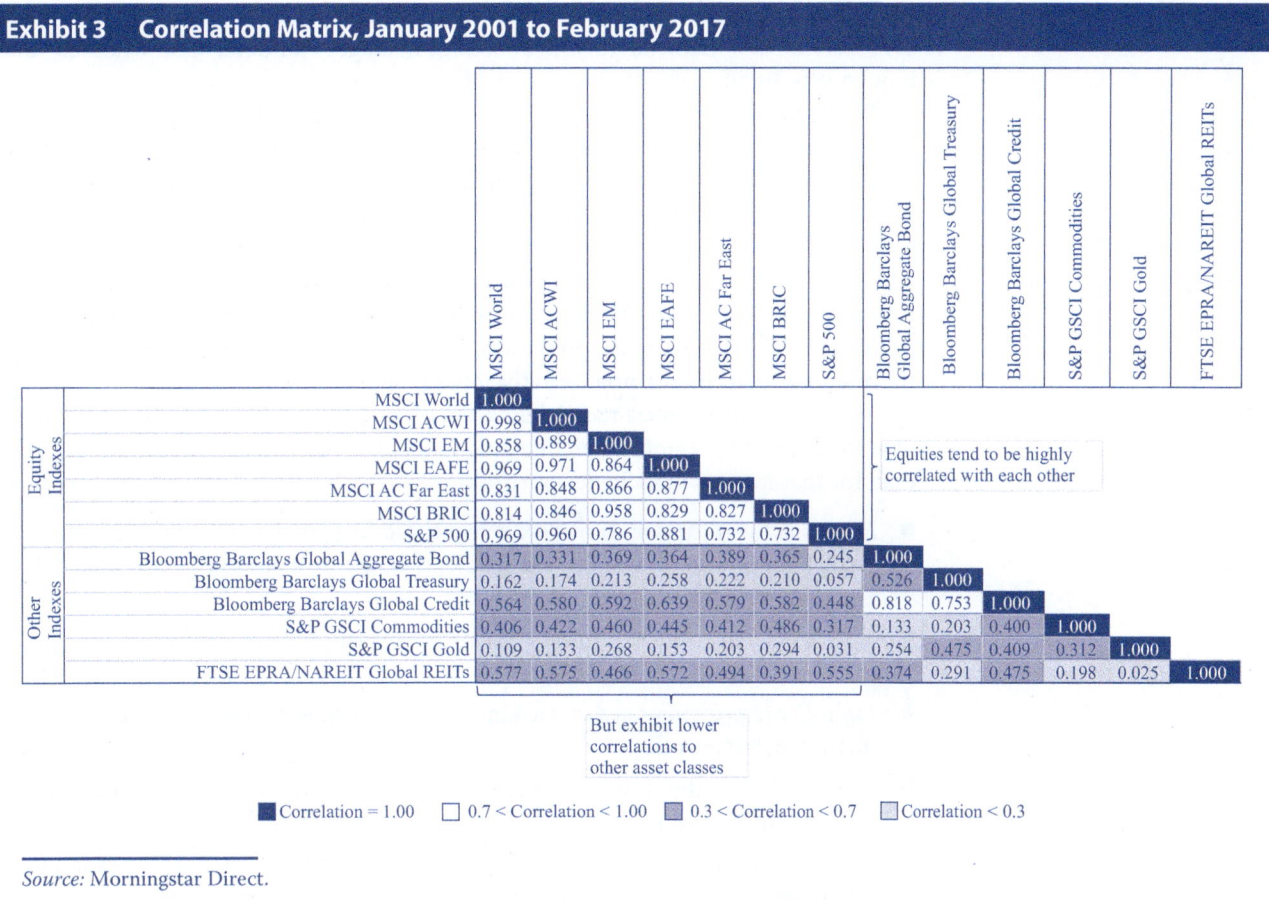

Exhibit 3 Correlation Matrix, January 2001 to February 2017

Source: Morningstar Direct.

1.1.4 Hedge Against Inflation

Some individual equities or sectors can provide some protection against inflation, although the ability to do so varies. For example, certain companies may be successful at passing along higher input costs (such as raw materials, energy, or wages) to customers. This ability to pass along costs to customers can protect a company's or industry's profit margin and cash flow and can be reflected in their stock prices. As another example, companies within sectors that produce broad-based commodities (e.g., oil or industrial metals producers) can more directly benefit from increases in commodity prices. Although individual equities or sectors can protect against inflation, the success of equities as an asset class in hedging inflation has been mixed. Certain empirical studies have indeed shown that real returns on equities and inflation have positive correlation over the long-term, thus in theory forming a hedge. However, the degree of correlation typically varies by country and is dependent on the time period assessed. In fact, for severe inflationary periods, some studies have shown that real returns on equities and inflation have been *negatively* correlated. When assessing the relationship between equity returns and inflation, investors should be aware that inflation is typically a lagging indicator of the business cycle, while equity prices are often a leading indicator.

1.1.5 Client Considerations for Equities in a Portfolio

The inclusion of equities in a portfolio can be driven by a client's goals or needs. A client's investment considerations are typically described in an investment policy statement (IPS), which establishes, among other things, a client's return objectives, risk tolerance, constraints, and unique circumstances. By understanding these client considerations, a financial adviser or wealth manager can determine whether—and how much—equities should be in a client's portfolio.

Equity investments are often characterized by such attributes as growth potential, income generation, risk and return volatility, and sensitivity to various macro-economic variables (e.g., energy prices, GDP growth, interest rates, and inflation). As a result, a portfolio manager can adapt such specific factors to an equity investor's investment goals and risk tolerance. For example, a risk-averse and conservative investor may prefer some exposure to well-established companies with strong and stable cash flow that pay meaningful dividends. Conversely, a growth-oriented investor with an aggressive risk tolerance may prefer small or large growth-oriented companies (e.g., those in the social media or alternative energy sectors).

Wealth managers and financial advisers often consider the following investment objectives and constraints when deciding to include equities (or asset classes in general, for that matter) in a client's portfolio:

- *Risk objective* addresses how risk is measured (e.g., in absolute or relative terms); the investor's willingness to take risk; the investor's ability to take risk; and the investor's specific risk objectives.
- *Return objective* addresses how returns are measured (e.g., in absolute or relative terms); stated return objectives.
- *Liquidity requirement* is a constraint in which cash is needed for anticipated or unanticipated events.
- *Time horizon* is the time period associated with an investment objective (e.g., short term, long term, or some combination of the two).
- *Tax concerns* include tax policies that can affect investor returns; for example, dividends may be taxed at a different rate than capital gains.
- *Legal and regulatory factors* are external factors imposed by governmental, regulatory, or oversight authorities.
- *Unique circumstances* are an investor's considerations other than liquidity requirements, time horizon, or tax concerns that may constrain portfolio choices. These considerations may include environmental, social, and governance (ESG) issues or religious preferences.

ESG considerations often occur at the request of clients because interest in sustainable investing has grown. With regard to equities, these considerations often determine the suitability of certain sectors or individual company stocks for designated investor portfolios. Historically, ESG approaches used by portfolio managers have largely represented **negative screening** (or exclusionary screening), which refers to the practice of excluding certain sectors or companies that deviate from accepted standards in such areas as human rights or environmental concerns. More recently, portfolio managers have increasingly focused on **positive screening** or **best-in-class** approaches, which attempt to identify companies or sectors that score most favorably with regard to ESG-related risks and/or opportunities. **Thematic investing** is another approach that focuses on investing in companies within a specific sector or following a specific theme, such as energy efficiency or climate change. **Impact investing** is a related approach that seeks to achieve targeted social or environmental objectives along with measurable financial returns through engagement with a company or by direct investment in projects or companies.

Equity Investment Universe

> ### EXAMPLE 1
>
> ### Roles of Equities
>
> Alex Chang, Lin Choi, and Frank Huber manage separate equity portfolios for the same investment firm. Chang's portfolio objective is conservative in nature, with a regular stream of income as the primary investment objective. Choi's portfolio is more aggressive in nature, with a long-term horizon and with growth as the primary objective. Finally, Huber's portfolio consists of wealthy entrepreneurs who are concerned about rising inflation and wish to preserve the purchasing power of their wealth.
>
> Discuss the investment approach that each portfolio manager would likely use to achieve his or her portfolio objectives.
>
> **Solution:**
>
> Given that his portfolio is focused on a regular stream of income, Chang is likely to focus on companies with regular dividend income. More specifically, Chang is likely to invest in large, well-established companies with stable or growing dividend payments. With a long-term horizon, Choi is most interested in capital appreciation of her portfolio, so she is likely to focus on companies with earnings growth and competitive success. Finally, Huber's clients are concerned about the effects of inflation, so he will likely seek to invest in shares of companies that can provide an inflation hedge. Huber would likely seek companies that can successfully pass on higher input costs to their customers, and he may also seek commodity producers that may benefit from rising commodity prices.

2. EQUITY INVESTMENT UNIVERSE

b describe how an equity manager's investment universe can be segmented;

Given the extensive range of companies in which an equity portfolio manager may invest, an important task for the manager is to segment companies or sectors according to similar characteristics. This segmentation enables portfolio managers to better evaluate and analyze their equity investment universe, and it can help with portfolio diversification. Several approaches to segmenting the equity investment universe are discussed in the following sections.

2.1 Segmentation by Size and Style

A popular approach to segmenting the equity universe incorporates two factors: (1) size and (2) style. Size is typically measured by market capitalization and often categorized by large cap, mid cap, and small cap. Style is typically classified as value, growth, or a combination of value and growth (typically termed "blend" or "core"). In addition, style is often determined through a "scoring" system that incorporates multiple metrics or ratios, such as price-to-book ratios, price-to-earnings ratios, earnings growth, dividend yield, and book value growth. These metrics are then typically "scored" individually for each company, assigned certain weights, and then aggregated. The result is a composite score that determines where the company's stock is positioned along the value–growth spectrum. A combination of growth and value style is not uncommon, particularly for large corporations that have both mature and higher growth business lines.

Exhibit 4 illustrates a common matrix that reflects size and style dimensions. Each category in the matrix can be represented by companies with considerably different business activities. For example, both a small, mature metal fabricating business and a small health care services provider may fall in the Small Cap Value category. In practice, individual stocks may not clearly fall into one of the size/style categories. As a result, the size/style matrix tends to be more of a scatter plot than a simple set of nine categories. An example of a scatter plot is demonstrated in Exhibit 5, which includes all listed equities on the New York Stock Exchange as of March 2017. Each company represents a single dot in Exhibit 5. This more granular representation enables the expansion of size and style categories, such as blue chip and micro-cap companies in size and deep value and high growth in style. It should be noted that Morningstar applies the term "core" for those stocks in which neither value nor growth characteristics dominate, and the term "blend" for those funds with a combination of both growth and value stocks or mostly core stocks.

Exhibit 4 Equity Size and Style Matrix

		Investment Style		
		Value	Core	Growth
Company Size (Market Cap)	Large Cap	Large Cap value	Large Cap core	Large Cap growth
	Mid Cap	Mid Cap value	Mid Cap core	Mid Cap growth
	Small Cap	Small Cap value	Small Cap core	Small Cap growth

Source: Morningstar.

Exhibit 5   Equity Size and Style Scatter Plot

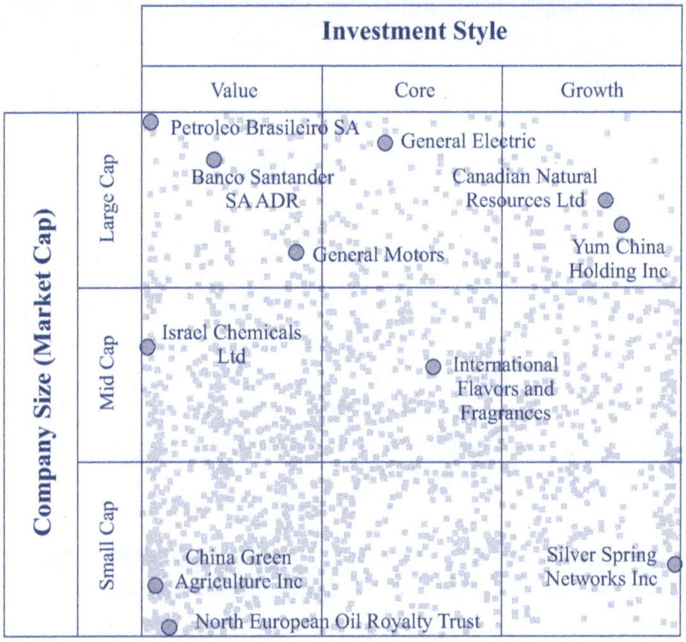

[Scatter plot with axes: Investment Style (Value, Core, Growth) on horizontal axis; Company Size (Market Cap) (Large Cap, Mid Cap, Small Cap) on vertical axis.

Labeled companies:
- Large Cap / Value: Petroleo Brasileiro SA; Banco Santander SA ADR
- Large Cap / Core: General Electric; General Motors
- Large Cap / Growth: Canadian Natural Resources Ltd; Yum China Holding Inc
- Mid Cap / Value: Israel Chemicals Ltd
- Mid Cap / Core: International Flavors and Fragrances
- Small Cap / Value: China Green Agriculture Inc; North European Oil Royalty Trust
- Small Cap / Growth: Silver Spring Networks Inc]

Source: Morningstar Direct.

Segmentation by size/style can provide several advantages for portfolio managers. First, portfolio managers can construct an overall equity portfolio that reflects desired risk, return, and income characteristics in a relatively straightforward and manageable way. Second, given the broad range of companies within each segment, segmentation by size/style results in diversification across economic sectors or industries. Third, active equity managers—that is, those seeking to outperform a given benchmark portfolio—can construct performance benchmarks for specific size/style segments. Generally, large investment management firms may have sizable teams dedicated toward specific size/style categories, while small firms may specialize in a specific size/style category, particularly mid-cap and small-cap companies, seeking to outperform a standard benchmark or comparable peer group.

The final advantage of segmentation by size/style is that it allows a portfolio to reflect a company's maturity and potentially changing growth/value orientation. Specifically, many companies that undertake an IPO (initial public offering) are small and in a growth phase, and thus they may fall in the small-cap growth category. If these companies can successfully grow, their size may ultimately move to mid cap or even large cap, while their style may conceivably shift from high growth to value or a combination of growth and value (e.g., a growth and income stock). Accordingly, over the life cycle of companies, investor preferences for these companies may shift increasingly from capital appreciation to dividend income. In addition, segmentation also helps fund managers adjust holdings over time—for example, when stocks that were previously considered to be in the growth category mature and possibly become value stocks. The key disadvantages of segmentation by size/style are that the categories may change over time and may be defined differently among investors.

2.2 Segmentation by Geography

Another common approach to equity universe segmentation is by geography. This approach is typically based on the stage of markets' macroeconomic development and wealth. Common geographic categories are *developed markets*, *emerging markets*, and *frontier markets*. Exhibit 6 demonstrates the commonly used geographic segmentation of international equity indexes according to MSCI. Other major index providers—such as FTSE, Standard & Poor's, and Russell—also provide similar types of international equity indexes.

Geographic segmentation is useful to equity investors who have considerable exposure to their domestic market and want to diversify by investing in global equities. A key weakness of geographic segmentation is that investing in a specific market (e.g., market index) may provide lower-than-expected exposure to that market. As an example, many large companies domiciled in the United States, Europe, or Asia may be global in nature as opposed to considerable focus on their domicile. Another key weakness of geographic segmentation is potential currency risk when investing in different global equity markets.

Exhibit 6   MSCI International Equity Indexes (as of November 2016)

Developed Markets

Americas	Europe and Middle East	Pacific
Canada	Austria	Australia
United States	Belgium	Hong Kong SAR
	Denmark	Japan
	Finland	New Zealand
	France	Singapore
	Germany	
	Ireland	
	Israel	
	Italy	
	Netherlands	
	Norway	
	Portugal	
	Spain	
	Sweden	
	Switzerland	
	United Kingdom	

Emerging Markets

Americas	Europe, Middle East, and Africa	Asia Pacific
Brazil	Czech Republic	Chinese mainland
Chile	Egypt	India
Colombia	Greece	Indonesia
Mexico	Hungary	Korea
Peru	Poland	Malaysia
	Qatar	Philippines
	Russia	Taiwan Region
	South Africa	Thailand
	Turkey	Pakistan
	United Arab Emirates	

Exhibit 6 (Continued)

Frontier Markets

Americas	Europe and CIS	Africa	Middle East	Asia
Argentina	Croatia	Kenya	Bahrain	Bangladesh
	Estonia	Mauritius	Jordan	Sri Lanka
	Lithuania	Morocco	Kuwait	Vietnam
	Kazakhstan	Nigeria	Lebanon	
	Romania	Tunisia	Oman	
	Serbia			
	Slovenia			

Notes:

1 The following markets are not included in the developed, emerging, or frontier indexes but have their own market-specific indexes: Saudi Arabia, Jamaica, Trinidad & Tobago, Bosnia Herzegovina, Bulgaria, Ukraine, Botswana, Ghana, Zimbabwe, and Palestine.

2 Pakistan was reclassified from the frontier market to the emerging market category as of May 2017.

3 CIS: Commonwealth of Independent States (formerly the USSR).

2.3 Segmentation by Economic Activity

Economic activity is another approach that portfolio managers may use to segment the equity universe. Most commonly used equity classification systems group companies into industries/sectors using either a *production-oriented* approach or a *market-oriented* approach. The production-oriented approach groups companies that manufacture similar products or use similar inputs in their manufacturing processes. The market-oriented approach groups companies based on the markets they serve, the way revenue is earned, and the way customers use companies' products. For example, using a production-oriented approach, a coal company may be classified in the basic materials or mining sector. However, using a market-oriented approach, this same coal company may be classified in the energy sector given the primary market (heating) for the use of coal. As another example, a commercial airline carrier may be classified in the transportation sector using the production-oriented approach, while the same company may be classified in the travel and leisure sector using the market-oriented approach.

Four main global classification systems segment the equity universe by economic activity: (1) the Global Industry Classification Standard (GICS); (2) the Industrial Classification Benchmark (ICB); (3) the Thomson Reuters Business Classification (TRBC); and (4) the Russell Global Sectors Classification (RGS). The GICS uses a market-oriented approach, while the ICB, TRBC, and RGS all use a production-oriented approach. These classification systems help standardize industry definitions so that portfolio managers can compare and analyze companies and industries/sectors. In addition, the classification systems are useful in the creation of industry performance benchmarks.

Exhibit 7 compares the four primary classification systems mentioned. Each system is classified broadly and then increasingly more granular to compare companies and their underlying businesses.

Exhibit 7 Primary Sector Classification Systems

Level/System	GICS	ICB	TRBC	RGS
1st	11 Sectors	10 Industries	10 Economic Sectors	9 Economic Sectors
2nd	24 Industry Groups	19 Super Sectors	28 Business Sectors	33 Sub-Sectors
3rd	68 Industries	41 Sectors	54 Industry Groups	157 Industries
4th	157 Sub-Industries	114 Sub-Sectors	136 Industries	Not Applicable

Source: Thomson Reuters, S&P/MSCI, FTSE/Dow Jones.

To illustrate how segmentation of the classification systems may be used in practice, Exhibit 8 demonstrates how GICS, perhaps the most prominent classification system, sub-divides selected sectors—in this case, Consumer Discretionary, Consumer Staples, and Information Technology—into certain industry group, industry, and sub-industry levels.

Exhibit 8 GICS Classification Examples

Sector	Consumer Discretionary	Consumer Staples	Information Technology
Industry Group Example	Automobiles & Components	Food, Beverage & Tobacco	Technology Hardware & Equipment
Industry Example	Automobiles	Beverages	Electronic Equipment, Instruments & Components
Sub-Industry Example	Motorcycle Manufacturers	Soft Drinks	Electronic Manufacturing Services

Source: MSCI.

As with other segmentation approaches mentioned previously, segmentation by economic activity enables equity portfolio managers to construct performance benchmarks for specific sectors or industries. Portfolio managers may also obtain better industry representation (diversification) by segmenting their equity universe according to economic activity. The key disadvantage of segmentation by economic activity is that the business activities of companies—particularly large ones—may include more than one industry or sub-industry.

> **EXAMPLE 2**
>
> ### Segmenting the Equity Investment Universe
>
> A portfolio manager is initiating a new fund that seeks to invest in the Chinese robotics industry, which is experiencing rapidly accelerating earnings. To help identify appropriate company stocks, the portfolio manager wants to select an approach to segment the equity universe.
>
> Recommend which segmentation approach would be most appropriate for the portfolio manager.

> **Solution:**
> Based on his desired strategy to invest in companies with rapidly accelerating (growing) earnings, the portfolio manager would most likely segment his equity universe by size/style. The portfolio manager would most likely use an investment style that reflects growth, with size (large cap, mid cap, or small cap) depending on the company being analyzed. Other segmentation approaches, including those according to geography and economic activity, would be less appropriate for the portfolio manager given the similar geographic and industry composition of the Chinese robotics industry.

2.4 Segmentation of Equity Indexes and Benchmarks

Segmentation of equity indexes or benchmarks reflects some of or all the approaches previously discussed in this section. For example, the MSCI Europe Large Cap Growth Index, the MSCI World Small Cap Value Index, the MSCI Emerging Markets Large Cap Growth Index, or the MSCI Latin America Midcap Index combine various geographic, size, and style dimensions. This combination of geography, size, and style also sometimes applies to individual countries—particularly those in large, developed markets.

A more focused approach to segmentation of equity indexes uses industries or sectors. Because many industries and sectors are global in scope, the most common types of these indexes are comprised of companies in different countries. A few examples include the following:

- Global Natural Resources—the *S&P Global Natural Resources Index* includes 90 of the largest publicly traded companies in natural resources and commodities businesses across three primary commodity-related sectors: agribusiness; energy; and metals and mining.
- Worldwide Oil and Natural Gas—the *MSCI World Energy Index* includes the large-cap and mid-cap segments of publicly traded oil and natural gas companies within the developed markets.
- Multinational Financials—the *Thomson Reuters Global Financials Index* includes the 100 largest publicly traded companies within the global financial services sector as defined by the TRBC classification system.

Finally, some indexes reflect specific investment approaches, such as ESG. Such ESG indexes are comprised of companies that reflect certain considerations, such as sustainability or impact investing.

INCOME ASSOCIATED WITH OWNING AND MANAGING AN EQUITY PORTFOLIO

3

c describe the types of income and costs associated with owning and managing an equity portfolio and their potential effects on portfolio performance;

Dividends are the primary source of income for equity portfolios. In addition, some portfolio managers may use securities lending or option-writing strategies to generate income. On the cost side, equity portfolios incur various fees and trading costs that adversely affect portfolio returns. The primary types of income and costs are discussed in this section.

3.1 Dividend Income

Investors requiring regular income may prefer to invest in stocks with large or frequent dividend payments, whereas growth-oriented investors may have little interest in dividends. Taxation is an important consideration for dividend income received, particularly for individuals. Depending on the country where the investor is domiciled, where dividends are issued, and the type of investor, dividends may be subject to withholding tax and/or income tax.

Beyond regular dividends, equity portfolios may receive **special dividends** from certain companies. Special dividends occur when companies decide to distribute excess cash to shareholders, but the payments may not be maintained over time. **Optional stock dividends** are another type of dividend in which shareholders may elect to receive either cash or new shares. When the share price used to calculate the number of stock dividend shares is established before the shareholder's election date, the choice between a cash or stock dividend may be important. This choice represents "optionality" for the shareholder, and the optionality has value. Some market participants, typically investment banks, may offer to purchase this "option," providing an additional, if modest, source of income to an equity investor.

3.2 Securities Lending Income

For some investors, **securities lending**—a form of collateralized lending—may be used to generate income for portfolios. Securities lending can facilitate short sales, which involve the sale of securities the seller does not own. When a securities lending transaction involves the transfer of equities, the transaction is generally known as **stock lending** and the securities are generally known as *stock loans*. Stock loans are collateralized with either cash or other high-quality securities to provide some financial protection to the lender. Stock loans are usually open-ended in duration, but the borrower must return the shares to the lender on demand.

Stock lenders generally receive a fee from the stock borrower as compensation for the loaned shares. Most stock loans in developed markets earn a modest fee, approximately 0.2–0.5% on an annualized basis. In emerging markets, fees are typically higher, often 1–2% annualized for large-cap stocks. In many equity markets, certain stocks—called "specials"—are in high demand for borrowing. These specials can earn fees that are substantially higher than average (typically 5–15% annualized), and in cases of extreme demand, they could be as high as 25–100% annually. However, such high fees do not normally persist for long periods of time.

In addition to fees earned, stock lenders can generate further income by reinvesting the cash collateral received (assuming a favorable interest rate environment). However, as with virtually any other investment, the collateral would be subject to market risk, credit risk, liquidity risk, and operational risk. The administrative costs of a securities lending program, in turn, will reduce the collateral income generated. Dividends on loaned stock are "manufactured" by the stock borrower for the stock lender—that is, the stock borrower ensures that the stock lender is compensated for any dividends that the lender would have received had the stock not been loaned.

Index funds are frequent stock lenders because of their large, long-term holdings in stocks. In addition, because index funds merely seek to replicate the performance of an index, portfolio managers of these funds are normally not concerned that borrowed stock used for short-selling purposes might decrease the prices of the corresponding equities. Large, actively managed pension funds, endowments, and institutional investors are also frequent stock lenders, although these investors are likely more concerned with the effect on their returns if the loaned shares are used to facilitate short-selling. The evidence on the impact of stock lending on asset prices has, however, been mixed (see, for example, Kaplan, Moskowitz, and Sensoy 2013).

3.3 Ancillary Investment Strategies

Additional income can be generated for an equity portfolio through a trading strategy known as **dividend capture**. Under this strategy, an equity portfolio manager purchases stocks just before their ex-dividend dates, holds these stocks through the ex-dividend date to earn the right to receive the dividend, and subsequently sells the shares. Once a stock goes ex-dividend, the share price should, in theory, decrease by the value of the dividend. In this way, capturing dividends would increase portfolio income, although the portfolio would, again in theory, experience capital losses of similar magnitude. However, the share price movement could vary from this theoretical assumption given income tax considerations, stock-specific supply/demand conditions, and general stock market moves around the ex-dividend date.

Selling (writing) options can also generate additional income for an equity portfolio. One such options strategy is writing a *covered call*, whereby the portfolio manager already owns the underlying stock and sells a call option on that stock. Another options strategy is writing a *cash-covered put* (also called a *cash-secured put*), whereby the portfolio manager writes a put option on a stock and simultaneously deposits money equal to the exercise price into a designated account. Under both covered calls and cash-covered puts, income is generated through the writing of options, but clearly the risk profile of the portfolio would be altered. For example, writing a covered call would limit the upside from share price appreciation of the underlying shares.

EXAMPLE 3

Equity Portfolio Income

Isabel Cordova is an equity portfolio manager for a large multinational investment firm. Her portfolio consists of several dividend-paying stocks, and she is interested in generating additional income to enhance the portfolio's total return. Describe potential sources of additional income for Cordova's equity portfolio.

Solution:

Cordova's primary source of income for her portfolio would likely be "regular" and, in some cases, special dividends from those companies that pay them. Another potential source of income for Cordova is securities (stock) lending, whereby eligible equities in her portfolio can be loaned to other market participants, including those seeking to sell short securities. In this case, income would be generated from fees received from the stock borrower as well as from reinvesting the cash collateral received. Another potential income-generating strategy available to Cordova is dividend capture, which entails purchasing stocks just before their ex-dividend dates, holding the stocks through the ex-dividend date to earn the right to receive the dividend, and subsequently selling the shares. Selling (writing) options, including covered call and cash-covered put (cash-secured put) strategies, is another way Cordova can generate additional income for her equity portfolio.

COSTS ASSOCIATED WITH OWNING AND MANAGING AN EQUITY PORTFOLIO

4

c   describe the types of income and costs associated with owning and managing an equity portfolio and their potential effects on portfolio performance;

Management fees are typically determined as a percentage of the funds under management (an *ad-valorem* fee) at regular intervals. For actively managed portfolios, the level of management fees involves a balance between fees that are high enough to fund investment research but low enough to avoid detracting too much from investor returns. Management fees for actively managed portfolios include direct costs of research (e.g., remuneration and expenses for investment analysts and portfolio managers) and the direct costs of portfolio management (e.g., software, trade processing costs, and compliance). For passively managed portfolios, management fees are typically low because of lower direct costs of research and portfolio management relative to actively managed portfolios.

4.1 Performance Fees

In addition to management fees, portfolio managers sometimes earn performance fees (also known as incentive fees) on their portfolios. Performance fees are generally associated with hedge funds and long/short equity portfolios, rather than long-only portfolios. These fees are an incentive for portfolio managers to achieve or outperform return objectives, to the benefit of both the manager and investors. As an example, a performance fee might represent 10–20% of any capital appreciation in a portfolio that exceeds some stated annual absolute return threshold (e.g., 8%). Several performance fee structures exist, although performance fees tend to be "upwards only"—that is, fees are earned by the manager when performance objectives are met, but fund investors are not reimbursed when performance is negative. However, performance fees could be reduced following a period of poor performance. Fee calculations also reflect high-water marks. A **high-water mark** is the highest value, net of fees, that the fund has reached. The use of high-water marks protects clients from paying twice for the same performance. For example, if a fund performed well in a given year, it might earn a performance fee. If the value of the same fund fell the following year, no performance fee would be payable. Then, if the fund's value increased in the third year to a point just below the value achieved at the end of the first year, no performance fee would be earned because the fund's value did not exceed the high-water mark. This basic fee structure is used by many alternative investment funds and partnerships, including hedge funds.

Investment managers typically present a standard schedule of fees to a prospective client, although actual fees can be negotiated between the manager and investors. For a fund, fees are established in the prospectus, although investors could negotiate special terms (e.g., a discount for being an early investor in a fund).

4.2 Administration Fees

Equity portfolios are subject to administration fees. These fees include the processing of corporate actions, such as rights issues; the measurement of performance and risk of a portfolio; and voting at company meetings. Generally, these functions are provided by an investment management firm itself and are included as part of the management fee.

Some functions, however, are provided by external parties, with the fees charged to the client in addition to management fees. These externally provided functions include:

- *Custody fees* paid for the safekeeping of assets by a custodian (often a subsidiary of a large bank) that is independent of the investment manager.

- *Depository fees* paid to help ensure that custodians segregate the assets of the portfolio and that the portfolio complies with any investment limits, leverage requirements, and limits on cash holdings.
- *Registration fees* that are associated with the registration of ownership of units in a mutual fund.

4.3 Marketing and Distribution Costs

Most investment management firms market and distribute their services to some degree. Marketing and distribution costs typically include the following:

- Costs of employing marketing, sales, and client servicing staff
- Advertising costs
- Sponsorship costs, including costs associated with sponsoring or presenting at conferences
- Costs of producing and distributing brochures or other communications to financial intermediaries or prospective clients
- "Platform" fees, which are costs incurred when an intermediary offers an investment management firm fund services on the intermediary's platform of funds (e.g., a "funds supermarket")
- Sales commissions paid to such financial intermediaries as financial planners, independent financial advisers, and brokers to facilitate the distribution of funds or investment services

When marketing and distribution services are performed by an investment management firm, the costs are likely included as part of the management fee. However, those marketing and distribution services that are performed by external parties (e.g., consultants) typically incur additional costs to the investor.

4.4 Trading Costs

Buying and selling equities incurs a series of trading (or transaction) costs. Some of these trading costs are explicit, including brokerage commission costs, taxes, stamp duties, and stock exchange fees. In addition, many countries charge a modest regulatory fee for certain types of equity trading.

In contrast to explicit costs, some trading costs are implicit in nature. These implicit costs include the following:

- Bid–offer spread
- Market impact (also called price impact), which measures the effect of the trade on transaction prices
- Delay costs (also called slippage), which arise from the inability to complete desired trades immediately because of order size or lack of market liquidity

In an equity portfolio, total trading costs are a function of the size of trades, the frequency of trading, and the degree to which trades demand liquidity from the market. Unlike many other equity portfolio costs, such as management fees, the total cost of trading is generally not revealed to the investor. Rather, trading costs are incorporated into a portfolio's total return and presented as overall performance data. One final trading cost relates to stock lending transactions that were previously discussed. Equity portfolio managers who borrow shares in these transactions must pay fees on shares borrowed.

4.5 Investment Approaches and Effects on Costs

Equity portfolio costs tend to vary depending on their underlying strategy or approach. As mentioned previously, passively managed strategies tend to charge lower management fees than active strategies primarily because of lower research costs to manage the portfolios. Passively managed equity portfolios also tend to trade less frequently than actively managed equity portfolios, with trading in passive portfolios typically involving rebalancing or changes to index constituents. Index funds, however, do face a "hidden" cost from potential predatory trading. As an illustration, a predatory trader may purchase (or sell short) shares prior to their effective inclusion (or deletion) from an index, resulting in price movement and potential profit for a predatory trader. Such predatory trading strategies can be regarded as a cost to investors in index funds, albeit a cost that is not necessarily evident to a portfolio manager or investor.

Some active investing approaches "demand liquidity" from the market. For example, in a momentum strategy, the investor seeks to buy shares that are already rising in price (or sell those that are already falling). In contrast, some active investing approaches are more likely to "provide liquidity" to the market, such as deep value strategies (i.e., those involving stocks that are deemed to be significantly undervalued). Investment strategies that involve frequent trading and demand liquidity are, unsurprisingly, likely to have higher trading costs than long-term, buy-and-hold investment strategies.

5 SHAREHOLDER ENGAGEMENT

d   describe the potential benefits of shareholder engagement and the role an equity manager might play in shareholder engagement;

Shareholder engagement refers to the process whereby investors actively interact with companies. Shareholder engagement often includes voting on corporate matters at general meetings as well as other forms of communication (e.g., quarterly investor calls or in-person meetings) between shareholders and representatives of a company. Generally, shareholder engagement concerns issues that can affect the value of a company and, by extension, an investor's shares.

When shareholders engage with companies, several issues may be discussed. Some of these issues include the following:

- *Strategy*—a company's strategic goals, resources, plans for growth, and constraints. Also of interest may be a company's research, product development, culture, sustainability and corporate responsibility, and industry and competitor developments. Shareholders may ask the company how it balances short-term requirements and long-term goals and how it prioritizes the interests of its various stakeholders.

- *Allocation of capital*—a company's process for selecting new projects as well as its mergers and acquisitions strategy. Shareholders may be interested to learn about policies on dividends, financial leverage, equity raising, and capital expenditures.

- *Corporate governance* and regulatory and political risk—including internal controls and the operation of its audit and risk committees.

- *Remuneration*—compensation structures for directors and senior management, incentives for certain behaviors, and alignment of interests between directors and shareholders. In some cases, investors may be able to influence future

remuneration structures. Such influence, especially regarding larger companies, often involves the use of remuneration consultants and an iterative process with large, long-term shareholders.
- *Composition of the board of directors*—succession planning, director expertise and competence, culture, diversity, and board effectiveness.

5.1 Benefits of Shareholder Engagement

Shareholder engagement can provide benefits for both shareholders and companies. From a company's perspective, shareholder engagement can assist in developing a more effective corporate governance culture. In turn, shareholder engagement may lead to better company performance to the benefit of shareholders (as well as other stakeholders).

Investors may also benefit from engagement because they will have more information about companies or the sectors in which companies operate. Such information may include a company's strategy, culture, and competitive environment within an industry. Shareholder engagement is particularly relevant for active portfolio managers given their objective to outperform a benchmark portfolio. By contrast, passive (or index) fund managers are primarily focused on tracking a given benchmark or index while minimizing costs to do so. Any process, such as shareholder engagement, that takes up management time (and adds to cost) would detract from the primary goal of a passive manager. This would be less of an issue for very large passively managed portfolios, where any engagement costs could be spread over a sizable asset base.

In theory, some investors could benefit from the shareholder engagement of others under the so-called "free rider problem." Specifically, assume that a portfolio manager using an active strategy actively engages with a company to improve its operations and was successful in increasing the company's stock price. The manager's actions in this case improved the value of his portfolio and also benefitted other investors who own the same stock in their portfolios. Investors who did not participate in shareholder engagement benefitted from improved performance but without the costs necessary for engagement.

In addition to shareholders, other stakeholders of a company may also have an interest in the process and outcomes of shareholder engagement. These stakeholders may include creditors, customers, employees, regulators, governmental bodies, and certain other members of society (e.g., community organizations and citizen groups). These other stakeholders can gain or lose influence with companies depending on the outcomes of shareholder engagement. For example, employees can be affected by cost reduction programs requested by shareholders. Another example is when creditors of a company are affected by a change in a company's vendor payment terms, which can impact the company's working capital and cash flow. Such external forces as the media, the academic community, corporate governance consultants, and proxy voting advisers can also influence the process of shareholder engagement.

Shareholders that also have non-financial interests, such as ESG considerations, may also benefit from shareholder engagement. However, these benefits are difficult to quantify. Empirical evidence relating shareholder returns to a company's adherence to corporate governance and ESG practices is mixed. This mixed evidence could be partly attributable to the fact that a company's management quality and effective ESG practices may be correlated with one another. As a result, it is often difficult to isolate non-financial factors and measure the direct effects of shareholder engagement.

5.2 Disadvantages of Shareholder Engagement

Shareholder engagement also has several disadvantages. First, shareholder engagement is time consuming and can be costly for both shareholders and companies. Second, pressure on company management to meet near-term share price or earnings targets could be made at the expense of long-term corporate decisions. Third, engagement can result in selective disclosure of important information to a certain subset of shareholders, which could lead to a breach of insider trading rules while in possession of specific, material, non-public information about a company. Finally, conflicts of interest can result for a company. For example, a portfolio manager could engage with a company that also happens to be an investor in the manager's portfolio. In such a situation, a portfolio manager may be unduly influenced to support the company's management so as not to jeopardize the company's investment mandate with the portfolio manager.

5.3 The Role of an Equity Manager in Shareholder Engagement

Active managers of equity portfolios typically engage, to some degree, with companies in which they currently (or potentially) invest. In fact, investment firms in some countries have legal or regulatory responsibilities to establish written policies on stewardship and/or shareholder engagement. Engagement activities for equity portfolio managers often include regular meetings with company management or investor relations teams. Such meetings can occur at any time but are often held after annual, semi-annual, or quarterly company results have been published.

For such non-financial issues as ESG, large investment firms, in particular, sometimes employ an analyst (or team of analysts) who focuses on ESG issues. These ESG-focused analysts normally work in conjunction with traditional fundamental investment analysts, with primary responsibility for shareholder voting decisions or environmental or social issues that affect equity investments. In lieu of—or in addition to—dedicated ESG analyst teams, some institutional investors have retained outside experts to assist with corporate governance monitoring and proxy voting. In response to this demand, an industry that provides corporate governance services, including governance ratings and proxy advice, has developed.

5.3.1 Activist Investing

A distinct and specialized version of engagement is known as activist investing. Activist investors (or activists) specialize in taking stakes in companies and creating change to generate a gain on the investment. Hedge funds are among the most common activists, possibly because of the potential for, in many cases, high performance fees. In addition, because hedge funds are subject to limited regulation, have fewer investment constraints, and can often leverage positions, these investors often have more flexibility as activists.

Engagement through activist investing can include meetings with management as well as shareholder resolutions, letters to management, presentations to other investors, and media campaigns. Activists may also seek representation on a company's board of directors as a way of exerting influence. Proxy contests are one method used to obtain board representation. These contests represent corporate takeover mechanisms in which shareholders are persuaded to vote for a group seeking a controlling position on a company's board of directors. Social media and other communication tools can help activists coordinate the actions of other shareholders.

5.3.2 *Voting*

The participation of shareholders in general meetings, also known as general assemblies, and the exercise of their voting rights are among the most influential tools available for shareholder engagement. General meetings enable shareholders to participate in discussions and to vote on major corporate matters and transactions that are not delegated to the board of directors. By engaging in general meetings, shareholders can exercise their voting rights on major corporate issues and better monitor the performance of the board and senior management.

Proxy voting enables shareholders who are unable to attend a meeting to authorize another individual (e.g., another shareholder or director) to vote on their behalf. Proxy voting is the most common form of investor participation in general meetings. Although most resolutions pass without controversy, sometimes minority shareholders attempt to strengthen their influence at companies via proxy voting. Occasionally, multiple shareholders may use this process to collectively vote their shares in favor of or in opposition to a certain resolution.

Some investors use external proxy advisory firms that provide voting recommendations and reduce research efforts by investors. Portfolio managers need not follow the recommendations of proxy advisory firms, but these external parties can highlight potential controversial issues. An investor's voting instructions are typically processed electronically via third-party proxy voting agents.

When an investor loans shares, the transaction is technically an assignment of title with a repurchase option; that is, the voting rights are transferred to the borrower. The transfer of voting rights with stock lending could potentially result in the borrower having different voting opinions from the lending investor. To mitigate this problem, some stock lenders recall shares ahead of voting resolutions to enable exercise of their voting rights. The downside of this action would be the loss of stock lending revenue during the period of stock loan recall and potential reputation risk as an attractive lender. Investors, in some cases, may borrow shares explicitly to exercise the voting rights attached. This process is called *empty voting*, whereby no capital is invested in the voted shares.

EXAMPLE 4

Shareholder Engagement

An investor manages a fund with a sizable concentration in the transportation sector and is interested in meeting with senior management of a small aircraft manufacturer. Discuss how the investor may benefit from his/her shareholder engagement activities, as well as from the shareholder engagement of other investors, with this manufacturer.

Solution:

The investor may benefit from information obtained about the aircraft manufacturer, such as its strategy, allocation of capital, corporate governance, remuneration of directors and senior management, culture, and competitive environment within the aerospace industry. The investor may also benefit as a "free rider," whereby other investors may improve the manufacturer's operating performance through shareholder engagement—to the benefit of all shareholders. Finally, if the investor has non-financial interests, such as ESG, he or she may address these considerations as part of shareholder engagement.

6 EQUITY INVESTMENT ACROSS THE PASSIVE-ACTIVE SPECTRUM

e   describe rationales for equity investment across the passive–active spectrum.

The debate between passive management and active management of equity portfolios has been a longstanding one in the investment community. In reality, the decision between passive management and active management is not an "either/or" (binary) alternative. Instead, equity portfolios tend to exist across a passive–active spectrum, ranging from portfolios that closely track an equity market index or benchmark to unconstrained portfolios that are not subject to any benchmark or index. In some cases, portfolios may resemble a "closet index" in which the portfolio is advertised as actively managed but essentially resembles a passively managed fund. For an equity manager (or investment firm), several rationales exist for positioning a portfolio along the passive–active spectrum. Each of these rationales is discussed further.

6.1 Confidence to Outperform

An active investment manager typically needs to be confident that she can adequately outperform her benchmark. This determination requires an understanding of the manager's equity investment universe as well as a competitive analysis of other managers that have a similar investment universe.

6.2 Client Preference

For equity portfolio managers, client preference is a primary consideration when deciding between passive or active investing. Portfolio managers must assess whether their passive or active investment strategies will attract sufficient funds from clients to make the initiatives viable. Another consideration reflects investors' beliefs regarding the potential for active strategies to generate positive alpha. For example, in some equity market categories, such as large-cap/developed markets, companies are widely known and have considerable equity analyst coverage. For such categories as these, investors often believe that potential alpha is substantially reduced because all publicly available information is efficiently disseminated, analyzed, and reflected in stock prices.

A comparison of passive and active equities is illustrated in Exhibit 9. The exhibit demonstrates the relative proportion of investment passive and active equities in US open-ended mutual funds and exchange-traded funds (ETFs) by equity category. Nearly all equities in some categories, such as foreign small/mid-cap growth, are managed on an active basis. Conversely, equities in other categories, such as large-cap blend, are predominantly managed on a passive basis.

Exhibit 9: Passive versus Active Equities in US Open-Ended Mutual Funds and ETFs

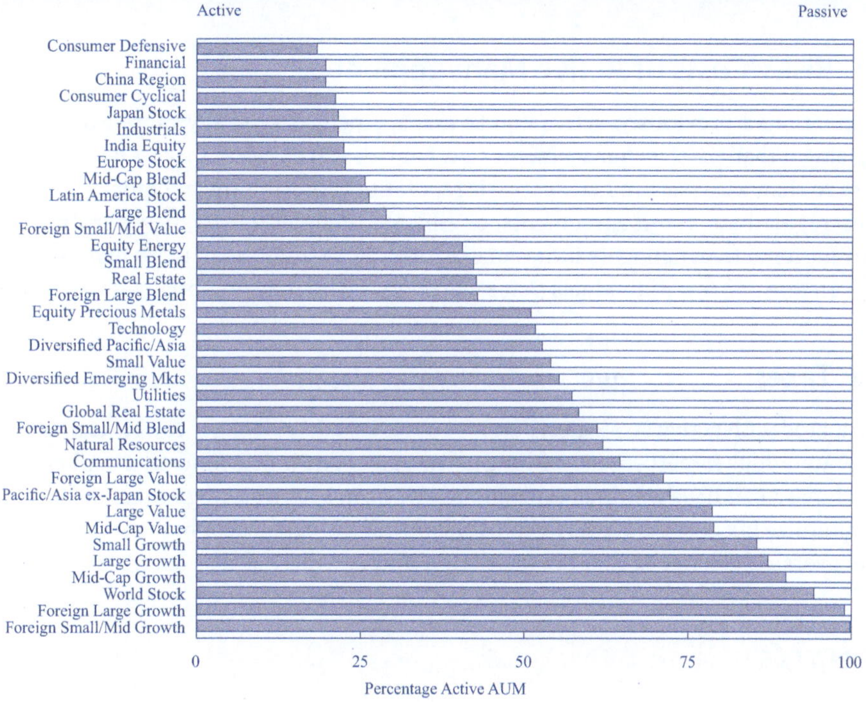

Source: Morningstar Direct. Data as of August 2016.

6.3 Suitable Benchmark

An investor or equity manager's choice of benchmark can play a meaningful role in the ability to attract new funds. This choice is particularly relevant in the institutional equity market, where asset owners (and their consultants) regularly screen new managers in desired equity segments. As part of the selection process in desired equity segments, active managers normally must have benchmarks with sufficient liquidity of underlying securities (thus maintaining a reasonable cost of trading). In addition, the number of securities underlying the benchmark typically must be broad enough to generate sufficient alpha. For this reason, many country or sector-specific investment strategies (e.g., consumer defensive companies) are managed passively rather than actively.

6.4 Client-Specific Mandates

Client-specific investment mandates, such as those related to ESG considerations, are typically managed actively rather than passively. This active approach occurs because passive management may not be particularly efficient or cost effective when managers must meet a client's desired holdings (or holdings to avoid). For example, a mandate to avoid investments in companies involved in certain "unacceptable" activities (e.g., the sale of military technology or weapons, tobacco/alcohol, or gambling) requires ongoing monitoring and management. As part of this *exclusionary (or negative) screening* process, managers need to determine those companies that are directly, as well as indirectly, involved in such "unacceptable" industries. Although ESG investing is typically more active than passive, several investment vehicles enable a portfolio manager to invest passively according to ESG-related considerations.

6.5 Risks/Costs of Active Management

As mentioned previously, active equity management is typically more expensive to implement than passive management. Another risk that active managers face—perhaps more so than with passive managers—is reputation risk from the potential violation of rules, regulations, client agreements, or ethical principles. Lastly, "key person" risk is relevant for active managers if the success of an investment manager's firm is dependent on one or a few individuals ("star managers") who may potentially leave the firm.

6.6 Taxes

Compared with active strategies, passive strategies generally have lower turnover and generate a higher percentage of long-term gains. An index fund that replicates its benchmark can have minimal rebalancing. In turn, active strategies can be designed to minimize tax consequences of gains/income at the expense of higher trading costs. One overall challenge is that tax legislation differs widely across countries.

EXAMPLE 5

Passive–Active Spectrum

James Drummond, an equity portfolio manager, is meeting with Marie Goudreaux, a wealthy client of his investment firm. Goudreaux is very cost conscious and believes that equity markets are highly efficient. Goudreaux also has a narrow investment focus, seeking stocks in specific country and industry sectors.

Discuss where Goudreaux's portfolio is likely to be positioned across the passive–active spectrum.

Solution:

Goudreaux's portfolio is likely to be managed passively. Because she believes in market efficiency, Goudreaux likely believes that Drummond's ability to generate alpha is limited. Goudreaux's cost consciousness also supports passive management, which is typically less expensive to implement than active management. Finally, Goudreaux's stated desire to invest in specific countries and sectors would likely be better managed passively.

SUMMARY

This reading provides an overview of the roles equity investments may play in the client's portfolio, how asset owners and investment managers segment the equity universe for purposes of defining an investment mandate, the costs and obligations

Summary

of equity ownership (including shareholder engagement) and issues relevant to the decision to pursue active or passive management of an equity portfolio. Among the key points made in this reading are the following:

- Equities can provide several roles or benefits to an overall portfolio, including capital appreciation, dividend income, diversification with other asset classes, and a potential hedge against inflation.

- The inclusion of equities in a portfolio can be driven by a client's goals or needs. Portfolio managers often consider the following investment objectives and constraints when deciding to include equities (or asset classes in general, for that matter) in a client's portfolio: *risk objective; return objective; liquidity requirement; time horizon; tax concerns; legal and regulatory factors*; and *unique circumstances.*

- Investors often segment the equity universe according to (1) size and style; (2) geography; and (3) economic activity.

- Sources of equity portfolio income include dividends; securities lending fees and interest; dividend capture; covered calls; and cash-covered puts (or cash-secured puts).

- Sources of equity portfolio costs include management fees; performance fees; administration fees; marketing/distribution fees; and trading costs.

- Shareholder engagement is the process whereby companies engage with their shareholders. The process typically includes voting on corporate matters at general meetings and other forms of communication, such as quarterly investor calls or in-person meetings.

- Shareholder engagement can provide benefits for both shareholders and companies. From a company's perspective, shareholder engagement can assist in developing a more effective corporate governance culture. In turn, shareholder engagement may lead to better company performance to the benefit of shareholders (as well as other stakeholders).

- Disadvantages of shareholder engagement include costs and time involved, pressure on a company to meet near-term share price or earnings targets, possible selective disclosure of information, and potential conflicts of interest.

- Activist investors (or activists) specialize in taking stakes in companies and creating change to generate a gain on the investment.

- The participation of shareholders in general meetings, also known as general assemblies, and the exercise of their voting rights are among the most influential tools available for shareholder engagement.

- The choice of using active management or passive management is not an "either/or" (binary) alternative but rather a decision involving a passive–active spectrum. Investors may decide to position their portfolios across the passive–active spectrum based on their confidence to outperform, client preference, suitable benchmarks, client-specific mandates, risks/costs of active management, and taxes.

REFERENCES

Chincarini, Ludwig, and Kim Daehwan. 2006. *Quantitative Equity Portfolio Management*. New York, NY: McGraw-Hill.

Kaplan, Steven, Tobias Moskowitz, and Berk Sensoy. 2013. "The Effects of Stock Lending on Security Prices: An Experiment." *Journal of Finance*, vol. 68, no. 5: 1891–1936.

McMillan, Michael, Jerald Pinto, Wendy Pirie, and Gerhard Van de Venter. 2011. *Investments: Principles of Portfolio and Equity Analysis*. CFA Institute Investment Series. Hoboken, NJ: John Wiley & Sons.

Weigand, Robert. 2014. *Applied Equity Analysis and Portfolio Management*. Hoboken, NJ: John Wiley & Sons.

Zhou, Xinfeng, and Sameer Jain. 2014. *Active Equity Management*. 1st ed. Cambridge, MA: MIT University Press.

PRACTICE PROBLEMS

The following information relates to questions 1–8

Three years ago, the Albright Investment Management Company (Albright) added four new funds—the Barboa Fund, the Caribou Fund, the DoGood Fund, and the Elmer Fund—to its existing fund offering. Albright's new funds are described in Exhibit 1.

Exhibit 1	Albright Investment Management Company New Funds
Fund	**Fund Description**
Barboa Fund	Invests solely in the equity of companies in oil production and transportation industries in many countries.
Caribou Fund	Uses an aggressive strategy focusing on relatively new, fast-growing companies in emerging industries.
DoGood Fund	Investment universe includes all US companies and sectors that have favorable environmental, social, and governance (ESG) ratings and specifically excludes companies with products or services related to aerospace and defense.
Elmer Fund	Investments selected to track the S&P 500 Index. Minimizes trading based on the assumption that markets are efficient.

Hans Smith, an Albright portfolio manager, makes the following notes after examining these funds:

Note 1 The fee on the Caribou Fund is a 15% share of any capital appreciation above a 7% threshold and the use of a high-water mark.

Note 2 The DoGood Fund invests in Fleeker Corporation stock, which is rated high in the ESG space, and Fleeker's pension fund has a significant investment in the DoGood Fund. This dynamic has the potential for a conflict of interest on the part of Fleeker Corporation but not for the DoGood Fund.

Note 3 The DoGood Fund's portfolio manager has written policies stating that the fund does not engage in shareholder activism. Therefore, the DoGood Fund may be a free-rider on the activism by these shareholders.

Note 4 Of the four funds, the Elmer Fund is most likely to appeal to investors who want to minimize fees and believe that the market is efficient.

Note 5 Adding investment-grade bonds to the Elmer Fund will decrease the portfolio's short-term risk.

Smith discusses means of enhancing income for the three funds with the junior analyst, Kolton Frey, including engaging in securities lending or writing covered calls. Frey tells Smith the following:

Statement 1   Securities lending would increase income through reinvestment of the cash collateral but would require the fund to miss out on dividend income from the lent securities.

Statement 2   Writing covered calls would generate income, but doing so would limit the upside share price appreciation for the underlying shares.

1   The Barboa Fund can be *best* described as a fund segmented by:
   A   size/style.
   B   geography.
   C   economic activity.

2   The Caribou Fund is *most likely* classified as a:
   A   large-cap value fund.
   B   small-cap value fund.
   C   small-cap growth fund.

3   The DoGood Fund's approach to the aerospace and defense industry is *best* described as:
   A   positive screening.
   B   negative screening.
   C   thematic investing.

4   The Elmer fund's management strategy is:
   A   active.
   B   passive.
   C   blended.

5   Based on Note 1, the fee on the Caribou Fund is *best* described as a:
   A   performance fee.
   B   management fee.
   C   administrative fee.

6   Which of the following notes about the DoGood Fund is correct?
   A   Only Note 2
   B   Only Note 3
   C   Both Note 2 and Note 3

7   Which of the notes regarding the Elmer Fund is correct?
   A   Only Note 4
   B   Only Note 5
   C   Both Note 4 and Note 5

8   Which of Frey's statements about securities lending and covered call writing is correct?
   A   Only Statement 1
   B   Only Statement 2
   C   Both Statement 1 and Statement 2

SOLUTIONS

1. C is correct. The Barboa Fund invests solely in the equity of companies in the oil production and transportation industries in many countries. The fund's description is consistent with the production-oriented approach, which groups companies that manufacture similar products or use similar inputs in their manufacturing processes.

   A is incorrect because the fund description does not mention the firms' size or style (i.e., value, growth, or blend). Size is typically measured by market capitalization and often categorized as large cap, mid-cap, or small cap. Style is typically classified as value, growth, or a blend of value and growth. In addition, style is often determined through a "scoring" system that incorporates multiple metrics or ratios, such as price-to-book ratios, price-to-earnings ratios, earnings growth, dividend yield, and book value growth. These metrics are then typically "scored" individually for each company, assigned certain weights, and then aggregated.

   B is incorrect because the fund is invested across many countries, which indicates that the fund is not segmented by geography. Segmentation by geography is typically based upon the stage of countries' macroeconomic development and wealth. Common geographic categories are developed markets, emerging markets, and frontier markets.

2. C is correct because the fund focuses on new companies that are generally classified as small firms, and the fund has a style classified as aggressive. A widely used approach to segment the equity universe incorporates two factors: size and style. Size is typically measured by market capitalization and often categorized as large cap, mid-cap, or small cap. Style is typically classified as value, growth, or a blend of value and growth.

3. B is correct. The DoGood fund excludes companies based on specified activities (e.g., aerospace and defense), which is a process of negative screening. Negative or exclusionary screening refers to the practice of excluding certain sectors or companies that deviate from accepted standards in areas such as human rights or environmental concerns

   A is incorrect because positive screening attempts to identify companies or sectors that score most favorably regarding ESG-related risks and/or opportunities. The restrictions on investing indicates that a negative screen is established.

   C is incorrect because thematic investing focuses on investing in companies within a specific sector or following a specific theme, such as energy efficiency or climate change. The DoGood Fund's investment universe includes all companies and sectors that have favorable ESG (no specific sectors or screens) but with specific exclusions.

4. B is correct. The fund is managed assuming that the market is efficient, and investments are selected to mimic an index. Compared with active strategies, passive strategies generally have lower turnover and generate a higher percentage of long-term gains. An index fund that replicates its benchmark can have minimal rebalancing.

5. A is correct. Performance fees serve as an incentive for portfolio managers to achieve or outperform return objectives, to the benefit of both the manager and investors. Several performance fee structures exist, although performance fees tend to be "upward only"—that is, fees are earned by the manager when performance objectives are met, but fund investors are not reimbursed when

performance is negative. Performance fees could be reduced following a period of poor performance, however. Fee calculations also reflect high-water marks. As described in Note 1, the fee for the Caribou Fund is a 15% share of any capital appreciation above a 7% threshold, with the use of a high-water mark, and is therefore a performance fee.

B is incorrect because management fees include direct costs of research (such as remuneration and expenses for investment analysts and portfolio managers) and the direct costs of portfolio management (e.g., software, trade processing costs, and compliance). Management fees are typically determined as a percentage of the funds under management.

C is incorrect because administrative fees include the processing of corporate actions such as rights issues and optional stock dividends, the measurement of performance and risk of a portfolio, and voting at company meetings. Generally, these functions are provided by an investment management firm itself and are included as part of the management fee.

6 B is correct because the fund becomes a free-rider if it allows other shareholders to engage in actions that benefit the fund, and therefore Note 3 is correct. In theory, some investors could benefit from the shareholder engagement of others under the so-called "free rider problem." Specifically, assume that a portfolio manager using an active strategy actively engages with a company to improve its operations and was successful in increasing the company's stock price. The manager's actions in this case improved the value of his portfolio and also benefitted other investors that own the same stock in their portfolios. Those investors that did not participate in shareholder engagement benefit from improved performance but without the costs necessary for engagement.

Note 2 is incorrect because a conflict of interest arises on the part of the DoGood Fund if it owns shares of a company that invests in the fund. Conflicts of interest can result for a company. For example, a portfolio manager could engage with a company that also happens to be an investor in the manager's portfolio. In such a situation, a portfolio manager may be unduly influenced to support the company's management so as not to jeopardize the company's investment mandate with the portfolio manager.

7 A is correct. For passively managed portfolios, management fees are typically low because of lower direct costs of research and portfolio management relative to actively managed portfolios. Therefore, Note 4 is correct.

Note 5 is incorrect because the predictability of correlations is uncertain.

8 B is correct. Writing covered calls also generates additional income for an equity portfolio, but doing so limits the upside from share price appreciation of the underlying shares. Therefore, Statement 2 is correct.

A is incorrect because dividends on loaned stock are "manufactured" by the stock borrower for the stock lender—that is, the stock borrower ensures that the stock lender is compensated for any dividends that the lender would have received had the stock not been loaned. Therefore, Statement 1 is incorrect. Frey is incorrect in stating that the funds would miss out on dividend income on lent securities.

READING
16

Passive Equity Investing

by David M. Smith, PhD, CFA, and Kevin K. Yousif, CFA

David M. Smith, PhD, CFA, is at the University at Albany, New York (USA). Kevin K. Yousif, CFA, is at LSIA Wealth & Institutional (USA).

LEARNING OUTCOMES	
Mastery	The candidate should be able to:
☐	a. discuss considerations in choosing a benchmark for a passively managed equity portfolio;
☐	b. compare passive factor-based strategies to market-capitalization-weighted indexing;
☐	c. compare different approaches to passive equity investing;
☐	d. compare the full replication, stratified sampling, and optimization approaches for the construction of passively managed equity portfolios;
☐	e. discuss potential causes of tracking error and methods to control tracking error for passively managed equity portfolios;
☐	f. explain sources of return and risk to a passively managed equity portfolio.

1. CHOOSING A BENCHMARK: INDEXES AS A BASIS FOR INVESTMENT

a discuss considerations in choosing a benchmark for a passively managed equity portfolio;

This reading provides a broad overview of passive equity investing, including index selection, portfolio management techniques, and the analysis of investment results.

Although they mean different things, passive equity investing and indexing have become nearly synonymous in the investment industry. Indexing refers to strategies intended to replicate the performance of benchmark indexes, such as the S&P 500 Index, the Topix 100, the FTSE 100, and the MSCI All-Country World Index. The main advantages of indexing include low costs, broad diversification, and tax efficiency. Indexing is the purest form of a more general idea: passive investing. Passive

© 2018 CFA Institute. All rights reserved.

investing refers to any rules-based, transparent, and investable strategy that does not involve identifying mispriced individual securities. Unlike indexing, however, passive investing can include investing in a changing set of market segments that are selected by the portfolio manager.

Studies over the years have reported support for passive investing. Renshaw and Feldstein (1960) observe that the returns of professionally managed portfolios trailed the returns on the principal index of that time, the Dow Jones Industrial Average. They also conclude that the index would be a good basis for what they termed an "unmanaged investment company." French (2008) indicates that the cost of passive investing is lower than the cost of active management.

Further motivation for passive investing comes from studies that examine the return and risk consequences of stock selection, which involves identifying mispriced securities. This differs from asset allocation, which involves selecting asset class investments that are, themselves, essentially passive indexed-based portfolios. Brinson, Hood, and Beebower (1986) find a dominant role for asset allocation rather than security selection in explaining return variability. With passive investing, portfolio managers eschew the idea of security selection, concluding that the benefits do not justify the costs.

The efficient market hypothesis gave credence to investors' interest in indexes by theorizing that stock prices incorporate all relevant information—implying that after costs, the majority of active investors could not consistently outperform the market. With this backdrop, investment managers began to offer strategies to replicate the returns of stock market indexes as early as 1971.

In comparison with passive investing strategies, active management of an investment portfolio requires a substantial commitment of personnel, technological resources, and time spent on analysis and management that can involve significant costs. Consequently, passive portfolio fees charged to investors are generally much lower than fees charged by their active managers. This fee differential represents the most significant and enduring advantage of passive management.

Another advantage is that passive managers seeking to track an index can generally achieve their objective. Passive managers model their clients' portfolios to the benchmark's constituent securities and weights as reported by the index provider, thereby replicating the benchmark. The skill of a passive manager is apparent in the ability to trade, report, and explain the performance of a client's portfolio. Gross-of-fees performance among passive managers tends to be similar, so much of the industry views passive managers as undifferentiated apart from their scope of offerings and client-servicing capabilities.

Investors of passively managed funds may seek market return, otherwise known as beta exposure, and do not seek outperformance, known as alpha. A focus on beta is based on a single-factor model: the capital asset pricing model.

Since the turn of the millennium, passive factor-based strategies, which are based on more than a single factor, have become more prevalent as investors gain a different understanding of what drives investment returns. These strategies maintain the low-cost advantage of index funds and provide a different expected return stream based on exposure to such factors as style, capitalization, volatility, and quality.

This reading contains the following sections. Sections 1–3 focus on how to choose a passive benchmark, including weighting considerations. Sections 4 and 5 look at how to gain exposure to the desired index, whether through a pooled investment, a derivatives-based approach, or a separately managed account. Section 6 describes passive portfolio construction techniques. Section 7 discusses how a portfolio manager can control tracking error against the benchmark, including the sources of tracking error. Section 8 introduces methods a portfolio manager can use to attribute the sources of return in the portfolio, including country returns, currency returns, sector returns, and security returns. This section also describes sources of portfolio risk. A summary of key points concludes the reading.

1.1 Choosing a Benchmark

Investors initially used benchmark indexes solely to compare the performance of an active portfolio manager against the performance of an unmanaged market portfolio. Indexes are now used as a basis for investment strategies. Many investment vehicles try to replicate index performance, which has contributed to a proliferation of indexes. Indeed, many indexes are developed specifically as a basis for new investment securities.

Successful investors choose their performance benchmarks with care. It is surprising that investors who spend countless hours analyzing the investment process and past performance of an active management strategy may accept a strategy based on a benchmark index without question. A comprehensive analysis of the creation methodology and performance of an index is just as important to investors as the analysis of an active strategy.

1.1.1 Indexes as a Basis for Investment

For an index to become the basis for an equity investment strategy, it must meet three initial requirements. It must be rules-based, transparent, and investable.

Examples of rules include criteria for including a constituent stock and the frequency with which weights are rebalanced. An active manager may use rules and guidelines, but it is often impossible for others to replicate the active manager's decision process. Index rules, on the other hand, must be objective, consistent, and predictable.

Transparency may be the most important requirement because passive investors expect to understand the rules underlying their investment choices. Benchmark providers disclose the rules used and constituents in creating their indexes without any black-box methodologies, which assures investors that indexes will continue to represent the intended strategy.

Equity index benchmarks are investable when their performance can be replicated in the market. For example, the FTSE 100 Index is an investable index because its constituent securities can be purchased easily on the London Stock Exchange. In contrast, most investors cannot track hedge fund-of-funds indexes, such as the HFRI series of indexes, because of the difficulty of buying the constituent hedge funds. Another example of a non-investable index is the Value Line Geometric Index, which is a multiplicative average price. In other words, the value of the index is obtained by multiplying the prices and taking a root corresponding to the number of stocks. This index is not useful for investing purposes because it cannot be replicated.

Certain features of individual securities make them non-investable as index constituents. Many stock indexes "free-float adjust" their shares outstanding, which means that they count only shares available for trade by the public, excluding those shares that are held by founders, governments, or other companies. When a company's shares that are floated in the market are a small fraction of the total shares outstanding, trading can result in disproportionate effects. Similarly, stocks for which trading volume is a small fraction of the total shares outstanding are likely to have low liquidity and commensurately high trading costs. Many indexes consequently require that stocks have float and average shares traded above a certain percent of shares outstanding.

Equity index providers include CRSP, FTSE Russell, Morningstar, MSCI, and S&P Dow Jones. These index providers publicize the rules underlying their indexes, communicate changes in the constituent securities, and report performance. For a fee, they may also provide data to investors who want to replicate the underlying basket of securities.

Index providers have taken steps to make their indexes more investable. One key decision concerns when individual stocks will migrate from one index to another. As a stock increases in market capitalization (market cap) over time, it might move from small-cap to mid-cap to large-cap status. Some index providers have adopted policies intended to limit stock migration problems and keep trading costs low for investors who replicate indexes. Among these policies are buffering and packeting. **Buffering** involves establishing ranges around breakpoints that define whether a stock belongs in one index or another. As long as stocks remain within the buffer zone, they stay in their current index. For example, the MSCI USA Large Cap Index contains the 300 largest companies in the US equity market. But a company currently in the MSCI USA Mid Cap Index must achieve a rank as the 200th largest stock to move up to the Large Cap Index. Similarly, a large-cap constituent must shrink and be the 451st largest stock to move down to the Mid Cap Index. Size rankings may change almost every day with market price movements, so buffering makes index transitions a more gradual and orderly process.

The effect of buffering is demonstrated with the MSCI USA Large Cap Index during the regularly scheduled May 2016 reconstitution. The MSCI USA Large Cap Index consists of stocks of US-based companies that meet the criterion to be considered for large cap. Further, the MSCI USA Large Cap Index is intended to represent the largest 70% of the market capitalization of the US equity market.

At each rebalance date, MSCI sets a cutoff value for the smallest company in the index and then sets the buffer value at 67% of the cutoff value. During the May 2016 rebalance, the cutoff market capitalization (market cap) of the smallest company in the index was USD 15,707 million; so, the buffer value was USD 10,524 million or approximately USD 10.5 billion.

Whole Foods Market, a grocery store operating primarily in the United States, had experienced a drop in market value from USD 15.3 billion in May of 2015 to USD 10.4 billion in May of 2016. The drop in value put the market cap of Whole Foods Market at a lower value than the acceptable buffer. That is, Whole Foods Market was valued at USD 10.4 billion, which was below the buffer point of USD 10.5 billion. Per the stated rules, Whole Foods Market was removed from the MSCI USA Large Cap Index and was added to the MSCI USA Mid Cap Index.

Packeting involves splitting stock positions into multiple parts. Let us say that a stock is currently in a mid-cap index. If its capitalization increases and breaches the breakpoint between mid-cap and large-cap indexes, a portion of the total holding is transferred to the large-cap index but the rest stays in the mid-cap index. On the next reconstitution date, if the stock value remains large-cap and all other qualifications are met, the remainder of the shares are moved out of the mid-cap and into the large-cap index. A policy of packeting can keep portfolio turnover and trading costs low. The Center for Research in Security Prices (CRSP) uses packeting in the creation of the CRSP family of indexes.

1.1.2 Considerations When Choosing a Benchmark Index

The first consideration when choosing a benchmark index is the desired *market exposure*, which is driven by the objectives and constraints in the investor's investment policy statement (IPS). For equity portfolios, the choices to be made include the market segment (broad versus sectors; domestic versus international), equity capitalization (large, mid, or small), style (value, growth, or blend/core), exposure, and other constituent characteristics (e.g., high or low momentum, low volatility, and quality) that are considered risk factors.

The choice of market depends on the investor's perspective. The investor's domicile, risk tolerance, liquidity needs, and legal considerations all influence the decision. For example, the decision will proceed differently for an Indian institutional investor than for a US-based individual investor. In India, the domestic equity universe is much smaller than in the United States, making the Indian investor more likely to invest globally. But a domestic investment does not carry with it the complexities of cross-border transactions.

A common way to implement the domestic/international investment decision is to use country indexes. Some indexes cover individual countries, and others encompass multiple country markets. For example, the global equity market can also be broken into geographic regions or based on development status (developed, emerging, or frontier markets). The US market is frequently treated as distinct from other developed markets because of its large size.

Another decision element is the *risk-factor exposure* that the index provides. As described later, equity risk factors can arise from several sources, including the holdings' market capitalization (the Size factor), investment style (growth vs. value, or the Value factor), price momentum (the Momentum factor), and liquidity (the Liquidity factor).

The Size factor is perhaps the best known of these. Market history and empirical studies show that small-cap stocks tend to be riskier and provide a higher long-term return than large-cap stocks. This return difference is considered a risk factor. To the extent that a benchmark's return is correlated with this risk factor, the benchmark has exposure to the Size factor. A similar argument applies to the Value factor, which is calculated as the return on value stocks less the return on growth stocks.

Practically speaking, some investors consider certain size ranges (e.g., small cap) to be more amenable to alpha generation using active management and others (e.g., large cap) amenable to lower-cost passive management. Size classifications range from mega cap to micro cap. Classifications are not limited to individual size categories. For example, many indexes seek to provide equity exposure to both small- and mid-cap companies ("smid-cap" indexes). Investors who desire exposure across the capitalization spectrum may use an "all-cap" index. Such indexes do not necessarily contain all stocks in the market; they usually just combine representative stocks from each of the size ranges. Note that a large-cap stock in an emerging market may have the same capitalization as a small-cap stock in a developed country. Accordingly, index providers usually classify company capitalizations in the context of the local market environment.

Equity benchmark selection also involves the investor's preference for exposure on the growth vs. value style spectrum. Growth stocks exhibit such characteristics as high price momentum, high P/Es, and high EPS growth. Value stocks, however, may exhibit high dividend yields, low P/Es, and low price-to-book value ratios. Depending on their basic philosophy and market outlook, investors may have a strong preference for growth or value.

Exhibit 1 shows the number of available total-return equity indexes[1] in various classifications available worldwide. Broad market exposure is provided by nearly two-thirds of all indexes, while the others track industry sectors. Developed market indexes are about twice as common as emerging-market indexes. The majority of broad market indexes cover the all-cap space or are otherwise focused on large-cap and mid-cap stocks.

Exhibit 1 Characteristics of Equity Indexes

Equity indexes	9,165

(continued)

---

[1] Total-return indexes account for both price and income (e.g., from cash dividends) returns to the constituent securities. The value of price-return indexes changes only because of return from the constituents' price changes.

Exhibit 1 (Continued)	
Broad market indexes	5,658
Sector indexes	3,479
Not classified	28
Of the 5,658 broad market indexes:	
Developed markets	2,903
Emerging markets	1,701
Developed & emerging markets	1,050
Not classified	4
Of the 5,658 broad market indexes:	
All-cap stocks	1,892
Large-cap stocks	121
Large-cap and mid-cap stocks	2,100
Mid-cap stocks	657
Mid- and small-cap stocks	39
Small-cap stocks	846
Not classified	3

Source: Morningstar Direct, May 2017.

Once the investor has settled on the market, capitalization, and style of benchmark, the next step is to explore the method used in constructing and maintaining the benchmark index.

2. CHOOSING A BENCHMARK: INDEX CONSTRUCTION METHODOLOGIES

a discuss considerations in choosing a benchmark for a passively managed equity portfolio;

Equity index providers differ in their stock inclusion methods, ranging from **exhaustive** to **selective** in their investment universes. Exhaustive stock inclusion strategies are those that select every constituent of a universe, while selective approaches target only those securities with certain characteristics. The CRSP US Total Market Index has perhaps the most exhaustive set of constituents in the US market. This market-cap-weighted index includes approximately 4,000 publicly traded stocks from across the market-cap spectrum. In contrast, the S&P 500 Index embodies a selective approach and aims to provide exposure to US large-cap stocks. Its constituent securities are selected using a committee process and are based on both size and broad industry affiliation.

The weighting method used in constructing an index influences its performance. One of the most common weighting methods is market-cap weighting. The equity market cap of a constituent company is its stock price multiplied by the number of shares outstanding. Each constituent company's weight in the index is calculated as its market capitalization divided by the total market capitalization of all constituents of the index. In the development of the capital asset pricing model, the capitalization-weighted market portfolio is mean–variance efficient, meaning that it offers the highest return for a given level of risk. To the extent a capitalization-weighted equity index is a reasonable proxy for the market portfolio, the tracking portfolio may be close to mean–variance efficient.

A further advantage of the capitalization-weighted approach is that it reflects a strategy's investment capacity. A cap-weighted index can be thought of as a liquidity-weighted index because the largest-cap stocks tend to have the highest liquidity and the greatest capacity to handle investor flows at a manageable cost. Many investor portfolios tend to be biased toward large-cap stocks and use benchmarks that reflect that bias.

The most common form of market-cap weighting is free-float weighting, which adjusts each constituent's shares outstanding for closely held shares that are not generally available to the investing public. The process to determine the free-float-adjusted shares outstanding relies on publicly available information to determine the holders of the shares and whether those shares would be available for purchase in the marketplace. One reason to adjust a company's share count may include strategic holdings by governments, affiliated companies, founders, and employees. Another less common reason is to account for limitations on foreign ownership of a company; these limitations typically represent rules that are generally set up by a governmental entity through regulation.

Adjusting a company's shares outstanding for float can be a complex task and often requires an index provider to reach out to the company's shareholder services unit or to rely on analytical judgements. Although all data used in determining a company's free-float-adjusted shares outstanding are public information, the various index providers often report a different number of shares outstanding for the same security. This variation in reported shares outstanding can often be attributed to small differences in their methodologies.

In a *price-weighted* index, the weight of each stock is its price per share divided by the sum of all share prices in the index. A price-weighted index can be interpreted as a portfolio that consists of one share of each constituent company. Although some price-weighted indexes, such as the Dow Jones Industrial Average and the Nikkei 225, have high visibility as indicators of day-to-day market movements, price-weighted investment approaches are not commonly used by portfolio managers. A stock split for any constituent of the index complicates the index calculation. The weight in the index of the stock that split decreases, and the index divisor decreases as well. With its divisor changed, the index ceases to be a simple average of the constituent stocks' prices. For price-weighted indexes, the assumption that the same number of shares is held in each component stock is a shortcoming, because very few market participants invest in that way.

Equally weighted indexes produce the least-concentrated portfolios. Such indexes have constituent weights of $1/n$, where n represents the number of stocks in the index. Equal weighting of stocks within an index is considered a naive strategy because it does not show preference toward any single stock. The reduction of single stock concentration risk and slow changing sector exposures make equal weighting attractive to many investors.

As noted by Zeng and Luo (2013), broad market equally weighted indexes are factor-indifferent and the weighting randomizes factor mispricing. Equal weighting also produces higher volatility than cap weighting, one reason being that it imparts a small-cap bias to the portfolio. Equal weights deviate from market weights most dramatically for large-cap indexes, which contain mega-cap stocks. Constrained market-cap ranges such as mid-cap indexes, even if market weighted, tend to have relatively uniform weights.

Equally weighted indexes require regular rebalancing because immediately after trading in the constituent stocks begins, the weights are no longer equal. Most investors use a regular reweighting schedule. Standard & Poor's offers its S&P 500 Index in an equally weighted format and rebalances the index to equal weights once each quarter. Therein would appear to lie a misleading aspect of equally weighted indexes. For a 91-day quarter, the index is not equally weighted for 90/91 = 99% of the time.

Another drawback of equal weighting is its limited investment capacity. The smallest-cap constituents of an equally weighted index may have low liquidity, which means that investors cannot purchase a large number of shares without causing price changes. Zeng and Luo (2013) address this issue by assuming that 10% of shares in the cap-weighted S&P 100 and 500 and 5% of shares in the cap-weighted S&P 400 and 600 indexes are currently held in cap-weighted indexing strategies without any appreciable liquidity problems. They then focus on the smallest-cap constituent of each index as of December 2012, and they determine the value that 10% (5%) of its market capitalization represents. Finally, they multiply this amount by the number of stocks in the index to estimate the total investment capacity for tracking each of the S&P equally weighted equity indexes. Zeng's and Luo's estimates are shown in Exhibit 2.

Exhibit 2: Estimated Investment Capacity of Equally Weighted (EW) Equity Indexes

Index	Capitalization Category	Estimated Capacity
S&P 100 EW	Mega cap	USD 176 billion
S&P 500 EW	Large cap	USD 82 billion
S&P 400 EW	Mid cap	USD 8 billion
S&P 600 EW	Small cap	USD 2 billion

Source: Zeng and Luo (2013).

Qin and Singal (2015) show that equally weighted portfolios have a natural advantage over cap-weighted portfolios. To the extent that any of the constituent stocks are mispriced, equally weighted portfolios will experience return superiority as the stock prices move up or down toward their correct intrinsic value. Because of the aforementioned need to rebalance back to equal weights, Qin and Singal find that the advantage largely vanishes when taxes and transaction costs are considered. However, based on their results, tax-exempt institutional investors could experience superior returns from equal weighting.

Other non-cap-weighted indexes are weighted based on such attributes as a company or stock's fundamental characteristics (e.g., sales, income, or dividends). Discussed in more detail later, fundamental weighting delinks a constituent stock's portfolio weight from its market value. The philosophy behind fundamental weighting is that although stock prices may become over- or undervalued, the market price will eventually converge to a level implied by the fundamental attributes.

Market-cap-weighted indexes and fundamentally weighted indexes share attractive characteristics, including low cost, rules-based construction, transparency, and investability. Their philosophies, however, are different. Market-cap-weighted portfolios are based on the efficient market hypothesis, while fundamentally weighted indexes look to exploit possible inefficiencies in market pricing.

An important concern in benchmark selection relates to how concentrated the index is. In this case, the concept of the effective number of stocks, which is an indication of portfolio concentration, can provide important information. An index that has a high degree of stock concentration or a low effective number of stocks may be relatively

Choosing a Benchmark: Index Construction Methodologies

undiversified. Woerheide and Persson (1993) show that the Herfindahl–Hirschman Index (HHI) is a valid measure of stock-concentration risk in a portfolio, and Hannam and Jamet (2017) demonstrate its use by practitioners. The HHI is calculated as the sum of the constituent weightings squared, as shown in Equation 1:

$$\text{HHI} = \sum_{i=1}^{n} w_i^2 \qquad (1)$$

where w_i is the weight of stock i in the portfolio.

The HHI can range in value from $1/n$, where n is equal to the number of securities held, to 1.0. An HHI of $1/n$ would signify an equally weighted portfolio, and a value of 1.0 would signify portfolio concentration in a single security.

Using the HHI, one can estimate the effective (or equivalent) number of stocks, held in equal weights, that would mimic the concentration level of the chosen index. The effective number of stocks for a portfolio is calculated as the reciprocal of the HHI, as shown in Equation 2.

$$\text{Effective number of stocks} = \frac{1}{\sum_{i=1}^{n} w_i^2} = 1/\text{HHI} \qquad (2)$$

Malevergne, Santa-Clara, and Sornette (2009) demonstrate that cap-weighted indexes have a surprisingly low effective number of stocks. Consider the NASDAQ 100, a US-based market-cap-weighted index consisting of 100 stocks. If the index were weighted uniformly, each stock's weight would be 0.01 (1%). In May 2017, the constituent weights ranged from 0.123 for Apple, Inc., to 0.0016 for Liberty Global plc, a ratio of 77:1. Weights for the top five stocks totaled almost 0.38 (38%), a significant allocation to those securities. Across all stocks in the index, the median weight was 0.0039 (that is, 0.39%). The effective number of stocks can be estimated by squaring the weights for the stocks, summing the results, and calculating the reciprocal of that figure. The squared weights for the NASDAQ 100 stocks summed to 0.0404, the reciprocal of which is 1/0.0404 = 24.75, the effective number of stocks. Thus, the 100 stocks in the index had a concentration level that can be thought of as being equivalent to approximately 25 stocks held in equal weights.

EXAMPLE 1

Effective Number of Stocks

A market-cap-weighted index contains 50 stocks. The five largest-cap stocks have weights of 0.089, 0.080, 0.065, 0.059, and 0.053. The bottom 45 stocks represent the remaining weight of 0.654, and the sum of the squares of those weights is 0.01405. What are the portfolio's Herfindahl–Hirschman Index and effective number of stocks held?

Solution:

The stocks, their weights, and their squared weights are shown in Exhibit 3.

Exhibit 3 Calculations for Effective Number of Stocks

Stock	Weight	Squared Weight
1	0.089	0.00792
2	0.080	0.00640
3	0.065	0.00423

(continued)

Exhibit 3 (Continued)

Stock	Weight	Squared Weight
4	0.059	0.00348
5	0.053	0.00281
Stocks 6–50	0.654	Sum of squared weights for stocks 6–50: 0.01405
Total for stocks 1–50	1.000	0.03889

The HHI is shown in the final row: 0.03889. The reciprocal of the HHI is 1/0.03889 = 25.71. Thus, the effective number of stocks is approximately 26. The fact that the portfolio weights are far from being a uniform 2% across the 50 stocks makes the effective number of stocks held in equal weights less than 26.

The stock market crises of 2000 and 2008 brought heightened attention to investment strategies that are defensive or volatility reducing. For example, some income-oriented investors are drawn to strategies that weight benchmark constituents based on the dividend yield of each stock. Volatility weighting calculates the volatility of each constituent stock and weights the index based on the inverse of each stock's relative volatility. A related method produces a minimum-variance index using mean–variance optimization.

Exhibit 4 shows the various methods for weighting the constituent securities of broad-based, non-industry-sector, total-return equity indexes.

Exhibit 4 Equity Index Constituent Weighting Methods

Weighting Method	Number of Indexes
Market-cap, free-float adjusted	5,182
Market-cap-weighted	169
Multi-factor-weighted	143
Equal-weighted	63
Dividend-weighted	36

Source: Morningstar Direct, May 2017.

Another consideration in how an index is constructed involves its periodic rebalancing and reconstitution schedule. Reconstitution of an index frequently involves the addition and deletion of index constituents, while rebalancing refers to the periodic reweighting of those constituents. Index reconstitution and rebalancing create turnover. The turnover for developed-market, large-cap indexes that are infrequently reconstituted tends to be low, while benchmarks constructed using stock selection rather than exhaustive inclusion have higher turnover. As seen in Exhibit 5, both rebalancing and reconstitution occur with varied frequency, although the former is slightly more frequent.

Exhibit 5 Index Rebalancing/Reconstitution Frequency for Broad Equity Market Total-Return Indexes

Frequency	Rebalancing	Reconstitution
Daily	3	2
Monthly	4	3
Quarterly	2,481	1,379
Semi-annually	2,743	3,855
Annually	260	308
As needed	74	13

Note: The totals for the Rebalancing and Reconstitution columns differ slightly, as does the index total in Exhibit 4.
Source: Morningstar Direct, May 2017.

The method of reconstitution may produce additional effects. When reconstitution occurs, index-tracking portfolios, mutual funds, and ETFs will want to hold the newly included names and sell the deleted names. The demand created by investors seeking to track an index can push up the stock prices of added companies while depressing the prices of the deleted ones. Research shows that this produces a significant price effect in each case. Depending on the reconstitution method used by index publishers, arbitrageurs may be able to anticipate the changes and front-run the trades that will be made by passive investors. In some cases, the index rules are written so that the decision to add or remove an index constituent is voted on by a committee maintained by the index provider. Where a committee makes the final decision, the changes become difficult to guess ahead of time. In other cases, investors know the precise method used for reconstitution so guessing is often successful.

Chen, Noronha, and Singal (2004) find that constituent changes for indexes that reconstitute using subjective criteria are often more difficult for arbitrageurs to predict than indexes that use objective criteria. Even indexes that use objective criteria for reconstitution often announce the changes several weeks before they are implemented. Stocks near the breakpoint between small-cap and large-cap indexes are especially vulnerable to reconstitution-induced price changes. The smallest-cap stocks in the Russell 1000 Large-Cap Index have a low weight in that cap-weighted index. After any of those stocks are demoted to the Russell 2000 Small-Cap Index, they are likely to have some of the highest weights. Petajisto (2010) shows that the process of moving in that direction tends to be associated with increases in stock prices, while movements into the large-cap index tend to have negative effects. He also concludes that transparency in reconstitution is a virtue rather than a drawback.

A final consideration is investability. As stated in a prior section, an effective benchmark must be investable in that its constituent stocks are available for timely purchase in a liquid trading environment. Indexes that represent the performance of a market segment that is not available for direct ownership by investors must be replicated through derivatives strategies, which for reasons explained later may be sub-optimal for many investors.

3 CHOOSING A BENCHMARK: FACTOR-BASED STRATEGIES

b compare passive factor-based strategies to market-capitalization-weighted indexing;

Traditional indexing generally involves tracking the returns to a market-cap-weighted benchmark index. Yet most benchmark returns are driven by factors, which are risk exposures that can be identified and isolated. An investor who wants access only to specific aspects of an index's return stream can invest in a subset of constituent securities that best reflect the investor's preferred risk factors, such as Size, Value, Quality, and Momentum. The goal of being exposed to one or more specific risk factors will also drive the choice of a benchmark index.

Factor-based strategies are an increasingly popular variation on traditional indexing, and they have important implications for benchmark selection. Some elaboration on the topic is warranted. The origin of passive factor-based strategies dates to at least the observation by Banz (1981) that small-cap stocks tend to outperform large-cap stocks. Work by Fama and French (2015) shows that at least five risk factors explain US equity market returns. Their asset pricing model incorporates the market risk premium from the CAPM plus factors for a company's size, book-to-market (value or growth style classification), operating profitability, and investment intensity. Consistent with prior research, they find a positive risk premium for small companies and value stocks over large companies and growth stocks. They measure operating profitability as the previous year's gross profit minus selling, general, and administrative expenses as well as interest expense—all divided by the beginning book value of equity. Investment intensity is measured as the growth rate in total assets in the previous year.

Although the concepts underlying passive factor investing, sometimes marketed as "smart beta," have been known for a long time, investors' use of the technique increased dramatically over time. There presently exist many passive investment vehicles and indexes that allow access to such factors as Value, Size, Momentum, Volatility, and Quality, which are described in Exhibit 6. Many investors use their beliefs about market conditions to apply factor tilts to their portfolios. This is the process of intentionally overweighting and underweighting certain risk factors. Passive factor-based strategies can be used in place of or to complement a market-cap-weighted indexed portfolio.

Exhibit 6 Common Equity Risk Factors

Factor	Description
Growth	Growth stocks are generally associated with high-performing companies with an above-average net income growth rate and high P/Es.
Value	Value stocks are generally associated with mature companies that have stable net incomes or are experiencing a cyclical downturn. Value stocks frequently have low price-to-book and price-to-earnings ratios as well as high dividend yields.
Size	A tilt toward smaller size involves buying stocks with low float-adjusted market capitalization.
Yield	Yield is identified as dividend yield relative to other stocks. High dividend-yielding stocks may provide excess returns in low interest rate environments.

Exhibit 6	(Continued)
Factor	**Description**
Momentum	Momentum attempts to capture further returns from stocks that have experienced an above-average increase in price during the prior period.
Quality	Quality stocks might include those with consistent earnings and dividend growth, high cash flow to earnings, and low debt-to-equity ratios.
Volatility	Low volatility is generally desired by investors seeking to lower their downside risk. Volatility is often measured as the standard deviation of stock returns.

Passive factor-based equity strategies use passive rules, but they frequently involve active decision making: Decisions on the timing and degree of factor exposure are being made. As Jacobs and Levy (2014) note, the difference between passive factor investing and conventional active management is that with the former, active management takes place up front rather than continuously. Relative to broad-market-cap-weighting, passive factor-based strategies tend to concentrate risk exposures, leaving investors exposed during periods when a chosen risk factor is out of favor. The observation that even strong risk factors experience periods of underperformance has led many investors toward multi-factor approaches. Passive factor-based strategies tend to be transparent in terms of factor selection, weighting, and rebalancing. Possible risks include ease of replication by other investors, which can produce overcrowding and reduce the realized advantages of a strategy.

Fundamental Factor Indexing

Capitalization weighting of indexes and index-tracking portfolios involve treating each constituent stock as if investors were buying all the available shares. Arnott, Hsu, and Moore (2005) developed an alternative weighting method based on the notion that if stock market prices deviate from their intrinsic value, larger-cap stocks will exhibit this tendency more than smaller-cap stocks. Thus, traditional cap weighting is likely to overweight overpriced stocks and underweight underpriced stocks. The combination is intended to make cap-weighting inferior to a method that does not use market prices as a basis for weighting.

The idea advanced by Arnott, Hsu, and Moore is to use a cluster of company fundamentals—book value, cash flow, revenue, sales, dividends, and employee count—as a basis for weighting each company. A separate weighting is developed for each fundamental measure. In the case of a large company, its sales might be 1.3% of the total sales for all companies in the index, so its weight for this criterion would be 0.013. For each company, the weightings are averaged across all of the fundamental measures, and those average values represent the weight of each stock in a "composite fundamentals" index.

The authors show that over a 43-year period, a fundamental index would have outperformed a related cap-weighted index by an average of almost 200 basis points per year. They hasten to add that the result should not necessarily be considered alpha, because the fundamental portfolio provides heightened exposure to the Value and Size factors.

Since the time of the seminal article's publication, fundamental-weighted indexing strategies for country markets as well as market segments have gained in popularity and attracted a large amount of investor funds.

No matter the style of a passive factor-based strategy, its ultimate goal is to improve upon the risk or return performance of the market-cap-weighted strategy. Passive factor-based approaches gain exposure to many of the same risk factors that active managers seek to exploit. The strategies can be return oriented, risk oriented, or diversification oriented.

Return-oriented factor-based strategies include dividend yield strategies, momentum strategies, and fundamentally weighted strategies. Dividend yield strategies can include dividend growth as well as absolute dividend yield. The low interest rate environment, which followed the 2008–2009 global financial crisis, led to an increase in dividend yield strategies as investors sought reliable income streams. An example index is the S&P 1500 High Yield Dividend Aristocrats Index. This index selects securities within the S&P 1500 that increased dividends in each of the past 20 years and then weights those securities by their dividend yield, with the highest dividend-yielding stocks receiving the highest weight.

Another return-oriented strategy is momentum, which is generally defined by the amount of a stock's excess price return relative to the market over a specified time period. Momentum can be determined in various ways. One example is MSCI's Momentum Index family, in which a stock's most recent 12-month and 6-month price performance are determined and then used to weight the securities in the index.[2]

Risk-oriented strategies take several forms, seeking to reduce downside volatility and overall portfolio risk. For example, risk-oriented factor strategies include volatility weighting, where all of an index's constituents are held and then weighted by the inverse of their relative price volatility. Price volatility is defined differently by each index provider, but two common methods include using standard deviation of price returns for the past 252 trading days (approximately one calendar year) or the weekly standard deviation of price returns for the past 156 weeks (approximately three calendar years).

Volatility weighting can take other forms as well. Minimum variance investing is another risk reducing strategy, and it requires access to a mean–variance optimizer. Minimum variance weights are those that minimize the volatility of the portfolio's returns based on historical price returns, subject to certain constraints on the index's construction. Constraints can include limitations on sector over/under weights, country selection limits, and limits on single stock concentration levels. Mean–variance optimizer programs can be accessed from such vendors as Axioma, BARRA, and Northfield.

Risk weighting has the advantages of being simple to understand and providing a way to reduce absolute volatility and downside returns. However, the development of these strategies is based on past return data, which may not reflect future returns. Thus, investors will not always achieve their objectives despite the strategy's stated goal.

Diversification-oriented strategies include equally weighted indexes and maximum-diversification strategies. Equal weighting is intuitive and is discussed elsewhere in the reading as having a low amount of single-stock risk. The low single-stock risk comes by way of the weighting structure of $1/n$, where n is equal to the number of securities held. Choueifaty and Coignard (2008) define maximum diversification by calculating a "diversification ratio" as the ratio of the weighted average volatilities divided by the portfolio volatility. Diversification strategies then can attempt to maximize future diversification by determining portfolio weights using past price return volatilities.

Portfolio managers who pursue factor-based strategies often use multiple benchmark indexes, including a factor-based index and a broad market-cap-weighted index. This mismatch in benchmarks can also produce an unintended mismatch in returns,

---

[2] The indexes are rebalanced semi-annually. More information can be found at www.msci.com/eqb/methodology/meth_docs/MSCI_Momentum_Indices_Methodology.pdf.

known as tracking error, from the perspective of the end investor who has modeled a portfolio against a broad market-cap-weighted index. Tracking error indicates how closely the portfolio behaves like its benchmark and is measured as the standard deviation of the differences between a portfolio's returns and its benchmark returns. The concept of tracking error is discussed in detail later.

Finally, passive factor-based strategies can involve higher management fees and trading commissions than broad-market indexing. Factor-based index providers and managers demand a premium price for the creation and management of these strategies, and those fees decrease performance. Also, commission costs can be higher in factor-based strategies than they are in market-cap-weighted strategies. All else equal, higher costs will lead to lower net performance.

Passive factor-based approaches may offer an advantage for those investors who believe it is prudent to seek out groups of stocks that are poised to have desirable return patterns. Active managers also believe in seeking those stocks, but active management brings the burden of higher fees that can eat into any outperformance. Active managers may also own stocks that are outside the benchmark and are, thus, incompatible with the investment strategy. In contrast, passive factor-based strategies can provide nearly pure exposure to specific market segments, and there are numerous benchmarks against which to measure performance. Fees are restricted because factor-based strategies are rules based and thus do not require constant monitoring. An investor's process of changing exposures to specific risk factors as market conditions change is known as factor rotation. With factor rotation, investors can use passive vehicles to make active bets on future market conditions.

APPROACHES TO PASSIVE EQUITY INVESTING: POOLED INVESTMENTS

4

c   compare different approaches to passive equity investing;

Passive equity investment strategies may be implemented using several approaches, from the do-it-yourself method of buying stocks to hiring a subadviser to create and maintain the investment strategy. Passively managed investment strategies can be replicated by any internal or external portfolio manager who has the index data, trading tools, and necessary skills. In contrast, actively managed funds each, in theory, have a unique investment strategy developed by the active portfolio manager.

This section discusses different approaches to gain access to an investment strategy's desired performance stream: pooled investments (e.g., mutual funds and exchange-traded funds), derivatives-based portfolios (using options, futures, and swaps contracts), and direct investment in the stocks underlying the strategy.

Some passive investments are managed to establish a target beta, and managers are judged on how closely they meet that target. Portfolio managers commonly use futures and open-end mutual funds to transform a position (in cash, for example) and obtain the desired equity exposure. This process is known as "equitizing." The choice of which method to use is largely determined by the financing costs of rolling the futures contracts over time.[3] With multinational indexes, it can be expedient to buy a set of complementary exchange-traded funds to replicate market returns for the various countries.

4.1 Pooled Investments

Pooled investments are the most convenient approach for the average investor because they are easy to purchase, hold, and sell. This section covers conventional open-end mutual funds and exchange-traded funds (ETFs).

The Qualidex Fund, started in 1970, was the first open-end index mutual fund available to retail investors. It was designed to track the Dow Jones Industrial Average. The Vanguard S&P 500 Index Fund, started in 1975, was the first retail fund to attract investors on a large scale. The primary advantage provided by a mutual fund purchase is its ease of investing and record keeping.

Investors who want to invest in a passively managed mutual fund must take the same steps as those investing in actively managed ones. First, a needs analysis must be undertaken to decide on the investor's return and risk objectives as well as investment constraints, and then to find a corresponding strategy. For example, risk-averse equity investors may seek a low volatility strategy, while investors looking to match the broad market may prefer an all-cap market-cap-weighted strategy. Once the need has been identified, it is likely that a mutual fund-based strategy can be built to match that need.

Traditional mutual fund shares can be purchased directly from the adviser who manages the fund, through a fund marketplace, or through an individual financial adviser. The process is the same for any mutual fund whether passively or actively managed. Investment companies generally have websites and call centers to help their prospective investors transact shares.

A fund marketplace is a brokerage company that offers funds from different providers. The advantage of buying a mutual fund from a fund marketplace is the ease of purchasing a mutual fund from different providers while maintaining a single account for streamlined record keeping.

A financial adviser can also help in purchasing a fund by offering the guidance needed to identify the strategy, providing the single account to house the fund shares, and gaining access to lower-cost share classes that may not be available to all investors.

No matter how mutual fund shares are purchased, the primary benefits of investing passively using mutual funds are low costs and the convenience of the fund structure. The manager of the passively managed fund handles all of the needed rebalancing, reconstitution, and other changes that are required to keep the investment portfolio in line with the index. Passively managed strategies require constant maintenance and care to reinvest cash from dividends and to execute the buys and sells required to match the additions and deletions of securities to the index. The portfolio manager of a passively managed mutual fund also has most of the same responsibilities as a direct investor. These include trading securities, managing cash, deciding how to proceed with corporate actions, voting proxies, and reporting performance. Moreover, index-replicating mutual funds bear costs in such areas as registration, custodial, and audit, which are similar to those for actively managed mutual funds.

---

[3] Rolling a futures contract involves closing out a contract prior to its last trading day before expiration while taking a similar position in the next month's contract. Contracts that are cash-settled are marked to market, and any resulting funds in the account are available as margin that is used to initiate a position in the next month's contract.

Record keeping functions for a mutual fund include maintaining a record of who owns the shares and when and at what price those shares were purchased. Record keepers work closely with both the custodian of the fund shares to ensure that the security is safely held in the name of the investor and the mutual fund sponsor who communicates those trades.

In the United States, mutual funds are governed by provisions of the Investment Company Act of 1940. In Europe, Undertakings for Collective Investment in Transferable Securities (UCITS) is an agreement among countries in the European Union that governs the management and sale of collective investment funds (mutual funds) across European borders.

ETFs are another form of pooled investment vehicle. The first ETF was launched in the Canadian market in 1990 to track the return of 35 large stocks listed on the Toronto Stock Exchange. ETFs were introduced in the US market in 1993. They are registered funds that can be bought and sold throughout the trading day and change hands like stocks. Advantages of the ETF structure include ease of trading, low management fees, and tax efficiency. Unlike with traditional open-end mutual funds, ETF shares can be bought by investors using margin borrowing; moreover, investors can take short positions in an ETF. ETFs offer flexibility in that they track a wide array of indexes.

ETFs have a unique structure that requires a fund manager as well as an authorized participant who can deliver the assets to the manager. The role of the authorized participant is to be the market maker for the ETF and the intermediary between investors and the ETF fund manager when shares are created or redeemed. To create shares of the ETF, the authorized participant delivers a basket of the underlying stocks to the fund manager and, in exchange, receives shares of the ETF that can be sold to the public. When an authorized participant needs to redeem shares, the process is reversed so that the authorized participant delivers shares of the ETF in exchange for a basket of the underlying stocks that can then be sold in the market.

The creation/redemption process is used when the authorized participant is either called upon to deliver new shares of the ETF to meet investor needs or when large redemptions are requested. The redemption process occurs when an authorized participant needs to reduce its exposure to the ETF holding and accepts shares of the underlying securities in exchange for shares of the ETF.

All else equal, taxable investors in an ETF will have a smaller taxable event than those in a similarly managed mutual fund. Managers of mutual funds must sell their portfolio holdings to fulfill shareholder redemptions, creating a taxable event where gains and losses are realized. ETFs have the advantage of accommodating those redemptions through an in-kind delivery of stock, which is the redemption process. Capital gains are not recorded when a redemption is fulfilled through an in-kind delivery of securities, so the taxable gain/loss passed to the investor becomes smaller.

Disadvantages of the ETF structure include the need to buy at the offer and sell at the bid price, commission costs, and the risk of an illiquid market when the investor needs to buy or sell the actual ETF shares.

ETFs that track indexes are used to an increasing degree by financial advisers to provide targeted exposure to different sectors of the investable market. Large investors find it more cost effective to build their own portfolios through replication, stratified sampling, and optimization, concepts to be introduced later. Other investors find ETFs to be a relatively low-cost method of tracking major indexes. Importantly, like traditional open-end mutual funds, ETFs are an integrated approach in that portfolio management and accounting are conducted by the fund adviser itself. A limitation is that there are far more benchmark indexes than ETFs, so not all indexes have an exchange-traded security that tracks them, although new ETFs are constantly being created. Exhibit 7 depicts the strong global trend in investor net flows into index-tracking equity ETFs since 1998. The exhibit does not reflect changes in value caused by market fluctuations, but rather purely investments and redemptions.

Exhibit 7 also shows that, over time, factor-based ETFs have become a large segment of the market. Factor-based ETFs provide exposure to such single factors as Size, Value, Momentum, Quality, Volatility, and Yield. Among the most important innovations are ETFs that track multiple factors simultaneously. For example, the iShares Edge MSCI Multifactor USA ETF emphasizes exposure to Size, Value, Momentum, and Quality factors. Meanwhile, the ETF attempts to maintain characteristics that are similar to the underlying MSCI USA Diversified Multiple-Factor Index, including industry sector exposure. As of 2017, the fund's expense ratio is 0.20% and it holds all 139 of the stocks in the index.

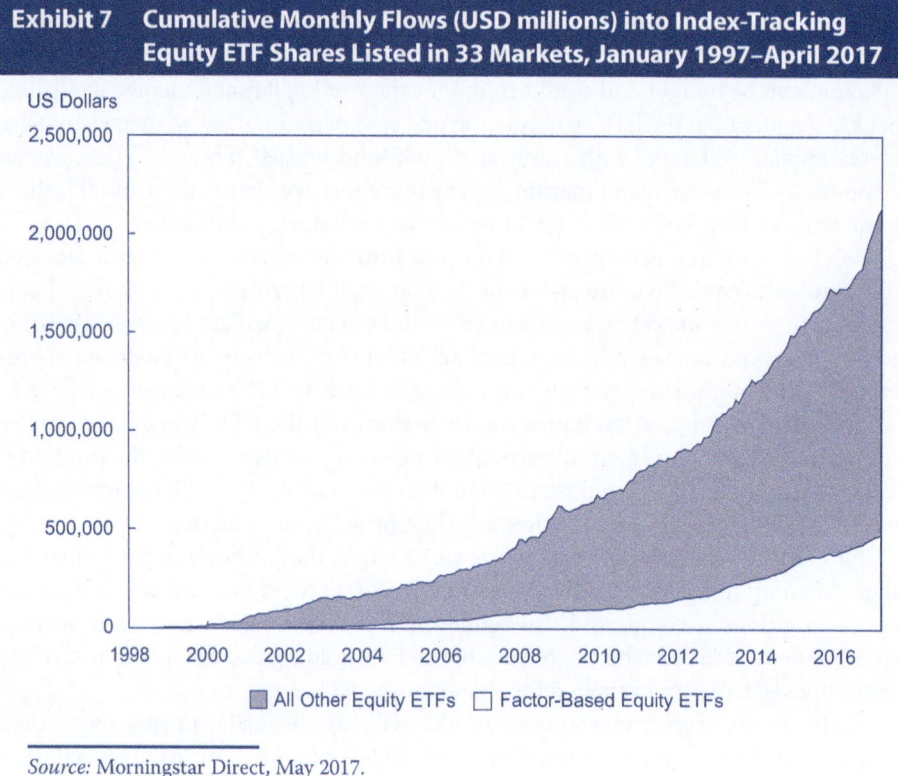

Exhibit 7 Cumulative Monthly Flows (USD millions) into Index-Tracking Equity ETF Shares Listed in 33 Markets, January 1997–April 2017

Source: Morningstar Direct, May 2017.

Exhibit 8 shows that, among 33 major exchange locations, the market value of equity ETFs that track indexes approaches USD 3 trillion. US exchanges have about one-third of the individual ETFs and more than 75% of the total market value as of May 2017. Japan, the United Kingdom, and Switzerland have more than half of the remaining market value. These numbers reflect purely passive ETFs, including factor-based securities.

Exhibit 8 Number of Index-Tracking Equity ETFs and Their Market Values (in USD millions) May 2017

Exchange Location	ETFs	Market Value
United States	1,104	2,236,166
Japan	99	200,965
United Kingdom	365	139,900
Switzerland	272	104,025
Germany	205	81,047

Exhibit 8   (Continued)

Exchange Location	ETFs	Market Value
France	260	66,680
Canada	252	47,625
Netherlands	24	22,350
South Korea	177	12,162
Hong Kong SAR	63	9,605
Italy	22	3,724
Singapore	41	3,451
Australia	55	2,873
Mexico	12	2,319
Sweden	4	1,922
Spain	6	1,654
Brazil	13	1,411
South Africa	27	1,347
New Zealand	11	566
Finland	1	234
Next 13 Locations	52	794
Total for 33 Locations	3,166	2,940,818

Source: Morningstar Direct, May 2017.

The decision of whether to use a conventional open-end mutual fund versus an ETF often comes down to cost and flexibility. Investors who seek to mimic an index must identify a suitable tracking security. According to Morningstar, in the United States, ETFs track 1,354 distinct equity indexes while conventional open-end mutual funds track only 184. Of the ETFs, 38 benchmarks are for price-only returns and the remainder are for total returns, which also include the return from reinvested dividends. Long-term investors benefit from the slightly lower expense ratios of ETFs than otherwise equivalent conventional open-end mutual funds. However, the brokerage fees associated with frequent investor trades into ETF shares can negate the expense ratio advantage and thus make ETFs less economical.

APPROACHES TO PASSIVE EQUITY INVESTING: DERIVATIVES-BASED APPROACHES & INDEX-BASED PORTFOLIOS

5

c   compare different approaches to passive equity investing;

Beyond purchasing a third-party-sponsored pooled investment and building it themselves, investors can access index performance through such derivatives as options, swaps, or futures contracts. Derivative strategies are advantageous in that they can be low cost, easy to implement, and provide leverage. However, they also present a new set of risks, including counterparty default risk for derivatives that are not traded on exchanges or cleared through a clearing house. Derivatives can also be relatively difficult to access for individual investors.

Options, swaps, and futures contracts can be found on many of the major indexes, such as the MSCI EAFE Index (EAFE stands for Europe, Australasia, and the Far East) and the S&P 500 Index. Options and futures are traded on exchanges and so are processed through a clearing house. This is important because a clearing house eliminates virtually all of the default risk present in having a contract with a single counterparty. Equity swaps, on the other hand, are generally executed with a single counterparty and so add the risk of default by that counterparty.

Derivatives allow for leverage through their notional value amounts. Notional value of the contracts can be many times greater than the initial cash outlay. However, derivatives expire, whereas stocks can be held indefinitely. The risk of an expiring options contract is a complete loss of the relatively small premium paid to acquire the exposure. Futures and swaps can be extended by "rolling" the contract forward, which means selling the expiring contract and buying a longer dated one.

Futures positions must be initiated with a futures commission merchant (FCM), a clearing house member assigned to trade on behalf of the investor. The FCM posts the initial margin required to open the position and then settles on a daily basis to comply with the maintenance margin required by the clearing house. The FCM also helps close the position upon expiration. However, futures accounts are not free of effort on the client's part. Having a futures account requires the management of daily cash flows, sometimes committing additional money and sometimes drawing it down.

It is uncommon for passive portfolio managers to use derivatives in the long term to synthetically mimic the return from physical securities. Derivatives are typically used to adjust a pre-existing portfolio to move closer to meeting its objectives. These derivative positions are often referred to as an **overlay**. A **completion overlay** addresses an indexed portfolio that has diverged from its proper exposure. A common example is a portfolio that has built up a surplus of cash from investor flows or dividends, causing the portfolio's beta to be significantly less than that of the benchmark. Using derivatives can efficiently restore the overall portfolio beta to its target. A **rebalancing overlay** addresses a portfolio's need to sell certain constituent securities and buy others. Particularly in the context of a mixed stock and bond portfolio, using equity index derivatives to rebalance toward investment policy target weights can be efficient and cost-effective. A **currency overlay** assists a portfolio manager in hedging the returns of securities that are held in a foreign currency back to the home country's currency.

Equity index derivatives offer several advantages over cash-based portfolio construction approaches. A passive portfolio manager can increase or decrease exposure to the entire index portfolio in a single transaction. Managers who want to make tactical adjustments to portfolio exposure often find derivatives to be a more efficient tool than cash-market transactions for achieving their goals. Many derivatives contracts are highly liquid, sometimes more so than the underlying cash assets. Especially in this case, portfolio exposures can be tactically adjusted quickly and at low cost.

For the longer term, strategic changes to portfolios are usually best made using cash instruments, which have indefinite expirations and do not necessitate rolling over expiring positions. Futures markets, for example, can impose position limits on such instruments that constrain the scale of use. Derivatives usage is also sometimes restricted by regulatory bodies or investment policy statement stipulations, so in this case cash could be a preferred approach. Finally, depending on the index that is being tracked by the passive portfolio manager, a suitable exchange-traded futures contract may not be available.

In addition to options, which have nonlinear payoffs[4], the two primary types of equity index derivatives contracts are futures and swaps. Equity index futures provide exposure to a specific index. Unlike many commodity futures contracts, index futures are cash-settled, which means the counterparties exchange cash rather than the underlying shares.

The buyer of an equity index futures contract obtains the right to buy the underlying (in this case, an index) on the expiration date of the contract at the futures price prevailing at the time the derivative was purchased. For exchange-traded futures, the buyer is required to post margin (collateral) in the account to decrease the credit risk to the exchange, which is the effective counterparty. For S&P 500 Index futures contracts as traded on the Chicago Mercantile Exchange, every USD change in the futures price produces a USD 250 change in the contract value (thus a "multiplier" of 250). On 4 August 2016, the September S&P 500 futures contract settled at a price of 2,159.30, after settling at 2,157 the day before. The change in contract value was thus 250 × USD (2,159.30 − 2,157) = USD 575.

Equity index futures contracts for various global markets are shown in Exhibit 9.

Exhibit 9 Representative Equity-Index Futures Contracts

Index Futures Contract	Market	Contract Currency and Multiplier
Americas		
Dow Jones mini	United States	USD 5
S&P 500	United States	USD 250
S&P 500 mini	United States	USD 50
NASDAQ 100 mini	United States	USD 20
Mexican IPC	Mexico	MXN 10
S&P/TSX Composite mini	Canada	CAD 5
S&P/TSX 60	Canada	CAD 200
Ibovespa	Brazil	BRL 1
Europe, Middle East, and Africa		
Euro STOXX 50	Europe	EUR 10
FTSE 100	United Kingdom	GBP 10
DAX 30	Germany	EUR 25
CAC 40	France	EUR 10
FTSE/Athens 20	Greece	EUR 5
OMX Stockholm 30	Sweden	SEK 100
Swiss Market	Switzerland	CHF 10
OMX Copenhagen 20	Denmark	DKK 100
PSI-20	Portugal	EUR 1
IBEX 35	Spain	EUR 10
WIG20	Poland	PLN 10
BIST 30	Turkey	TRY 100

(continued)

---

4 The nonlinearity of option payoffs arises because all prices of the underlying that cause the option to be out-of-the-money at expiration produce zero payoff for the investor who holds the option. When an option is in the money, the investor holding it experiences a linearly increasing payoff at all prices of the underlying in that range. In the case of futures and swaps, the payoffs are two-sided and linear for price changes in the underlying that are in the investor's favor as well as those that are against the investor.

Exhibit 9   (Continued)

Index Futures Contract	Market	Contract Currency and Multiplier
FTSE/JSE Top 40	South Africa	ZAR 10
Asia Pacific		
S&P/ASX 200	Australia	AUD 25
CSI 300	Chinese mainland	CNY 300
Hang Seng	Hong Kong SAR	HKD 50
H-Shares	Hong Kong SAR	HKD 50
Nifty 50	India	INR 50
Nikkei 225	Japan	JPY 1,000
Topix	Japan	JPY 10,000
KOSPI 200	Korea	KRW 500,000

Source: Please see www.investing.com/indices/indices-futures, May 2017.

Given that futures can be traded using only a small amount of margin, it is clear that futures provide a significant degree of potential leverage to a portfolio. Leverage can be considered either a positive or negative characteristic, depending on the manner with which the derivative instrument is used. Unlike some institutional investors' short-sale constraints on stock positions, many investors do not face constraints on opening a futures position with a sale of the contracts. Among other benefits of futures is the high degree of liquidity in the market, as evidenced by low bid–ask spreads. Both commission and execution costs also tend to be low relative to the exposure achieved. The low cost of transacting makes it easy for portfolio managers to use futures contracts to modify the equity risk exposure of their portfolios.

Equity index futures do come with some disadvantages. Futures are used by index fund managers because the instruments are expected to move in line with the underlying index. To the extent that the futures and spot prices do not move in concert, the portfolio may not track the benchmark perfectly. The extent to which futures prices do not move with spot prices is known as basis risk. Basis risk results from using a hedging instrument that is imperfectly matched to the investment being hedged. Basis risk can arise when the underlying securities pay dividends, while the futures contract tracks only the price of the underlying index. The difference can be partially mitigated when futures holders combine that position with interest-bearing securities.

As noted, futures account holders also must post margin. The margin amount varies by trading exchange. In the case of an ASX-200 futures contract, the initial margin required by the Sydney Futures Exchange in January 2017 for an overnight position is AUD 6,700. The minimum maintenance margin for one contract is AUD 5,300.

By way of example, assume an investor buys an ASX-200 futures contract priced at AUD 5,700, and the futures contract has a multiplier of 25. The investor controls AUD 142,500 [= 25 × AUD 5,700] in value. This currency amount is known as the contract unit value. With the initial margin of AUD 6,700 and a maintenance margin of AUD 5,300, a margin call will be triggered if the contract unit value decreases by more than AUD 1,400. A decrease of AUD 1,400 in the margin is associated with a contract unit value of AUD 142,500 – AUD 1,400 = AUD 141,100. This corresponds to an ASX-200 futures price of AUD 5,644 [= AUD 141,100/25]. Thus, a futures price decrease of 0.98% [= (AUD 5,644 – AUD 5,700)/AUD 5,700] is associated with a decrease in the margin account balance of 20%. This example demonstrates how even a small change in the index value can result in a margin call once the mark-to-market process occurs.

Another derivatives-based approach is the use of equity index swaps. Equity index swaps are negotiated arrangements in which two counterparties agree to exchange cash flows in the future. For example, consider an investor who has a EUR 20 million notional amount and wants to be paid the return on her benchmark index, the Euro STOXX 50, during the coming year. In exchange, the investor agrees to pay a floating rate of return of Libor + 0.20% per year, with settlement occurring semi-annually. Assuming a six-month stock index return of 2.3% and annualized Libor of 0.18% per year, the first payment on the swap agreement would be calculated as follows. The investor would receive EUR 20 million × 0.023 = EUR 460,000. The investor would be liable to the counterparty for EUR 20 million × (0.0018 + 0.0020) × (180/360) = EUR 38,000; so, when the first settlement occurs the investor would receive EUR 460,000 − EUR 38,000 = EUR 422,000. In this case, the payment received by the passive portfolio manager is from the first leg of the swap, and the payment made by that manager is from the second leg. Libor is used in this example, but the second leg can also involve the return on a different index, stock, or other asset, or even a fixed currency amount per period.

Disadvantages of swaps include counterparty, liquidity, interest rate, and tax policy risks. Relatively frequent settlement decreases counterparty risk and reduces the potential loss from a counterparty's failure to perform. Equity swaps tend to be nonmarketable instruments, so once the agreement is made there is not a highly liquid market that allows them to be sold to another party (though it is usually possible to go back to the dealer and enter into an offsetting position). Although the equity index payment recipient is an equity investor, this investor must deliver an amount linked to Libor; the investor bears interest rate risk. One prime motivation for initiating equity swaps is to avoid paying high taxes on the full return amount from an equity investment. This advantage is dependent on tax laws remaining favorable, which means that equity swaps carry tax policy risk.

There are a number of advantages to using an equity swap to gain synthetic exposure to index returns. Exchange-traded futures contracts are available only on a limited number of equity indexes. Yet as long as there is a willing counterparty, a swap can be initiated on virtually any index. So swaps can be customized with respect to the underlying as well as to settlement frequency and maturity. Although most swap agreements are one year or shorter in maturity, they can be negotiated for as long a tenor as the counterparties are willing. If a swap is used, it is not necessary for an investor to pay transaction costs associated with buying all of the index constituents. Like futures, a swap can help a portfolio manager add leverage or hedge a portfolio, which is usually done on a tactical or short-term basis.

5.1 Separately Managed Equity Index-Based Portfolios

Building an index-based equity portfolio as a separately managed portfolio requires a certain set of capabilities and tools. An equity investor who builds an indexed portfolio will need to subscribe to certain data on the index and its constituents. The investor also requires a robust trading and accounting system to manage the portfolio, broker relationships to trade efficiently and cheaply, and compliance systems to meet applicable laws and regulations.

The data subscription can generally be acquired directly from the index provider and may be offered on a daily or less-frequent basis. Generally, the data are provided for analysis only and a separate license must be purchased for index replication strategies. The index subscription data should include company and security identifiers, weights, cash dividend, return, and corporate action information. Corporate actions can include stock dividends and splits, mergers and acquisitions, liquidations, and other reasons for index constituent inclusion and exclusion. These data are generally provided in electronic format and can be delivered via file downloads or fed through a portfolio manager's analytical systems, such as Bloomberg or FactSet. The data are then used as the basis for the indexed portfolio.

Certain trading systems, such as those provided by Charles River Investment Management Solution, SS&C Advent (through Moxy), and Eze Castle Integration, allow the manager to see her portfolio and compare it to the chosen benchmark. Common features of trading systems include electronic communication with multiple brokers and exchanges, an ability to record required information on holdings for taxable investors, and modeling tools so that a portfolio can be traded to match its benchmark.

Accounting systems should be able to report daily performance, record historical transactions, and produce statements. Portfolio managers rely heavily on their accounting systems and teams to help them understand the drivers of portfolio performance.

Broker relationships are an often-overlooked advantage of portfolio managers that are able to negotiate better commission rates. Commissions are a negative drag on a portfolio's returns. The commission rates quoted to a manager can differ on the basis of the type of securities being traded, the size of the trade, and the magnitude of the relationship between the manager and broker.

Finally, compliance tools and teams are necessary. Investors must adhere to a myriad of rules and regulations, which can come from client agreements and regulatory bodies. Sanctions for violating compliance-related rules can range from losing a client to losing the registration to participate in the investment industry; thus, a robust compliance system is essential to the success of an investment manager.

Compliance rules can be company-wide or specific to an investor's account. Company-wide rules take such forms as restricting trades in stocks of affiliated companies. Rules specific to an account involve such matters as dealing with a directed broker or steps to prevent cash overdrafts. Compliance rules should also be written to prohibit manager misconduct, such as front-running in a personal account prior to executing client trades.

To ensure that their portfolios closely match the return stream of the chosen index, indexed portfolio managers must review their holdings and their weightings versus the index each day. Although a perfect match is a near impossibility because of rounding errors and trading costs, the manager must always weigh the benefits and costs of maintaining a close match.

To establish the portfolio, the manager creates a trading file and transmits the file to an executing broker, who buys the securities using a program trade. **Program trading** is a strategy of buying or selling many stocks simultaneously. Index portfolio managers may trade thousands of positions in a single trade file and are required to deliver the orders and execute the trades quickly. The creation of trades may be done on something as rudimentary as an Excel spreadsheet, but it is more likely to be created on an order management system (OMS), such as Charles River

Portfolio managers use their OMS to model their portfolios against the index, decide which trades to execute, and transmit the orders. Transmitting an order in the United States is generally done on a secure communication line, such as through FIX Protocol. FIX Protocol is an electronic communication protocol to transmit the orders from the portfolio manager to the broker or directly to the executing market place. The orders are first transmitted via FIX Protocol to a broker who executes the trade and then delivers back pricing and settlement instructions to the OMS. International trading is usually communicated using a similar protocol through SWIFT. SWIFT stands for "Society for Worldwide Interbank Financial Telecommunication," and is a service that is used to securely transmit trade instructions.

Index-based strategies seek to replicate an index that is priced at the close of business each day. Therefore, most index-based trade executions take place at the close of the business day using market-on-close (MOC) orders. Matching the trade execution to the benchmark price helps the manager more closely match the performance of the index.

Beyond the portfolio's initial construction, managers maintain the portfolio by trading any index changes, such as adds/deletes, rebalances, and reinvesting cash dividend payments. These responsibilities require the manager to commit time each day to oversee the portfolio and create the necessary trades. Best practice would be to review the portfolio's performance each day and its composition at least once a month.

Dividends paid over time can accumulate to significant amounts that must be reinvested into the securities in the index. Index fund managers must determine when the cash paid out by dividends should be reinvested and then create trades to purchase the required securities.

PASSIVE PORTFOLIO CONSTRUCTION

d compare the full replication, stratified sampling, and optimization approaches for the construction of passively managed equity portfolios;

This section discusses the principal approaches that equity portfolio managers use when building a passive-indexed portfolio by transacting in individual securities. The three approaches are full replication, stratified sampling, and optimization. According to Morningstar, among index-tracking equity ETF portfolios globally:

- 38% of funds (representing 42% of July 2016 assets) use full replication,
- 41% of funds (representing 54% of assets) use stratified sampling or optimization techniques, and
- 21% of funds (representing only about 4% of assets) use synthetic replication, using over-the-counter derivatives).

6.1 Full Replication

Full replication in index investing occurs when a manager holds all securities represented by the index in weightings that closely match the actual index weightings. Advantages of full replication include the fact that it usually accomplishes the primary goal of matching the index performance, and it is easy to comprehend. Full replication, however, requires that the asset size of the mandate is sufficient and that the index constituents are available for trading.

Not all indexes lend themselves to full replication. For example, the MSCI ACWI Investable Markets Index consists of over 8,000 constituents,[5] but not all securities need be held to closely match the characteristics and performance of that index. Other indexes, such as the S&P 500, have constituents that are readily available for trading and can be applied to portfolios as small as USD 10 million.

With respect to the choice between index replication versus sampling, as the number of securities held increases, tracking error decreases because the passive portfolio gets closer to replicating the index perfectly. Yet as the portfolio manager adds index constituent stocks that are smaller and more thinly traded than average, trading costs

---

5 The MSCI ACWI Investable Markets Index captures large, mid-, and small-cap stocks across developed and emerging market countries and represents 8,609 securities as of April 2016.

increase. The trading costs can take the form of brokerage fees and upward price pressure as a result of the portfolio's purchases. These transaction costs can depress performance and start to impose a small negative effect on tracking effectiveness. As the portfolio manager moves to the least liquid stocks in the index, transaction costs begin to dominate and tracking error increases again. Thus, for an index that has some constituent securities that are relatively illiquid, the conceptual relationship between tracking error and the number of securities held is U-shaped. The relation can be depicted as shown in Exhibit 10.

Exhibit 10   Relation Between Tracking Error and Transaction Costs versus Number of Benchmark Index Constituent Stocks Held

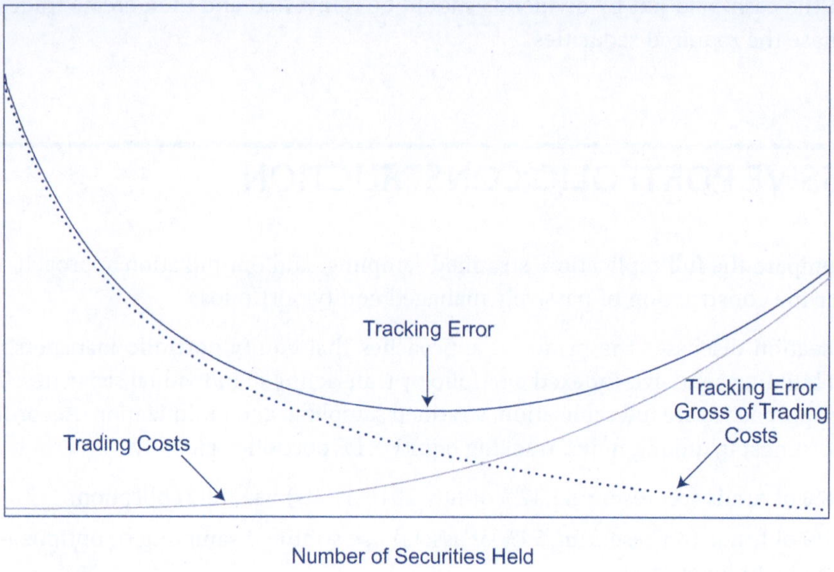

Source: Author team.

Many managers attempt to match an index's characteristics and performance through a full replication technique, but how does a manager create the portfolio? As mentioned in a prior section, the passive equity manager needs data from the index provider to construct the portfolio. This includes the constituent stocks, their relevant identifiers (ticker, CUSIP, SEDOL, or ISIN), shares outstanding, and price. Additional data, such as constituents' dividends paid and total return, facilitate management of the portfolio.

The manager then uses the index data to create the portfolio by replicating as closely as possible the index constituents and weights. The portfolio construction method may vary by investor, but the most common method is to import the provided data into a data compiler such as Charles River, Moxy, or some other external or internally created OMS. The imported data show the manager the trades that are needed to match the index. Exhibit 11 contains an example for a portfolio that has an initial investment of USD 10 million.

Passive Portfolio Construction

Exhibit 11 Sample Index Portfolio Positions and Transactions

Identifier	Security Description	Price	Current Weight	Model Weight	Current Weight – Model Weight = Variance	Current Shares	New Shares	Shares to Trade
Cash	Cash	1	50%	0%	50%	5,000,000	0	–5,000,000
SECA	Security 1	100	50%	50%	0%	50,000	50,000	0
SECB	Security 2	50	0%	50%	–50%	0	100,000	100,000

Exhibit 11 shows a current portfolio made up of one security and a cash holding that needs to be traded to match a two-security index. The index becomes the model for the portfolio, and that model is used to match the portfolio. This type of modeling can easily and cheaply be conducted using spreadsheet and database programs, such as Excel and Access. However, the modeling is only a part of the portfolio management process.

The OMS should also be programmed to provide the investor with pre-trade compliance to check for client-specific restrictions, front-running issues, and other compliance rules. The OMS is also used to deliver the buy and sell orders for execution using FIX or SWIFT Protocol, as described previously.

After initial creation of the indexed portfolio, the manager must maintain the portfolio according to any changes in the index. The changes are announced publicly by the index provider. Index fund managers use those details to update their models in the OMS and to determine the number of shares to buy or sell. A fully replicated portfolio must make those changes in a timely manner to maintain its performance tracking with the index. Again, a perfectly replicated index portfolio must trade at the market-on-close price where available to match the price used by the index provider in calculating the index performance.

6.2 Stratified Sampling

Despite their preference to realize the benefits of pure replication of an index, portfolio managers often find it impractical to hold all the constituent securities. Some equity indexes have a large number of constituents, and not all constituents offer high trading liquidity. This can make trading expensive, especially if a portfolio manager needs to scale up the portfolio. Brokerage fees can also become excessive if the number of constituents is large.

Holding a limited sample of the index constituents can produce results that track the index return and risk characteristics closely. But such sampling is not done randomly. Rather, portfolio managers use stratified sampling. To stratify is to arrange a population into distinct strata or subgroupings. Arranged correctly, the various strata will be mutually exclusive and also exhaustive (a complete set), and they should closely match the characteristics and performance of the index. Common stratification approaches include using industry membership and equity style characteristics. Investors who use stratified sampling to track the S&P 500 commonly assign each stock to one of the eleven sectors designated by the Global Industry Classification Standard (GICS). For multinational indexes, stratification is often done first on the basis of country affiliation. Indexes can be stratified along multiple dimensions (e.g., country affiliation and then industry affiliation) within each country. An advantage of stratifying along multiple dimensions is closer index tracking.

In equity indexing, stratified sampling is most frequently used when the portfolio manager wants to track indexes that have many constituents or when dealing with a relatively low level of assets under management. Indexes with many constituents are usually multi-country or multi-cap indexes, such as the S&P Global Broad Market Index that consists of more than 11,000 constituents. Most investors are reluctant to trade and maintain 11,000 securities when a significantly smaller number of constituents would achieve most portfolios' tracking objectives. Regardless of the stratified sampling approach used, passive equity managers tend to weight portfolio holdings proportionately to each stratum's weight in the index.

> **EXAMPLE 2**
>
> ### Stratified Sampling
>
> A portfolio manager responsible for accounts of high-net-worth individuals is asked to build an index portfolio that tracks the S&P 500 Value Index, which has more than 300 constituents. The manager and the client agree that the minimum account size will be USD 750,000, but the manager explains to the client that full replication is not feasible at a reasonable cost because of the mandate size. How can the manager use stratified sampling to achieve her goal of tracking the S&P 500 Value Index?
>
> ### Solution:
>
> The manager recommends that the client set a maximum number of constituents (for example, 200) to limit the average lot size and to reduce commission costs. Next, the manager seeks to identify the constituents to hold based on their market capitalization. That is, the manager selects the 200 securities with the largest market capitalizations. Then the manager seeks to more closely match the performance of the index by matching the sector weightings of the sampled portfolio to the sector weightings of the index. After comparing sector weights, the manager reweights the sampled portfolio. Using this method of stratified sampling meets the manager's stated goal of closely tracking the performance of the index at a reasonable cost.

6.3 Optimization

Optimization approaches for index portfolio construction, such as full replication and stratified sampling, have index-tracking goals. Optimization typically involves maximizing a desirable characteristic or minimizing an undesirable characteristic, subject to one or more constraints. For an indexed portfolio, optimization could involve minimizing index tracking error, subject to the constraint that the portfolio holds 50 constituent securities or fewer. The desired output from the optimization process is identification of the 50 securities and their weights that results in the lowest possible tracking error. The number of security holdings is not the only possible constraint. Other common constraints include limiting portfolio membership to stocks that have a market capitalization above a certain specified level, style characteristics that mimic those of the benchmark, restricting trades to round lots, and using only stocks that will keep rebalancing costs low.

Roll (1992) and Jorion (2003) demonstrate that running an optimization to minimize tracking error can lead to portfolios that are mean–variance inefficient versus the benchmark. That is, the optimized portfolio may exhibit higher risk than the benchmark it is being optimized against. They show that a useful way to address this problem is to add a constraint on total portfolio volatility. Accordingly, the manager of an optimized passive fund would aim to make its total volatility equal to that of the benchmark index.

Fabozzi, Focardi, and Kolm (2010) note that in practice, passive portfolio managers often conduct a mean–variance optimization using all the index constituents, the output from which shows highly diverse weightings for the stocks. Given that investing in the lowest-weight stocks may involve marginal transaction costs that exceed marginal diversification benefits, in a second, post-optimization stage, the managers may then delete the lowest-weighted stocks.

Optimization can be conducted in conjunction with stratified sampling or alone. Optimization programs, when run without constraints, do not consider country or industry affiliation but rather use security level data. Optimization requires an analyst who has a high level of technical sophistication, including familiarity with computerized optimization software or algorithms, and a good understanding of the output.

Advantages of optimization involve a lower amount of tracking error than stratified sampling. Also, the optimization process accounts explicitly for the covariances among the portfolio constituents. Although two securities from different industry sectors may be included in a passive portfolio under stratified sampling, if their returns move strongly together, one will likely be excluded from an optimized portfolio.

Usually the constituents and weights of an optimized portfolio are determined based on past market data; however, returns, variances, and correlations between securities tend to vary over time. Thus, the output from an optimization program may apply only to the period from which the data are drawn and not to a future period. Even if current results apply to the future, they might not be applicable for long. This means that optimization would need to be run frequently and adjustments made to the portfolio, which can be costly.

6.4 Blended Approach

For indexes that have few constituent securities or for which the constituents are homogeneous, full replication is typically advisable. When the reverse is true, sampling or optimization are likely to be the preferred methods. But such indexes as the Russell 3000, the S&P 1500, and the Wilshire 5000 span the capitalization spectrum from large to small. For these indexes, the 1,000 or so largest constituents are quite liquid, which means that brokerage fees, bid–ask spreads, and trading costs are low. For the largest-cap portion of an indexed portfolio, full replication is a sensible and desirable approach. For the index constituents that have smaller market capitalizations or less liquidity, however, a stratified sampling or optimization approach can be useful for all the reasons mentioned previously in this section. Thus, an indexed portfolio can actually be managed using a blended approach consisting of full replication for more-liquid issues and one of the other methods for less-liquid issues.

TRACKING ERROR MANAGEMENT

e discuss potential causes of tracking error and methods to control tracking error for passively managed equity portfolios;

As discussed previously, managers of passive strategies use a variety of approaches to track indexes in cost-efficient ways. To the extent the portfolio manager's skills are ineffective, tracking error results. This section discusses the measurement and management of tracking error.

7.1 Tracking Error and Excess Return

Tracking error and excess return are two measures that enable investors to differentiate performance among passive portfolio managers. Tracking error indicates how closely the portfolio behaves like its benchmark and measures a manager's ability to replicate the benchmark return. Tracking error is calculated as the standard deviation of the difference between the portfolio return and its benchmark index return. Excess return measures the difference between the portfolio returns and benchmark returns. Tracking error for portfolio p then can be expressed by Equation 3.

$$\text{Tracking error}_p = \sqrt{\text{Variance}_{(R_p - R_b)}} \qquad (3)$$

where R_p is the return on the portfolio and R_b is the return on the benchmark index. Excess return for portfolio p is calculated as in Equation 4.

$$\text{Excess return}_p = R_p - R_b \qquad (4)$$

Tracking error and excess return are distinct measures; the terms should not be used interchangeably. Tracking error measures the manager's ability to closely track the benchmark over time. In principle, a manager whose return is identical to that of the index could have arrived at that point by lagging and subsequently leading the index, producing a net difference of zero. But being a standard deviation, tracking error cannot be zero in cases such as the one described. Excess returns can be positive or negative and tell the investor how the manager performed relative to the benchmark. Tracking error, which is a standard deviation, is always presented as a non-negative number.

Index fund managers endeavor to have low tracking error and excess returns that are not negative. Low tracking error is important in measuring the skill of the index fund manager because the investor's goal is to mimic the return stream of the index. Avoiding negative excess returns versus the benchmark is also important because the manager will want to avoid underperforming the stated index.

Tracking error varies according to the manager's approach to tracking the index. An index that contains a large number of constituents will tend to create higher tracking error than those with fewer constituents. This is because a large number of constituents may prevent the manager from fully replicating the index.

For an index fund, the degree of tracking error fluctuates over time. Also, the value will differ depending on whether the data frequency is daily or less frequent.

EXAMPLE 3

Tracking Error and Excess Return

Exhibit 12 illustrates key portfolio metrics for three of the older and larger conventional open-end funds in the Australian and South Korean markets. Based on the levels of tracking error and excess return figures provided in the exhibit, explain whether the funds are likely replicating or sampling.

Exhibit 12 Major Conventional Index Mutual Funds in Australia and South Korea

Fund Name (Holdings)	Holdings	Annual Management Fee (bps)	3-Year Annualized Tracking Error	3-Year Annualized Excess Return
Australian market benchmark for the following funds is the S&P/ASX 300 Index. Number of securities in the index: 300.				
BlackRock Indexed Australian Equity Fund	296	20	0.0347%	−0.1684%
Macquarie True Index Australian Shares	259	0	0.0167%	0.0111%
Vanguard Australian Shares Index	293	18	0.1084%	−0.1814%
South Korean market benchmark for the funds below is the KRX KOSPI 200 Korea Index. Number of securities in the index: 200.				
KB Star Korea Index Equity CE	190	36	1.2671%	0.3356%
KIM Cruise Index F2.8 Equity-Deriv A	178	9	1.5019%	1.7381%
Samsung Index Premium Equity-Deriv A	204	40	1.3325%	1.1097%

Solution:

Based on the number of stocks in the fund compared to the index constituent number, it appears most funds are attempting to replicate. Two of the funds (Macquarie True Index and KIM Cruise Index) have 80% to 90% of the stocks in the index, which indicates they are more likely to be using sampling. One fund (Samsung Index Premium) actually holds more than the index, which can happen if buffering is used. No fund contains the same number of stocks as constituents in the index. Thus, it is not surprising that the funds failed to track their respective indexes perfectly. On an annualized basis, tracking error for the Australian funds is less than one-tenth the level of the Korean funds. However, the Korean funds' excess return—which is fund return less the benchmark index return—is positive in all three cases. The negative excess returns for two of the Australian funds are relatively close and possibly attributable to their management fees of 18–20 basis points.

7.2 Potential Causes of Tracking Error and Excess Return

Tracking error in an indexed equity fund can arise for several reasons. A major reason involves the fees charged. Although tracking error is expressed as an absolute value, fees are always negative because they represent a cost and drive down the excess return. Therefore, higher fees will contribute to lower excess returns and higher tracking error.

A second issue to consider is the number of securities held by the portfolio versus the benchmark index. Stock indexes that are liquid and investable may be fully replicated, while indexes with hard-to-find securities or a great number of securities are sampled. Sampled portfolios typically report greater tracking error than those that are fully replicated.

The intra-day trading of the constituent stocks of an indexed portfolio also presents an important issue to consider when attributing tracking error. The effect of intra-day trading can be positive or negative for a portfolio's returns compared to its benchmark index. The price levels used to report index returns are struck at the close of the trading day, so any securities that are bought or sold at a different price than that of the index will contribute to portfolio tracking error. Index fund managers can minimize this type of tracking error by transacting at the market-on-close price or as near to the closing time as feasible.

A secondary component of trading costs that contributes to tracking error is the trading commission paid to brokers. Commission costs make excess returns more negative and also affect tracking error. According to Perold and Salomon (1991), the trading cost for passive portfolio managers is likely to be lower than the trading cost for active managers who are suspected by their counterparties to possess an information advantage.

Another issue to consider is the cash holding of the portfolio. Equity indexes do not have a cash allocation, so any cash balance creates tracking error for the index fund manager. Cash can be accumulated in the portfolio from a variety of sources, such as dividends received, sale proceeds, investor contributions, and other sources of income. Cash flows from investors and from the constituent companies may not be invested immediately, and investing them often entails a commission cost. Both may affect tracking error. The tracking error caused by temporarily uninvested cash is known as **cash drag**. The effect of cash drag on portfolio value is negative when the market is rising and positive when it is falling.

Hill and Cheong (1996) discuss how to equitize a portfolio that would otherwise suffer from cash drag. One method is to use futures contracts. ETFs have been used widely for this purpose. Some portfolio managers establish a futures commission merchant relationship to offset their cash positions with a futures contract that represents the replicated index. When a manager does this, she will calculate the accrued dividends as well to hedge the dividend drag, which is cash drag attributable to accrued cash dividends paid to shareholders.

7.3 Controlling Tracking Error

The process of controlling tracking error involves trade-offs between the benefits and costs of maintaining complete faithfulness to the benchmark index, as illustrated in Exhibit 10. Portfolio managers who are unconstrained would keep the number of constituent securities and their weights as closely aligned to the benchmark index as possible. Even so, trading costs and other fees cause actual investment performance to deviate from index performance. Passive investing does not mean that the fund does not trade. Managers trade to accommodate inflows and outflows of cash from investors, to reinvest dividends, and to reflect changes in constituents of the underlying index.

As discussed in Section 7.2, most passive portfolio managers attempt to minimize cash held because a cash position generally creates undesirable tracking error. To keep tracking error low, portfolio managers need to invest cash flows received at the same valuations used by the benchmark index provider. Of course, because this is not always feasible, portfolio managers aim to maintain a beta of 1.0 relative to the benchmark index, while keeping other risk factor exposures similar to those of the index.

8. SOURCES OF RETURN AND RISK IN PASSIVE EQUITY PORTFOLIOS

f   explain sources of return and risk to a passively managed equity portfolio.

Sources of Return and Risk in Passive Equity Portfolios

Indexed portfolios began as a representation of market performance, and some investors accept the returns of the indexed portfolio without judgment. However, understanding both positive and negative sources of return through attribution analysis is an important step in the passive equity investment process.

8.1 Attribution Analysis

An investor has many choices across the investable spectrum of assets. An investor must first choose between stocks, bonds, and other asset classes and then partition each asset class by its sub-categories. In partitioning stocks, the process begins with choosing what countries to invest in, what market-cap sizes and investment style to use, and whether to weight the constituents using market cap or an alternative weighting method.

The return on an indexed portfolio can come from any of the aforementioned criteria. Return analyses are conducted ex-post, which means that the returns of the portfolio are studied after they have been experienced.

The sources of return for an equity index replication portfolio are the same as for any actively managed fund and include company-specific returns, sector returns, country returns, and currency returns. Beyond the traditional methods of grouping the risk and returns of the indexed portfolio, portfolio managers can group their indexed portfolios according to the stated portfolio objective. For example, a high dividend yield indexed portfolio may be grouped against the broad market benchmark by dividend yield. A low volatility portfolio could be grouped by volatility buckets to show how the lowest volatility stocks performed in the indexed portfolio as well as the broad market.

Most portfolio managers will rely on their portfolio attribution system to help them in understanding the sources of return. Index fund managers who track a broad market index need to understand what factors are driving the returns of that portfolio and its underlying index. Index fund managers of passive factor-based strategies should understand both the sources of return for their indexed portfolios and how those returns relate to the broad market index from which the constituents were chosen. In this way, passive factor-based strategies are very similar to actively managed funds in the sense that they are actively chosen.

Exhibit 13 shows an example of a portfolio attribution analysis using annual returns. Portfolio X is an index fund that seeks to replicate the performance of its benchmark. The manager of Portfolio X confirms that the portfolio, which has a return of 5.62%, is closely replicating the performance of the benchmark, which has a return of 5.65%.

Using Exhibit 13, the manager analyzes the relative sector weights and sources of the three basis points of return difference. A portfolio that is within three basis points of its benchmark index is undoubtedly tracking the index closely. Beyond seeking the source of the tracking error, the portfolio manager will also seek to understand the source of the positive returns.

Exhibit 13 Example of Sector Attribution Analysis (All figures in %)

Sector	Sector Return (A)	Portfolio X Sector Weight (B)	Portfolio X Contribution to Return (C) = (A) × (B)	Benchmark for Portfolio X Sector Weight (D)	Benchmark for Portfolio X Contribution to Return (E) = (A) × (D)	Attribution Analysis Difference (F) = (C) − (E)
Total	5.62	100.00	5.62	100.00	5.65	−0.03
Telecom. Services	16.94	2.25	0.38	2.34	0.40	−0.02
Utilities	15.45	12.99	2.01	13.03	2.01	−0.01
Consumer Discretionary	12.09	3.89	0.47	3.90	0.47	0.00
Materials	9.61	2.08	0.20	2.08	0.20	0.00
Information Technology	7.03	2.82	0.20	2.85	0.20	0.00
Consumer Staples	6.82	15.07	1.03	15.09	1.03	0.00
Industrials	3.93	16.08	0.63	16.15	0.63	0.00
Financials	0.50	19.85	0.10	19.32	0.10	0.00
Health Care	0.31	12.70	0.04	12.77	0.04	0.00
Real Estate	0.80	5.04	0.04	5.23	0.04	0.00
Energy	7.21	7.23	0.52	7.24	0.52	0.00
[Cash]	0.00	0.00	0.00	0.00	0.00	0.00

Attribution analyses like the one in Exhibit 13 can be structured in many ways. This analysis is grouped by economic sector. Sector attribution can help an investor develop expectations about how a portfolio might perform in different market conditions. For example, during an era of low interest rates, high-dividend stocks such as utilities are likely to outperform while financial stocks such as banks are likely to underperform, other things held equal. To the extent the portfolio holds financial stocks in a lower concentration than the benchmark, the portfolio will likely outperform if interest rates stay low.

Column A in Exhibit 13 shows the total return for each sector. For example, the Telecommunications sector posted a return of 16.94% over this period.

Column B shows Portfolio's X's sector weight. The portfolio is heavily invested in Financials, because this is the largest sector in the benchmark index.

Column C shows each sector's contribution to the overall return of Portfolio X, obtained by multiplying each sector weight in Portfolio X by the sector's total return. The sum of the eleven sectors' contributions to return is equal to the total return of the portfolio.

Column D shows the benchmark's sector weights.

Column E shows the contribution to return of each sector held by the benchmark, obtained by multiplying each sector's weight in the benchmark by the sector's total return. The sum of the eleven sectors' contributions to return is equal to the total return of the benchmark.

Finally, column F shows the difference in contribution to returns between Portfolio X and the benchmark. Column F is the difference between columns C and E.

Portfolio X has 15.07% invested in Consumer Staples, which compares to the benchmark index's 15.09% weight in that sector. The negligible underweighting combined with a sector return of 6.82% enabled the portfolio to closely match the contribution to return of the portfolio to that of the index.

The Telecommunications and Utilities sectors were the best-performing sectors over the period. Telecommunications and Utilities holdings made up 15.24% of the portfolio's holdings and contributed 2.39 percentage points (or 239 basis points) of the 5.62% total return.

Companies in the Telecommunications and Utilities sectors are high-dividend payers and are positively affected by falling interest rates. Given this information, the manager could then connect the positive performance of the sectors to the prevailing interest rate environment. The manager would also note in the attribution analysis that the same interest rate environment, in part, caused the Financials sector to underperform the market. These opposing forces act as a good hedge against interest rate movements in either direction and are part of a robust portfolio structure.

The portfolio manager of the strategy may use the attribution analysis to determine the sources of tracking error. In this case, the analysis confirmed that the portfolio is meeting its goal of closely tracking the composition and performance of its benchmark. Further, the portfolio manager is able to determine the sources of return, which in this case are in large part from the high-dividend-yielding Telecommunications and Utilities sectors.

8.2 Securities Lending

Investors who hold long equity positions usually keep the shares in their brokerage accounts, so they are ready to sell when the time arises. But there is a demand for those shares independent of fellow investors who may wish to buy them. Investors who want to sell short may need to borrow the shares, and they are willing to pay for the right to borrow. The securities-lending income received by long portfolio managers can be a valuable addition to portfolio returns. At the very least, the proceeds can help offset the other costs of managing the portfolio. In the case of low-cost indexed portfolios, securities lending income can actually make net expenses negative—meaning that in addition to tracking the benchmark index, the portfolio earns a return in excess of the index.

An investor who wants to lend securities often uses a lending agent. In the case of institutional investors (e.g., mutual funds, pension funds, and hedge funds), the custodian (i.e., custody bank) is frequently used. Occasionally, the asset management firm will offer securities lending services. Two legal documents are usually put in place, including a securities lending authorization agreement between the lender and the agent and a master securities lending agreement between the agent and borrowers.

The lending agent identifies a borrower who posts collateral (typically 102–105% of the value of the securities). When the collateral is in securities rather than cash, the lending agent holds them as a guarantee. The lending agent evaluates the collateral daily to ensure that it is sufficient. When the collateral is in the form of cash, the lending agent invests it in money market instruments and receives interest income. In this case, the borrower sometimes receives a rebate that partially defrays its lost interest income. Regardless, the borrower pays a fee to the lender when borrowing the securities, and the lender typically splits part of this fee with the lending agent.

According to the International Securities Lending Association (2016), the 30 June 2016 global value of securities made available for lending by institutional investors was EUR 14 trillion. Of this, EUR 1.9 trillion in value was actually loaned, 53% of which was in equity securities. Of global securities on loan, US and Canadian lenders represented 67% of value. Mutual funds and pension funds accounted for 66% of the total value of equity securities loaned. In North America, cash represents approximately 70% of all collateral; in Europe, noncash collateral is more than 80% of the total. ISLA reports that over 60 countries have issued formal legal opinions on the responsibilities of securities lending counterparties.

Securities lending carries risks that can offset the benefits. The main risks are the credit quality of the borrower (credit risk) and the value of the posted collateral (market risk), although liquidity risk and operational risk are additional considerations. Lenders are permitted to sell loaned securities at any time under the normal course of the portfolio management mandate, and the borrowed shares must be returned in time for normal settlement of that sale. However, there is no guarantee that the borrower can deliver on a timely basis.

An additional risk is that lenders can invest cash held as collateral; and if a lender elects to invest the cash in long-term or risky securities, the collateral value is at risk of erosion. As long as the cash is invested in low-risk securities, risk is kept low. Typically, an agreed return on the invested cash is rebated by the lender to the borrower. Similarly, borrowers must pay cash to lenders in lieu of any cash dividends received because the dividends paid by the issuers of the shares will go to the holders. According to Duffie, Gârleanu, and Pedersen (2002), institutional investors such as index mutual funds and pension funds are viewed as preferred lenders because they are long-term holders of shares and unlikely to claim their shares back abruptly from borrowers.

The example of Sigma Finance Company illustrates collateral investment risk. Sigma Finance was a structured investment vehicle that primarily held long-term debt financed by short-term borrowings, and profit came from the interest differential. During the credit 2008–2009 global financial crisis, Sigma was downgraded by the rating agencies and lost its ability to borrow in the short-term markets, which led to default. Investors in Sigma's credit offerings, many of them security lenders, suffered substantial losses because of the default.

Borrowers take formal legal title to the securities, receive all cash flows and voting rights, and pay an annualized cost of borrowing (typically 2–10%). The borrowing cost depends on the borrower's credit quality and how difficult it is to borrow the security in question. Some securities are widely recognized as "easy to borrow" (ETB).

A popular exchange-traded fund (ETF) represents a good example of how securities lending revenue can provide a benefit to investment beneficiaries. As of 31 March 2016, the USD 25.344 billion iShares Russell 2000 ETF had loaned out USD 4.273 billion in securities to 19 counterparties. This amount was 100% collateralized with cash. An affiliated party, BlackRock Institutional Trust Company, served as the securities lending agent in exchange for 4 basis points of collateral investment fees annually, totaling USD 29 million for the year ending 31 March 2016. IWM's net securities lending income for the year was slightly above USD 10 million, which nearly offset the approximately USD 14 million in investment advisory fees charged by the portfolio managers.

8.3 Investor Activism and Engagement by Passive Managers

Institutional investors, especially index fund managers, are among the largest shareholders of many companies. The shares that they vote can have a large influence on corporate elections and outcomes of the proxy process. Their status as large shareholders often gives such investors access to private meetings with corporate management to discuss their concerns and preferences regarding corporate policies on board structure and composition, management compensation, operational risk management, the integrity of accounting statements, and other matters. Goldstein (2014) reports that in a survey, about two-thirds of public companies indicate investor engagement in 2014 was higher than it had been three years earlier. The typical points of contact were investor relations specialists, general counsel/corporate secretary, the board chair, and the CEO or CFO of the company. The respondents also reported that engagement is now covering more topics, but the subject matter is not principally financial. Governance policies, executive compensation, and social, environmental, and strategy issues are dominant.

Ferguson (2010) argues that institutional investors—who are themselves required to act in a fiduciary capacity—have a key responsibility to carry out their duties as voting shareholders. Lambiotte, Gibney, and Hartley (2014) assert that if done in an enlightened way, voting and engagement with company management by passive investors can be a return-enhancing activity. Many hedge funds and other large investors even specialize in activism to align governance in their invested companies with shareholder interests.

Activist investors are usually associated with active portfolio management. If their activism efforts do not produce the desired result, they can express their dissatisfaction by selling their shares. In contrast, passive investors hold index-constituent stocks directly or indirectly. If they are attempting to match an index's performance, they do not have the flexibility to sell. Yet both types of investors usually have the opportunity to vote their shares and participate in governance improvements.

Why should governance matter for passive investors in broadly diversified portfolios? Across such portfolios, governance quality is broadly diversified; moreover, by definition, passive investors do not try to select the best-performing companies or avoid the worst. However, corporate governance improvements are aimed at improving the effectiveness of the operations, management, and board oversight of the business. If the resulting efficiency improvements are evidenced in higher returns to index-constituent stocks, the index performance rises and so does the performance of an index-tracking portfolio. Thus, a goal of activism is to increase returns.

Passive investors may even have a higher duty than more-transient active managers to use their influence to improve governance. As long as a stock has membership in the benchmark index, passive managers can be considered permanent shareholders. Such investors might benefit from engaging with company management and boards, even outside the usual proxy season. Reinforcing the concept of permanence, some companies even give greater voting rights to long-term shareholders. Dallas and Barry (2016) examine 12 US companies with voting rights that increase to four, five, or even ten votes per share if the holding period is greater than three and sometimes four years.

Most passive managers have a fiduciary duty to their clients that includes the obligation to vote proxy ballots on behalf of investors. Although shareholder return can be enhanced by engagement, the costs of these measures must also be considered. Among the more significant costs are staff resources required to become familiar with key issues and to engage management, regulators, and other investors. Researching and voting thousands of proxy ballots becomes problematic for many managers. They frequently hire a proxy voting service, such as Institutional Shareholder Services or Broadridge Financial Services, to achieve their goal of voting the proxy ballots in their clients' favor.

Although a strong argument can be made in favor of even passive managers voting their shares in an informed way and pursuing governance changes when warranted, potential conflicts of interest may limit investors' propensity to challenge company management. Consider the hypothetical case of a large financial firm that earns substantial fees from its business of administering corporate retirement plans, including the pension plan of Millheim Corp. Let us say that the financial firm also manages index funds, and Millheim's stock is one of many index constituents. If Millheim becomes the target of shareholder activism, the financial firm's incentives are structured to support Millheim's management on any controversial issue.

Some may question the probable effectiveness of activist efforts by passive investors. Management of the company targeted by activist investors is likely to see active portfolio managers as skillful and willing users of the proxy process to effect changes and accordingly will respond seriously. In contrast, passive investors are required to hold the company's shares to fulfill their tracking mandate (without the flexibility to sell or take a short position), and management may be aware of this constrained position and thus take passive investors' activist activities less seriously.

SUMMARY

This reading explains the rationale for passive investing as well as the construction of equity market indexes and the various methods by which investors can track the indexes. Passive portfolio managers must understand benchmark index construction and the advantages and disadvantages of the various methods used to track index performance.

Among the key points made in this reading are the following:

- Active equity portfolio managers who focus on individual security selection have long been unsuccessful at beating benchmarks and have charged high management fees to their end investors. Consequently, passive investing has increased in popularity.

- Passive equity investors seek to track the return of benchmark indexes and construct their portfolios to reflect the characteristics of the chosen benchmarks.

- Selection of a benchmark is driven by the equity investor's objectives and constraints as presented in the investment policy statement. The benchmark index must be rules-based, transparent, and investable. Specific important characteristics include the domestic or foreign market covered, the market capitalization of the constituent stocks, where the index falls in the value–growth spectrum, and other risk factors.

- The equity benchmark index weighting scheme is another important consideration for investors. Weighting methods include market-cap weighting, price weighting, equal weighting, and fundamental weighting. Market cap-weighting has several advantages, including the fact that weights adjust automatically.

- Index rebalancing and reconstitution policies are important features. Rebalancing involves adjusting the portfolio's constituent weights after price changes, mergers, or other corporate events have caused those weights to deviate from the benchmark index. Reconstitution involves deleting names that are no longer in the index and adding names that have been approved as new index members.

- Increasingly, passive investors use index-based strategies to gain exposure to individual risk factors. Examples of known equity risk factors include Capitalization, Style, Yield, Momentum, Volatility, and Quality.

- For passive investors, portfolio tracking error is the standard deviation of the portfolio return net of the benchmark return.

- Indexing involves the goal of minimizing tracking error subject to realistic portfolio constraints.

- Methods of pursuing passive investing include the use of such pooled investments as mutual funds and exchange-traded funds (ETFs), a do-it-yourself approach of building the portfolio stock-by-stock, and using derivatives to obtain exposure.

- Conventional open-end index mutual funds generally maintain low fees. Their expense ratios are slightly higher than for ETFs, but a brokerage fee is usually required for investor purchases and sales of ETF shares.

- Index exposure can also be obtained through the use of derivatives, such as futures and swaps.

- Building a passive portfolio by full replication, meaning to hold all the index constituents, requires a large-scale portfolio and high-quality information about the constituent characteristics. Most equity index portfolios are managed using either a full replication strategy to keep tracking error low, are sampled to keep trading costs low, or use optimization techniques to match as closely as possible the characteristics and performance of the underlying index.

- The principal sources of passive portfolio tracking error are fees, trading costs, and cash drag. Cash drag refers to the dilution of the return on the equity assets because of cash held. Cash drag can be exacerbated by the receipt of dividends from constituent stocks and the delay in getting them converted into shares.

- Portfolio managers control tracking error by minimizing trading costs, netting investor cash inflows and redemptions, and using equitization tools like derivatives to compensate for cash drag.

- Many index fund managers offer the constituent securities held in their portfolios for lending to short sellers and other market participants. The income earned from lending those securities helps offset portfolio management costs, often resulting in lower net fees to investors.

- Investor activism is engagement with portfolio companies and recognizing the primacy of end investors. Forms of activism can include expressing views to company boards or management on executive compensation, operational risk, board governance, and other value-relevant matters.

- Successful passive equity investment requires an understanding of the investor's needs, benchmark index construction, and methods available to track the index.

REFERENCES

Arnott, Robert, Jason Hsu, and Philip Moore. 2005. "Fundamental Indexation." *Financial Analysts Journal*, vol. 61, no. 2: 83–99.

Banz, Rolf W. 1981. "The Relationship between Return and Market Value of Common Stocks." *Journal of Financial Economics*, vol. 9, no. 1: 3–18.

Brinson, Gary P., L. Randolph Hood, and Gilbert L. Beebower. 1986. "Determinants of Portfolio Performance." *Financial Analysts Journal*, vol. 42, no. 4: 39–44.

Chen, Honghui, Gregory Noronha, and Vijay Singal. 2004. "The Price Response to S&P 500 Index Additions and Deletions: Evidence of Asymmetry and a New Explanation." *Journal of Finance*, vol. 63, no. 4: 1537–1573.

Choueifaty, Yves, and Yves Coignard. 2008. "Toward Maximum Diversification." *Journal of Portfolio Management*, vol. 35, no. 1: 40–51.

Dallas, Lynne, and Jordan M. Barry. 2016. "Long-Term Shareholders and Time-Phased Voting." *Delaware Journal of Corporate Law*, vol. 40, no. 2: 541–646.

Duffie, Darrell, Nicolae Gârleanu, and Lasse Heje Pedersen. 2002. "Securities Lending, Shorting, and Pricing." *Journal of Financial Economics*, vol. 66, no. 2–3: 307–339.

Fabozzi, Frank J., Sergio M. Focardi, and Petter N. Kolm. 2010. *Quantitative Equity Investing: Techniques and Strategies*. Hoboken, NJ: John Wiley & Sons.

Fama, Eugene F., and Kenneth R. French. 2015. "A Five-Factor Asset Pricing Model." *Journal of Financial Economics*, vol. 116, no. 1: 1–22.

Ferguson, Roger W., Jr 2010. "Riding Herd on Company Management." *Wall Street Journal* (27 April).

French, Kenneth R. 2008. "The Cost of Active Investing." *Journal of Finance*, vol. 63, no. 4: 1537–1573.

Goldstein, Marc. 2014. "Defining Engagement: An Update on the Evolving Relationship between Shareholders, Directors, and Executives." Institutional Shareholder Services for the Investor Responsibility Research Center Institute: 1–48.

Hannam, Richard, and Frédéric Jamet. 2017. "IQ Insights: Equal Weighting and Other Forms of Size Tilting." SSGA white paper (January).

Hill, Joanne M., and Rebecca K. Cheong. 1996. "Minimizing Cash Drag with S&P 500 Index Tools." Goldman Sachs New York working paper.

International Securities Lending Association. 2015. "Establishing an Agency Securities Lending Program." ISLA white paper available at www.isla.co.uk.

International Securities Lending Association. 2016. "ISLA Securities Lending Market Report" (September): http://www.isla.co.uk/wp-content/uploads/2016/10/ISLA-SL-REPORT-9-16-final.pdf.

Jacobs, Bruce I., and Kenneth N. Levy. 2014. "Smart Beta versus Smart Alpha." *Journal of Portfolio Management*, vol. 40, no. 4: 4–7.

Jorion, Philippe. 2003. "Portfolio Optimization with Tracking-Error Constraints." *Financial Analysts Journal*, vol. 59, no. 5: 70–82.

Lambiotte, Clay, Paul Gibney, and Joel Hartley. 2014. "Activist Equity Investing: Unlocking Value by Acting as a Catalyst for Corporate Change." LCP: Insight-Clarity-Advice. Lane, Clark, and Peacock LLP (August): 1–2.

Malevergne, Yannick, Pedro Santa-Clara, and Didier Sornette. 2009. "Professor Zipf Goes to Wall Street." NBER Working Paper 15295 (August).

MSCI. 2017. "MSCI US Equity Indexes Methodology":www.msci.com/eqb/methodology/meth_docs/MSCI_Feb17_USEI_Methodology.pdf.

Perold, André, and Robert S. Salomon, Jr. 1991. "The Right Amount of Assets under Management." *Financial Analysts Journal*, vol. 47, no. 3: 31–39.

Petajisto, Antti. 2010. "The Index Premium and Its Hidden Cost for Index Funds." NYU Stern Working paper.

Podkaminer, Gene. 2015. "The Education of Beta—Revisited." Callan Investments Institute white paper.

Qin, Nan, and Vijay Singal. 2015. "Investor Portfolios When Stocks Are Mispriced: Equally-Weighted or Value-Weighted?" Virginia Tech working paper.

Renshaw, Edward F., and Paul J. Feldstein. 1960. "The Case for an Unmanaged Investment Company." *Financial Analysts Journal*, vol. 16, no. 1: 43–46.

Roll, Richard. 1992. "A Mean/Variance Analysis of Tracking Error." *Journal of Portfolio Management*, vol. 18, no. 4: 13–22.

Soe, Aye M., and Ryan Poirer. 2016. "SPIVA U.S. Scorecard." S&P Dow Jones Indices Report.

Woerheide, Walt, and Don Persson. 1993. "An Index of Portfolio Diversification." *Financial Services Review*, vol. 2, no. 2: 73–85.

Zeng, Liu, and Frank Luo. 2013. "10 Years Later: Where in the World Is Equal Weight Indexing Now?" Standard & Poor's white paper.

PRACTICE PROBLEMS

The following information relates to questions 1–8

Evan Winthrop, a senior officer of a US-based corporation, meets with Rebecca Tong, a portfolio manager at Cobalt Wealth Management. Winthrop recently moved his investments to Cobalt in response to his previous manager's benchmark-relative underperformance and high expenses.

Winthrop resides in Canada and plans to retire there. His annual salary covers his current spending needs, and his vested defined benefit pension plan is sufficient to meet retirement income goals. Winthrop prefers passive exposure to global equity markets with a focus on low management costs and minimal tracking error to any index benchmarks. The fixed-income portion of the portfolio may consist of laddered maturities with a home-country bias.

Tong proposes using an equity index as a basis for an investment strategy and reviews the most important requirements for an appropriate benchmark. With regard to investable indexes, Tong tells Winthrop the following:

Statement 1   A free-float adjustment to a market-capitalization weighted index lowers its liquidity.

Statement 2   An index provider that incorporates a buffering policy makes the index more investable.

Winthrop asks Tong to select a benchmark for the domestic stock allocation that holds all sectors of the Canadian equity market and to focus the portfolio on highly liquid, well-known companies. In addition, Winthrop specifies that any stock purchased should have a relatively low beta, a high dividend yield, a low P/E, and a low price-to-book ratio (P/B).

Winthrop and Tong agree that only the existing equity investments need to be liquidated. Tong suggests that, as an alternative to direct equity investments, the new equity portfolio be composed of the exchange-traded funds (ETFs) shown in Exhibit 1.

Exhibit 1   Available Equity ETFs

Equity Benchmark	ETF Ticker	Number of Constituents	P/B	P/E	Fund Expense Ratio
S&P/TSX 60	XIU	60	2.02	17.44	0.18%
S&P 500	SPY	506	1.88	15.65	0.10%
MSCI EAFE	EFA	933	2.13	18.12	0.33%

Winthrop asks Tong about the techniques wealth managers and fund companies use to create index-tracking equity portfolios that minimize tracking error and costs. In response, Tong outlines two frequently used methods:

Method 1   One process requires that all index constituents are available for trading and liquid, but significant brokerage commissions can occur when the index is large.

Method 2   When tracking an index with a large number of constituents and/or managing a relatively low level of assets, a relatively straightforward and technically unsophisticated method can be used to build a passive portfolio that requires fewer individual securities than the index and reduces brokerage commission costs.

Tong adds that portfolio stocks may be used to generate incremental revenue, thereby partially offsetting administrative costs but potentially creating undesirable counterparty and collateral risks.

After determining Winthrop's objectives and constraints, the CAD147 million portfolio's new strategic policy is to target long-term market returns while being fully invested at all times. Tong recommends quarterly rebalancing, currency hedging, and a composite benchmark composed of equity and fixed-income indexes. Currently the USD is worth CAD1.2930, and this exchange rate is expected to remain stable during the next month. Exhibit 2 presents the strategic asset allocation and benchmark weights.

Exhibit 2   Composite Benchmark and Policy Weights

Asset Class	Benchmark Index	Policy Weight
Canadian equity	S&P/TSX 60	40.0%
US equity	S&P 500	15.0%
International developed markets equity	MSCI EAFE	15.0%
Canadian bonds	DEX Universe	30.0%
Total portfolio		100.0%

In one month, Winthrop will receive a performance bonus of USD5,750,000. He believes that the US equity market is likely to increase during this timeframe. To take advantage of Winthrop's market outlook, he instructs Tong to immediately initiate an equity transaction using the S&P 500 futures contract with a current price of 2,464.29 while respecting the policy weights in Exhibit 2. The S&P 500 futures contract multiplier is 250, and the S&P 500 E-mini multiplier is 50.

Tong cautions Winthrop that there is a potential pitfall with the proposed request when it comes time to analyze performance. She discloses to Winthrop that equity index futures returns can differ from the underlying index, primarily because of corporate actions such as the declaration of dividends and stock splits.

1 Which of Tong's statements regarding equity index benchmarks is (are) correct?

  A Only Statement 1

  B Only Statement 2

  C Both Statement 1 and Statement 2

2 To satisfy Winthrop's benchmark and security selection specifications, the Canadian equity index benchmark Tong selects should be:

  A small-capitalization with a core tilt.

  B large-capitalization with a value tilt.

  C mid-capitalization with a growth tilt.

Practice Problems

3 Based on Exhibit 1 and assuming a full-replication indexing approach, the tracking error is expected to be highest for:
   A XIU.
   B SPY.
   C EFA.

4 Method 1's portfolio construction process is *most likely*:
   A optimization.
   B full replication.
   C stratified sampling.

5 Method 2's portfolio construction process is *most likely*:
   A optimization.
   B full replication.
   C stratified sampling.

6 The method that Tong suggests to add incremental revenue is:
   A program trading.
   B securities lending.
   C attribution analysis.

7 In preparation for receipt of the performance bonus, Tong should immediately:
   A buy two US E-mini equity futures contracts.
   B sell nine US E-mini equity futures contracts.
   C buy seven US E-mini equity futures contracts.

8 The risk that Tong discloses regarding the equity futures strategy is *most likely*:
   A basis risk.
   B currency risk.
   C counterparty risk.

The following information relates to questions 9–14

The Mackenzie Education Foundation funds educational projects in a four-state region of the United States. Because of the investment portfolio's poor benchmark-relative returns, the foundation's board of directors hired a consultant, Stacy McMahon, to analyze performance and provide recommendations.

McMahon meets with Autumn Laubach, the foundation's executive director, to review the existing asset allocation strategy. Laubach believes the portfolio's underperformance is attributable to the equity holdings, which are allocated 55% to a US large-capitalization index fund, 30% to an actively managed US small-cap fund, and 15% to an actively managed developed international fund.

Laubach states that that the board is interested in following a passive approach for some or all of the equity allocation. In addition, the board is open to approaches that could generate returns in excess of the benchmark for part of the equity allocation. McMahon suggests that the board consider following a passive factor-based momentum strategy for the allocation to international stocks.

McMahon observes that the benchmark used for the US large-cap equity component is a price-weighted index containing 150 stocks. The benchmark's Herfindahl–Hirschman Index (HHI) is 0.0286.

McMahon performs a sector attribution analysis based on Exhibit 1 to explain the large-cap portfolio's underperformance relative to the benchmark.

Exhibit 1 Trailing 12-Month US Large-Cap Returns and Foundation/Benchmark Weights

Sector	Sector Returns	Foundation Sector Weights	Benchmark Sector Weights
Information technology	10.75%	18.71%	19.06%
Consumer staples	12.31%	16.52%	16.10%
Energy	8.63%	9.38%	9.53%
Utilities	−3.92%	8.76%	8.25%
Financials	7.05%	6.89%	6.62%

The board decides to consider adding a mid-cap manager. McMahon presents candidates for the mid-cap portfolio. Exhibit 2 provides fees and cash holdings for three portfolios and an index fund.

Exhibit 2 Characteristics of US Mid-Cap Portfolios and Index Fund

	Portfolio 1	Portfolio 2	Portfolio 3	Index Fund
Fees	0.10%	0.09%	0.07%	0.03%
Cash holdings	6.95%	3.42%	2.13%	0.51%

9 Compared with broad-market-cap weighting, the international equity strategy suggested by McMahon is *most likely* to:
  A concentrate risk exposure.
  B be based on the efficient market hypothesis.
  C overweight stocks that recently experienced large price decreases.

10 The international strategy suggested by McMahon is *most likely* characterized as:
  A risk based.
  B return oriented.
  C diversification oriented.

11 The initial benchmark used for the US large-cap allocation:
  A is unaffected by stocks splits.
  B is essentially a liquidity-weighted index.
  C holds the same number of shares in each component stock.

12 Based on its HHI, the initial US large-cap benchmark *most likely* has:
  A a concentration level of 4.29.
  B an effective number of stocks of approximately 35.

Practice Problems

    C individual stocks held in approximately equal weights.

13 Using a sector attribution analysis based on Exhibit 1, which US large-cap sector is the primary contributor to the portfolio's underperformance relative to the benchmark?

    A Utilities

    B Consumer staples

    C Information technology

14 Based on Exhibit 2, which portfolio will *most likely* have the lowest tracking error?

    A Portfolio 1

    B Portfolio 2

    C Portfolio 3

SOLUTIONS

1. B is correct. The three requirements for an index to become the basis for an equity investment strategy are that the index be (a) rules based, (b) transparent, and (c) investable. Buffering makes index benchmarks more investable (Statement 2) by making index transitions a more gradual and orderly process.

   A is incorrect because basing the index weight of an individual security solely on the total number of shares outstanding without using a free-float adjustment may make the index less investable. If a stock market cap excludes shares held by founders, governments, or other companies, then the remaining shares more accurately reflect the stock's true liquidity. Thus a free-float adjustment (Statement 1) to a market index more accurately reflects its actual liquidity (it does not lower its liquidity). Many indexes require that individual stocks have float and average shares traded above a certain percentage of shares outstanding.

2. B is correct. To address Winthrop's concerns (sector diversification, liquidity, risk, dividend yield, P/E, and P/B), the Canadian equity index benchmark should consist of large-capitalization stocks with a value tilt. A large-capitalization index contains the largest-cap stocks, which tend to have the highest liquidity. Value stocks tend to exhibit high dividend yields and low P/E and P/B ratios.

   A is incorrect because small-capitalization stocks tend to be riskier than large-capitalization stocks. Winthrop has a preference for low-beta (risk) stocks.

   C is incorrect because a growth index will not address Winthrop's preference for a low P/E. Growth stocks exhibit characteristics such as high price momentum, high P/Es, and high EPS growth.

3. C is correct. An index that contains a large number of constituents will tend to create higher tracking error than one with fewer constituents. Based on the number of constituents in the three indexes (S&P/TSX 60 has 60, S&P 500 has 506, and MSCI EAFE has 933), EFA (the MSCI EAFE ETF) is expected to have the highest tracking error. Higher expense ratios (XIU: 0.18%; SPY: 0.10%; and EFA: 0.33%) also contribute to lower excess returns and higher tracking error, which implies that EFA has the highest expected tracking error.

4. B is correct. Full replication occurs when a manager holds all securities represented by the index in weightings that closely match the actual index weightings. Thus it requires that all index constituents are liquid and available for trading, and the asset size of the mandate must also be sufficient. Significant brokerage commissions can occur, however, when the index is large.

5. C is correct. Stratified sampling methods are most frequently used when a portfolio manager is tracking an index that has a large number of constituents, or when managing a relatively low level of assets. Brokerage fees can become excessive when the number of constituents in the index is large.

   A is incorrect because optimization does not involve simple techniques. Optimization requires a high level of technical sophistication, including familiarity with computerized optimization software or algorithms, and a good understanding of the output.

   B is incorrect because full replication occurs when a manager holds all (not fewer) securities represented by the index in weightings that closely match actual index weightings. Full replication techniques require that the mandate's

Solutions

asset size is sufficient and that the index constituents are available for trading. Full replication can create significant brokerage commissions when the index is large.

6. B is correct. Securities lending is typically used to offset the costs associated with portfolio management. By lending stocks, however, the investor is exposed to the credit quality of the stocks' borrower (counterparty or credit risk) and to risks involved with the posted collateral (market risk).

   A is incorrect because program trading is a strategy of buying or selling many stocks simultaneously. It is used primarily by institutional investors, typically for large-volume trades. Orders from the trader's computer are entered directly into the market's computer system and executed automatically.

   C is incorrect because attribution analysis is not a method of generating incremental revenue. Attribution analysis is a method that helps the manager understand the sources of return.

7. C is correct. The amount of the performance bonus that will be received in one month (USD5,750,000) needs to be invested passively based upon the strategic allocation recommended by Tong. Using the strategic allocation of the portfolio, 15% (USD862,500.00) should be allocated to US equity exposure using the S&P 500 E-mini contract, which trades in US dollars. Because the futures price is 2,464.29 and the S&P 500 E-mini multiplier is 50, the contract unit value is USD123,214.50 (2,464.29 × 50).

   The correct number of futures contracts is (5,750,000.00 × 0.15)/123,214.50 = 7.00.

   Therefore, Tong will buy seven S&P 500 E-mini futures contracts.

8. A is correct. Basis risk results from using a hedging instrument that is imperfectly matched to the investment being hedged. Basis risk can arise when the underlying securities pay dividends, because the futures contract tracks only the price of the underlying index. Stock splits do not affect investment performance comparisons.

9. A is correct. Compared with broad-market-cap weighting, passive factor-based strategies tend to concentrate risk exposure, leaving investors vulnerable during periods when the risk factor (e.g., momentum) is out of favor.

10. B is correct. McMahon suggests that the foundation follow a passive factor-based momentum strategy, which is generally defined by the amount of a stock's excess price return relative to the market during a specified period. Factor-based momentum strategies are classified as return oriented.

11. C is correct. The initial benchmark used for the US large-cap allocation is a price-weighted index. In a price-weighted index, the weight of each stock is its price per share divided by the sum of all the share prices in the index. As a result, a price-weighted index can be interpreted as a portfolio composed of one share of each constituent security.

12. B is correct. The HHI measures stock concentration risk in a portfolio, calculated as the sum of the constituent weightings squared:

$$\text{HHI} = \sum_{i=1}^{n} w_i^2$$

Using the HHI, one can estimate the effective number of stocks, held in equal weights, that would mimic the concentration level of the respective index. The effective number of stocks for a portfolio is calculated as the reciprocal of the

HHI. The HHI is 0.0286; the reciprocal (1/0.0286) is 34.97. Therefore, the effective number of stocks to mimic the US large-cap benchmark is approximately 35.

13 C is correct. Below is the attribution analysis for selected sectors of the US large-cap portfolio.

Sector	Sector Return (A)	US Large-Cap Core Portfolio		Large-Cap Benchmark		Attribution Analysis
		Sector Weight (B)	Contribution to Return (C) = (A) × (B)	Sector Weight (D)	Contribution to Return (E) = (A) × (D)	Difference (F) = (C) − (E)
Information technology	10.75%	18.71%	2.01%	19.06%	2.05%	−0.04%
Consumer staples	12.31%	16.52%	2.03%	16.10%	1.98%	0.05%
Energy	8.63%	9.38%	0.81%	9.53%	0.82%	−0.01%
Utilities	−3.92%	8.76%	−0.34%	8.25%	−0.32%	−0.02%
Financials	7.05%	6.89%	0.49%	6.62%	0.47%	0.02%

Based on this analysis, the US large-cap portfolio's information technology sector is the primary contributor to the portfolio's disappointing equity returns because it provided the largest negative differential relative to the benchmark, with a differential of −0.04%. Although the information technology sector had a positive return, this sector was underweighted relative to the benchmark, resulting in a negative contribution to the portfolio's returns.

14 C is correct. Of the three portfolios, Portfolio 3 has the lowest cash holding and the lowest fees. As a result, Portfolio 3 has the potential for the lowest tracking error compared with the other proposed portfolios.

PORTFOLIO MANAGEMENT
STUDY SESSION

8

Equity Portfolio Management (2)

This study session takes an in-depth look at active equity portfolio management. It begins with a discussion of quantitative and fundamental equity strategies, including the underlying rationale for the investment approach and how they are created, whether top-down or bottom-up. Factor-based investing, as well as key specialized equity strategies such as activist investing and statistical arbitrage, are explored. The study session concludes with a discussion of issues important in active equity portfolio construction, including active share, active risk, risk budgeting, and constraints on portfolio construction.

READING ASSIGNMENT

Reading 17	Active Equity Investing: Strategies by Bing Li, PhD, CFA, Yin Luo, CPA, PStat, CFA, and Pranay Gupta, CFA
Reading 18	Active Equity Investing: Portfolio Construction by Jacques Lussier, PhD, CFA, and Marc R. Reinganum, PhD

READING
17

Active Equity Investing: Strategies

by Bing Li, PhD, CFA, Yin Luo, CPA, PStat, CFA, and Pranay Gupta, CFA

Bing Li, PhD, CFA, is at Yuanyin Asset Management (Hong Kong SAR). Yin Luo, CPA, PStat, CFA, is at Wolfe Research LLC (USA). Pranay Gupta, CFA, is at Allocationmetrics Limited (USA).

LEARNING OUTCOMES	
Mastery	The candidate should be able to:
☐	a. compare fundamental and quantitative approaches to active management;
☐	b. analyze bottom-up active strategies, including their rationale and associated processes;
☐	c. analyze top-down active strategies, including their rationale and associated processes;
☐	d. analyze factor-based active strategies, including their rationale and associated processes;
☐	e. analyze activist strategies, including their rationale and associated processes;
☐	f. describe active strategies based on statistical arbitrage and market microstructure;
☐	g. describe how fundamental active investment strategies are created;
☐	h. describe how quantitative active investment strategies are created;
☐	i. discuss equity investment style classifications.

INTRODUCTION

1

This reading provides an overview of active equity investing and the major types of active equity strategies. The reading is organized around a classification of active equity strategies into two broad approaches: fundamental and quantitative. Both approaches aim at outperforming a passive benchmark (for example, a broad equity market index), but they tend to make investment decisions differently. Fundamental approaches stress the use of human judgment in processing information and making investment decisions, whereas quantitative approaches tend to rely more heavily on

© 2018 CFA Institute. All rights reserved.

rules-based quantitative models. As a result, some practitioners and academics refer to the fundamental, judgment-based approaches as "discretionary" and to the rules-based, quantitative approaches as "systematic."

This reading is organized as follows. Section 2 introduces fundamental and quantitative approaches to active management. Sections 3–9 discuss bottom-up, top-down, factor-based, and activist investing strategies. Section 10 describes the process of creating fundamental active investment strategies, including the parameters to consider as well as some of the pitfalls. Section 11 describes the steps required to create quantitative active investment strategies, as well as the pitfalls in a quantitative investment process. Section 12 discusses style classifications of active strategies and the uses and limitations of such classifications. A summary of key points completes the reading.

2. APPROACHES TO ACTIVE MANAGEMENT

a compare fundamental and quantitative approaches to active management

Active equity investing may reflect a variety of ideas about profitable investment opportunities. However, with regard to how these investment ideas are implemented—for example, how securities are selected—active strategies can be divided into two broad categories: fundamental and quantitative. Fundamental approaches are based on research into companies, sectors, or markets and involve the application of analyst discretion and judgment. In contrast, quantitative approaches are based on quantitative models of security returns that are applied systematically with limited involvement of human judgment or discretion. The labels *fundamental* and *quantitative* in this context are an imperfect shorthand that should not be misunderstood. The contrast with quantitative approaches does not mean that fundamental approaches do not use quantitative tools. Fundamental approaches often make use of valuation models (such as the free cash flow model), quantitative screening tools, and statistical techniques (e.g., regression analysis). Furthermore, quantitative approaches often make use of variables that relate to company fundamentals. Some investment disciplines may be viewed as hybrids in that they combine elements of both fundamental and quantitative disciplines. In the next sections, we examine these two approaches more closely.

Fundamental research forms the basis of the fundamental approach to investing. Although it can be organized in many ways, fundamental research consistently involves and often begins with the analysis of a company's financial statements. Through such an analysis, this approach seeks to obtain a detailed understanding of the company's current and past profitability, financial position, and cash flows. Along with insights into a company's business model, management team, product lines, and economic outlook, this analysis provides a view on the company's future business prospects and includes a valuation of its shares. Estimates are typically made of the stock's intrinsic value and/or its relative value compared to the shares of a peer group or the stock's own history of market valuations. Based on this valuation and other factors (including overall portfolio considerations), the portfolio manager may conclude that the stock should be bought (or a position increased) or sold (or a position reduced). The decision can also be stated in terms of overweighting, market weighting, or underweighting relative to the portfolio's benchmark.

In the search for investment opportunities, fundamental strategies may have various starting points. Some strategies start at a top or macro level—with analyses of markets, economies, or industries—to narrow the search for likely areas for profitable active investment. These are called top-down strategies. Other strategies, often referred to as bottom-up strategies, make little or no use of macro analysis and instead rely on individual stock analysis to identify areas of opportunity. Research distributed by investment banks and reports produced by internal analysts, organized by industry or economic sector, are also potential sources of investment ideas. The vetting of such ideas may be done by portfolio managers, who may themselves be involved in fundamental research, or by an investment committee.

Quantitative strategies, on the other hand, involve analyst judgment at the design stage, but they largely replace the ongoing reliance on human judgment and discretion with systematic processes that are often dependent on computer programming for execution. These systematic processes search for security and market characteristics and patterns ("factors") that have predictive power in order to identify securities or trades that will earn superior investment returns, in the sense of expected added value relative to risk or expected return relative to a benchmark—for example, an index benchmark or peer benchmark.

Factors that might be considered include valuation (e.g., earnings yield), size (e.g., market capitalization), profitability (e.g., return on equity), financial strength (e.g., debt-to-equity ratio), market sentiment (e.g., analyst consensus on companies' long-term earnings growth), industry membership (e.g., stocks' GICS classification), and price-related attributes (e.g., price momentum). While a wide range of security characteristics have been used to define "factors," some factors (e.g., the aforementioned size, valuation, momentum, and profitability) have been shown to be positively associated with a long-term return premium. We call these *rewarded* factors. Many other factors are used in portfolio construction but have not been empirically proven to offer a persistent return premium, and are thus called *unrewarded* factors.

Once a pattern or relationship between a given variable (or set of variables) and security prices has been established by analysis of past data, a quantitative model is used to predict future expected returns of securities or baskets of securities. Security selection then flows from expected returns, which reflect securities' exposures to the selected variables with predictive power. From a quantitative perspective, investment success depends not on individual company insights but on model quality.

Exhibit 1 presents typical differences between the main characteristics of fundamental and quantitative methodologies.

Exhibit 1 Differences between Fundamental and Quantitative Approaches

	Fundamental	Quantitative
Style	Subjective	Objective
Decision-making process	Discretionary	Systematic, non-discretionary
Primary resources	Human skill, experience, judgment	Expertise in statistical modeling
Information used	Research (company/industry/economy)	Data and statistics
Analysis focus	Conviction (high depth) in stock-, sector-, or region-based selection	A selection of variables, subsequently applied broadly over a large number of securities
Orientation to data	Forecast future corporate parameters and establish views on companies	Attempt to draw conclusions from a variety of historical data
Portfolio construction	Use judgment and conviction within permissible risk parameters	Use optimizers

In the following section, we take a closer look at some of the distinguishing characteristics listed in Exhibit 1 and how they are evolving with the advent of new technologies available to investors.

2.1 Differences in the Nature of the Information Used

To contrast the information used in fundamental and quantitative strategies, we can start by describing typical activities for fundamental investors with a bottom-up investment discipline. Bottom-up fundamental analysts research and analyze a company, using data from company financial statements and disclosures to assess attributes such as profitability, leverage, and absolute or peer-relative valuation. They typically also assess how those metrics compare to their historical values to identify trends and scrutinize such characteristics as the company's management competence, its future prospects, and the competitive position of its product lines. Such analysts usually focus on the more recent financial statements (which include current and previous years' accounting data), notes to the financial statements and assumptions in the accounts, and management discussion and analysis disclosures. Corporate governance is often taken into consideration as well as wider environmental, social, and governance (ESG) characteristics.

Top-down fundamental investors' research focuses first on region, country, or sector information (e.g., economic growth, money supply, and market valuations). Some of the data used by fundamental managers can be measured or expressed numerically and therefore "quantified." Other items, such as management quality and reputation, cannot.

Quantitative approaches often use large amounts of historical data from companies' financial reports (in addition to other information, such as return data) but process those data in a systematic rather than a judgmental way. Judgment is used in model building, particularly in deciding which variables and signals are relevant. Typically, quantitative approaches use historical stock data and statistical techniques to identify variables that may have a statistically significant relationship with stock returns; then these relationships are used to predict individual security returns. In contrast to the fundamental approach, the quantitative approach does not normally consider information or characteristics that cannot be quantified. In order to minimize survivorship and look-ahead biases, historical data used in quantitative research should include stocks that are no longer listed, and accounting data used should be the original, unrestated numbers that were available to the market at that point in time.

Investment Process: Fundamental vs. Quantitative

The goal of the investment process is to construct a portfolio that best reflects the stated investment objective and risk tolerance, with an optimal balance between expected return and risk exposure, subject to the constraints imposed by the investment policy. The investment processes under both fundamental and quantitative approaches involve a number of considerations, such as the methodology and valuation process, which are the subject of this reading. Other considerations, such as portfolio construction and risk management, trade execution, and ongoing performance monitoring, are the subjects of subsequent curriculum readings.

	Fundamental	**Quantitative**
Methodology	Determine methodology to evaluate stocks (bottom-up or top-down, value or growth, income or deep value, intrinsic or relative value, etc.)	Define model to estimate expected stock returns (choose time-series macro-level factors or cross-sectional stock-level factors, identify factors that have a stable positive information coefficient IC, use a factor combination algorithm, etc.)
Valuation process	▪ Prescreen to identify potential investment candidates with stringent financial and market criteria ▪ Perform in-depth analysis of companies to derive their intrinsic values ▪ Determine buy or sell candidates trading at a discount or premium to their intrinsic values	▪ Construct factor exposures across all shares in the same industry ▪ Forecast IC and/or its volatility for each factor by using algorithms (such as artificial intelligence or time-series analysis) or fundamental research ▪ Combine factor exposures to estimate expected returns
Portfolio construction and rebalancing	▪ Allocate assets by determining industry and country/region exposures ▪ Set limits on maximum sector, country, and individual stock positions ▪ Determine buy-and-sell list ▪ Monitor portfolio holdings continuously	▪ Determine which factors to underweight or overweight ▪ Use risk model to measure *ex ante* active risk ▪ Run portfolio optimization with risk model, investment, and risk constraints, as well as the structure of transaction costs ▪ Rebalance at regular intervals

2.2 Differences in the Focus of the Analysis

Fundamental investors usually focus their attention on a relatively small group of stocks and perform in-depth analysis on each one of them. This practice has characteristically given fundamental (or "discretionary") investors an edge of depth in understanding individual companies' businesses over quantitative (or "systematic") investors, who do not focus on individual stocks. Quantitative investors instead usually focus on factors across a potentially very large group of stocks. Therefore, fundamental investors tend to take larger positions in their selected stocks, while quantitative investors tend to focus their analysis on a selection of factors but spread their selected factor bets across a substantially larger group of holdings.[1]

2.3 Difference in Orientation to the Data: Forecasting Fundamentals vs. Pattern Recognition

Fundamental analysis places an emphasis on forecasting future prospects, including the future earnings and cash flows of a company. Fundamental investors use judgment and in-depth analysis to formulate a view of the company's outlook and to identify the catalysts that will generate future growth. They rely on knowledge, experience, and their ability to predict future conditions in a company to make investment decisions. Conceptually, the fundamental approach aims at forecasting forward parameters in order to make investment decisions. That said, many fundamental investors use a

---

[1] The implications for portfolio risk of using individual stocks or factors will be considered in the reading on portfolio construction.

quantitative component in their investment process, such as a quantitative screen or a commercial quantitative risk model such as those produced by Axioma, MSCI, Northfield, and Bloomberg.

In contrast, the quantitative approach aims to predict future returns using conclusions derived from analyzing historical data and patterns therein. Quantitative investors construct models by back-testing on historical data, using what is known about or has been reported by a company, including future earnings estimates that have been published by analysts, to search for the best company characteristics for purposes of stock selection. Once a model based on historical data has been finalized, it is applied to the latest available data to determine investment decisions. While the process is distinct from the fundamental approach, the active return and risk profiles of many fundamentals managers have been explained or replicated using well-known quantitative factors. See, for example, Ang, Goetzman, and Schaefer 2009 and Frazzini, Kabiller, and Pedersen 2013.

Forestalling Look-Ahead Bias

Satyam Computers is an India-based company that provides IT consulting and solutions to its global customers. In the eight years preceding 2009, Satyam overstated its revenues and profits and reported a cash holdings total of approximately $1.04 billion that did not exist. The falsification of the accounts came to light in early 2009, and Satyam was removed from the S&P CNX Nifty 50 index on 12 January.

If a quantitative analyst runs a simulation benchmarked against the S&P CNX Nifty 50 index on 31 December 2008, he or she should include the 50 stocks that were in the index on 31 December 2008 and use only the data for the included stocks that were available to investors as of that date. The analyst should therefore include Satyam as an index constituent and use the original accounting data that were published by the company at that time. While it was subsequently proved that these accounting data were fraudulent, this fact was not known to analysts and investors on 31 December 2008. As a result, it would not have been possible for any analyst to incorporate the true accounting data for Satyam on that date.

2.4 Differences in Portfolio Construction: Judgment vs. Optimization

Fundamental investors typically select stocks by performing extensive research on individual companies, which results in a list of high-conviction stocks. Thus, fundamental investors see risk at the company level. There is a risk that the assessment of the company's fair value is inaccurate, that the business's performance will differ from the analyst's expectations, or that the market will fail to recognize the identified reason for under- or overvaluation. Construction of a fundamental portfolio therefore often depends on judgment, whereby the absolute or index-relative sizes of positions in stocks, sectors, or countries are based on the manager's conviction of his or her forecasts. The portfolio must, of course, still comply with the risk parameters set out in the investment agreements with clients or in the fund prospectus.

In quantitative analysis, on the other hand, the risk is that factor returns will not perform as expected. Because the quantitative approach invests in baskets of stocks, the risks lie at the portfolio level rather than at the level of specific stocks. Construction of a quantitative portfolio is therefore generally done using a portfolio optimizer, which controls for risk at the portfolio level in arriving at individual stock weights.

The two approaches also differ in the way that portfolio changes or rebalancings are performed. Managers using a fundamental approach usually monitor the portfolio's holdings continuously and may increase, decrease, or eliminate positions at any time. Portfolios managed using a quantitative approach are usually rebalanced at regular intervals, such as monthly or quarterly. At each interval, the program or algorithm, using pre-determined rules, automatically selects positions to be sold, reduced, added, or increased.

> **EXAMPLE 1**
>
> ### Fundamental vs. Quantitative Approach
>
> Consider two equity portfolios with the same benchmark index, the MSCI Asia ex Japan. The index contains 627 stocks as of December 2016. One portfolio is managed using a fundamental approach, while the other is managed using a quantitative approach. The fundamental approach–based portfolio is made up of 50 individually selected stocks, which are reviewed for potential sale or trimming on an ongoing basis. In the fundamental approach, the investment universe is first pre-screened by valuation and by the fundamental metrics of earnings yield, dividend yield, earnings growth, and financial leverage. The quantitative approach–based portfolio makes active bets on 400 stocks with monthly rebalancing. The particular approach used is based on a five-factor model of equity returns.
>
> Contrast fundamental and quantitative investment processes with respect to the following:
>
> 1 Constructing the portfolio
> 2 Rebalancing the portfolio
>
> **Solution to 1:**
>
> Fundamental: Construct the portfolio by overweighting stocks that are expected to outperform their peers or the market as a whole. Where necessary for risk reduction, underweight some benchmark stocks that are expected to underperform. The stocks that fell out in the pre-screening process do not have explicit forecasts and will not be included in the portfolio.
>
> Quantitative: Construct the portfolio by maximizing the objective function (such as portfolio alpha or information ratio) with risk models.
>
> **Solution to 2:**
>
> Fundamental: The manager monitors each stock continuously and sells stocks when their market prices surpass the target prices (either through appreciation of the stock price or through reduction of the target price due to changes in expectations).
>
> Quantitative: Portfolios are usually rebalanced at regular intervals, such as monthly.

BOTTOM-UP STRATEGIES

3

b   analyze bottom-up active strategies, including their rationale and associated processes

Equity investors have developed many different techniques for processing all the information necessary to arrive at an investment decision. Multiple approaches may be taken into account in formulating an overall opinion of a stock; however, each analyst will have his or her own set of favorite techniques based on his or her experience and judgment. Depending on the specifics of the investment discipline, most fundamental and quantitative strategies can be characterized as either bottom-up or top-down.

3.1 Bottom-Up Strategies

Bottom-up strategies begin the asset selection process with data at the individual asset and company level, such as price momentum and profitability. Bottom-up quantitative investors harness computer power to apply their models to this asset- and company-level information (with the added requirement that the information be quantifiable). The balance of this section illustrates the bottom-up process as used by fundamental investors. These investors typically begin their analysis at the company level before forming an opinion on the wider sector or market. The ability to identify companies with strong or weak fundamentals depends on the analyst's in-depth knowledge of each company's industry, product lines, business plan, management abilities, and financial strength. After identifying individual companies, the bottom-up approach uses economic and financial analysis to assess the intrinsic value of a company and compares that value with the current market price to determine which stocks are undervalued or overvalued. The analyst may also find companies operating efficiently with good prospects even though the industry they belong to is deteriorating. Similarly, companies with poor prospects may be found in otherwise healthy and prosperous industries.

Fundamental investors often focus on one or more of the following parameters for a company, either individually or in relation to its peers:

- business model and branding
- competitive advantages
- company management and corporate governance

Valuation is based on either a discounted cash flow model or a preferred market multiple, often earnings-related. We address each of these parameters and valuation approaches in turn.

Business Model and Branding. The business model of a company refers to its overall strategy for running the business and generating profit. The business model details how a company converts its resources into products or services and how it delivers those products or services to customers. Companies with a superior business model compete successfully, have scalability, and generate significant earnings. Further, companies with a robust and adaptive business model tend to outperform their peers in terms of return on shareholder equity. The business model gives investors insight into a company's value proposition, its operational flow, the structure of its value chain, its branding strategy, its market segment, and the resulting revenue generation and profit margins. This insight helps investors evaluate the sustainability of the company's competitive advantages and make informed investment decisions.

Corporate branding is a way of defining the company's business for the market in general and retail customers in particular and can be understood as the company's identity as well as its promise to its customers. Strong brand names convey product quality and can give the company an edge over its competitors in both market share and profit margin. It is widely recognized that brand equity plays an important role in the determination of product price, allowing companies to command price premiums after controlling for observed product differentiation. Apple in consumer technology and BMW in motor vehicles, for example, charge more for their products, but customers are willing to pay the premium because of brand loyalty.

Competitive Advantages. A competitive advantage typically allows a company to outperform its peers in terms of the return it generates on its capital. There are many types of competitive advantage, such as access to natural resources, superior technology, innovation, skilled personnel, corporate reputation, brand strength, high entry barriers, exclusive distribution rights, and superior product or customer support.

For value investors, who search for companies that appear to be trading below their intrinsic value (often following earnings disappointments), it is important to understand the sustainability of the company's competitive position when assessing the prospects for recovery.

Company Management. A good management team is crucial to a company's success. Management's role is to allocate resources and capital to maximize the growth of enterprise value for the company's shareholders. A management team that has a long-term rather than a short-term focus is more likely to add value to an enterprise over the long term.

To evaluate management effectiveness, one can begin with the financial statements. Return on assets, equity, or invested capital (compared either to industry peers or to historical rates achieved by the company) and earnings growth over a reasonable time period are examples of indicators used to gauge the value added by management.

Qualitative analysis of the company's management and governance structures requires attention to (1) the alignment of management's interests with those of shareholders to minimize agency problems; (2) the competence of management in achieving the company's objectives (as described in the mission statement) and long-term plans; (3) the stability of the management team and the company's ability to attract and retain high-performing executives; and (4) increasingly, risk considerations and opportunities related to a company's ESG attributes. Analysts also monitor management insider purchases and sales of the company's shares for potential indications of the confidence of management in the company's future.

The above qualitative considerations and financial statement analysis will help in making earnings estimates, cash flow estimates, and evaluations of risk, providing inputs to company valuation. Fundamental strategies within the bottom-up category may use a combination of approaches to stock valuation. Some investors rely on discounted cash flow or dividend models. Others focus on relative valuation, often based on earnings-related valuation metrics such as a P/E, price to book (P/B), and enterprise value (EV)/EBITDA. A conclusion that a security's intrinsic value is different from its current market price means the valuation is using estimates that are different from those reflected in current market prices. Conviction that the analyst's forecasts are, over a particular time period, more accurate than the market's is therefore important, as is the belief that the market will reflect the more accurate estimates within a time frame that is consistent with the strategy's investment horizon.

Bottom-up strategies are often broadly categorized as either value-based (or value-oriented) or growth-based (or growth-oriented), as the following section explains.

3.1.1 Value-Based Approaches

Benjamin Graham is regarded as the father of value investing. Along with David Dodd, he wrote the book *Security Analysis* (1934), which laid the basic framework for value investing. Graham posited that buying earnings and assets relatively inexpensively afforded a "margin of safety" necessary for prudent investing. Consistent with that idea, value-based approaches aim to buy stocks that are trading at a significant discount to their estimated intrinsic value. Value investors typically focus on companies with attractive valuation metrics, reflected in low earnings (or asset) multiples. In their view, investors' sometimes irrational behavior can make stocks trade below the intrinsic value based on company fundamentals. Such opportunities may arise due to a variety of behavioral biases and often reflect investors' overreaction to negative news. Various styles of value-based investing are sometimes distinguished; for example, "relative value" investors purchase stocks on valuation multiples that are high relative to historical levels but that compare favorably to those of the peer group.

3.1.1.1 Relative Value

Investors who pursue a relative value strategy evaluate companies by comparing their value indicators (e.g., P/E or P/B multiples) to the average valuation of companies in the same industry sector with the aim of identifying stocks that offer value relative to their sector peers. As different sectors face different market structures and different competitive and regulatory conditions, average sector multiples vary.

Exhibit 2 lists the key financial ratios for sectors in the Hang Seng Index on the last trading day of 2016. The average P/E for companies in the energy sector is almost five times the average P/E for those in real estate. A consumer staples company trading on a P/E of 12 would appear undervalued relative to its sector, while a real estate company trading on the same P/E multiple of 12 would appear overvalued relative to its sector.

Exhibit 2 Key Financial Ratios of Hang Seng Index (30 December 2016)

	Weight	Dividend Yield	Price-to-Earnings Ratio (P/E)	Price-to-Cash-Flow Ratio (P/CF)	Price-to-Book Ratio (P/B)	Total Debt to Common Equity (%)	Current Ratio
Hang Seng Index	100.0	3.5	12.2	6.1	1.1	128.4	1.3
Consumer discretionary	2.9	4.1	21.3	12.5	3.0	26.3	1.4
Consumer staples	1.6	2.6	16.8	14.3	3.3	62.1	1.4
Energy	7.0	2.6	39.5	3.7	0.9	38.5	1.0
Financials	47.5	4.3	10.1	5.0	1.1	199.8	1.1
Industrials	5.5	3.8	11.8	6.0	0.9	158.7	1.2
Information technology	11.4	0.6	32.7	19.9	8.2	60.2	1.0
Real estate	10.6	3.9	8.3	8.0	0.7	30.3	2.5
Telecommunication services	7.8	3.2	13.3	4.6	1.4	11.5	0.7
Utilities	5.6	3.7	14.2	10.8	1.7	47.0	1.3

Source: Bloomberg.

Investors usually recognize that in addition to the simple comparison of a company's multiple to that of the sector, one needs a good understanding of why the valuation is what it is. A premium or discount to the industry may well be justified by the company's fundamentals.

3.1.1.2 Contrarian Investing

Contrarian investors purchase and sell shares against prevailing market sentiment. Their investment strategy is to go against the crowd by buying poorly performing stocks at valuations they find attractive and then selling them at a later time, following what they expect to be a recovery in the share price. Companies in which contrarian managers invest are frequently depressed cyclical stocks with low or even negative earnings or low dividend payments. Contrarians expect these stocks to rebound once the company's earnings have turned around, resulting in substantial price appreciation.

Contrarian investors often point to research in behavioral finance suggesting that investors tend to overweight recent trends and to follow the crowd in making investment decisions. A contrarian investor attempts to determine whether the valuation of an individual company, industry, or entire market is irrational—that is, undervalued or overvalued at any time—and whether that irrationality represents an exploitable mispricing of shares. Accordingly, contrarian investors tend to go against the crowd.

Both contrarian investors and value investors who do not describe their style as contrarian aim to buy shares at a discount to their intrinsic value. The primary difference between the two is that non-contrarian value investors rely on fundamental metrics to make their assessments, while contrarian investors rely more on market sentiment and sharp price movements (such as 52-week high and low prices as sell and buy prices) to make their decisions.

3.1.1.3 High-Quality Value Some value-based strategies give valuation close attention but place at least equal emphasis on financial strength and demonstrated profitability. For example, one such investment discipline requires a record of consistent earnings power, above-average return on equity, financial strength, and exemplary management. There is no widely accepted label for this value style, the refinement of which is often associated with investor Warren Buffett.[2]

3.1.1.4 Income Investing The income investing approach focuses on shares that offer relatively high dividend yields and positive dividend growth rates. Several rationales for this approach have been offered. One argument is that a secure, high dividend yield tends to put a floor under the share price in the case of companies that are expected to maintain such a dividend. Another argument points to empirical studies that demonstrate the higher returns to equities with these characteristics and their greater ability to withstand market declines.

3.1.1.5 Deep-Value Investing A value investor with a deep-value orientation focuses on undervalued companies that are available at extremely low valuation relative to their assets (e.g., low P/B). Such companies are often those in financial distress. The rationale is that market interest in such securities may be limited, increasing the chance of informational inefficiencies. The deep-value investor's special area of expertise may lie in reorganizations or related legislation, providing a better position from which to assess the likelihood of company recovery.

3.1.1.6 Restructuring and Distressed Investing While the restructuring and distressed investment strategies are more commonly observed in the distressed-debt space, some equity investors specialize in these disciplines. Opportunities in restructuring and distressed investing are generally counter cyclical relative to the overall economy or to the business cycle of a particular sector. A weak economy generates increased incidence of companies facing financial distress. When a company is having difficulty meeting its short-term liabilities, it will often propose to restructure its financial obligations or change its capital structure.

Restructuring investors seek to purchase the debt or equity of companies in distress. A distressed company that goes through restructuring may still have valuable assets, distribution channels, or patents that make it an attractive acquisition target. Restructuring investing is often done before an expected bankruptcy or during the bankruptcy process. The goal of restructuring investing is to gain control or substantial influence over a company in distress at a large discount and then restructure it to restore a large part of its intrinsic value.

---

[2] See Greenwald, Kahn, Sonkin, and Biema (2001).

Effective investment in a distressed company depends on skill and expertise in identifying companies whose situation is better than the market believes it to be. Distressed investors assume that either the company will survive or there will be sufficient assets remaining upon liquidation to generate an appropriate return on investment.

3.1.1.7 Special Situations The "special situations" investment style focuses on the identification and exploitation of mispricings that may arise as a result of corporate events such as divestitures or spinoffs of assets or divisions or mergers with other entities. In the opinion of many investors such situations represent short-term opportunities to exploit mispricing that result from such special situations. According to Greenblatt (2010), investors often overlook companies that are in such special situations as restructuring (involving asset disposals or spinoffs) and mergers, which may create opportunities to add value through active investing. To take advantage of such opportunities, this type of investing requires specific knowledge of the industry and the company, as well as legal expertise.

3.1.2 Growth-Based Approaches

Growth-based investment approaches focus on companies that are expected to grow faster than their industry or faster than the overall market, as measured by revenues, earnings, or cash flow. Growth investors usually look for high-quality companies with consistent growth or companies with strong earnings momentum. Characteristics usually examined by growth investors include historical and estimated future growth of earnings or cash flows, underpinned by attributes such as a solid business model, cost control, and exemplary management able to execute long-term plans to achieve higher growth. Such companies typically feature above-average return on equity, a large part of which they retain and reinvest in funding future growth. Because growth companies may also have volatile earnings and cash flows going forward, the intrinsic values calculated by discounting expected future cash flows are subject to relatively high uncertainty. Compared to value-focused investors, growth-focused investors have a higher tolerance for above-average valuation multiples.

GARP (growth at a reasonable price) is a sub-discipline within growth investing. This approach is used by investors who seek out companies with above-average growth that trade at reasonable valuation multiples, and is often referred to as a hybrid of growth and value investing. Many investors who use GARP rely on the P/E-to-growth (PEG) ratio—calculated as the stock's P/E divided by the expected earnings growth rate (in percentage terms)—while also paying attention to variations in risk and duration of growth.

EXAMPLE 2

Characteristic Securities for Bottom-Up Investment Disciplines

The following table provides information on four stocks.

Company	Price	12-Month Forward EPS	3-Year EPS Growth Forecast	Dividend Yield	Industry Sector	Sector Average P/E
A	50	5	20%	1%	Industrial	10
B	56	2	2%	0%	Information technology	35

Company	Price	12-Month Forward EPS	3-Year EPS Growth Forecast	Dividend Yield	Industry Sector	Sector Average P/E
C	22	10	–5%	2%	Consumer staples	15
D	32	2	2%	8%	Utilities	16

Using only the information given in the table above, for each stock, determine which fundamental investment discipline would most likely select it.

Solution:

- Company A's forward P/E is 50/5 = 10, and its P/E-to-growth ratio (PEG) is 10/20 = 0.5, which is lower than the PEGs for the other companies (28/2 = 14 for Company B, negative for Company C, and 16/2 = 8 for Company D). Given the favorable valuation relative to growth, the company is a good candidate for investors who use GARP.

- Company B's forward P/E is 56/2 = 28, which is lower than the average P/E of 35 for its sector peers. The company is a good candidate for the relative value approach.

- Company C's forward P/E is 22/10 = 2.2, which is considered very low in both absolute and relative terms. Assuming the investor pays attention to company circumstances, the stock could be a good candidate for the deep-value approach.

- Company D's forward P/E is 32/2 = 16, which is the same as its industry average. Company D's earnings are growing slowly at 2%, but the dividend yield of 8% appears high. This combination makes the company a good candidate for income investing.

EXAMPLE 3

Growth vs. Value

Tencent Holdings Limited is a leading provider of value-added internet services in China. The company's services include social networks, web portals, e-commerce, and multiplayer online games.

Exhibit 3 shows an excerpt from an analyst report on Tencent published following the release of the company's Q3 2016 results on 16 November 2016.

Exhibit 3   Financial Summary and Valuation for Tencent Holdings Limited

Market Data: 16 November 2016			2014	2015	2016E	2017E	2018E
Closing price	196.9	Revenue (RMB millions)	78,932	102,863	150,996	212,471	276,538
Price target	251.5	YOY (%)	30.60	30.32	46.79	40.71	30.15
HSCEI	9,380	Net income (RMB millions)	23,810	28,806	42,292	56,533	68,994
HSCCI	3,669	YOY (%)	53.49	21.85	46.76	32.87	22.04
52-Week high/low	132.10/220.8	EPS (RMB)	2.58	3.10	4.56	6.05	7.39

(continued)

Exhibit 3 (Continued)

Market Data: 16 November 2016			2014	2015	2016E	2017E	2018E
Market cap (USD millions)	240,311	Diluted EPS (RMB)	2.55	3.06	4.51	5.99	7.31
Market cap (HKD millions)	1,864,045	ROE (%)	29.09	23.84	26.11	26.18	24.71
Shares outstanding (millions)	9,467	Debt/Assets (%)	52.02	60.20	61.33	61.26	60.37
Exchange rate (RMB/HKD)	0.8857	Dividend yield (%)	0.20	0.20	0.28	0.38	0.46
		P/E	54.78	55.17	38.27	28.80	23.60
		P/B	22.31	19.35	13.39	9.99	7.54
		EV/EBITDA	40.79	35.88	28.06	20.09	15.39

Notes: Market data are quoted in HKD; the company's filing is in RMB. Diluted EPS is calculated as if all outstanding convertible securities (such as convertible preferred shares, convertible debentures, stock options, and warrants) were exercised. P/E is calculated as closing price divided by each year's EPS.
Source: SWS Research.

From the perspective of the date of Exhibit 3:

1 Which metrics would support a decision to invest by a growth investor?
2 Which characteristics would a growth investor tend to weigh less heavily than a high-quality value investor?

Solution to 1:

A growth investor would focus on the following:

- The year-over-year change in revenue exceeded 30% in 2014 and 2015 and is expected to accelerate over 2016–2018.
- Past and expected net income growth rates are also high.

Solution to 2:

A growth investor would tend to be less concerned about the relatively high valuation levels (high P/E, P/B, and EV/EBITDA) and low dividend yield.

4 TOP-DOWN STRATEGIES

c analyze top-down active strategies, including their rationale and associated processes

As the name suggests, in contrast to bottom-up strategies, top-down strategies use an investment process that begins at a top or macro level. Instead of focusing on individual company- and asset-level variables in making investment decisions, top-down portfolio managers study variables affecting many companies, such as the macroeconomic environment, demographic trends, and government policies. These managers often use instruments such as futures contracts, ETFs, swaps, and custom baskets of individual stocks to capture macro dynamics and generate portfolio return. Some bottom-up stock pickers also incorporate top-down analysis as part of their process for arriving at investment decisions. A typical method of incorporating both top-down macroeconomic and bottom-up fundamental processes is to have the portfolio strategist set the target country and sector weights. Portfolio managers then construct stock portfolios that are consistent with these preset weights.

4.1 Country and Geographic Allocation to Equities

Investors using country allocation strategies form their portfolios by investing in different geographic regions depending on their assessment of the regions' prospects. For example, the manager may have a preference for a particular region and may establish a position in that region while limiting exposure to others. Managers of global equity funds may, for example, make a decision based on a tradeoff between the US equity market and the European equity market, or they may allocate among all investable country equity markets using futures or ETFs. Such strategies may also seek to track the overall supply and demand for equities in regions or countries by analyzing the aggregate volumes of share buybacks, investment fund flows, the volumes of initial public offerings, and secondary share issuance.

The country or geographic allocation decision itself can be based on both top-down macroeconomic and bottom-up fundamental analysis. For example, just as economic data for a given country are available, the market valuation of a country can be calculated by aggregating all company earnings and market capitalization.

4.2 Sector and Industry Rotation

Just as one can formulate a strategy that allocates to different countries or regions in an investment universe, one can also have a view on the expected returns of various sectors and industries across borders. Industries that are more integrated on a global basis—and therefore subject to global supply and demand dynamics—are more suitable to global sector allocation decisions. Examples of such industries include information technology and energy. On the other hand, sectors and industries that are more local in nature to individual countries are more suitable to sector allocation within a country. Examples of these industries are real estate and consumer staples. The availability of sector and industry ETFs greatly facilitates the implementation of sector and industry rotation strategies for those portfolio managers who cannot or do not wish to implement such strategies by investing in individual stocks.

As with country and geographic allocation, both top-down macroeconomic and bottom-up fundamental variables can be used to predict sector/industry returns. Many bottom-up portfolio managers also add a top-down sector overlay to their portfolios.

4.3 Volatility-Based Strategies

Another category of top-down equity strategies is based on investors' view on volatility and is usually implemented using derivative instruments. Those managers who believe they have the skill to predict future market volatility better than option-implied volatility (reflected, for example, in the VIX Index) can trade the VIX futures listed on the CBOE Futures Exchange (CFE), trade instruments such as index options, or enter into volatility swaps (or variance swaps).

Let's assume that an investor predicts a major market move, not anticipated by others, in the near term. The investor does not have an opinion on the direction of the move and only expects the index volatility to be high. The investor can use an index straddle strategy to capitalize on his or her view. Entering into an index straddle position involves the purchase of call and put options (on the same underlying index) with the same strike price and expiry date. The success of this long straddle strategy depends on whether or not volatility turns out to be higher than anticipated by the market; the strategy incurs losses when the market stays broadly flat. Exhibit 4 shows the payoff of such an index straddle strategy. The maximum loss of the long straddle is limited to the total call and put premiums paid.

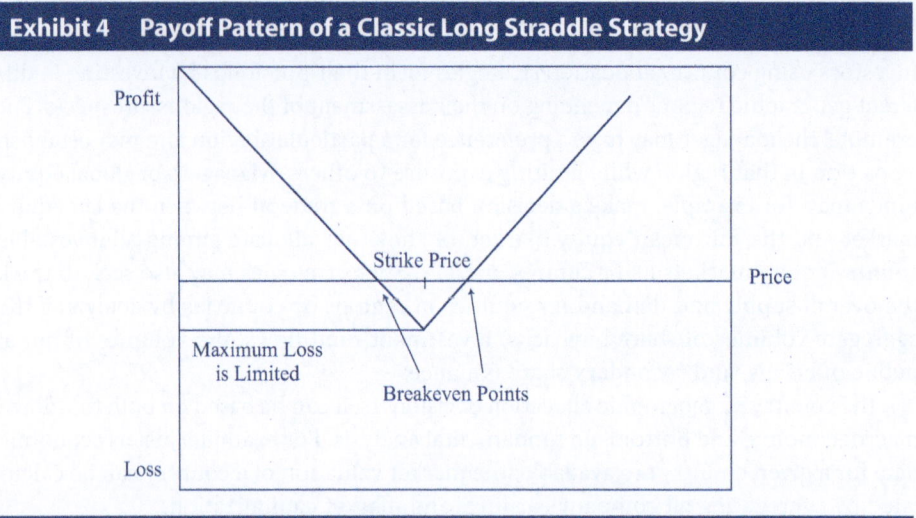

Exhibit 4 Payoff Pattern of a Classic Long Straddle Strategy

4.4 Thematic Investment Strategies

Thematic investing is another broad category of strategies. Thematic strategies can use broad macroeconomic, demographic, or political drivers, or bottom-up ideas on industries and sectors, to identify investment opportunities. Disruptive technologies, processes, and regulations; innovations; and economic cycles present investment opportunities and also pose challenges to existing companies. Investors constantly search for new and promising ideas or themes that will drive the market in the future.

It is also important to determine whether any new trend is structural (and hence long-term) or short-term in nature. Structural changes can have long-lasting impacts on the way people behave or a market operates. For example, the development of smartphones and tablets and the move towards cloud computing are probably structural changes. On the other hand, a manager might attempt to identify companies with significant sales exposure to foreign countries as a way to benefit from short-term views on currency movements. The success of a structural thematic investment depends equally on the ability to take advantage of future trends and the ability to avoid what will turn out to be merely fashionable for a limited time, unless the strategy specifically focuses on short-term trends. Further examples of thematic investment drivers include new technologies, mobile communication and computing devices, clean energy, fintech, and advances in medicine.

Implementation of Top-Down Investment Strategies

A global equity portfolio manager with special insights into particular countries or regions can tactically choose to overweight or underweight those countries or regions on a short-term basis. Once the country or region weights are determined by a top-down process, the portfolio can be constructed by selecting stocks in the relevant countries or regions.

A portfolio manager with expertise in identifying drivers of sector or industry returns will establish a view on those drivers and will set weights for those sectors in a portfolio. For example, the performance of the energy sector is typically driven by the price of crude oil. The returns of the materials sector rest on forecasts for commodity prices. The consumer and industrials sectors require in-depth knowledge of the customer–supplier chains and a range of other dynamics. Once a view is established on the return and risk of each sector, a manager can then decide which industries to invest in and what weightings to assign to those industries relative to the benchmark.

The significant growth of passive factor investing—sometimes marketed as "smart beta" products—has given portfolio managers more tools and flexibility for investing in different equity styles. One can exploit the fact, for example, that high-quality stocks tend to perform well in recessions, or that cyclical deep-value companies are more likely to deliver superior returns in a more "risk-on" environment, in which the market becomes less risk-averse. For example, where the investment mandate permits, top-down managers can choose among different equity style ETFs and structured products to obtain risk exposures that are consistent with their views on different stages of the economic cycle or their views on market sentiment.

Portfolio Overlays

Bottom-up fundamental strategies often lead to unintended macro (e.g., sector or country) risk exposures. However, bottom-up fundamental investors can incorporate some of the risk control benefits of top-down investment strategies via portfolio overlays. (A **portfolio overlay** is an array of derivative positions managed separately from the securities portfolio to achieve overall portfolio characteristics that are desired by the portfolio manager.) The fundamental investor's sector weights, for example, may vary from the benchmark's weights as a result of the stock selection process even though the investor did not intend to make sector bets. In that case, the investor may be able to adjust the sector weights to align with the benchmark's weights via long and short positions in derivatives. In this way, top-down strategies can be effective in controlling risk exposures. Overlays can also be used to attempt to add active returns that are not correlated with those generated by the underlying portfolio strategy.

FACTOR-BASED STRATEGIES: OVERVIEW

5

d   analyze factor-based active strategies, including their rationale and associated processes

A factor is a variable or characteristic with which individual asset returns are correlated. It can be broadly defined as any variable that is believed to be valuable in ranking stocks for investment and in predicting future returns or risks. A wide range of security characteristics have been used to define "factors." Some factors (most commonly, size, value, momentum, and quality) have been shown to be positively associated with a long-term return premium and are often referred to as *rewarded* factors. In fact, hundreds of factors have been identified and used in portfolio construction, but a large number have not been empirically proven to offer a persistent return premium (some call these *unrewarded* factors).

Broadly defined, a factor-based strategy aims to identify significant factors that can predict future stock returns and to construct a portfolio that tilts towards such factors. Some strategies rely on a single factor, are transparent, and maintain a relatively stable exposure to that factor with regular rebalancing (as is explained in the curriculum reading on passive equity investing). Other strategies rely on a selection of factors. Yet other strategies may attempt to time the exposure to factors, recognizing that factor performance varies over time.

For new factor ideas, analysts and managers of portfolios that use factor strategies often rely on academic research, working papers, in-house research, and external research performed by entities such as investment banks. The following exhibits illustrate how some of the traditional style factors performed in recent decades, showing the varying nature of returns. Exhibit 5 shows the cumulative performance of large-cap versus small-cap US equities, using the S&P 500 and Russell 2000 total return indexes. Exhibit 6 presents the total returns of value (Russell 1000 Value Index) versus growth (Russell 1000 Growth Index) styles. Over the 28 years from January 1988 to April 2016, small-cap stocks earned marginally higher returns than large-cap stocks, but with significantly higher risk. Value and growth styles produce about the same return, but growth equities seem to be slightly more volatile (see Exhibit 7).

Equity style rotation strategies, a subcategory of factor investing, are based on the belief that different factors—such as size, value, momentum, and quality—work well during some time periods but less well during other time periods. These strategies use an investment process that allocates to stock baskets representing each of these styles when a particular style is expected to offer a positive excess return compared to the benchmark. While style rotation as a strategy can be used in both fundamental and quantitative investment processes, it is generally more in the domain of quantitative investing. Unlike sector or country allocation, discussed earlier, the classification of securities into style categories is less standardized.

Exhibit 5 Large-Cap vs. Small-Cap Equities

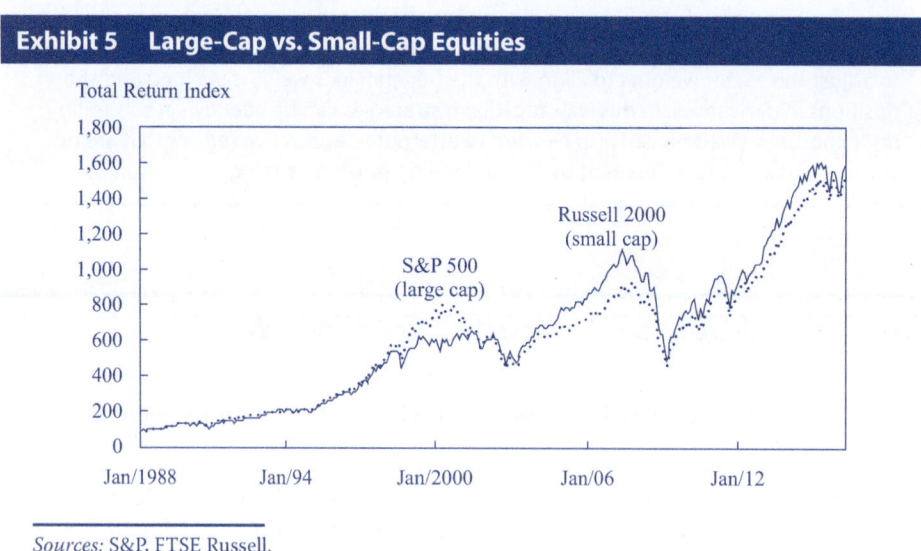

Sources: S&P, FTSE Russell.

Factor-Based Strategies: Overview

Exhibit 6 Value vs. Growth Equities

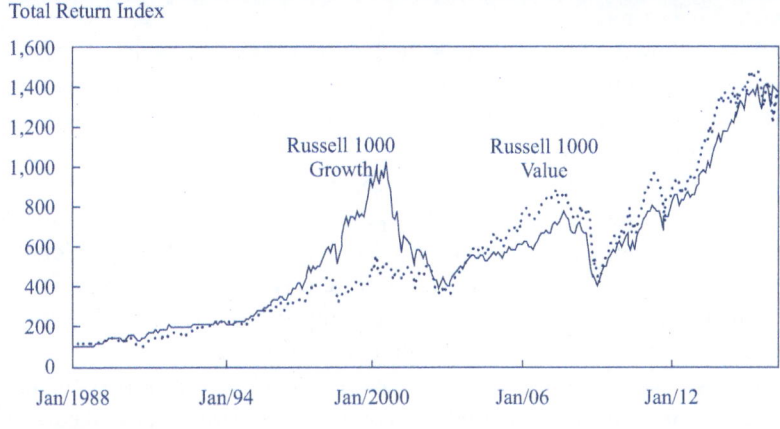

Sources: S&P, FTSE Russell.

Exhibit 7 Summary Statistics

	S&P 500	Russell 2000	Russell 1000 Value	Russell 1000 Growth
Annual return (%)	10.7	11.1	10.9	10.7
Annual volatility (%)	14.4	18.7	14.2	16.4
Sharpe Ratio	0.74	0.59	0.77	0.65

Sources: S&P, FTSE Russell.

The most important test, however, is the "smell" test: Does the factor make intuitive sense? A factor can often pass statistical backtesting, but if it does not make common sense—if justification for the factor's efficacy is lacking—then the manager may be data-mining. Investors should always remember that impressive performance in backtesting does not necessarily imply that the factor will continue to add value in the future.

> An important step is choosing the appropriate investment universe. Practitioners mostly define their investment universe in terms of well-known broad market indexes—for the United States, for example, the S&P 500, Russell 3000, and MSCI World Index. Using a well-defined index has several benefits: Such indexes are free from look-ahead and survivorship biases, the stocks in the indexes are investable with sufficient liquidity, and the indexes are also generally free from foreign ownership restrictions.

The most traditional and widely used method for implementing factor-based portfolios is the hedged portfolio approach, pioneered and formulated by Fama and French (1993). In this approach, after choosing the factor to be scrutinized and ranking the investable stock universe by that factor, investors divide the universe into groups referred to as *quantiles* (typically quintiles or deciles) to form quantile portfolios. Stocks are either equally weighted or capitalization weighted within each quantile. A long/short hedged portfolio is typically formed by going long the best quantile and shorting the worst quantile. The performance of the hedged long/short portfolio is then tracked over time.

There are a few drawbacks to this "hedged portfolio" approach. First, the information contained in the middle quantiles is not utilized, as only the top and bottom quantiles are used in forming the hedged portfolio. Second, it is implicitly assumed that the relationship between the factor and future stock returns is linear (or at least monotonic), which may not be the case.[3] Third, portfolios built using this approach tend to be concentrated, and if many managers use similar factors, the resulting portfolios will be concentrated in specific stocks. Fourth, the hedged portfolio requires managers to short stocks. Shorting may not be possible in some markets and may be overly expensive in others. Fifth, and most important, the hedged portfolio is not a "pure" factor portfolio because it has significant exposures to other risk factors.

Exhibit 8 shows the performance of a factor called "year-over-year change in debt outstanding." The factor is calculated by taking the year-over-year percentage change in the per share long-term debt outstanding on the balance sheet, using all stocks in the Russell 3000 universe. The portfolio is constructed by buying the top 10% of companies that reduce their debt and shorting the bottom 10% of companies that issue the most debt. Stocks in both the long and short portfolios are equally weighted.[4] The bars in the chart indicate the monthly portfolio returns. The average monthly return of the strategy is about 0.22% (or 2.7% per year), and the Sharpe ratio is 0.53 over the test period. All cumulative performance is computed on an initial investment in the factor of $100, with monthly rebalancing and excluding transaction costs.

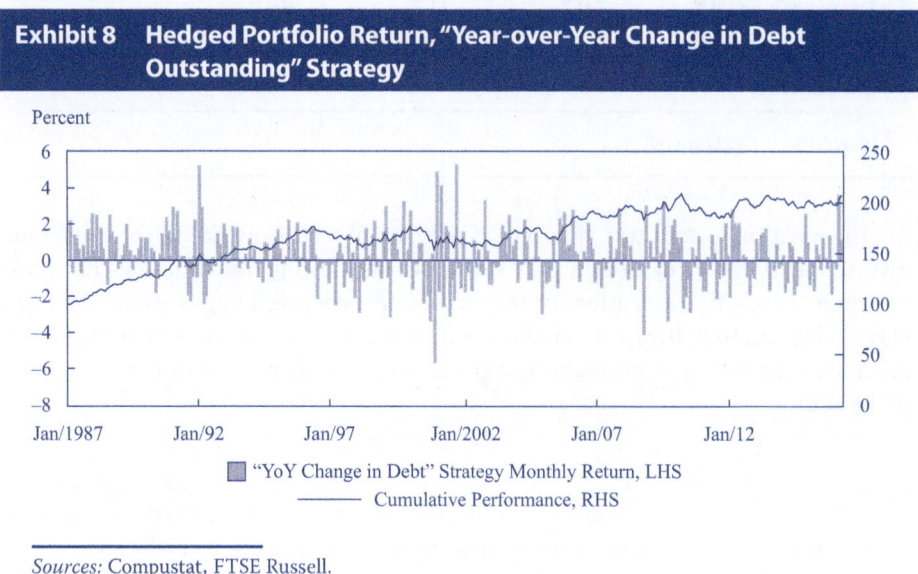

Exhibit 8 Hedged Portfolio Return, "Year-over-Year Change in Debt Outstanding" Strategy

Sources: Compustat, FTSE Russell.

Exhibit 9 shows the average monthly returns of the 10 decile portfolios. It shows that companies with the highest year-over-year increase in debt financing (D10 category) marginally underperform companies with the lowest year-over-year increase in debt financing (average monthly return of 0.6% versus average monthly return of 0.8%). However, it can also be seen that the best-performing companies are the ones with reasonable financial leverage in Deciles 3 to 6. A long/short hedged portfolio

---

[3] The payoff patterns between factor exposures and future stock returns are becoming increasingly non-linear, especially in the United States and Japan.
[4] Stocks can also be weighted based on their market capitalization.

approach based on the 1st and 10th deciles (as illustrated in Exhibit 9) would not take advantage of this information, as stocks in these deciles would not be used in such a portfolio. Portfolio managers observing this pattern concerning the different deciles could change the deciles used in the strategy if they believed the pattern would continue into the future.

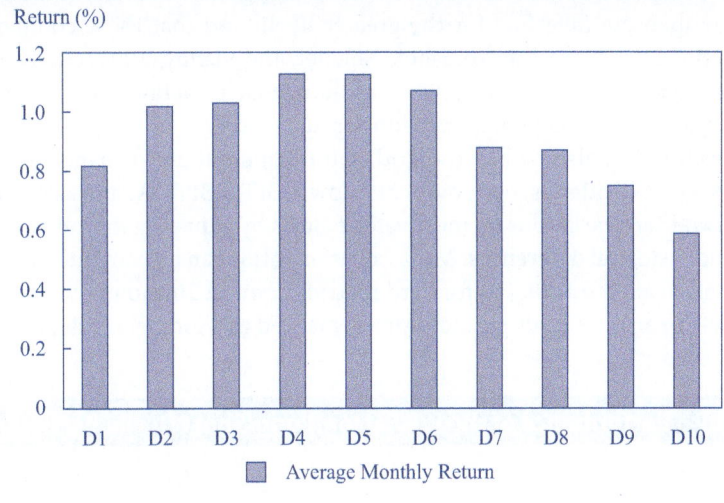

Exhibit 9: Average Decile Portfolio Return Based on Year-over-Year Change in Debt Outstanding

Sources: Compustat, FTSE Russell.

For investors who desire a long-only factor portfolio, a commonly used approach is to construct a factor-tilting portfolio, where a long-only portfolio with exposures to a given factor can be built with controlled tracking error. The factor-tilting portfolio tracks a benchmark index closely but also provides exposures to the chosen factor. In this way, it is similar to an enhanced indexing strategy.

A "factor-mimicking portfolio," or FMP, is a theoretical implementation of a pure factor portfolio. An FMP is a theoretical long/short portfolio that is dollar neutral with a unit exposure to a chosen factor and no exposure to other factors. Because FMPs invest in almost every single stock, entering into long or short positions without taking into account short availability issues or transaction costs, they are very expensive to trade. Managers typically construct the pure factor portfolio by following the FMP theory but adding trading liquidity and short availability constraints.

FACTOR-BASED STRATEGIES: STYLE FACTORS

d analyze factor-based active strategies, including their rationale and associated processes

Factors are the raw ingredients of quantitative investing and are often referred to as signals. Quantitative managers spend a large amount of time studying factors. Traditionally, factors have been based on fundamental characteristics of underlying companies. However, many investors have recently shifted their attention to unconventional and unstructured data sources in an effort to gain an edge in creating strategies.

6.1 Value

Value is based on Graham and Dodd's (1934) concept and can be measured in a number of ways. The academic literature has a long history of documenting the value phenomenon. Basu (1977) found that stocks with low P/E or high earnings yield tend to provide higher returns. Fama and French (1993) formally outlined value investing by proposing the book-to-market ratio as a way to measure value and growth.

Although many academics and practitioners believe that value stocks tend to deliver superior returns, there has been considerable disagreement over the explanation of this effect. Fama and French (1992, 1993, 1996) suggested that the value premium exists to compensate investors for the greater likelihood that these companies will experience financial distress. Lakonishok, Shleifer, and Vishny (1994) cited behavioral arguments, suggesting that the effect is a result of behavioral biases on the part of the typical investor rather than compensation for higher risk.

Value factors can also be based on other fundamental performance metrics of a company, such as dividends, earnings, cash flow, EBIT, EBITDA, and sales. Investors often add two more variations on most value factors by adjusting for industry (and/or country) and historical differences. Most valuation ratios can be computed using either historical (also called *trailing*) or forward metrics. Exhibit 10 shows the performance of the price-to-earnings multiple factor implemented as a long/short decile portfolio.

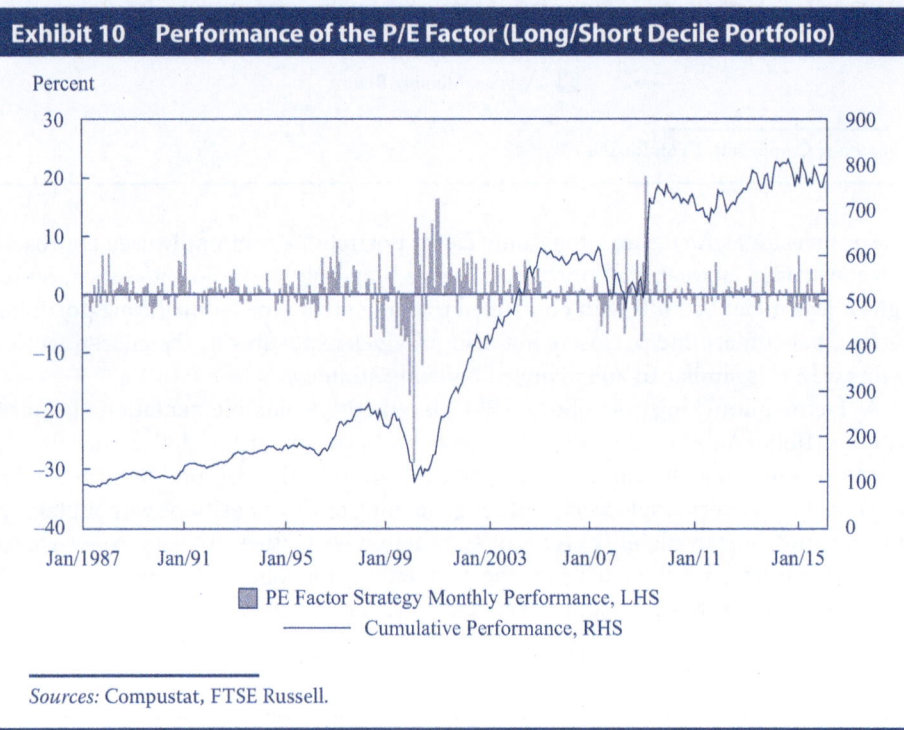

Exhibit 10 Performance of the P/E Factor (Long/Short Decile Portfolio)

Sources: Compustat, FTSE Russell.

6.2 Price Momentum

Researchers have also found a strong price momentum effect in almost all asset classes in most countries. In fact, value and price momentum have long been the two cornerstones of quantitative investing.

Jegadeesh and Titman (1993) first documented that stocks that are "winners" over the previous 12 months tend to outperform past "losers" (those that have done poorly over the previous 12 months) and that such outperformance persists over the following 2 to 12 months. The study focused on the US market during the 1965–1989 period.

The authors also found a short-term reversal effect, whereby stocks that have high price momentum in the previous month tend to underperform over the next 2 to 12 months. This price momentum anomaly is commonly attributed to behavioral biases, such as overreaction to information.[5] It is interesting to note that since the academic publication of these findings, the performance of the price momentum factor has become much more volatile (see Exhibit 11). Price momentum is, however, subject to extreme tail risk. Over the three-month March–May 2009 time period, the simple price momentum strategy (as measured by the long/short decile portfolio) lost 56%. For this data period, some reduction in downside risk can be achieved by removing the effect of sector exposure from momentum factor returns: We will call this modified version the "sector-neutralized price momentum factor."[6] The results are shown in Exhibits 12 and 13 for US, European, and Japanese markets.

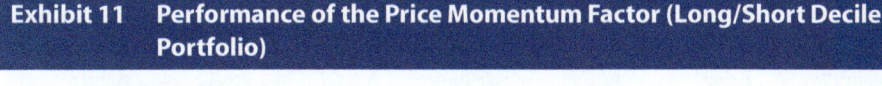

Exhibit 11 Performance of the Price Momentum Factor (Long/Short Decile Portfolio)

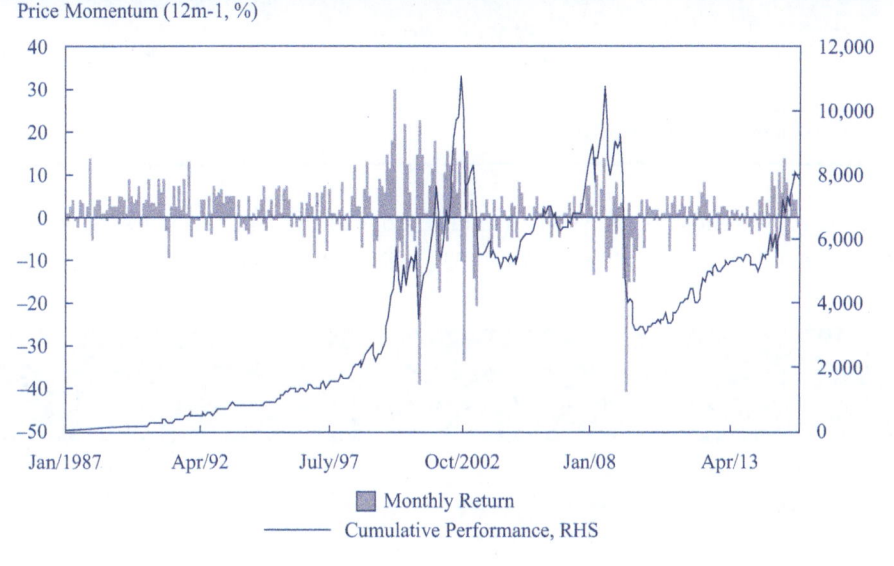

Sources: Compustat, FTSE Russell.

---

[5] Behavioral biases are covered in the Level III readings on behavioral finance.
[6] The methods for removing sector exposure are beyond the scope of this reading.

Exhibit 12 Performance of the Sector-Neutralized Price Momentum Factor (Long/Short Decile Portfolio)

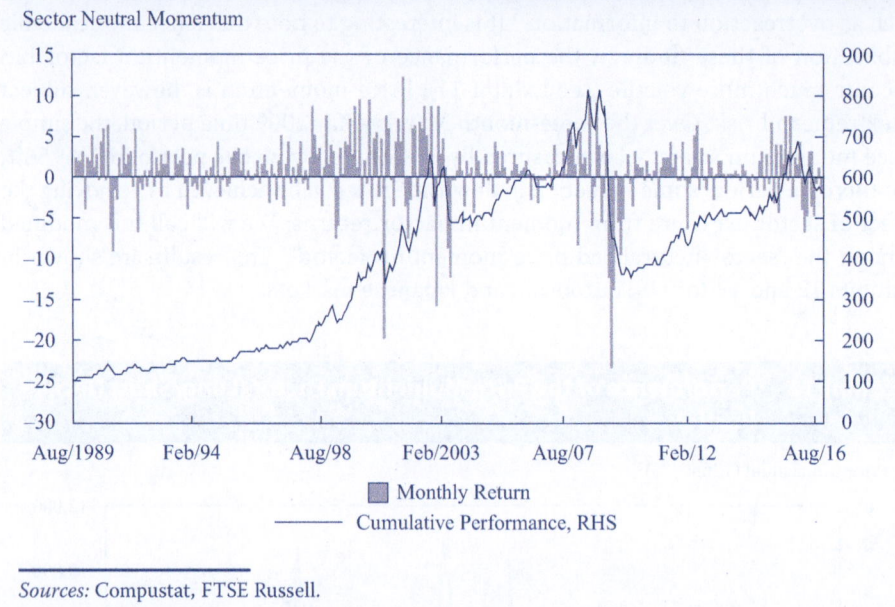

Sources: Compustat, FTSE Russell.

Exhibit 13 extends the analysis to include European and Japanese markets, where a similar effect on downside risk can be shown to have been operative over the period.

Exhibit 13 Performance of the Sector-Neutralized Price Momentum Factor in US, European, and Japanese Markets (Long/Short Decile Portfolio)

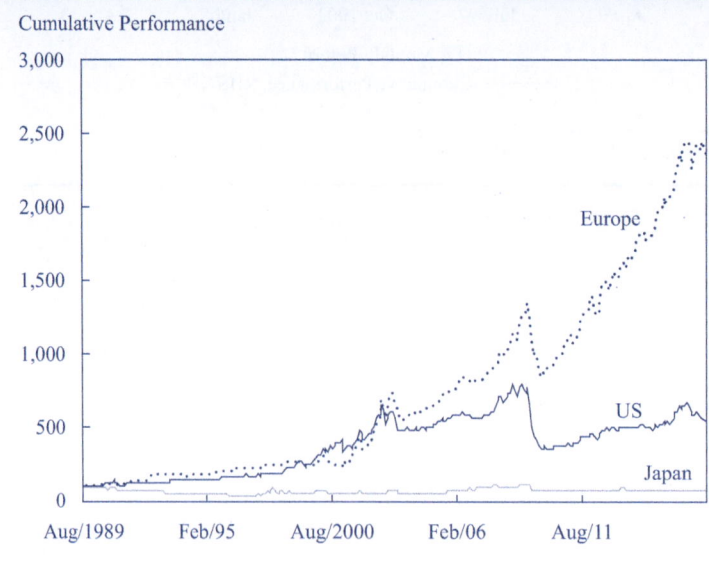

Sources: Compustat, FTSE Russell.

Factor-Based Strategies: Style Factors

> **EXAMPLE 4**
>
> ### Factor Investing
>
> A quantitative manager wants to expand his current strategy from US equities into international equity markets. His current strategy uses a price momentum factor. Based on Exhibit 13:
>
> 1. State whether momentum has been a factor in European and Japanese equity returns overall in the time period examined.
> 2. Discuss the potential reasons why neutralizing sectors reduces downside risk.
>
> #### Solution to 1:
>
> As shown in Exhibit 13, price momentum has performed substantially better in Europe than in the United States. On the other hand, there does not appear to be any meaningful pattern of price momentum in Japan. Exhibit 13 suggests that the price momentum factor could be used for a European portfolio but not for a Japanese portfolio. However, managers need to perform rigorous backtesting before they can confidently implement a factor model in a market that they are not familiar with. Managers should be aware that what appears to be impressive performance in backtests does not necessarily imply that the factor will continue to add value in the future.
>
> #### Solution to 2:
>
> Using the simple price momentum factor means that a portfolio buys past winners and shorts past losers. The resulting portfolio could have exposure to potentially significant industry bets. Sector-neutral price momentum focuses on stock selection without such risk exposures and thus tends to reduce downside risk.

6.3 Growth

Growth is another investment approach used by some style investors. Growth factors aim to measure a company's growth potential and can be calculated using the company's historical growth rates or projected forward growth rates. Growth factors can also be classified as short-term growth (last quarter's, last year's, next quarter's, or next year's growth) and long-term growth (last five years' or next five years' growth). While higher-than-market or higher-than-sector growth is generally considered to be a possible indicator for strong future stock price performance, the growth of some metrics, such as assets, results in weaker future stock price performance.

Exhibit 14 shows the performance of the year-over-year earnings growth factor. The exhibit is based on a strategy that invests in the top 10% of companies with the highest year-over-year growth in earnings per share and shorts all the stocks in the bottom 10%.

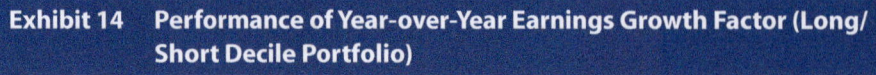

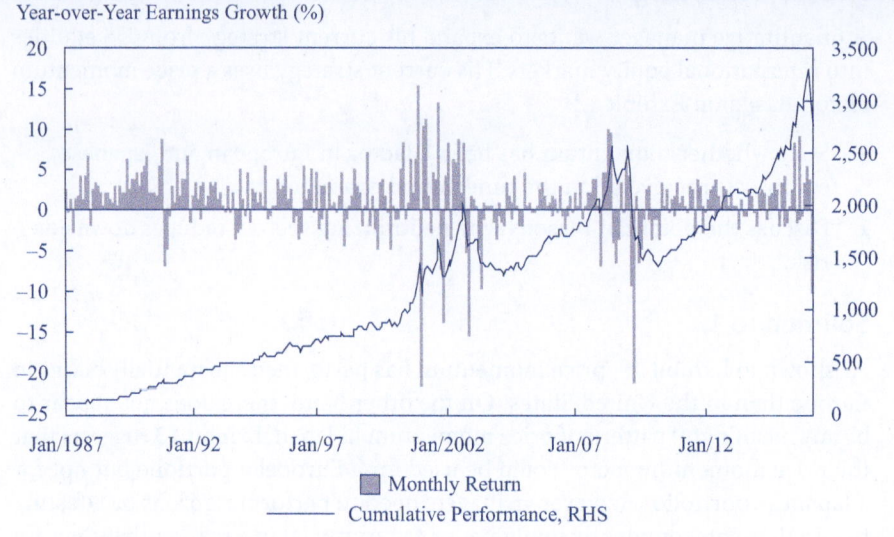

Sources: Compustat, FTSE Russell.

6.4 Quality

In addition to using accounting ratios and share price data as fundamental style factors, investors have continued to create more complex factors based on the variety of accounting information available for companies. One of the best-known examples of how in-depth accounting knowledge can impact investment performance is Richard Sloan's (1996) seminal paper on earnings quality, with its proposition of the accruals factor. Sloan suggests that stock prices fail to reflect fully the information contained in the accrual and cash flow components of current earnings.[7] The performance of the accruals anomaly factor, however, appears to be quite cyclical.

---

[7] Sloan (1996) argues that in the long term, cash flows from operations and net income (under accruals-based accounting) should converge and be consistent. In the short term, they could diverge. Management has more discretion in accruals-based accounting; therefore, the temporary divergence between cash flows and net income reflects how conservative a company chooses to be in reporting its net income.

Exhibit 15: Performance of Earnings Quality Factor

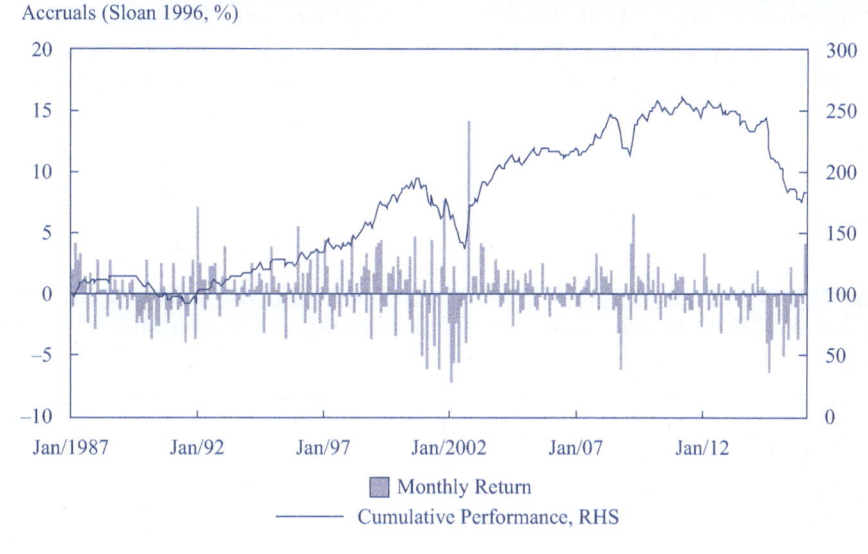

Sources: Compustat, FTSE Russell.

In addition to the accruals anomaly, there are many other potential factors based on a company's fundamental data, such as profitability, balance sheet and solvency risk, earnings quality, stability, sustainability of dividend payout, capital utilization, and management efficiency measures. Yet another, analyst sentiment, refers to the phenomenon of sell-side analysts revising their forecasts of corporate earnings estimates, which is called *earnings revision*. More recently, with the availability of more data, analysts have started to include cash flow revisions, sales revisions, ROE revisions, sell-side analyst stock recommendations, and target price changes as variables in the "analyst sentiment" category.

A new and exciting area of research involves news sentiment. Rather than just relying on the output of sell-side analysts, investors could use natural language processing (NLP) algorithms to analyze the large volume of news stories and quantify the news sentiment on stocks.

FACTOR-BASED STRATEGIES: UNCONVENTIONAL FACTORS

d   analyze factor-based active strategies, including their rationale and associated processes

With the rapid growth in technology and computational algorithms, investors have been embracing big data. "Big data" is a broad term referring to extremely large datasets that may include structured data—such as traditional financial statements and market data—as well as unstructured or "alternative" data that has previously not been widely used in the investment industry because it lacks recognizable structure. Examples of such alternative data include satellite images, textual information, credit card payment information, and the number of online mentions of a particular product or brand.

Exhibit 16 shows the performance (as measured by the long/short quintile portfolio) of a factor based on customer–supplier chain data.[8] The signal is based on the trailing one-month stock price return of a company's largest customer. Stocks are ranked by largest customer performance, and the portfolio goes long the top quintile and shorts the lowest quintile. The positions are held until the following month's stock ranking and rebalancing. The intuition is that the positive performance of customers is likely to benefit the supplier company in subsequent periods. Indeed, compared to many traditional factors, the supply-chain signal seems to have shown more consistent returns, especially in recent years.

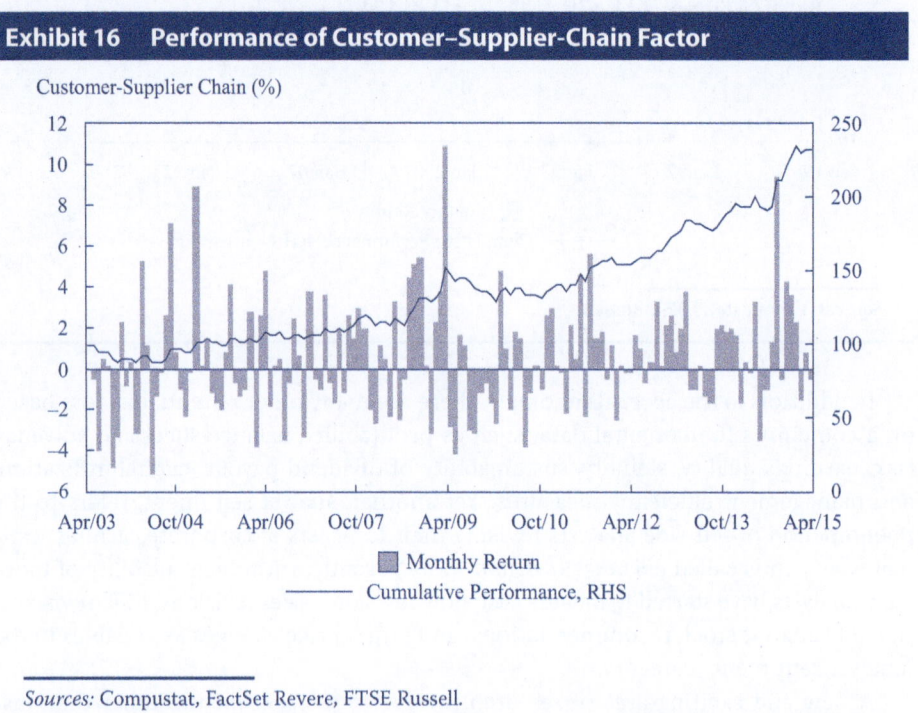

Exhibit 16 Performance of Customer–Supplier-Chain Factor

Sources: Compustat, FactSet Revere, FTSE Russell.

Portfolio construction is covered in the curriculum reading titled "Active Equity Portfolio Construction."

EXAMPLE 5

Researching Factor Timing

An analyst is exploring the relationship between interest rates and style factor returns for the purpose of developing equity style rotation strategies for the US equity market. The analysis takes place in early 2017. The first problem the analyst addresses is how to model the interest rate variable. The data in Exhibit 17 show an apparent trend of declining US government bond yields over the last 30 years. Trends may or may not continue into the future. The analyst decides

---

8 These data can be obtained from FactSet Revere's historical point-in-time supply chain dataset.

to normalize the yield data so that they do not incorporate a prediction on continuation of the trend and makes a simple transformation by subtracting the yield's own 12-month moving average:

$$\text{Normalized yield}_t = \text{Nominal yield}_t - \frac{1}{12}\sum_{\tau=1}^{12}\text{Nominal yield}_{t-\tau+1}$$

The normalized yield data are shown in Exhibit 18. Yields calculated are as of the beginning of the month. Do the fluctuations in yield have any relationship with style factor returns? The analyst explores possible contemporaneous (current) and lagged relationships by performing two regressions (using the current month's and the next month's factor returns, respectively) against the normalized long-term bond yield:

$$f_{i,t} = \beta_{i,0} + \beta_{i,1}\text{Normalized yield}_t + \varepsilon_{i,t}$$

and

$$f_{i,t+1} = \beta_{i,0} + \beta_{i,1}\text{Normalized yield}_t + \varepsilon_{i,t}$$

where $f_{i,t}$ is the return of style factor i at time t and $f_{i,t+1}$ is the subsequent (next) month's return to style factor i. The first regression reveals the contemporaneous relationship between interest rate and factor performance—that is, how well the current interest rate relates to the current factor performance. The second equation states whether the current interest rate can predict the next month's factor return. Exhibit 19 shows the findings.

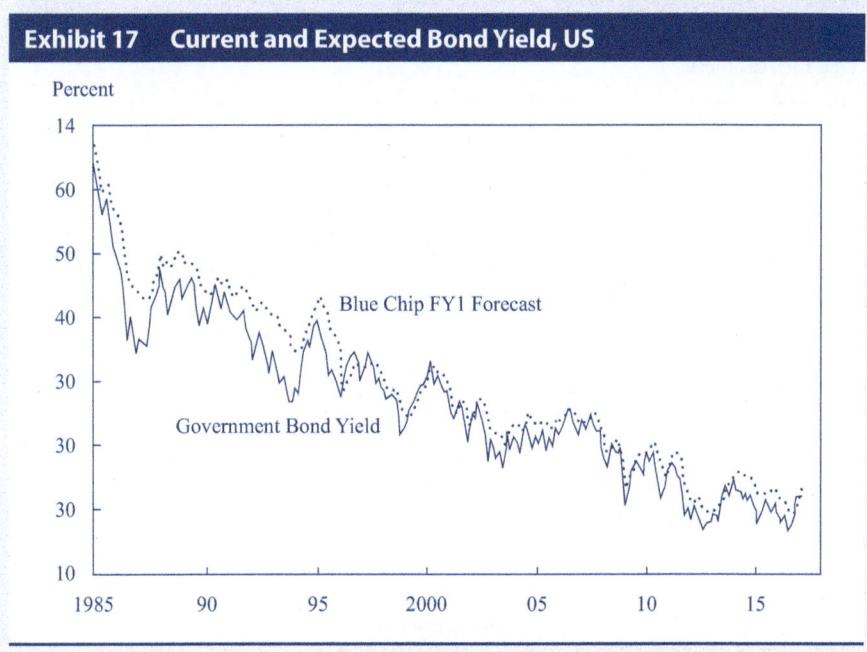

Exhibit 17   Current and Expected Bond Yield, US

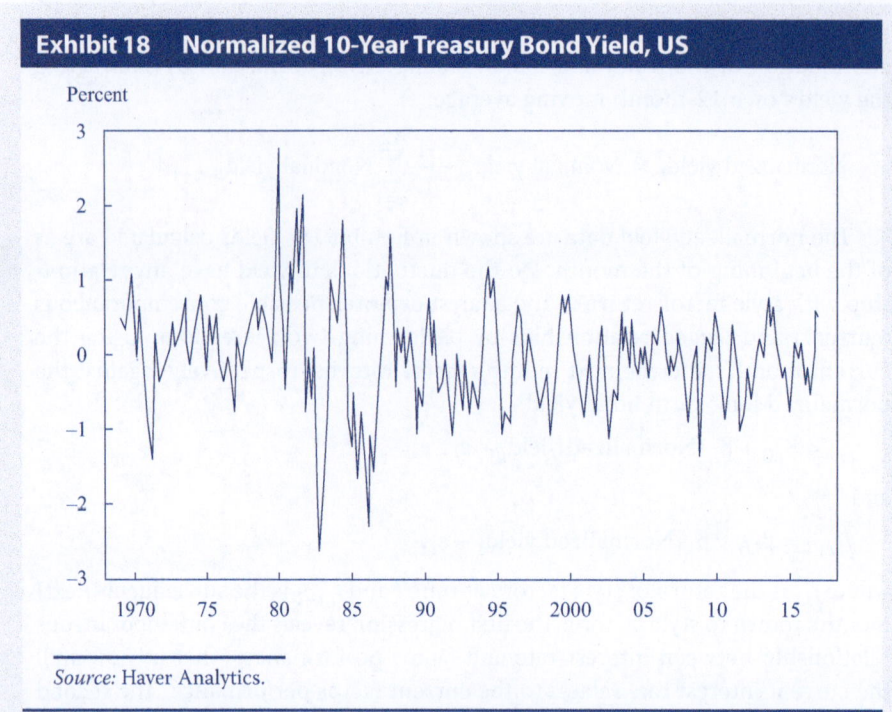

Exhibit 18   Normalized 10-Year Treasury Bond Yield, US

Source: Haver Analytics.

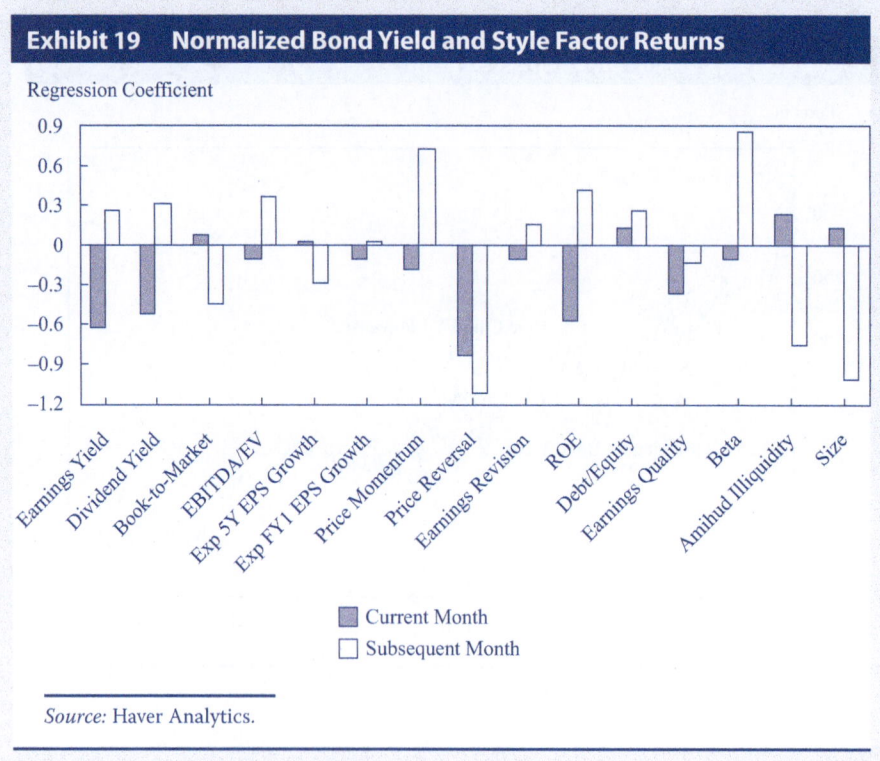

Exhibit 19   Normalized Bond Yield and Style Factor Returns

Source: Haver Analytics.

Using only the information given, address the following:

1   Interpret Exhibit 19.

2 Discuss the relevance of contemporaneous and forward relationships in an equity factor rotation strategy.

3 What concerns could the analyst have in relation to an equity factor rotation strategy, and what possible next steps could the analyst take to address those concerns?

Solution to 1:

Exhibit 19 suggests an inverse relationship between concurrent bond yields and returns to the dividend yield, price reversal, and ROE factors. For some factors (such as earnings quality), the relationship between bond yields and forward (next month's) factor returns is in the same direction as the contemporaneous relationship.

Solution to 2:

Attention needs to be given to the timing relationship of variables to address this question. A contemporaneous style factor return becomes known as of the end of the month. If the known value of bond yields at the beginning of the month is correlated with factor returns, the investor may be able to gain some edge relative to investors who do not use that information. The same conclusion holds concerning the forward relationship. If the contemporaneous variable were defined so that it is realized at the same time as the variable we want to predict, the forward but not the contemporaneous variable would be relevant.

Solution to 3:

The major concern is the validity of the relationships between normalized interest rates and the style variables. Among the steps the analyst can take to increase his or her conviction in the relationships' validity are the following:

- Establish whether the relationships have predictive value out of sample (that is, based on data not used to model the relationship).
- Investigate whether or not there are economic rationales for the relationships such that those relationships could be expected to persist into the future.

Exhibit 19 shows both weak relationships (e.g., for earnings revision) and strong relationships (e.g., for size and beta) in relation to the subsequent month's returns. This fact suggests some priorities in examining this question.

ACTIVIST STRATEGIES

e analyze activist strategies, including their rationale and associated processes

Activist investors specialize in taking stakes in listed companies and advocating changes for the purpose of producing a gain on the investment. The investor may wish to obtain representation on the company's board of directors or use other measures in an effort to initiate strategic, operational, or financial structure changes. In some cases, activist investors may support activities such as asset sales, cost-cutting measures, changes to management, changes to the capital structure, dividend increases, or share buybacks. Activists—including hedge funds, public pension funds, private investors, and others—vary greatly in their approaches, expertise, and investment horizons. They may also seek different outcomes. What they have in common is that they advocate for change in their target companies.

Shareholder activism typically follows a period of screening and analysis of opportunities in the market. The investor usually reviews a number of companies based on a range of parameters and carries out in-depth analysis of the business and the opportunities for unlocking value. Activism itself starts when an investor buys an equity stake in the company and starts advocating for change (i.e., pursuing an activist campaign). These equity stakes are generally made public. Stakes above a certain threshold must be made public in most jurisdictions. Exhibit 20 shows a typical activist investing process. The goal of activist investing could be either financial gain (increased shareholder value) or a non-financial cause (e.g., environmental, social, and governance issues). Rather than pursuing a full takeover bid, activist investors aim to achieve their goals with smaller stakes, typically of less than 10%. Activist investors' time horizon is often shorter than that of buy-and-hold investors, but the whole process can last for a number of years.

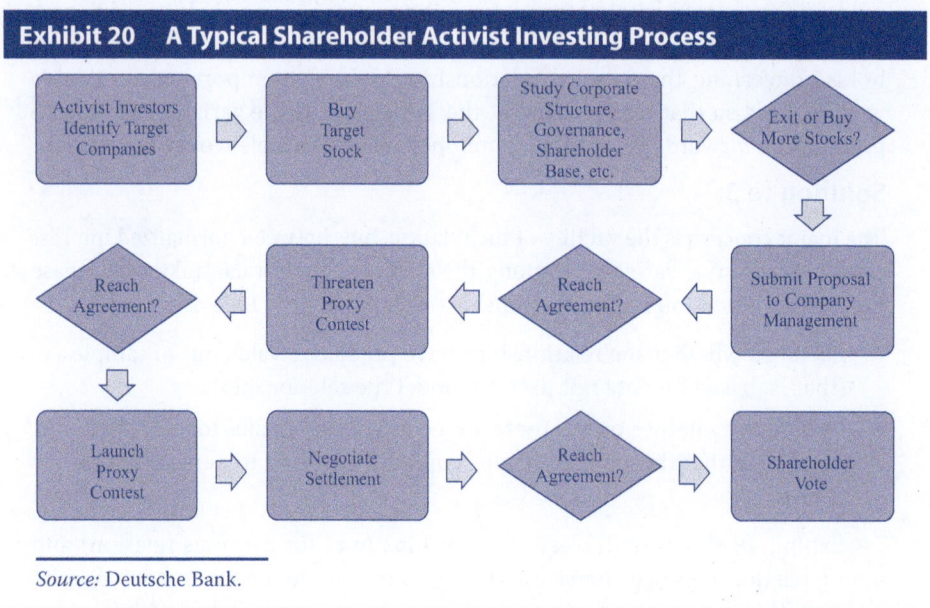

Exhibit 20   A Typical Shareholder Activist Investing Process

Source: Deutsche Bank.

8.1 The Popularity of Shareholder Activism

Shareholder (or investor) activism is by no means a new investment strategy. Its foundations go back to the 1970s and 1980s, when investors known as corporate raiders took substantial stakes in companies in order to influence their operations, unlock value in the target companies, and thereby raise the value of their shares. Proponents of activism argue that it is an important and necessary activity that helps monitor and discipline corporate management to the benefit of all shareholders. Opponents argue that such interventionist tactics can cause distraction and negatively impact management performance.

Activist hedge funds—among the most prominent activist investors—saw growing popularity for a number of years, with assets under management (AUM) reaching $50 billion in 2007[9] before falling sharply during the global financial crisis. Activist

---

[9] Hedge Fund Research.

hedge fund investing has since strongly recovered, with AUM close to $120 billion in 2015.[10] The activity of such investors can be tracked by following the activists' announcements that they are launching a campaign seeking to influence companies. Exhibit 21 shows the number of activist events reported by the industry. Hedge funds that specialize in activism benefit from lighter regulation than other types of funds, and their fee structure, offering greater rewards, justifies concerted campaigns for change at the companies they hold. The popularity and viability of investor activism are influenced by the legal frameworks in different jurisdictions, shareholder structures, and cultural considerations. The United States has seen the greatest amount of activist activity initiated by hedge funds, individuals, and pension funds, but there have been a number of activist events in Europe too. Other regions have so far seen more limited activity on the part of activist investors. Cultural reasons and more concentrated shareholder ownership of companies are two frequently cited explanations.

Exhibit 21 Number of Global Activist Events

Source: Thomson Reuters Activism database.

8.2 Tactics Used by Activist Investors

Activists use a range of tactics on target companies in order to boost shareholder value. These tactics include the following:

- Seeking board representation and nominations
- Engaging with management by writing letters to management calling for and explaining suggested changes, participating in management discussions with analysts or meeting the management team privately, or launching proxy contests whereby activists encourage other shareholders to use their proxy votes to effect change in the organization
- Proposing significant corporate changes during the annual general meeting (AGM)
- Proposing restructuring of the balance sheet to better utilize capital and potentially initiate share buybacks or increase dividends

---

10 See "Activist Funds: An Investor Calls," *Economist* (7 February 2015).

- Reducing management compensation or realigning management compensation with share price performance
- Launching legal proceedings against existing management for breach of fiduciary duties
- Reaching out to other shareholders of the company to coordinate action
- Launching a media campaign against existing management practices
- Breaking up a large conglomerate to unlock value

The effectiveness of shareholder activism depends on the response of the existing management team and the tools at that team's disposal. In many countries, defense mechanisms can be employed by management or a dominant shareholder to hinder activist intervention. These techniques include multi-class share structures whereby a company founder's shares are typically entitled to multiple votes per share; "poison pill" plans allowing the issuance of shares at a deep discount, which causes significant economic and voting dilution; staggered board provisions whereby a portion of the board members are not elected at annual shareholders meetings and hence cannot all be replaced simultaneously; and charter and bylaw provisions and amendments.

8.3 Typical Activist Targets

Activist investors look for specific characteristics in deciding which companies to target. Exhibit 22 shows the characteristics of target companies relative to the market as a whole. The exhibit provides a measure of these characteristics on the event day as well as a year before the announcement, giving a flavor of the dynamics of these attributes. It shows that, on average,[11] target companies feature slower revenue and earnings growth than the market, suffer negative share price momentum, and have weaker-than-average corporate governance.[12] By building stakes and initiating change in underperforming companies, activists hope to unlock value. In addition, by targeting such companies, activist investors are more likely to win support for their actions from other shareholders and the wider public. Traditionally, the target companies have been small and medium-sized listed stocks. This has changed as a number of larger companies have become subject to activism.[13]

---

[11] The fundamental characteristics of all companies in the investment universe (i.e., the Russell 3000) are standardized using z-scores (by subtracting the mean and dividing by the standard deviation) every month from 1988 until 2015. Thus, we can compare the average exposure to each fundamental characteristic over time.

[12] We normalize all target and non-target companies' factor exposures using z-scores (i.e., subtracting the sample mean and dividing by the sample standard deviation).

[13] Trian Fund Management proposed splitting PepsiCo into standalone public companies; Third Point called for leadership change at Yahoo!.

Exhibit 22 Fundamental Characteristics of Target Companies

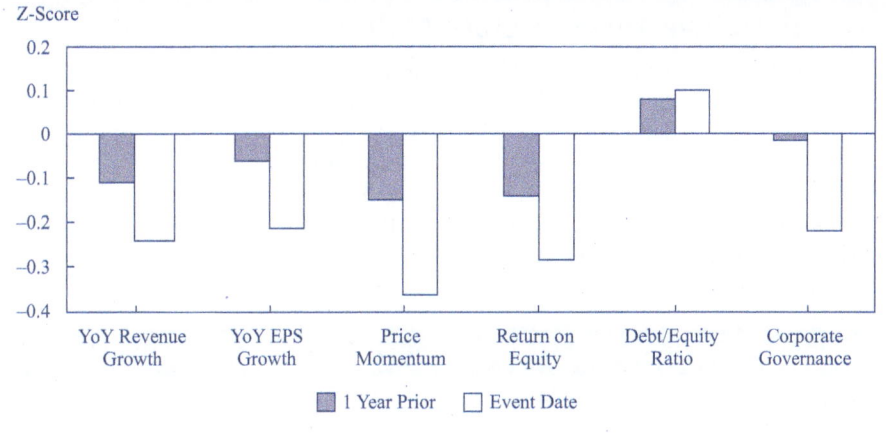

Sources: Capital IQ, Compustat, FTSE Russell, MSCI, S&P.

Do Activists Really Improve Company Performance?

Exhibit 23 shows that, on average, fundamental characteristics of targeted companies do improve in subsequent years following activists' efforts, with evidence that revenue and earnings growth increase, profitability improves, and corporate governance indicators become more robust. There is evidence, however, that the financial leverage of such companies increases significantly.

Exhibit 23 Fundamentals of Target Companies Improve

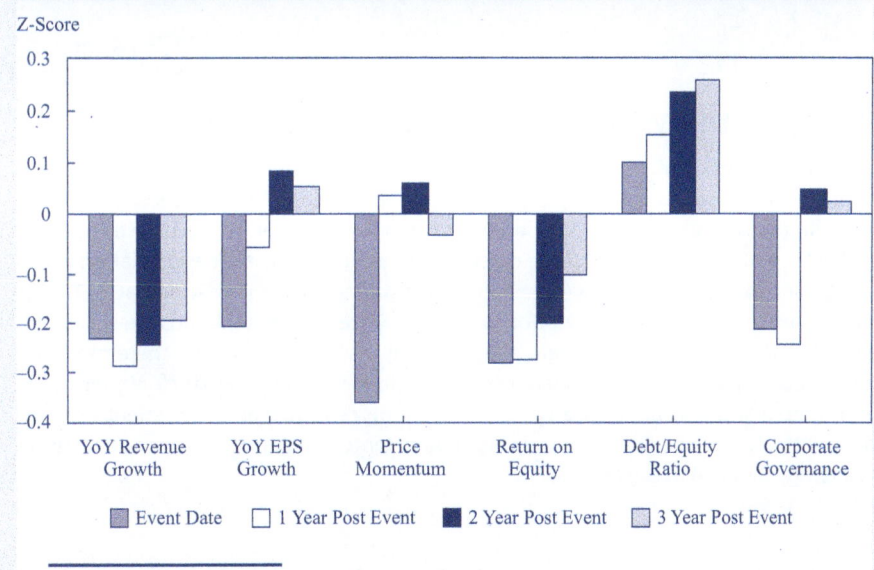

Note: Data are for US companies, 1988–2015.
Sources: Capital IQ, Compustat, FTSE Russell, MSCI, S&P.

Do Activist Investors Generate Alpha?

Activist hedge funds are among the major activist investors. Based on the HFRX Activist Index, in the aggregate, activist hedge funds have delivered an average annual return of 7.7% with annual volatility of 13.7% and therefore a Sharpe ratio of 0.56—slightly higher than the Sharpe ratio of the S&P 500 Index of 0.54 (see Exhibit 24). However, it is difficult to conclude how much value activist investors add because the HFRX index does not include a large enough number of managers. Furthermore, managers themselves vary in their approaches and the risks they take.

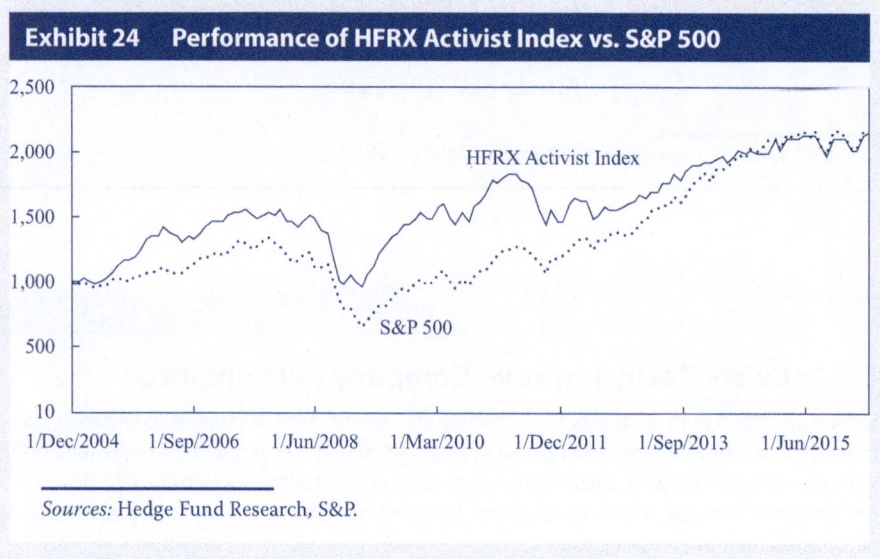

Exhibit 24 Performance of HFRX Activist Index vs. S&P 500

Sources: Hedge Fund Research, S&P.

How Does the Market React to Activist Events?

Investors have generally reacted positively to activism announcements: On average, target company stocks go up by 2% on the announcement day (based on all activist events in the Thomson Reuters Corporate Governance Intelligence database from 1987 to 2016).[14] Interestingly, the positive reaction comes on top of stock appreciation prior to activism announcements (see Exhibit 25). According to the model of Maug (1998), activist investors trade in a stock prior to the announcement to build up a stake, assert control, and profit from the value creation. It may also be argued that there must be information leakage about the activists' involvement, driving the stock higher even before the first public announcement. There is a modest post-announcement drift: In the month after the activist announcement date, target share prices move up by 0.6%, on average, relative to the market.

---

14 All returns are excess returns, adjusted for the market and sector. For details, see Jussa, Webster, Zhao, and Luo (2016).

Activist Strategies

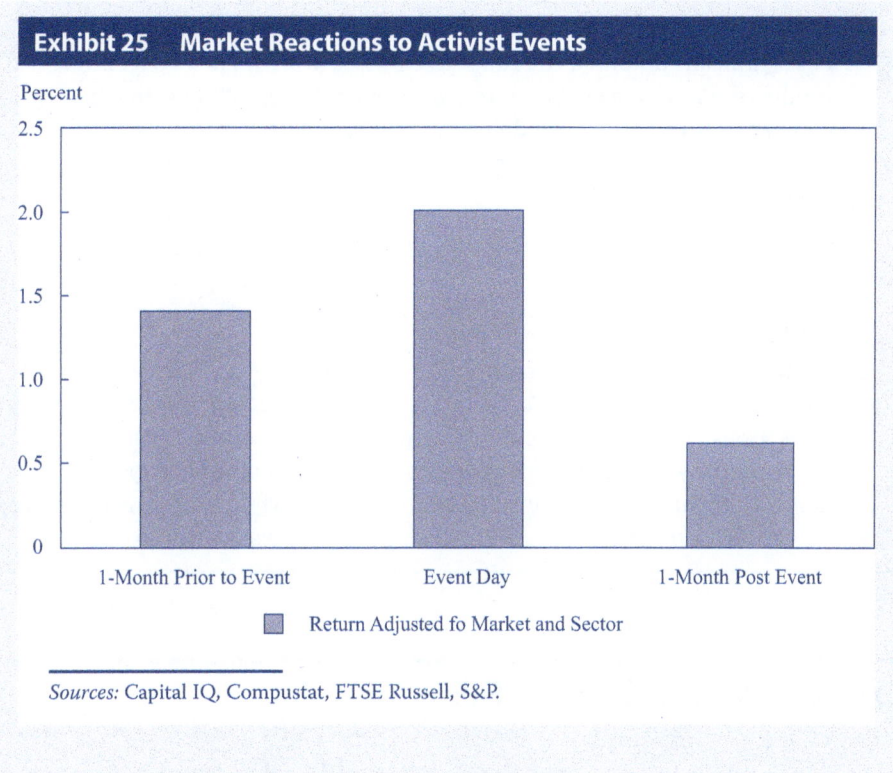

Exhibit 25 Market Reactions to Activist Events

Sources: Capital IQ, Compustat, FTSE Russell, S&P.

EXAMPLE 6

Activist Investing

Kendra Cho is an analyst at an investment firm that specializes in activist investing and manages a concentrated portfolio of stocks invested in listed European companies. Cho and her colleagues hope to identify and buy stakes in companies with the potential to increase their value through strategic, operational, or financial change. Cho is considering the following three companies:

- Company A is a well-established, medium-sized food producer. Its profitability, measured by operating margins and return on assets, is ahead of industry peers. The company is recognised for its high corporate governance standards and effective communication with existing and potential investors. Cho's firm has invested in companies in this sector in the past and made gains on those positions.

- Company B is a medium-sized engineering business that has experienced a significant deterioration in profitability in recent years. More recently, the company has been unable to pay interest on its debt, and its new management team has recognized the need to restructure the business and negotiate with its creditors. Due to the company's losses, Cho cannot use earnings-based price multiples to assess upside potential, but based on sales and asset multiples, she believes there is significant upside potential in the stock if the company's current difficulties can be overcome and the debt can be restructured.

- Company C is also a medium-sized engineering business, but its operating performance, particularly when measured by the return on assets, is below that of the rest of the industry. Cho has identified a number of company assets that are underutilised. She believes that the management has significant potential to reduce fixed-asset investments, concentrate production in fewer facilities, and dispose of assets, in line with what the company's peers have been doing. Such steps could improve asset turnover and make it possible to return capital to shareholders through special dividends.

Identify the company that is most appropriate for Cho to recommend to the fund managers:

Solution:

Company C is the most appropriate choice. The company offers upside potential because of its ability to improve operating performance and cash payout using asset disposals, a strategy being implemented by other companies in its sector. Neither Company A nor Company B offers an attractive opportunity for activist investing: Company A is already operating efficiently, while Company B is more suitable for investors that focus on restructuring and distressed investing.

9 OTHER ACTIVE STRATEGIES

f describe active strategies based on statistical arbitrage and market microstructure

There are many other strategies that active portfolio managers employ in an attempt to beat the market benchmark. In this section, we explain two other categories of active strategies that do not fit neatly into our previous categorizations—namely, statistical arbitrage and event-driven strategies. Both rely on extensive use of quantitative data and are usually implemented in a systematic, rules-based way but can also incorporate the fund manager's judgment in making investment decisions.

9.1 Strategies Based on Statistical Arbitrage and Market Microstructure

Statistical arbitrage (or "stat arb") strategies use statistical and technical analysis to exploit pricing anomalies. Statistical arbitrage makes extensive use of data such as stock price, dividend, trading volume, and the limit order book for this purpose. The analytical tools used include (1) traditional technical analysis, (2) sophisticated time-series analysis and econometric models, and (3) machine-learning techniques. Portfolio managers typically take advantage of either mean reversion in share prices or opportunities created by market microstructure issues.

Pairs trading is an example of a popular and simple statistical arbitrage strategy. Pairs trading uses statistical techniques to identify two securities that are historically highly correlated with each other. When the price relationship of these two securities deviates from its long-term average, managers that expect the deviation to be temporary go long the underperforming stock and simultaneously short the outperforming stock. If the prices do converge to the long-term average as forecast, the investors close the trade and realize a profit. This kind of pairs trading therefore bets on a mean-reversion pattern in stock prices. The biggest risk in pairs trading and most other mean-reversion strategies is that the observed price divergence is not

Other Active Strategies

temporary; rather, it might be due to structural reasons.[15] Because risk management is critical for the success of such strategies, investors often employ stop-loss rules to exit trades when a loss limit is reached.

The most difficult aspect of a pairs-trading strategy is the identification of the pairs of stocks. This can be done either by using a quantitative approach and creating models of stock prices or by using a fundamental approach to judge the two stocks whose prices should move together for qualitative reasons.

Consider Canadian National Railway (CNR) and Canadian Pacific Railway (CP). These are the two dominant railways in Canada. Their business models are fairly similar, as both operate railway networks and transport goods throughout the country. Exhibit 26 shows that the prices of the two stocks have been highly correlated.[16] The y-axis shows the log price differential, referred to as the spread.[17] The exhibit also shows the moving average of the spread computed on a rolling 130-day window and bands at two standard deviations above and two standard deviations below the moving average. A simple pairs-trading strategy would be to enter into a trade when the spread is more than (or less than) two standard deviations from the moving average. The trade would be closed when the spread reaches the moving average again. Exhibit 26 shows the three trades based on our decision rules. The first trade was opened on 2 October 2014, when the spread between CNR and CP crossed the −2 standard deviation mark.[18] This trade was closed on 18 November 2014, when the spread reached the moving average. The first trade was profitable, and the position was maintained for slightly more than a month. The second trade was also profitable but lasted much longer. After the third trade was entered on 21 July 2015, however, there was a structural break, in that CP's decline further intensified while CNR stayed relatively flat; therefore, the spread continued to narrow. The loss on the third trade could have been significantly greater than the profits made from the first two transactions if the positions had been closed prior to mean reversion in the spring of 2016. This example highlights the risk inherent in mean-reversion strategies.

---

15 For example, the outperformance of one stock might be due to the fact that the company has developed a new technology or product that cannot be easily replicated by competitors.
16 The correlation coefficient between the two stocks was 69% based on daily returns from 2 January 2014 to 26 May 2016.
17 ln(Price of CNR/Price of CP).
18 The position is long CNR and short CP.

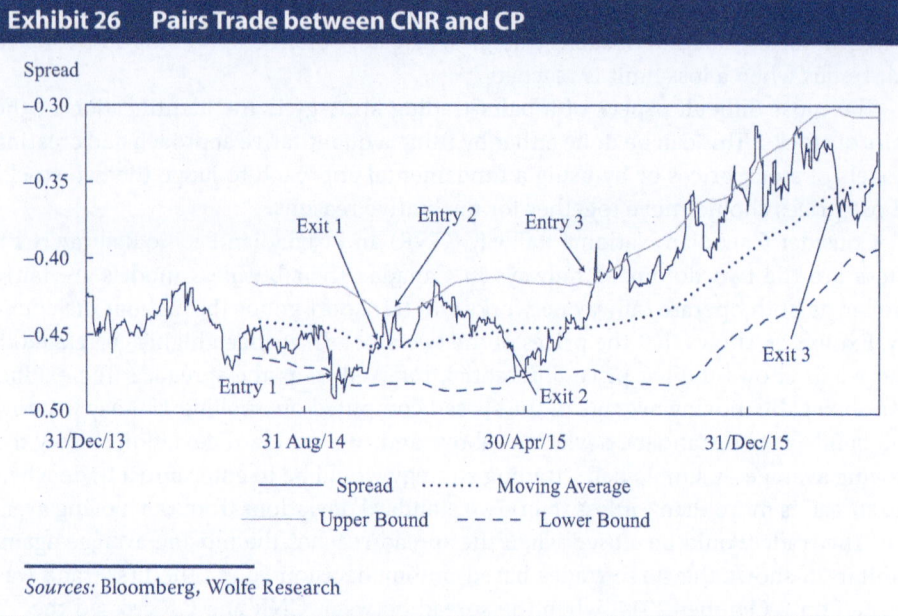

Exhibit 26 Pairs Trade between CNR and CP

Sources: Bloomberg, Wolfe Research

In the United States, many market microstructure–based arbitrage strategies take advantage of the NYSE Trade and Quote (TAQ) database and often involve extensive analysis of the limit order book to identify very short-term mispricing opportunities. For example, a temporary imbalance between buy and sell orders may trigger a spike in share price that lasts for only a few milliseconds. Only those investors with the analytical tools and trading capabilities for high-frequency trading are in a position to capture such opportunities, usually within a portfolio of many stocks designed to take advantage of very short-term discrepancies.

EXAMPLE 7

An analyst is asked to recommend a pair of stocks to be added to a statistical arbitrage fund. She considers the following three pairs of stocks:

- Pair 1 consists of two food-producing companies. Both are mature companies with comparable future earnings prospects. Both typically trade on similar valuation multiples. The ratio of their share prices shows mean reversion over the last two decades. The ratio is currently more than one standard deviation above its moving average.

- Pair 2 consists of two consumer stocks: One is a food retailer, and the other is a car manufacturer. Although the two companies operate in different markets and have different business models, statistical analysis performed by the analyst shows strong correlation between their share prices that has persisted for more than a decade. The stock prices have moved significantly in opposite directions in recent days. The analyst, expecting mean reversion, believes this discrepancy represents an investment opportunity.

- Pair 3 consists of two well-established financial services companies with a traditional focus on retail banking. One of the companies recently saw the arrival of a new management team and an increase in acquisition activity in corporate and investment banking—both new business areas for the company. The share price fell sharply on news of these changes. The price ratio of the two banks now deviates significantly from the moving average.

> Based on the information provided, select the pair that would be most suitable for the fund.
>
> **Solution:**
>
> Pair 1 is the most suitable for the fund. The companies' share prices have been correlated in the past, with the share price ratio reverting to the moving average. They have similar businesses, and there is no indication of a change in either company's strategies, as there is for Pair 3. By contrast with the price ratio for Pair 1, the past correlation of share prices for Pair 2 may have been spurious and is not described as exhibiting mean reversion.

9.2 Event-Driven Strategies

Event-driven strategies exploit market inefficiencies that may occur around corporate events such as mergers and acquisitions, earnings or restructuring announcements, share buybacks, special dividends, and spinoffs.

Risk arbitrage associated with merger and acquisition (M&A) activity is one of the most common examples of an event-driven strategy.

In a cash-only transaction, the acquirer proposes to purchase the shares of the target company for a given price. The stock price of the target company typically remains below the offered price until the transaction is completed. Therefore, an arbitrageur could buy the stock of the target company and earn a profit if and when the acquisition closes.

In a share-for-share exchange transaction, the acquirer uses its own shares to purchase the target company at a given exchange ratio. A risk arbitrage trader normally purchases the target share and simultaneously short-sells the acquirer's stock at the same exchange ratio. Once the acquisition is closed, the arbitrageur uses his or her long positions in the target company to exchange for the acquirer's stocks, which are further used to cover the arbitrageur's short positions.

The first challenge in managing risk arbitrage positions is to accurately estimate the risk of the deal failing. An M&A transaction, for example, may not go through for numerous reasons. A regulator may block the deal because of antitrust concerns, or the acquirer may not be able to secure the approval from the target company's shareholders. If a deal fails, the price of the target stock typically falls sharply, generating significant loss for the arbitrageur. Hence, this strategy has the label "risk arbitrage."

Another important consideration that an arbitrageur has to take into account is the deal duration. At any given point in time, there are many M&A transactions outstanding, and the arbitrageur has to decide which ones to participate in and how to weight each position, based on the predicted premium and risk. The predicted premium has to be annualized to enable the arbitrageur to compare different opportunities. Therefore, estimating deal duration is important for accurately estimating the deal premium.

CREATING A FUNDAMENTAL ACTIVE INVESTMENT STRATEGY

10

g   describe how fundamental active investment strategies are created

Fundamental (or discretionary) investing remains one of the prevailing philosophies of active management. In the following sections, we discuss how fundamental investors organize their investment processes.

10.1 The Fundamental Active Investment Process

The broad goal of active management is to outperform a selected benchmark on a risk-adjusted basis, net of fees and transaction costs. Value can be added at different stages of the investment process. For example, added value may come from the use of proprietary data, from special skill in security analysis and valuation, or from insight into industry/sector allocation.

Many fundamental investors use processes that include the following steps:

1. Define the investment universe and the market opportunity—the perceived opportunity to earn a positive risk-adjusted return to active investing, net of costs—in accordance with the investment mandate. The market opportunity is also known as the investment thesis.
2. Prescreen the investment universe to obtain a manageable set of securities for further, more detailed analysis.
3. Understand the industry and business for this screened set by performing:
   - industry and competitive analysis and
   - analysis of financial reports.
4. Forecast company performance, most commonly in terms of cash flows or earnings.
5. Convert forecasts to valuations and identify *ex ante* profitable investments.
6. Construct a portfolio of these investments with the desired risk profile.
7. Rebalance the portfolio with buy and sell disciplines.

The investment universe is mainly determined by the mandate agreed on by the fund manager and the client. The mandate defines the market segments, regions, and/or countries in which the manager will seek to add value. For example, if an investment mandate specifies Hong Kong's Hang Seng Index as the performance benchmark, the manager's investment universe will be primarily restricted to the 50 stocks in that index. However, an active manager may also include non-index stocks that trade on the same exchange or whose business activities significantly relate to this region. It is important for investors who seek to hold a diversified and well-constructed portfolio to understand the markets in which components of the portfolio will be invested. In addition, a clear picture of the market opportunity to earn positive active returns is important for active equity investment. The basic question is, what is the opportunity and why is it there? The answer to this two-part question can be called the investment thesis. The "why" part involves understanding the economic, financial, behavioral, or other rationale for a strategy's profitability in the future.

Practically, the investment thesis will suggest a set of characteristics that tend to be associated with potentially profitable investments. The investor may prescreen the investment universe with quantitative and/or qualitative criteria to obtain a manageable subset that will be analyzed in greater detail. Prescreening criteria can often be associated with a particular investment style. A value style manager, for example, may first exclude those stocks with high P/E multiples and high debt-to-equity ratios. Growth style managers may first rule out stocks that do not have high enough historical or forecast EPS growth. Steps 3 to 5 cover processes of in-depth analysis described in the Level II CFA Program readings on industry and company analysis and equity valuation. Finally, a portfolio is constructed in which stocks that have high upside potential are overweighted relative to the benchmark and stocks that are expected to underperform the benchmark are underweighted, not held at all, or (where relevant) shorted.[19]

As part of the portfolio construction process (step 6), the portfolio manager needs to decide whether to take active exposures to particular industry groups or economic sectors or to remain sector neutral relative to the benchmark. Portfolio managers may have top-down views on the business trends in some industries. For example, innovations in medical technology may cause an increase in earnings in the health care sector as a whole, while a potential central bank interest rate hike may increase the profitability of the banking sector. With these views, assuming the changed circumstances are not already priced in by the market, a manager could add extra value to the portfolio by overweighting the health care and financial services sectors. If the manager doesn't have views on individual sectors, he or she should, in theory, establish a neutral industry position relative to the benchmark in constructing the portfolio. However, a manager who has very strong convictions on the individual names in a specific industry may still want to overweight the industry that those names belong to. The potential high excess return from overweighting individual stocks can justify the risk the portfolio takes on the active exposure to that industry.

In addition to the regular portfolio rebalancing that ensures that the investment mandate and the desired risk exposures are maintained, a stock sell discipline needs to be incorporated into the investment process. The stock sell discipline will enable the portfolio to take profit from a successful investment and to exit from an unsuccessful investment at a prudent time.

In fundamental analysis, each stock is typically assigned a target price that the analyst believes to be the fair market value of the stock. The stock will be reclassified from undervalued to overvalued if the stock price surpasses this target price. Once this happens, the upside of the stock is expected to be limited, and holding that stock may not be justified, given the potential downside risk. The sell discipline embedded within an investment process requires the portfolio manager to sell the stock at this point. In practice, recognizing that valuation is an imprecise exercise, managers may continue to hold the stock or may simply reduce the size of the position rather than sell outright. This flexibility is particularly relevant when, in relative valuation frameworks where the company is being valued against a peer group, the valuations of industry peers are also changing. The target price of a stock need not be a constant but can be updated by the analyst with the arrival of new information. Adjusting the target price downward until it is lower than the current market price would also trigger a sale or a reduction in the position size.

Other situations could arise in which a stock's price has fallen and continues to fall for what the analyst considers to be poorly understood reasons. If the analyst remains positive on the stock, he or she should carefully consider the rationale for maintaining the position; if the company fundamentals indeed worsened, the analyst must also consider his or her own possible behavioral biases. The portfolio manager needs to have the discipline to take a loss by selling the stock if, for example, the price touches some pre-defined stop-loss trigger point. The stop-loss point is intended to set the maximum loss for each asset, under any conditions, and limit such behavioral biases.

---

[19] A portfolio that is benchmarked against an index that contains hundreds or thousands of constituents will most likely have zero weighting in most of them.

> **EXAMPLE 8**
>
> **Fundamental Investing**
>
> A portfolio manager uses the following criteria to prescreen his investment universe:
>
> 1. The year-over-year growth rate in earnings per share from continuing operations has increased over each of the last four fiscal years.
> 2. Growth in earnings per share from continuing operations over the last 12 months has been positive.
> 3. The percentage difference between the actual announced earnings and the consensus earnings estimate for the most recent quarter is greater than or equal to 10%.
> 4. The percentage change in stock price over the last four weeks is positive.
> 5. The 26-week relative price strength is greater than or equal to the industry's 26-week relative price strength.
> 6. The average daily volume for the last 10 days is in the top 50% of the market.
>
> Describe the manager's investment mandate.
>
> **Solution:**
>
> The portfolio manager has a growth orientation with a focus on companies that have delivered EPS growth in recent years and that have maintained their earnings and price growth momentum. Criterion 1 specifies accelerating EPS growth rates over recent fiscal years, while criterion 2 discards companies for which recent earnings growth has been negative. Criterion 3 further screens for companies that have beaten consensus earnings expectations—have had a positive earnings surprise—in the most recent quarter. A positive earnings surprise suggests that past earnings growth is continuing. Criteria 4 and 5 screen for positive recent stock price momentum. Criterion 6 retains only stocks with at least average market liquidity. Note the absence of any valuation multiples among the screening criteria: A value investor's screening criteria would typically include a rule to screen out issues that are expensively valued relative to earnings or assets.

10.2 Pitfalls in Fundamental Investing

Pitfalls in fundamental investing include behavioral biases, the value trap, and the growth trap.

10.2.1 Behavioral Bias

Fundamental, discretionary investing in general and stock selection in particular depend on subjective judgments by portfolio managers based on their research and analysis. However, human judgment, though potentially more insightful than a purely quantitative method, can be less rational and is often susceptible to human biases. The CFA Program curriculum readings on behavioral finance divide behavioral biases into two broad groups: cognitive errors and emotional biases. Cognitive errors are basic statistical, information-processing, or memory errors that cause a decision to deviate from the rational decisions of traditional finance, while emotional biases arise spontaneously as a result of attitudes and feelings that can cause a decision to deviate from the rational decisions of traditional finance. Several biases that are relevant to active fundamental equity management are discussed here.

Creating a Fundamental Active Investment Strategy

10.2.1.1 Confirmation Bias A cognitive error, confirmation bias—sometimes referred to as "stock love bias"—is the tendency of analysts and investors to look for information that confirms their existing beliefs about their favorite companies and to ignore or undervalue any information that contradicts their existing beliefs. This behavior creates selective exposure, perception, and retention and may be thought of as a selection bias. Some of the consequences are a poorly diversified portfolio, excessive risk exposure, and holdings in poorly performing securities. Actively seeking out the opinions of other investors or team members and looking for information from a range of sources to challenge existing beliefs may reduce the risk of confirmation bias.

10.2.1.2 Illusion of Control The basic philosophy behind active equity management is that investors believe they can control or at least influence outcomes. Skilled investors have a healthy confidence in their own ability to select stocks and influence outcomes, and they expect to outperform the market. The illusion of control bias refers to the human tendency to overestimate these abilities. Langer (1983) defines the illusion of control bias as "an expectancy of a personal success probability inappropriately higher than the objective probability would warrant." The illusion of control is a cognitive error.

Having an illusion of control could lead to excessive trading and/or heavy weighting on a few stocks. Investors should seek contrary viewpoints and set and enforce proper trading and portfolio diversification rules to try to avoid this problem.

10.2.1.3 Availability Bias Availability bias is an information-processing bias whereby individuals take a mental shortcut in estimating the probability of an outcome based on the availability of the information and how easily the outcome comes to mind. Easily recalled outcomes are often perceived as being more likely than those that are harder to recall or understand. Availability bias falls in the cognitive error category. In fundamental equity investing, this bias may reduce the investment opportunity set and result in insufficient diversification as the portfolio manager relies on familiar stocks that reflect a narrow range of experience. Setting an appropriate investment strategy in line with the investment horizon, as well as conducting a disciplined portfolio analysis with a long-term focus, will help eliminate any short-term over-emphasis caused by this bias.

10.2.1.4 Loss Aversion Loss aversion is an emotional bias whereby investors tend to prefer avoiding losses over achieving gains. A number of studies on loss aversion suggest that, psychologically, losses are significantly more powerful than gains. In absolute value terms, the utility derived from a gain is much lower than the utility given up in an equivalent loss.

Loss aversion can cause investors to hold unbalanced portfolios in which poorly performing positions are maintained in the hope of potential recovery and successful investments are sold (and the gains realized) prematurely in order to avoid further risk. A disciplined trading strategy with firmly established stop-loss rules is essential to prevent fundamental investors from falling into this trap.

10.2.1.5 Overconfidence Bias Overconfidence bias is an emotional bias whereby investors demonstrate unwarranted faith in their own intuitive reasoning, judgment, and/or cognitive abilities. This overconfidence may be the result of overestimating knowledge levels, abilities, and access to information. Unlike the illusion of control bias, which is a cognitive error, overconfidence bias is an illusion of exaggerated knowledge and abilities. Investors may, for example, attribute success to their own ability rather than to luck. Such bias means that the portfolio manager underestimates risks and overestimates expected returns. Regularly reviewing actual investment records and seeking constructive feedback from other professionals can help investors gain awareness of such self-attribution bias.

10.2.1.6 Regret Aversion Bias An emotional bias, regret aversion bias causes investors to avoid making decisions that they fear will turn out poorly. Simply put, investors try to avoid the pain of regret associated with bad decisions. This bias may actually prevent investors from making decisions. They may instead hold on to positions for too long and, in the meantime, lose out on profitable investment opportunities.

A carefully defined portfolio review process can help mitigate the effects of regret aversion bias. Such a process might, for example, require investors to periodically review and justify existing positions or to substantiate the decision not to have exposure to other stocks in the universe.

10.2.2 *Value and Growth Traps*

Value- and growth-oriented investors face certain distinctive risks, often described as "traps."

10.2.2.1 The Value Trap A value trap is a stock that appears to be attractively valued—with a low P/E multiple (and/or low price-to-book-value or price-to-cash-flow multiples)—because of a significant price fall but that may still be overpriced given its worsening future prospects. For example, the fact that a company is trading at a low price relative to earnings or book value might indicate that the company or the entire sector is facing deteriorating future prospects and that stock prices may stay low for an extended period of time or decline even further. Often, a value trap appears to be such an attractive investment that investors struggle to understand why the stock fails to perform. Value investors should conduct thorough research before investing in any company that appears to be cheap so that they fully understand the reasons for what appears to be an attractive valuation. Stock prices generally need catalysts or a change in perceptions in order to advance. If a company doesn't have any catalysts to trigger a reevaluation of its prospects, there is less of a chance that the stock price will adjust to reflect its fair value. In such a case, although the stock may appear to be an attractive investment because of a low multiple, it could lead the investor into a value trap.

HSBC Holdings is a multinational banking and financial services holding company headquartered in London. It has a dual primary listing on the Hong Kong Stock Exchange (HKSE) and the London Stock Exchange (LSE) and is a constituent of both the Hang Seng Index (HSI) and the FTSE 100 Index (UKX).

The stock traded on the HKSE at a price of over $80 at the end of 2013 and dropped below $50 in mid-June 2016. It declined by 43.7% in two and a half years, while the industry index (the Hang Seng Financial Index) lost only 5.4% over the same period. At the start of the period, HSBC Holdings looked cheap compared to peers and its own history, with average P/E and P/B multiples of 10.9x and 0.9x, respectively. Despite appearing undervalued, the stock performed poorly over the subsequent two-and-a-half-year period (see Exhibit 27) for reasons that included the need for extensive cost cutting. The above scenario is an illustration of a value trap.

Creating a Fundamental Active Investment Strategy

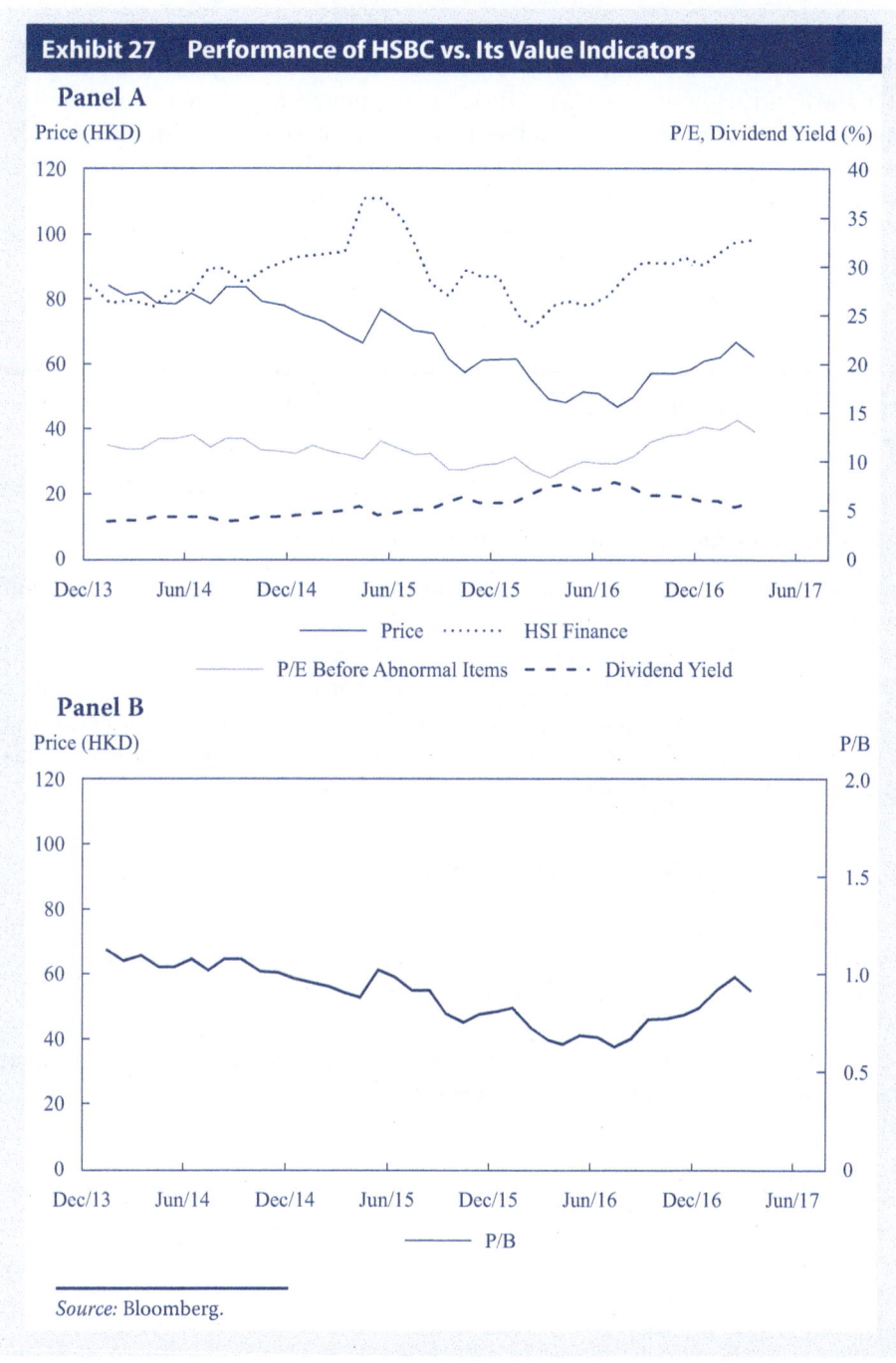

Exhibit 27 Performance of HSBC vs. Its Value Indicators

Source: Bloomberg.

10.2.2.2 The Growth Trap Investors in growth stocks do so with the expectation that the share price will appreciate when the company experiences above-average earnings (or cash flow) growth in the future. However, if the company's results fall short of these expectations, stock performance is affected negatively. The stock may also turn out to have been overpriced at the time of the purchase. The company may deliver above-average earnings or cash flow growth, in line with expectations, but the share price may not move any higher due to its already high starting level. The above circumstances are known as a growth trap. As with the value trap in the case of value stocks, the possibility of a growth trap should be considered when investing in what are perceived to be growth stocks.

Investors are often willing to justify paying high multiples for growth stocks in the belief that the current earnings are sustainable and that earnings are likely to grow fast in the future. However, neither of these assumptions may turn out to be true: The company's superior market position may be unsustainable and may last only until its competitors respond. Industry-specific variables often determine the pace at which new entrants or existing competitors respond and compete away any supernormal profits. It is also not uncommon to see earnings grow quickly from a very low base only to undergo a marked slowdown after that initial expansion.

11. CREATING A QUANTITATIVE ACTIVE INVESTMENT STRATEGY

h   describe how quantitative active investment strategies are created

Quantitative active equity investing began in the 1970s and became a mainstream investment approach in the subsequent decades. Many quantitative equity funds suffered significant losses in August 2007, an event that became known as the "quant meltdown." The subsequent global financial crisis contributed to growing suspicions about the sustainability of quantitative investing. However, both the performance and the perception of quantitative investing have recovered significantly since 2012 as this approach has regained popularity.

11.1 Creating a Quantitative Investment Process

Quantitative (systematic, or rules-based) investing generally has a structured and well-defined investment process. It starts with a belief or hypothesis. Investors collect data from a wide range of sources. Data science and management are also critical for dealing with missing values and outliers. Investors then create quantitative models to test their hypothesis. Once they are comfortable with their models' investment value, quantitative investors combine their return-predicting models with risk controls to construct their portfolios.

11.1.1 Defining the Market Opportunity (Investment Thesis)

Like fundamental active investing, quantitative active investing is based on a belief that the market is competitive but not necessarily efficient. Fund managers use publicly available information to predict future returns of stocks, using factors to build their return-forecasting models.

11.1.2 Acquiring and Processing Data

Data management is probably the least glamorous part of the quantitative investing process. However, investors often spend most of their time building databases, mapping data from different sources, understanding the data availability, cleaning up the data, and reshaping the data into a usable format. The most commonly used data in quantitative investing typically fall into the following categories:

- **Company mapping** is used to track many companies over time and across data vendors. Each company may also have multiple classes of shares. New companies go public, while some existing companies disappear due to bankruptcies, mergers, or takeovers. Company names, ticker symbols, and other identifiers can also change over time. Different data vendors have their own unique identifiers.

Creating a Quantitative Active Investment Strategy

- **Company fundamentals** include company demographics, financial statements, and other market data (e.g., price, dividends, stock splits, trading volume). Quantitative portfolio managers almost never collect company fundamental data themselves. Instead, they rely on data vendors, such as Capital IQ, Compustat, Worldscope, Reuters, FactSet, and Bloomberg.
- **Survey data** include details of corporate earnings, forecasts and estimates by various market participants, macroeconomic variables, sentiment indicators, and information on funds flow.
- **Unconventional data,** or unstructured data, include satellite images, measures of news sentiment, customer–supplier chain metrics, and corporate events, among many other types of information.

Data are almost never in the format that is required for quantitative investment analysis. Hence, investors spend a significant amount of time checking data for consistency, cleaning up errors and outliers, and transforming the data into a usable format.

11.1.3 Back-testing the Strategy

Once the required data are available in the appropriate form, strategy back-testing is undertaken. Back-testing is a simulation of real-life investing. For example, in a standard monthly back-test, one can build a portfolio based on a value factor as of a given month-end—perhaps 10 years ago—and then track the return of this portfolio over the subsequent month. Investors normally repeat this process (i.e., rebalance the portfolio) according to a predefined frequency or rule for multiple years to evaluate how such a portfolio would perform and assess the effectiveness of a given strategy over time.

11.1.3.1 Information Coefficient
Under the assumption that expected returns are linearly related to factor exposures, the correlation between factor exposures and their holding period returns for a cross section of securities has been used as a measure of factor performance in quantitative back-tests. This correlation for a factor is known in this context as the factor's information coefficient (IC). An advantage of the IC is that it aggregates information about factors from all securities in the investment universe, in contrast to an approach that uses only the best and worst deciles (a quantile-based approach), which captures only the top and bottom extremes.

The Pearson IC is the simple correlation coefficient between the factor scores (essentially standardized exposures) for the current period's and the next period's stock returns. As it is a correlation coefficient, its value is always between −1 and +1 (or, expressed in percentage terms, between −100% and +100%). The higher the IC, the higher the predictive power of the factor for subsequent returns. As a simple rule of thumb, in relation to US equities, any factor with an average monthly IC of 5%–6% is considered very strong. The coefficient is sensitive to outliers, as is illustrated below.

A similar but more robust measure is the Spearman rank IC, which is often preferred by practitioners. The Spearman rank IC is essentially the Pearson correlation coefficient between the ranked factor scores and ranked forward returns.

In the example shown in Exhibit 28 for earnings yield, the Pearson IC is negative at −0.8%, suggesting that the signal did not perform well and was negatively correlated with the subsequent month's returns. Looking more carefully, however, we can see that the sample factor is generally in line with the subsequent stock returns, with the exception of Stock I, for which the factor predicts the highest return but which turns out to be the worst performer. A single outlier can therefore turn what may actually be a good factor into a bad one, as the Pearson IC is sensitive to outliers. In contrast, the Spearman rank IC is at 40%, suggesting that the factor has strong predictive power for subsequent returns. If three equally weighted portfolios had been constructed, the long basket (Stocks G, H, and I) would have outperformed the short basket (Stocks A, B, and C) by 56 bps in this period.

Exhibit 28 Pearson Correlation Coefficient IC and Spearman Rank IC

Stock	Factor Score	Subsequent Month Return (%)	Rank of Factor Score	Rank of Return
A	−1.45	−3.00%	9	8
B	−1.16	−0.60%	8	7
C	−0.60	−0.50%	7	6
D	−0.40	−0.48%	6	5
E	0.00	1.20%	5	4
F	0.40	3.00%	4	3
G	0.60	3.02%	3	2
H	1.16	3.05%	2	1
I	1.45	−8.50%	1	9
Mean	0.00	−0.31%		
Standard deviation	1.00	3.71%		
Pearson IC		−0.80%		
Spearman rank IC				40.00%
Long/short tercile portfolio return				0.56%

Note: The portfolio is split into terciles, with each tercile containing one-third of the stocks.
Source: QES (Wolfe Research).

11.1.3.2 Creating a Multifactor Model   After studying the efficacy of single factors, managers need to decide which factors to include in a multifactor model. Factor selection and weighting is a fairly complex subject. Managers can select and weight each factor using either qualitative or systematic processes. For example, Qian, Hua, and Sorensen (2007) propose treating each factor as an asset; therefore, factor weighting becomes an asset allocation decision. A standard mean–variance optimization can also be used to weight factors. Deciding on which factors to include and their weight is a critical piece of the strategy. Investors should bear in mind that factors may be effective individually but not add material value to a factor model because they are correlated with other factors.

11.1.4 *Evaluating the Strategy*

Once back-testing is complete, the performance of the strategy can be evaluated. An out-of-sample back-test, in which a different set of data is used to evaluate the model's performance, is generally done to confirm model robustness. However, even strategies with great out-of-sample performance may perform poorly in live trading. Managers generally compute various statistics—such as the *t*-statistic, Sharpe ratio, Sortino ratio, VaR, conditional VaR, and drawdown characteristics—to form an opinion on the outcome of their out-of-sample back-test.

Creating a Quantitative Active Investment Strategy

11.1.5 Portfolio Construction Issues in Quantitative Investment

Most quantitative managers spend the bulk of their time searching for and exploring models that can predict stock returns, and may overlook the importance of portfolio construction to the quantitative investment process. While portfolio construction is covered in greater detail in other readings, the following aspects are particularly relevant to quantitative investing:

- **Risk models:** Risk models estimate the variance–covariance matrix of stock returns—that is, the risk of every stock and the correlation among stocks. Directly estimating the variance–covariance matrix using sample return data typically is infeasible and suffers from significant estimation errors.[20] Managers generally rely on commercial risk model vendors[21] for these data.

- **Trading costs:** There are two kinds of trading costs—explicit (e.g., commissions, fees, and taxes) and implicit (e.g., bid–ask spread and market impact). When two stocks have similar expected returns and risks, normally the one with lower execution costs is preferred.[22]

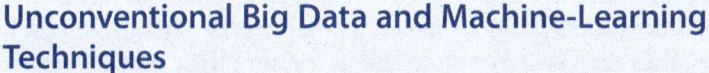

Unconventional Big Data and Machine-Learning Techniques

Rohal, Jussa, Luo, Wang, Zhao, Alvarez, Wang, and Elledge (2016) discuss the implications and applications of big data and machine-learning techniques in investment management. The rapid advancement in computing power today allows for the collection and processing of data from sources that were traditionally impossible or overly expensive to access, such as satellite images, social media, and payment-processing systems.

Investors now have access to data that go far beyond the traditional company fundamentals metrics. There are also many data vendors providing increasingly specialized or unique data content. Processing and incorporating unconventional data into existing investment frameworks, however, remains a challenge. With the improvements in computing speed and algorithms, significant successes in machine-learning techniques have been achieved. Despite concerns about data mining, machine learning has led to significant improvement in strategy performance.

11.2 Pitfalls in Quantitative Investment Processes

All active investment strategies have their pros and cons. There are many pitfalls that investors need to be aware of when they assess any quantitative strategy. Wang, Wang, Luo, Jussa, Rohal, and Alvarez (2014) discuss some of the common issues in quantitative investing in detail.

11.2.1 Survivorship Bias, Look-Ahead Bias, Data Mining, and Overfitting

Survivorship bias is one of the most common issues affecting quantitative decision making. While investors are generally aware of the problem, they often underestimate its significance. When back-tests use only those companies that are currently in business today, they ignore the stocks that have left the investment universe due

---

20 One problem with a sample covariance matrix is the curse of dimensionality. For a portfolio of N assets, we need to estimate $N \times (N + 1)/2$ parameters—that is, $N \times (N - 1)/2$ covariance parameters and N estimates of stock-specific risk. For a universe of 3,000 stocks, we would have to estimate about 4.5 million parameters.
21 MSCI Barra and Axioma are examples of data providers.
22 Trading costs are covered in depth in separate curriculum readings.

to bankruptcy,[23] delisting, or acquisition. This approach creates a bias whereby only companies that have survived are tested and it is assumed that the strategy would never have invested in companies that have failed. Survivorship bias often leads to overly optimistic results and sometimes even causes investors to draw wrong conclusions.

The second major issue in back-testing is look-ahead bias. This bias results from using information that was unknown or unavailable at the time an investment decision was made. An example of this bias is the use of financial accounting data for a company at a point in time before the data were actually released by the company.

In computer science, data mining refers to automated computational processes for discovering patterns in large datasets, often involving sophisticated statistical techniques, computation algorithms, and large-scale database systems. In finance, data mining can refer to such a process and can introduce a bias that results in model overfitting. It can be described as excessive search analysis of past financial data to uncover patterns and to conform to a pre-determined model for potential use in investing.

11.2.2 Turnover, Transaction Costs, and Short Availability

Back-testing is often conducted in an ideal, but unrealistic world without transaction costs, constraints on turnover, or limits on the availability of long and short positions. In reality, managers may face numerous constraints, such as limits on turnover and difficulties in establishing short positions in certain markets. Depending on how fast their signal decays, they may or may not be able to capture their model's expected excess return in a live trading process.

More importantly, trading is not free. Transaction costs can easily erode returns significantly. An example is the use of short-term reversal as a factor: Stocks that have performed well recently (say, in the last month) are more likely to revert (underperform) in the subsequent month. This reversal factor has been found to be a good stock selection signal in the Japanese equity market (before transaction costs). As shown in Exhibit 29, in a theoretical world with no transaction costs, a simple long/short strategy (buying the top 20% dividend-paying stocks in Japan with the worst performance in the previous month and shorting the bottom 20% stocks with the highest returns in the previous month) has generated an annual return of 12%, beating the classic value factor of price to book. However, if the transaction cost assumption is changed from 0 bps to 30 bps per trade, the return of the reversal strategy drops sharply, while the return of the price-to-book value strategy drops only modestly.

---

[23] In the United States, companies may continue to trade after filing for bankruptcy as long as they continue to meet listing requirements. However, their stocks are normally removed from most equity indexes.

Creating a Quantitative Active Investment Strategy

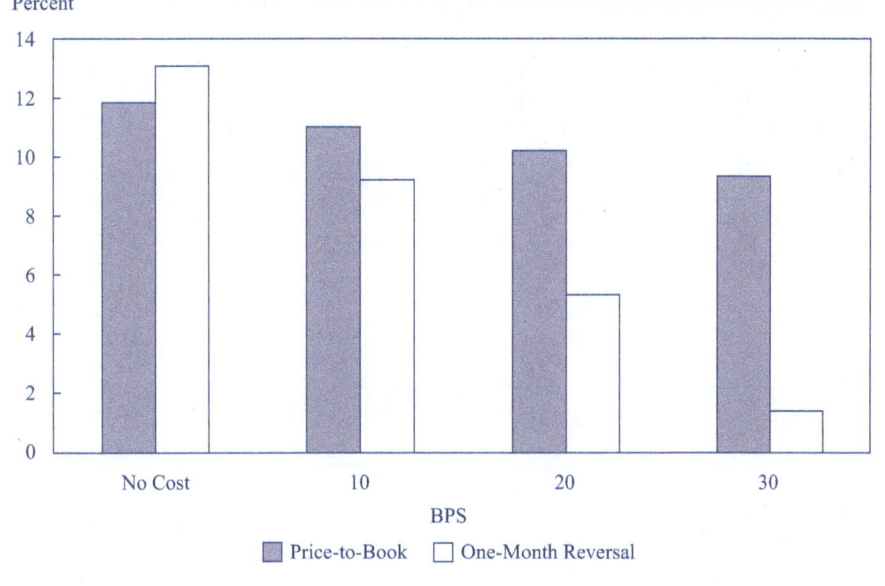

Exhibit 29 Annualized Returns with Different Transaction Cost Assumptions

Sources: Compustat, Capital IQ, Thomson Reuters.

Quant Crowding

In the first half of 2007, despite some early signs of the US subprime crisis, the global equity market was relatively calm. Then, in August 2007, many of the standard factors used by quantitative managers suffered significant losses,[24] and quantitative equity managers' performance suffered. These losses have been attributed to crowding among quantitative managers following similar trades (see Khandani and Lo 2008). Many of these managers headed for the exit at the same time, exacerbating the losses.

How can it be concluded that the August 2007 quant crisis was due to crowding? More importantly, how can crowding be measured so that the next crowded trade can be avoided? Jussa et al (2016a) used daily short interest data from Markit's securities finance database to measure crowding. They proposed that if stocks with poor price momentum are heavily shorted[25] relative to outperforming stocks, it indicates that many investors are following a momentum style. Hence, momentum as an investment strategy might get crowded. A measure of crowding that may be called a "crowding coefficient" can be estimated by regressing short interest on price momentum. Details of such regression analysis are beyond the scope of this reading.[26] As shown in Exhibit 30, the level of crowding for momentum reached a local peak in mid-2007. In the exhibit, increasing values of the crowding coefficient indicate greater crowding in momentum strategies.

---

[24] The average performance of many common factors was strong and relatively stable in 2003–2007. Actually, value and momentum factors suffered more severe losses in late 2002 and around March 2009.
[25] Short interest can be defined as the ratio of the number of stocks shorted to the number of stocks in the available qnventory for lending.
[26] For more on this subject, see Jussa, Rohal, Wang, Zhao, Luo, Alvarez, Wang, and Elledge (2016) and Cahan and Luo (2013).

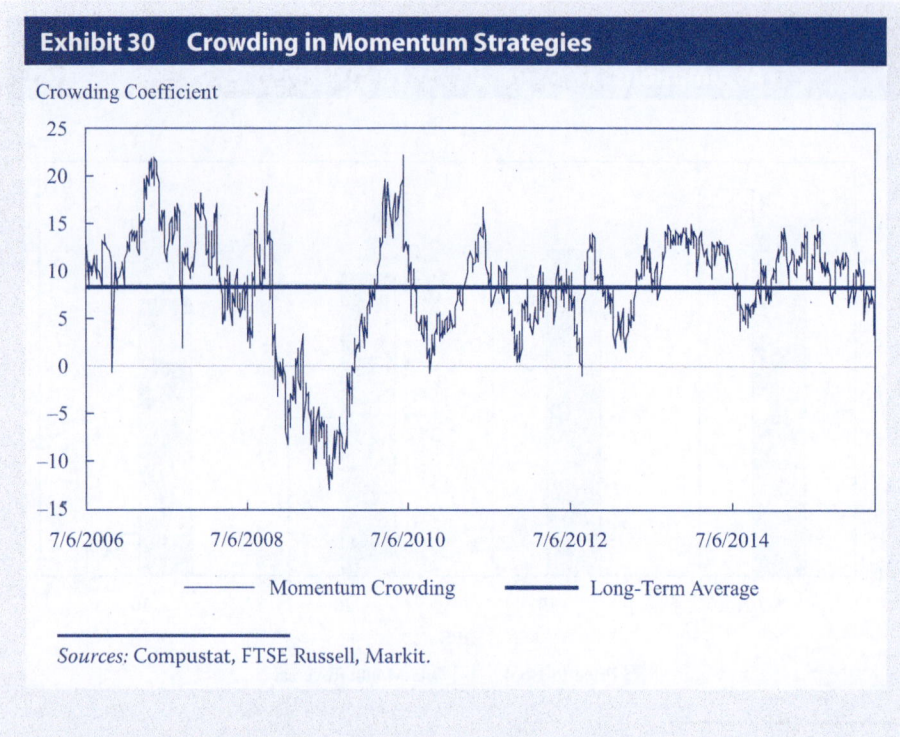

EXAMPLE 9

How to Start a Quantitative Investment Process

An asset management firm that traditionally follows primarily a fundamental value investing approach wants to diversify its investment process by incorporating a quantitative element. Discuss the potential benefits and hurdles involved in adding quantitative models to a fundamental investment approach.

Solution:

Quantitative investing is based on building models from attributes of thousands of stocks. The performance of quantitative strategies is generally not highly correlated with that of fundamental approaches. Therefore, in theory, adding a quantitative overlay may provide some diversification benefit to the firm.

In practice, however, because the processes behind quantitative and fundamental investing tend to be quite different, combining these two approaches is not always straightforward. Quantitative investing requires a large upfront investment in data, technology, and model development. It is generally desirable to use factors and models that are different from those used by most other investors to avoid potential crowded trades.

Managers need to be particularly careful with their back-testing so that the results do not suffer from look-ahead and survivorship biases. Transaction costs and short availability (if the fund involves shorting) should be incorporated into the back-testing.

EQUITY INVESTMENT STYLE CLASSIFICATION

i. discuss equity investment style classifications

An investment style classification process generally splits the stock universe into two or three groups, such that each group contains stocks with similar characteristics. The returns of stocks within a style group should therefore be correlated with one another, and the returns of stocks in different style groups should have less correlation. The common style characteristics used in active management include value, growth, blend (or core), size, price momentum, volatility, income (high dividend), and earnings quality. Stock membership in an industry, sector, or country group—for example, the financial sector or emerging markets—is also used to classify the investment style. Exhibit 31 lists a few mainstream categories of investment styles in use today.

Exhibit 31 Examples of Investment Styles

Characteristics based	Value, Growth or Blend/Core
	Capitalization
	Volatility
Membership based	Sector
	Country
	Market (developed or emerging)
Position based	Long/short (net long, short, or neutral)

Investment style classification is important for asset owners who seek to select active strategies. It allows active equity managers with similar styles to be compared with one another. Further, comparing the active returns or positions of a manager with those of the right style index can provide more information about the manager's active strategy and approach. A manager's portfolio may appear to have active positions when compared with the general market benchmark index; however, that manager may actually follow a style index and do so passively. Identifying the actual investment style of equity managers is important for asset owners in their decision-making process.

12.1 Different Approaches to Style Classification

Equity styles are defined by pairs of common attributes, such as value and growth, large cap and small cap, high volatility and low volatility, high dividend and low dividend, or developed markets and emerging markets. Style pairs need not be mutually exclusive. Each pair interprets the stock performance from a different perspective. A combination of several style pairs may often give a more complete picture of the sources of stock returns.

Identifying the investment styles of active managers helps to reveal the sources of added value in the portfolio. Modern portfolio theory advocates the use of efficient portfolio management of a diversified portfolio of stocks and bonds. Gupta, Skallsjö, and Li (2016) detail how the concept of diversification, when extended to different strategies and investment processes, can have a significant impact on the risk and reward of an investor's portfolio. A portfolio's risk–return profile is improved not only by including multiple asset classes but also by employing managers with different investment styles. An understanding of the investment style of a manager helps in evaluating the manager and confirming whether he or she sticks with the claimed investment style or deviates from it.

Two main approaches are often used in style analysis: a holdings-based approach and a returns-based approach. Each approach has its own strengths and weaknesses.

12.1.1 Holdings-Based Approaches

An equity investment style is actually the aggregation of attributes from individual stocks in the portfolio. Holdings-based approaches to style analysis are done bottom-up, but they are executed differently by the various commercial investment information providers. Using different criteria or different sources of underlying value and growth numbers may lead to slightly different classifications for stocks and therefore may result in different style characterizations for the same portfolio. In the style classification process followed by Morningstar and Thomson Reuters Lipper, the styles of individual stocks are clearly defined in that a stock's attribute for a specific style is 1 if it is included in that style index; otherwise, it is 0. The methodology used by MSCI and FTSE Russell, on the other hand, assumes that a stock can have characteristics of two styles, such as value and growth, at the same time. This methodology uses a multifactor approach to assign style inclusion factors to each stock. So a particular stock can belong to both value and growth styles by a pre-determined fraction. A portfolio's active exposure to a certain style equals the sum of the style attributes from all the individual stocks, weighted by their active positions.

The Morningstar Style Box

The Morningstar Style Box first appeared in 1992 to help investors and advisers determine the investment style of a fund. In a style box, each style pair splits the stock universe into two to three groups, such as value, core (or "blend"), and growth. The same universe can be split by another style definition—for example, large cap, mid cap, and small cap. The Morningstar Style Box splits the stock universe along both style dimensions, creating a grid of nine squares. It uses holdings-based style analysis and classifies about the same number of stocks in each of the value, core, and growth styles. Morningstar determines the value and growth scores by using five stock attributes (see Exhibit 33). The current Morningstar Style Box, as shown in Exhibit 32, is a nine-square grid featuring three stock investment styles for each of three size categories: large, mid, and small. Two of the three style categories are "value" and "growth," common to both stocks and funds. However, the third, central column is labeled "core" for stocks (i.e., those stocks for which neither value nor growth characteristics dominate) and "blend" for funds (meaning that the fund holds a mixture of growth and value stocks).

Equity Investment Style Classification

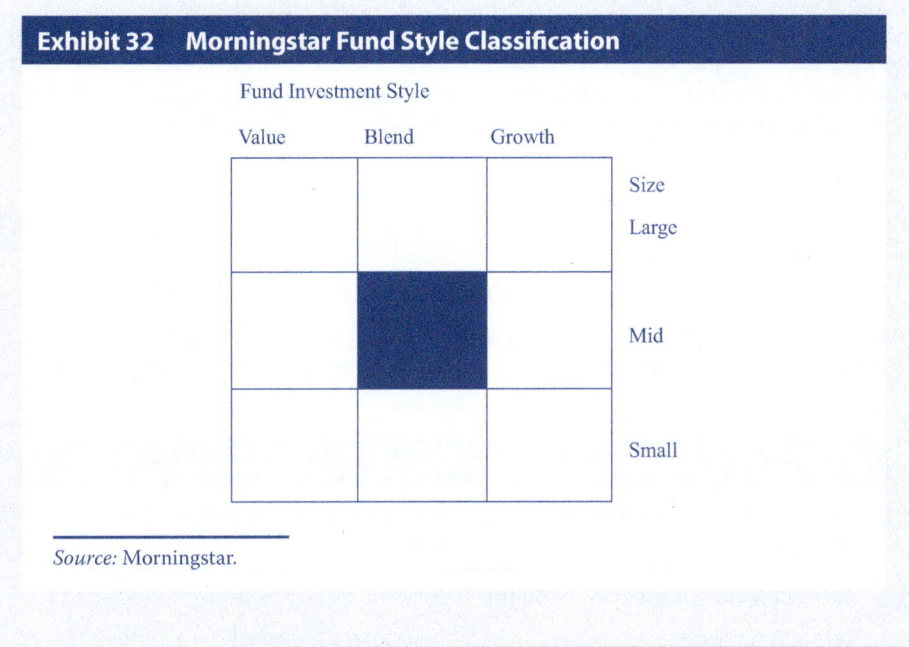

Exhibit 32   Morningstar Fund Style Classification

Source: Morningstar.

12.1.1.1 Large-Cap, Mid-Cap, and Small-Cap Classifications   The size classification is determined by the company's market capitalization. There is no consensus on what the size thresholds for the different categories should be, and indeed, different data and research providers use different criteria for size classification purposes. Large-cap companies tend to be well-established companies with a strong market presence, good levels of information disclosure, and extensive scrutiny by the investor community and the media. While these attributes may not apply universally across different parts of the world, large-cap companies are recognized as being lower risk than smaller companies and offering more limited future growth potential. Small-cap companies, on the other hand, tend to be less mature companies with potentially greater room for future growth, higher risk of failure, and a lower degree of analyst and public scrutiny.

Mid-cap companies tend to rank between the two other groups on many important parameters, such as size, revenues, employee count, and client base. In general, they are in a more advanced stage of development than small-cap companies but provide greater growth potential than large-cap companies.

There is no consensus on the boundaries that separate large-, mid-, and small-cap companies. One practice is to define large-cap stocks as those that account for the top ~70% of the capitalization of all stocks in the universe, with mid-cap stocks representing the next ~20% and small-cap stocks accounting for the balance.

12.1.1.2 Measuring Growth, Value, and Core Characteristics   Equity style analysis starts with assigning a style score to each individual stock. Taking the value/growth style pair as an example, each stock is assigned a value score based on the combination of several value and growth characteristics or factors of that stock. The simplest value scoring model uses one factor, price-to-book ratio, to rank the stock. The bottom half of the stocks in this ranking (smaller P/Bs) constitute the value index, while the stocks ranked in the top half (higher P/Bs) constitute the growth index. Weighting the stocks by their market capitalization thus creates both a value index and a growth index, with the condition that each style index must represent 50% of the market capitalization of all stocks in the target universe. A comprehensive value scoring model may use more factors in addition to price to book, such as price to earnings, price to sales, price to cash flow, return on equity, dividend yield, and so on. The combination of these factors through a predefined process, such as assigning a fixed weight to each selected factor, generates the value score. The value score is usually a number between 0 and

1, corresponding to 0% and 100% contribution to the value index. Depending on the methodologies employed by the vendors, the value score may be a fraction. A security with a value score of 0.6 will have 60% of its market capitalization allocated to the value index and the remaining 40% to the growth index.

Morningstar's Classification Criteria for Value Stocks

For each stock, Morningstar assigns a growth score and a value score, each based on five components that are combined with pre-determined weights, as shown in Exhibit 33.

Exhibit 33   Morningstar Value and Growth Scoring Scheme

Value Score Components and Weights		Growth Score Components and Weights	
Forward-looking measures	50.0%	*Forward-looking measures*	50.0%
*Price to projected earnings		*Long-term projected earnings growth	
Historical measures	50.0%	*Historical measures*	50.0%
*Price to book	12.5%	*Historical earnings growth	12.5%
*Price to sales	12.5%	*Sales growth	12.5%
*Price to cash flow	12.5%	*Cash flow growth	12.5%
*Dividend yield	12.5%	*Book value growth	12.5%

The scores are scaled to a range of 0 to 100, and the difference between the stock's growth and value scores is called the net style score. If this net style score is strongly negative, approaching –100, the stock's style is classified as value. If the result is strongly positive, the stock is classified as growth. If the scores for value and growth are similar in strength, the net style score will be close to zero and the stock will be classified as core. On average, value, core, and growth stocks each account for approximately one-third of the total capitalization in a given row of the Morningstar Style Box.

MSCI World Value and Growth Indexes

MSCI provides a range of indexes that include value and growth. In order to construct those indexes, the firm needs to establish the individual stocks' characteristics. The following (simplified) process is used to establish how much of each stock's market capitalization should be included in the respective indexes.

The value investment style characteristics for index construction are defined using three variables: book-value-to-price ratio, 12-month forward-earnings-to-price ratio, and dividend yield. The growth investment style characteristics for index construction are defined using five variables: long-term forward EPS growth rate, short-term forward EPS growth rate, current internal growth rate, long-term historical EPS growth trend, and long-term historical sales-per-share growth trend. *Z*-scores for each variable are calculated and aggregated for each security to determine the security's overall style characteristics. For example, a stock is assigned a so-called "value inclusion factor" of

Equity Investment Style Classification

0.6, which means that the stock could have both value and growth characteristics and contributes to the performance of the value and growth indexes by 60% and 40%, respectively. Exhibit 34 shows the cumulative return of the MSCI World Value and MSCI World Growth indexes since 1975.

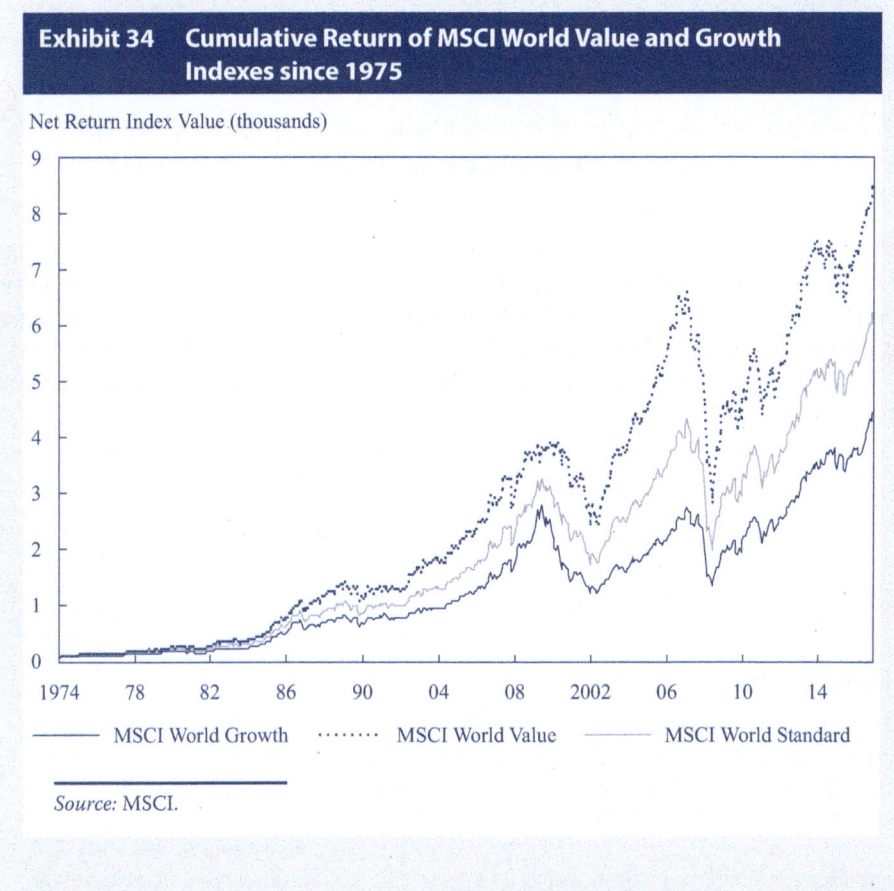

Exhibit 34 Cumulative Return of MSCI World Value and Growth Indexes since 1975

Source: MSCI.

12.1.2 Returns-Based Style Analysis

Many investment managers do not disclose the full details of their portfolios, and therefore a holdings-based approach cannot be used to assess their strategies. The investment style of these portfolio managers is therefore analyzed by using a returns-based approach to compare the returns of the employed strategy to those of a set of style indexes.

The objective of a returns-based style analysis is to find the style concentration of underlying holdings by identifying the style indexes that provide significant contributions to fund returns with the help of statistical tools. Such an analysis attributes fund returns to selected investment styles by running a constrained multivariate regression:[27]

$$r_t = \alpha + \sum_{s=1}^{m} \beta^s R_t^s + \varepsilon_t$$

---

[27] Sharpe (1992).

where

r_t = the fund return within the period ending at time t

R_t^s = the return of style index s in the same period

β^s = the fund exposure to style s (with constraints $\sum_{s=1}^{m} \beta^s = 1$ and $\beta^s > 0$ for a long-only portfolio)

α = a constant often interpreted as the value added by the fund manager

ε_t = the residual return that cannot be explained by the styles used in the analysis

The key inputs to a returns-based style analysis are the historical returns for the portfolio and the returns for the style indexes. The critical part, however, is the selection of the styles used, as stock returns can be highly correlated within the same sector, across sectors, and even across global markets. If available, the manager's own description of his or her style is a good starting point for determining the investment styles that can be used.

Commercial investment information providers, such as Thomson Reuters Lipper and Morningstar, perform the role of collecting and analyzing fund data and classifying the funds into style groups.

Data Sources

The success of a returns-based style analysis depends, to some extent, on the choice of style indexes. The component-based style indexes provided by investment information providers enable analysts to identify the style that is closest to the investment strategy employed by the fund manager.

Thomson Reuters Lipper provides mutual and hedge fund data as well as analytical and reporting tools to institutional and retail investors. All funds covered by Lipper are given a classification based on statements in the funds' prospectuses. Funds that are considered "diversified," because they invest across economic sectors and/or countries, also have a portfolio-based classification. Exhibit 35 shows the Lipper fund classifications for US-listed open-end equity funds.

Equity Investment Style Classification

Exhibit 35 Lipper's Style Classification

	OPEN-END EQUITY FUNDS		
	General Domestic Equity	**World Equity**	**Sector Equity**
Prospectus-Based Classifications	**All** prospectus-based classifications in this group are considered diversified.	**Some** prospectus-based classifications in this group are considered diversified (global and international types only).	**No** prospectus-based classifications in this group are considered diversified.
	Capital Appreciation	Gold	Health/Biotech
	Growth	European Region	Natural Resources
	Micro Cap	Pacific Region	Technology
	Mid Cap	Japan	Telecom
	Small Cap	Pacific ex-Japan	Utilities
	Growth & Income	China	Financial Services
	S&P 500	Emerging Markets	Real Estate
	Equity	Latin America	Specialty & Miscellaneous
	Income	Global	
		Global Small Cap	
		International	
		International Small Cap	

(continued)

Exhibit 35 (Continued)

	OPEN-END EQUITY FUNDS		
	General Domestic Equity	**World Equity**	**Sector Equity**
Portfolio-Based Classifications	Large-Cap Growth Large-Cap Core Large-Cap Value Multi-Cap Growth Multi-Cap Core Multi-Cap Value Mid-Cap Growth Mid-Cap Core Mid-Cap Value Small-Cap Growth Small-Cap Core Small-Cap Value S&P 500 Equity Income	Global Large-Cap Growth Global Large-Cap Core Global Large-Cap Value Global Multi-Cap Growth Global Multi-Cap Core Global Multi-Cap Value Global Small-/Mid-Cap Growth Global Small-/Mid-Cap Core Global Small-/Mid-Cap Value International Large-Cap Growth International Large-Cap Core International Large-Cap Value International Multi-Cap Growth International Multi-Cap Core International Multi-Cap Value International Small-/Mid-Cap Growth International Small-/Mid-Cap Core International Small-/Mid-Cap Value	

Source: Thomson Reuters Lipper.

12.1.3 *Manager Self-Identification*

Equity strategy investment styles result from the active equity manager's employment of a particular strategy to manage the fund. The fund's investment strategy is usually described in the fund prospectus and can be used to identify the fund's investment objective. This objective can be regarded as the manager's self-identification of the investment style.

Returns-based or holdings-based style analysis is commonly used to identify the investment style—such as value/growth or large cap/small cap—and to determine whether it corresponds to the manager's self-identified style. Some other styles, however, cannot be easily identified by such methods. For example, the styles of equity hedge funds, equity income funds, and special sector funds can be more efficiently identified using a combination of manager self-identification and holdings- or returns-based analysis.

Some equity hedge fund styles are non-standard and do not fit into any of the established style categories. Examples include long/short equity, equity market neutral, and dedicated short bias. For such funds, the investment objective is often laid out in the prospectus, which explains the fund's investment strategy. The prospectus becomes the key source of information for those assigning styles to such funds.

12.2 Strengths and Limitations of Style Analysis

Holdings-based style analysis is generally more accurate than returns-based analysis because it uses the actual portfolio holdings. Portfolio managers (and those who assess their strategies and performance) can see how each portfolio holding contributes to the portfolio's style, verify that the style is in line with the stated investment philosophy, and take action if they wish to prevent the portfolio's style from moving away from its intended target. Unlike returns-based style analysis, holdings-based style analysis is able to show the styles that any portfolio is exposed to, thus providing input for style allocation decisions.

Holdings-based style analysis requires the availability of all the portfolio constituents as well as the style attributes of each stock in the portfolio. While this information may be accessible for current portfolios, an analyst who wants to track the historical change in investment styles may face some difficulty. In this case, point-in-time databases are required for both the constituents of the fund and the stocks' style definitions.

As investment style research uses statistical and empirical methods to arrive at conclusions, it can produce inaccurate results due to limitations of the data or flaws in the application design. Kaplan (2011) argued that most returns-based style analysis models impose unnecessary constraints that limit the results within certain boundaries, making it difficult to detect more aggressive positions, such as deep value or micro cap. Furthermore, the limited availability of data on derivatives often makes holdings-based style analysis less effective for funds with substantial positions in derivatives. It is therefore important to understand the strengths and limitations of style analysis models in order to interpret the results correctly. Morningstar studies have concluded that holdings-based style analysis generally produces more accurate results than returns-based style analysis, although there may be exceptions. Ideally, practitioners should use both approaches: Returns-based models can often be more widely applied, while holdings-based models allow deeper style analysis.

Variation of Fund Characteristics within a Style Classification

Consider the Morningstar Style Box, in which funds are classified along two dimensions: value/growth and size (market capitalization). Within the same value style box, funds can be classified as large cap or small cap. To keep the classification map simple and concise, Morningstar omits other styles and characteristics, such as performance volatility and sector or market/region exposure. It is important to note that style classification provides only a reference to the key investment styles that may contribute to performance. The funds within the same style classification can be quite different in other characteristics, which may also contribute to fund returns and lead to differences in performance.

EXAMPLE 10

Equity Investment Styles

Consider an actively managed equity fund that has a five-year track record. An analyst performed both holdings-based and returns-based style analysis on the portfolio. She used the current portfolio holdings to perform the holdings-based style analysis and five-year historical monthly returns to carry out the returns-based analysis. The analyst found the following:

- Holdings-based style analysis on the current portfolio shows that the fund has value and growth exposures of 0.85 and 0.15, respectively.
- Returns-based style analysis with 60 months' historical returns shows that the value and growth exposures of the fund are equal to 0.4 and 0.6, respectively.

Explain possible reason(s) for the inconsistency between the holdings-based and returns-based style analyses.

Solution:

Some active equity managers may maintain one investment style over time in the belief that that particular style will outperform the general market. Others may rotate or switch between styles to accommodate the then-prevailing investment thesis. Returns-based style analysis regresses the portfolio's historical returns against the returns of the corresponding style indexes (over 60 months in this example). Its output indicates the average effect of investment styles employed during the period. While the holdings-based analysis suggests that the current investment style of the equity fund is value oriented, the returns-based analysis indicates that the style actually employed was likely in the growth category for a period of time within the past five years.

SUMMARY

This reading discusses the different approaches to active equity management and describes how the various strategies are created. It also addresses the style classification of active approaches.

- Active equity management approaches can be generally divided into two groups: fundamental (also referred to as discretionary) and quantitative (also known as systematic or rules-based). Fundamental approaches stress the use of human judgment in arriving at an investment decision, whereas quantitative approaches stress the use of rules-based, quantitative models to arrive at a decision.

Summary

- The main differences between fundamental and quantitative approaches include the following characteristics: approach to the decision-making process (subjective versus objective); forecast focus (stock returns versus factor returns); information used (research versus data); focus of the analysis (depth versus breadth); orientation to the data (forward looking versus backward looking); and approach to portfolio risk (emphasis on judgment versus emphasis on optimization techniques).
- The main types of active management strategies include bottom-up, top-down, factor-based, and activist.
- Bottom-up strategies begin at the company level, and use company and industry analyses to assess the intrinsic value of the company and determine whether the stock is undervalued or overvalued relative to its market price.
- Fundamental managers often focus on one or more of the following company and industry characteristics: business model and branding, competitive advantages, and management and corporate governance.
- Bottom-up strategies are often divided into value-based approaches and growth-based approaches.
- Top-down strategies focus on the macroeconomic environment, demographic trends, and government policies to arrive at investment decisions.
- Top-down strategies are used in several investment decision processes, including the following: country and geographic allocation, sector and industry rotation, equity style rotation, volatility-based strategies, and thematic investment strategies.
- Quantitative equity investment strategies often use factor-based models. A factor-based strategy aims to identify significant factors that drive stock prices and to construct a portfolio with a positive bias towards such factors.
- Factors can be grouped based on fundamental characteristics—such as value, growth, and price momentum—or on unconventional data.
- Activist investors specialize in taking meaningful stakes in listed companies and influencing those companies to make changes to their management, strategy, or capital structures for the purpose of increasing the stock's value and realizing a gain on their investment.
- Statistical arbitrage (or "stat arb") strategies use statistical and technical analysis to exploit pricing anomalies and achieve superior returns. Pairs trading is an example of a popular and simple statistical arbitrage strategy.
- Event-driven strategies exploit market inefficiencies that may occur around corporate events such as mergers and acquisitions, earnings announcements, bankruptcies, share buybacks, special dividends, and spinoffs.
- The fundamental active investment process includes the following steps: define the investment universe; prescreen the universe; understand the industry and business; forecast the company's financial performance; convert forecasts into a target price; construct the portfolio with the desired risk profile; and rebalance the portfolio according to a buy and sell discipline.
- Pitfalls in fundamental investing include behavioral biases, the value trap, and the growth trap.
- Behavioral biases can be divided into two groups: cognitive errors and emotional biases. Typical biases that are relevant to active equity management include confirmation bias, illusion of control, availability bias, loss aversion, overconfidence, and regret aversion.

- The quantitative active investment process includes the following steps: define the investment thesis; acquire, clean, and process the data; backtest the strategy; evaluate the strategy; and construct an efficient portfolio using risk and trading cost models.

- The pitfalls in quantitative investing include look-ahead and survivorship biases, overfitting, data mining, unrealistic turnover assumptions, transaction costs, and short availability.

- An investment style generally splits the stock universe into two or three groups, such that each group contains stocks with similar characteristics. The common style characteristics used in active management include value, size, price momentum, volatility, high dividend, and earnings quality. A stock's membership in an industry, sector, or country group is also used to classify the investment style.

- Two main approaches are often used in style analysis: a returns-based approach and a holdings-based approach. Holdings-based approaches aggregate the style scores of individual holdings, while returns-based approaches analyze the investment style of portfolio managers by comparing the returns of the strategy to those of a set of style indexes.

REFERENCES

Ang, A., W. Goetzmann, and S. Schaefer. 2009. *"Evaluation of Active Management of the Norwegian Government Pension Fund - Global."* (14 December). https://www.regjeringen.no/globalassets/upload/fin/statens-pensjonsfond-eksterne-rapporter-og-brev/ags-report.pdf

Basu, S. 1977. "Investment Performance of Common Stocks in Relation to Their Price-Earnings Ratios: A Test of the Efficient Market Hypothesis." *Journal of Finance* 32 (3): 663–82.

Cahan, R., and Y. Luo. 2013. "Standing Out From the Crowd: Measuring Crowding in Quantitative Strategies." *Journal of Portfolio Management* 39 (4): 14–23.

Fama, E., and K. R. French. 1992. "The Cross-Section of Expected Stock Returns." *Journal of Finance* 47 (2): 427–65.

Fama, E., and K. R. French. 1993. "Common Risk Factors in the Returns on Stocks and Bonds." *Journal of Financial Economics* 33 (1): 3–56.

Fama, E., and K. R. French. 1996. "Multifactor Explanations of Asset Pricing Anomalies." *Journal of Finance* 51 (1): 55–84.

Frazzini, A., and D. Kabiller, .and L. Pedersen. 2013. *"Buffett's Alpha."* NBER Working Paper 19681. 10.3386/w19681

Graham, B., and D. L. Dodd. 1934. *Security Analysis*. New York: McGraw-Hill.

Greenblatt, J. 2010. *The Little Book That Still Beats the Market*. Hoboken, NJ: John Wiley & Sons.

Greenwald, B., J. Kahn, P. Sonkin, and M. Biema. 2001. *Value Investing: From Graham to Buffett and Beyond*. Hoboken, NJ: John Wiley & Sons.

Gupta, P., S. Skallsjö, and B. Li. 2016. *Multi-Asset Investing: A Practitioner's Framework*. Chichester, UK: John Wiley & Sons.

Jegadeesh, N., and S. Titman. 1993. "Returns to Buying Winners and Selling Losers: Implications for Stock Market Efficiency." *Journal of Finance* 48 (1): 65–91.

Jussa, J., G. Rohal, S. Wang, G. Zhao, Y. Luo, M. Alvarez, A. Wang, and D. Elledge. 2016a. "Strategy Crowding." Deutsche Bank (16 May).

Jussa, J., K. Webster, G. Zhao, and Y. Luo. 2016b. *"Activism, Alpha and Action Heroes."* Deutsche Bank (6 January).

Kaplan, P. 2011. *Frontiers of Modern Asset Allocation*. Hoboken, NJ: John Wiley & Sons.

Khandani, A., and A. Lo. 2008. *"What Happened to the Quants in August 2007? Evidence from Factors and Transactions Data."* NBER Working Paper 14465.

Lakonishok, J., A. Shleifer, and R. W. Vishny. 1994. "Contrarian Investment, Extrapolation, and Risk." *Journal of Finance* 49 (5): 1541–78.

Langer, E. J. 1983. *The Psychology of Control*. Beverly Hills, CA: Sage Publications.

Maug, E. 1998. "Large Shareholders as Monitors: Is There a Trade-Off between Liquidity and Control?" *Journal of Finance* 53 (1): 65–98.

Qian, E. E., R. H. Hua, and E. H. Sorensen. 2007. *Quantitative Equity Portfolio Management: Modern Techniques and Applications*. Boca Raton, FL: Chapman & Hall/CRC.

Rohal, G., J. Jussa, Y. Luo, S. Wang, G. Zhao, M. Alvarez, A. Wang, and D. Elledge. 2016. "Big Data in Investment Management." Deutsche Bank (17 February).

Sharpe, W. F. 1992. "Asset Allocation, Management Style, and Performance Measurement." *Journal of Portfolio Management* 18 (2): 7–19.

Sloan, R. G. 1996. "Do Stock Prices Fully Reflect Information in Accruals and Cash Flows about Future Earnings?" *Accounting Review* 71 (3): 289–315.

Wang, S., A. Wang, Y. Luo, J. Jussa, G. Rohal, and M. Alvarez. 2014. *Seven Sins of Quantitative Investing*. Deutsche Bank Market Research (September).

PRACTICE PROBLEMS

The following information relates to questions 1–6

James Leonard is a fund-of-funds manager with Future Generation, a large sovereign fund. He is considering whether to pursue more in-depth due diligence processes with three large-cap long-only funds proposed by his analysts. Although the funds emphasize different financial metrics and use different implementation methodologies, they operate in the same market segment and are evaluated against the same benchmark. The analysts prepared a short description of each fund, presented in Exhibit 1.

Exhibit 1	Description of Each Candidate Fund
Fund	**Description**
Furlings	Furlings Investment Partners combines sector views and security selection. The firm's head manager uses several industry and economic indicators identified from his own experience during the last two decades, as well as his personal views on market flow dynamics, to determine how to position the fund on a sector basis. Sector deviations from the benchmark of 10% or more are common and are usually maintained for 12 to 24 months. At the same time, sector managers at Furlings use their expertise in dissecting financial statements and their understanding of the corporate branding and competitive landscape within sectors to build equally weighted baskets of securities within sectors. Each basket contains their 7 to 10 highest-conviction securities, favoring firms that have good governance, strong growth potential, competitive advantages such as branding, and attractive relative valuations. The Furlings master fund holds approximately 90 securities.
Asgard	Asgard Investment Partners is a very large asset manager. It believes in investing in firms that have a strong business model and governance, reasonable valuations, solid capital structures with limited financial leverage, and above-average expected earnings growth for the next three years. Although the Asgard master fund invests in fewer than 125 securities, each sector analyst builds financial models that track as many as 50 firms. To support them in their task, analysts benefit from software developed by the Asgard research and technology group that provides access to detailed market and accounting information on 5,000 global firms, allowing for the calculation of many valuation and growth metrics and precise modeling of sources of cash-flow strengths and weaknesses within each business. Asgard analysts can also use the application to back-test strategies and build their own models to rank securities' attractiveness according to their preferred characteristics. Security allocation is determined by a management team but depends heavily on a quantitative risk model developed by Asgard. Asgard has a low portfolio turnover.
Tokra	Tokra Capital uses a factor-based strategy to rank securities from most attractive to least attractive. Each security is scored based on three metrics: price to book value (P/B), 12-month increase in stock price, and return on assets. Tokra's managers have a strong risk management background. Their objective is to maximize their exposure to the most attractive securities using a total scoring approach subject to limiting single-security concentration below 2%, sector deviations below 3%, active risk below 4%, and annual turnover less than 40%, while having a market beta close to 1. The master fund holds approximately 400 positions out of a possible universe of more than 2,000 securities evaluated.

When Leonard's analysts met with Asgard, they inquired whether its managers engage in activist investing because Asgard's portfolio frequently holds significant positions, because of their large asset size, and because of their emphasis on strong governance and their ability to model sources of cash-flow strengths and weaknesses within each business. The manager indicated that Asgard engages with companies from a long-term shareholder's perspective, which is consistent with the firm's low portfolio turnover, and uses its voice, and its vote, on matters that can influence companies' long-term value.

Leonard wants to confirm that each manager's portfolios are consistent with its declared style. To this end, Exhibit 2 presents key financial information associated with each manager's portfolio and also with the index that all three managers use.

Exhibit 2 Key Financial Data

Fund	Index	Furlings	Asgard	Tokra
Dividend/price (trailing 12-month)	2.3%	2.2%	2.2%	2.6%
P/E (trailing 12-month)	26.5	24.7	26.6	27.3
Price/cash flows (12-month forward)	12.5	13.8	12.5	11.6
P/B	4.8	4.30	4.35	5.4
Average EPS growth (three to five years forward)	11.9%	11.0%	13.1%	10.8%
Net income/assets	2.8%	4.5%	4.3%	3.2%
Average price momentum (trailing 12 months)	10.5%	14.0%	10.0%	12.0%

1 Which fund manager's investing approach is most consistent with fundamental management?
   A Furlings
   B Asgard
   C Tokra

2 Which of the following statements about the approaches and styles of either Furlings, Asgard, or Tokra is incorrect?
   A Furlings is a top-down sector rotator with a value orientation within sectors.
   B Asgard is a bottom-up manager with a GARP (growth at a reasonable price) style.
   C Tokra is a factor-based manager using value, growth, and profitability metrics.

3 Which manager is most likely to get caught in a value trap?
   A Furlings
   B Asgard
   C Tokra

4 Which activist investing tactic is Asgard *least likely* to use?
   A Engaging with management by writing letters to management, calling for and explaining suggested changes, and participating in management discussions with analysts or meeting the management team privately
   B Launching legal proceedings against existing management for breach of fiduciary duties
   C Proposing restructuring of the balance sheet to better utilize capital and potentially initiate share buybacks or increase dividends

Practice Problems

5 Based on the information provided in Exhibits 1 and 2, which manager's portfolio characteristics is most likely at odds with its declared style?
   A   Furlings
   B   Asgard
   C   Tokra

6 Leonard is looking at the style classification from Asgard as reported by Morningstar and Thomson Reuters Lipper. He is surprised to find that Asgard is classified as a blend fund by Morningstar and a value fund by Lipper. Which of the following statements is correct?
   A   Although the Morningstar methodology classifies securities as either value, growth, or core, the Lipper methodology assumes a stock can have the characteristics of many styles. This approach can result in a different classification for the same portfolio.
   B   The Lipper methodology can only lead to a value or growth classification. It does not offer a core/blend component.
   C   The Morningstar methodology classifies securities as either value, growth, or core by looking at the difference between their respective growth and value scores. It is possible that the Asgard funds hold a balanced exposure to both value and growth and/or core stocks.

The following information relates to questions 7–14

Aleksy Nowacki is a new portfolio manager at Heydon Investments. The firm currently offers a single equity fund, which uses a top-down investment strategy based on fundamentals. Vicky Knight, a junior analyst at Heydon, assists with managing the fund.

Nowacki has been hired to start a second fund, the Heydon Quant Fund, which will use quantitative active equity strategies. Nowacki and Knight meet to discuss distinct characteristics of the quantitative approach to active management, and Knight suggests three such characteristics:

Characteristic 1	The focus is on factors across a potentially large group of stocks.
Characteristic 2	The decision-making process is systematic and non-discretionary.
Characteristic 3	The approach places an emphasis on forecasting the future prospects of underlying companies.

Nowacki states that quantitative investing generally follows a structured and well-defined process. Knight asks Nowacki:

"What is the starting point for the quantitative investment process?"

The new Heydon Quant Fund will use a factor-based strategy. Nowacki assembles a large dataset with monthly standardized scores and monthly returns for the strategy to back-test a new investment strategy and calculates the information coefficient. $FS(t)$ is the factor score for the current month, and $FS(t + 1)$ is the score for the next month. $SR(t)$ is the strategy's holding period return for the current month, and $SR(t + 1)$ is the strategy's holding period return for the next month.

As an additional step in back-testing of the strategy, Nowacki computes historical price/book ratios (P/Bs) and price/earnings ratios (P/Es) using calendar year-end (31 December) stock prices and companies' financial statement data for the same calendar year. He notes that the financial statement data for a given calendar year are not typically published until weeks after the end of that year.

Because the Heydon Quant Fund occasionally performs pairs trading using statistical arbitrage, Nowacki creates three examples of pairs trading candidates, presented in Exhibit 1. Nowacki asks Knight to recommend a suitable pair trade.

Exhibit 1 Possible Pairs Trades Based on Statistical Arbitrage

Stock Pair	Current Price Ratio Compared with Long-Term Average	Historical Price Ratio Relationship	Historical Correlation between Returns
1 and 2	Not significantly different	Mean reverting	High
3 and 4	Significantly different	Mean reverting	High
5 and 6	Significantly different	Not mean reverting	Low

Knight foresees a possible scenario in which the investment universe for the Heydon Quant Fund is unchanged but a new factor is added to its multifactor model. Knight asks Nowacki whether this scenario could affect the fund's investment-style classifications using either the returns-based or holdings-based approaches.

7 Which of the following asset allocation methods would **not** likely be used by Nowacki and Knight to select investments for the existing equity fund?
   A Sector and industry rotation
   B Growth at a reasonable price
   C Country and geographic allocation

8 Relative to Heydon's existing fund, the new fund will *most likely*:
   A hold a smaller number of stocks.
   B rebalance at more regular intervals.
   C see risk at the company level rather than the portfolio level.

9 Which characteristic suggested by Knight to describe the quantitative approach to active management is *incorrect*?
   A Characteristic 1
   B Characteristic 2
   C Characteristic 3

10 Nowacki's *most appropriate* response to Knight's question about the quantitative investment process is to:
   A back-test the new strategy.
   B define the market opportunity.
   C identify the factors to include and their weights.

11 In Nowacki's back-testing of the factor-based strategy for the new fund, the calculated information coefficient should be based on:
   A $FS(t)$ and $SR(t)$.
   B $FS(t)$ and $SR(t + 1)$.

Practice Problems

    C $SR(t)$ and $FS(t + 1)$.

12 Nowacki's calculated price/book ratios (P/Bs) and price/earnings ratios (P/Es), in his back-testing of the new strategy, are a problem because of:

    A   data mining.

    B   look-ahead bias.

    C   survivorship bias.

13 Based on Exhibit 1, which stock pair should Knight recommend as the best candidate for statistical arbitrage?

    A   Stock 1 and Stock 2

    B   Stock 3 and Stock 4

    C   Stock 5 and Stock 6

14 The *most appropriate* response to Knight's question regarding the potential future scenario for the Heydon Quant Fund is:

    A   only the returns-based approach.

    B   only the holdings-based approach.

    C   both the returns-based approach and the holdings-based approach.

The following information relates to questions 15–19

Jack Dewey is managing partner of DC&H, an investment management firm, and Supriya Sardar is an equity analyst with the firm. Dewey recently took over management of the firm's Purity Fund. He is developing a fundamental active investment process for managing this fund that emphasizes financial strength and demonstrated profitability of portfolio companies. At his previous employer, Dewey managed a fund for which his investment process involved taking active exposures in sectors based on the macroeconomic environment and demographic trends.

Dewey and Sardar meet to discuss developing a fundamental active investment process for the Purity Fund. They start by defining the investment universe and market opportunity for the fund, and then they pre-screen the universe to obtain a manageable set of securities for further, more detailed analysis. Next, Dewey notes that industry and competitive analysis of the list of securities must be performed. He then asks Sardar to recommend the next step in development of the fundamental active management process.

During the next few months, Dewey rebalances the Purity Fund to reflect his fundamental active investment process. Dewey and Sardar meet again to discuss potential new investment opportunities for the fund. Sardar recommends the purchase of AZ Industrial, which she believes is trading below its intrinsic value, despite its high price-to-book value (P/B) relative to the industry average.

Dewey asks Sardar to perform a bottom-up style analysis of the Purity Fund based on the aggregation of attributes from individual stocks in the portfolio. Dewey plans to include the results of this style analysis in a profile he is preparing for the fund.

15 In managing the fund at his previous employer, Dewey's investment process can be *best* described as:

    A   an activist strategy.

    B   a top-down strategy.

    C a bottom-up strategy.

16 Sardar's recommendation for the next step should be to:
- **A** review results from back-testing the strategy.
- **B** make recommendations for rebalancing the portfolio.
- **C** forecast companies' performances and convert those forecasts into valuations.

17 Based upon Dewey's chosen investment process for the management of the Purity Fund, rebalancing of the fund will *most likely* occur:
- **A** at regular intervals.
- **B** in response to changes in company-specific information.
- **C** in response to updated output from optimization models.

18 Which investment approach is the *most likely* basis for Sardar's buy recommendation for AZ Industrial?
- **A** Relative value
- **B** High-quality value
- **C** Deep-value investing

19 The analysis performed by Sardar on the Purity Fund can be *best* described as being based on:
- **A** a holdings-based approach.
- **B** manager self-identification.
- **C** a returns-based style analysis.

SOLUTIONS

1. **A is correct.** Furlings combines a top-down and bottom-up approach, but in both cases, the allocation process is significantly determined according to the managers' discretion and judgement. There is a strong emphasis on understanding financial reporting, and the sector managers focus on a relatively small number for firms. They also extend their analysis to other areas associated with fundamental management, such as valuation, competitive advantages, and governance. Finally, Furlings's top-down process depends largely on the views and experience of its head manager.

   B is incorrect. Asgard has many of the attributes associated with a fundamental manager. It invests in a relatively small number of securities and focuses on the companies' business model, valuations, and future growth prospects. Because of the scope of the securities coverage by each manager, however, Asgard depends heavily on technology and tools to support screening and ranking of securities attractiveness. Each manager can use his judgement to build his own quantitative models. Furthermore, the allocation process, although overlaid by a management team, also depends heavily on technology. Asgard has characteristics of both fundamental and quantitative managers.

   C is incorrect. Tokra exhibits the characteristics of a quantitative manager. The firm uses quantitative metrics to rank securities based on valuation, profitability, and momentum criteria and uses portfolio optimization to determine the final allocation. Tokra holds many positions typical of quantitative approaches.

2. **C is an incorrect statement.** Although Tokra is a factor manager, and although it uses a value proxy such as P/B and a profitability proxy such as return on assets, it does not use a growth proxy such as earnings growth over the last 12 or 36 months but rather a price momentum proxy.

   A is a correct statement. Furlings is a top-down manager. It makes significant sector bets based on industry and economic indicators derived from the head manager's experience, and it does select its securities within sectors while considering relative valuation.

   B is a correct statement. Asgard favors securities that have reasonable valuations and above-average growth prospects. It has a bottom-up approach and builds its portfolio starting at the security level.

3. **C is the correct answer.** A value trap occurs when a stock that appears to have an attractive valuation because of a low P/E and/or P/B multiple (or other relevant value proxies) appears cheap only because of its worsening growth prospects. Although a pitfall such as value trap is more common in fundamental investing, a quantitative process that relies on historical information and does not integrate future expectations about cash flows or profitability may be unable to detect a value trap.

   A is an incorrect answer. Although Furlings is a top-down manager, its sector portfolios are built through investing in a small number of high-conviction securities after its analysts have dissected the financial statements and analyzed the competitive landscape and growth prospects. Managers at Furlings are more likely than managers at Tokra to be aware of the significant deteriorating prospects of a security they are considering for investment.

   B is an incorrect answer. One of Asgard's investment criteria is identifying firms that have good potential cash flow growth over the next three years. The firm has access to database and support tools, allowing its analysts to evaluate many potential growth metrics. Managers at Asgard are more likely than managers at Tokra to be aware of the significant deteriorating prospects of a security they are considering for investment.

4   B is the correct answer. Asgard invests in firms that have strong business models and good governance. Also, it approaches investing as a long-term investor looking to use its voice to improve the company's asset management. Asgard is unlikely to use an aggressive posturing or to invest or stay invested in companies with weak governance or where managers may be in breach of fiduciary duties.

A is an incorrect answer. Engaging in positive conversations with management of companies with which Asgard has invested reflects a use of its voice to improve these companies' long-term value.

C is an incorrect answer. Because Asgard is strong at modeling sources of cash flows and is known for investing in companies with a strong capital structure, it would be consistent for Asgard to propose ways to optimize the capital structure and shareholders' compensation.

5   C is the correct answer. Tokra indicates that it emphasizes three metrics: P/B, 12-month price momentum, and return on assets. Although the portfolio consists of securities that have stronger momentum than those of the index on average, and although the ratio of net income to assets is also favorable, the average P/B is somehow higher than that of the index. Although this scenario could normally be explained by an emphasis on specific sectors with a higher P/B than other sectors, the low level of sector deviation tolerated within the strategy weakens that explanation. This should be explored with Tokra's managers.

A is an incorrect answer. Furlings is a top-down sector rotator with a value orientation within sectors. The lower P/B and P/E and higher net income over assets are consistent with a relative value orientation. Because Furlings can take significant positions in specific sectors, however, there could be other circumstances in which the portfolio would have a higher P/B and/or P/E and or a lower net income /assets than the index if the fund were to emphasize sectors having such characteristics. Yet, this would not necessarily imply that the firm does not favor the most attractive relative valuations within sectors.

B is an incorrect answer. Asgard invests in firms that offer reasonable valuations and above-average expected cash flow growth during the next three years. The data, such as P/B and average expected three-year profit growth, are consistent with its declared style. Again, it is not necessarily inconsistent to emphasize these aspects while investing in a portfolio that has a lower dividend yield, slightly higher P/E, and lower price momentum.

6   C is a correct answer. Morningstar calculates a score for value and growth on a scale of 0 to 100 using five proxy measures for each. The value score is subtracted from the growth score. A strongly positive net score leads to a growth classification, and a strongly negative score leads to a value classification. A score relatively close to zero indicates a core classification. To achieve a blend classification, the portfolio must have a balanced exposure to stocks classified as value and growth, a dominant exposure to stocks classified as core, or a combination of both.

A is an incorrect answer. Both Morningstar and Lipper classify individual stocks in a specific style category. Neither assumes a security can belong to several styles in specific proportion.

B is an incorrect answer. The Lipper methodology does have a core classification. It sums the Z-score of six portfolio characteristics over several years to determine an overall Z-score that determines either a value, core, or growth classification.

7 B is correct. The firm currently offers a single equity fund, which uses a top-down investment strategy. Country and geographic allocation and sector and industry rotation are both top-down strategies that begin at the top or macro level and are consistent with the fund's top-down investment strategy. Growth at a reasonable price (GARP), however—a growth-based approach—is a bottom-up asset selection strategy that begins with data at the company level. Therefore, Nowacki and Knight likely would not use the GARP approach to select investments for the existing equity fund, which uses a top-down investment strategy. A is incorrect because sector and industry rotation is a top-down strategy, consistent with the fund's top-down approach. C is incorrect because country and geography selection is a top-down strategy, consistent with the fund's top-down approach.

8 B is correct. Portfolios managed using a quantitative approach are usually rebalanced at regular intervals, such as monthly or quarterly. In contrast, portfolios managed using a fundamental approach usually monitor the portfolio's holdings continuously and may increase, decrease, or eliminate positions at any time.

Also, the focus of a quantitative approach is on factors across a potentially large group of stocks, whereas fundamental strategies focus on a relatively small group of stocks. Consequently, Heydon's new quantitative fund will likely hold a larger number of stocks than the existing equity fund.

Finally, managers following a fundamental approach typically select stocks by performing extensive research on individual companies; thus, fundamental investors see risk at the company level. In contrast, with a quantitative approach, the risk is that factor returns will not perform as expected. Because the quantitative approach invests in baskets of stocks, the risks lie at the portfolio level rather than at the level of specific stocks (company level). Consequently, Nowacki's new quantitative fund will likely see risk at the portfolio level, rather than the company level as the existing equity fund does.

9 C is correct. Quantitative analysis uses a company's history to arrive at investment decisions. The quantitative decision-making process is systematic and non-discretionary (whereas the fundamental decision-making process is more discretionary), and the focus of the quantitative approach is on factors across a potentially large group of stocks (whereas fundamental strategies focus on a relatively small group of stocks). In contrast, fundamental analysis (not quantitative analysis) emphasizes forecasting future prospects, including the future earnings and cash flows of a company.

10 B is correct. The first step in creating a quantitative, active strategy is to define the market opportunity or investment thesis. Then, relevant data is acquired, processed, and transformed into a usable format. This step is followed by back-testing the strategy, which involves identifying the factors to include as well as their weights. Finally, the strategy performance should be evaluated using an out-of-sample back-test.

11 B is correct. The purpose of back-testing is to identify correlations between the current period's factor scores, $FS(t)$, and the next period's holding period strategy returns, $SR(t + 1)$.

12 B is correct. Look-ahead bias results from using information that was unknown or unavailable at the time the investment decision was made. An example of this bias is using financial accounting data for a company at a point before the

data were actually released by the company. Nowacki computed historical P/Bs and P/Es using calendar year-end (31 December) stock prices and companies' financial statement data for the same calendar year, even though the financial statement data for that calendar year were likely unavailable at year-end.

Data mining refers to automated computational procedures for discovering patterns in large datasets, which can introduce a bias known as overfitting. Survivorship bias occurs when back-testing uses companies that are in business today but ignores companies that have left the investment universe.

13 B is correct. Knight should recommend the Stock 3 and Stock 4 pair trade. Two stocks make for an ideal pairs trade if (1) the current price ratio differs from its long-term average and shows historical mean reversion and (2) the two stocks' returns are highly correlated. The relationship between Stock 3 and Stock 4 meets these conditions.

14 C is correct. Because the Heydon Quant Fund would be changing its factor model by adding a new factor, the correlations of the fund's returns with the factors would likely change and the returns-based style would change. Even though the investment universe is unchanged, the portfolio holdings would likely change and the holdings-based style classification would also will be affected.

15 B is correct. At his previous firm, Dewey managed a fund for which his investment process involved taking active exposures in sectors based on the macroeconomic environment and demographic trends. An investment process that begins at a top, or macro level, is a top-down strategy. Top-down portfolio strategies study variables affecting many companies or whole sectors, such as the macroeconomic environment, demographic trends, and government policies. This approach differs from bottom-up strategies, which focus on individual company variables in making investment decisions. It also differs from activist strategies, which take stakes in listed companies and advocate changes for the purpose of producing a gain on the investment.

16 C is correct. The steps to developing a fundamental active investment process are as follows:

1 Define the investment universe and the market opportunity—the perceived opportunity to earn a positive risk-adjusted return to active investing, net of costs—in accordance with the investment mandate. The market opportunity is also known as the investment thesis.

2 Prescreen the investment universe to obtain a manageable set of securities for further, more detailed analysis.

3 Understand the industry and business for this screened set by performing industry and competitive analysis and analyzing financial reports.

4 Forecast company performance, most commonly in terms of cash flows or earnings.

5 Convert forecasts to valuations and identify *ex ante* profitable investments.

6 Construct a portfolio of these investments with the desired risk profile.

7 Rebalance the portfolio with buy and sell disciplines.

So, Sardar should recommend that the next step in the development of the fundamental active management process be forecasting companies' performances and converting those forecasts into valuations.

17 B is correct. Managers using an active fundamental investment process, like Dewey's, usually monitor the portfolio's holdings continuously and may rebalance at any time. In contrast, portfolios using a quantitative approach are usually rebalanced at regular intervals, such as monthly or quarterly, or in response

to updated output from optimization models. A is incorrect because portfolios using a quantitative (not fundamental) active approach are usually rebalanced at regular intervals, such as monthly or quarterly. C is incorrect because construction of a quantitative portfolio (not a fundamental portfolio) typically involves using a portfolio optimizer, which controls for risk at the portfolio level in arriving at individual stock weights and leads to rebalancing decisions.

18. B is correct. Dewey has developed a fundamental active investment process for the Purity Fund that emphasizes financial strength and demonstrated profitability. High-quality value investors focus on companies' intrinsic values that are supported by attractive valuation metrics, with an emphasis on financial strength and demonstrated profitability. In their view, investors sometimes behave irrationally, making stocks trade at prices very different from intrinsic value based on company fundamentals. A is incorrect because investors who pursue a relative value strategy evaluate companies by comparing their value indicators (e.g., P/E or P/B multiples) with the average valuation of companies in the same industry sector, in an effort to identify stocks that offer value relative to their sector peers. AZ Industrial is trading at a high P/B relative to the industry average, which is contrary to relative value and suggests that the relative value approach was not the basis for Sardar's buy recommendation. C is incorrect because a deep-value investing approach focuses on undervalued companies that are available at extremely low valuation relative to their assets. Such companies are often those in financial distress, which is not reflective of financial strength or demonstrated profitability. Therefore, Sardar's buy recommendation was not based on a deep-value investing orientation.

19. A is correct. Dewey asks Sardar to perform a bottom-up style analysis of the Purity Fund based on the aggregation of attributes from individual stocks in the portfolio, which describes a holdings-based approach to style analysis. The overall equity investment style is an aggregation of attributes from individual stocks in the portfolio, weighted by their positions.

READING
18

Active Equity Investing: Portfolio Construction

by Jacques Lussier, PhD, CFA, and Marc R. Reinganum, PhD

Jacques Lussier, PhD, CFA (Canada). Marc R. Reinganum, PhD (USA).

LEARNING OUTCOMES	
Mastery	The candidate should be able to:
☐	a. describe elements of a manager's investment philosophy that influence the portfolio construction process;
☐	b. discuss approaches for constructing actively managed equity portfolios;
☐	c. distinguish between Active Share and active risk and discuss how each measure relates to a manager's investment strategy;
☐	d. discuss the application of risk budgeting concepts in portfolio construction;
☐	e. discuss risk measures that are incorporated in equity portfolio construction and describe how limits set on these measures affect portfolio construction;
☐	f. discuss how assets under management, position size, market liquidity, and portfolio turnover affect equity portfolio construction decisions;
☐	g. evaluate the efficiency of a portfolio structure given its investment mandate;
☐	h. discuss the long-only, long extension, long/short, and equitized market-neutral approaches to equity portfolio construction, including their risks, costs, and effects on potential alphas.

INTRODUCTION 1

Active equity investing is based on the concept that a skilled portfolio manager can both identify and differentiate between the most attractive securities and the least attractive securities—typically relative to a pre-specified benchmark. If this is the case, why is a portfolio—a collection of securities—even necessary? Why shouldn't

© 2018 CFA Institute. All rights reserved.

the portfolio manager just identify the most attractive security and invest all assets in this one security? Or in a long/short context, why not buy the "best" security and sell the "worst" one? Although very simple, this one-stock approach is not likely to be optimal or even feasible. No manager has perfect foresight, and his predictions will likely differ from realized returns. What he predicted would be the "best security" may quite likely turn out *not* to be the best. Active equity portfolio managers, even those with great skill, cannot avoid this risk. Security analysis is the process for ranking the relative attractiveness of securities, whereas portfolio construction is about selecting the securities to be included and carefully determining what percentage of the portfolio is to be held in each security—balancing superior insights regarding predicted returns against some likelihood that these insights will be derailed by events unknown or simply prove to be inaccurate.

Active managers rely on a wide array of investment strategies and methodologies to build portfolios of securities that they expect to outperform the benchmark. The challenges faced by active managers are similar whether they manage long-only traditional strategies, systematic/quantitative strategies, or long/short opportunistic strategies. Managers may differ in their investment style, operational complexity, flexibility of investment policy, ability to use leverage and short positions, and implementation methodologies, but predictions about returns and risk are essential to most active equity management styles.

In Section 2, we introduce the "building blocks" of portfolio construction, and in Sections 3–5, we discuss the different approaches to portfolio construction. In Sections 6–9, we discuss risk budgeting concepts relevant to portfolio construction and the measures used to evaluate portfolio risk. Section 10 looks at how issues of scale may affect portfolio construction. Section 11 addresses the attributes of a well-constructed portfolio. Section 12 looks at certain specialized equity strategies and how their approaches to portfolio construction may differ from a long-only equity strategy. The reading concludes with a summary.

2 BUILDING BLOCKS OF ACTIVE EQUITY PORTFOLIO CONSTRUCTION

a describe elements of a manager's investment philosophy that influence the portfolio construction process

Investors who pursue active management are looking to generate portfolio returns in excess of benchmark returns (adjusted for all costs) for an appropriate level of risk. The excess return—also called **active return** (R_A)—of an actively managed portfolio is driven by the difference in weights between the active portfolio and the benchmark. It can be mathematically expressed as

$$R_A = \sum_{i=1}^{N} \Delta W_i R_i \tag{1}$$

where

R_i = the return on security i and

ΔW_i = the difference between the portfolio weights W_{Pi} and the benchmark weights W_{Bi}. ΔW_i is also referred to as the active weight.

An active manager will generate positive active returns if:

The gains generated by		The losses generated by
■ overweighting the securities that outperform the benchmark and	are, on average, >	■ underweighting the securities that outperform the benchmark and
■ underweighting the securities that underperform the benchmark.		■ overweighting the securities that underperform the benchmark.

2.1 Fundamentals of Portfolio Construction

Conceptually, a manager can generate active returns by

- strategically adjusting the active weights of the securities to create long-term exposures to rewarded risks that are different from those of his benchmark;
- tactically adjusting the active weights of the securities using his skills/expertise in identifying mispricing in securities, sectors, rewarded risks, and so on, to generate alpha that cannot be explained by long-term exposure to rewarded risks; and
- assuming excessive idiosyncratic risk that may result in lucky or unlucky returns.

Historically, any excess return over the benchmark was often termed "alpha." More sophisticated investors then moved to evaluating managers on the basis of excess *risk-adjusted* returns, where risk was assessed relative to a cap-weighted index. The information ratio became an important measure of the manager's value-added. Today, research supports the argument that much of what was historically viewed as alpha is, in fact, "alternative beta"—exposure to rewarded risks (often referred to as "priced factors" or "rewarded factors") that can be obtained at much lower cost.[1] In this reading, we use "rewarded factors" as a generic term that refers specifically to investment risks for which investors expect to be compensated through a long-run return premium, such as exposure to market risk and liquidity risk. The existence of numerous rewarded factors is well documented in the literature and supported by strong empirical evidence. The recognition of this phenomenon is fundamentally altering the investment management industry, with large asset owners negotiating fee structures that compensate active managers for returns above and beyond those that can be generated by simple exposure to rewarded factors.[2]

These three sources of active return remain the same whether a manager follows a fundamental/discretionary or quantitative/systematic approach, a bottom-up or top-down strategy, or a style such as value or growth at a reasonable price. Of course, the proportion of return sourced from exposure to rewarded factors, alpha, and luck will vary among managers and portfolio management approaches. Equation 2 expresses the decomposition of *ex post* active returns in terms of these components:

$$R_A = \sum (\beta_{pk} - \beta_{bk}) \times F_k + (\alpha + \varepsilon) \quad (2)$$

---

[1] Kahn and Lemmon (2016); Bender, Hammond, and Mok (2014).
[2] Rewarded factors were discussed in the Level II reading "An Introduction to Multifactor Models." For example, Fama and French (1992) introduced a three-factor model that includes Market, Size, and Value, which was complemented with Momentum by Carhart (1997). However, there are potentially many more factors, such as liquidity, low beta, and credit. There are also factors related to surprises in macroeconomic variables, such as interest rates, inflation, and business cycles, although academicians have had much more difficulty identifying reliable return premiums to these types of macroeconomic factors.

where

β_{pk} = the sensitivity of the portfolio (p) to each rewarded factor (k)
β_{bk} = the sensitivity of the benchmark to each rewarded factor[3]
F_k = the return of each rewarded factor
($\alpha + \varepsilon$) = the part of the return that cannot be explained by exposure to rewarded factors. The volatility of this component is very much dependent on how a manager sizes individual positions in his portfolio. The alpha (α) is the active return of the portfolio that can be attributed to the specific skills/strategies of the manager—skills such as security selection and factor timing. ε is the idiosyncratic return, often resulting from a random shock, such as a company announcing unexpected earnings. It could also be called noise or luck (good or bad). Although managers generate returns above or below those that can be explained by the exposure to rewarded factors, it is very difficult to isolate how much of this return differential can be attributed to alpha/skill or to noise/luck.[4]

Although not all active managers expressly employ a factor methodology in creating active returns, the growth of exchange-traded funds, coupled with the disappointing after-fee performance of many active managers, is expanding the factor-based view of the investment landscape. It is important to understand the components of active returns (exposure to rewarded risks, alpha, and luck) and how Equation 2 explicitly or implicitly relates to various management styles and approaches.

To illustrate, let's consider two hypothetical managers: a systematic manager (Quanto) and a discretionary manager (Evolo). Each claims to have a "Value" orientation.

Quanto estimates the "Value" characteristics of each security in his investment universe using such proxies as the ratios of price to book and forward earnings to price. He then uses a systematic allocation methodology that determines the specific active weights that can be expected to deliver the desired exposure to the Value factor. Quanto holds a large number of securities to limit the impact of idiosyncratic risks on performance. Quanto attempts to outperform the benchmark by choosing factor exposures that differ from those of the benchmark.

Evolo has developed a comprehensive measure of value using a forward-looking free cash flow model. This allows Evolo to compare her own estimates of security valuation to the current market price for each security covered by the firm. The manager uses her judgment to determine the appropriate active weights based on her own level of confidence in each estimate. She runs a concentrated portfolio because she believes she has an edge in setting the appropriate active weights.

Although Evolo is not using a systematic approach to determine the active security weights and the overall portfolio exposure to the Value factor, she is driven by a Value philosophy and is exposed to the Value factor. Her returns will be driven in part by this factor exposure, even if she has never seen Equation 2. Indeed, if her portfolio is not exposed to the Value factor, clients and consultants may question her claim to run a value-oriented portfolio. If Evolo has developed a better Value proxy than her competitors and if she is skilled at identifying the best and worst securities and setting

---

[3] Because the investable universe as a whole (the market) is usually much larger than the investment universe defined by any single benchmark, most benchmarks have an inherent exposure to the Market factor different from one and some net exposure (different from zero) to other rewarded factors.
[4] If one observes only a small number of active returns, it may be difficult to infer whether the active return is zero or significantly different from zero given the likely volatility of realized active returns.

appropriate active weights, part of her active return will be attributed to her alpha skills. Because Evolo runs a more concentrated portfolio, the portion of her active performance attributed to idiosyncratic risk will likely be greater.

2.2 Building Blocks Used in Portfolio Construction

This section introduces the three main building blocks of portfolio construction—*rewarded factor weightings*, *alpha skills*, and *position sizing* (shown in Exhibit 1)—and explains how each relates to the three broad sources of active returns. A fourth critical component of portfolio construction, *breadth of expertise*, is necessary to assemble these three building blocks into a successful portfolio construction process.

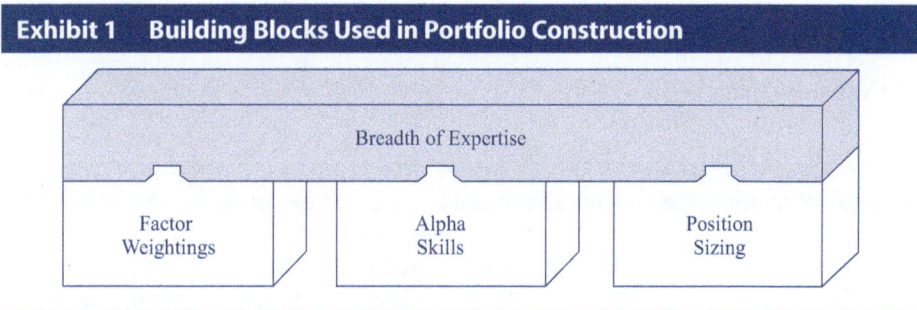

Exhibit 1   Building Blocks Used in Portfolio Construction

2.2.1 First Building Block: Overweight or Underweight Rewarded Factors

Let's begin by considering the market portfolio as our benchmark. The market portfolio encompasses all securities, and the weight of each security is proportional to its market capitalization. Our benchmark would have an exposure (or beta, β) of 1 to the Market factor and no net exposure to other rewarded factors, such as Size, Value, and Momentum.[5]

However, most individual securities have a β less than or greater than 1 to the Market factor and most will also have a non-zero exposure to the other factors. Indeed, one way an active manager can try to add value over and above the market portfolio is to choose, explicitly or implicitly, exposures to rewarded risks that differ from those of the market.

Practically speaking, most investors use narrower market proxies as a benchmark: the S&P 500 Index for a US mandate, the FTSE 100 Index for a UK mandate, or the MSCI All Country World Index (ACWI)[6] for a global mandate, for example. These indexes, although quite broad, do not include all securities that are publicly traded. Thus, these well-known indexes may not have a β of exactly 1 to the Market factor and could very well have a net exposure to other rewarded factors. For example, although most large-cap indexes usually have a β close to 1 to the Market factor, they usually have a negative sensitivity to the Size factor, indicating their large-cap tilt. When a manager is creating an exposure to a rewarded risk, the exposure must be established relative to that of his benchmark to achieve an expected excess return.

---

[5] Market is a long-only factor, whereas other factors, such as Size and Value, are defined as long/short factors. Hence, the exposure of the market portfolio to the Market factor should be 1, whereas the exposure of the market portfolio to other factors should be 0.
[6] The MSCI ACWI is a cap-weighted index that represents sources of equity returns from 23 developed and 24 emerging markets.

The growing understanding of rewarded factors is profoundly changing the view of active and passive investing. There are many investment products that allow investors to directly access such factors as Value, Size, Momentum, and Quality, and the bar for active managers is rising: An active value manager not only needs to outperform a passive value benchmark but may also need to outperform a rules-based value-tilted product. In the following discussion, we illustrate the concept of returns to factors and the application of this concept to portfolio management.

Exhibit 2 illustrates the factor exposures of the Russell 1000 Index, the Russell 1000 Value Index, and a discretionary mid-cap value fund (using the four Fama–French and Carhart factors). The performance of the actively managed fund is presented before the deduction of fees to make the comparison with benchmark returns fair.

The average monthly performance of each factor from February 1990 to December 2016 is specified in the last column.[7] All four factors showed positive returns over the period. Most regression coefficients are statistically significant at the 5% level (not shown); the momentum coefficients of the Russell 1000 and the Russell 1000 Value are the exceptions.

Exhibit 2 Risk Factor Exposure (February 1990–December 2016)

	Russell 1000 Index	Russell 1000 Value Index	Value Fund	Factor Performance US Market
Monthly performance in excess of the risk-free rate	0.64%	0.66%	0.40%	—
	β to specified factor:			
Market*	0.99	0.92	0.90	0.64%
Size	−0.16	−0.23	0.13	0.16%
Value	0.02	0.41	0.59	0.18%
Momentum	−0.01	0.13	0.09	0.61%
"Alpha" (monthly)	0.05%	−0.05%	−0.35%	—
R^2	0.99	0.95	0.74	

* As mentioned in footnote 3, the Market factor is built from a much larger universe of securities than are traditional benchmarks, such as the Russell 1000. Therefore, we should not expect the β of indexes to the Market factor to be necessarily equal to one.
Note: All data are measured in US dollars.
Sources: Factor data for the United States are from AQR Capital Management, market data are from Bloomberg, and calculations are from the authors.

The Russell 1000 Index has a Market β close to 1, a negative exposure to the Size factor (indicating it has a large-cap tilt), and almost no sensitivity to the Value and Momentum factors. This is what we would expect for a capitalization-weighted large-cap index. In comparison, the Russell 1000 Value Index has a lower Market β and a significant exposure to the Value factor, also in line with expectations. Finally, the mid-cap value fund has positive exposure to the Size factor (consistent with its mid-cap tilt) and a very significant exposure to the Value factor.

---

[7] Pricing and accounting data used by AQR are from the union of the CRSP tape and the Compustat/Xpressfeed Global database. The data include all available common stocks in the merged CRSP/Xpressfeed data.

In these regression specifications, there is still a component of return that cannot be explained by the rewarded factors alone. It is often labeled "alpha." This may be true alpha, or it may be simply noise/luck. The two indexes have a relatively small alpha, whereas the value fund has a significantly negative alpha of –0.35% per month. An alpha of this magnitude is unlikely to be explained by a small misspecification in the factor model. An investor considering this fund would need to investigate the causes of this negative alpha.

In Exhibit 3, we show the sources of performance of each product in terms of its exposure to each of the four factors and its respective alpha. In all cases, the Market factor is the dominant source of performance. The Value and Momentum factors did contribute positively to performance for the Russell 1000 Value, but much of this performance was lost because of the large-cap tilt and the negative alpha. The value fund did get a significant performance boost from the Value tilt, but much of it was lost to the very poor alpha in this period.

Exhibit 3 Sources of Performance (February 1990–December 2016)

Source of Performance	Russell 1000	Russell 1000 Value	Value Fund
Market	0.63%	0.59%	0.57%
Size	–0.03%	–0.04%	0.02%
Value	0.00%	0.08%	0.11%
Momentum	–0.01%	0.08%	0.05%
Alpha	0.05%	–0.05%	–0.35%
Total monthly performance	0.64%	0.66%	0.40%

Source: Calculations by authors.

These examples illustrate the components of Equation 2. Irrespective of the manager's investment approach—whether she explicitly targets factors or focuses only on securities she believes to be attractively priced—her portfolio performance can be analyzed in terms of factors. Some portion of returns will not be explained by factors, which may be attributable to

- the unique skills and strategies of the manager (alpha),
- an incomplete factor model that ignores relevant factors, or
- exposure to idiosyncratic risks that either helped or hurt performance.

The next section discusses the alpha skills building block.

2.2.2 Second Building Block: Alpha Skills

In principle, there are many approaches that can be used to generate alpha, but in practice, generating positive alpha in a zero-sum game environment (before fees) is a challenge.[8] Furthermore, the alpha generated by active managers must be sufficient to cover the higher fees usually associated with active management.

---

[8] Investing is often considered a zero-sum game (before fees) because all investors in aggregate own the market. Assuming all investors in a specific market (such as US equity) have a similar and appropriate benchmark, for each investor that outperforms the benchmark by $1, there would be another investor or group of investors that underperforms the benchmark by $1. Hence, in a zero-sum game, we can outperform only at the expense of someone else. The average level of expertise of market participants in that market does not change this observation. Although beyond the scope of this reading, if different investors use different benchmarks, the zero-sum game analogy may not be appropriate.

Let's initially consider rewarded factors. With exposures to rewarded factors increasingly accessible via rule-based indexes, simple static exposure to known rewarded factors is no longer widely considered a source of alpha. However, successfully timing that exposure *would* be a source of alpha. For example, some managers believe part of their skill emanates from an understanding of when rewarded factor returns might be greater than or less than their average returns (factor timing). Hence, in periods when the market return is negative, a manager with an exposure (β) to the Market factor substantially less than 1 will outperform the market and will probably also outperform many other managers. Similarly, a beta greater than 1 in a rising market would drive strong portfolio performance relative to the market. Exposure to the Market factor can be adjusted by investing in securities having, on average, Market betas less than or greater than 1.

The same can be said for the other rewarded factors. Exhibit 4 shows the cumulative value of $100 invested in both the Russell 1000 Growth Index and the Russell 1000 Value Index over a 10-year period ending in 2006. The Value index produced superior performance over the full 10-year time span, although it underperformed the growth index in 1998 and 1999. A manager skilled at timing his exposure to the Value factor would have owned the Growth index until the late 1990s and the Value index afterward, outperforming a manager with static exposure to the Value factor. However, as we have indicated, factor timing is difficult, and there is no consensus on the ability to generate alpha from factor timing.[9]

Exhibit 4   Cumulative Value—Russell 1000 Growth and Russell 1000 Value

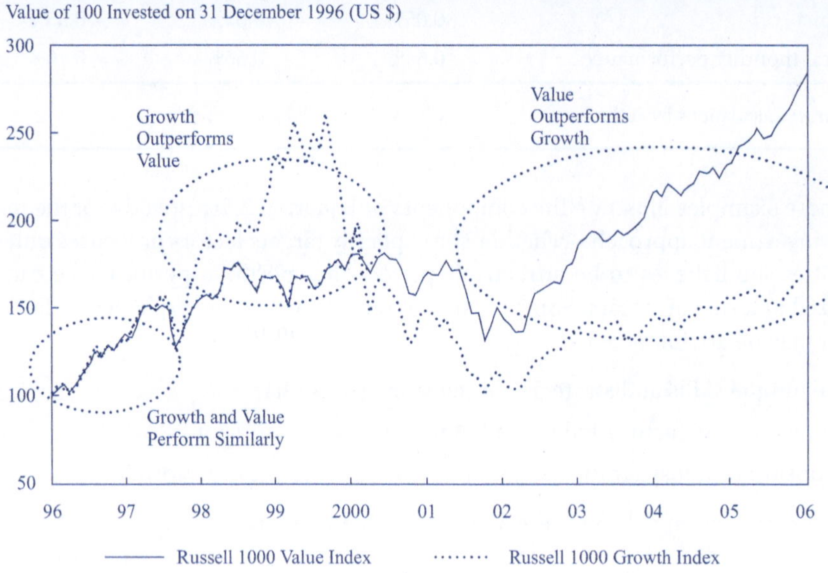

Source: Langlois and Lussier (2017, p. 44).

In principle, alpha can also be generated from timing exposure to *unrewarded* factors, such as regional exposure, sector exposure, the price of commodities, or even security selection. For example, there is no theoretical basis supporting an expectation that a portfolio with greater-than-benchmark sensitivity to oil prices will be rewarded in the long term. Oil price fluctuations are certainly a risk, but oil price is not a rewarded factor. However, a manager who held a very specific view about the

---
9 See Asness (2017).

Building Blocks of Active Equity Portfolio Construction

future of oil prices and correctly anticipated the decline in the price of oil that started in June 2014 and ended in March 2016 would have had a strong incentive to reduce his exposure to the energy sector and especially to smaller, less integrated, and more indebted energy companies, which performed poorly as a result of the price movement. A discretionary manager might refer to these as *thematic exposures.* Although oil prices are not a rewarded "factor," his skill in timing that exposure would have been amply rewarded. The literature thus far has found little evidence of an ability to consistently time rewarded factors, but it is conceivable that a skillful manager could have identified a factor that has yet to be recognized by the academic or investment community.

In summary, active returns arising from skillful timing of exposure to rewarded factors, unrewarded factors, or even other asset classes (such as cash) constitute a manager's alpha—the second building block.

2.2.3 Third Building Block: Sizing Positions

Position sizing is about balancing managers' confidence in their alpha and factor insights while mitigating idiosyncratic risks. Although position sizing influences all three components of Equation 2, its most dramatic impact is often on idiosyncratic risk. For example, consider a manager seeking to create a greater exposure to the Value and Size factors. She could achieve the same average exposure (beta) to these factors by allocating her portfolio to 20 securities or 200 securities. However, the level of idiosyncratic risk and the potential impact of luck on performance will be much greater in the concentrated portfolio. In concentrated portfolios, the volatility of the active return $\left(\sigma_{R_A}\right)$ attributed to idiosyncratic risks (σ_ε) will likely be more significant. In other words, there may be greater deviations between realized portfolio returns and expected returns.

A manager's choices with respect to portfolio concentration are a function of his beliefs regarding the nature of his investment skill. The factor-oriented manager believes that she is skilled at properly setting and balancing her exposure to rewarded factors. She targets specific exposure to factors (the $\sum\left(\beta_{pk} - \beta_{bk}\right) \times F_k$ part of Equation 2) and maintains a diversified portfolio to minimize the impact of idiosyncratic risk. The stock picker believes that he is skilled at forecasting security-specific performance over a specific horizon and expresses his forward-looking views using a concentrated portfolio, assuming a higher degree of idiosyncratic risk (the $\alpha + \varepsilon$ part of Equation 2).

Diversification, Volatility, and Idiosyncratic risk

The stock picker must carefully consider influences that can substantially alter the absolute or relative risk profile of his portfolio. Consider, for example, the absolute volatility of the Russell 1000 Index and its underlying securities over the 12 months ending in October 2016. During this period:

- the index had an annualized daily volatility of 15.7%;
- the weighted average volatility of all securities in the index was substantially higher, about 26.7%;
- the average volatility of the 100 smallest securities in the index was approximately 41%;
- the average volatility of the 100 largest securities in the index was approximately 24%.

This disparity in individual stock volatility illustrates the potential of diversification. A concentrated portfolio is unlikely to achieve the low volatility of the Russell 1000 unless the manager specifically emphasizes investing in stocks that have a lower average volatility than that of the average security in the index.

Exhibit 5 illustrates the effect of diversification on total portfolio risk at two different levels of average individual stock volatility. (We use the standard deviation of returns as our measure of risk here.) Total portfolio volatility is a function of the average individual stock volatility and the number of securities in the portfolio. The calculations assume an average cross correlation of 0.24, consistent with the historical average correlation for Russell 1000 securities since 1979.

Exhibit 5   Total Portfolio Volatility as a Function of Concentration and Single Stock Volatility[10]

	Single Stock Volatility	
	25%	30%
Number of Securities	Portfolio Volatility	
10	14.1%	16.9%
30	12.9%	15.5%
50	12.6%	15.2%
100	12.4%	14.9%
500	12.3%	14.7%

Examining this table closely, we can see that diversification is a powerful tool but that it has its limitations. Even the most diversified portfolio of high-volatility stocks (the 500-stock portfolio with an average single-stock volatility of 30%) cannot achieve the same level of volatility inherent in the portfolios of lower-volatility stocks. Even the most concentrated portfolio of lower-volatility stocks displays a portfolio volatility lower than that of the highly diversified portfolio of higher-volatility stocks.

The concentrated portfolio, however, bears higher idiosyncratic risk, which can substantially influence portfolio performance. The manager's choices with respect to the magnitude of his active weights and the volatility of the securities with the highest active weights will be significant determinants of the portfolio's active return and active risk.

Active risk is a measure of the volatility of portfolio returns relative to the volatility of benchmark returns. It is expressed as follows:

$$\text{Active risk}\left(\sigma_{R_A}\right) = \sqrt{\frac{\sum_{t=1}^{T}(R_{At})^2}{T-1}} \quad (3)$$

where R_{At} represents the active return at time t and T equals the number of return periods. Active risk is often referred to as "tracking error."

All else being equal, a 1.0% allocation to a security that has a 0.2% weighting in the benchmark (Security A) will have a greater effect on the active risk of the portfolio than a 2.0% allocation to a security that has a 2.5% weighting in the benchmark (Security B). Despite the overall smaller position size of Security A, the active decision the manager made with respect to the weighting of Security A (an 80 bp difference from the

---

[10] This is a simplified example of Markowitz portfolio diversification where securities are equally weighted and all securities have the same volatility and cross correlation:

$$\sigma_p = \sqrt{\frac{1}{n}\sigma^2 + \frac{(n-1)}{n}\sigma^2 C},$$

where n is the number of securities, σ^2 is the equal variance of all securities, and C is the cross correlation between them.

> benchmark weight) is significantly larger than the active decision with respect to the weight of Security B (a 50 bp difference). If Security A also has a higher volatility than Security B, the effect of the active decision will be magnified.
>
> Similarly, all else equal, an active weight of 1.0% on a single security will have a greater impact on active risk than will an active weight of 0.2% on five separate securities. The imperfect cross correlations of active returns of the basket of five stocks would contribute to lowering the level of active risk.

To summarize, a manager's choice with respect to position sizing is influenced by her investment approach and the level of confidence she places on her analytic work. On the one hand, the stock picker with high confidence in her analysis of individual securities may be willing to assume high levels of idiosyncratic risk. This is consistent with her emphasis on the "$\alpha + \varepsilon$" part of Equation 2. On the other hand, a manager focused on creating balanced exposures to rewarded factors is unlikely to assume a high level of idiosyncratic risk and is, therefore, quite likely to construct a highly diversified portfolio of individual securities.

2.2.4 Integrating the Building Blocks: Breadth of Expertise

The three foregoing building blocks encompass all of Equation 2, which we used to describe the sources of a manager's active returns:

- exposure to rewarded risks,
- timing of exposures to rewarded and unrewarded risks, and
- position sizing and its implications for idiosyncratic risk.

A manager may be more or less successful at combining these three sources of return into a portfolio. Success is a function of a manager's breadth of expertise. Broader expertise may increase the manager's likelihood of generating consistent, positive active returns.

The importance of breadth of expertise is implicit in the fundamental law of active management (covered extensively in the Level II reading "Analysis of Active Portfolio Management"), which implies that confidence in a manager's ability to outperform his benchmark increases when that performance can be attributed to a larger sample of independent decisions. Independent decisions are not the same thing as individual securities. Independent decisions are uncorrelated decisions, much like two uncorrelated stocks are diversifying. Thus, overweighting both General Motors and Toyota, two auto companies, relative to their benchmark weights are not fully independent decisions because much of their respective returns are driven by common influences—the strength of consumer spending, the price of gasoline, and the price of steel and aluminum, for example. In evaluating portfolio construction, one must distinguish between the nominal number of decisions a manager makes about his active weights and the effective number of independent decisions. Without truly independent decisions, performance may be influenced more significantly by common exposures to specific factors.[11] According to the fundamental law, the expected active portfolio return $E(R_A)$ is determined by the following:[12]

$$E(R_A) = IC\sqrt{BR}\sigma_{R_A}TC \qquad (4)$$

where

IC = Expected **information coefficient** of the manager—the extent to which a manager's forecasted active returns correspond to the managers realized active returns

BR = **Breadth**—the number of truly independent decisions made each year

TC = **Transfer coefficient**, or the ability to translate portfolio insights into investment decisions without constraint (a truly unconstrained portfolio would have a transfer coefficient of 1)

σ_{R_A} = the manager's active risk

For example, assuming an active risk of 6% (which many institutional investors would consider to be high), a transfer coefficient of 0.25 (representative of a constrained long-only investor), and an information coefficient of 0.10, the manager could expect to generate an active return of 15 bps yearly, on average, if she makes a single independent decision. If the manager wanted to achieve excess return of 1%, she would need to make approximately 40 fully independent decisions. Even if a manager does have positive information and transfer coefficients, it does not necessarily follow that excess return will be positive every year. A horizon of many years is required to have a reasonable probability of generating the expected excess return. However, a larger number of independent decisions will increase the probability of outperforming over a shorter horizon.

What is the implication of making multiple independent decisions? Assume two managers hold similarly diversified portfolios in terms of the number of securities and that both managers have outperformed the market over a specific period. Manager A has a pure value style and favors securities that have a low price-to-book ratio (a single valuation metric), whereas Manager B has a multidimensional, factor-based approach. Manager B's approach includes considerations related to valuation, price momentum, growth, balance sheet sustainability, quality of management, and so on, and considers a much larger set of metrics for each dimension (such as several metrics for valuation). Manager A's performance is largely attributed to a single dimension: his narrowly defined value bias. Although he holds 100 securities, he did not make 100 independent decisions.[13]

---

[11] Although the fundamental law is an interesting concept for illustrating the main drivers of positive expected active returns, investment decisions are rarely truly independent. When using specific metrics to determine how to allocate to securities, managers emphasize securities that have common characteristics they deem to be relevant. The process by which managers determine their allocation to securities will affect the degree of independence of investment decisions. In other words, investing in the 100 securities among 1,000 that have the lowest price-to-book ratio does not lead to 100 independent decisions. Furthermore, we should not assume that the information coefficient of the manager is insensitive to the number of securities in his portfolio.

[12] The basic fundamental law was initially introduced by Grinold (1989) but was further expanded into the full fundamental law with the addition of the transfer coefficient by Clarke, de Silva, and Thorley (2002).

[13] Consider an active manager who has a value and momentum style. Value is measured by the price-to-book ratio, and momentum is measured over a single historical period, such as $P_{t-1\ month}/P_{t-12\ months}$. Assume that his exposure to these two factors explains more than 60% of his excess return (consistent with a study by Bender, Hammond, and Mok, 2014). The portfolio exposure to these two risk factors has, therefore, had greater bearing on excess returns than have the security selection skills of the manager.

Building Blocks of Active Equity Portfolio Construction

Manager B may not have 100 independent decisions embedded in her portfolio, but she likely has more than Manager A. Thus, the historical performance of Manager B may be a more reliable indicator of her ability to outperform in the future because her portfolio construction process integrates several dimensions and metrics, as well as their interactions. Her performance is less likely to be explained by how the market has recently favored a specific management style.

Let's take this example a bit further. Suppose Manager A makes 20 independent decisions and Manager B makes 40 independent decisions. Assume they both have the same information coefficient (0.2), the same active risk (4%), and the same transfer coefficient (0.6). What would be the expected active return of each manager? Using Equation 4:

Manager A $0.2 \times \sqrt{20} \times 4\% \times 0.6 = 2.15\%$

Manager B $0.2 \times \sqrt{40} \times 4\% \times 0.6 = 3.04\%$

What if Manager A's information coefficient was only 0.1? How many independent decisions would the manager need to make to generate the same 2.15% expected active return?

Manager A: $0.1 \times \sqrt{x} \times 4\% \times 0.6 = 2.15\%$

$x \approx 80$

Assuming Manager A maintains a concentrated portfolio of twenty securities, what information coefficient would be required for Manager A to match the expected performance of Manager B?

Manager A: $x \times \sqrt{20} \times 4\% \times 0.6 = 3.04\%$

$x \approx 0.28$

Equation 4 illustrates the importance of breadth of expertise. As a practical matter, long-term success is not achieved by being right all the time but, rather, by being right often through small victories achieved consistently over long periods.

EXAMPLE 1

The Building Blocks of Asset Management

Proteus was launched as an asset management firm 20 years ago, after receiving assets of $100 million from a seed investor. Today, the firm has grown into a large organization with more than $30 billion in assets. Although the investment process has evolved, the firm has remained true to its core philosophy. It has also delivered strong risk-adjusted performance to its investors.

Proteus's emphasis has always been to invest in quality companies, appropriately priced, which are benefiting from positive and sustained price momentum. Although fairly agnostic in terms of portfolio weights compared with benchmark weights, the managers of Proteus believe in avoiding extreme views. For example, sector deviations are limited to between 80% and 120% of benchmark weights plus or minus 500 bps; for example, a sector with a 20% weight in the index could have a weight in the portfolio ranging from 11% [(0.8 × 20%) − 5%] to 29% [(1.2 × 20%) + 5%]. An individual security position can be no more than the lesser of (1) 10 times its weight in the index or (2) its weight in the index + 1%. On average, Proteus's portfolios hold between 120 and 150 securities. The active risk is above 5%.

> As the firm grew in experience, research, and resources, the process of defining and measuring what is a quality company, appropriately priced, and benefiting from positive momentum evolved. Initially, the firm avoided companies that were the most indebted within their sector and favored those that generated strong cash flows to sales. It also favored companies that had a lower price-to-book value and had positive price momentum in the last 12 months.
>
> Today, Proteus still emphasizes quality, valuation, and price momentum but has considerably improved how those characteristics are measured and weighed. It now evaluates 45 metrics related to the financial health of the companies, the quality of its financial reporting, its valuation within its sector, and its short- and medium-term price momentum. It also developed its own weighting mechanism to appropriately weight each metric. The managers at Proteus believe their competitive advantage is the effort they invest in identifying, measuring, and weighing these metrics.
>
> Discuss the contributions of rewarded factors, alpha skills, position sizing, and breadth of expertise for Proteus.
>
> **Solution:**
>
> Overall, Proteus has integrated all the primary dimensions of the investment process.
>
> - Rewarded factors: Proteus recognizes the existence of rewarded factors, and it has significantly enhanced its measures of Quality, Value, and Momentum over time.
> - Alpha skills: Given the commercial success of Proteus as a firm, we might safely assume that there is an alpha component in the process.
> - Position sizing: Position size limits are integrated into the investment process to ensure diversification limits idiosyncratic risks.
> - Breadth of expertise: Proteus has 20 years of experience refining and improving an investment process based on a consistent investment philosophy.

3. THE IMPLEMENTATION PROCESS: PORTFOLIO CONSTRUCTION APPROACHES

b discuss approaches for constructing actively managed equity portfolios

Portfolio construction is part art and part science. It is about investment philosophy and the implementation of that philosophy. It requires an understanding of the technical principles of portfolio construction, filtered through a manager's core beliefs regarding her ability to add value using the building blocks discussed earlier:

- *Factor exposures:* How does she create her factor exposures? Does the manager believe she is skilled at extracting return premiums from rewarded factors? Or are her exposures to rewarded factors a residual of her in-depth research into the securities' fundamentals?
- *Timing:* Does she believe that she has skill in generating alpha through timing of portfolio exposures to rewarded and unrewarded factors or to security selection uncorrelated with exposures to either rewarded or unrewarded factors?

The Implementation Process: Portfolio Construction Approaches

- *Position sizing:* How does she size portfolio positions? Is she confident about her expected return forecasts, and therefore runs a high-conviction portfolio? Or does she seek to reduce idiosyncratic risk by running a highly diversified portfolio?
- *Breadth or depth:* Does she rely on a specialized but narrower skill set or on a greater breadth of expertise?

A manager's portfolio construction process should reflect her beliefs with respect to the nature of her skills in each of these areas. The majority of investment approaches can be classified as either

- *systematic or discretionary* (the degree to which a portfolio construction process is subject to a set of predetermined rules or is left to the discretionary views of the manager)

and

- *bottom-up or top-down* (the degree to which security-specific factors, rather than macroeconomic factors, drive portfolio construction).

In addition, these approaches can vary in the extent to which they are *benchmark aware* versus *benchmark agnostic*. Each manager's investment approach is implemented within a framework that specifies the acceptable levels of active risk and **Active Share** relative to a clearly articulated benchmark. (Active Share is a measure of how similar a portfolio is to its benchmark.) A manager may emphasize these dimensions to varying degrees as he attempts to differentiate his portfolio from the benchmark.

3.1 The Implementation Process: The Choice of Portfolio Management Approaches

We previously identified three primary building blocks that managers can use in constructing a portfolio that reflects their core beliefs. Let's look at these in a little more detail, beginning with the systematic–discretionary continuum.

3.1.1 Systematic vs. Discretionary

How are a manager's beliefs regarding rewarded factor exposures, timing of factor exposures, exposure to unrewarded factors, and willingness to assume idiosyncratic risk reflected in a systematic investment process and in a discretionary investment process?

- Systematic strategies are more likely to be designed around the construction of portfolios seeking to extract return premiums from a balanced exposure to known, rewarded factors.
- Discretionary strategies search for active returns by building a greater depth of understanding of a firm's governance, business model, and competitive landscape, through the development of better factor proxies (e.g., a better definition of Quality), or through successful timing strategies. Factor timing is a challenging endeavor, and few factor-based systematic strategies have integrated a factor timing approach.
- Systematic strategies typically incorporate research-based rules across a broad universe of securities. For example, a simple systematic value methodology could filter out the 50% of securities that have the highest price-to-book ratio and then equally weight the remaining securities, leading to small individual portfolio positions. A more comprehensive approach might integrate a much larger number of considerations and balance total portfolio risk equally across them.

- Discretionary strategies integrate the judgment of the manager, usually on a smaller subset of securities. While a discretionary value manager might also rely on financial metrics to estimate the value characteristics of each security, she is likely to use her judgment to evaluate the relative importance of this information and assign appropriate weights to each security. A discretionary manager is also likely to integrate nonfinancial variables to the equation, such as the quality of management, the competitive landscape, and the pricing power of the firm. (Systematic strategies also integrate judgment, but their judgment is largely expressed up front through the design of the strategy and the learning process that comes with its implementation.)
- Systematic strategies seek to reduce exposure to idiosyncratic risk and often use broadly diversified portfolios to achieve the desired factor exposure while minimizing security-specific risk.
- Discretionary strategies are generally more concentrated portfolios, reflecting the depth of the manager's insights on company characteristics and the competitive landscape.
- Systematic strategies are typically more adaptable to a formal portfolio optimization process. The systematic manager must, however, carefully consider the parameters of that optimization. What objective function is he seeking to maximize (information ratio, Sharpe ratio, index or factor exposure, etc.) or minimize (volatility, downside risk, etc.)? Will elements of his investment style (such as performance and valuation metrics) be incorporated into the objective function or into the constraints?
- Discretionary portfolio managers typically use a less formal approach to portfolio construction, building a portfolio of securities deemed attractive, subject to a set of agreed-upon risk constraints.

Bridging the Divide

The philosophical divide between systematic and discretionary managers seems to be shrinking. Systematic and discretionary strategies were commonly differentiated in terms of their breadth and depth (discretionary managers conducting more in-depth research on a sub-set of the securities universe) and systematic managers having more breadth (less in-depth research across the entire universe of securities). Although this remains generally true today, research and technology have been narrowing the gap. Advancements in and the accessibility of technology, together with the greater range of quality data available, are allowing discretionary managers to extend their in-depth analyses across a broader universe of securities. Technology also allows systematic managers to design strategies that can capture risk premiums in rewarded factors, a source of active returns that was previously considered to be part of the alpha of discretionary managers.

3.1.2 Bottom-Up vs. Top-Down

A top-down approach seeks to understand the overall geo-political, economic, financial, social, and public policy environment and then project how the expected environment will affect countries, asset classes, sectors, and then securities. An investment manager who projects that growth companies will outperform value companies, that financials will outperform industrials, that the US market will outperform the European market, that oil prices will increase, or that cash will outperform equity and then targets individual securities and/or a cash/stock allocation to reflect these views is following a top-down approach.

A manager following a bottom-up approach develops his understanding of the environment by first evaluating the risk and return characteristics of individual securities. The aggregate of these risk and return expectations implies expectations for the overall economic and market environment. An investment manager who expects Ford to outperform GM, AstraZeneca (a bio-pharmaceutical company) to outperform Ford, and Sony to outperform AstraZeneca and builds a portfolio based on these stock-specific forecasts is following a bottom-up approach. Although the resulting portfolio will contain an implicit expectation for sector, style, and country performance, this is nonetheless a bottom-up approach.

- Both top-down and bottom-up strategies typically rely on returns from factors. However, top-down managers are more likely to emphasize macro factors, whereas bottom-up managers emphasize security-specific factors.

- A top-down investment process contains an important element of factor timing. A manager who opportunistically shifts the portfolio to capture returns from rewarded or unrewarded factors, such as country, sectors, and styles, is following a top-down investment process. They may also embrace the same security characteristics sought by bottom-up managers as they translate their macro views into security-specific positions. A top-down investment process is also more likely to raise cash opportunistically when the overall view of the Market factor is unfavorable.

- Bottom-up managers may embrace such styles as Value, Growth at Reasonable Price, Momentum, and Quality. These strategies are often built around documented rewarded factors, whether explicitly or implicitly.

- A top-down manager is likely to run a portfolio concentrated with respect to macro factor exposures. Bottom-up managers and top-down managers can run portfolios that are either diversified or concentrated in terms of securities. Both a bottom-up stock picker and a top-down sector rotator can run concentrated portfolios. Both a bottom-up value manager and a top-down risk allocator can run diversified portfolios.

Some managers will incorporate elements of both top-down and bottom-up investment approaches.

3.1.3 A Summary of the Different Approaches

While most managers make some use of all the building blocks, we can make some general assertions about the relative importance and use of these building blocks to each of the implementation choices. They are summarized in the four quadrants of Exhibit 6.

Exhibit 6 Approaches and Their Use of Building Blocks

	Top-Down	
Systematic	• Emphasizes macro factors • Factor timing • Diversified	• Emphasizes macro factors • Factor timing • Diversified or concentrated depending on strategy and style
	• Emphasizes security specific factors • No factor timing • Diversified	• Emphasizes firm specific characteristics or factors • Potential factor timing • Diversified or concentrated depending on strategy and style
	Bottom-Up	**Discretionary**

- Exposure to rewarded factors can be achieved with either a systematic or discretionary approach.
- Bottom-up managers first emphasize security-specific factors, whereas top-down managers first emphasize macro factors.
- Factor timing is more likely to be implemented among discretionary managers, especially those with a top-down approach.
- Systematic managers are unlikely to run concentrated portfolios. Discretionary managers can have either concentrated or diversified portfolios, depending on their strategy and portfolio management style.
- In principle, a systematic top-down manager would emphasize macro factors and factor timing and would have diversified portfolios. However, there are few managers in this category.

4 THE IMPLEMENTATION PROCESS: MEASURES OF BENCHMARK-RELATIVE RISK

b discuss approaches for constructing actively managed equity portfolios

c contrast Active Share with active risk and discuss how each measure relates to a manager's investment strategy

Managers have very specific beliefs about the level of security concentration and the absolute or relative risk that they (and their investors) are willing to tolerate. Relative risk is measured with respect to the benchmark that the manager has adopted as representative of his investment universe. We know that a manager must have active weights different from zero in order to outperform his benchmark. How do we measure these weights?

The Implementation Process: Measures of Benchmark-Relative Risk

There are two measures of benchmark-relative risk used to evaluate a manager's success—Active Share and active risk—and they do not always move in tandem. A manager can pursue a higher Active Share without necessarily increasing active risk (and vice versa).

Active Share is easier to calculate than active risk; one only needs to know the weight of each security in the portfolio and the weight of the security in the benchmark. The formula for Active Share is shown in Equation 5. It measures the extent to which the number and sizing positions in a manager's portfolio differ from the benchmark.

$$\text{Active Share} = \frac{1}{2}\sum_{i=1}^{n}\left|\text{Weight}_{portfolio,i} - \text{Weight}_{benchmark,i}\right| \quad (5)$$

where n represents the total number of securities that are in either the portfolio or the benchmark.

The Active Share calculation involves no statistical analysis or estimation; it is simple arithmetic. Active Share is a measure of the differentiation of the holdings of a portfolio from the holdings of a chosen benchmark portfolio. It measures the proportion of a portfolio's holdings that is different from the benchmark for that portfolio. The Active Share is 0 for a portfolio that matches the benchmark and 100% for a portfolio that shares no investments with those of the benchmark. The percentage of portfolio assets deployed in the same way as the benchmark is equal to 100% minus the portfolio's Active Share. For example, an Active Share of 80% implies that 20% of the portfolio capital was invested in a similar way as the index. There are only two sources of Active Share:

- Including securities in the portfolio that are not in the benchmark
- Holding securities in the portfolio that are in the benchmark but at weights different than the benchmark weights

If two portfolios are managed against the same benchmark (and if they invest only in securities that are part of the benchmark), the portfolio with fewer securities will have a higher level of Active Share than the highly diversified portfolio. A portfolio manager has complete control over his Active Share because he determines the weights of the securities in his portfolio.

Active risk is a more complicated calculation. Like Active Share, active risk depends on the differences between the security weights in the portfolio and the security weights in the benchmark. There are two different measures of active risk. One is realized active risk, which is the actual, historical standard deviation between the portfolio return and the benchmark return as described in Equation 3. This number relies on historical returns and is easy to calculate. But portfolio construction is a forward-looking exercise, and in this context, the relevant measure is predicted active risk, which requires a forward-looking estimate of correlations and variances.[14] As the accuracy of the forward-looking estimates of correlations and variances improves, the likelihood of better portfolio outcomes also improves.

---

14 To generate estimates of future volatility and correlations, different levels of sophistication can be considered. Although several methodologies are available, two dominant methodologies are exponentially weighted moving average (EWMA) and generalized autoregressive conditional heteroskedasticity (GARCH). EWMA applies greater weights to recent return observations, allowing for a more accurate representation of the near-term volatility environment. However, EWMA does not allow for regression to the mean to occur. More specifically, abnormally high or low levels of volatility in financial markets are expected to eventually normalize toward a long-term mean. The family of GARCH models integrates the benefits of EWMA and regression to the mean. The efficiency of risk forecasting and its implementation are illustrated in Langlois and Lussier (2017, pp. 82–85).

The variance–covariance matrix of returns is very important in the calculation of active risk. Although portfolios that have higher active risk tend to have higher Active Share (and vice versa), this is not always the case. For example, underweighting one bank stock to overweight another bank stock will likely have less effect on active risk than underweighting one bank stock and overweighting an information technology stock. Active risk is affected by the degree of cross correlation, but Active Share is not. Active Share is not concerned with the efficiency of diversification.[15] If the extent of underweighting and overweighting is the same in the bank/bank over-/underweight and in the bank/technology over-/underweight, the effect on Active Share would be identical. The effect on active risk would be different, however, because the correlation of the bank/technology pair is most likely lower than the correlation of the bank/bank pair. This highlights an important difference in Active Share versus active risk. A portfolio manager can completely control Active Share, but she cannot completely control active risk because active risk depends on the correlations and variances of securities that are beyond her control. Recall that in Equation 2, we decomposed active return into returns to factors, alpha, and idiosyncratic risk.

$$\sigma_{R_A} = \sqrt{\sigma^2\left(\sum\left(\beta_{pk} - \beta_{bk}\right) \times F_k\right) + \sigma_e^2} \tag{6}$$

Here, we show that the active *risk* of a portfolio $\left(\sigma_{R_A}\right)$ is a function of the *variance* attributed to the factor exposure $\sigma^2\left(\sum\left(\beta_{pk} - \beta_{bk}\right) \times F_k\right)$ and of the *variance* attributed to the idiosyncratic risk $\left(\sigma_e^2\right)$.[16] Although realized active risk will almost never be identical to predicted active risk, existing risk forecasting methodologies allow the manager to predict active risk over a short horizon with a high level of accuracy. Managers can then control the level of active risk through portfolio structure.

Sapra and Hunjan (2013) derived a relationship between active risk, Active Share, and factor exposure for an unconstrained investor, assuming a single-factor model. They found that

- high net exposure to a risk factor will lead to a high level of active risk, irrespective of the level of idiosyncratic risk;
- if the factor exposure is fully neutralized, the active risk will be entirely attributed to Active Share;
- the active risk attributed to Active Share will be smaller if the number of securities is large and/or average idiosyncratic risk is small; and
- the level of active risk will rise with an increase in factor and idiosyncratic volatility (such as occurred in 2008).[17]

These observations are very intuitive: Active risk increases when a portfolio becomes more uncorrelated with its benchmark. As discussed previously, although overweighting or underweighting GM relative to Ford will generate some Active Share, it will

---

15 Active Share is often used to determine how much fees an investor is paying for active management. For example, if two managers charge asset management fees of 0.5%, the manager with an Active Share of 0.80 offers twice as much "active" management per unit of fees as a manager with an Active Share of 0.40.
16 The variance attributed to alpha returns is embedded in the variance of idiosyncratic risks.
17 In 2008, markets were faced with the worst crisis of confidence and liquidity since the Great Depression. This situation triggered a deep global recession and rising unemployment and debt levels. The Market factor performed poorly, but the onset of the economic decline, the Lehman Brothers' bankruptcy on 15 September 2008, and the exposure of financial firms to weak mortgage and leveraged credit led to poor performance of value stocks and, consequently, of the Value factor. Furthermore, the forced deleveraging of many trades/strategies led to the biggest decline of the Momentum factor in more than 70 years.

typically not generate much active risk. However, overweighting or underweighting energy firms versus financial firms, small-cap firms versus large-cap firms, or growth firms versus value firms will certainly contribute more to active risk.

So how do we use these two measures to discriminate between different portfolio management approaches and management styles? Using the observations from Sapra and Hunjan (2013), we could characterize a manager as

- factor neutral, factor diversified, or factor concentrated and as
- diversified (with low security concentration and low idiosyncratic risk) or concentrated (with high security concentration and high idiosyncratic risk).[18]

Exhibit 7 illustrates how various combinations of factor exposure and idiosyncratic risk affect Active Share and active risk.[19]

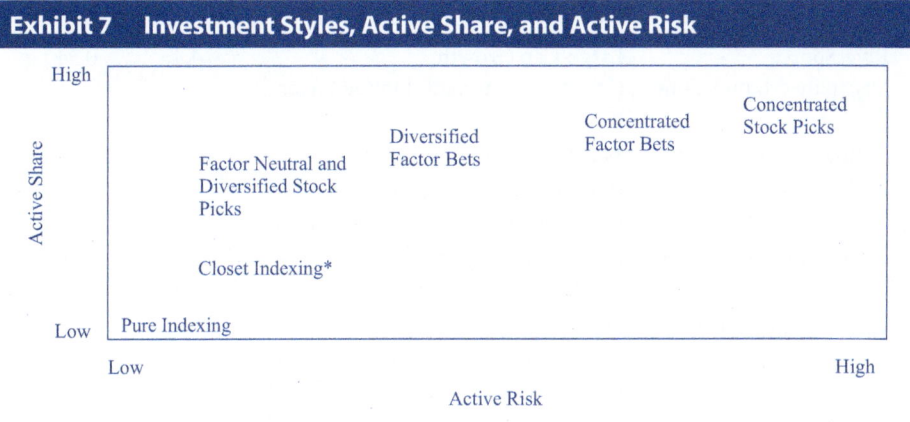

Exhibit 7   Investment Styles, Active Share, and Active Risk

*A **closet indexer** is defined as a fund that advertises itself as being actively managed but is substantially similar to an index fund in its exposures.

Using this framework, we can classify most equity strategies in terms of active risk and Active Share by analyzing the specific management style of the manager. For example, most multi-factor products have a low concentration among securities, often holding more than 250 positions (the purpose of these products is to achieve a balanced exposure to risk factors and minimize idiosyncratic risks). They are diversified across factors and securities. Thus, they typically have a high Active Share, such as 0.70, but they have reasonably low active risk (tracking error), often in the range of ±3%.

The concentrated stock picker, in contrast, has both a high Active Share (typically above 0.90) and a high active risk (such as 8%–12% or higher).[20] (The average active manager owns about 100 stocks, and fewer than 20% of managers own more than 200 stocks.) It follows, then, that the level of idiosyncratic risk in the average active discretionary portfolio is greater than that of the average multi-factor fund, with its 250+ positions. Therefore, on average, we could expect the portfolio of a typical discretionary manager to display higher active risk.

Consequently, a manager can increase his degree of control over the level of Active Share and/or active risk in his portfolio by decreasing his security concentration. For example, it would not be uncommon for a sector rotator—typically a high-active-risk

---

18 See Ceria (2015).
19 Factor portfolios usually have low security concentration.
20 See Yeung, Pellizzari, Bird, and Abidin (2012).

strategy—to have an active risk above 8%. If he chooses to run a concentrated portfolio, he might also have high Active Share. Or he can diversify his portfolio and reduce his Active Share.[21]

Petajisto (2013) provided examples of funds of different styles and their corresponding active risk and Active Share; see Exhibit 8A. The risk tolerance and portfolio construction approach of each manager is partially revealed by his Active Share and active risk. Exhibit 8B presents the same information but plots it in the Active Share/active risk dimension using the format of Exhibit 7.

Exhibit 8A Active Risk, Active Share, and Portfolio Styles, 2009

Name of Fund	Style/Comments	Active Risk	Active Share
Vanguard Index Fund	Indexed	0.0%	0.00
RiverSource Disciplined Equity Fund	Large-Cap Growth (Small active weight, limited factor timing)	4.4%	0.54
T. Rowe Price Mid-Cap Value Fund	Mid-Cap Value (Limited active weights on sectors but significant stock picking)	5.4%	0.93
AIM Constellation Fund	Large-Cap Growth (Significant sector bets)	9.7%	0.66
GMO Quality Fund	Mega-Cap Core (Timing on a number of factors and cash)	12.9%	0.65
Sequoia	Stock Picker (Highly concentrated positions)	14.1%	0.97

Source: Petajisto (2013).

Exhibit 8B Active Risk, Active Share, and Portfolio Styles

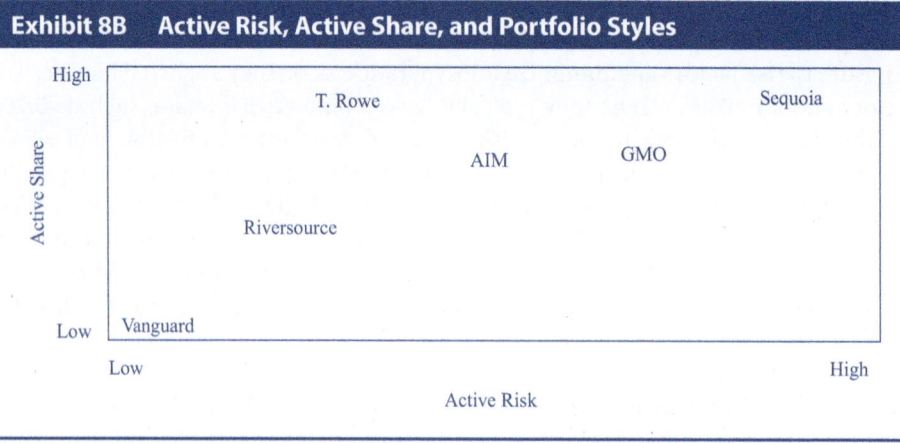

---

[21] It is important to use an appropriate index when calculating the level of Active Share. A manager whose investment universe is the S&P 500 could see her Active Share increase by approximately 12% if the Russell 1000 index was used to compute the Active Share. By default, a portfolio of 500 stocks will have high Active Share if Active Share is measured against the Russell 1000 Index.

The Implementation Process: Measures of Benchmark-Relative Risk

Active risk and Active Share provide information about the level of managers' activism against their benchmark, but there is little research on the relative efficiency of different asset management styles translating higher active risk or Active Share into higher active returns. However, many investors are using Active Share to assess the fees that they pay per unit of active management. For example, a fund with an Active Share of 0.25 (a closet indexer) would be considered expensive relative to a fund with an Active Share of 0.75 if both funds were charging the same fees.

Not all investment products neatly fall into the categorization we have just presented. Niche equity strategies, such as statistical arbitrage, event-driven investing, and activist investing, focus on generating alpha returns generally without regard to factor exposures or factor timing. These strategies do, however, typically assume a high level of idiosyncratic risk.

EXAMPLE 2

Portfolio Construction—Approaches and Return Drivers

1. You are evaluating two equity managers. Explain how Manager A, with his high level of Active Share, is able to achieve such a low active risk. What are the implications for Manager B's performance relative to that of Manager A?

	Manager A	Manager B
Active Share	0.73	0.71
Active risk	2.8%	6.0%
Number of positions	120	125

2. Discuss the drivers of return for Managers A and B.

	Manager A	Manager B	Factor Returns
Monthly performance in excess of the risk-free rate	0.65%	0.65%	
"Alpha" (monthly)	0.00%	0.20%	
Beta to:			
Market*	0.99	1.05	0.45%
Size	0	−0.2	0.20%
Value	0.15	0.05	0.35%
Momentum	0.25	0	0.60%
R-squared	0.99	0.78	

* Market factor is built from a much larger universe of securities than traditional benchmarks such as the Russell 1000. Therefore, we should not expect the β of indexes to the Market factor to be necessarily equal to one.

3. Based on the information provided below regarding four managers benchmarked against the MSCI World Index, identify the manager most likely to be a:

   a closet indexer.

   b concentrated stock picker.

   c diversified multi-factor investor.

d sector rotator.

Justify your response.

Manager Constraints:	A	B	C	D
Target active risk	10%	1%	4%	7%
Max. sector deviations	0%	3%	10%	15%
Max. risk contribution, single security	5%	1%	1%	3%

4 Discuss the main differences between top-down and bottom-up portfolio management approaches and how they relate to two of the building blocks: exposure to rewarded factors and alpha.

Solution to 1:

Managers A and B have a similar number of positions and similar Active Share. Manager B has much higher active risk. A high Active Share says only that a manager's security-level weights are quite different from those of the index. A 0.5% underallocation to one security and a 0.5% over-allocation to another security will have the same impact on Active Share whether these two securities are in the same sector or in different sectors. Given similar levels of Active Share, it is likely that Manager B's active risk is driven by active decisions at the sector level rather than at the security level. Clearly, they implement very different investment strategies. Although we cannot draw a direct conclusion about the ability of Manager B to outperform Manager A, we can assume that the realized outcomes of Manager B are likely to be much more dispersed about the benchmark (both in positive and negative directions) given the higher level of active risk.

Solution to 2:

Both managers generated the same absolute return, but they achieved their performance in very different ways. All of Manager A's performance can be explained from exposure to rewarded factors. There is no alpha, and the high R^2 shows that the four factors explain much of the monthly variability in returns. Manager A did outperform the Market factor by 20 bps (0.65% − 0.45%). The excess return can be attributed to the significant exposure (0.25) to the strong-performing Momentum factor (0.60%). Exposure to the Value factor explains the balance.

Manager B generated significant alpha (20 bps per month). The relatively low R^2 indicates that much of the variability of returns is unexplained by the factors. Manager B's performance must, therefore, be attributed to either her alpha skills or idiosyncratic risks that favored the manager's investment approach during the period.

Solution to 3:

Manager B is a closet indexer. The low targeted active risk combined with the narrow sector deviation constraint indicates that the manager is making very few active bets.

Manager A is likely a concentrated stock picker. The 10% active risk target indicates a willingness to tolerate significant performance deviations from the market. The 5% limit on a single security's contribution to portfolio risk indicates he is willing to run a concentrated portfolio. The unwillingness to take sector deviations combined with the high tolerance for idiosyncratic risk indicates that the manager likely focuses on stock selection and is, therefore, a stock picker.

Manager C limits single-security risk contribution to no more than 1%, which implies a highly diversified portfolio. The significant sector deviations despite this high diversification are often indicative of a multi-factor manager. The relatively low tracking error further supports the argument that Manager C is a multi-factor manager.

Manager D has characteristics consistent with a sector rotator. The significant active risk and high tolerance for sector deviations and security concentration are what one would expect to find with a sector rotator.

Solution to 4:

Factor exposure.

Bottom-up managers look at characteristics of securities to build their portfolios. The factor exposure inherent in their portfolios may be intentional, or it may be a by-product of their security selection process. Top-down managers articulate a macro view of the investment universe and build a portfolio emphasizing the macro factors that reflect those views. Although their macro views could then be translated into security views using a bottom-up approach, their performance will likely be dominated by their macro-level factor exposures.

Alpha.

In the context of Equation 2, the alpha of bottom-up managers is most likely attributable to their security selection skills. Some portion of their active return can also be explained through exposure to rewarded factors. Top-down managers' alphas are largely derived from factor timing.

5. THE IMPLEMENTATION PROCESS: OBJECTIVES AND CONSTRAINTS

b   discuss approaches for constructing actively managed equity portfolios

c   contrast Active Share with active risk and discuss how each measure relates to a manager's investment strategy

The simplest conceptual way to think about portfolio construction is to view it as an optimization problem. A standard optimization problem has an objective function and a set of constraints. The objective function defines the desired goal while the constraints limit the actions one can take to achieve that goal. Portfolio managers are trying to achieve desirable outcomes within the bounds of permissible actions. The nature of the objective function and the nature and specifics of the constraints can be indicative of an investment manager's philosophy and style.

A common objective function in portfolio management is to maximize a risk-adjusted return. If risk is being measured by predicted active risk, then the objective function is seeking to maximize the information ratio (the ratio of active return to active risk). If risk is being measured by predicted portfolio volatility, then the objective function is seeking to maximize the Sharpe ratio (the ratio of return in excess of the risk-free rate to portfolio volatility). Ideally, these objective functions would specify *net* returns—adjusted for the costs associated with implementation.

Typical constraints in the portfolio optimization problem may include limits on geographic, sector, industry, and single-security exposures and may also specify limits on transaction costs (to limit turnover and/or help manage liquidity issues). They may also include limits on exposure to specific factors; for example, the investment process may specify a required minimum market capitalization for any single security or a minimum weighted average capitalization for the portfolio as a whole. Or it may specify a maximum price-to-book ratio for any single security or a maximum weighted average price-to-book ratio for the portfolio. Constraints can be defined relative to the benchmark or without regard to it. Setting constraints that properly express the risk dimensions being monitored, the desired level of risk taking, and the preferred portfolio structure while still allowing sufficient flexibility to achieve the risk and return goals is a challenging task. In principle, the active equity manager's portfolio is the final blend that maximizes the objective function subject to the portfolio constraints.

Not all portfolio managers engage in such a formalistic, scientific approach to portfolio construction. The objectives and constraints of systematic managers are explicitly specified, whereas those of discretionary managers are less explicitly specified. However, most managers at least conceptually optimize their portfolios using the expected returns for each security, their own view of risk, and constraints imposed by the stated portfolio construction process or by the client. For our purposes, it is useful to frame the problem in this technical manner to provide a framework for discussion of the portfolio construction process.

Objectives and constraints may be stated in absolute terms or relative to a benchmark. Exhibit 9 illustrates two generic objective functions—one that is absolute and one that is relative. Each is subject to a few specific constraints.

Exhibit 9 Objective Functions and Constraints

	Absolute Framework	Relative Framework
Objective Function:	Maximize Sharpe Ratio	Maximize Information Ratio
Constraint		
Individual security weights (w)	$w_i \leq 2\%$	$|w_{ip} - w_{ib}| \leq 2\%$
Sectors weights (S)	$S_i \leq 20\%$	$|S_{ip} - S_{ib}| \leq 10\%$
Portfolio volatility (σ)	$\sigma_p < 0.9\, \sigma_b$	—
Active risk (TE)	—	$TE \leq 5\%$
Weighted average capitalization (Z)	$Z \geq 20\text{bn}$	$Z \geq 20\text{bn}$

- The absolute approach seeks to maximize the Sharpe ratio; the relative approach seeks to maximize the information ratio.
- The absolute approach limits any single security position to no more than 2% of the portfolio and any single sector to no more than 20% of the portfolio; the relative approach imposes a constraint that a security must remain within ±2% of its index weight and sector weights must remain within ±10% of the index weights.
- The absolute approach imposes a portfolio volatility limit equal to 90% of the estimated benchmark volatility and imposes a minimum weighted average security capitalization of $20 billion; the relative approach imposes a 5% active risk limit and the same capitalization constraint.
- Managers can also combine relative and absolute constraints in the same framework, such as limiting sector deviations against a benchmark while imposing absolute limits on security positions.

The Implementation Process: Objectives and Constraints

Other optimization approaches specify their objectives in terms of the risk metrics, such as portfolio volatility, downside risk, maximum diversification, and drawdowns. These approaches do not integrate an explicit expected return component. However, they do implicitly create an exposure to risk factors. For example, products built using a risk-based objective function (such as minimum variance or maximum diversification)[22] often exhibit a Market beta below 1.0 and have a statistically significant exposure to the Value factor and to the low-minus-high-β factor.[23] This occurs because an objective function that seeks to manage or minimize risk will tend to favor value and low-beta securities.

Finally, not all objective functions are explicitly concerned with risk or returns. For example, Equation 7 shows an explicit objective function that might be specified by a quantitative manager seeking to maximize exposure to rewarded factors:

$$\text{MAX}\left(\sum_{i=1}^{N} \frac{1}{3}\text{Size}_i + \frac{1}{3}\text{Value}_i + \frac{1}{3}\text{Momentum}_i\right) \quad (7)$$

where Size_i, Value_i, and Momentum_i are standardized[24] proxy measures of Size, Value, and Momentum for security i.[25] The portfolio may also be subject to additional constraints similar to those in Exhibit 9.

Of course, articulating an explicit objective of maximizing the Sharpe ratio or the information ratio or minimizing a given risk measure implies that we have information about expected returns and expected risk. Some managers—typically discretionary managers—do not make explicit return and risk forecasts and instead seek to "maximize" their exposure to securities having specific characteristics. Embedded in their investment process is an implicit return-to-risk objective.

For example, the objective function of a discretionary manager may be expressed in a mission statement such as: "We are a deep value manager in large-cap US equity with a concentrated, best ideas style." They then identify securities possessing deep value characteristics (as they define value). The portfolio construction process will balance security concentration and sector exposure as the manager seeks to maximize the return at an acceptable level of risk. The allocation may be driven by the manager's judgment about the risk and return trade-offs, or a formal risk management protocol may be used to drive the allocation process, or a feedback mechanism may be put in place to ensure that constraints are being respected as the portfolio is being assembled or rebalanced by the manager.

When an explicit objective function is not used, many heuristic methodologies can be considered to determine security weighting in a portfolio. We list a few examples below.

- Identify securities that have the desired characteristics and weight them relative to their scoring on these characteristics. For example, a security with a price-to-book ratio of 8 would have half the weight of a security with a price-to-book ratio of 4.

---

[22] The maximum diversification concept seeks to maximize the ratio of the average volatility of securities within a portfolio to portfolio volatility. It does not seek to achieve the lowest volatility, but rather, it seeks to maximize the benefits that diversification can bring.

[23] The low-minus-high-β factor compensation is justified as a structural impediment. Frazzini and Pederson (2014) expanded on an idea raised by Fischer Black (1972). They made the argument that investors looking for higher returns but who are constrained by borrowing limits bid up the prices of high-β securities.

[24] Because it can be unwise to compare securities of different size, price-to-book ratio, and other metrics across sectors or countries, proxies of factors are often standardized by sectors or countries.

[25] For example, a manager could rank securities per these three measures and determine a score for each security. For example, a small firm with a high book-to–price ratio and positive price momentum would score higher than a large firm with a low book-to-price ratio and negative price momentum. Other approaches could be used to attribute scores on each factor.

- Identify securities that have the desired characteristics and weight them per their ranking or risk on these characteristics. For example, if there are five securities ranked on their price-to-book ratios, the security with the lowest price-to-book ratio would constitute 33% of the portfolio value [5/(5 + 4 + 3 + 2 + 1)] and the security with the highest price-to-book ratio would constitute 6.7% of the portfolio value [1/(5 + 4 + 3 + 2 + 1)].
- Identify stocks that have the desired characteristics, rank them according to how strongly they adhere to these characteristics, select the top x% of these stocks, and assign them portfolio weights based on one of several methodologies, such as equal weight, equal risk, scoring, or ranking on these characteristics. For example, if there are 1,000 securities in an index, the 500 securities with the lowest price-to-book ratios could be selected. Each security would then be weighted using the chosen methodology.

Although these alternative methodologies may be intuitively appealing, they may not allocate active risk as efficiently as a formal optimization framework would. The constraints and objective function will be strongly reflective of the philosophy and style of a manager. For example, a stock picker is likely to have fewer and more permissive constraints on security weights than a multi-factor manager seeking to minimize idiosyncratic risks. A manager specializing in sector rotation will have more permissive constraints with respect to sector concentration than a value manager.

EXAMPLE 3

Approaches to Portfolio Construction

Marc Cohen is a portfolio manager whose primary skill is based on having a good understanding of rewarded sources of risk. He does not believe in factor timing. Sophie Palmer is a portfolio manager who believes she has skill in anticipating shifts in sector performance. She does not profess to have skill in individual security selection but tolerates significant deviations in sector exposure. Sean Christopher is a stock picker running a high-turnover strategy based on recent movements in market price among the Russell 1000 stock universe. He is highly sector and size agnostic and has significant active risk. Discuss the expected profile of each manager in terms of

- the sensitivity of their performance to risk factors,
- the level of security concentration, and
- the contribution of idiosyncratic risk to the total active risk of their portfolios.

Solution:

We should be able to explain a large part of Cohen's excess return using the performance of rewarded factors. We would not expect alpha to be a significant component of his performance. His exposure to risk factors would be relatively stable across time periods because he does not believe in factor timing. Because his primary emphasis is on long-term exposure to risk factors, he would hold a highly diversified portfolio to minimize idiosyncratic risk. As a multi-factor manager running a diversified portfolio, his active risk should be relatively low.

Palmer's performance is likely to be explained by tactical exposures to sectors, which we have said are unrewarded risks, rather than static exposures to known rewarded factor returns. Her excess performance against her benchmark will likely be attributed to alpha. With no professed skill in security selection, she is likely to hold a large number of securities in each sector to minimize

The Implementation Process: Objectives and Constraints

idiosyncratic risk. The active risk arising from her sector weightings will overshadow the active risk from security weightings. Her active risk is likely to be higher than that of Marc Cohen.

Christopher's portfolio is more difficult to assess. His focus on recent price movements indicates a sensitivity to the Momentum factor, although the sensitivity to this factor may depend on the time horizons and methodologies he uses to measure price momentum. He is size agnostic and may at times have exposure to the Size factor, a smaller-cap bias. With the information given, we cannot make an inference regarding the diversification of his portfolio. As a discretionary manager, he is to run a concentrated portfolio in order to more closely monitor his positions. However, if he makes extensive use of quantitative tools in monitoring his portfolio, he may be able to hold a more diversified portfolio. His active risk will be high, and his performance is likely to have a significant alpha component, whether positive or negative.

EXAMPLE 4

Approaches to Portfolio Construction

Manager A uses a scoring process and seeks to maximize the portfolio score based on the factor characteristics of individual securities. His purpose is not to time factor exposure but to achieve an appropriate diversification of factor risks. His approach is fully systematic, and he has a tracking error constraint of less than 4%. No one position can be greater than 2%, irrespective of its benchmark weight.

Manager B has a strong fundamental process based on a comprehensive understanding of the business model and competitive advantages of each firm. However, Manager B also uses sophisticated models to make explicit three-year forecasts of the growth of free cash flow to determine the attractiveness of each security's current valuation. A committee of portfolio managers meets once a month to debate the portfolio allocation. The manager has a large staff of portfolio managers and analysts and thus can maintain wide coverage of companies within each industry. Individual positions are constrained to the lower of (1) benchmark weight + 2% or (2) five times the benchmark weight.

Manager C specializes in timing sector exposure and has little appetite for idiosyncratic risks within sectors. Using technical analyses and econometric methodologies, she produces several types of forecasts. The manager uses this information to determine appropriate sector weights. The risk contribution from any single sector is limited to 30% of total portfolio risk. The final decision on sector allocations rests with the manager.

Discuss each manager's implementation approach, security selection approach, portfolio concentration, objective function, and constraints.

Solution:

Manager A is best characterized as a systematic, bottom-up manager.

- *Implementation approach.* An implementation approach that is fully quantitative (allocations are unaffected by a portfolio manager's judgment) is systematic.
- *Security selection approach.* A scoring process that ranks individual securities based on their factor characteristics is a bottom-up approach.

- *Concentration.* Although the limit of no more than 2% of the portfolio in any single position means the portfolio could hold as few as 50 securities, the tracking error constraint of 4% indicates that the portfolio is likely diversified.
- *Objective function.* A process that aims to maximize the portfolio's score based on the factor characteristics of single securities is an example of an explicit objective function.
- *Constraints.* The tracking error constraint of less than 4% is a relative constraint function. The limit on any single position to no more than 2% of the portfolio is an absolute—not a relative—constraint. It does not depend on benchmark weights.

The following table summarizes this information for all three managers:

	Manager A	Manager B	Manager C
Implementation approach	Systematic	Discretionary	Discretionary
Security selection approach	Bottom-up	Bottom-up	Top-down
Portfolio concentration	Diversified	Diversified	Security diversified Factor concentrated
Objective function	Explicit	Explicit	Explicit
Constraints	Relative and absolute	Relative	Absolute

6. ABSOLUTE VS. RELATIVE MEASURES OF RISK

d discuss the application of risk budgeting concepts in portfolio construction

e discuss risk measures that are incorporated in equity portfolio construction and describe how limits set on these measures affect portfolio construction

Risk budgeting is a process by which the total risk appetite of the portfolio is allocated among the various components of portfolio choice. As an example, if the portfolio manager has an *ex ante* active risk budget explicitly provided by the client, with risk budgeting, she seeks to optimize the portfolio's exposures relative to the benchmark to ensure that the choices she makes among stocks, sectors, or countries make efficient use of the active risk budget. But *ex ante* active risk is just one possible measure of risk. An effective risk management process requires that the portfolio manager do the following:

- Determine which type of risk measure is most appropriate to her strategy.
  - For example, a long/short equity manager benchmarked against a cash plus target will usually prefer an absolute risk measure (such as total volatility of portfolio returns), whereas a long-only equity manager benchmarked against a capitalization-weighted index may prefer a relative risk measure (such as active risk).
- Understand how each aspect of the strategy contributes to its overall risk.

- Total portfolio variance may be dominated by exposure to rewarded risk factors or by allocations to countries, sectors, or securities. If these exposures are dynamic, the timing of portfolio exposures also introduces risk. An important step in risk budgeting is to understand what drives a portfolio's risk and to ensure the portfolio has the right kinds of specific risks.
- Determine what level of risk budget is appropriate.
  - Targeted levels of risk vary widely among managers and strategies. Although there are general principles that limit the level of advisable risk in a specific strategy, it is also very much a policy issue.
- Properly allocate risk among individual positions/factors.
  - Whether the risk measure is absolute or relative, managers must efficiently allocate their targeted risk budget.

6.1 Absolute vs. Relative Measures of Risk

The choice between an absolute and a relative risk portfolio management orientation is driven by the mandate of the manager and the goals of investors. If the mandate is to outperform a market index over a horizon, such as three years, then the manager will focus on active risk. If the investment objective is expressed in terms of total returns, then the manager will likely focus on the volatility of portfolio returns.

Managers' beliefs about how they add value can influence the choice between an absolute and a relative risk measure. Some managers may believe that the benchmark-relative constraints so common in the world of investment management today inhibit the ability of their investment approach to realize its full potential. To address this issue, they may prefer either an absolute risk measure or a relative risk measure with a wide range of allowed deviations. An absolute risk measure is just that: Whatever the risk threshold, the portfolio risk must remain at or below that level. The manager is free to construct his portfolio without regard to the characteristics of the benchmark. A relative risk measure with wide bands around a central target implies a benchmark-relative approach with significant degrees of freedom to diverge from the characteristics of the benchmark. Ultimately, however, risk and reward will be measured relative to that benchmark. Although some large institutional investors have adopted investment strategies in recent years that are agnostic to the benchmark (an absolute/total return approach) or have had a very high active risk target in a benchmark-relative framework, most assets under management are managed under benchmark-relative mandates. Irrespective of whether a manager focuses on absolute risk or relative risk, the risks he chooses to take should be related to his perceived skills. All other risk should be diversified or minimized. For example,

- market timers should be concerned with timing their factor exposure,
- sector rotators should be concerned with timing their sector exposure, and
- multi-factor managers should be concerned with balancing their factor exposure.

The first step in determining how risk should be allocated is understanding the generic drivers of absolute and relative portfolio risk.

6.1.1 Causes and Sources of Absolute Risk

We start with the following fundamental principles:

- If a manager adds a new asset (such as a security) to his portfolio that has a higher covariance with the portfolio than most current securities, total portfolio risk will rise. (A high covariance with the existing portfolio can be driven by a high variance or a higher correlation of the new security with the portfolio.)
- If a manager replaces an existing security with another security that has a higher covariance with the portfolio than that of the security being replaced, total portfolio risk will rise.

These principles also work in reverse. Consider the three-asset portfolio in Exhibit 10.

Exhibit 10 Absolute Risk Attribution

| | Portfolio Weight | Standard Deviation | Correlation | | | Portfolio Risk Attribution | |
| | | | Asset A | Asset B | Asset C | Contribution to Portfolio Variance | |
						Absolute	%
Asset A	40%	20%	1	0.40	0.20	0.008416	59.22%
Asset B	50%	12%	0.40	1	0.20	0.005592	39.35%
Asset C	10%	6%	0.20	0.20	1	0.000204	1.44%
Portfolio	100%	11.92%	0.88	0.78	0.20	0.014212	100%

| | Covariance | | |
	Asset A	Asset B	Asset C
Asset A	0.040000	0.009600	0.002400
Asset B	0.009600	0.014400	0.001440
Asset C	0.002400	0.001440	0.003600
Portfolio	0.020926	0.011129	0.001427

Portfolio variance is a function of the individual asset returns and the covariance of returns between assets. In this example, the total variance is 0.014212, which equates to a portfolio standard deviation of 11.92%. Equation 8a expresses the calculation of total portfolio variance (V_p), and Equation 8b determines the contribution of each asset to portfolio variance (CV_i).

$$V_p = \sum_{i=1}^{n}\sum_{j=1}^{n} x_i x_j C_{ij} \tag{8a}$$

$$CV_i = \sum_{j=1}^{n} x_i x_j C_{ij} = x_i C_{ip} \tag{8b}$$

where

x_j = the asset's weight in the portfolio
C_{ij} = the covariance of returns between asset i and asset j
C_{ip} = the covariance of returns between asset i and the portfolio

Absolute vs. Relative Measures of Risk

In other words, the contribution of an asset to total portfolio variance is equal to the product of the weight of the asset and its covariance with the entire portfolio. For example, Asset A's contribution to total portfolio variance is calculated as follows:

Weight of Asset A × Weight of Asset A × Covariance of Asset A with Asset A	0.40 × 0.40 × 0.04
+ Weight of Asset A × Weight of Asset B × Covariance of Asset B with Asset A	+ 0.40 × 0.50 × 0.0096
+ Weight of Asset A × Weight of Asset C × Covariance of Asset C with Asset A	+ 0.40 × 0.10 × 0.0024
= Asset A's contribution to total portfolio variance	= 0.008416

The proportion of total portfolio variance contributed by Asset A is, therefore, 0.008416/0.014212 = 59.22%. Asset A, which has an allocation of 40%, accounts for nearly 60% of total portfolio variance. This is not surprising, because the correlation of Asset A with the portfolio is 0.88. Asset B contributes 39.35% of total portfolio variance, and Asset C contributes 1.44%.

As you read the foregoing discussion, you naturally thought of Assets A, B, and C as securities, but the "assets" might also be sectors, countries, or pools of assets representing risk factors (Value versus Growth, Small versus Large). Hence, if a manager specializes in sector rotation and replaces an allocation to one sector with an allocation to another sector having a higher covariance with the portfolio, total portfolio risk will increase.

We have explained risk by looking at how a single asset contributes to total portfolio variance, but a manager might also seek to understand how his portfolio variance can be attributed to factor exposures versus that which is unexplained by these factors. As we noted earlier, the risks a manager chooses to take should be related to his perceived skills. If the manager's skills can be attributed to certain factors, then he would want to minimize the level of portfolio risk not explained by those factors. The segmentation of absolute portfolio variance into these two components—variance attributed to factor exposure and variance unexplained—is expressed by Equation 9:[26]

$$V_p = \text{Var}\left(\sum_{i=1}^{K}(\beta_{ip} \times F_i)\right) + \text{Var}(\varepsilon_p) \quad (9)$$

If the manager's portfolio were the market portfolio, all the variance of the portfolio returns would be explained by a beta of 1 to the Market factor. Idiosyncratic risks would be fully diversified. However, as we move away from the market portfolio, total portfolio variance will be influenced by other factor exposures and other risks unexplained by factors.[27]

Exhibit 11 presents the risk factor attribution (as measured by the variance of returns) of the three products presented earlier in Exhibit 2: the Russell 1000 Index, the Russell 1000 Value Index, and a Value fund. Exhibit 11 shows that more than 100% of the absolute risk of the Russell 1000 Index is explained by the Market factor. The size exposure (the large-cap tilt of the Russell 1000 relative to the market) has a slight negative contribution to total risk.

The risk of the Russell 1000 Value Index is also dominated by the Market factor, and unsurprisingly, the Value factor explains 12.5% of total risk.

---

26 Equation 9 is the same general formulation as Equation 6. However, Equation 6 was concerned with active risk.
27 There are two ways of determining the portion of the variance of returns attributed to factors versus idiosyncratic risk. One approach consists of simply calculating each period's returns attributed to factors (the sum of the product of factor coefficients and the factor returns, which is the first term of Equation 9) and then calculating the variance of the calculated return series. This is variance attributed to factors. It can then be compared with the actual portfolio variance. A second approach identifies the variance contribution of each individual factor. However, it requires the variance–covariance matrix of factors and the vector of factor coefficients.

The Value fund appears to have much idiosyncratic risk. Its sensitivity to the Market factor is only 57.7%, whereas the Value factor accounts for 18.1% of total risk. Overall, the four factors account for slightly more than 74% of total portfolio risk, and almost 26% remains unexplained. The percentage of total variance that is explained corresponds to the R^2 of the regressions as reported in Exhibit 2.

Exhibit 11 Absolute Risk Factor Attribution, February 1990–December 2016[28]

	Russell 1000 Index	Russell 1000 Value Index	Value Fund
Market	100.4%	88.9%	57.7%
Size	−1.8%	−1.6%	1.8%
Value	0.2%	12.5%	18.1%
Momentum	0.5%	−5.2%	−3.5%
Total explained risk	99.3%	94.6%	74.1%
Total unexplained risk	0.7%	5.4%	25.9%
Total absolute risk (standard deviation annualized)	14.5%	14.2%	18.0%

Source: Calculations by authors.

6.1.2 Causes and Sources of Relative/Active Risk

Relative risk becomes an appropriate measure when the manager is concerned with her performance relative to a benchmark. One measure of relative risk is the variance of the portfolio's active return (AV_p):

$$AV_p = \sum_{i=1}^{n}\sum_{j=1}^{n}(x_i - b_i)(x_j - b_j)RC_{ij} \quad (10a)$$

where

x_i = the asset's weight in the portfolio
b_i = the benchmark weight in asset i
RC_{ij} = the covariance of relative returns between asset i and asset j

The contribution of each asset to the portfolio active variance (CAV_i) is

$$CAV_i = (x_i - b_i)RC_{ip} \quad (10b)$$

where RC_{ip} is the covariance of relative returns between asset i and the portfolio.

If you are assessing risk using a relative risk construct, you can no longer assume that a lower-risk asset reduces active risk or that a higher-risk asset increases it. In fact, depending on the composition of the benchmark, a lower-risk asset could increase active risk whereas a higher-risk asset might reduce it.

Let's consider a simple example. Assume a benchmark is composed of a 50/50 allocation to two equity indexes. The portfolio is composed of allocations to these two indexes and to a third asset—cash. What happens to the active risk of the portfolio if, instead of a 50/50 allocation to the two indexes, the portfolio allocation is 40/40

---

[28] The Market factor is built from a much larger universe of securities than traditional benchmarks, such as the Russell 1000. Therefore, we should not expect the β of indexes to the Market factor to necessarily equal one.

Absolute vs. Relative Measures of Risk

and 20% in cash? The benchmark is still 50/50. Let's look at the contribution of the active weights to the active variance of the portfolio. Exhibit 12 presents the relevant information and the results.

Exhibit 12   Relative Risk Attribution

	Benchmark Weight	Portfolio Weight	Standard Deviation	Active Risk	Correlation of Active Returns			Variance of Active Returns Attributed to Each Asset
					Index A	Index B	Cash	
Index A	50%	40%	16%	5.0%	1.00	−1.00	−0.69	14.3%
Index B	50%	40%	10%	5.0%	−1.00	1.00	0.69	−14.3%
Cash	0%	20%	0.5%	12.0%	−0.69	0.69	1.00	100%
Total	100%	100%		2.4%	−0.69	0.69	1.00	100%

Index A and Index B have absolute volatilities of 16% and 10%, respectively, whereas cash has a very low volatility. The manager is concerned with active risk, however, not portfolio volatility. Both Index A and Index B have an active risk of 5% against the 50/50 benchmark. Cash has higher active risk because it has a low correlation with the equity benchmark.

Exhibit 12 shows that the correlations of active returns between the benchmark and Index A and between the benchmark and Index B are both −1.0. This is not a coincidence; it must be so. Because the benchmark comprises just these two indexes, any outperformance of one index relative to the benchmark must be offset by underperformance of the other index. Similarly, cash has a positive correlation of relative returns with one index and a negative relative correlation with the other.

This example illustrates that this portfolio's risk (defined here as variance of active returns) can be attributed entirely to the allocation to cash, which is a low-risk asset—in an absolute sense. Hence, in the context of relative measures of risk, what matters is not the volatility of an asset but its relative (active) volatility. Introducing a low-volatility asset within a portfolio benchmarked against a high-volatility index would increase the active risk. Similarly, introducing a high-volatility asset to a portfolio might lower the active risk if the asset has a high covariance with the benchmark. These principles hold whether allocating among countries, sectors, securities, or other factors.

Exhibit 13 is similar to Exhibit 11, but it considers the attribution of active risk rather than absolute risk. It shows how much of the active risk of each product can be attributed to the four factors and how much remains unexplained. The Russell 1000 Index has some active risk (though very low, at 2% annualized). The active risk of the Russell 1000 Value Index and the Value fund are higher, at 6.0% and 11.4%, respectively.[29]

The Market factor does not explain much of the active risk; the very action of building a portfolio that is structurally different from the market creates the active risk. The two indexes have a significant portion of their active risk explained by the four rewarded factors. More than half of the active risk of the Russell 1000 Index is generated from the larger-cap tilt of the index. About 37% of the active risk remains unexplained. More than half of the active risk of the Russell 1000 Value Index is generated from the value tilt of the index. About 31% of the active risk remains unexplained. Finally, the Value fund has significant active risk (11.4%). Virtually all of this risk can

---

[29] For a detailed explanation of risk decomposition, see MacQueen (2007).

be attributed the Value factor. In this case, though, nearly two-thirds of the active risk remains unexplained. An investor would want to investigate more carefully what is driving the active risk of the value manager.

Exhibit 13   Active Risk Factor Attribution, February 1990–December 2016

	Russell 1000	Russell 1000 Value	Value Fund
Total active risk	2.0%	6.0%	11.4%
Risk Factor Contribution to Active Risk			
Market	3.0%	6.0%	1.2%
Size	56.4%	15.4%	0.8%
Value	3.0%	53.9%	38.4%
Momentum	0.5%	−5.4%	−4.1%
Total explained risk	62.8%	69.9%	36.4%
Total unexplained risk	37.2%	31.1%	63.6%

Source: Calculations by authors.

7. DETERMINING THE APPROPRIATE LEVEL OF RISK

d   discuss the application of risk budgeting concepts in portfolio construction

e   discuss risk measures that are incorporated in equity portfolio construction and describe how limits set on these measures affect portfolio construction

Listed below are representative examples of risk targets for different mandates:

- a market-neutral hedge fund targeting an absolute risk of 10%,
- a long-only equity manager targeting an active risk of something less than 2% (a closet indexer),
- a long-only manager targeting active risk of 6%–10% (benchmark agnostic), and
- a benchmark-agnostic equity manager targeting an absolute risk equal to 85% of the index risk.

Establishing the appropriate level of absolute or relative risk is a subjective exercise, highly sensitive to managers' investment style and their conviction in their ability to add value using the various levers at their disposal. Managers with similar investment approaches may have very different risk appetites. This has implications for portfolio structure, portfolio turnover, and other facets of portfolio implementation. Managers must clearly communicate to investors their overall risk orientation, and investors must understand the implications of this risk orientation. This does not mean that a strategy can or should be executed at any level of risk. Here are three scenarios that give some insights into practical risk limits:

- portfolios may face implementation constraints that degrade the information ratio if active risk increases beyond a specific level;

- portfolios with high absolute risk targets face limited diversification opportunities, which may lead to a decrease in the Sharpe ratio; and
- there is a level of leverage beyond which volatility reduces expected compounded returns.

7.1 Implementation constraints

Consider two managers (A and B), each with a relative risk focus. Irrespective of the targeted level of active risk, the managers seek to use that risk efficiently. They are concerned with the ratio of active return to active risk—the information ratio. Assume that their portfolios have the same information ratio but different levels of active risk. If the investor is willing to tolerate the higher level of active risk, Manager A might proportionately scale up his active risk to match the active risk level of Manager B. He would accomplish this by scaling up his active weights, which would increase Manager A's excess returns while maintaining the same information ratio. This scenario is illustrated in Exhibit 14.

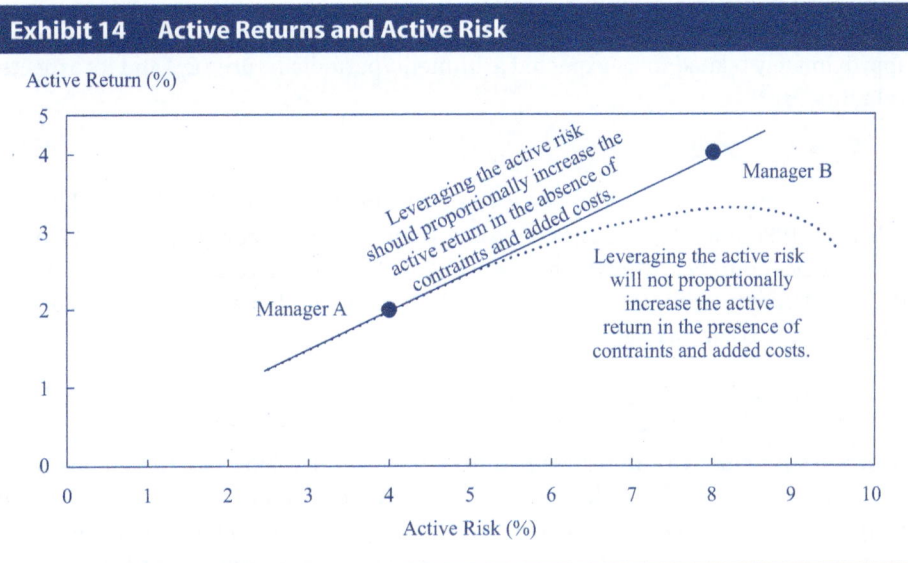

Exhibit 14 Active Returns and Active Risk

However, there may be constraints that prevent Manager A from scaling his active weights. For example, if the investment policy does not allow short positions, he may be unable to increase underweights. If the policy does not allow leverage, he may be unable to increase overweights. If some of the security positions have poor liquidity, leveraging these positions may be imprudent and may also have a trading cost impact. If the policy restricts maximum position sizes, Manager A may be unable to proportionately scale his active risk.[30]

---

[30] This constraint is also implicit in the full fundamental law of active management, which expresses the main sources of active returns. The transfer coefficient represents the ability to translate portfolio insights into investment decisions without constraint. If a manager is limited in his ability to implement his strategy, the transfer coefficient will decline. If he attempts to maintain the same level of active risk, his information ratio will also decline. In this case, there is an optimal/maximum level of active risk.

7.2 Limited diversification opportunities

Consider a manager with a high absolute risk target. Despite his higher risk tolerance, he still strives to use risk efficiently. We know, though, that twice the absolute risk will not lead to twice the return: The mathematics of the Markowitz efficient investment frontier clearly shows that the relationship between return and risk is concave. Expected returns increase with risk but at a declining pace. Portfolios with higher risk/return targets eventually run out of high-return investment opportunities and lose the ability to diversify efficiently, thereby reducing the Sharpe ratio.

7.3 Leverage and its implications for risk

Sharpe demonstrated that if there is a risk-free rate at which investors can borrow or lend, there is a linear relationship between absolute risk and return in a one-period setting. Managers can scale expected returns and absolute risk up or down proportionately and maintain a constant, optimal Sharpe ratio. A manager could choose to leverage her portfolio to extend the implementation limits of a strategy. However, as we show below, leverage eventually leads to a reduction of expected compounded return in a multi-period setting.

We know that the expected compounded/geometric return of an asset (R_g) is approximately related to its expected arithmetic/periodic return (R_a) and its expected volatility (σ):[31]

$$R_g = R_a - \sigma^2/2 \tag{11}$$

For example, let's consider again the performance of the Russell 1000 between February 1990 and December 2016. The average monthly compounded return was 0.789%, the monthly arithmetic return was 0.878%, and the volatility, as measured by the standard deviation of return, was 4.199%. Applying Equation 11, we obtain the compounded return as follows:

$$R_g = 0.878\% - \frac{4.199\%^2}{2} = 0.790\%$$

which is very close to the realized compounded return. Now, what happens to the relationship between the arithmetic return and the compounded return when leverage is used? Let's consider an asset with a 20% standard deviation and a 10% expected arithmetic return. This asset has an expected compounded return of 8%:

$$10\% - 20\%^2/2 = 8\%$$

Ignoring the cost of funding, if we leverage the asset by a factor of 2, the expected compounded return increases to 12%:

$$2 \times 10\% - (2 \times 20\%)^2/2 = 12\%$$

If we leverage the asset by a factor of 3, however, there is no additional improvement in return:

$$3 \times 10\% - (3 \times 20\%)^2/2 = 12\%$$

If we incorporate the cost of funding leverage, the active return is reduced while the volatility remains proportional to the amount of leverage. The Sharpe ratio will decline even faster. For example, using the same example, we could show that a portfolio with a leverage of 3× would have the same expected return as an unlevered portfolio if the cost of funding leverage were 2%:

$$(3 \times 10\% - 2 \times 2\%) - (3 \times 20\%)^2/2 = 8\%$$

---

[31] The arithmetic return and the geometric returns are the same only when there is no volatility.

Furthermore, if the realized volatility is significantly greater than expected, such as in crisis time, the combined impact of volatility and leverage on compounded return could be dramatic.

The information ratio and the Sharpe ratio will not always be degraded by a reasonable rise in active or absolute risk, and a reasonable level of leverage can increase expected compounded return. The appropriate tactics must be evaluated by the manager in the context of his investment approach and investors' expectations.

ALLOCATING THE RISK BUDGET

d discuss the application of risk budgeting concepts in portfolio construction

e discuss risk measures that are incorporated in equity portfolio construction and describe how limits set on these measures affect portfolio construction

We have explained how absolute and relative risk are determined by the position sizing of assets/factors (absolute or relative) and by the covariance of assets/factors with the portfolio (absolute or relative). By understanding both components (position sizing and covariance), a manager can determine the contribution of each position (whether a factor, country, sector, or security) to the portfolio's variance or active variance.

Let's consider a benchmark-agnostic US sector rotator. Although he himself is benchmark agnostic, his client is going to evaluate his performance relative to *some* benchmark—one that represents the universe of securities he typically draws from. The nature of his strategy indicates that he will likely exhibit a high level of active risk. In assessing whether he has effectively used this risk budget, the client will look to decompose the sources of realized risk: How much is attributable to market risk and other risk factors? How much is attributable to other decisions, such as sector and security allocation? If the manager runs a concentrated portfolio, we should expect sector and security allocation to be the main source of active risk. Although all these aspects may not be explicit elements of his portfolio construction process, because his effectiveness will be evaluated using these metrics, he would be well served to understand their contributions to his risk and return.

A fund's style and strategy will also dictate much of the structure of its risk budget. We explore this further with an examination of the three US equity managers presented in Exhibit 15A. All managers draw their securities from a universe of large-cap and mid-cap securities defined by the Russell 1000, which has a weighted average market capitalization of approximately $133 billion. The first two managers believe their skill is their ability to create balanced exposures to rewarded risk factors. The third specializes in sector timing, but he also makes significant use of cash positions. The first two managers have many securities in their portfolios, which suggests that their active risk is unlikely to be driven by idiosyncratic risks related to security concentration. Their low level of security concentration is consistent with their respective investment style.

The third manager runs a highly concentrated portfolio. As a sector rotator, he is exposed to significant unrewarded risk related to his sector views and to idiosyncratic risk related to his security views. A sector rotator could choose to run either a diversified portfolio or a highly concentrated portfolio within sectors. Manager C chose the latter. A greater concentration of risk implicitly leads to a greater sensitivity to unrewarded factors and idiosyncratic risks.

Exhibit 15A Comparative Sources of Risk, Drivers of Return

	Manager A	Manager B	Manager C
Investment Approach:	Factor Diversified	Factor Diversified	Sector Rotator
Number of securities	251	835	21
Weight of top 5 securities	6.54%	3.7%	25.1%
Cash and bond position	0.8%	0.0%	21.3%
Weighted average capitalization ($ billions)	33.7	21.3	164.0
Market beta	0.90	0.97	1.28
Absolute risk	10.89%	10.87%	11.69%
Active risk	3.4%	3.6%%	4.5%
Active Share	0.76	0.63	0.87
Average sector deviation	3.6%	3.9%	5.6%
Source of risk: Market	98.0%	99.2%	69.2%
Source of risk: Sectors	−0.8%	−3.8%	11.6%
Source of risk: Styles	1.8%	4.2%	9.7%
Unexplained	1.0%	0.4%	9.5%

Note: Manager C owns 49 positions, but several of these positions are cash and bond related.
Source: Bloomberg.

None of the managers is tightly tracking the benchmark; active risk exceeds 3% for all three. Somewhat surprisingly, the active risk of the sector rotator (4.5%) is only slightly greater than that for the other managers, especially given that the rotator has 25.1% of his portfolio invested in the top five positions and holds 21.3% in cash and bonds.[32] The large position in cash and bonds may also explain why the absolute volatility is not higher. We can see, however, that the sector rotator is taking less of a size bet: The weighted average capitalization of his portfolio is close to that of the index, whereas the weighted average capitalization of the two factor managers is quite low. This smaller size bet is likely what has constrained the active risk of the sector rotator.

Although managers may view their investment process and evaluation of securities as benchmark agnostic, the outcomes may, in fact, be similar to the benchmark along critical dimensions, such as active risk. The portfolio construction process of multi-factor managers often leads to a balanced exposure to risk factors, constraining active risk. The sector rotator has a higher level of active risk, but not dramatically so. The returns of the sector rotator are more driven by concentrated sector and style exposures than are the returns of the multi-factor managers. These differences are likely to influence returns over shorter horizons. Two strategies with similar active risk may have very different patterns of realized returns. When evaluating an investment manager, the asset owner needs to understand the drivers of active risk that can lead to differences in realized portfolio returns over time.

The strategy and portfolio structure of Manager C is also revealed by the sources of absolute risk. The risk attribution in Exhibit 15 not only considers the Market factor but also adds a sector factor and a style factor.

---

[32] The active risk is calculated from daily data over a one-year horizon. This calculation usually leads to a lower active risk than would be obtained from monthly data over a longer period.

Allocating the Risk Budget

The exposures of Managers A and B are dominated by the Market factor. Manager B's active risk, however, can be explained in part by the sector and style factors: The sector exposure reduces risk by 3.8%, and the style exposure increases it by 4.2%.

Let's look more closely at the risk profile of Manager C in Exhibit 15B.

Exhibit 15B

Investment Approach:	Sector Rotator	Manager C — Risk Positioning Relative to Managers A and B
Number of securities	21	Very concentrated; high levels of security-specific risk
Weight of top 5 securities	25.1%	
Cash and bond position	21.3%	Large cash position dampens overall portfolio volatility
Weighted average capitalization ($ billions)	164.0	Much closer to the capitalization of the index
Market beta	1.28	Significantly higher, consistent with the absolute risk measures
Absolute risk	11.69%	Absolute risk only slightly higher, likely dampened by the large cash position
Active risk	4.5%	Higher
Active Share	0.87	High, consistent with the level of security concentration
Average sector deviation	5.6%	Higher, consistent with willingness to take sector bets
Source of risk: Market	69.2%	Significantly less exposure to the Market factor, consistent with a concentrated, high-Active-Share manager
Source of risk: Sectors	11.6%	Significantly more Sector risk
Source of risk: Styles	9.7%	Significantly more Style risk
Unexplained	9.5%	Significantly higher proportion of risk is unexplained

Taken together, these measures indicate a benchmark-agnostic strategy with significant and concentrated security, sector, and style exposures.

EXAMPLE 5

Application of Risk Budgeting Concepts

1. Using the information in Exhibit 15, discuss key differences in the risk profiles of Manager A and Manager C.

2. The table below presents the risk factor coefficients of a four-factor model and the factor variance–covariance matrix of a manager running a low-risk strategy. All data are monthly. The monthly standard deviation of the manager's return is 3.07%. What portion of the total portfolio risk is explained by the Market factor?

| | Coefficients | Variance/Covariance of Returns | | | |
		Market	Size	Value	Momentum
Market	0.733	0.00178	0.00042	0.00066	−0.00062
Size	−0.328	0.00042	0.00048	0.00033	−0.00035
Value	0.045	0.00066	0.00033	0.00127	−0.00140
Momentum	0.042	−0.00062	−0.00035	−0.00140	0.00214

3 If a manager benchmarked against the FTSE 100 makes a significant allocation to cash, how will that allocation affect the portfolio's absolute risk and active risk?

4 Manager A has been running a successful strategy achieving a high information ratio with a relatively low active risk of 3.4%. The manager is considering offering a product with twice the active risk. What are the obstacles that may make it difficult for the manager to maintain the same information ratio?

Solution to 1:

Manager C holds significantly fewer positions than Manager A, and the weight of his top five securities is nearly four times that of Manager B. This indicates a willingness to assume a much higher level of idiosyncratic risk. This observation is reinforced by Manager C's higher Active Share and higher proportion of unexplained risk. The Market beta of Manager C is significantly greater, and the risk decomposition indicates that Manager C appears more willing to make sector and style bets. Finally, the absolute risk of Manager's C portfolio is higher, even though it appears that he makes greater use of lower-risk bond and cash positions.

Solution to 2:

91% of total portfolio risk is explained by the Market factor. From Equation 8b (repeated below), the contribution of an asset to total portfolio variance is equal to the product of the weight of the asset and its covariance with the entire portfolio. To calculate the variance attributed to the Market factor,

$$CV_i = \sum_{j=1}^{n} x_i x_j C_{ij} = x_i C_{ip} \tag{8b}$$

where

x_j = the asset's weight in the portfolio
C_{ij} = the covariance of returns between asset i and asset j
C_{ip} = the covariance of returns between asset i and the portfolio

Therefore, the variance attributed to the Market factor is

(0.733 × 0.00178 × 0.733) + (0.733 × 0.00042 × −0.328) + (0.733 × 0.00066 × 0.045) + (0.733 × −0.00062 × 0.042) = 0.000858

Divide this result by the portfolio variance of returns:

$0.000858/3.07\%^2$ = 0.000858/0.000942 = 91% of total portfolio variance is explained by the Market factor.

Solution to 3:

Cash has a low volatility and a low correlation of returns with any asset. Therefore, it will contribute to a reduction in absolute risk. However, because cash has a low correlation with other assets, it will contribute to an increase in active risk.

Solution to 4:

If the manager is running a long-only portfolio without leverage, she is likely able to increase her exposure to securities she wants to overweight, but she may be limited in her ability to reduce exposure to securities she wishes to avoid or underweight. Increased exposure to the most desirable securities (in her view) will lead to increased security concentration and may substantially increase active risk. The manager risks a degradation of her information ratio if there is not a

> corresponding increase in her active return. If the manager can short, she will be able to increase underweighting when desired (assuming the securities can be easily borrowed). Although leverage can increase total exposure and reduce concentration issues, its impact on volatility may be substantial, and the additional return enabled by leverage may be eroded by the impact of the increased volatility on compounded returns and the other associated costs.

ADDITIONAL RISK MEASURES USED IN PORTFOLIO CONSTRUCTION AND MONITORING

d   discuss the application of risk budgeting concepts in portfolio construction

e   discuss risk measures that are incorporated in equity portfolio construction and describe how limits set on these measures affect portfolio construction

9.1 Heuristic Constraints

Risk constraints imposed as part of the portfolio construction process may be either formal or heuristic. Heuristic constraints appear as controls imposed on the permissible portfolio composition through some exogenous classification structure. Such constraints are often based on experience or practice, rather than empirical evidence of their effectiveness. These risk controls may be used to limit

- exposure concentrations by security, sector, industry, or geography;
- net exposures to risk factors, such as beta, size, value, and momentum;
- net exposures to currencies;
- degree of leverage;
- degree of illiquidity;
- turnover/trading-related costs;
- exposures to reputational and environmental risks, such as actual or potential carbon emissions; and
- other attributes related to an investor's core concerns.

A major concern of any portfolio manager is a risk that is unknown or unexpected. Risk constraints are one way that managers try to limit the portfolio losses from unexpected events. Listed below are sample heuristic constraints that may be used by a portfolio manager:

- Any single position is limited to the lesser of
  - five times the weight of the security in the benchmark or
  - 2%.
- The portfolio must have a weighted average capitalization of no less than 75% of that of the index.
- The portfolio may not size any position such that it exceeds two times the average daily trading volume of the past three months.
- The portfolio's carbon footprint must be limited to no more than 75% of the benchmark's exposure.

Such heuristic constraints as these may limit active managers' ability to fully exploit their insights into expected returns, but they might also be viewed as safeguarding against overconfidence and hubris.

Managing risk through portfolio characteristics is a "bottom-up" risk management process. Managers that rely on such an approach express their risk objectives through the heuristic characteristics of their portfolios. The resulting statistical risk measures of such portfolios do not drive the portfolio construction process but are an outcome of those heuristic characteristics. For example, if a manager imposes maximum sector deviations of ±3% and limits security concentration to no more than the index weight + 1% or twice the weight of any security in the index, then we could expect the active risk of that portfolio to be small even if no constraint on active risk is explicitly imposed. The portfolio construction process ensures that the desired heuristic risk is achieved. Continuous monitoring is necessary to determine whether the evolution of market prices causes a heuristic constraint to be breached or nearly breached.

Managers will often impose constraints on the heuristic characteristics of their portfolios even if they also use more formal statistical measures of risk. The investment policy of most equity products, for example, will usually specify constraints on allocations to individual securities and to sectors or, for international mandates, regions. Some may also have constraints related to liquidity and capitalization. Even managers with a low-volatility mandate will have security and sector constraints to avoid unbalanced and concentrated portfolio solutions that may have significant idiosyncratic risk or allocations that are unduly influenced by estimation error.

9.2 Formal Constraints

Formal risk measures are distinct from these heuristic controls. They are often statistical in nature and directly linked to the distribution of returns for the portfolio.

Formal measures of risk include the following:

- Volatility
- Active risk
- Skewness
- Drawdowns
- Value at risk (VaR)
- Conditional Value at risk (CVaR)
- Incremental Value at risk (IVaR)
- Marginal Value at risk (MVaR)

A major difference between formal and heuristic risk measures is that formal measures require a manager to estimate or predict risk. For example, a formal risk measure might be that predicted active risk be no more than, say, 5%. With the benefit of hindsight, one can always calculate the historical active risk, but in portfolio construction, the forward-looking view of risk and active risk is what matters: Portfolio decisions are based on these forward-looking estimates. If predicted risk deviates substantially from realized risk, it is likely that portfolio performance will be quite different than expected. In times of crisis or financial stress, predicted and realized risks could diverge very significantly.

Exhibit 16 presents five different risk measures for the same three products discussed in Exhibit 15. Four one-day VaR measures are presented: VaR and CVaR at two different levels of probability (1% and 5%).

Additional Risk Measures Used in Portfolio Construction and Monitoring

Exhibit 16 Risk Measures

Risk Measure	Manager A Factor Diversified	Manager B Factor Diversified	Manager C Sector Rotator
Absolute risk	10.89%	10.87%	11.69%
Active risk	3.4%	3.6%%	4.5%
VaR (5%)	1.08%	1.11%	1.20%
VaR (1%)	1.77%	1.77%	1.87%
CVaR (5%)	1.50%	1.53%	1.65%
CVaR (1%)	2.21%	2.24%	2.41%

Source: Bloomberg.

In this example, Manager A has a 5% probability of realizing a one-day loss greater than 1.08% and a 1% probability of a loss greater than 1.77%. If we look at the distribution of losses beyond the 5% and 1% probability levels, the averages of the tail losses (CVaR) are 1.50% and 2.21%, respectively. Despite the high security concentration, the loss estimates of Manager C are not much higher than those of Managers A and B, most likely because of the large position in cash and bonds.

Risk Measures

- Volatility is the standard deviation of portfolio returns.
- Active risk is the standard deviation of the differences between a portfolio's returns and its benchmark's returns. It is also called *tracking error* or *tracking risk*.
- Skewness is a measure of the degree to which return expectations are non-normally distributed. If a distribution is positively skewed, the mean of the distribution is greater than its median (more than half of the deviations from the mean are negative and less than half are positive) and the average magnitude of positive deviations is larger than the average magnitude of negative deviations. Negative skew indicates that the mean of the distribution lies below its median and the average magnitude of negative deviations is larger than the average magnitude of positive deviations.
- Drawdown measures the portfolio loss from its high point until it begins to recover.
- VaR is the minimum loss that would be expected a certain percentage of the time over a specific period of time (e.g., a day, a week, a month) given the modeled market conditions. It is typically expressed as the minimum loss that can be expected to occur 5% of the time.
- CVaR is the average loss that would be incurred if the VaR cutoff is exceeded. It is also sometimes referred to as the **expected tail loss** or **expected shortfall**. It is not technically a VaR measure.
- IVaR is the change in portfolio VaR when adding a new position to a portfolio, thereby reducing the position size of current positions.
- MVaR reflects the effect of a very small change in the position size. In a diversified portfolio, marginal VaR may be used to determine the contribution of each asset to the overall VaR.

Formal risk constraints may be applied as part of a portfolio optimization process (as is common with systematic strategies) or using an iterative feedback mechanism to determine whether the portfolio would remain within the risk tolerance limits given the proposed change (an approach more common among discretionary managers).

All risk measures, whether formal or heuristic, can be expressed on an absolute basis or relative to a benchmark. For example, a benchmark-aware long-only equity manager may limit sector deviations to 5%, whereas a long/short hedge fund manager concerned with the overall diversification of his portfolio may limit any given sector exposure to no more than 30% of his gross exposure. Similarly, a long-only equity manager may limit active risk to 5%, whereas a long/short equity manager may limit overall portfolio volatility to 10%. In many cases, the investment policy imposes both formal and heuristic constraints on a portfolio. Exhibit 17 illustrates a product for which the investment policy statement considers constraints on both types of risk measures.

Exhibit 17 Sample Investment Policy Risk Constraints

The MSCI Diversified Multi-Factor Index

This index uses an optimization process to maximize the exposure score to several risk factors. The index seeks to achieve this objective while controlling for several portfolio and risk characteristics, such as the following:

- Weight of index constituents: maximum of weight in the parent (capitalization-weighted) index + 2% or 10 times weight in the parent index
- Sector weights: restricted to a 5% deviation against the parent index
- Exposure to style factors, such as growth and liquidity: restricted to a 0.25 standard deviation from the parent index
- Limit on volatility: restricted to a 0.25 standard deviation from the parent index

9.3 The Risks of Being Wrong

The consequences of being wrong about risk expectations can be significant but even more so when a strategy is leveraged. In 2008, for example, a hedge fund owned a two-times levered portfolio of highly rated mortgage-related securities. Although the specific securities were not materially exposed to subprime mortgages, concerns about the economy and poor market liquidity led to a steep decline in the prices of these securities. Prices quickly recovered, but the presence of the 2× leverage combined with an unprecedented price decline led to a forced liquidation of the assets just a few days before prices recovered. The manager and his investors lost all capital.

Similarly, a pension fund created an indexed equity position by combining an investment of short-term highly rated (AAA) commercial paper with an equivalent notional position in equity derivatives (a receiver swap on a large-cap equity index), creating a synthetic indexed equity position. In principle, this pension fund believed it owned the equivalent of an index equity position. However, as the liquidity crisis worsened in 2008 and early 2009, the pension fund was faced with a substantial decline in equity markets *and* a simultaneous spike in the perceived riskiness of the short-term commercial paper. The equity derivatives position and the commercial paper each lost 50% of their value, creating a paper loss equivalent to 100% of the invested capital. Although both components eventually recovered, such unexpected losses can lead to a forced liquidation of all or part of the portfolio in an unfavorable market environment, crystalizing the losses.

Exhibit 18 illustrates the time-varying volatility of the S&P 500. Although volatility remains in a range of 10%–20% most of the time, periods of much higher volatility are observed: in 1973–1974 during the first oil shock, in 1987 during the October crisis, in 2000–2002 when technology stocks collapsed, and during the 2008 liquidity crisis. Effective risk management requires the manager to account for the fact that unexpected volatility can derail the investment strategy. Furthermore, spikes in volatility can also be sector specific—the technology sector in the early 2000s and the energy sector in 2014 and 2015. Therefore, what may seem to be an acceptable sector deviation limit in normal times may be the source of significant active losses in a different environment. Some managers may tighten risk constraints in more volatile periods to protect the portfolio against excessive variability.

Despite these "tail events," risk can usually be managed efficiently. The dotted line in Exhibit 18[33] shows the realized volatility of a portfolio dynamically allocated between the S&P 500 Index and short-term bonds. The portfolio targets a 10% annualized volatility.[34] The realized volatility stayed very close to the target.

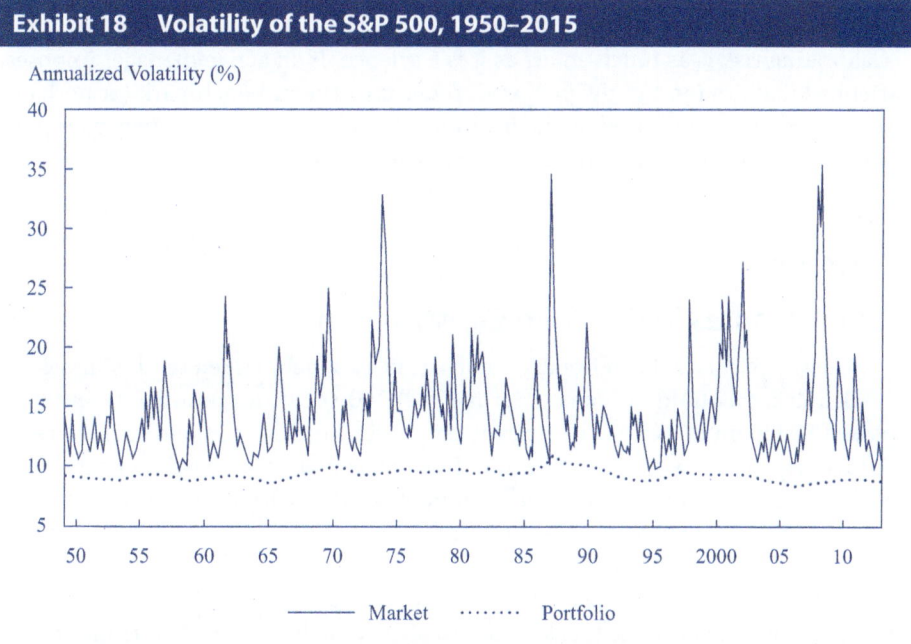

Exhibit 18 Volatility of the S&P 500, 1950–2015

The statistical risk measures used in equity portfolio construction often depend on the style of management. A benchmark-agnostic manager with an absolute return philosophy is less likely to be concerned with active risk but is much more likely to be concerned with drawdowns. A long/short equity manager who neutralizes market risk but is exposed to other risk premiums is likely to target a volatility within a specific range.

---

33 Langlois and Lussier (2017).
34 The management of this portfolio required forecasts of volatility and correlation for both assets. The same general techniques described in footnote 15 were used.

Portfolios with a very limited number of securities may be more difficult to manage using formal risk measures because estimation errors in portfolio risk parameters are likely to be higher: The dispersion in possible outcomes may be wide, and the distributions may not easily conform to standard assumptions underlying many of the formal risk measures.

This does not mean, however, that these measures cannot be used on an *ex ante* basis. It merely suggests that they should be used with an understanding of their limitations. For example, VaR is particularly useful to a pension plan sponsor that has a multi-asset-class portfolio and needs to measure its exposure to a variety of risk factors (Simons, 2000). However, this information may be less useful to an equity manager holding only 40 equity positions. Measures of risk and their efficacy must be appropriate to the nature and objective of the portfolio mandate.

Formal, statistical measures of risk are often not outlined in investment policy statements even if the manager is actively tracking such risks and using such measures to adjust security weights. One reason may be the difficulty in measuring and forecasting such measures as volatility and value at risk. The resultant answers are likely to be different depending on what methodology is used. Even if the historical measures were in alignment with one another, what happened in the past will not necessarily be indicative of what is to come. When formal, statistical measures of risk are used by managers, they are typically expressed as a soft target, such as, "We are targeting a 10%–12% annualized volatility."

Calibrating risk is as much an art as it is a science. If an active manager imposes restrictions that are too tightly anchored to her investment benchmark (or perhaps these restrictions are imposed by the investor), the resulting portfolio may have performance that too closely mirrors that of the benchmark.

EXAMPLE 6

Risk Measures in Portfolio Construction

Matthew Rice runs a discretionary equity strategy benchmarked on the Russell 1000 Index. His fund contains approximately 80 securities and has recently passed $2 billion in assets. His strategy emphasizes quality companies that are attractively priced within their sector. This determination is based on careful analyses of the balance sheet, free cash flows, and quality of management of the companies they invest in. Rice is not benchmark agnostic, but his strategy does require the ability to tolerate some sector deviations because attractive positions are sometimes concentrated in three or four sectors. Rice is supported by a team of six analysts but makes all final allocation decisions. Historically, no single position or bet has dominated the performance of the fund. However, Rice believes there is no point in holding a position so small that it will barely affect excess returns even if it is successful. Rice does not believe in taking aggressive views. His investors do not expect him to have the active risk of a sector rotator. The portfolio has lower turnover than that of most of his peers. Single positions can easily remain in the portfolio for two or three years.

1 What heuristic constraints could be appropriate for such a fund?
2 What role might such statistical measures as VaR or active risk play in the management of Rice's fund?

Solution to 1:

Because no single position or bet has dominated historical returns, a heuristic constraint on maximum position size is a logical one. Given that his portfolio is built around a relatively small number of positions (80), single positions might be constrained to no more than 3%. Given his view on small position sizes, a minimum position size of 0.5% might also be appropriate.

Rice's strategy requires some active risk, but he could not tolerate the sector deviations taken by a sector rotator. A sector constraint in the range of ±5%–7.5% relative to the index is appropriate for his strategy.

The fund's benchmark incorporates many mid-cap securities. With $2 billion in assets, a single position can be as small as $10 million (0.5%) but as high as perhaps $60 million (3%). Positions on the higher end of this range could represent a large portion of the average daily trading of some mid-cap securities, which range in size from $2 billion to $10 billion. The fund's long investment horizon means that trading into and out of a position can be stretched over days or even weeks. Nevertheless, it could make sense to consider a constraint that accounts for the size (capitalization) of individual securities and their trading volume, such as not owning more than five times the capitalization weight in the index of any security.

Solution to 2:

Discretionary managers usually do not use statistical measures as hard constraints, but they can be used as guidelines in the portfolio management process. A fund that contains only 80 positions out of a universe of 1,000 possible securities and takes views across capitalization and sectors is likely to see significant variability in its active risk or VaR over time. Although Rice is not very sensitive to what happens in the short run (he is a long-term investor), statistical measures can be used to monitor changes in the risks within his portfolio. If these risk exposures deviate from his typical risk exposures, it might signal a need to investigate the sources of such changes and initiate some portfolio changes if those exposures are unwanted.

IMPLICIT COST-RELATED CONSIDERATIONS IN PORTFOLIO CONSTRUCTION

10

f discuss how assets under management, position size, market liquidity, and portfolio turnover affect equity portfolio construction decisions

There are numerous costs that can affect the net performance of an investment product. The same investment strategy can easily cost twice as much to manage if a manager is not careful with her implementation approach. Assets under management (AUM) will affect position size. Position size and the liquidity of the securities in the portfolio will affect the level of turnover that can be sustained at an acceptable level of costs.[35] Although smaller-AUM funds may pay more in explicit costs (such as broker commissions), these funds may incur lower implicit costs (such as delay and market

---

35 The portfolio turnover ratio is a measure of the fund's trading activity. It is computed by taking the lesser of purchases or sales and dividing by average monthly net assets.

impact) than large-AUM funds. Overall, smaller funds may be able to sustain greater turnover and still deliver superior performance. A manager needs to carefully weigh both explicit and implicit costs in his implementation approach.

Thoughtful portfolio management requires a manager to balance the potential benefits of turnover against the costs of turnover. When considering a rebalancing or restructuring of the portfolio, the benefits of the post-trade risk/return position must justify the costs of getting there.

This section concerns the implicit costs of implementing an active strategy and implementation issues related to asset under management, position sizing, turnover, and market liquidity. Explicit costs, such as broker commissions, financial transaction taxes, custody/safekeeping fees, and transaction processing, are covered in other parts of the CFA Program curriculum.

10.1 Implicit Costs—Market Impact and the Relevance of Position Size, Assets under Management, and Turnover

The price movement (or market impact) resulting from a manager's purchase or sale of a security can materially erode a manager's alpha. Market impact is a function of the liquidity and trade size of the security. A manager's investment approach and style will influence the extent to which he is exposed to market impact costs. A manager whose strategy demands immediacy in execution or requires a higher portfolio turnover is likely to incur higher market impact costs relative to a manager who patiently trades into a position. A manager who believes her investment insights will be rewarded over a longer-term investment horizon may be able to mitigate market impact costs by slowly building up positions as liquidity becomes available. A manager whose trades contain "information" is more vulnerable to market impact costs. A trade contains information when the manager's decision to buy or sell the security signals to the market that something has changed. If a discretionary manager with sizable assets under management begins to buy a stock, the trade signals to other market participants that there is likely to be upward pressure on the stock price as the manager builds the position. Some market participants may try to "front-run" the manager, buying up known supply to sell it to the manager at a higher price. If that same manager begins to sell his position following a company "event," it signals to the market that the manager's view on the stock has changed and he is likely to be selling off his position, putting downward pressure on the price. Assets under management, portfolio turnover, and the liquidity of the underlying assets all affect the potential market impact costs.

Consider the relationship between the size of a security, as measured by its capitalization, and a manager's ability to trade in this security, as measured by its average daily trading volume. Exhibit 19 presents the capitalization and average daily trading volume of the Russell 1000 companies in declining order of their capitalization. The figure is built using a moving average of the capitalization of groups of 20 companies. The first point on the graph shows the average capitalization and trading volume of the largest 20 companies by capitalization. The next point on the graph presents the same information for the averages of the companies ranking 2nd to 21st in terms of capitalization, and so on.

Exhibit 19 Capitalization and Trading Volume (in $) of the Russell 1000 Companies in Declining Order of Capitalization

Source: Data from Bloomberg.

Two observations are warranted. First, the distribution of market cap is skewed: The average capitalization declines quickly. The combined capitalization of the top 500 companies is more than seven times that of the bottom 500 companies. Second, smaller-capitalization companies have lower daily trading volume (in dollars). However, smaller-cap companies trade a greater percentage of their capitalization. The smallest 900 companies within the index trade nearly two times more volume—as a percentage of their market capitalization—than the 100 largest companies (e.g., the 900 smallest companies on average trade 1% of their market cap daily, whereas the 100 largest companies trade 0.5% of their market cap daily). Nevertheless, the lower absolute level of average trading volume of the smaller securities can be a significant implementation hurdle for a manager running a strategy with significant assets under management and significant positive active weights on smaller companies.

For example, let's assume the smallest company within an index has a capitalization of $2 billion and that 1% of its capitalization trades each day on average—about $20 million. Let's also assume that a manager has a policy not to own a position that constitutes more than 10% of the average trading volume of a security and that no position in the portfolio can be larger than 2% of total assets. If this manager has $200 million under management, the allocation constraint indicates that he could own as much as $4 million of that security ($200 million × 2% = $4 million), but the liquidity constraint limits the position to $2 million ($20 million × 10%). Thus, the position size is limited to about 1.0% of the fund's assets. A $1 billion fund with similar constraints would be limited to the same $2 million position, a much smaller position size relative to his total portfolio.

A $100 million fund can typically implement its strategy with very few obstacles arising from trading volume and position size constraints. However, the manager of a $5 billion fund could not effectively operate with the same constraints. A 2% position in a $5 billion fund is $100 million, yet only approximately 35% of the securities in the Russell 1000 have an average daily trading volume greater than $100 million. The trading volume constraint significantly limits the manager's opportunity set. A large-AUM fund can address this issue in several ways:

- It may establish position limits on individual securities that consider their respective market-cap weights on both an absolute and relative basis. For example, it may limit the allocation to the lesser of market-cap weight + 1% (100 bps) or 10 times the market-cap weight allocation of the security within the index. In other words, the position limit would be related to the market cap of each security.

- It may establish position limits based on the average daily trading volume of a security. For example, it may limit the position size to, say, no more than 10 days of average trading volume.

- It may build a rebalancing strategy into the investment process that anticipates a longer rebalancing period or that gradually and consistently rebalances over time, assuming the performance of the strategy is not affected by the implementation delay.

The challenges are even greater for small-cap funds. The weighted average capitalization of the Russell 2000 Index is only $2.2 billion, and nearly 60% of the companies in the index have a market capitalization below $1 billion (as of March 2017). The average market cap of companies over this $1 billion market-cap threshold is only $1.2 billion. The average daily volume of these "larger" companies is approximately 2% of their market capitalization—less than $25 million. Approximately 75% of securities within the index have a lower average daily trading volume.

A small-cap manager with the same limits on position size relative to trading volume as the manager above would have an average position size of no more than $2.5 million, based on average daily trading volume. A strategy rooted in a smaller number of securities—say, 40—may find it difficult to run a $100 million fund and may have to concentrate its allocation among the 25% largest securities in the index or accept a lower turnover. Although a strategy with a larger number of securities—say, 200—would be able to support a substantially higher level of AUM, it may still be constrained to concentrate its exposure among the larger and more liquid securities. Small-cap funds with capacities of $1 billion or greater may very well need to hold 400 securities or more.

The strategy of the manager must be consistent with the feasibility of implementing it. A high-turnover strategy with a significant allocation to smaller securities will at some point reach a level of AUM at which the strategy becomes difficult to implement successfully. The level of idiosyncratic risk inherent in the strategy will also play a role in the suitable level of AUM. A manager targeting low levels of idiosyncratic risk in his portfolio is likely to have more securities and smaller position sizes and could, therefore, conceivably support a higher level of AUM.

10.2 Estimating the Cost of Slippage

Slippage is often measured as the difference between the execution price and the midpoint of the bid and ask quotes at the time the trade was first entered.[36] It incorporates both the effect of volatility/trend costs and market impact. (Volatility/trend costs are the costs associated with buying in a rising market and selling in a declining market.) This measure provides an estimate of the cost to execute a transaction when the order is executed in a single trade.

When a larger trade is executed in increments over multiple days, the estimate of market impact costs for later trades does not account for the impact of earlier trades on subsequent execution prices. Depending on the size of the trade, the manager's own sell (buy) orders may put downward (upward) pressure on the security's price, thereby increasing the effective cost of implementation. Large institutional investors today will often try to camouflage the potential size of their trade by breaking a trade

---
36 See Taleb (1997).

Implicit Cost-Related Considerations in Portfolio Construction

into many smaller trades or by trading in "unlit" venues. Unlit venues allow buyers and sellers to trade anonymously with one another. Dark pools and crossing networks are examples of unlit venues.[37]

Studies have shown that small-cap stocks have consistently had higher effective trading costs than large-cap stocks and that illiquidity can be very cyclical, increasing prior to the beginning of a recession and decreasing prior to the end of a recession.[38] It is difficult to quantify this cost, but we know intuitively that a given trading volume causes a larger price move for a less liquid asset.[39] The larger a trade size relative to a stock's average daily volume is, the more likely it is that the trade will affect prices. Thus, a fund with a focus on large-cap stocks can support a higher level of AUM than can a similar-strategy fund focused on small-cap stocks. A fund focused on small-cap stocks must either limit its AUM, hold a more diversified portfolio, limit turnover, or devise a trading strategy to mitigate market impact costs.

Exhibit 20 provides estimates of the average slippage for several markets in 2016 and for the last two quarters of 2009. The table also presents the information per capitalization segment for the US market alone. There are four conclusions we can draw:

- Slippage costs are usually more important than commission costs.
- Slippage costs are greater for smaller-cap securities than for large-cap securities.
- Slippage costs are not necessarily greater in emerging markets.
- Slippage costs can vary substantially over time, especially when market volatility is higher.

---

37 If a large institution wants to sell a big block of stock but doesn't want to alert other market participants about the pending activity, it may choose to trade anonymously. Unlit venues—private trading venues where transactions are completed "in the dark" (without full transparency)—have become a powerful force in financial markets.
38 Hasbrouck (2009) and Amihud (2002).
39 Ilmanen (2011).

Exhibit 20 Average Slippage by Cap Size and Country

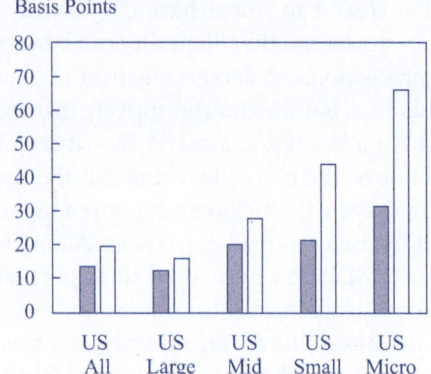

A. US Market by Cap Size

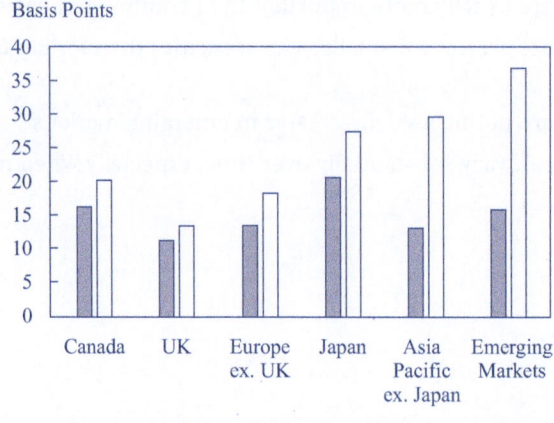

B. By Country

■ 2016   □ Q3 and Q4 2009

Source: ITG, "Global Cost Review Q4/2016" (2017).

Slippage cost can be managed with a strategic approach to implementation. Smaller-AUM managers have an advantage in this respect. For example, two hypothetical $100 million trades were sent to an execution platform that provides estimates of trading costs. The first trade mirrored the Russell 1000. The second trade bought just 250 securities in the same Russell 1000 universe, but the weighted average capitalization was only $26 billion (versus $133 billion for the index). Assuming the trading was accomplished in the course of a single day, the first trade had an estimated implementation cost of just 1 bp, whereas the second trade incurred implementation costs of 3%.

For some strategies, the true cost of slippage may be the opportunity cost of not being able to implement the strategy as assets grow. Investors choose a given fund based on the manager's stated strategy and implementation approach. If this approach is modified as the manager's level of AUM grows, it may have unanticipated consequences for expected risks and returns to investors. In these situations, the manager must either inform investors of changes being made to the strategy and its implementation or they must limit the size of the fund assets—that is, close the fund to new investors or new contributions from existing investors. Managers need to very carefully think about capacity as a new product is launched; although historical results based

Implicit Cost-Related Considerations in Portfolio Construction

on a lower level of AUM may attract attention and clients, if the strategy cannot be scaled for the larger AUM, the product delivered to clients may be different from the strategy they thought they were investing in.

A study by Frazzini, Israel, and Moskowitz (2012) examined the scalability of well-known factor-based strategies, such as Size, Value, Momentum, and Short-Term Reversal, and considered the price impact of implementing such strategies. The study covered 19 developed markets over the period 1998–2001. It concluded that strategies based on Value could support significant scale. However, scaling up Size and especially Short-Term Reversal led to a steeper decline in performance and an increase in tracking error. Clearly, investors need to monitor a strategy's capacity by observing the evolution of portfolio turnover and portfolio characteristics, such as an increasing allocation to larger-cap stocks.[40]

EXAMPLE 7

Issues of Scale

1. Stephen Lo has been the sole portfolio manager of the Top Asia Fund since its inception 20 years ago. He is supported by a group of analysts. The fund has been highly successful as it grew from assets of less than $30 million in his first year to more than $7 billion. As a potential investor in the Top Asia Fund, you have been asked to determine how Lo has been able to generate his performance and whether his style has evolved over the years. You prepared the following analysis of the return and risk characteristics of the fund for its first five years and last five years of existence.

   Discuss the evolution of the fund's characteristics and its implications for Lo's success as a manager.

Top Asia Fund Characteristics	First Five Years	Last Five Years
Average assets ($ millions)	200	5,000
Average number of positions	80	300
Market Beta	0.90	0.91
Size coefficient	0.30	−0.10
Value coefficient	0.25	0.24
Momentum coefficient	0.20	0.10
Portfolio turnover	100%	30%
Alpha (gross of fees)	2.5%	0.40%

2. Andrew Isaac runs a $100 million diversified equity portfolio (about 200 positions) using the the Russell 1000 as his investable universe. The total capitalization of the index is approximately $20 trillion. Isaac's strategy is very much size agnostic. He consistently owns securities along the entire size spectrum of permissible securities. The strategy was designed with the following constraints:

   - No investment in any security whose index weight is less than 0.015% (approximately 15% of the securities in the index)

---

[40] Peter Lynch, while managing the highly successful Magellan Fund, generated a 2% gross *monthly* alpha on average (less than $1 million per month) assets under management of $40 million during his first five years of tenure and a 0.20% alpha per month during his last five years on assets of about $10 billion (more than $20 million per month). It is likely that the portfolio management approach evolved as the asset base grew.

- Maximum position size equal to the lesser of 10× the index weight or the index weight plus 150 bps
- No position size that represents more than 5% of the security's average daily trading volume (ADV) over the trailing three months

The smaller securities in Isaac's permissible universe trade about 1% of shares outstanding daily. At what level of AUM is Isaac's strategy likely to be affected by the liquidity and concentration constraints?

Solution to 1:

AUM grew rapidly over the past 20 years. The number of positions in the portfolio nearly quadrupled while assets grew by a factor of 25. Still, there are aspects of his style that have not changed: He is still very much a value manager investing in lower-beta securities. However, the portfolio no longer has a small-cap tilt, and the exposure to the momentum factor has also declined. It is likely that these are both byproducts of the increase in AUM; for example, a large fund has greater difficulty executing in small-cap securities. This last point is supported by the decline in portfolio turnover. The decline in alpha indicates that the growth in AUM has altered the implementation of the investment approach.

Solution to 2:

Based on the index capitalization of $20 trillion, the size constraint indicates that the smallest stocks in his portfolio will have a minimum market cap of about $3 billion (0.015% × $20 trillion). The ADV of the stocks at the lower end of his capitalization constraint would be about $30 million (1% × $3 billion). Because Isaac does not want to represent more than 5% of any security's ADV, the maximum position size for these smaller-cap stocks is about $1.5 million (5% × $30 million). It appears that Isaac's strategy will not be constrained until the portfolio reaches about $1 billion in size ($1.5 million ÷ 0.15% = $1 billion). If the level of AUM exceeds $1 billion, his position size constraints will require the portfolio to hold a larger number of smaller-cap positions. There is room to grow this strategy.

11. THE WELL-CONSTRUCTED PORTFOLIO

g   evaluate the efficiency of a portfolio structure given its investment mandate

A well-constructed portfolio should deliver results consistent with investors' risk and return expectations. It will not guarantee excess return relative to the appropriate benchmark, especially over a shorter horizon, but it will be designed to deliver the risk characteristics desired by the manager and promised to investors. The well-constructed portfolio possesses

- a clear investment philosophy and a consistent investment process,
- risk and structural characteristics as promised to investors,
- a risk-efficient delivery methodology, and
- reasonably low operating costs given the strategy.

Investors and managers may have different requirements with respect to the characteristics they seek in a well-structured portfolio. For some managers, substantial diversification is required, whereas others seek a high-conviction, less diversified strategy.

The Well-Constructed Portfolio

Some investors require formal and heuristic risk metrics that are tightly constrained, and others tolerate more permissive risk limits. A well-structured portfolio must, at the very least, deliver the promised characteristics in a cost- and risk-efficient way.

Consider the following large-cap US equity products, Product A and Product B. Between January 1999 and September 2016, the two products had similar annualized absolute volatility, 15.1% and 15.2%, and similar active risk, 4.9% and 4.8%. However, they differ on other dimensions. Exhibit 21 presents the factor exposure of each product using a six-factor model. The factors are Market, Size, Value, Momentum, Betting against Beta (BAB), and Quality. The exhibit also shows the volatility of each factor. Exhibit 22 illustrates the contribution to the total variance of each product originating from these factors, as well as the portion of total variance that remains unexplained. Other characteristics are also presented.[41]

Exhibit 21 Factor Exposure, January 1999–September 2016

Factor	Product A	Product B	Factor Volatility
Market	0.92	1.08	15.8%
Size	−0.29	0.04	9.7%
Value	0.33	0.06	14.7%
Momentum	0.04	0.06	19.2%
BAB	0.02	0.09	14.4%
Quality	0.03	0.23	11.4%

Sources: Data are from Bloomberg and AQR.

Exhibit 22 Risk Characteristics

	Factor Risk Contribution	
Factor	Product A	Product B
Market	87.4%	105.9%
Size	−2.3%	0.6%
Value	14.0%	1.2%
Momentum	−2.7%	−2.0%
BAB	−0.4%	−2.0%
Quality	−1.6%	−10.5%
Unexplained	5.5%	6.8%
Total	100%	100%

	Other Characteristics	
Number of securities	≈320	≈120
Annualized active risk	4.9%	4.8%

(continued)

---

41 The style of a particular product may evolve over time because of changes in investment philosophy and even changes in the product management team. Although the two products presented in Exhibits 21 and 22 were selected for the consistency of their respective approaches over time, when the period covers several decades, it would be prudent to do factor analyses over several sub periods to determine whether changes in management style did, in fact, occur.

Exhibit 22 (Continued)

	Other Characteristics	
Active Share	0.43	0.80
Annualized volatility	15.1%	15.2%
Maximum drawdown	54.6%	51.8%

Since the two products have similar volatility and active risk, what opinion can we form about the risk efficiency of each product?

Product A exhibits the following relevant characteristics:

- A Market β slightly less than 1
- A large-cap bias (a negative coefficient on the Size factor)
- A very large exposure to the Value factor
- Greater security-level diversification than Product B
- Market risk representing only 87.4% of the total portfolio risk
- A significant portion of the absolute risk attributed to the Value factor

The relevant characteristics for Product B are:

- A Market β slightly more than 1
- A more balanced exposure to all factors
- A large exposure to the Quality factor (although the factor itself has a relatively low volatility)
- Active Share nearly double that of Product A
- Modestly lower drawdowns
- More than 100% of its absolute risk attributed to the Market factor

Thus, Product B's emphasis on quality companies having a high return on equity, a low debt-to-equity ratio, and a low earnings variability is a likely explanation for absolute and relative risk measures that are not significantly different from those of Manager A. That Product B can achieve this level of risk efficiency with less than half the number of securities held by Product A indicates that risk management is an important component of the portfolio construction process of Product B. Although there is no guarantee that a more efficiently risk-structured portfolio will outperform, Product B outperformed Product A by more than 3.1% annually over the period.

In a well-constructed portfolio, we would be looking for risk exposures that are aligned with investor expectations and constraints and low idiosyncratic risk (unexplained) relative to total risk. If two products have comparable factor exposures, the product with a lower absolute volatility and lower active risk will likely be preferred (assuming similar costs). If two products have similar active and absolute risks, the portfolios have similar costs, and the alpha skills of the managers are similar, the product having a higher Active Share is preferable, because it leverages the alpha skills of the manager and will have higher expected returns.

Finally, the "risk efficiency" of any given portfolio approach should be judged in the context of the investor's total portfolio. The active risk of a concentrated stock picker should be higher than that of a diversified factor investor, and the concentrated stock picker may have a lower information ratio. Yet both managers could be building a well-structured portfolio relative to their mandate. It is important to consider the diversification effect of a manager's portfolio on the total portfolio of the investor to arrive at an appropriate solution.

EXAMPLE 8

The Well-Structured Portfolio

David Larrabee is CIO of a pension fund with $5 billion in assets. The fund has 60% of its assets invested in equities with more than 10 managers. Larrabee is considering creating a core equity position that would represent 65% of all equity assets. The remaining 35% would then be allocated to approximately five active satellite (non-core) managers. The core position would be invested in a customized passive portfolio designed specifically for the pension fund using a well-documented construction and rebalancing process. The portfolio would be implemented by a known counterparty at a low cost (less than 10 bps). The main specifications for the custom portfolio were the following:

- Investable universe composed of securities within the MSCI World Index
- Low volatility achieved through an optimization process
- High payout yield (dividend and share repurchase)
- No fewer than 250 securities
- No position greater than 2%
- Average portfolio turnover less than 50% annually

Larrabee understands that a low-volatility objective usually leads to portfolios with large-cap, Value, and Quality biases.

Exhibits 23 and 24 present the results of a pro forma analysis of the custom portfolio. The portfolio was simulated over a period of 12 years. Exhibit 23 presents some key risk and structural characteristics, as well as the average active sector exposure. Exhibit 24 presents the results of factor analyses for both the MSCI World and the custom portfolio.

Exhibit 23

	MSCI World	Custom Portfolio
Return annualized	7.0%	8.45%
Volatility annualized	11.3%	9.0%
Active risk	—	6.0%
Number of securities	1,700	325
Turnover	2.4%	35%
Dividend yield	2.6%	3.6%
Average Active Sector Exposure		
Energy	—	−2.00%
Materials	—	−1.50%
Industrials	—	−1.50%
Consumer discretionary	—	3.00%
Consumer staples	—	4.20%
Health care	—	2.40%
Financials	—	−1.00%
Information technology	—	−10.00%

(continued)

Exhibit 23 (Continued)

	MSCI World	Custom Portfolio
Telecommunication services	—	3.20%
Utilities	—	3.20%

Exhibit 24

	Factor Exposure		Factor Relative Risk Attribution	
	MSCI World	Custom Portfolio	MSCI World	Custom Portfolio
Alpha (annualized)	−1.0%	−3.1%	—	—
Market	1.00	0.84	103%	105%
Size	−0.13	−0.26	−1%	−1%
Value	0.06	0.30	2%	10%
Momentum	0.02	0.02	−1%	−3%
BAB	0.01	0.32	0%	2%
Quality	0.10	0.54	−4%	−22%
Unexplained	—	—	1%	9%

Larrabee has hired you to advise him on the proposed core product. Considering the information provided,

1. Does the pro forma custom portfolio meet the specifications of a well-structured portfolio, and are there any characteristics of this product that concern you?

2. If the custom portfolio were implemented, what recommendations would you make to Larrabee in terms of the style of the satellite managers or in general?

Solution to 1:

The proposed solution is aligned with many of the characteristics of a well-constructed portfolio. It is based on a consistent investment process, and it appears to meet the requirements of the investor: It has significantly lower volatility than the MSCI World and a significantly higher dividend yield (although we do not have the information on the payout yield), the portfolio has a low security concentration, and the estimated turnover is lower than the required limit. It can also be implemented at a low cost. The factor analysis also confirms what we could expect from a high-payout/low-volatility portfolio. The Market beta is significantly below 1, the negative Size coefficient indicates a larger-capitalization bias, and finally, the portfolio has a Value and Quality bias. The risk attribution analysis indicates that the exposure to Quality companies is largely responsible for reducing the total risk of the portfolio.

> However, there are some aspects of the portfolio that create some concerns. Although the custom portfolio meets all of Larrabee's specified objectives, the portfolio construction process leads to a high tracking error (active risk). Given the size of this allocation relative to the total equity portfolio, this poses a problem. Some of this tracking error may be attributed to a significant underallocation to the information technology sector. Finally, although the portfolio would have generated an excess return on average over the past 12 years, the alpha is negative. Understanding the source of this negative alpha is essential. In this instance, the excess return was achieved largely through a very high and intentional exposure to rewarded factors, such as Value, BAB, and Quality, which may not have been rewarded over the simulated period.
>
> **Solution to 2:**
>
> The first recommendation would be to investigate further the source of the significant negative alpha. Because the excess performance is so strongly explained by exposure to specific factors, we should be concerned about how the portfolio would perform if factor returns were to decline. Is there a systemic reason that can explain this observation? Secondly, if tracking error is a concern, it is important to identify satellite managers whose active returns have a low correlation with the core mandate, perhaps even a lower active risk. Finally, considering the importance of the information technology sector, it could be prudent to hire a manager that has a strong technology orientation. The objective is not necessarily to maintain a technology exposure equal to that of the MSCI World Index but perhaps to lower the consistent underexposure to a more reasonable level. At the very least, these structural biases should be continuously monitored.

LONG/SHORT, LONG EXTENSION, AND MARKET-NEUTRAL PORTFOLIO CONSTRUCTION

h discuss the long-only, long extension, long/short, and equitized market-neutral approaches to equity portfolio construction, including their risks, costs, and effects on potential alphas

Long/short, long extension, and market-neutral portfolio approaches are all variations on a theme: Each is predicated on the belief that research insights can be exploited not only in the pursuit of stocks that are expected to perform well but also to profit from the negative insights gathered during the research process. "Long/short" is the most encompassing term and can include long extension and market-neutral products. Most commonly, the term "long/short" refers to strategies that are relatively unconstrained in the extent to which they can lever both positive and negative insights.

Long extension strategies are constrained long/short strategies. The capital committed by the client is invested similarly to a manager's long-only strategy but levered to some extent to exploit the manager's insights on projected losers as well as winners. A typical long-extension strategy is constrained to have a net exposure of 100%; for example, 130% of the capital is invested long and 30% of the capital is invested short, for a net exposure of 100%—the same as it would be in a long-only portfolio. There may or may not be a relationship between the long and the short portfolios.

Market-neutral strategies are long/short portfolios constructed in a manner to ensure that the portfolio's exposures to a wide variety of risk factors is zero. In addition, these portfolios may be neutralized against a wide variety of other risk factors.

12.1 The Merits of Long-Only Investing

An investor's choice of whether to pursue a long-only strategy or some variation of a long/short strategy is likely to be influenced by several considerations:

- Long-term risk premiums
- Capacity and scale (the ability to invest assets)
- Limited legal liability and risk appetite
- Regulatory constraints
- Transactional complexity
- Management costs
- Personal ideology

12.1.1 Long-term risk premiums

A major motivation for investors to be long only is the generally accepted belief that there is a positive long-run premium to be earned from bearing market risk. Investors may also believe that risk premiums can be earned from other sources of risk, such as Size, Value, or Momentum. To capture these risk premiums, investors must over time own (go net "long") the underlying securities that are exposed to these risks. Although risk premiums have been shown to earn a return in the long run, realized risk premium returns can be negative in the short run; the market can and does experience returns less than the risk-free rate, and recall the earlier discussion regarding the cyclicality of the Size, Value, and Momentum factors. For investors with shorter-term investment horizons, the potential benefits of a positive expected risk premium over the long run may not offset the potential risk of market declines or other reversals. These investors may pursue an approach other than strictly long-only investing and may prefer to short-sell some securities.

12.1.2 Capacity and scalability

Long-only investing, particularly strategies that focus on large-cap stocks, generally offers greater investment capacity than other approaches. For example, the MSCI ACWI has a total market cap of nearly $37 trillion, and the 10 largest companies are worth $3.4 trillion.[42] For large institutional investors, such as pension plans, there are no effective capacity constraints in terms of the total market cap available for long-only large-cap investing. Long-only strategies may face capacity constraints, however, if they focus on smaller and illiquid stocks or employ a strategy reliant on a high level of portfolio turnover. Unlike long-only strategies, the capacity of short-selling strategies is limited by the availability of securities to borrow.

12.1.3 Limited legal liability

Common stocks are limited liability financial instruments. The lowest a stock price can fall to is zero, so the maximum amount that a long-only investor in a common stock can lose is the amount of money that she invested in the stock. Thus, long-only investing puts a firm floor on how much an investor can lose. In contrast, a short-seller's potential losses are unlimited in principle. The short-seller loses money as the stock price rises, and there is no ceiling limiting the price increase. This type of "naked"

---

[42] Market cap is not necessarily the same as shares available for general investors, because some shares may be closely held and not traded. Most index providers now calculate "float," which represents shares the public can trade.

short-selling is quite risky. To offset this risk, investors often combine a short-selling strategy with a long-only strategy. Indeed, long/short strategies are often less risky than long-only or short-only strategies.

12.1.4 Regulatory

Some countries ban short-selling activities. Others have temporarily restricted or banned short-selling. For example, on 18 September 2008, the UK Financial Services Authority (FSA) temporarily prohibited the short-selling of financial companies to protect the integrity of the financial system. The US Securities and Exchange Commission (SEC) followed suit the next day. Additionally, many countries that allow short-selling prohibit or restrict naked short-selling, a practice consisting of short-selling a tradable asset without first borrowing the security or ensuring that it can be borrowed.

12.1.5 Transactional complexity

The mechanics of long-only investing are relatively simple and easy to understand. The investment manager instructs a broker (or uses an electronic platform) to buy stock XYZ. The broker executes the trade on the client's behalf and arranges for the security to be delivered to the client's account. Typically, a custodial bank sits between the investment adviser and the client. In this case, the custodian would deliver the cash for the stock and take possession of the shares of XYZ stock. If the shares are held in a custodial bank, the adviser can liquidate the position at any time (a caveat is that to exercise this flexibility completely, the custodian must be instructed not to lend out the shares). In long-only investing, buying and selling stocks are straightforward, intuitive transactions.

A short-selling transaction is more complex. The investor first needs to find shares of stock to borrow. Although many stocks are easy to borrow, others may be hard to locate, and the cost to borrow these shares can be much higher. Investors must also provide collateral to ensure that they can repay the borrowed stock if the price moves up. Borrowed stock may also be recalled at an inopportune time for the short-seller.

In many regions, regulated investment entities must use a custodian for all the transactions. When a custodian is involved, complicated three-party agreements (between the fund, prime broker, and custodian) are required. The agreements govern the buying and selling of securities as well as the management of collateral. An investor who does not use a custodian is exposed to counterparty risk—the collateral is often held in a general operating account of a prime broker. If the prime broker goes bankrupt, the collateral can vanish (which happened to many investors in the Lehman Brothers bankruptcy). Operational risk is significantly greater with long/short investing.

12.1.6 Management costs

Long-only investing is less expensive, both in terms of management fees and from an operational perspective. Managers of long/short products often charge fees that are a multiple of what long-only managers typically charge. Three categories of long/short products are active extension, market neutral, and directional.[43] As of 2016, management fees on active extension strategies usually range from 0.50% to 1.5%, whereas market-neutral and directional strategies typically charge hedge fund fixed fees of 1%–2% and performance fees of 20%. It follows, then, that the investor in a long/short product must have a high degree of confidence in the manager's ability to extract premiums or generate alpha relative to lower-fee, long-only managers.

---

43 See Pavilion (2011).

12.1.7 Personal ideology

Some investors may express a preference for long-only investment for ideological reasons. They may feel that directly gaining from the losses of others is morally wrong, as might be the case in short-selling. Some investors may believe that short-selling requires significantly greater expertise than long-only investing and that such expertise is not reliably available or consistent. And some might argue that short-selling requires significant leverage to achieve the targeted long-term expected return, and they may be unwilling to assume this risk. In short, some investors may "just say no" to anything other than long-only investing.

12.2 Long/Short Portfolio Construction

Investors may be interested in long/short strategies for a variety of reasons. For example, the conviction of negative views can be more strongly expressed when short-selling is permitted than in a long-only approach. In addition, short-selling can help reduce exposures to sectors, regions, or general market movements and allow managers to focus on their unique skill set. Finally, the full extraction of the benefits of risk factors requires a long/short approach (i.e., short large cap and long small cap, short growth and long value, short poor price momentum and long high price momentum, etc.). Long-only investors can profit from only part of the opportunity set.

There are many different styles of long/short strategies, each driven by its own investment thesis. Exhibit 25 presents a range of possible options to structure a long/short portfolio. Implementation of long/short strategies varies with their intended purpose. In a long-only portfolio construction process, the weights assigned to every asset must be greater than or equal to 0 and the weights must sum to 1. In the long/short approach, position weights can be negative and the weights are not necessarily constrained to sum to 1. Some long/short portfolios may even have aggregate exposure of less than 1. The absolute value of the longs minus the absolute value of the shorts is called the portfolio's *net exposure*. The sum of the longs plus the absolute value of the shorts is called the portfolio's *gross exposure*.

A comprehensive use of long/short strategies can also be found in the design of equal-risk-premium products. Such products seek to extract return premiums from rewarded factors, often across asset classes. To do so, the manager must create long/short sub-portfolios extracting these premiums (such as Size, Value, Momentum, and Low Beta) and combine these sub-portfolios using weightings that ensure each component will contribute the same amount of risk to the overall portfolio. The combination may be levered across all sub-portfolios to achieve a specific volatility level. In other words, the manager is using long and short positions as well as leverage (or deleveraging) to achieve the most efficient combination of rewarded factors.

Exhibit 25 Illustrative Long/Short Portfolio Structures (as a percentage of capital)

	Long Positions	Short Positions	Cash	Gross Exposure	Net Exposure
Long only	100	0	0	100	100
130/30 long extension	130	30	0	160	100
Market neutral – low risk	50	50	100	100	0
Market neutral – higher risk	100	100	100	200	0

Exhibit 25   (Continued)

	Long Positions	Short Positions	Cash	Gross Exposure	Net Exposure
Directional – low risk	80	40	60	120	40
Net short	40	100	160	140	−60

Long/short managers typically define their exposure constraints as part of the portfolio construction process. For example, many equity hedge funds have a strategy of targeting a gross exposure (long plus short) of 150%–200% while targeting a net exposure (long minus short) of 0%–60%. A net exposure greater than zero implies some positive exposure to the Market factor. Regardless of the investment approach, all long/short strategies must establish parameters regarding the desired level of gross and net exposure, and these parameters will provide the investor with meaningful information about the manager's strategy and its expected risk profile.

12.3 Long Extension Portfolio Construction

Long extension strategies are a hybrid of long-only and long/short strategies. They are often called "enhanced active equity" strategies. A particular enhanced active equity strategy called "130/30" was popular until the market decline during the global financial crisis.[44] This strategy is making inroads again as investors better understand the potential pitfalls of shorting and are seeking more return in a low interest rate environment. A 130/30 strategy builds a portfolio of long positions worth 130% of the wealth invested in the strategy—that is, 1.3 times the amount of capital. At the same time, the portfolio holds short positions worth 30% of capital. The long and short positions combined equal 100% of capital. In essence, the short positions are funding the excess long positions, and the resulting gross leverage (160% = 130% + 30%) potentially allows for greater alpha and a more efficient exposure to rewarded factors. Unlike leverage incurred via cash borrowing in a long-only portfolio, which can be used only to exploit *long* insights, the long/short approach allows the portfolio to benefit not only from insights on companies that are forecasted to perform well (the long positions) but also from insights on companies forecasted to perform poorly (the short positions). In theory, this strategy offers the opportunity to magnify total returns. Of course, the long/short approach could also lead to greater losses if the manager is simultaneously wrong on both his long and short picks.

Another benefit of the 130/30 strategy is that long-only managers are limited in their ability to underallocate to securities that have a small initial allocation in the benchmark. For example, if Security X has a 0.25% allocation within the benchmark, a long-only manager can express a negative view on the stock only to the extent of its 0.25% benchmark weight by omitting the security from the portfolio. A 130/30 strategy affords the possibility of sizing the underweight in line with the manager's expectations for the stock. This ability allows the strength of the positive and negative views to be expressed more symmetrically.

---

[44] 130/30 strategies can accentuate losses. For example, Value strategies performed poorly during the financial crisis of 2007–2008, whereas Momentum strategies performed poorly after March 2009, as the equity markets rebounded. Many 130/30 products were built on these rewarded factors and performed poorly.

12.4 Market-Neutral Portfolio Construction

Market-neutral portfolio construction is a specialized form of long/short portfolio construction. At a very simple, naive level, one might think that in this strategy, the dollars invested in long securities are identical to the dollars associated with short-selling—that is, a portfolio with zero net investment, often called "dollar neutral." But dollar neutral is not the same thing as market neutral, because the economic drivers of returns for the long side may not be the same as the economic drivers for the short side.

True market-neutral strategies hedge out most market risk. They are often employed when the investor wants to remove the effects of general market movements from returns to explicitly focus on the manager's skill in forecasting returns of stocks, sectors, factors, or geographic regions. In essence, the investor wants to remove the "noise" that market movements can create to better focus on the creation of positive abnormal returns. In isolation, this strategy could be considered risky. For example, if stock prices appreciate rapidly (and historically, stock prices do rise), then the investor would miss out on this appreciation. However, some investors might add this type of strategy to their overall portfolio to increase diversification and at least partially offset losses in other parts of the portfolio when stock prices decline.

Market-neutral portfolio construction attempts to exactly match and offset the systematic risks of the long positions with those of the short positions. For example, if one uses beta as the measure of systematic risk, then a market-neutral portfolio, using longs and shorts, would have a Market beta of zero. A simple example of zero-beta investment would be a fund that is long $100 of assets with a Market beta of 1 and short $80 of assets with a Market beta of 1.25. This concept can be extended to include other systematic factors that influence returns, such as Size, Value, and Momentum. In other words, the market-neutral concept can be implemented for a variety of risk factors. The main constraint is that in aggregate, the targeted beta(s) of the portfolio be zero.

A market-neutral strategy is still expected to generate a positive information ratio. Although market neutral may seek to eliminate market risk and perhaps some other risks on an *ex ante* basis, the manager cannot eliminate all risks. If she could—and did—the expected return would likely be equal to the risk-free rate minus the manager's fees. The objective is to neutralize the risks for which the manager believes she has no comparative forecasting advantage, thus allowing the manager to concentrate on her very specific skills.

Given that market-neutral strategies seek to remove major sources of systematic risk from a portfolio, these strategies are usually less volatile than long-only strategies. They are often considered absolute return strategies because their benchmarks might be fixed-income instruments. Even if a market-neutral strategy is not fully successful in its implementation, the correlation of market-neutral strategies with other types of strategies is typically quite low. Thus, some market-neutral strategies may serve more of a diversification role in a portfolio, rather than a high-return-seeking role.

A specific form of market-neutral strategy is pairs trading, where an investor will go long one security in an industry and short another security in the same industry, trying to exploit what the investor perceives as "mispricing." A more quantitatively oriented form of pairs trading called *statistical arbitrage* ("stat arb") uses statistical techniques to identify two securities that are historically highly correlated with each other. When the price correlation of these two securities deviates from its long-term average (and if the manager believes that the deviation is temporary), the manager will go long the underperforming stock and simultaneously short the outperforming stock. If the prices do converge to the long-term average as forecasted, the manager will close the trade and realize a profit.

In other variations of market-neutral investing, one might find portfolios constructed with hundreds of securities identified using systematic multi-factor models that evaluate all securities in the investable universe. The manager will buy the most favorably ranked securities and short the least favorably ranked ones. The manager may impose constraints on exposures of the longs and the shorts to keep gross and net exposures at the desired levels.

Market-neutral strategies have two inherent limitations:

1. Practically speaking, it is no easy task to maintain a beta of zero. Not all risks can be efficiently hedged, and correlations between exposures are continually shifting.
2. Market-neutral strategies have a limited upside in a bull market unless they are "equitized." Some investors, therefore, choose to index their equity exposure and overlay long/short strategies. In this case, the investor is not abandoning equity-like returns and is using the market-neutral portfolio as an overlay.

12.5 Benefits and Drawbacks of Long/Short Strategies

Long/short strategies offer the following benefits:

- Ability to more fully express short ideas than under a long-only strategy
- Efficient use of leverage and of the benefits of diversification
- Greater ability to calibrate/control exposure to factors (such as Market and other rewarded factors), sectors, geography, or any undesired exposure (such as, perhaps, sensitivity to the price of oil)

We've explored the first two benefits of long/short portfolio construction listed above. Let's look more closely at the last one.

A fully invested long-only strategy will be exposed to market risk. To reduce the level of market risk, the manager must either concentrate holdings in low-beta stocks or hold a portion of the assets in cash, an asset that produces minimal return. Conversely, to increase the level of market risk, the long-only manager must own high-beta stocks or use financial leverage; the cost of leverage will reduce future returns. Practically speaking, the portfolio beta of a long-only manager is likely constrained within a range of, say, 0.8–1.2. In contrast, a long/short manager has much more flexibility in adjusting his level of market exposure to reflect his view on the current opportunities.

In long-only portfolios, total portfolio risk is dominated by the Market factor, and the Market factor is a long-only factor. However, all other factor returns can be thought of as long/short portfolios: *Size* is long small cap and short large cap, *Value* is long value and short growth, *Momentum* is long positive momentum and short less positive or negative momentum, and so on. Just like with beta, the ability to tilt a portfolio in favor of these other factors or diversify efficiently across factors is structurally restricted in a long-only portfolio. Because the average of cross correlations among rewarded factors is close to zero or even negative, efficiently allocating across factors could bring significant diversification benefits. But the ability to reduce overall risk and to distribute sources of risk more evenly cannot be optimally achieved without short-selling.

Strategies that short securities contain the following inherent risks, which must be understood:

1. Unlike a long position, a short position will move against the manager if the price of the security increases.
2. Long/short strategies sometimes require significant leverage. Leverage must be used wisely.

3   The cost of borrowing a security can become prohibitive, particularly if the security is hard to borrow.

4   Collateral requirements will increase if a short position moves against the manager. In extreme cases, the manager may be forced to liquidate some favorably ranked long positions (and short positions that might eventually reverse) if too much leverage has been used. The manager may also fall victim to a short squeeze. A short squeeze is a situation in which the price of the stock that has been shorted has risen so much and so quickly that many short investors may be unable to maintain their positions in the short run in light of the increased collateral requirements. The "squeeze" is worsened as short-sellers liquidate their short position, buying back the security and possibly pushing the price even higher.

As previously indicated, to short-sell securities, investors typically rely on a prime broker who can help them locate the securities they wish to borrow. But the prime broker will require collateral from the short-sellers to assure the lenders of these securities that their contracts will be honored. The higher the relative amount of short-selling in a portfolio, the greater the amount of collateral required. A portfolio with 20% of capital invested short may be required to put up collateral equal to 40% of the short positions, whereas a portfolio with 100% of capital invested short could be required to put up collateral equal to 200% of the short positions. In addition, different types of assets are weighed differently in the calculation of collateral value. For example, a US Treasury bill may be viewed as very safe collateral and accorded 100% of its value toward the required collateral. In contrast, a high-yield bond or some other asset with restricted liquidity would have only a portion of its market value counted toward the collateral requirement.

These collateral requirements are designed to protect the lender in the event of adverse price movements. When stock prices are rising rapidly, the lender may recall all the borrowed shares, fearing that the borrower's collateral will be wiped out. If this were to happen, the leveraged long/short manager would be forced to close out his short positions at an inopportune time, leaving significant profits on the table. In the end, long/short investing is a compromise between return impacts, sources of risk, and costs, as illustrated in the table below.

Benefits	Costs
■ Short positions can reduce market risk. ■ Shorting potentially expands benefits from other risk premiums and alpha. ■ The combination of long and short positions allows for a greater diversification potential.	■ Short positions might reduce the market return premium. ■ Shorting may amplify the active risk (but please note that it does note have to do so). ■ There are higher implementation costs and greater complexity associated with shorting and leverage relative to a long-only approach.

EXAMPLE 9

Creating a 130/30 Strategy

Alpha Prime has been managing long-only equity portfolios for more than 15 years. The firm has a systematic investment process built around assessing security valuation and price momentum. Each company is attributed a standardized score (F_k) that is based on a combination of quantitative and fundamental metrics. Positions are selected from among those securities with a positive standardized score and are weighted based on the strength of that score. The security weightings within sectors can be significantly different from those of the benchmark, but the portfolio's sector weightings adhere closely to the benchmark weights. Investment decisions are made by the portfolio management team and are re-evaluated monthly. A constrained optimization process is used to guide investment decision making. Listed below are the objective function and the primary constraints used by the firm.

- *Objective function:* Maximize the portfolio factor score
- *Total exposure constraint:* Sum of portfolio weights must = 1
- *Individual security constraint:* Minimum weight of 0% and maximum weight of 3%
- *Sector constraint:* Benchmark weight ±5%
- *Constraint on active risk (TE):* Active risk less than 5%

The managers at Alpha Prime have realized that their investment process can also generate a negative signal, indicating that a security is likely to underperform. However, the signal is not quite as reliable or stable when it is used for this purpose. There is much more noise around the performance of the expected losers than there is around the performance of the winners. Still, the signal has value.

1. You are asked to draft guidelines for the creation of a 130/30 strategy. What changes to the objective function and to each of the constraints would you recommend?
2. Discuss the potential challenges of incorporating short positions into the portfolio strategy.

Solution to 1:

- *Objective function:* The objective function would remain the same. Securities with a positive standardized score would be eligible for positive weights, and securities with a negative standardized factor score would receive negative weights (the fund would short these securities).
- *Total exposure constraint:* The portfolio now needs a constraint for gross exposure and one for net exposure. The net exposure constraint in a 130/30 product is constrained to 100%. (The notional value of the longs minus the absolute value of the shorts must be equal to 1.) The portfolio's gross exposure constraint is implicit in the nature of the 130/30 product. (The notional value of the longs plus the absolute value of the shorts cannot exceed 160%.)
- *Individual security constraint:* To take advantage of the negative signals from the model, the portfolio must allow shorting. The minimum weight constraint must be relaxed. Given the issues associated with short-selling, the firm's relative inexperience in this area, and the lower reliability of the short signal, the maximum short position size should be smaller than the maximum long position size. One might recommend that the initial short constraint be set at 1%. Position limits on the long side could stay the same, but that would likely lead to more long positions, given the increase in long exposure to 130%. The manager must assess whether to expand the number of securities held in the portfolio or to raise the maximum position size limit.

- *Sector constraint:* There is no need to change the aggregate sector constraint. The manager now has the ability to offset any overweight on the long side with a short position that would bring the portfolio's exposure to that sector back within the current constraint.

- *Tracking error target:* Sector deviations have a greater bearing on active risk than do security-level differences. Alpha Prime's sector bets are very limited; thus, no change in the tracking error constraint is necessary. The ability to short gives them greater opportunity to exploit investment ideas without changing the firm's approach to sector weightings.

Solution to 2:

Shorting adds complexity to both the operational and the risk aspects of portfolio management. Operationally, the firm must establish relationships with one or more prime brokers and ensure that adequate collateral for the short positions remains available. Some securities can be difficult to borrow, and the cost of borrowing some stocks can be prohibitive. This may inhibit Alpha Prime's ability to implement its short ideas and will raise the operational costs of running the portfolio. In addition, shorting introduces a new type of risk: A short transaction has no loss limit. If the stock moves against the manager in the short run, the manager may have to close the position before he is proven right.

EXAMPLE 10

Long Only vs. Long/Short

Marc Salter has been running a long-only unlevered factor-based strategy in the US market for more than five years. He has delivered a product that has all the expected exposure to rewarded risk factors promised to investors. Salter just met with a pension fund investor looking at a multi-factor based approach. However, the pension fund manager indicates they are also considering investing with a competitor that runs a leveraged long/short factor-based strategy. It appears the competitor's product has a significantly higher information ratio. The product of the competitor neutralizes market risk and concentrates on exposure to other rewarded factors.

1 Why would the competitor's long/short product have a higher information ratio?
2 What are its drawbacks?

Solution to 1:

Factor returns are usually built from a long portfolio having the desired factor characteristic against a short portfolio that does not. A long-only factor investor is limited in his ability to short (relative to the benchmark) positions that do not have the desired characteristics. Adding the ability to leverage negative as well as positive research insights should improve the transfer coefficient and increase the potential to generate better excess returns.

In addition, in a long-only strategy, the Market factor dominates all other risks. Adding the ability to short could facilitate a more balanced distribution of risk. Given the similar volatilities and low cross correlations among factors, the more balanced distribution of risk can be expected to reduce the tracking error of the strategy, thereby improving the information ratio.

> **Solution to 2:**
> Multi-factor products often contain several hundred securities, some of which may be difficult to borrow. The complexity of shorting across this large number of names combined with higher management fees and implementation costs may necessitate more implementation constraints on the short side.
>
> Removing the risk associated with the Market factor implies that the long/short product would most likely be used as an overlay on long-only mandates. The mandate may also be leveraged (more than 1× long and 1× short) to maximize the potential return per dollar of capital. For example, equal-risk-premium products (that remove the effect of the Market factor) often need three units of leverage long and short to achieve a 10% absolute risk target. Some investors may be uncomfortable with such leverage.

SUMMARY

Active equity portfolio construction strives to make sure that superior insights about forecasted returns get efficiently reflected in realized portfolio performance. Active equity portfolio construction is about thoroughly understanding the return objectives of a portfolio, as well as its acceptable risk levels, and then finding the right mix of securities that balances predicted returns against risk and other impediments that can interfere with realizing these returns. These principles apply to long-only, long/short, long-extension, and market-neutral approaches. Below, we highlight the discussions of this reading.

- The four main building blocks of portfolio construction are the following:
  - Overweight, underweight, or neutralize rewarded factors: The four most recognized factors known to offer a persistent return premium are Market, Size, Value, and Momentum.
  - Alpha skills: Timing factors, securities, and markets. Finding new factors and enhancing existing factors.
  - Sizing positions to account for risk and active weights.
  - Breadth of expertise: A manager's ability to consistently outperform his benchmark increases when that performance can be attributed to a larger sample of independent decisions. Independent decisions are uncorrelated decisions.
- Managers can rely on a combination of approaches to implement their core beliefs:
  - Systematic vs. discretionary
    - Systematic strategies incorporate research-based rules across a broad universe of securities.
    - Discretionary strategies integrate the judgment of the manager on a smaller subset of securities.
  - Bottom up vs. top down
    - A bottom-up manager evaluates the risk and return characteristics of individual securities. The aggregate of these risk and return expectations implies expectations for the overall economic and market environment.

- A top-down manager starts with an understanding of the overall market environment and then projects how the expected environment will affect countries, asset classes, sectors, and securities.
    - Benchmark aware vs. benchmark agnostic
- Portfolio construction can be framed as an optimization problem using an objective function and a set of constraints. The objective function of a systematic manager will be specified explicitly, whereas that of a discretionary manager may be set implicitly.
- Risk budgeting is a process by which the total risk appetite of the portfolio is allocated among the various components of portfolio choice.
- Active risk (tracking error) is a function of the portfolio's exposure to systematic risks and the level of idiosyncratic, security-specific risk. It is a relevant risk measure for benchmark-relative portfolios.
- Absolute risk is the total volatility of portfolio returns independent of a benchmark. It is the most appropriate risk measure for portfolios with an absolute return objective.
- Active Share measures the extent to which the number and sizing of positions in a manager's portfolio differ from the benchmark.
- Benchmark-agnostic managers usually have a greater level of Active Share and most likely have a greater level of active risk.
- An effective risk management process requires that the portfolio manager
    - determine which type of risk measure is most appropriate,
    - understand how each aspect of the strategy contributes to its overall risk,
    - determine what level of risk budget is appropriate, and
    - effectively allocate risk among individual positions/factors.
- Risk constraints may be either formal or heuristic. Heuristic constraints may impose limits on
    - concentration by security, sector, industry, or geography;
    - net exposures to risk factors, such as Beta, Size, Value, and Momentum;
    - net exposures to currencies;
    - the degree of leverage;
    - the degree of illiquidity;
    - exposures to reputational/environmental risks, such as carbon emissions; and
    - other attributes related to an investor's core concerns.
- Formal risk constraints are statistical in nature. Formal risk measures include the following:
    - Volatility—the standard deviation of portfolio returns
    - Active risk—also called *tracking error* or *tracking risk*
    - Skewness—a measure of the degree to which return expectations are non-normally distributed
    - Drawdown—a measure of portfolio loss from its high point until it begins to recover
    - Value at risk (VaR)—the minimum loss that would be expected a certain percentage of the time over a certain period of time given the modeled market conditions, typically expressed as the minimum loss that can be expected to occur 5% of the time

- CVaR (expected tail loss or expected shortfall)—the average loss that would be incurred if the VaR cutoff is exceeded
- IVaR—the change in portfolio VaR when adding a new position to a portfolio
- MVaR—the effect on portfolio risk of a change in the position size. In a diversified portfolio, it may be used to determine the contribution of each asset to the overall VaR.

■ Portfolio management costs fall into two categories: explicit costs and implicit costs. Implicit costs include delay and slippage.

■ The costs of managing assets may affect the investment strategy and the portfolio construction process.
- Slippage costs are significantly greater for smaller-cap securities and during periods of high volatility.
- A strategy that demands immediate execution is likely to incur higher market impact costs.
- A patient manager can mitigate market impact costs by slowly building up positions as liquidity becomes available, but he exposes himself to greater volatility/trend price risk.

■ A well-constructed portfolio exhibits
- a clear investment philosophy and a consistent investment process,
- risk and structural characteristics as promised to investors,
- a risk-efficient delivery methodology, and
- reasonably low operating costs.

■ Long/short investing is a compromise between
- reducing risk and not capturing fully the market risk premium,
- expanding the return potential from alpha and other risk premiums at the potential expense of increasing active risk, and
- achieving greater diversification and higher costs and complexity.

REFERENCES

Amihud, Yakov. 2002. "Illiquidity and Stock Returns: Cross-Section and Time-Series Effects." *Journal of Financial Markets*, vol. 5, no. 1: 31–56.

Asness, Cliff. 2017. "Factor Timing Is Hard." *Cliff's Perspective*, AQR.

Bender, Jennifer, P. Brett Hammond, and William Mok. 2014. "Can Alpha Be Captured by Risk Premia?" *Journal of Portfolio Management*, vol. 40, no. 2 (Winter): 18–29.

Black, Fischer. 1972. "Capital Market Equilibrium with Restricted Borrowing." *Journal of Business*, vol. 45, no. 3: 444–455.

Carhart, Mark M. 1997. "On Persistence in Mutual Fund Performance." *Journal of Finance*, vol. 52: 57–82.

Ceria, Sebastian. 2015. "Active Is as Active Does: Active Share vs. Tracking Error." FactSet 2015 Symposium (March).

Clarke, Roger, Harindra de Silva, and Steven Thorley. 2002. "Portfolio Constraints and the Fundamental Law of Active Management." *Financial Analysts Journal*, vol. 58, no. 5 (September/October): 48–66.

Fama, Eugene F., and Kenneth French. 1992. "The Cross-Section of Expected Stock Returns." *Journal of Finance*, vol. 47, no. 2 (June): 427–465.

Frazzini, Andrea, and Lasse Heje Pedersen. 2014. "Betting against Beta." *Journal of Financial Economics*, vol. 111, no. 1: 1–25.

Frazzini, Andrea, Ronen Israel, and Tobias Moskowitz. 2012. "Trading Costs of Asset Pricing Anomalies." Fama–Miller Center for Research in Finance, University of Chicago Booth School of Business Paper 14–05.

Grinold, R.C. 1989. "The Fundamental Law of Active Management." *Journal of Portfolio Management*, vol. 15: 30–37.

Hasbrouck, Joel. 2009. "Trading Costs and Returns for US Equities: Estimating Effective Costs from Daily Date." *Journal of Finance*, vol. 64, no. 3: 1445–1477.

Ilmanen, Antti. 2011. *Expected Returns: An Investor's Guide to Harvesting Market Rewards*. New York: John Wiley & Sons.

Kahn, Ronald N., and Michael Lemmon. 2016. "The Asset Manager's Dilemma: How Smart Beta Is Disrupting the Investment Management Industry." *Financial Analysts Journal*, vol. 72, no. 1 (January/February): 15–20.

Langlois, Hugues, and Jacques Lussier. 2017. *Rational Investing: The Subtleties of Asset Management*. New York: Columbia Business School Publishing.

MacQueen, Jason. 2007. "Portfolio Risk Decomposition (and Risk Budgeting)." Series of talks presented by R-Squared Risk Management Limited.

Pavilion. 2011. "Long/Short as Long-Only Equity Replacement—Evaluation of Long/Short Strategies: Active Extension, Equity Market Neutral and Directional" (November–December).

Petajisto, Antti. 2013. "Active Share and Mutual Fund Performance." *Financial Analysts Journal*, vol. 69, no. 4 (July/August): 73–93.

Sapra, Steve, and Manny Hunjan. 2013. "Active Share, Tracking Error and Manager Style." PIMCO Quantitative Research and Analytics (October).

Simons, Katerina. 2000. "The Use of Value at Risk by Institutional Investors." *New England Economic Review*, November/December: 21–30.

Taleb, Nassim Nicolas. 1997. *Dynamic Hedging: Managing Vanilla and Exotic Options*. New York: John Wiley & Sons.

Yeung, Danny, Paolo Pellizzari, Ron Bird, and Sazali Abidin. 2012. "Diversification versus Concentration . . . and the Winner Is?" Working Paper 18, University of Technology, Sydney (September).

PRACTICE PROBLEMS

The following information relates to questions 1–8

Monongahela Ap is an equity fund analyst. His manager asks him to evaluate three actively managed equity funds from a single sponsor, Chiyodasenko Investment Corp. Ap's assessments of the funds based on assets under management (AUM), the three main building blocks of portfolio construction, and the funds' approaches to portfolio management are presented in Exhibit 1. Selected data for Fund 1 is presented in Exhibit 2.

Exhibit 1 Ap's Assessments of Funds 1, 2, and 3

Fund	Fund Category	Fund Size (AUM)	Number of Securities	Description
1	Small-cap stocks	Large	Small	Fund 1 focuses on skillfully timing exposures to factors, both rewarded and unrewarded, and to other asset classes. The fund's managers use timing skills to opportunistically shift their portfolio to capture returns from factors such as country, asset class, and sector. Fund 1 prefers to make large trades.
2	Large-cap stocks	Large	Large	Fund 2 holds a diversified portfolio and is concentrated in terms of factors. It targets individual securities that reflect the manager's view that growth firms will outperform value firms. Fund 2 builds up its positions slowly, using unlit venues when possible.
3	Small-cap stocks	Small	Large	Fund 3 holds a highly diversified portfolio. The fund's managers start by evaluating the risk and return characteristics of individual securities and then build their portfolio based on their stock-specific forecasts. Fund 3 prefers to make large trades.

Exhibit 2 Selected Data for Fund 1

Factor	Market	Size	Value	Momentum
Coefficient	1.080	0.098	−0.401	0.034
Variance of the market factor return and covariances with the market factor return	0.00109	0.00053	0.00022	−0.00025
Portfolio's monthly standard deviation of returns				3.74%

Ap learns that Chiyodasenko has initiated a new equity fund. It is similar to Fund 1 but scales up active risk by doubling all of the active weights relative to Fund 1. The new fund aims to scale active return linearly with active risk, but implementation is problematic. Because of the cost and difficulty of borrowing some securities, the new fund cannot scale up its short positions to the same extent that it can scale up its long positions.

Ap reviews quarterly holdings reports for Fund 3. In comparing the two most recent quarterly reports, he notices differences in holdings that indicate that Fund 3 executed two trades, with each trade involving pairs of stocks. Initially, Fund 3 held active positions in two automobile stocks—one was overweight by 1 percentage point (pp), and the other was underweight by 1pp. Fund 3 traded back to benchmark weights on those two stocks. In the second trade, Fund 3 selected two different stocks that were held at benchmark weights, one energy stock and one financial stock. Fund 3 overweighted the energy stock by 1pp and underweighted the financial stock by 1pp.

In Fund 3's latest quarterly report, Ap reads that Fund 3 implemented a new formal risk control for its forecasting model that constrains the predicted return distribution so that no more than 60% of the deviations from the mean are negative.

1. Based on Exhibit 1, the main building block of portfolio construction on which Fund 1 focuses is *most likely*:
   A alpha skills.
   B position sizing.
   C rewarded factor weightings.

2. Which fund in Exhibit 1 *most likely* follows a bottom-up approach?
   A Fund 1
   B Fund 2
   C Fund 3

3. Which fund in Exhibit 1 *most likely* has the greatest implicit costs to implement its strategy?
   A Fund 1
   B Fund 2
   C Fund 3

4. Based on Exhibit 2, the portion of total portfolio risk that is explained by the market factor in Fund 1's existing portfolio is *closest* to:
   A 3%.
   B 81%.
   C 87%.

5. Relative to Fund 1, Chiyodasenko's new equity fund will *most likely* exhibit a lower:
   A information ratio.
   B idiosyncratic risk.
   C collateral requirement.

6. As a result of Fund 3's two trades, the portfolio's active risk *most likely*:
   A decreased.
   B remained unchanged.
   C increased.

7. What was the effect of Fund 3's two trades on its active share? Fund 3's active share:

Practice Problems

    A decreased.

    B remained unchanged.

    C increased.

8 Which risk measure does Fund 3's new risk control explicitly constrain?

    A Volatility

    B Skewness

    C Drawdown

The following information relates to questions 9–15

Ayanna Chen is a portfolio manager at Aycrig Fund, where she supervises assistant portfolio manager Mordechai Garcia. Aycrig Fund invests money for high-net-worth and institutional investors. Chen asks Garcia to analyze certain information relating to Aycrig Fund's three sub-managers, Managers A, B, and C.

Manager A has $250 million in assets under management (AUM), an active risk of 5%, an information coefficient of 0.15, and a transfer coefficient of 0.40. Manager A's portfolio has a 2.5% expected active return this year.

Chen directs Garcia to determine the maximum position size that Manager A can hold in shares of Pasliant Corporation, which has a market capitalization of $3.0 billion, an index weight of 0.20%, and an average daily trading volume (ADV) of 1% of its market capitalization.

Manager A has the following position size policy constraints:

- Allocation: No investment in any security may represent more than 3% of total AUM.
- Liquidity: No position size may represent more than 10% of the dollar value of the security's ADV.
- Index weight: The maximum position weight must be less than or equal to 10 times the security's weight in the index.

Manager B holds a highly diversified portfolio that has balanced exposures to rewarded risk factors, high active share, and a relatively low active risk target.

Selected data on Manager C's portfolio, which contains three assets, is presented in Exhibit 1.

Exhibit 1   Selected Data on Manager C's Portfolio

	Portfolio Weight	Standard Deviation	Covariance Asset 1	Asset 2	Asset 3
Asset 1	30%	25.00%	0.06250	0.01050	0.00800
Asset 2	45%	14.00%	0.01050	0.01960	0.00224
Asset 3	25%	8.00%	0.00800	0.00224	0.00640

Chen considers adding a fourth sub-manager and evaluates three managers' portfolios, Portfolios X, Y, and Z. The managers for Portfolios X, Y, and Z all have similar costs, fees, and alpha skills, and their factor exposures align with both Aycrig's and investors' expectations and constraints. The portfolio factor exposures, risk contributions, and risk characteristics are presented in Exhibits 2 and 3.

Exhibit 2 Portfolio Factor Exposures and Factor Risk Contribution

	Factor Exposure			Factor Risk Contribution		
	Portfolio X	Portfolio Y	Portfolio Z	Portfolio X	Portfolio Y	Portfolio Z
Market	1.07	0.84	1.08	103%	82%	104%
Size	−0.13	0.15	−0.12	−2%	7%	−3%
Value	0.04	0.30	0.05	−5%	18%	−6%
Momentum	0.08	0.02	0.07	7%	−3%	7%
Quality	0.10	0.35	0.11	−4%	−21%	−5%
Unexplained	—	—	—	1%	17%	3%
Total	n/a	n/a	n/a	100%	100%	100%

Exhibit 3 Portfolio Risk Characteristics

	Portfolio X	Portfolio Y	Portfolio Z
Annualized volatility	10.50%	13.15%	15.20%
Annualized active risk	2.90%	8.40%	4.20%
Active share	0.71	0.74	0.63

Chen and Garcia next discuss characteristics of long–short and long-only investing. Garcia makes the following statements about investing with long–short and long-only managers:

Statement 1 A long–short portfolio allows for a gross exposure of 100%.

Statement 2 A long-only portfolio generally allows for greater investment capacity than other approaches, particularly when using strategies that focus on large-cap stocks.

Chen and Garcia then turn their attention to portfolio management approaches. Chen prefers an approach that emphasizes security-specific factors, engages in factor timing, and typically leads to portfolios that are generally more concentrated than those built using a systematic approach.

9 The number of truly independent decisions Manager A would need to make in order to earn her expected active portfolio return this year is *closest* to:

   A 8.

   B 11.

   C 69.

10 Which of the following position size policy constraints is the most restrictive in setting Manager A's maximum position size in shares of Pasliant Corporation?

Practice Problems

    A Liquidity

    B Allocation

    C Index weight

11 Manager B's portfolio is *most likely* consistent with the characteristics of a:

    A pure indexer.

    B sector rotator.

    C multi-factor manager.

12 Based on Exhibit 1, the contribution of Asset 2 to Manager C's portfolio variance is *closest to*:

    A 0.0025.

    B 0.0056.

    C 0.0088.

13 Based on Exhibits 2 and 3, which portfolio *best* exhibits the risk characteristics of a well-constructed portfolio?

    A Portfolio X

    B Portfolio Y

    C Portfolio Z

14 Which of Garcia's statements regarding investing with long–short and long-only managers is correct?

    A Only Statement 1

    B Only Statement 2

    C Both Statement 1 and Statement 2

15 Chen's preferred portfolio management approach would be *best* described as:

    A top down.

    B systematic.

    C discretionary.

SOLUTIONS

1. A is correct. The three main building blocks of portfolio construction are alpha skills, position sizing, and rewarded factor weightings. Fund 1 generates active returns by skillfully timing exposures to factors, both rewarded and unrewarded, and to other asset classes, which constitute a manager's alpha skills.

2. C is correct. Bottom-up managers evaluate the risk and return characteristics of individual securities and build portfolios based on stock-specific forecasts; Fund 3 follows this exact approach. Example views of bottom-up managers include expecting one auto company to outperform another, expecting a pharmaceutical company to outperform an auto company, and expecting a technology company to outperform a pharmaceutical company. Both bottom-up and top-down managers can be either diversified or concentrated in terms of securities.

3. A is correct. Because Fund 1 has a large AUM but focuses on small-cap stocks, holds a relatively small number of securities in its portfolio, and prefers to make large trades, Fund 1 likely has the highest implicit costs. Each of these characteristics serves to increase the market impact of its trades. Market impact is a function of the security's liquidity and trade size. The larger a trade size relative to a stock's average daily volume, the more likely it is that the trade will affect prices. The relatively low level of trading volume of small-cap stocks can be a significant implementation hurdle for a manager running a strategy with significant assets under management and significant positive active weights on smaller companies.

4. C is correct. The portion of total portfolio risk explained by the market factor is calculated in two steps. The first step is to calculate the contribution of the market factor to total portfolio variance as follows:

$$CV\text{market factor} = \sum_{j=1}^{n} x_{market\ factor} x_j C_{mf,j} = x_{market\ factor} \sum_{j=1}^{n} x_j C_{mf,j}$$

where

$CV_{market\ factor}$ = contribution of the market factor to total portfolio variance
$x_{market\ factor}$ = weight of the market factor in the portfolio
x_j = weight of factor j in the portfolio
$C_{mf,j}$ = covariance between the market factor and factor j

The variance attributed to the market factor is as follows:

$CV_{market\ factor}$ = (1.080 × 0.00109 × 1.080) + (1.080 × 0.00053 × 0.098) + (1.080 × 0.00022 × –0.401) + (1.080 × –0.00025 × 0.034)

$CV_{market\ factor}$ = 0.001223

The second step is to divide the resulting variance attributed to the market factor by the portfolio variance of returns, which is the square of the standard deviation of returns:

Portion of total portfolio risk explained by the market factor = $0.001223/(0.0374)^2$

Portion of total portfolio risk explained by the market factor = 87%

Solutions 385

5   A is correct. As the new fund scales up active risk by doubling active weights, it will face implementation constraints that will prevent it from increasing the weights of many of its short positions. The information ratio (IR) is defined as the ratio of active return to active risk. If there were no constraints preventing the new fund from scaling up active weights, it could scale up active risk by scaling up active weights, proportionally increase active return, and keep the IR unchanged. Implementation constraints experienced by the new fund, however, such as the cost and difficulty in borrowing securities to support the scaled-up short positions, will prevent the active return from proportionally increasing with the active risk. Therefore, the IR would most likely be lower for the new fund than for Fund 1. As the following chart illustrates, as active risk is scaled up, implementation constraints create diminishing returns to scale for active returns, thereby degrading the IR.

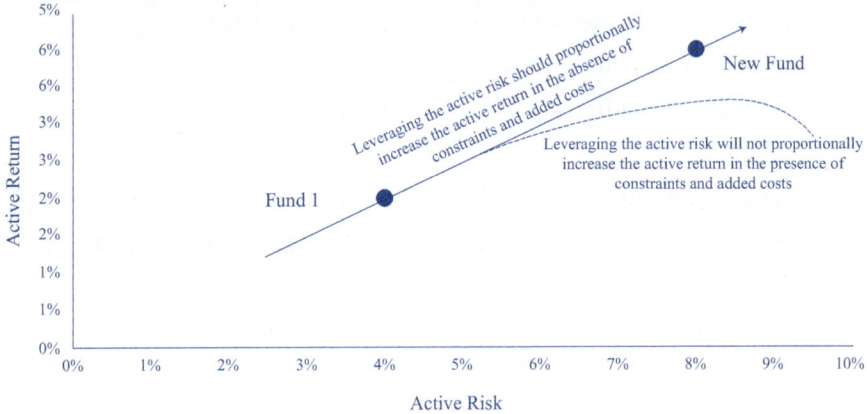

6   C is correct. Active risk is affected by the degree of cross-correlation. The correlation of two stocks in different sectors is most likely lower than the correlation of two stocks in the same sector. Therefore, the correlation of the energy/financial pair is most likely lower than that of the automobile/automobile pair. Because both positions were implemented as an overweight and underweight, the lower correlation of the two stocks in the new position should contribute more to active risk than the two-stock position that it replaced.

7   B is correct. Active share changes only if the total of the absolute values of the portfolio's active weights changes. For the two trades in Fund 3, both the initial position and the new position involved two stocks such that one was 1pp underweighted and the other was 1pp overweighted. Although the active weights of particular securities did change between the initial position and the new position, the total absolute active weights did not change. Therefore, the portfolio's active share did not change.

8   B is correct. Skewness measures the degree to which return expectations are non-normally distributed. If a distribution is positively skewed, the mean of the distribution is greater than its median—more than half of the deviations from the mean are negative and less than half are positive—and the average magnitude of positive deviations is larger than the average magnitude of negative deviations. Negative skew indicates that that the mean of the distribution lies below its median, and the average magnitude of negative deviations is larger than the average magnitude of positive deviations. Fund 3's new risk control constrains its model's predicted return distribution so that no more than 60% of the deviations from the mean are negative. This is an explicit constraint on skewness.

9   C is correct. The breadth (number of truly independent decisions made each year by the manager) required to earn the expected portfolio active return of 2.5% per year is approximately 69 decisions, calculated as follows:

$$E(R_A) = IC \times \sqrt{BR} \times \sigma_{R_A} \times TC$$
$$E(R_A) = 0.15 \times \sqrt{BR} \times 5\% \times 0.40 = 2.5\%$$
$$2.5\% = 0.15 \times \sqrt{BR} \times 5\% \times 0.40$$
$$\sqrt{BR} = \frac{2.5\%}{0.3\%} = 8.33$$
$$BR = 69.44$$

10 A is correct. The maximum position size in shares of Pasliant Corporation (PC) is determined by the constraint with the lowest dollar amount. The maximum position size for PC under each constraint is calculated as follows:

   Liquidity Constraint

   Dollar value of PC traded daily = PC market cap × Average daily trading volume

   Dollar value of PC traded daily = $3 billion × 1.0% = $30 million

   Liquidity constraint = Dollar value of PC traded daily × Liquidity % threshold

   Liquidity constraint = $30 million × 10% = $3 million

   Allocation Constraint

   Allocation constraint = AUM × Maximum position size threshold

   Allocation constraint = $250 million × 3.0% = $7.5 million

   Index Weight Constraint

   Index weight constraint = AUM × (Index weight × 10)

   Index weight constraint = $250 million × (0.20% × 10) = $5.0 million

   The liquidity constraint of $3.0 million is less than both the $5.0 million index weight constraint and the $7.5 million allocation constraint. Therefore, the maximum allowable position size that Manager A may take in PC is $3.0 million.

11 C is correct. Most multi-factor products are diversified across factors and securities and typically have high active share but have reasonably low active risk (tracking error), often in the range of 3%. Most multi-factor products have a low concentration among securities in order to achieve a balanced exposure to risk factors and minimize idiosyncratic risks. Manager B holds a highly diversified portfolio that has balanced exposures to rewarded risk factors, a high active share, and a relatively low target active risk—consistent with the characteristics of a multi-factor manager.

12 B is correct. The contribution of an asset to total portfolio variance equals the summation of the multiplication between the weight of the asset whose contribution is being measured, the weight of each asset (x_j), and the covariance between the asset being measured and each asset (C_{ij}), as follows:

$$\text{Contribution of each asset to portfolio variance} = CV_i = \sum_{j=1}^{n} x_i x_j C_{ij}$$

The contribution of Asset 2 to portfolio variance is computed as the sum of the following products:

Weight of Asset 2 × Weight of Asset 1 × Covariance of asset 2 with Asset 1, plus	0.45 × 0.30 × 0.01050
Weight of Asset 2 × Weight of Asset 2 × Covariance of Asset 2 with Asset 2, plus	0.45 × 0.45 × 0.01960
Weight of Asset 2 × Weight of Asset 3 × Covariance of Asset 2 with Asset 3	0.45 × 0.25 × 0.00224
= Asset 2's contribution to total portfolio variance	0.005639

13 A is correct. Well-constructed portfolios should have low idiosyncratic (unexplained) risk relative to total risk. Portfolio Y exhibits extremely high unexplained risk relative to total risk, and Portfolios X and Z have low unexplained risk relative to total risk. Therefore, Portfolio Y may be eliminated.

Portfolios X and Z have comparable factor exposures. In comparing portfolios with comparable factor exposures, the portfolio with lower absolute volatility and lower active risk will likely be preferred, assuming similar costs. Portfolio X has lower absolute volatility and lower active risk than Portfolio Z, although both have similar costs.

Finally, for managers with similar costs, fees, and alpha skills, if two products have similar active and absolute risks, the portfolio having a higher active share is preferred. Portfolio X has lower absolute volatility, lower active risk, and higher active share than Portfolio Z. As a result, Portfolio X best exhibits the risk characteristics of a well-constructed portfolio.

14 C is correct. Both Statement 1 and Statement 2 are correct.

Statement 1 is correct because, similar to a long-only portfolio, a long–short portfolio can be structured to have a gross exposure of 100%. Gross exposure of the portfolio is calculated as the sum of the long positions and the absolute value of the short positions, expressed as percentages of the portfolio's capital.

Gross exposure = Long positions + |Short positions|

Gross exposure long-only portfolio = 100% (Long positions) + 0% (Short positions) = 100%

Gross exposure long–short portfolio = 50% (Long positions) + |−50%| (Short positions) = 100%

Statement 2 is correct because long-only investing generally offers greater investment capacity than other approaches, particularly when using strategies that focus on large-cap stocks. For large institutional investors such as pension plans, there are no effective capacity constraints in terms of the total market cap available for long-only investing.

15 C is correct. Chen prefers an approach that emphasizes security-specific factors, engages in factor timing, and typically leads to portfolios that are generally more concentrated than those built using a systematic approach. These characteristics reflect a discretionary bottom-up portfolio management approach.

Glossary

Absolute return benchmark A minimum target return that an investment manager is expected to beat.

Accounting defeasance Also called in-substance defeasance, accounting defeasance is a way of extinguishing a debt obligation by setting aside sufficient high-quality securities to repay the liability.

Accumulation phase Phase where the government predominantly contributes to a sovereign wealth pension reserve fund.

Active management A portfolio management approach that allows risk factor mismatches relative to a benchmark index causing potentially significant return differences between the active portfolio and the underlying benchmark.

Active return Portfolio return minus benchmark return.

Active risk The annualized standard deviation of active returns, also referred to as *tracking error* (also sometimes called *tracking risk*).

Active risk budgeting Risk budgeting that concerns active risk (risk relative to a portfolio's benchmark).

Active share A measure of how similar a portfolio is to its benchmark. A manager who precisely replicates the benchmark will have an Active Share of zero; a manager with no holdings in common with the benchmark will have an Active Share of one.

Activist short selling A hedge fund strategy in which the manager takes a short position in a given security and then publicly presents his/her research backing the short thesis.

After-tax excess return Calculated as the after-tax return of the portfolio minus the after-tax return of the associated benchmark portfolio.

Agency trade A trade in which the broker is engaged to find the other side of the trade, acting as an agent. In doing so, the broker does not assume any risk for the trade.

Alpha decay In a trading context, alpha decay is the erosion or deterioration in short term alpha after the investment decision has been made.

Alternative trading systems (ATS) Non-exchange trading venues that bring together buyers and sellers to find transaction counterparties. Also called *multilateral trading facilities (MTF)*.

Anchoring and adjustment An information-processing bias in which the use of a psychological heuristic influences the way people estimate probabilities.

Anchoring and adjustment bias An information-processing bias in which the use of a psychological heuristic influences the way people estimate probabilities.

Anomalies Apparent deviations from market efficiency.

Arithmetic attribution An attribution approach which explains the arithmetic difference between the portfolio return and its benchmark return. The single-period attribution effects sum to the excess return, however, when combining multiple periods, the sub-period attribution effects will not sum to the excess return.

Arrival price In a trading context, the arrival price is the security price at the time the order was released to the market for execution.

Asset location The type of account an asset is held within, e.g., taxable or tax deferred.

Asset-only With respect to asset allocation, an approach that focuses directly on the characteristics of the assets without explicitly modeling the liabilities.

Asset swap spread (ASW) The spread over MRR on an interest rate swap for the remaining life of the bond that is equivalent to the bond's fixed coupon.

Asset swaps Convert a bond's fixed coupon to MRR plus (or minus) a spread.

Authorized participants Institutional investors who create and redeem ETF shares using an OTC primary market with an ETF sponsor.

Availability bias An information-processing bias in which people take a heuristic approach to estimating the probability of an outcome based on how easily the outcome comes to mind.

Back-fill bias The distortion in index or peer group data which results when returns are reported to a database only after they are known to be good returns.

Barbell A fixed-income investment strategy combining short- and long-term bond positions.

Base With respect to a foreign exchange quotation of the price of one unit of a currency, the currency referred to in "one unit of a currency."

Base-rate neglect A type of representativeness bias in which the base rate or probability of the categorization is not adequately considered.

Basis risk The risk resulting from using a hedging instrument that is imperfectly matched to the investment being hedged; in general, the risk that the basis will change in an unpredictable way.

Bear flattening A decrease in the yield spread between long- and short-term maturities across the yield curve, which is largely driven by a rise in short-term bond yields-to-maturity.

Bear spread An option strategy that becomes more valuable when the price of the underlying asset declines, so requires buying one option and writing another with a *lower* exercise price. A put bear spread involves buying a put with a higher exercise price and selling a put with a lower exercise price. A bear spread can also be executed with calls.

Bear steepening An increase in the yield spread between long- and short-term maturities across the yield curve, which is largely driven by a rise in long-term bond yields-to-maturity.

Behavioral finance macro A focus on market level behavior that considers market anomalies that distinguish markets from the efficient markets of traditional finance.

Behavioral finance micro A focus on individual level behavior that examines the behavioral biases that distinguish individual investors from the rational decision makers of traditional finance.

Bequest The transferring, or bequeathing, of assets in some other way upon a person's death. Also referred to as a testamentary bequest or testamentary gratuitous transfer.

Best-in-class An ESG implementation approach that seeks to identify the most favorable companies and sectors based on ESG considerations. Also called *positive screening*.

Bid price In a price quotation, the price at which the party making the quotation is willing to buy a specified quantity of an asset or security.

Breadth The number of truly independent decisions made each year.

Buffering Establishing ranges around breakpoints that define whether a stock belongs in one index or another.

Bull flattening A decrease in the yield spread between long- and short-term maturities across the yield curve, which is largely driven by a decline in long-term bond yields-to-maturity.

Bull spread An option strategy that becomes more valuable when the price of the underlying asset rises, so requires buying one option and writing another with a *higher* exercise price. A call bull spread involves buying a call with a lower exercise price and selling a call with a higher exercise price. A bull spread can also be executed with puts.

Bull steepening An increase in the yield spread between long- and short-term maturities across the yield curve, which is largely driven by a decline in short-term bond yields-to-maturity.

Bullet A fixed-income investment strategy that focuses on the intermediate term (or "belly") of the yield curve.

Business cycle Fluctuations in GDP in relation to long-term trend growth, usually lasting 9-11 years.

Butterfly spread A measure of yield curve shape or curvature equal to double the intermediate yield-to-maturity less the sum of short- and long-term yields-to-maturity.

Butterfly strategy A common yield curve shape strategy that combines a long or short bullet position with a barbell portfolio in the opposite direction to capitalize on expected yield curve shape changes.

Calendar rebalancing Rebalancing a portfolio to target weights on a periodic basis; for example, monthly, quarterly, semiannually, or annually.

Calendar spread A strategy in which one sells an option and buys the same type of option but with different expiration dates, on the same underlying asset and with the same strike. When the investor buys the more distant (near-term) call and sells the near-term (more distant) call, it is a long (short) calendar spread.

Canada model Characterized by a high allocation to alternatives. Unlike the endowment model, however, the Canada model relies more on internally managed assets. The innovative features of the Canada model are the: a) reference portfolio, b) total portfolio approach, and c) active management.

Capital gain or loss For tax purposes equals the selling price (net of commissions and other trading costs) of the asset less its tax basis.

Capital market expectations (CME) Expectations concerning the risk and return prospects of asset classes.

Capital needs analysis See *capital sufficiency analysis*.

Capital sufficiency analysis The process by which a wealth manager determines whether a client has, or is likely to accumulate, sufficient financial resources to meet his or her objectives; also known as *capital needs analysis*.

Capture ratio A measure of the manager's gain or loss relative to the gain or loss of the benchmark.

Carhart model A four factor model used in performance attribution. The four factors are: market (RMRF), size (SMB), value (HML), and momentum (WML).

Carry trade A trading strategy that involves buying a security and financing it at a rate that is lower than the yield on that security.

Carry trade across currencies A strategy seeking to benefit from a positive interest rate differential across currencies by combining a short position (or borrowing) in a low-yielding currency and a long position (or lending) in a high-yielding currency.

Cash drag Tracking error caused by temporarily uninvested cash.

Cash flow matching Immunization approach that attempts to ensure that all future liability payouts are matched precisely by cash flows from bonds or fixed-income derivatives.

Cash-secured put An option strategy involving the writing of a put option and simultaneously depositing an amount of money equal to the exercise price into a designated account (this strategy is also called a fiduciary put).

CDS curve Plot of CDS spreads across maturities for a single reference entity or group of reference entities in an index.

Cell approach See *stratified sampling*.

Charitable gratuitous transfers Asset transfers to not-for-profit or charitable organizations. In most jurisdictions charitable donations are not subject to a gift tax and most jurisdictions permit income tax deductions for charitable donations.

Charitable remainder trust A trust setup to provide income for the life of named-beneficiaries. When the last named-beneficiary dies any remaining assets in this trust are distributed to the charity named in the trust, hence the term *charitable remainder* trust.

Closet indexer A fund that advertises itself as being actively managed but is substantially similar to an index fund in its exposures.

Cognitive cost The effort involved in processing new information and updating beliefs.

Cognitive dissonance The mental discomfort that occurs when new information conflicts with previously held beliefs or cognitions.

Cognitive errors Behavioral biases resulting from faulty reasoning; cognitive errors stem from basic statistical, information processing, or memory errors.

Collar An option position in which the investor is long shares of stock and then buys a put with an exercise price below the current stock price and writes a call with an exercise price above the current stock price. Collars allow a shareholder to acquire downside protection through a protective put but reduce the cash outlay by writing a covered call.

Completion overlay A type of overlay that addresses an indexed portfolio that has diverged from its proper exposure.

Completion portfolio Is an index-based portfolio that when added to a given concentrated asset position creates an overall portfolio with exposures similar to the investor's benchmark.

Conditional value at risk (CVaR) Also known as expected loss The average portfolio loss over a specific time period conditional on that loss exceeding the value at risk (VaR) threshold.

Glossary

Confirmation bias A belief perseverance bias in which people tend to look for and notice what confirms their beliefs, to ignore or undervalue what contradicts their beliefs, and to misinterpret information as support for their beliefs.

Conjunction fallacy An inappropriate combining of probabilities of independent events to support a belief. In fact, the probability of two independent events occurring in conjunction is never greater than the probability of either event occurring alone; the probability of two independent events occurring together is equal to the multiplication of the probabilities of the independent events.

Conservatism bias A belief perseverance bias in which people maintain their prior views or forecasts by inadequately incorporating new information.

Contingent immunization Hybrid approach that combines immunization with an active management approach when the asset portfolio's value exceeds the present value of the liability portfolio.

Controlled foreign corporation (CFC) A company located outside a taxpayer's home country in which the taxpayer has a controlling interest as defined under the home country law.

Covered call An option strategy in which a long position in an asset is combined with a short position in a call on that asset.

Covered interest rate parity The relationship among the spot exchange rate, the forward exchange rate, and the interest rate in two currencies that ensures that the return on a hedged (i.e., covered) foreign risk-free investment is the same as the return on a domestic risk-free investment. Also called *interest rate parity*.

Credit cycle The expansion and contraction of credit over the business cycle, which translates into asset price changes based on default and recovery expectations across maturities and rating categories.

Credit default swap (CDS) basis Yield spread on a bond, as compared to CDS spread of same tenor.

Credit loss rate The realized percentage of par value lost to default for a group of bonds equal to the bonds' default rate multiplied by the loss severity.

Credit migration The change in a bond's credit rating over a certain period.

Credit valuation adjustment (CVA) The present value of credit risk for a loan, bond, or derivative obligation.

Cross-currency basis swap An interest rate swap involving the periodic exchange of floating payments in one currency for another based upon respective market reference rates with an initial and final exchange of notional principal.

Cross hedge A hedge involving a hedging instrument that is imperfectly correlated with the asset being hedged; an example is hedging a bond investment with futures on a non-identical bond.

Cross-sectional consistency A feature of expectations setting which means that estimates for all classes reflect the same underlying assumptions and are generated with methodologies that reflect or preserve important relationships among the asset classes, such as strong correlations. It is the internal consistency across asset classes.

Cross-sectional momentum A managed futures trend following strategy implemented with a cross-section of assets (within an asset class) by going long those that are rising in price the most and by shorting those that are falling the most. This approach generally results in holding a net zero (market-neutral) position and works well when a market's out- or underperformance is a reliable predictor of its future performance.

Currency overlay A type of overlay that helps hedge the returns of securities held in foreign currency back to the home country's currency.

Currency overlay programs A currency overlay program is a program to manage a portfolio's currency exposures for the case in which those exposures are managed separately from the management of the portfolio itself.

Custom security-based benchmark Benchmark that is custom built to accurately reflect the investment discipline of a particular investment manager. Also called a *strategy benchmark* because it reflects a manager's particular strategy.

Decision price In a trading context, the decision price is the security price at the time the investment decision was made.

Decision-reversal risk The risk of reversing a chosen course of action at the point of maximum loss.

Decumulation phase Phase where the government predominantly withdraws from a sovereign wealth pension reserve fund.

Dedicated short-selling A hedge fund strategy in which the manager takes short-only positions in equities deemed to be expensively priced versus their deteriorating fundamental situations. Short exposures may vary only in terms of portfolio sizing by, at times, holding higher levels of cash.

Default intensity POD over a specified time period in a reduced form credit model.

Default risk Likelihood that a borrower will default or fail to meet its obligation to make full and timely payments of principal and interest according to the terms of a debt obligation.

Deferred annuity An annuity that enables an individual to purchase an income stream that will begin at a later date.

Defined benefit A retirement plan in which a plan sponsor commits to paying a specified retirement benefit.

Defined contribution A retirement plan in which contributions are defined but the ultimate retirement benefit is not specified or guaranteed by the plan sponsor.

Delay cost The (trading related) cost associated with not submitting the order to the market in a timely manner.

Delta The change in an option's price in response to a change in price of the underlying, all else equal.

Delta hedging Hedging that involves matching the price response of the position being hedged over a narrow range of prices.

Demand deposits Accounts that can be drawn upon regularly and without notice. This category includes checking accounts and certain savings accounts that are often accessible through online banks or automated teller machines (ATMs).

Diffusion index An index that measures how many indicators are pointing up and how many are pointing down.

Direct market access (DMA) Access in which market participants can transact orders directly with the order book of an exchange using a broker's exchange connectivity.

Disability income insurance A type of insurance designed to mitigate earnings risk as a result of a disability in which an individual becomes less than fully employed.

Discount margin The discount (or required) margin is the yield spread versus the MRR such that the FRN is priced at par on a rate reset date.

Discretionary portfolio management An arrangement in which a wealth manager has a client's pre-approval to execute investment decisions.

Discretionary trust A trust that enables the trustee to determine whether and how much to distribute based on a beneficiary's general welfare.

Disposition effect As a result of loss aversion, an emotional bias whereby investors are reluctant to dispose of losers. This results in an inefficient and gradual adjustment to deterioration in fundamental value.

Dividend capture A trading strategy whereby an equity portfolio manager purchases stocks just before their ex-dividend dates, holds these stocks through the ex-dividend date to earn the right to receive the dividend, and subsequently sells the shares.

Domestic asset An asset that trades in the investor's domestic currency (or home currency).

Domestic currency The currency of the investor, i.e., the currency in which he or she typically makes consumption purchases, e.g., the Swiss franc for an investor domiciled in Switzerland.

Domestic-currency return A rate of return stated in domestic currency terms from the perspective of the investor; reflects both the foreign-currency return on an asset as well as percentage movement in the spot exchange rate between the domestic and foreign currencies.

Double taxation A term used to describe situations in which income is taxed twice. For example, when corporate earnings are taxed at the company level and then that portion of earnings paid as dividends is taxed again at the investor level.

Drawdown A decline in value (represented by a series of negative returns only) following a peak fund valuation.

Drawdown duration The total time from the start of the drawdown until the cumulative drawdown recovers to zero.

Due diligence Investigation and analysis in support of an investment action, decision, or recommendation.

Duration matching Immunization approach based on the duration of assets and liabilities. Ideally, the liabilities being matched (the liability portfolio) and the portfolio of assets (the bond portfolio) should be affected similarly by a change in interest rates.

Duration times spread Weighting of spread duration by credit spread in order to incorporate the empirical observation that spread changes for lower-rated bonds tend to be consistent on a percentage, rather than absolute, basis.

Duration Times Spread (DTS) Weighting of spread duration by credit spread to incorporate the empirical observation that spread changes for lower-rated bonds tend to be consistent on a percentage rather than absolute basis.

Dynamic asset allocation A strategy incorporating deviations from the strategic asset allocation that are motivated by longer-term valuation signals or economic views than usually associated with tactical asset allocation.

Dynamic hedge A hedge requiring adjustment as the price of the hedged asset changes.

Earnings risk The risk associated with the earning potential of an individual.

Econometrics The application of quantitative modeling and analysis grounded in economic theory to the analysis of economic data.

Economic balance sheet A balance sheet that provides an individual's total wealth portfolio, supplementing traditional balance sheet assets with human capital and pension wealth, and expanding liabilities to include consumption and bequest goals. Also known as *holistic balance sheet*.

Economic indicators Economic statistics provided by government and established private organizations that contain information on an economy's recent past activity or its current or future position in the business cycle.

Economic net worth The difference between an individual's assets and liabilities; extends traditional financial assets and liabilities to include human capital and future consumption needs.

Effective federal funds (FFE) rate The fed funds rate actually transacted between depository institutions, not the Fed's target federal funds rate.

Emotional biases Behavioral biases resulting from reasoning influenced by feelings; emotional biases stem from impulse or intuition.

Empirical duration Estimation of the price-yield relationship using historical bond market data in statistical models.

Endowment bias An emotional bias in which people value an asset more when they hold rights to it than when they do not.

Endowment model Characterized by a high allocation to alternative investments (private investments and hedge funds), significant active management, and externally managed assets.

Enhanced indexing approach Maintains a close link to the benchmark but attempts to generate a modest amount of outperformance relative to the benchmark.

Enhanced indexing strategy Method investors use to match an underlying market index in which the investor purchases fewer securities than the full set of index constituents but matches primary risk factors reflected in the index.

Equity monetization A group of strategies that allow investors to receive cash for their concentrated stock positions without an outright sale. These transactions are structured to avoid triggering the capital gains tax.

Estate Consists of all of the property a person owns or controls, which may consist of financial assets (e.g., bank accounts, stocks, bonds, business interests), tangible personal assets (e.g., artwork, collectibles, vehicles), immovable property (e.g., residential real estate, timber rights), and intellectual property (e.g., royalties).

Estate planning The process of preparing for the disposition of one's estate upon death and during one's lifetime.

Estate tax Levied on the total value of a deceased person's assets and paid out of the estate before any distributions to beneficiaries.

Evaluated pricing See *matrix pricing*.

Excess return Used in various senses appropriate to context: 1) The difference between the portfolio return and the benchmark return; 2) The return in excess of the risk-free rate.

Excess spread Credit spread return measure that incorporates both changes in spread and expected credit losses for a given period.

Exchange fund A partnership in which each of the partners have each contributed low cost-basis stock to the fund. Used in the United Sates as a mechanism to achieve a tax-free exchange of a concentrated asset position.

Execution cost The difference between the (trading related) cost of the real portfolio and the paper portfolio, based on shares and prices transacted.

Exhaustive An index construction strategy that selects every constituent of a universe.

Expected shortfall The average loss conditional on exceeding the VaR cutoff; sometimes referred to as *conditional VaR* or *expected tail loss*.

Expected tail loss See *expected shortfall*.

Extended portfolio assets and liabilities Assets and liabilities beyond those shown on a conventional balance sheet that are relevant in making asset allocation decisions; an example of an extended asset is human capital.

Factor-model-based benchmarks Benchmarks constructed by examining a portfolio's sensitivity to a set of factors, such as the return for a broad market index, company earnings growth, industry, or financial leverage.

Family constitution Typically a non-binding document that sets forth an agreed-upon set of rights, values, and responsibilities of the family members and other stakeholders. Used by many wealth- and business-owning families as the starting point of conflict resolution procedures.

Family governance The process for a family's collective communication and decision making designed to serve current and future generations based on the common values of the family.

Financial capital The tangible and intangible assets (excluding human capital) owned by an individual or household.

Fixed trust Distributions to beneficiaries of a fixed trust are specified in the trust document to occur at certain times or in certain amounts.

Forced heirship Is the requirement that a certain proportion of assets must pass to specified family members, such as a spouse and children.

Foreign assets Assets denominated in currencies other than the investor's home currency.

Foreign currency Currency that is not the currency in which an investor makes consumption purchases, e.g., the US dollar from the perspective of a Swiss investor.

Foreign-currency return The return of the foreign asset measured in foreign-currency terms.

Forward rate bias An empirically observed divergence from interest rate parity conditions that active investors seek to benefit from by borrowing in a lower-yield currency and investing in a higher-yield currency.

Foundation A legal entity available in certain jurisdictions. Foundations are typically set up to hold assets for a specific charitable purpose, such as to promote education or for philanthropy. When set up and funded by an individual or family and managed by its own directors, it is called a *private foundation*. The term *family foundation* usually refers to a private foundation where donors or members of the donors' family are actively involved.

Framing An information-processing bias in which a person answers a question differently based on the way in which it is asked (framed).

Framing bias An information-processing bias in which a person answers a question differently based on the way in which it is asked (framed).

Fulcrum securities Partially-in-the-money claims (not expected to be repaid in full) whose holders end up owning the reorganized company in a corporate reorganization situation.

Full replication approach When every issue in an index is represented in the portfolio, and each portfolio position has approximately the same weight in the fund as in the index.

Fund-of-funds A fund of hedge funds in which the fund-of-funds manager allocates capital to separate, underlying hedge funds (e.g., single manager and/or multi-manager funds) that themselves run a range of different strategies.

Funding currencies The low-yield currencies in which borrowing occurs in a carry trade.

G-spread Yield spread for a fixed-rate bond over a government benchmark.

Gamblers' fallacy A misunderstanding of probabilities in which people wrongly project reversal to a long-term mean.

Gamma The change in an option's delta for a change in price of the underlying, all else equal.

General account Account holding assets to fund future liabilities from traditional life insurance and fixed annuities, the products in which the insurer bears all the risks—particularly mortality risk and longevity risk.

Generation-skipping tax Taxes levied in some jurisdictions on asset transfers (gifts) that skip one generation such as when a grandparent transfers assets to their grandchildren. (see related Gift Tax).

Gift tax Depending on the tax laws of the country, assets gifted by one person to another during the giftor's lifetime may be subject to a gift tax.

Goals-based With respect to asset allocation or investing, an approach that focuses on achieving an investor's goals (for example, related to supporting lifestyle needs or aspirations) based typically on constructing sub-portfolios aligned with those goals.

Goals-based investing An investment industry term for approaches to investing for individuals and families focused on aligning investments with goals (parallel to liability-driven investing for institutional investors).

Green bonds Fixed-income instruments issued by private or public sector borrowers that directly fund ESG initiatives.

Grinold–Kroner model An expression for the expected return on a share as the sum of an expected income return, an expected nominal earnings growth return, and an expected repricing return.

Halo effect An emotional bias that extends a favorable evaluation of some characteristics to other characteristics.

Hard-catalyst event-driven approach An event-driven approach in which investments are made in reaction to an already announced corporate event (mergers and acquisitions, bankruptcies, share issuances, buybacks, capital restructurings, re-organizations, accounting changes) in which security prices related to the event have yet to fully converge.

Hazard rate The conditional POD, or the likelihood that default will occur given that it has not already occurred in a prior period.

Health insurance A type of insurance used to cover health care and medical costs.

Health risk The risk associated with illness or injury.

Hedge ratio The relationship of the quantity of an asset being hedged to the quantity of the derivative used for hedging.

Herding When a group of investors trade on the same side of the market in the same securities, or when investors ignore their own private information and act as other investors do.

High-water mark A specified net asset value level that a fund must exceed before performance fees are paid to the hedge fund manager.

Hindsight bias A bias with selective perception and retention aspects in which people may see past events as having been predictable and reasonable to expect.

Holdings-based attribution A "buy and hold" attribution approach which calculates the return of portfolio and benchmark components based upon the price and foreign exchange rate changes applied to daily snapshots of portfolio holdings.

Holdings-based style analysis A bottom-up style analysis that estimates the risk exposures from the actual securities held in the portfolio at a point in time.

Holistic balance sheet See *economic balance sheet*.

Home bias A preference for securities listed on the exchanges of one's home country.

Home-country bias The favoring of domestic over non-domestic investments relative to global market value weights.

Home currency See *domestic currency*.

Human capital An implied asset; the net present value of an investor's future expected labor income weighted by the probability of surviving to each future age. Also called *net employment capital*.

I-spread (interpolated spread) Yield spread measure using swaps or constant maturity Treasury YTMs as a benchmark.

Illusion of control A bias in which people tend to believe that they can control or influence outcomes when, in fact, they cannot. Illusion of knowledge and self-attribution biases contribute to the overconfidence bias.

Illusion of control bias A bias in which people tend to believe that they can control or influence outcomes when, in fact, they cannot. Illusion of knowledge and self-attribution biases contribute to the overconfidence bias.

Immediate annuity An annuity that provides a guarantee of specified future monthly payments over a specified period of time.

Immunization An asset/liability management approach that structures investments in bonds to match (offset) liabilities' weighted-average duration; a type of dedication strategy.

Impact investing Investment approach that seeks to achieve targeted social or environmental objectives along with measurable financial returns through engagement with a company or by direct investment in projects or companies.

Implementation shortfall (IS) The difference between the return for a notional or paper portfolio, where all transactions are assumed to take place at the manager's decision price, and the portfolio's actual return, which reflects realized transactions, including all fees and costs.

Implied volatility The outlook for the future volatility of the underlying asset's price. It is the value (i.e., standard deviation of underlying's returns) that equates the model (e.g., Black–Scholes–Merton model) price of an option to its market price.

Implied volatility surface A three-dimensional plot, for put and call options on the same underlying asset, of days to expiration (x-axis), option strike prices (y-axis), and implied volatilities (z-axis). It simultaneously shows the volatility skew (or smile) and the term structure of implied volatility.

Incremental VaR (or partial VaR) The change in the minimum portfolio loss expected to occur over a given time period at a specific confidence level resulting from increasing or decreasing a portfolio position.

Information coefficient Formally defined as the correlation between forecast return and actual return. In essence, it measures the effectiveness of investment insight.

Inheritance tax Paid by each individual beneficiary of a deceased person's estate on the value of the benefit the individual received from the estate.

Input uncertainty Uncertainty concerning whether the inputs are correct.

Interaction effect The attribution effect resulting from the interaction of the allocation and selection decisions.

Intertemporal consistency A feature of expectations setting which means that estimates for an asset class over different horizons reflect the same assumptions with respect to the potential paths of returns over time. It is the internal consistency over various time horizons.

Intestate A person who dies without a valid will or with a will that does not dispose of their property are considered to have died intestate.

Intrinsic value The difference between the spot exchange rate and the strike price of a currency option.

Investment currencies The high-yielding currencies in a carry trade.

Investment policy statement A written planning document that describes a client's investment objectives and risk tolerance over a relevant time horizon, along with the constraints that apply to the client's portfolio.

Investment style A natural grouping of investment disciplines that has some predictive power in explaining the future dispersion of returns across portfolios.

Irrevocable trust The person whose assets are used to create the trust gives up the right to rescind the trust relationship and regain title to the trust assets.

Key person risk The risk that results from over-reliance on an individual or individuals whose departure would negatively affect an investment manager.

Key rate duration A method of measuring interest rate sensitivities of a fixed-income instrument or portfolio to shifts in key points along the yield curve.

Knock-in/knock-out Features of a vanilla option that is created (or ceases to exist) when the spot exchange rate touches a pre-specified level.

Leading economic indicators A set of economic variables whose values vary with the business cycle but at a fairly consistent time interval before a turn in the business cycle.

Liability-based mandates Mandates managed to match or cover expected liability payments (future cash outflows) with future projected cash inflows.

Liability-driven investing An investment industry term that generally encompasses asset allocation that is focused on funding an investor's liabilities in institutional contexts.

Liability driven investing (LDI) model In the LDI model, the primary investment objective is to generate returns sufficient to cover liabilities, with a focus on maximizing expected surplus return (excess return of assets over liabilities) and managing surplus volatility.

Liability glide path A specification of desired proportions of liability-hedging assets and return-seeking assets and the duration of the liability hedge as funded status changes and contributions are made.

Liability insurance A type of insurance used to manage liability risk.

Liability-relative With respect to asset allocation, an approach that focuses directly only on funding liabilities as an investment objective.

Liability risk The possibility that an individual or household may be held legally liable for the financial costs associated with property damage or physical injury.

Life-cycle finance A concept in finance that recognizes as an investor ages, the fundamental nature of wealth and risk evolves.

Life insurance   A type of insurance that protects against the loss of human capital for those who depend on an individual's future earnings.

Life settlement   The sale of a life insurance contract to a third party. The valuation of a life settlement typically requires detailed biometric analysis of the individual policyholder and an understanding of actuarial analysis.

Limited-life foundations   A type of foundation where founders seek to maintain control of spending while they (or their immediate heirs) are still alive.

Liquidity budget   The portfolio allocations (or weightings) considered acceptable for the liquidity categories in the liquidity classification schedule (or time-to-cash table).

Liquidity classification schedule   A liquidity management classification (or table) that defines portfolio liquidity "buckets" or categories based on the estimated time it would take to convert assets in that particular category into cash.

Longevity risk   The risk of outliving one's financial resources.

Loss-aversion bias   A bias in which people tend to strongly prefer avoiding losses as opposed to achieving gains.

Loss severity   Also known as loss given default (LGD). The amount of loss if a default occurs, usually expressed as a percentage in annual terms.

Macro attribution   Attribution at the sponsor level.

Manager peer group   See *manager universe*.

Manager universe   A broad group of managers with similar investment disciplines. Also called *manager peer group*.

Matrix pricing   An approach for estimating the prices of thinly traded securities based on the prices of securities with similar attributions, such as similar credit rating, maturity, or economic sector. Also called *evaluated pricing*.

Matrix pricing (or evaluated pricing)   Methodology for pricing infrequently traded bonds using bonds from similar issuers and actively traded government benchmarks to establish a bond's fair value.

Mental accounting bias   An information-processing bias in which people treat one sum of money differently from another equal-sized sum based on which mental account the money is assigned to.

Micro attribution   Attribution at the portfolio manager level.

Minimum-variance hedge ratio   A mathematical approach to determining the optimal cross hedging ratio.

Mission-related investing   Aims to direct a significant portion of assets in excess of annual grants into projects promoting a foundation's mission.

Model uncertainty   Uncertainty as to whether a selected model is correct.

Mortality table   A table that indicates individual life expectancies at specified ages.

Multi-class trading   An equity market-neutral strategy that capitalizes on misalignment in prices and involves buying and selling different classes of shares of the same company, such as voting and non-voting shares.

Multi-manager fund   Can be of two types—one is a multi-strategy fund in which teams of portfolio managers trade and invest in multiple different strategies within the same fund; the second type is a fund of hedge funds (or fund-of-funds) in which the manager allocates capital to separate, underlying hedge funds that themselves run a range of different strategies.

Multi-strategy fund   A fund in which teams of portfolio managers trade and invest in multiple different strategies within the same fund.

Multilateral trading facilities   (MTF) See *Alternative trading systems (ATS)*.

Negative butterfly   An increase in the butterfly spread due to lower short- and long-term yields-to-maturity and a higher intermediate yield-to-maturity.

Negative screening   An ESG implementation approach that excludes certain sectors or companies that deviate from an investor's accepted standards.

Non-deliverable forwards   Forward contracts that are cash settled (in the non-controlled currency of the currency pair) rather than physically settled (the controlled currency is neither delivered nor received).

Nonstationarity   A characteristic of series of data whose properties, such as mean and variance, are not constant through time. When analyzing historical data it means that different parts of a data series reflect different underlying statistical properties.

Norway model   Characterized by an almost exclusive reliance on public equities and fixed income (the traditional 60/40 equity/bond model falls under the Norway model), with largely passively managed assets and with very little to no allocation to alternative investments.

OAS duration   The change in bond price for a given change in OAS.

Offer price   The price at which a counterparty is willing to sell one unit of the base currency.

Opportunity cost   The (trading related) cost associated with not being able to transact the entire order at the decision price.

Option-adjusted spread (OAS)   A generalization of the Z-spread yield spread calculation that incorporates bond option pricing based on assumed interest rate volatility.

Optional stock dividends   A type of dividend in which shareholders may elect to receive either cash or new shares.

Options on bond futures contracts   Instruments that involve the right, but not the obligation, to enter into a bond futures contract at a pre-determined strike (bond price) on a future date in exchange for an up-front premium.

Overbought   When a market has trended too far in one direction and is vulnerable to a trend reversal, or correction.

Overconfidence bias   A bias in which people demonstrate unwarranted faith in their own intuitive reasoning, judgments, and/or cognitive abilities.

Overlay   A derivative position (or positions) used to adjust a pre-existing portfolio closer to its objectives.

Oversold   The opposite of overbought; see *overbought*.

Packeting   Splitting stock positions into multiple parts.

Pairs trading   An equity market-neutral strategy that capitalizes on the misalignment in prices of pairs of similar under- and overvalued equities. The expectation is the differential valuations or trading relationships will revert to their long-term mean values or their fundamentally-correct trading relationships, with the long position rising and the short position declining in value.

Parameter uncertainty   Uncertainty arising because a quantitative model's parameters are estimated with error.

Participant/cohort option   Pools the DC plan member with a cohort that has a similar target retirement date.

Participant-switching life-cycle options   Automatically switch DC plan members into a more conservative asset mix as their age increases. There may be several automatic de-risking switches at different age targets.

Passive investment In the fixed-income context, it is investment that seeks to mimic the prevailing characteristics of the overall investments available in terms of credit quality, type of borrower, maturity, and duration rather than express a specific market view.

Passive management A buy-and-hold approach to investing in which an investor does not make portfolio changes based upon short-term expectations of changing market or security performance.

Percent-range rebalancing An approach to rebalancing that involves setting rebalancing thresholds or trigger points, stated as a percentage of the portfolio's value, around target values.

Performance attribution Attribution, including return attribution and risk attribution; often used as a synonym for return attribution.

Permanent life insurance A type of life insurance that provides lifetime coverage.

Portfolio overlay An array of derivative positions managed separately from the securities portfolio to achieve overall intended portfolio characteristics.

Position delta The overall or portfolio delta. For example, the position delta of a covered call, consisting of long 100 shares and short one at-the-money call, is +50 (= +100 for the shares and -50 for the short ATM call).

Positive butterfly A decrease in the butterfly spread due to higher short- and long-term yields-to-maturity and a lower intermediate yield-to-maturity.

Positive screening An ESG implementation approach that seeks to identify the most favorable companies and sectors based on ESG considerations. Also called *best-in-class*.

Post-liquidation return Calculates the return assuming that all portfolio holdings are sold as of the end date of the analysis and that the resulting capital gains tax that would be due is deducted from the ending portfolio value.

Potential capital gain exposure (PCGE) Is an estimate of the percentage of a fund's assets that represents gains and measures how much the fund's assets have appreciated. It can be an indicator of possible future capital gain distributions.

Premature death risk The risk of an individual dying earlier than anticipated; sometimes referred to as *mortality risk*.

Present value of distribution of cash flows methodology Method used to address a portfolio's sensitivity to rate changes along the yield curve. This approach seeks to approximate and match the yield curve risk of an index over discrete time periods.

Principal trade A trade in which the market maker or dealer becomes a disclosed counterparty and assumes risk for the trade by transacting the security for their own account. Also called *broker risk trades*.

Probability of default The likelihood that a borrower defaults or fails to meet its obligation to make full and timely payments of principal and interest.

Probate The legal process to confirm the validity of the will so that executors, heirs, and other interested parties can rely on its authenticity.

Program trading A strategy of buying or selling many stocks simultaneously.

Progressive tax rate schedule A tax regime in which the tax rate increases as the amount of income or wealth being taxed increases.

Property insurance A type of insurance used by individuals to manage property risk.

Property risk The possibility that a person's property may be damaged, destroyed, stolen, or lost.

Protective put An option strategy in which a long position in an asset is combined with a long position in a put on that asset.

Pure indexing Attempts to replicate a bond index as closely as possible, targeting zero active return and zero active risk.

Put spread A strategy used to reduce the upfront cost of buying a protective put, it involves buying a put option and writing another put option.

Qualified dividends Generally dividends from shares in domestic corporations and certain qualified foreign corporations which have been held for at least a specified minimum period of time.

Quantitative market-neutral An approach to building market-neutral portfolios in which large numbers of securities are traded and positions are adjusted on a daily or even an hourly basis using algorithm-based models.

Quoted margin The yield spread over the MRR established upon issuance of an FRN to compensate investors for assuming an issuer's credit risk.

Re-base With reference to index construction, to change the time period used as the base of the index.

Realized volatility Historical volatility, the square root of the realized variance of returns, which is a measure of the range of past price outcomes for the underlying asset.

Rebalancing In the context of asset allocation, a discipline for adjusting the portfolio to align with the strategic asset allocation.

Rebalancing overlay A type of overlay that addresses a portfolio's need to sell certain constituent securities and buy others.

Rebalancing range A range of values for asset class weights defined by trigger points above and below target weights, such that if the portfolio value passes through a trigger point, rebalancing occurs. Also known as a corridor.

Rebate rate The portion of the collateral earnings rate that is repaid to the security borrower by the security lender.

Reduced form credit models Credit models that solve for default probability over a specific time period using observable company-specific variables such as financial ratios and macroeconomic variables.

Reduced-form models Models that use economic theory and other factors such as prior research output to describe hypothesized relationships. Can be described as more compact representations of underlying structural models. Evaluate endogenous variables in terms of observable exogenous variables.

Regime The governing set of relationships (between variables) that stem from technological, political, legal, and regulatory environments. Changes in such environments or policy stances can be described as changes in regime.

Regret The feeling that an opportunity has been missed; typically an expression of *hindsight bias*.

Regret-aversion bias An emotional bias in which people tend to avoid making decisions that will result in action out of fear that the decision will turn out poorly.

Relative value A concept that describes the selection of the most attractive individual securities to populate the portfolio with, using ranking and comparing.

Relative value volatility arbitrage A volatility trading strategy that aims to source and buy cheap volatility and sell more expensive volatility while netting out the time decay aspects normally associated with options portfolios.

Glossary

Relative VaR The minimum portfolio loss expected to occur over a given time period at a specific confidence level based on a portfolio containing active positions minus benchmark holdings.

Repo rate The interest rate on a repurchase agreement.

Representativeness bias A belief perseverance bias in which people tend to classify new information based on past experiences and classifications.

Repurchase agreements In repurchase agreements, or *repos*, a security owner agrees to sell a security for a specific cash amount while simultaneously agreeing to repurchase the security at a specified future date (typically one day later) and price.

Request for quote (RFQ) A non-binding quote provided by a market maker or dealer to a potential buyer or seller upon request. Commonly used in fixed income markets these quotes are only valid at the time they are provided.

Reserve portfolio The component of an insurer's general account that is subject to specific regulatory requirements and is intended to ensure the company's ability to meet its policy liabilities. The assets in the reserve portfolio are managed conservatively and must be highly liquid and low risk.

Resistance levels Price points on dealers' order boards where one would expect to see a clustering of offers.

Return attribution A set of techniques used to identify the sources of the excess return of a portfolio against its benchmark.

Returns-based attribution An attribution approach that uses only the total portfolio returns over a period to identify the components of the investment process that have generated the returns. The Brinson–Hood–Beebower approach is a returns-based attribution approach.

Returns-based benchmarks Benchmarks constructed by examining a portfolio's sensitivity to a set of factors, such as the returns for various style indexes (e.g., small-cap value, small-cap growth, large-cap value, and large-cap growth).

Returns-based style analysis A top-down style analysis that involves estimating the sensitivities of a portfolio to security market indexes.

Reverse repos Repurchase agreements from the standpoint of the lender.

Revocable trust The person whose assets are used to create the trust retains the right to rescind the trust relationship and regain title to the trust assets.

Risk attribution The analysis of the sources of risk.

Risk aversion The degree of an investor's unwillingness to take risk; the inverse of risk tolerance.

Risk budgeting The establishment of objectives for individuals, groups, or divisions of an organization that takes into account the allocation of an acceptable level of risk.

Risk capacity The ability to accept financial risk.

Risk perception The subjective assessment of the risk involved in the outcome of an investment decision.

Risk premium An extra return expected by investors for bearing some specified risk.

Risk reversal A strategy used to profit from the existence of an implied volatility skew and from changes in its shape over time. A combination of long (short) calls and short (long) puts on the same underlying with the same expiration is a long (short) risk reversal.

Risk tolerance The capacity to accept risk; the level of risk an investor (or organization) is willing and able to bear.

Sample-size neglect A type of representativeness bias in which financial market participants incorrectly assume that small sample sizes are representative of populations (or "real" data).

Scenario analysis What-if analysis that involves changing multiple assumptions at the same time in order to evaluate the change in an investment's value.

Seagull spread An extension of the risk reversal foreign exchange option strategy that limits downside risk.

Securities lending A form of collateralized lending that may be used to generate income for portfolios.

Selective An index construction methodology that targets only those securities with certain characteristics.

Self-attribution bias A bias in which people take personal credit for successes and attribute failures to external factors outside the individual's control.

Self-control bias A bias in which people fail to act in pursuit of their long-term, overarching goals because of a lack of self-discipline.

Separate accounts Accounts holding assets to fund future liabilities from variable life insurance and variable annuities, the products in which customers make investment decisions from a menu of options and themselves bear investment risk.

Sharpe ratio The average return in excess of the risk-free rate divided by the standard deviation of return; a measure of the average excess return earned per unit of standard deviation of return. Also known as the *reward-to-variability ratio*.

Short-biased A hedge fund strategy in which the manager uses a less extreme version of dedicated short-selling. It involves searching for opportunities to sell expensively priced equities, but short exposure may be balanced with some modest value-oriented, or index-oriented, long exposure.

Shortfall probability The probability of failing to meet a specific liability or goal.

Shrinkage estimation Estimation that involves taking a weighted average of a historical estimate of a parameter and some other parameter estimate, where the weights reflect the analyst's relative belief in the estimates.

Single-manager fund A fund in which one portfolio manager or team of portfolio managers invests in one strategy or style.

Smart beta Involves the use of transparent, rules-based strategies as a basis for investment decisions.

Smart order routers (SOR) Smart systems used to electronically route small orders to the best markets for execution based on order type and prevailing market conditions.

Social proof A bias in which individuals tend to follow the beliefs of a group.

Soft-catalyst event-driven approach An event-driven approach in which investments are made proactively in anticipation of a corporate event (mergers and acquisitions, bankruptcies, share issuances, buybacks, capital restructurings, re-organizations, accounting changes) that has yet to occur.

Special dividends A dividend paid by a company that does not pay dividends on a regular schedule, or a dividend that supplements regular cash dividends with an extra payment.

Spread duration The change in bond price for a given change in yield spread. Also referred to as *OAS duration* when the option-adjusted spread (OAS) is the yield measure used.

Staged diversification strategy The simplest approach to managing the risk of a concentrated position involves selling the concentrated position over some period of time, paying associated tax, and reinvesting the proceeds in a diversified portfolio.

Static hedge A hedge that is not sensitive to changes in the price of the asset hedged.

Status quo bias An emotional bias in which people do nothing (i.e., maintain the "status quo") instead of making a change.

Stock lending Securities lending involving the transfer of equities.

Stop-losses A trading order that sets a selling price below the current market price with a goal of protecting profits or preventing further losses.

Stops Stop-loss orders involve leaving bids or offers away from the current market price to be filled if the market reaches those levels.

Straddle An option combination in which one buys *both* puts and calls, with the same exercise price and same expiration date, on the same underlying asset. In contrast to this long straddle, if someone *writes* both options, it is a short straddle.

Strangle A variation on a straddle in which the put and call have different exercise prices; if the put and call are held long, it is a long strangle; if they are held short, it is a short strangle.

Stratified sampling A sampling method that guarantees that subpopulations of interest are represented in the sample. Also called *representative sampling* or *cell approach*.

Structural credit models Credit models that apply market-based variables to estimate the value of an issuer's assets and the volatility of asset value.

Structural models Models that specify functional relationships among variables based on economic theory. The functional form and parameters of these models are derived from the underlying theory. They may include unobservable parameters.

Structural risk Risk that arises from portfolio design, particularly the choice of the portfolio allocations.

Stub trading An equity market-neutral strategy that capitalizes on misalignment in prices and entails buying and selling stock of a parent company and its subsidiaries, typically weighted by the percentage ownership of the parent company in the subsidiaries.

Support levels Price points on dealers' order boards where one would expect to see a clustering of bids.

Surplus The difference between the value of assets and the present value of liabilities. With respect to an insurance company, the net difference between the total assets and total liabilities (equivalent to policyholders' surplus for a mutual insurance company and stockholders' equity for a stock company).

Surplus portfolio The component of an insurer's general account that is intended to realize higher expected returns than the reserve portfolio and so can assume some liquidity risk. Surplus portfolio assets are often managed aggressively with exposure to alternative assets.

Survivorship bias Bias that arises in a data series when managers with poor track records exit the business and are dropped from the database whereas managers with good records remain; when a data series of a given date reflects only entitites that have survived to that date.

Swaption This instrument grants a party the right, but not the obligation, to enter into an interest rate swap at a pre-determined strike (fixed swap rate) on a future date in exchange for an up-front premium.

Synthetic long forward position The combination of a long call and a short put with identical strike price and expiration, traded at the same time on the same underlying.

Synthetic short forward position The combination of a short call and a long put at the same strike price and maturity (traded at the same time on the same underlying).

Tactical asset allocation Asset allocation that involves making short-term adjustments to asset class weights based on short-term predictions of relative performance among asset classes.

Tax alpha Calculated by subtracting the pre-tax excess return from the after-tax excess return, the tax alpha isolates the benefit of tax management of the portfolio.

Tax avoidance The legal activity of understanding the tax laws and finding approaches that avoid or minimize taxation.

Tax basis In many cases, the tax basis is the amount that was paid to acquire an asset, or its 'cost' basis, and serves as the foundation for calculating a capital gain or loss.

Tax-deferred account An account where investments and contributions may be made on a pre-tax basis and investment returns accumulate on a tax-deferred basis until funds are withdrawn, at which time they are taxed at ordinary income tax rates.

Tax-efficiency ratio (TER) Is calculated as the after-tax return divided by the pre-tax return. It is used to understand if a fund is appropriate for the taxable account of a client.

Tax-efficient decumulation strategy Is the process of taking into account the tax considerations involved in deploying retirement assets to support spending needs over a client's remaining lifetime during retirement.

Tax-efficient strategy An investment strategy that is designed to give up very little of its return to taxes.

Tax evasion The illegal concealment and non-payment of taxes that are otherwise due.

Tax-exempt account An account on which no taxes are assessed during the investment, contribution, or withdrawal phase, nor are they assessed on investment returns.

Tax haven A country or independent area with no or very low tax rates for foreign investors.

Tax loss harvesting Selling securities at a loss to offset a realized capital gain or other income. The rules for what can be done vary by jurisdiction.

Tax lot accounting Important in tax loss harvesting strategies to identify the cost of securities sold from a portfolio that has been built up over time with purchases and sales over time. Tax lot accounting keeps track of how much was paid for an investment and when it was purchased for the portfolio. Not allowed in all jurisdictions.

Taxable account An account on which the normal tax rules of the jurisdiction apply to investments and contributions.

Taylor rule A rule linking a central bank's target short-term interest rate to the rate of growth of the economy and inflation.

Temporary life insurance A type of life insurance that covers a certain period of time, specified at purchase. Commonly referred to as "term" life insurance.

Term deposits Interest-bearing accounts that have a specified maturity date. This category includes savings accounts and certificates of deposit (CDs).

Glossary

Term structure of volatility The plot of implied volatility (y-axis) against option maturity (x-axis) for options with the same strike price on the same underlying. Typically, implied volatility is not constant across different maturities – rather, it is often in contango, meaning that the implied volatilities for longer-term options are higher than for near-term ones.

Territorial tax systems Jurisdictions operate where only locally-sourced income is taxed.

Testamentary bequest See *Bequest*.

Testamentary gratuitous transfer See *Bequest*.

Testator The person who authored the will and whose property is disposed of according to the will.

Thematic investing An investment approach that focuses on companies within a specific sector or following a specific theme, such as energy efficiency or climate change.

Theta The daily change in an option's price, all else equal. Theta measures the sensitivity of the option's price to the passage of time, known as time decay.

Time deposits Interest-bearing accounts that have a specified maturity date. This category includes savings accounts and certificates of deposit (CDs).

Time-series estimation Estimators that are based on lagged values of the variable being forecast; often consist of lagged values of other selected variables.

Time-series momentum A managed futures trend following strategy in which managers go long assets that are rising in price and go short assets that are falling in price. The manager trades on an absolute basis, so be net long or net short depending on the current price trend of an asset. This approach works best when an asset's own past returns are a good predictor of its future returns.

Time-to-cash table See *liquidity classification schedule*.

Time value The difference between the market price of an option and its intrinsic value, determined by the uncertainty of the underlying over the remaining life of the option.

Total factor productivity A variable which accounts for that part of Y not directly accounted for by the levels of the production factors (K and L).

Total return payer Party responsible for paying the reference obligation cash flows and return to the receiver but that is also compensated by the receiver for any depreciation in the index or default losses incurred by the portfolio.

Total return receiver Receives both the cash flows from the underlying index and any appreciation in the index over the period in exchange for paying the MRR plus a predetermined spread.

Total return swap A swap in which one party agrees to pay the total return on a security. Often used as a credit derivative, in which the underlying is a bond.

Tracking error The standard deviation of the differences between a portfolio's returns and its benchmark's returns; a synonym of active risk. Also called *tracking risk*.

Tracking risk The standard deviation of the differences between a portfolio's returns and its benchmark's returns; a synonym of active risk. Also called *tracking error*.

Trade urgency A reference to how quickly or slowly an order is executed over the trading time horizon.

Transactions-based attribution An attribution approach that captures the impact of intra-day trades and exogenous events such as a significant class action settlement.

Transfer coefficient The ability to translate portfolio insights into investment decisions without constraint.

Trigger points In the context of portfolio rebalancing, the endpoints of a rebalancing range (corridor).

Trust A legal is a vehicle through which an individual (called a settlor) entrusts certain assets to a trustee (or trustees) who manages the assets for the benefit of assigned beneficiaries. A trust may be either a testamentary trust—a trust created through the testator's will—or a living or inter-vivos trust—a trust created during the settlor's lifetime.

Uncovered interest rate parity The proposition that the expected return on an uncovered (i.e., unhedged) foreign currency (risk-free) investment should equal the return on a comparable domestic currency investment.

Unsmoothing An adjustment to the reported return series if serial correlation is detected. Various approaches are available to unsmooth a return series.

Value at risk (VaR) A measure of the minimum portfolio loss expected to occur over a given time period at a specific confidence level.

Variance notional The notional amount of a variance swap; it equals vega notional divided by two times the volatility strike price [i.e., (vega notional)/(2 × volatility strike)].

Vega The change in an option's price for a change in volatility of the underlying, all else equal.

Vega notional The trade size for a variance swap, which represents the average profit and loss of the variance swap for a 1% change in volatility from the strike.

Vesting A term indicating that employees only become eligible to receive a pension after meeting certain criteria, typically a minimum number of years of service.

Volatility clustering The tendency for large (small) swings in prices to be followed by large (small) swings of random direction.

Volatility skew The skewed plot (of implied volatility (y-axis) against strike price (x-axis) for options on the same underlying with the same expiration) that occurs when the implied volatility increases for OTM puts and decreases for OTM calls, as the strike price moves away from the current price.

Volatility smile The U-shaped plot (of implied volatility (y-axis) against strike price (x-axis) for options on the same underlying with the same expiration) that occurs when the implied volatilities priced into both OTM puts and calls trade at a premium to implied volatilities of ATM options.

Will (or Testament) A document that outlines the rights others will have over one's property after death.

Withholding taxes Taxes imposed on income in the country in which an investment is made without regard for offsetting investment expenses or losses that may be available from the taxpayer's other investment activities.

Worldwide tax system Jurisdictions that tax all income regardless of its source.

Yield spread The simple difference between a bond's YTM and the YTM of an on-the-run government bond of similar maturity.

Z-score Credit risk model that uses financial ratios and market-based information weighted by coefficients to create a composite score used to classify firms based on the likelihood of financial distress.

Zero-discount margin (Z-DM) A yield spread calculation for FRNs that incorporates forward MRR.

Zero-volatility spread (Z-spread) Constant yield spread over a government (or interest rate swap) spot curve.